COGNITIVE AND NEUROSCIENTIFIC ASPECTS OF HUMAN LOVE

A GUIDE FOR MARRIAGE AND COUPLES COUNSELING

PSYCHOLOGY OF EMOTIONS, MOTIVATIONS AND ACTIONS SERIES

Psychology of Aggression
James P. Morgan (Editor)
2004. ISBN 1-59454-136-1

New Research on the Psychology of Fear
Paul L. Gower (Editor)
2005. ISBN: 1-59454-334-8

Impulsivity: Causes, Control and Disorders
George H. Lassiter (Editor)
2009. ISBN: 978-60741-951-8

Handbook of Stress: Causes, Effects and Control
Pascal Heidenreich and Isidor Prüter (Editors)
2009. ISBN: 978-1-60741-858-0

Handbook of Aggressive Behavior Research
Caitriona Quin and Scott Tawse (Editors)
2009. ISBN: 978-1-60741-583-1

Handbook of Aggressive Behavior Research
Caitriona Quin and Scott Tawse (Editors)
2009. ISBN: 978-1-61668-572-0
(Online Book)

The Psychology of Pessimism
Daniel X. Choi; Ravi B. DeSilva and John R. T. Monson
2010. ISBN: 978-1-60876-802-8

Psychological Well-Being
Ingrid E. Wells (Editor)
2010. ISBN: 978-1-61668-180-7

Psychological Well-Being
Ingrid E. Wells (Editor)
2010. ISBN: 978-1-61668-804-2
(Online Book)

Psychology of Denial
Sofía K. Ogden and Ashley D. Biebers (Editors)
2010. ISBN: 978-1-61668-094-7

Psychology of Neuroticism and Shame
Raymond G. Jackson (Editor)
2010. ISBN: 978-1-60876-870-7

Psychology of Hate
Carol T. Lockhardt (Editor)
2010. ISBN: 978-1-61668-050-3

Bio-Psycho-Social Perspectives on Interpersonal Violence
Martha Frias-Armenta and Victor Corral-Verdigp (Editors)
2010. ISBN: 978-1-61668-159-3

Psychology of Risk Perception
Joana G. Lavino and Rasmus B. Neumann (Editors)
2010. ISBN: 978-1-60876-960-5

Psychology of Persuasion
Janos Csapó and Andor Magyar (Editors)
2010. ISBN: 978-1-60876-590-4

Psychology of Happiness
Anna Mäkinen and Paul Hájek (Editors)
2010. ISBN: 978-1-60876-555-3

**Personal Strivings as a Predictor of
Emotional Intelligence**
Ferenc Margitics and Zsuzsa Pauwlik
2010. ISBN: 978-1-60876-620-8

Psychology of Thinking
David A. Contreras (Editor)
2010. ISBN: 978-1-61668-934-6

Psychology of Thinking
David A. Contreras (Editor)
2010. ISBN: 978-1-61728-029-0
(Online Book)

Psychology of Expectations
Pablo León and Nino Tamez (Editors)
2010. ISBN: 978-1-60876-832-5

**Cognitive and Neuroscientific
Aspects of Human Love:
A Guide for Marriage
and Couples Counseling**
*Wiiliam A. Lambos
and William G. Emener*
2010. ISBN: 978-1-61668-281-1

Psychology of Intuition
*Bartoli Ruelas
and Vanessa Briseño (Editors)*
2010. ISBN: 978-1-60876-899-8

**Extraverted and Energized: Review
and Tests of Stress Moderation
and Mediation**
Dave Korotkov
2010. ISBN: 978-1-61668-325-2

**Extraverted and Energized: Review
and Tests of Stress Moderation
and Mediation**
Dave Korotkov
2010. ISBN: 978-1-61668-703-8
(Online Book)

**Emotion's Effects on Attention
and Memory: Relevance to
Posttraumatic Stress Disorder**
*Katherine Mickley Steinmetz
and Elizabeth Kensinger*
2010. ISBN: 978-1-61668-239-2

**Emotion's Effects on Attention
and Memory: Relevance to
Posttraumatic Stress Disorder**
*Katherine Mickley Steinmetz
and Elizabeth Kensinger*
2010. ISBN: 978-1-61668-532-4
(Online Book)

**Friendships: Types, Cultural,
Psychological and Social Aspects**
Joan C. Tolle (Editors)
2010. ISBN: 978-1-61668-008-4

**Friendships: Types, Cultural,
Psychological and Social Aspects**
Joan C. Toller (Editor)
2010. ISBN: 978-1-61668-386-3
(Online Book)

**Reputation and the Evolution of
Generous Behavior**
Pat Barclay
2010. ISBN: 978-1-61668-153-1

**Reputation and the Evolution of
Generous Behavior**
Pat Barclay
2010. ISBN: 978-1-61668-402-0
(Online Book)

Smoking as a Risk Factor for Suicide
Maurizio Pompili
2010. ISBN: 978-1-61668-507-2

Smoking as a Risk Factor for Suicide
Maurizio Pompili
2010. ISBN: 978-1-61668-817-2
(Online Book)

**Creativity: Fostering, Measuring
and Contexts**
Alessandra M. Corrigan Editor)
2010. ISBN: 978-1-61668-807-3

**Creativity: Fostering, Measuring
and Contexts**
Alessandra M. Corrigan Editor)
2010. ISBN: 978-1-61728-067-2
(Online Book)

**Personality Traits: Classifications,
Effects and Changes**
John Paul Villanueva (Editor)
2010. ISBN: 978-1-61668-619-2

PSYCHOLOGY OF EMOTIONS, MOTIVATIONS AND ACTIONS SERIES

COGNITIVE AND NEUROSCIENTIFIC ASPECTS OF HUMAN LOVE

A GUIDE FOR MARRIAGE AND COUPLES COUNSELING

WILLIAM A. LAMBOS

AND

WILLIAM G. EMENER

Nova Science Publishers, Inc.
New York

For permission to use material from this book please contact us:
Telephone 631-231-7269; Fax 631-231-8175
Web Site: http://www.novapublishers.com

NOTICE TO THE READER

The Publisher has taken reasonable care in the preparation of this book, but makes no expressed or implied warranty of any kind and assumes no responsibility for any errors or omissions. No liability is assumed for incidental or consequential damages in connection with or arising out of information contained in this book. The Publisher shall not be liable for any special, consequential, or exemplary damages resulting, in whole or in part, from the readers' use of, or reliance upon, this material. Any parts of this book based on government reports are so indicated and copyright is claimed for those parts to the extent applicable to compilations of such works.

Independent verification should be sought for any data, advice or recommendations contained in this book. In addition, no responsibility is assumed by the publisher for any injury and/or damage to persons or property arising from any methods, products, instructions, ideas or otherwise contained in this publication.

This publication is designed to provide accurate and authoritative information with regard to the subject matter covered herein. It is sold with the clear understanding that the Publisher is not engaged in rendering legal or any other professional services. If legal or any other expert assistance is required, the services of a competent person should be sought. FROM A DECLARATION OF PARTICIPANTS JOINTLY ADOPTED BY A COMMITTEE OF THE AMERICAN BAR ASSOCIATION AND A COMMITTEE OF PUBLISHERS.

LIBRARY OF CONGRESS CATALOGING-IN-PUBLICATION DATA
Cognitive and neuroscientific aspects of human love : a guide for marriage and couples counseling / William A. Lambos, William G. Emener.
   p. cm.
Includes bibliographical references and index.
ISBN 978-1-61668-281-1 (hbk.)
1. Marital psychotherapy. 2. Marriage counseling. 3. Couples therapy. 4. Love. I. Emener, William G. (William George) II. Title.
RC488.5.L3487 2009
616.89'1562--dc22
                2009051295

Published by Nova Science Publishers, Inc. † *New York*

CONTENTS

List of Tables   *xxvii*

List of Figures   *xiii*

List of Counselor-Client Dialogues   *xvii*

Dedication   *xix*

Acknowledgements   *xxi*

Foreword   *xxiii*

Prologue   **xxvii**

Chapter 1	**Foundations and Basic Concepts**	**1**
	Perspectives and Approaches: Neuroscientific, Cognitive, and Interpersonal Domains	1
	Counseling and Therapy	3
	Marriage and Family Therapy Versus Marriage and Couples Counseling	4
	The Roles of Culture and other Concomitants in Loving Relationships	5
	A Brief Tour of the Brain	5
	Chapter Summary	8
Chapter 2	**Theories of Counseling and Couples Counseling**	**11**
	Psychodynamic Theories	13
	Behavioral and Ethological Theories	14
	Existential and Humanistic Approaches	17
	Gestalt and Phenomenological Theories	18
	Transactional and Interpersonal Models	19
	Cognitive-Behavioral Theories	20
	Making Sense of it all: "The Magic Number Three"	21
	Theories of Counseling – A Multi-Dimensional Approach	23
	Chapter Summary	24
Chapter 3	**Love, Loving and Romance**	**27**
	What is Love?	28
	Why we Love: Analyses of Love in Three Domains	29

	Whom do we Love?	32
	Chapter Summary	34
Chapter 4	**Analytics: Individual Issues**	**35**
	Behavior Analysis	35
	Self Analysis	42
	Self Identity	51
	Chapter Summary	55
Chapter 5	**Analytics: Relationship Analysis**	**57**
	A House Built on one Stilt or Many Stilts	58
	Dependence and Independence	60
	Public Space and Private Space	62
	Loving Roles we Play	64
	Little Things Mean a lot	66
	Being Loved and Feeling Loved	67
	Relationship Pros and Cons	68
	Love Triangle	69
	Unconditional Love	71
	Forgetting and Forgiving	72
	Promoting Relationship Happiness	73
	Chapter Summary	75
Chapter 6	**The Past**	**77**
	A Relationship's Past, Present and Future	78
	The Interaction Effect of your Pasts	80
	Mom and Dads – Our Primary Teachers	82
	Learned Interpersonal Needs	84
	Past People, Characteristics and Relationships:	
	The "Self-Fulfilling Prophecy"	85
	Dysfunctional Relationships and Living Parallel Lives	87
	Secrets and the Past	88
	Only-Child Issues	91
	Recycling One's Abusive Relationship History	92
	Chapter Summary	93
Chapter 7	**The Individual and the Couple**	**95**
	Congruence and Balance	95
	Rational Versus Irrational Thinking I: The A-B-C's of Happiness	105
	Rational Versus Irrational Thinking II:	
	Needs, Wants And Expectations	107
	Rational Versus Irrational Thinking III: Dichotomous Thinking	115
	Feelings and Emotions	120
	Chapter Summary	128
Chapter 8	**The Couple and the Individual**	**131**
	Outside Factors	132
	Other People	142

	Boundaries and Control	148
	Chapter Summary	157
Chapter 9	**The Couple in the World**	**159**
	Monetary and Equity Issues	160
	Matters of Time and Timing	168
	Patterns and Trends	176
	Chapter Summary	186
Chapter 10	**When the Individual Impacts the Relationship**	**189**
	Guilt and Shame	190
	Fears and Phobias	197
	Depression and Anxiety	205
	Grieving	212
	Anger	220
	Addictions, Obsessions and Compulsions	223
	Chapter Summary	224
Chapter 11	**When the Relationship Impacts the Individual**	**227**
	Lifestyle Choices And Relationships	228
	Problems Relating to one's Significant Other	236
	Separation and Divorce	244
	Chapter Summary	255
Chapter 12	**Relationship Skills**	**257**
	Empathy and Listening Skills	259
	Coping Skills	264
	Skills for Different Relationship Stages	265
	Co-, In-, and Inter-Dependence	268
	Chapter Summary	271
Chapter 13	**Relationships in the New Millennium**	**273**
	The Internet : The Good, The Bad and the Ugly	275
	Relationships and the Twenty-Four Hour Work Cycle	283
	Managing Relationships when Time is Compressed	285
	Managing Relationships During Economic Duress	288
	Chapter Summary	290
Chapter 14	**When your Client Seeks your Help**	**293**
	Clients' Questions and Presenting Problems	296
	Intake Information	299
	Observation	305
	Goals of Couples and Marital Counseling	305
	Rules Of Engagement: Conjoint Versus Individual Sessions	307
	Clients' Wants and Willingness to Work	308
	Clients' Expectations	310
	Counseling Intervention Strategies	316
	Advising your Couple: When to come, when to Stop and when to come Back	322

	Chapter Summary	327
Chapter 15	**Ethics and Professionalism**	**329**
	Professionalism in Human Services	329
	Human Service Regulatory Mechanisms	330
	Autonomy and Professional Behavior	332
	Professional Codes of Ethics	333
	The Role(s) of Knowledge in a Professional's Decision-Making	338
	Your "Professional Self-Concept"	339
	Chapter Summary	340

Epilogue	**343**
References	*349*
Appendix A. A Categorical/Annotated List of Bibliotherapeutic Self-Help Books	*359*
Appendix B. A Categorical/Annotated List of Videotherapeutic Movies	*371*
About the Authors	*381*
Subject Index	*383*

LIST OF TABLES

Table 2.1. Six Theoretical Approaches to Counseling and
Their Respective Notable Representatives, Central Tenets,
Assumptions, and Status in the Counseling Profession   **12**

Table 15.1. Selected Sources of Professional Human Service Ethical Codes   **334**

LIST OF FIGURES

Figure 1.1. A view of the Human Brain from the side (called a sagittal view). 7

Figure 2.1. A Two Dimensional Organization of Counseling Theories. 23

Figure 3.1. A 2008 Lamborghini Countach. 29

Figure 4.1. Relationships among what I "Say" and "Don't Say," and what I "Do" and "Don't Do." 37

Figure 4.2. Recommendations for Being More Consistent in a Relationship. 38

Figure 4.3. Learned Escape Behavior and Learned Avoidant Behavior. 40

Figure 4.4. Physical Attributes and Attractiveness Issues. 46

Figure 4.5. Uni-Trackers and Multi-Trackers. 47

Figure 4.6. High Maintenance and Low-Maintenance People. 49

Figure 4.7. Living an Unbalanced Life without a Special Someone. 52

Figure 5.1. A "House" Built on one Stilt Compared to a "House" Built on Many Stilts. 59

Figure 5.2. Relationships among Compliance and Anti-Compliance, and Dependance and Independence. 61

Figure 5.3. Public Space, Private Space and Together Space. 63

Figure 5.4. Loving Roles We Play. 64

Figure 5.5. Three Lists to Assess Relationship Pros and Cons. 69

Figure 5.6. The Love Triangle. 70

Figure 6.1. In a Relationship for Fear of Being Alone. 86

Figure 7.1. How we relate to each other. Affectively, Behaviorally and Cognitively. 96

Figure 7.2. Linkages Among Feelings, Thoughts and Actions. 99

Figure 7.3. Our Feelings, Thoughts and Actions Toward Self, the Other Person and our Relationship. 100

Figure 7.4. A Need for Balance in our Lives.   **101**

Figure 7.5. Relationships Among Old Experiences and
        Responses to New Experiences.   **103**

Figure 7.6. My Social Self, My Ideal Self and My Real Self.   **104**

Figure 7.7. The "A-B-Cs" of Happiness.   **105**

Figure 7.8. Differences Between Rational and Irrational Beliefs.   **107**

Figure 7.9. Understanding Our "Our Roles" and How
        We Meet Our Needs and Wants.   **109**

Figure 7.10. Specifying How and with Whom we Meet our Needs and Wants.   **111**

Figure 7.11. Dichotomous Thinking and the Development of a "Middle Range."   **116**

Figure 7.12. How We Spend Our Time.   **117**

Figure 7.13. People Are either "Good" or "Bad."   **119**

Figure 7.14. All or Nothing Relationships.   **120**

Figure 7.15. Areas in Need for Resolution and Serenity.   **125**

Figure 7.16. Confronting the Fear and Pain.   **128**

Figure 8.1. Primary, Immediate and Future Families.   **133**

Figure 8.2. Illustration of a Blended Family.   **137**

Figure 8.3. Impact of a Disability on Chris and Mildred's Relationship.   **140**

Figure 8.4. A Third Person in a Two-Seater.   **144**

Figure 8.5. Example of a "Transition Person".   **145**

Figure 8.6. Establishing Values in a Loving Relationship.   **150**

Figure 8.7. Active and Passive Control.   **154**

Figure 8.8. Internal and External Control.   **155**

Figure 9.1. You Can't Create Time – Just Allocate it.   **170**

Figure 9.2. Priorities Change Over Time.   **172**

Figure 9.3. Learned Response Patterns.   **178**

Figure 10.1. Guilt versus Toxic Shame.   **194**

Figure 10.2. Fear of Losing Me.   **203**

Figure 10.3. Michelle's Commitment Phobia.   **204**

Figure 10.4. Grieving Can Sneak Back on You on Occasions.   **216**

Figure 10.5. The Stalls in Your Barn.   **217**

Figure 11.1. Individual and Collective Lifestyles.   **232**

Figure 11.2. Communication Styles.   234

Figure 11.3. Stages of Kevin's Divorce and the Effects of Time.   253

Figure 11.4. Jill's Divorce Process Over Time.   254

Figure 12.1. Empathic Understanding.   260

Figure 12.2. Areas of Focus During Three Loving Relationship Stages.   266

Figure 14.1. Couples and Marriage Counseling Intake Form, Page 1.   300

Figure 14.1. Couples and Marriage Counseling Intake Form, Page 2.   301

Figure 14.1. Couples and Marriage Counseling Intake Form, Page 3.   302

Figure 14.1. Couples and Marriage Counseling Intake Form, Page 4.   303

Figure 14.1. Couples and Marriage Counseling Intake Form, Page 5.   304

Figure 14.2. Going Ahead – Not Back to Where You Were.   306

Figure 14.3. Stages of Change Efforts.   311

Figure 14.4. Progress May Be Slow and Gradual.   312

Figure 14.5. Realistic Expectations: Behaviors and Emotions.   314

Figure 14.6. The Downside of an Upswing.   315

Figure 14.7. When to Come Back.   323

Figure 14.8. Real (Psychological) Versus Social ("As If") Recovery.   325

LIST OF COUNSELOR-CLIENT DIALOGUES

Dialogue 4.1	Multi-Trackers and Uni-Trackers.	47
Dialogue 4.2	High Maintenance and Low Maintenance People.	49
Dialogue 5.1	A House Built on One or Many Stilts.	58
Dialogue 5.2	Dependence and Independence.	61
Dialogue 5.3	Loving Role We Play.	64
Dialogue 6.1	The Interaction Effect of Your Pasts.	80
Dialogue 6.2	Learned Interpersonal Needs.	84
Dialogue 7.1	Linkages: Feelings, Thoughts and Actions.	97
Dialogue 7.2	New Experiences – Old Feelings.	101
Dialogue 8.1	Internal and External Control.	155
Dialogue 9.1	Equitable Equity.	163
Dialogue 9.2	Patterns are like Addictions.	182
Dialogue 10.1	Guilt and Existential Guilt.	191
Dialogue 10.2	Healthy Shame and Toxic Shame.	195
Dialogue 10.3	Helplessness and Hopelessness.	210
Dialogue 11.1	Individual Lifestyles and Relationship Lifestyles.	230
Dialogue 12.1	Empathy and Listening Skills.	261
Dialogue 13.1	Internet Dating… The Ugly.	281
Dialogue 13.2	Relationships and the Twenty-Four Hour Work Cycle.	284

DEDICATION

One of our mentors wrote

"The gift of wisdom is a reward,

not an entitlement – it has to be earned."

It is in this spirit that we dedicate this book to all of

our past and current clients, working with whom,

over the years, enabled us to earn much wisdom –

wisdom that not only greatly assisted us in

our professional work but throughout

our personal lives as well.

ACKNOWLEDGMENTS

First and foremost, as you already may have seen and surmised, we extend a hearty "Thank-you!" to all of our past and current clients, who over the years taught us much wisdom – wisdom that not only greatly assisted us in our professional work but our personal lives as well.

To assist you in your use of bibliotherapy and videotherapy with your individual clients and couples, at the end of this book there are two lists: (1) *Appendix A.* – a categorical/annotated list of 86 bibliotherapeutic self-help books published since 2000; and (2) *Appendix B.* – a categorical/annotated list of 61 videotherapeutic movies. Simply said, this special and unique feature of this book indeed would not be as thorough and complete if it were not for the valuable assistance of three top-notch professionals: Ardis Hanson, Director, Claudia J. Dold, Assistant Librarian, and Emelda Curry, Research Librarian, of the Research Library in The Louis de la Parte Florida Mental Health Institute at the University of South Florida.

In many ways, the high level veracity and integrity of the content this book enjoys is because of the exceptional field-review editing done on an earlier draft of the book manuscript. Commensurately, we shall forever be grateful to Barbara LoFrisco, Nicole M. Stratis Kratimenos and Andrea Malas for their timely and diligent attention to detail and real-world issues. In a nutshell – Barb, Nicole and Andrea, "We owe ya!"

And just when we thought we had a "perfect book manuscript," we smiled in great appreciation for the exceptional wordsmith skills of Dr. Brian Downing, a professional copyeditor extraordinaire. "Thank you Brian!"

Our respective families – children, grandchildren and loved ones – have been respectfully caring and compassionate when over the past few months we replied to many of their requests with, "Okay, as soon as I finish editing this chapter." Their unerring love did not go unnoticed and to all of them we extend our sincerest appreciation.

And let us not forget our debt of gratitude to Scott Johnson, who took the time from his busy schedule to review our work and write an insightful and eloquent Foreword. Thank you, Scott... may we say, "You nailed it!"

Bill Lambos individually wishes to extend his deepest thanks to two of his mentors. To Dr. Elkhonon Goldberg, the finest practicing neuropsychologist in America today, no amount of thanks is sufficient to express the impact you have had on Bill Lambos's thinking and career. Bill feels he simply could not have been the success he is without Elkhonon's careful guidance. And to Dr. Vincent Parr, thank you for sharing your enthusiasm and dedication to the theories and practices of Rational Emotive Behavioral Therapy, and to mentoring Bill through the world of rational theory. Bill knows that without the insights gained from his association and friendship with these two individuals, this book could not have become what it is.

As Bill Emener looks back over his shoulder at his 39-year career as a full-time professor, he continues to acknowledge and appreciate two pivotal individuals who significantly influenced him – especially regarding this book. The day he graduated from the University of Georgia, his major professor and close friend, Dr. Thomas L. Porter said, "Bill, at the end of the day, as a university professor, the only two things that will matter is what you leave in the hearts and minds of your students and on the bookshelves in the library." A few years later, his colleague, fellow psychologist and close friend, Dr. David E. Stenmark, said to Bill, "You know so much about loving relationships and are an excellent couples therapist – you need to be teaching and writing about what you know and do." His deepest appreciation of and for these two, now-deceased individuals withstanding, Bill also believes that Tom and David would be proud of him.

A special and genuine "Thank you" is well deserved by Mr. Frank Columbus, President, and Maya Columbus, Director of Acquisitions, and their staff at Nova Science Publishers – especially our "go-to" person at nova, Donna Dennis, Senior Editor. Individually and collectively, they not only offered numerous words of wisdom along the way and helped us with deadlines while maintaining the highest of standards, but they did it with class and epitomized the essence of first-class professionals in the world of publishing.

Bill and *Bill*
Tampa, Florida
January, 2010

FOREWORD

Therapists and counselors typically have many unusual experiences over the years, but most of us have not had the pleasure of meeting a professional hit man, nor of telling him we wouldn't try to help him feel less guilty about his work. If you do encounter a murderer for hire in your career as a therapist, however, you may be better off having read the book you are now holding, by Bill Lambos and Bill Emener.

Students, teachers, or clinicians unswervingly committed to the view that mental health professionals should never take an "expert" stance – that is, act as if their training gives them insight clients often will lack, or that their professional experience may be useful in guiding clients' progress – should close this book now. For these authors clearly believe that their knowledge of the process of counseling couples and individuals struggling with forming and maintaining intimate relationships is both hard won and valuable for others – a view not always endorsed by therapeutic schools which promote "co-constructing" therapy with our clients, or adopting "not knowing" approaches to our work.

Advocates of "not knowing" models may see many of the insights and interventions Drs. Lambos and Emener offer here as "uncollaborative" and "hierarchical" – the therapist knows better than the client – and they will be correct to view them that way. Like almost anyone who writes a book – including those who write books about how therapists shouldn't come across as "experts" – the authors believe they have important advice to offer, advice they undoubtedly wish they'd had when they began their therapeutic careers.

One of the most important pieces of that advice they implicitly and explicitly give is that no matter how many people are in the room, we are *always* working with our clients' relationships. Their examples of couples counseling range from the traditional therapist plus two partners in the room to one client dealing with their intimate connections to two parents in the counseling session with children – yet all are approached here as relational work of some sort.

Another critical piece of advice is that relationships are relationships are relationships– a point it may be easy to miss, since the writers don't spend as much time as some readers would undoubtedly wish talking about what have come to be called "contextual variables" – things like gender, ethnicity, race, age, sexual orientation, culture. There are good books out there that talk about such things (and an awful lot of bad ones masquerading as good) but the writers here take one fundamental premise as gospel: humans, no matter their gender, sexual attractions, race, religion, etc... have pretty similar wants and needs when it comes to connecting with other humans.

There's no such thing, for example, as one of my international family therapy students once wrote, as "European" heartache or "Asian" happiness. And as Drs. Lambos and Emener might add, given their emphasis on how everyone's brains and hearts interact – there's no such thing in any meaningful sense as an "African American" amygdala, a "female" hippocampus, or a "gay" or "lesbian" medulla – things you might not realize if you've spent too much time following the nightly news. We all want to be loved and want to love, and it isn't an easy process for anyone.

Moreover, that process is constantly in flux, as circumstances around us shift and whirl. These authors talk about that – the life stage influences on all of us, the effects of others in our lives, our own pasts and families of origin – even the way the internet or the Great Recession seem to be impacting how we connect with significant others – in a way few other works have tackled so well.

The authors also avoid much of the ubiquitous nonsense about relationships that contemporary life seems flooded with. You won't find such laughably stupid ideas here as "men have more affairs than women" – how could they if they are having sex together? Or the howler that men have affairs for the sake of the sex but women have affairs for the attention. No one who's ever heard Hank Williams' "I'm So Lonesome I Could Cry" or Nina Simon's "I Want a Little Sugar in My Bowl" could buy that for a second.

Mercifully, as the title of their book suggests, they have tried to ground their points in genuinely observable, scientifically defensible truths about the human brain and the human heart rather than contemporary prejudice.

They also have tried and to a great extent succeeded in avoiding arbitrary therapeutic theoretical biases. While clearly favoring a rational emotive framework laced with heavy doses of cognitive behavioral theory, they make room for transgenerational and structural perspectives, intrapsychic views, and even, in some of their well chosen dialogues, narrative approaches – though some readers may have to work a bit to see how they all fit.

They don't cover everything perfectly. They omit the not uncommon fact that seemingly "betrayed" partners in couples experiencing affairs often have colluded in or even nurtured their partners' extradyadic involvements for a variety of logical reasons – it can be much easier than dealing with the problems of the dyad itself – and they might have said a little more about how for some people good relationships can be a goal wholly in themselves – Margaret Mead, for example, is alleged to have said that all three of her marriages were "very successful."

But there isn't a lot that should be important to beginning students of couples work – or experienced therapists for that matter – that is missing here. As I read these pages I constantly found myself thinking not only of many of my old cases but of my own relationships and family, and found myself telling my wife – one of the best couples therapists walking – I thought she would not only enjoy this book, but that the two of us would learn things about our own connections in these pages.

There are also wonderful examples of the use of diagrams and sketches in therapy, simple drawings that can clearly transform how clients see themselves and their partners. One almost wishes the authors had written a chapter on how they come up with them.

One premise of higher learning is that other people have things to teach us we are unlikely to learn simply through our own trial and error or contemplation. On that score this book is a gem. With a number of other good works for anyone who works with couples, it is a rich contribution to our field.

Scott Johnson, PhD
Licensed Marriage and Family Therapist
Associate Director, Office of Recovery & Support
Associate Professor & Director
Marriage and Family Therapy Doctoral Program
Family Therapy Center of Virginia Tech University

PROLOGUE

Your authors occasionally enjoy recalling and sharing the paths each of our lives took that led us to become psychologists who work with couples and professionally prepare others to do the same. We often marvel at how two such different sets of experiences, both professionally and personally, could allow two such different individuals to arrive at the same place. William A. Lambos, Ph.D., hereinafter "Bill," did his doctoral work in experimental psychology with a minor concentration in computer science. Bill's dissertation concerned mechanisms of Pavlovian conditioning in animals – which hardly seems relevant to whatever it is that an effective couples counselor ought to know. Following many years working as a consultant in areas at the intersection of psychology and computer science (such as human factors engineering and artificial intelligence software development), Bill decided he'd had enough of machines and wanted a second career in the helping professions. Taking on a substantial commitment to clinical retraining, this Bill found himself one day as a graduate student in a seminar class called "Marriage and Couples Counseling: Theory and Techniques", taught by one William G. Emener, Ph.D., hereinafter also "Bill". Confusion as to which Bill is which is prevented wherever possible throughout the book, but at some point we hope our readers will agree that it doesn't really matter.

The first Bill (Lambos) aced the course (of course), graduated from the Master's program in Rehabilitation and Mental Health Counseling at the University of South Florida, and went on to attain licensure as a clinical psychologist (in California) and to do a post-doctoral specialization in clinical neuropsychology. Some years later, while at a conference in Catalina Island (off the California coast), Bill Lambos's cell phone rang. The call was from his former professor and now colleague, Bill Emener. To make a (very) long story short, Bill Emener asked Bill Lambos if he would like to be coauthor for a rewrite of the same book on loving relationships Bill Emener used as the textbook in that graduate seminar. Lambos, who, despite his concentration in neuroscience continued to do couples counseling in his clinical practice, said "Sure, why not?" Three (or more) years and two self-help books later, you hold one of the results of that Tampa-Catalina Island telephone conversation in your hands.

As it turned out, and as we hope you will agree, Lambos and Emener work well together not only as a writing team, but as two individuals whose distinctively different backgrounds allow for a broader approach to the subject of counseling than is usually possible. Lambos stands with one foot firmly grounded in the brain. Emener has a foot standing solidly on matters of mind. Most importantly, each of us stands with the other foot firmly resting on that most vital organ – the heart.

William A. Lambos and William G. Emener

Therefore, in many ways, what we bring to this book is an extension of us, Drs. Emener and Lambos, the professionals, *and* Bill Emener and Bill Lambos, the persons, the human beings. On the professional side, we have been professional counselors, rehabilitation counselor educators, university-based researchers and scholars for over 37 years. Between us, we also have been licensed psychologists in three different states for thirty-three years. Each of us has dated, married, divorced, remarried; and each has children whom we lovingly watch grow and experience their own loving relationships. As you shall see, throughout the book we share some relevant aspects of our own, unique experiences and trust that you will enjoy the personal side roads along the way. Importantly, we have been fortunate enough to experience both the knowledge derived through scientific inquiry and scholarly learning, and to see how it translates into clinical practice and becomes an integral part of the lore of the professions of counseling and psychotherapy. What emerge are sets of "common knowledge" among clinicians. Thus, we would like to suggest that this book is truly an extension of us and of our lives. In addition to a blending of our professional and personal lives, each of our experiences has also been unique in the same way that every loving relationship, like every snowflake, is unique unto itself and will never exist in exactly the same way again. In many ways we simply do not know, nor can we pinpoint where many of the ideas in this book have come from. Thus, let's just consider this book to be a culmination and sharing of the significant aspects of loving relationships that we two have gleaned during our journeys through life.

ABOUT THIS BOOK

We would like to talk with you for a moment about the purposes of this book. We have read and written many books over the course of our lives, and during the past 15 years our readings and writings have included an increasing number of the popular, self-help types of books. We began our journey writing such a book, intended for the general public, and when it grew too large for a single self-help book, we split it into two. Having finished that project, we wanted to take what seemed like the logical next step in our journey.

We wanted, in particular, to extend our self-help books and to create a textbook for the student of clinical psychology, mental health counseling, marriage and family counseling or clinical social work that draws from cognitive aspects (the mind) and from neuroscientific aspects (the brain) and relates them to the art and science of assisting couples with their loving relationships (the heart). Although it is by no means our intention to bore the student with endless conceptual approaches and the technical data with which they are associated in the research literature, we cannot escape the need for theory and research background. Nor can we, as two professional counselors whom have truly come to appreciate what the brain has to teach us about matters of the heart, avoid at least occasional forays into neuroscience. But rest assured, this is neither a book *about* theories of counseling nor *about* neuroscience *per se*. It is, rather, a book about how knowing something about these subjects can help you, the student, become an effective and supportive professional therapist to couples and individuals who seek your help about their loving relationships.

Above all, we want to use shine a spotlight on some of the significant and critical issues in loving relationships that we have learned from working with our clients. As stated, both of us have worked extensively with couples over the years. These include married couples working on marital issues, individuals engaged to be married or in exclusive, "significant-other" relationships, and individuals who were separated, widowed or divorced yet trying to deal with numerous aspects of their love life and their relationships. Each of us has spent months carefully going through all of our notes from more than 300 clients with whom we worked over a 15-year period as psychologists. We made very careful notes on what we talked about with clients and what critical aspects of loving relationships were important to them in their lives. As a matter of fact, we find ourselves caught up in the observation that many of the aspects of loving relationships gleaned from these case histories have been true for the majority of the thousands of individuals with whom we have worked over the past 35 years. As you will see, we occasionally talk about our own lives throughout the book as well. Collectively, we trust that you will find these experiences to embody a wealth of knowledge that will be helpful to you.

> Little toes curled around each other
> Sheepish grins of peace, tranquility, and serenity
> Rose petal pecks on the lips
> Falling back in awe, all aglow
>
> A sunset shared is more than a sunset

FOUNDATIONS AND BASIC CONCEPTS

He or she who folds parachutes for a living should be willing to jump once in a while.

This is a book about the human experience of love. In particular, its focus is on guiding present and future professional counselors, psychologists, marriage and family therapists and social workers to provide counseling and therapy services to their clients with problems and difficulties in their loving relationships. While there are many books available that are designed to meet this purpose, we are taking a different approach: to incorporate an understanding of how the brain and other aspects of neuroscience, as well as the latest data on cognitive functioning, can help our understanding of human love. As human service professions such as mental health counseling and clinical psychology are changing, we felt the need has arisen to explore how these new areas of knowledge can impact the practice of couples counseling to the benefit of our clients. The following will make this clearer.

PERSPECTIVES AND APPROACHES: NEUROSCIENTIFIC, COGNITIVE, AND INTERPERSONAL DOMAINS

Until recently, books such as this one typically would discuss theories of personality or human behavior, and then go on to discuss how couples counseling or therapy might be conducted from each of the perspectives respectively described. For example, the authors might discuss psychodynamic approaches first, and then show how a therapist trained in this approach would approach a therapy session with a couple whose issue lent itself to analysis in Freudian or Adlerian terms. In turn, the same approach would be used for other theories of counseling, such as behavioral and cognitive approaches.

At times, the traditional approach described above will be used in this book, but our goal is to broaden the approach in significant ways as well. As noted, one addition is a discussion of the neuroscience – the relevant aspects of brain function – that underlies the human experience of love. However, the student of clinical psychology, mental health and/or marriage and family therapy need not worry about this too much. Before breaking into a cold sweat and looking for an alternative course in your department's curriculum, rest assured that this is not a course in advanced neuroscience. Such material will be introduced only as it is directly relevant to the topics addressed and in a reader friendly and readily comprehensible fashion, even for those students with minimal backgrounds in the biological bases of behavior.

In the 21st Century, the broad fields of clinical mental health and neuropsychology, nonetheless, are beginning to merge, and the current counselor must adapt to this reality. Moreover, as the student shall see throughout this book, the brain has much to teach us about love. Although it is natural for mental health counselors and psychologists to focus on the *mental* aspects of counseling, the fully informed counselor or therapist can no longer afford to ignore the *brain* bases of mental life. Not only will the counselor's understanding of his or her client's issues and presenting conditions be more complete, but suggestions for treatment interventions often will be more effective as well. As far as we know, this is the first textbook on the topic of couples counseling to incorporate this approach, and we are confident that the student will not only benefit from the inclusion of such material but also appreciate and enjoy it.

Of course, neuroscience alone can take us only so far. No method of brain imaging allows us to determine what the observed person is thinking, and no explanation of neural activity, brain waves or transmitter substances can account for the contents of consciousness. Mental life has not been reduced to brain activity (nor, in our opinion, will it ever be). Rather, to understand and have a more meaningful impact on the behavior and happiness of an individual or a couple with loving relationship problems and difficulties, you also must be aware of the basis of their *thoughts* (cognitions) and *feelings* (emotions). To address these latter aspects of loving relationships, we herein include the more traditional approach based on theories of counseling, with an emphasis on cognitive-behavioral approaches.

We also cannot ignore issues that are best understood from the level of interpersonal interactions between an individual and his or her partner and their families, friends, co-workers and others. We humans are social animals, and one cannot hope to understand or intervene in loving relationships without recognizing the roles others' thoughts, feelings and behaviors have on our own. This level of understanding loving relationships and, indeed, the human experience of love itself, is based on what is usually characterized as "interactional psychology," and stems from a traditional set of approaches to marriage and family therapy that together fall under the rubric of *systems theory*. We therefore now have "a stool with three legs" as it were: (1) neuropsychological; (2) cognitive-behavioral; and (3) interactional and systems-based. Together these legs – these foundational pillars – will be shown to nicely support and organize a very large body of data and theories on the subject of human love and relationships. We promise you that our approach, although a novel one, will allow you to organize and understand this large body of material with far greater ease and efficiency than would otherwise be possible.

Lastly, while it is true that our approach to understanding and counseling those in loving relationships will recognize the roles of neuroscientific, cognitive and interpersonal factors that enable us to understand such relationships, it is also true that the choice of topics in this book did not come from such considerations alone. Rather, in many ways, what we bring to this book is an extension of us, Drs. Lambos and Emener, the professionals, and Bill Lambos and Bill Emener, the persons, the human beings. As we noted in the Prologue, we have been professional counselors, rehabilitation counselor educators, university-based researchers and scholars over the past 40 or more years. Between us, we also have been Licensed Psychologists in three different states for 33 years. Each of us has dated, married, divorced, remarried and have children whom we lovingly watch grow and experience their own loving relationships. Throughout this book we share some relevant aspects of our own, unique experiences and trust that you will enjoy the personal side roads along the way.

More than anything else, we want to shine a spotlight on some of the significant and critical issues in adult loving relationships that we have learned from working with clients. Our work as Licensed Psychologists, counselors and therapists for over three decades has often been focused on working with couples. These include married couples working on their relationship issues, individuals engaged to be married or in exclusive, committed, "significant-other" relationships, and individuals who were "separated," "widowed" or "divorced" yet trying to deal with numerous aspects of their loving and their loving relationships. To reiterate once more from the Prologue, each of us has spent months carefully going through all of our files from more than 300 clients with whom we worked over a 15-year period as psychologists. Of course, given the sensitivity of the topics addressed in client sessions, and the ethical imperative of client-therapist confidentiality, all the names and identifying information were changed. Any similarities to specific individuals by name would be purely coincidental.

As we reviewed our files, we made very careful notes – what we talked about with clients and what critical aspects of loving relationships were important to them in their lives. As a matter of fact, we find ourselves caught up in the observation that many of the aspects of adult loving relationships gleaned from these files have been true for the majority of the thousands of individuals with whom we have worked over the past 40 or more years. We trust that you will find these experiences to embody a wealth of knowledge that will be helpful to you in preparing for your career as a licensed professional providing counseling to individuals and couples having love relationship problems.

COUNSELING AND THERAPY

Having described how this book differs from others, we, your authors, now wish to define the terms "Counseling" and "Therapy" as we understand and use them throughout the book. The terms "Counseling" and "Therapy" (or "Psychotherapy") have evolved in their use over the last 20 years considerably, to the point where they now may or may not mean different things to different people.

"Psychotherapy," or what Freud (1961, 1964) referred to as "the talking cure," was once confined to the domain of medical doctors, typically neurologists retrained as psychiatrists. Following World War II, however, the need to provide psychological services for returning soldiers was too great for the number of available psychiatrists to handle, and psychologists (who held doctorates, not medical degrees) were added to the list of professions allowed to provide psychotherapy (but not to prescribe medications, which to this day remains the province of medical doctors). During the 1960s and 1970s, professions such as mental health counseling and social work argued that their training also enabled them to perform those interventions normally classified as psychotherapy and successively petitioned for licensure and recognition to provide such services. They succeeded. Meanwhile, psychiatrists focused their practices more on medication management, and clinical psychologists turned to specializing in the assessment and testing of mental health functioning and psychopathology.

Today, there are at least five groups of licensed professionals (psychiatrists, psychologists, mental health counselors, marriage and family therapists, and clinical social workers) who may legally use the term "psychotherapy" to describe at least some of the services they provide (Emener, Richard & Bosworth, 2009a). Among these, the terms "counseling," "therapy" and "psychotherapy" have become largely interchangeable and frequently are now used synonymously. This is also how we use them in this book.

MARRIAGE AND FAMILY THERAPY VERSUS MARRIAGE AND COUPLES COUNSELING

As stated above, this book uses the terms counseling, therapy and psychotherapy more or less interchangeably, even though they still convey slightly different things to different people. Nonetheless, we do make an important distinction between marriage and family therapy on the one hand, and marriage or couples counseling on the other. As we shall show in greater detail in the following chapter, no reasonable consideration of mental health issues or treatment approaches can ignore the significant role played by family members of an individual or a couple, or to the workings of the family *as a system*. There is a rich history of theories of counseling based on family factors, and the contributions made by some of those writing and practicing in this area have had enormous impact. Approaches with labels such as "systemic family therapy," "strategic family therapy" and "experiential family therapy" have been the subjects of dozens, if not hundreds, of textbooks and thousands of journal articles. The pioneering giants of this field such as Virginia Satir (1968), Carl Whitaker (1972), Jay Haley (1984, 1987) and others too numerous to list, were afforded due status and recognition and continue to play an influential role in systems-based approaches to family analysis and intervention.

The latter subject of this section – marriage or couples counseling – refers to a rather different activity, however. This approach is distinguished by its focus on the loving relationship between two individuals, on what we will often refer to as *the dyad*. Although family factors are properly recognized as playing important roles, the primary level of analysis remains, and is in some ways confined to, the interactional dynamic of the couple itself. This topic is the primary subject of our book.

This is an appropriate time to define our terms. What do we mean by *loving relationship*? The Greeks talked about the difference between eros (a love of self), philio (a brotherly/sisterly type of love) and agape love (a spiritually bonded type of love). While we truly believe that all loving relationships involve some aspects of eros, philio and agape types of love, the primary phenomena addressed in this book focuses on "agape intended" relationships of adults. As his name reflects, Dr. Lambos is of Greek lineage and grew up in an ethnic family that used these Greek terms as household words.

Given that our focus is on the couple – on the *dyad* and its constituents – what are the components of the dyad? It is important to realize that every relationship has not two but three components: each of two people *and* their relationship. At first glance, this may seem confusing. As we shall see time and again throughout this book relationships have characteristics that transcend and exist independently of the people involved in them. Therefore, to be an effective couples or marriage counselor, one has to have the ability to analyze the relationship separately from the individuals. As Dr. Scott Johnson, the 2007-2008 President of the American Association for Marriage and Family Therapy, pointedly stated, "Beyond the number of people in the room with the therapist, marriage and family therapy is unique for its premise that the behavior of individuals cannot be separated from the context of their relationships. What we often call dysfunctional behavior in individuals is in many cases influenced or caused by basic problems in those relationships themselves" (Johnson, 2009, p. 128). (This will become clearer when we examine the topic of relationship analysis in Chapter 5.)

THE ROLES OF CULTURE AND OTHER CONCOMITANTS IN LOVING RELATIONSHIPS

From time to time, loving relationships tend to have special considerations such as status, gender, race, age and culture. In the area of status, it could be suggested that during the courtship, engagement, marriage, separation and/or divorce stages there are special characteristics and features. It also has been our experience that many of the critical issues of heterosexual relationships are also equally vibrant and important in gay relationships. Some theorists have suggested that there are some differences between "same race" and "interracial" relationships. From the perspective of age, it could be suggested that there are some age-specific issues in loving relationships. We do not argue against any of this. Similarly, we agree that there are some cultural peculiarities pertinent to loving relationships. (If you saw the film *My Big Fat Greek Wedding*, what you saw was not entirely an exaggeration.) Nonetheless, please remember that we wrote this book with a specific focus on those aspects of loving relationships that tend to transcend issues of status, gender, socio-economics, ethnicity, age and culture. For this reason, we will make due note of cultural and normative aspects of dyadic interactions when they play a role in a given situation or example under discussion. But to the extent possible, it is our goal to address relationship issues that cut across and transcend the specific contributions of ethnicity, gender identification, socioeconomic variables, age and other such ideographic factors.

A BRIEF TOUR OF THE BRAIN

As we noted above and shall see in far greater detail in Chapter 3, the philosophy of the Ancient Greeks still influences how *love* is defined. Here we mention them again, for another reason entirely. It turns out that two of the greatest thinkers in ancient Athens – Aristotle, Plato's student, and Hippocrates, the founder of modern medicine – disagreed as to which organ of the body was responsible for, or the seat of, thoughts and emotions. Aristotle held the so-called *cardiocentric* view that the heart was the seat of the soul and that the brain played little, if any, significant role in either mental or emotional life.

It is easy to imagine why he guessed this to be so. Anyone who has ever experienced strong emotion – especially love – knows how the heart seems to soar in ecstasy or to writhe in pain as a result of experiencing various aspects of love. Our language today still refers to "heartache" and "broken hearts" when describing the emotions of unrequited love. When we experience the powerful and even overwhelming emotions associated with romantic love, it is from the heart that they seem to emanate. And yet, Hippocrates, who spent much more of his time than did Aristotle actually examining and treating the sick, knew more about what parts of the body accounted for life's sensations, perceptions, thoughts and emotional experiences. Hippocrates was the first among ancients to propose a *cephalocentric*, or brain-centered, view of inner life and bodily functioning. One of our favorite quotes about the brain attributed to Hippocrates is:

> Men ought to know that from the brain, and from the brain only, arise our pleasures, joys, laughter, and jests as well as our sorrows, pains, griefs and tears... it is the same thing which makes us mad or delirious, inspires us with dread and fear, whether by night or by day, brings us sleeplessness, inopportune mistakes, aimless anxieties, absent-mindedness and acts that are contrary to habit... (Jones, 1923)

Hippocrates's depth of insight was staggering, given how little was known at the time about brain organization and function. Indeed, the most basic fact about the brain – that the fundamental building block of the nervous system is the nerve cell or *neuron* – was not proved to the satisfaction of modern scientists until the late 1800s! It is not an exaggeration to posit that today more is learned about the brain each decade than the sum total of all the knowledge that existed about it in all of previous history. Moreover, what we have *yet to learn* dwarfs by many orders of magnitude that which we are confident we know.

Fortunately, we do know a great deal of relevant information about brain function, so much so that we can at least begin to simplify the topic and condense this understanding for the benefit of the student of counseling and therapy. As noted above, this is not a neuroscience textbook. Nonetheless, a bird's-eye view of brain function will guide us toward a deeper understanding and appreciation of love and relationships. It provides context, a set of "hooks" if you will, on which to hang seemingly unrelated aspects of the experience of human love and, in so doing, helps in understanding what is surely a topic equally as complex as that of the brain – the basis of human love.

The best way of appreciating this is to learn just enough about the brain to see why emotion and physiology are so central to the human experience. Despite being the most complex structure in the known universe, with its billions of nerve cells and trillions of connections among them, the brain is functionally divided into a much smaller subset of parts. As depicted in Figure 1.1, looking at the head from the side (i.e., looking at it from the perspective of the ear), there are three main parts or areas of interest. These are not the same as the "lobes" you may have heard of. Roughly speaking, the back half of the brain is designed to recognize, identify and recall what we have previously learned about the outside world. Think of this area as the "world parser" or "world identifier." The front of the brain – the so-called "executive brain" (Goldberg, 2002, 2005) – is charged with making decisions that enable us to meet our needs, including the need to maintain successful relationships and terminate unsuccessful ones. This executive part of the brain constantly receives information about what is happening in the outside world (from the back part), compares it to our memories of what we identify, and then has the job of acting on that information or, as turns out to be the case 99% of the time, just ignoring it. This filtering is an often underappreciated function of the brain – imagine if you were compelled to attend to the sound of the air conditioning system all day long!

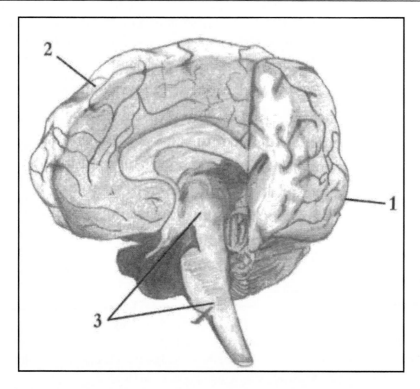

Figure 1.1. A view of the Human Brain from the side (called a sagittal view).

Finally, between the back and front halves and below the ear lie the centers of arousal and emotion – the brain stem and the so-called *limbic system*. This latter part of the brain (1) regulates the activation and attention (generalized arousal) necessary to deal with the task at hand, and then (2) assigns values such as "good or bad," "I want it!" or "Ugh... get away!" to what the back of the brain detects in the world and how we remember its previous impact on us. The front of the brain uses these values in every step of the decision-making process. The interaction of the limbic system with the upper portions of the brain stem (in particular, an important area called the ventral tegmentum) also controls our level of arousal, from deep sleep to hyper-focus and concentration.

Pulling this together, the "values" assigned to what we sense in the world determine how aroused we need to be in order to properly react to sensory input. For example, when the limbic system senses something dangerous "out there" (e.g., a poisonous spider), we become very physiologically aroused and take immediate steps to get away from it (or perhaps to freeze in place so it might not see us). When the limbic system determines that the thing out there is desirable (i.e., that gorgeous single-looking guy at the bar), we similarly become aroused and take steps to approach it ("Hi there, handsome!").

In both cases, as well as the vast majority of instances in between the really bad and really good, we cannot make even the simplest decision whether to freeze/avoid, approach or ignore what we sense in the world without this limbic value processing. Thus, there could never truly be a Mr. Spock or a Mr. Data – such a being could never decide how to react to the world using logic alone. Living organisms simply cannot make sense of their environment without assigning it values. And in the human experience, those values constitute arousal and emotions.

Now you may be ready to ask, "Okay, so how does this help me understand loving relationships?" Good question! The answer is that some combination of our genes and our lifetime of experiences determines how we value every aspect of both ourselves and the people with whom we relate. This in turn determines our level of arousal. Both the "good versus bad value" and the "level of arousal we feel" are central in determining the decisions we make in responding to other people and their actions.

Think for a moment about other people you know who are particularly adept at interacting successfully with others – the "people persons." Whether they are really good at the bar scene or highly effective leaders in business or politics, what they have in common is that they have learned how to sense what others want or need of them and how to appropriately respond to get what they are looking for. They do this well because (1) they have learned to regulate their level of arousal so that it is always appropriate for the situation, and (2) they have a great deal of knowledge about both themselves and the others with whom they relate. It sounds simple, but as most of us know, relating successfully with other people is as much an art as it is a science, and a big part of the art comes from self-knowledge and the ability to control one's own arousal and emotions.

So much for the science lesson – at least for now. The main point of this section is that for students who want to understand why they or a client may feel a certain way, this offers a simple yet intuitive explanation. And what about controlling and altering these emotions? Well, that's what much of the rest of this book addresses, beginning with the next chapter, which examines the important subject of theories of counseling.

CHAPTER SUMMARY

We trust that the student of couples counseling has by this point gained a working foundation for our further exploration of the topics of Human Love and Human Loving Relationships.

As we have seen, our journey through the areas of love, loving relationships and couples counseling will be guided by three important perspectives: (1) the neuroscientific; (2) the cognitive; and (3) the interpersonal. Although none of these perspectives, individually or collectively, are offered as the sole basis of explanation for love, loving relationships and counseling people with problems and difficulties in these areas, they indeed serve two extremely helpful purposes for the student: (1) from a pragmatic point of view, they work and can be very useful; and (2) they provide a good foundation upon which the student can, and over time probably will, develop his or her own approach to counseling individuals and couples in the area of loving. Please remember that when you study and learn the principles and techniques in this book and use them to understand and help others, you simultaneously will come to understand yourself more richly *and* ultimately help yourself – especially if you invest yourself in the concepts and considerations, professionally and personally.

CHAPTER 1 DISCUSSION QUESTIONS

1) In terms of your basic approaches to understanding human beings, how much importance do you put on their cognitions, emotions and behavior?
2) In your own words, what are the differences between "counseling" and "therapy?"
3) In addition to status, gender, race, age and culture, what other concomitants do you consider to be important in understanding individual clients and couples?
4) In your own words, what are the differences between "counseling" and "couples counseling?"
5) To what extent do you consider *love* a matter of the brain and/or a matter of the heart?

THEORIES OF COUNSELING
AND COUPLES COUNSELING

In the previous chapter we alluded to theories of counseling as one of the pertinent aspects of our approach to understanding and appreciating loving relationships and providing efficient and effective counseling to individuals and couples with relationship problems and difficulties. Furthermore, just as this is not a text on neuroscience, neither is it a textbook about theories of personality or counseling. On the other hand, as we have seen with regard to the brain, counseling theories provide efficient ways of organizing and remembering what is known about complex subjects, and can, when properly presented, actually help and advance one's understanding and ability to remember very complex sets of ideas. And let's not forget: loving relationships indeed entail numerous challenging complexities.

As a student of counseling or psychology, it is unlikely that this is the first time you will have encountered the material in this section. We nonetheless trust what follows serves as a "refresher" and will help you to remember these theories when we refer to them throughout the remainder of the book.

Over the years, therapists have classified theories about marriage and family therapy in a number of ways – especially with regard to counseling couples, and marriage and family therapy (Goldenberg & Goldenberg, 2004; Gurman & Kniskern, 1981; Johnson, 2009). Nonetheless, in view of the variety of professionals who provide such professional services in today's world, Table 2.1 identifies the major theories of counseling or personality, a representative list of the individuals most often identified with them, their central tenets or assumptions and their status in the counseling and clinical mental health professions. A brief review of Table 2.1 may prove useful before reading further about these approaches. As the Table shows, we conceptually group theories of counseling into six broad categories: (1) psychodynamic; (2) behavioral/ethological; (3) existential and humanistic; (4) gestalt and phenomenological; (5) interpersonal and transactional; finally, several of these have since merged to become the leading theory of counseling as it is practiced in the current era – namely; and (6) the cognitive-behavioral approach.

Table 2.1.

Six Theoretical Approaches to Counseling and Their Respective Notable Representatives, Central Tenets, Assumptions, and Status in the Counseling Profession.

Theoretical Approach	Notable Representatives	Central Tenets/Assumptions	Status in the Counseling Profession
1. Psychodynamic	Alfred Alder Sigmund Freud Carl Jung	People will seek to reduce tension caused by unmet needs	Not practiced much today in clinical mental health counseling
2. Behavioral and Ethological	B.F. Skinner Ivan Pavlov John Watson	The environment accounts for human behaviors	Not much impact on clinical mental health counseling
3. Existential and Humanistic	Victor Frankl Carl Rogers	Individuals create the meaning and essence of their lives based on subjectivity and perception	Contributes well to couples counseling
4. Gestalt and Phenomenological	Paul Goodman Fritz Perls Laura Perls	Emphasizes personal responsibility, seeks to re-establish coherence between behaviors and underlying perception	Appealing to those who believe in relationships based on total honesty, not used in system-based or cognitive behavioral approaches
5. Transactional and Interpersonal	Eric Berne Harry Stack Sullivan	Emphasizes the individual's interactions with one another via transactions.	Powerful approach used in couples and marriage counseling as well as relationship analysis
6. Cognitive-Behavioral	Aaron Beck Albert Ellis	Feelings and actions are caused by the individual's system of beliefs about the world	Most widely practiced and generally accepted approach to counseling today.

PSYCHODYNAMIC THEORIES

These are the oldest theories of counseling and personality, and are historically attributed to Sigmund Freud (1961, 1964), Carl Jung (1972), and Alfred Adler (1999). Freud was trained as a medical doctor – a neurologist in particular – during a time when very little was known about the brain. He decided that studying the brain and the nervous system would not help him to treat many of his clients, who presented with what came to be known as psychological symptoms (from the Greek word *psyche*, or "the soul, mind, spirit, breath, life, the invisible animating principle or entity which occupies and directs the physical body" [personified in mythology as Psykhe, the lover of Eros]). He therefore abandoned the study of the nervous system and developed an alternative approach to human behavior based on aspects of how the parts of the *psyche* interacted to account for development and adult behavior. This approach came to be called *psychodynamic*, because it related to the ever-changing interaction of parts of the psyche.

Briefly, according to Freud (1961), the psyche is composed of three basic structures: the id, ego and superego. The *id* is the source of instinctual drives that propel or motivate human behavior at the most fundamental level. According to the good doctor, unmet instinctual needs create tension that people will seek to reduce, and which accounts for much adult behavior – especially relationship-oriented behavior. Because the id operates at the level of instinct, it is said to operate on the pleasure principle. The *ego* is the part of the mind that interacts with the world and our memories of it, and is therefore said to operate on the reality principle – its job is to satisfy the id within the confines of external reality. The ego represents much of the contents of conscious awareness, though by no means all, as much remains unconscious and hidden from awareness. Finally, the *superego* operates on the conscience principle and keeps the id and ego in check and in line with morals and values as defined by the culture of the society in which people grow and develop.

Because his approach asserts that the parts of the psyche or mind are fixed and must interact in circumscribed ways, Freud's theory provides a very deterministic view of human nature in which adult plasticity is not given a central role. This may explain why it is not practiced much today outside of one or two areas of the United States. However, the student of counseling or psychology should never sell Freud's contributions short. He was the "eight-hundred pound gorilla" among early psychologists, a giant, and his was the first modern theory to recognize the notion, and role, of unconscious motivation in understanding human behavior. Furthermore, Freud's theory shares much more in common with the modern neuroscientific perspective of brain function described in the previous chapter, at least at the highest level of organization, than most neuroscientists will admit.

In the previous chapter, we also learned that the modern view of functional areas of the brain includes (a) an arousal and emotional center (the brain stem and limbic system), (b) a world-parser and memory store (to identify and categorize objects in the world), and (c) an executive area (the pre-frontal cortex) which responds to the other two and ultimately decides upon appropriate behaviors. Sound familiar? The analogy between these brain areas and the id, ego and superego is too compelling, in our opinion, to overlook. Yet, we can assure you that the mapping of the brain was in no way directed by Freud's ideas (at least not consciously).

Freud's contemporaries and students include Carl Jung and Alfred Adler, who each made various adjustments and additions to his theory. Jung (1972) focused on intergenerational memories (so-called "archetypes"), which overlap to no small degree with phylogenetic memories stored in a limbic brain structure called the amygdala. Adler (1999) added the importance of birth order and parenting variables and important ideas regarding differentiation and personal autonomy, in particular overcoming self-conceptions based on inferiority and replacing them with those based upon superiority.

BEHAVIORAL AND ETHOLOGICAL THEORIES

Around the same time Freud and his colleagues were developing the psychodynamic approach, scientists working mostly with animal subjects were creating the foundations of a very different approach to explaining human behavior, particularly with respect to love and relationships.

Pioneers in animal behavior studies in laboratory environments such as Ivan Pavlov (Mackintosh, 1983), John Watson (1924/1925, 1928) and B.F. Skinner (1969) studied the determinants of animal behavior and went on to postulate explanations of human behavior based on their studies and findings. Unlike Freud and his followers, the behavior theorists look largely to the current environment to explain and account for human behaviors, including thoughts and feelings. What characterizes behavioral theories (as well as ethological approaches, which we shall examine shortly), is a belief in a process of *natural selection*, broadly defined. Such explanations are often referred to as various types of Darwinian theories, in which the strong, successful or useful survive and the unsuccessful die out. Of course, Darwin (Dennett, 1995) applied his model only to the origins of existing and/or extinct biological species. Darwinian models extend his central mechanism to other entities, be they individual behaviors, genetic traits or even neuronal processes.

Extending Darwin's basic idea to *behaviors* as opposed to living organisms simply involves postulating that during the lifetime of an individual, those behaviors that lead to positive consequences are strengthened and occur more frequently, whereas unproductive or unsuccessful behaviors tend not to be repeated (they "die out," as it were). This broader application of natural selection also guides much work in neuroscience. For example, the Nobel Laureate Gerald Edelman (1987) used the notion of "survival of the fittest" at the level of individual neurons (or clusters of related neurons) to explain why some nerve cells and their connections to neighboring neurons are strengthened and become "etched" in our neural circuitry while others die out or become idle. Once again, we see the recurring overlap of analogies between underlying explanations of mind, brain and behavior that are central to the approach to understanding of human love advocated throughout this book.

To return to the behavioral school of counseling theories, most students reading this book will recall that several mechanisms of learning were proposed and used, in turn, to explain higher human functions, including relationship behavior. These mechanisms of learning include *simple stimulus-driven processes* such as sensitization and habituation, to forms of *associative learning* based on the formation of stimulus-stimulus associations (i.e. the bell and the meat powder in Pavlov's experiments), and further yet to the associations between *operant (voluntary) behavior and its consequences* (rewards and/or punishments), explored at great length by B. F. Skinner and his colleagues.

While it is sometimes said that although Behaviorism went on to become a school of psychology, it also has had considerably less impact on clinical mental health counseling than most of the other theories we will review here (for other theories, consult Patterson & Watkins, 1997). The same is also often said about ethologically oriented approaches to behavior from areas such as sociobiology and behavior genetics (Dennett, 1995). Let us assume for the moment that this reflects reality (although later we will challenge the *a priori* assumption underlying it). If it were true, as it certainly appears to be to any student in a clinical psychology or mental health counseling program in the current era, why should it be so?

The reasons have little to do with human psychology and behavior *per se* and a lot to do with the politics of both the funding of scientific research and the licensing of mental health professionals. This can be summed up with the term "turf wars." Behavioral and ethological theories, often based as they were on either laboratory animal experiments or naturalistic observations of lower species in the wild, were studied not by those who practiced in the fields of physical and mental health care, but by *experimental* psychologists who had little or no professional contact with patients (or even, in many cases, human subjects). Although some behavioral psychologists would later become clinical practitioners, they constituted a minority of licensed mental health providers and were rarely accepted among the ranks of clinicians in other disciplines of clinical mental health. There were two consequences of this historical divide, neither unexpected. The first, as mentioned, was that experimental behavioral and ethological psychologists were treated with suspicion by most of those in clinical practice and their influence was limited. The second consequence was that the great majority of clinical psychologists and counselors were not adequately schooled in the tenets and principles of either behavioral or ethological principles of psychology. This remains just as true today as it was 30 years ago. One of the co-authors of this book (Dr. Lambos) was trained first as an experimental psychologist, then later trained in clinical psychology, and finally in clinical neuropsychology. Dr. Lambos has yet, in many years of clinical practice, met a single licensed clinician with even a rudimentary understanding of subjects like the relationship between classical and operant conditioning, schedules of reinforcement, learning and extinction curves, hierarchies of reward systems or most of the rest of behavioral psychology's most basic concepts. For the sociobiologists, who focused their studies almost entirely on concepts such as mate selection and reproductive behavior in the natural environment, and whose work would therefore be expected to be especially relevant to understanding human relationships, the situation is even worse! Dr. Lambos doubts that even 3% of licensed clinicians in mental health practice can define the term sociobiology or name the National Medal of Science winner most closely associated with it (Edward O. Wilson, of Harvard University; see Wilson, 1975, 2000). And among the estimated 3% who can name him, the majority will probably assert that his work has been "discredited."[1] Interestingly, the

---

[1] Dr. Wilson's website, found as of this writing at http://www.hup.harvard.edu/catalog/WILSOR.html, includes the following paragraph: "When this classic work was first published in 1975, it created a new discipline and started a tumultuous round in the age-old nature versus nurture debate. Although voted by officers and fellows of the international Animal Behavior Society the most important book on animal behavior of all time, *Sociobiology* is probably more widely known as the object of bitter attacks by social scientists and other

other co-author of this book (Dr. Emener) was first trained as a rehabilitation counselor and then as a counseling psychologist; throughout his formal training and during his 40+ years as a rehabilitation professional and licensed psychologist, he also witnessed Dr. Lambos' aforementioned observations.

What is most disappointing about this state of affairs is that the two areas of behavioral psychology and behavior genetics have an astonishing amount to offer to the study of loving relationships. For example, sociobiological studies of the consequences of the differences in biological investment in reproduction by males versus females (of virtually every species) provide illuminating explanations of the differences in male and female sexual behavior – including human behavior. Basically, in all but a very few primitive species, females invest much more in the process of sexual reproduction than do males. This means that males must compete with each other for access to scarcer viable females. Thus, males of almost all species are, stereotypically, larger and more aggressive than females – they are often "fighting for the girl." Males also have more to gain from a strategy of multiple reproductive acts with many females, which is why females often choose to mate only with the males who are most willing to fight (and wait) for them. Females, on the other hand, can reproduce much less frequently due to longer gestation periods, a limited supply of eggs, and the necessity to feed and defend for themselves *and* their offspring while carrying their developing offspring. In short, females are looking for and are willing to "hold out for," males "willing to commit" that have resources to offer them and their future offspring (homes, food, and in the case of most humans, money). Males spend much of their time competing with other males for such resources, so they can attract the most desirable females. Such analogies can be deeply compelling and enlightening – especially when studying the nature of adult loving relationships.

Many students in clinical training, nonetheless, find such explanations abhorrent and mechanistic. Such individuals say behavioral and ethological theories fail to recognize what is "special" about human beings – for example our rational and logical abilities, the human compassion we so often display toward others in need, and in some cases, our being in possession of a soul and having a relationship to transcendental and spiritual matters that we do not share with animals.

The student reading this text must decide some of these matters for him- or herself. Philosophically as well as pedagogically, your authors take a rather pragmatic approach to the entire matter, choosing to see what every theoretical perspective has to offer and leaving the choice of fitness to the reader. Despite the rancor that has come to characterize this area, for those with an eclectic and inclusive orientation such as the authors of this textbook, the sweetest victories are often those in which the adversary has lost the battle without knowing it! Recall that at the beginning of this section, we stated that we would assume "for the moment" that explanations based on behavioral and ethological approaches have had little impact on the current practice of clinical psychology and mental health counseling. Now we can re-examine even that assumption and show it to be false. For while the labels for theories of counseling may have changed, their underlying assumptions have remained much the same, and those are the same assumptions proffered by behavioral psychology, behavior genetics and neuroscience.

---

scholars who opposed its claim that human social behavior, indeed human nature, has a biological foundation. The controversy surrounding the publication of the book reverberates to the present day."

EXISTENTIAL AND HUMANISTIC APPROACHES

In stark contrast to both psychodynamic and behavioral/ethological theories of personality and counseling, the Existential school and its offspring, Humanistic Psychology, explicitly reject the assumptions of their predecessors as unacceptably negative and overly mechanistic and/or deterministic (Aanstoos, Serlin & Greening, 2000). Like many theories of personality, Existentialism's roots lay in philosophy, in particular the works of Søren Kierkegaard, Jean-Paul Sartre, Friedrich Nietzsche and Martin Heidegger. These thinkers posited that individuals create the meaning and essence of their lives, as opposed to relying upon deities or authorities, or having it defined for them by philosophical or theological doctrines. In the 20th century, the Nazi concentration camp survivor and psychologist Viktor Frankl (1946, 1984) wrote a seminal book on Existential Psychology called *Man's Search for Meaning*, and went on to found a new approach to psychotherapy based on it, called "Logotherapy."

Shortly thereafter, starting in the late 1940s, three other figures adopted and extended the assumptions of the Existential approach and went on to form the school of Humanistic Psychology. These three, whose names should be familiar to every student of psychology regardless of their background or theoretical orientation, remain influential and their works are required reading for every introductory course in Personality or Counseling Psychology. They are Abraham Maslow (1943, 1954, 1970), Carl Rogers (1951, 1961) and Rollo May (1953, 1992).

Aside from the rejection of determinism, what makes the Humanistic Approach unique and distinguishes it from other approaches within psychology are (1) its emphasis on *subjective meaning*, as well as (2) a shift in emphasis for *positive growth and the maintenance of well-being* (dare we say "wellness?") rather than focusing on pathology (in this sense, the Humanistic school anticipates and predates more recent approaches of Positivistic Psychology advanced by Martin Seligman (2006) and Albert Bandura (1997). Whereas most psychologists posit that behavior can be understood only objectively, say by an impartial observer, the humanists argue that this requires the belief that individuals are incapable of understanding their own behavior, a point of view they explicitly reject. Instead, humanists such as Rogers (1951, 1961) insist that the meaning of behavior is essentially personal and subjective in nature. In responding to critics who have complained that this approach is inherently unscientific, the humanists further contend that this argument amounts to a straw man, because ultimately, all individuals are subjective; to Rogers, what makes science reliable is not that scientists are purely objective (they aren't), but that the nature of observed events can be agreed upon by different observers, or what Rogers called "intersubjective verification."

Humanistic psychology, with its emphasis on subjectivity and perception as more important than objective reality, lends itself well to couples counseling. As any therapist who spends time in the therapy room with a couple quickly learns, perception (of the situation, of one's significant other and/or of the relationship itself) readily trumps all else. As Dr. Emener is fond of paraphrasing Vince Lombardi when teaching the students enrolled in his couples counseling course, "Perception isn't everything, it's the only thing."

GESTALT AND PHENOMENOLOGICAL THEORIES

The term "Gestalt" (German for "whole" or "pattern") is used in two very different senses in modern psychology, and the student of the Gestalt School of Therapy needs to understand the difference. The first of these, referred to as "Gestalt Psychology," refers to theories of the mind and brain that propose that the brain's underlying operational principle is holistic, parallel and analog, with self-organizing tendencies; or, that the whole is different than the sum of its parts (Sternberg, 2003). This is a fascinating area of theories, especially for the psychologist with experimental and neuropsychological training, and although we are tempted to describe this psychophysiological approach to human behavior and cognition in detail, it would amount to an unnecessary detour and a digression that would take us too far afield of our subject matter, theories of human loving relationships.

It is the second use of the term "Gestalt" to which we refer in the title of this section, which is the subject of *Gestalt Therapy*, as advanced between 1950 and the 1970s primarily by Fritz Perls, his wife Laura Perls, and the American sociologist and activist Paul Goodman (Woldt & Toman, 2005). Fritz Perls, like Freud, was trained as a medical doctor but found medicine offered no insights to patients with psychological or mental illnesses. He was greatly influenced by Freud's writings, although he never studied with him. Perls believed that the treatment of psychic disturbances required focusing on the individual's experience in the present moment, on the therapist-client relationship, and in view of the environmental and the sociological contexts in which these things took place. He was among the earliest psychologists to pay close attention to the self-regulating adjustments people make as a result of their overall situation. Gestalt therapy also emphasizes personal responsibility (Levitsky & Simkin, 1972).

Gestalt Therapy, as developed by Perls and his followers, is based on the "Phenomenological Method." For this reason, this and similar approaches are sometimes categorized as "Phenomenological Approaches" to counseling and therapy. According to Perls and his followers, the goal of a phenomenological exploration is awareness – of both self and context – which works systematically to reduce the effects of bias through repeated observations and inquiry. The phenomenological method comprises a series of steps that begin with the therapist setting aside his or her initial biases and prejudices in order to suspend expectations and assumptions. During the second stage (sometimes referred to as "the rule of description"), the therapist occupies him- or herself with the process of describing, instead of trying to explain the client's issues, feelings and/or behavior. In the final stage, the so-called "rule of horizontalization" is applied, in which the therapist seeks to treat each item of description as having equal value or significance. Thus, a Gestalt therapist utilizing the phenomenological method might find him- or herself typically saying something like, "You are saying you are happy in your marriage but I notice you are tapping your foot and shifting your position on the couch whenever you say this. Perhaps you are not being honest with yourself about your marriage – maybe you're even being totally phony about it." Clients first experiencing Gestalt Therapy may, due to this type of approach, find the therapist inappropriate, unsupportive and/or outright rude. The therapist trained in Gestalt Therapy will defend the approach by claiming that he or she, when applying the phenomenological method, is merely seeking to re-establish coherence between the subject's overt behaviors and their underlying perceptions of them, which may be unconscious or hidden from the client's own understanding. Therapeutic advances are achieved when this coherence is restored and when the client can therefore be said to have attained greater *authenticity*. Levitsky and Simkin (1972) summed up the process as follows:

> If we were to choose one key idea to stand as a symbol for the Gestalt approach, it might well be the concept of authenticity, the quest for authenticity...If we regard therapy and the therapist in the pitiless light of authenticity, it becomes apparent that the therapist cannot teach what he does not know...A therapist with some experience really knows within himself that he is communicating to his patient his [the therapist's] own fears as well as his courage, his defensiveness as well as his openness, his confusion as well as his clarity. The therapist's awareness, acceptance, and sharing of these truths can be a highly persuasive demonstration of his own authenticity. Obviously such a position is not acquired overnight. It is to be learned and relearned ever more deeply not only throughout one's career but throughout one's entire life. (pp. 251-252)

Gestalt therapy remains attractive to some clients and couples, especially those who believe that the only healthy relationships are those based on total honesty. Although not as commonly used as systems-based or cognitive behavioral approaches today, it remains an active and vibrant school of counseling with much to be said in its favor. For a couple with little or no tolerance for euphemism or ambiguity (i.e., "B.S.") in fixing their relationship, it remains an attractive approach.

TRANSACTIONAL AND INTERPERSONAL MODELS

Transactional Analysis, commonly known as "TA," is an integrative approach to the theory of psychology and psychotherapy. It contains elements of psychoanalytic, humanist and cognitive approaches, and was first developed by the Canadian-born U.S. psychiatrist Eric Berne (1964) during the late 1950s. Developed for the mass audience of "Pop Psychology" consumers of self-help books, where it has had much popular appeal, it remains a serious approach to understanding human relationships. The seminal work in TA is Berne's 1964 best-selling book, *Games People Play*.

TA is based on three "ego states" – the Parent, the Child and the Adult – as well as on the interactions among individuals ("transactions") occupying any of these states at a given time. Thus the theory, according to Berne, is not only "post-Freudian" but "extra-Freudian" in that it deliberately abandons interactions among an individual's psychic components (id, ego and superego) in favor of individuals' interactions (in the three ego states) with one another via transactions. Given that Berne was trained as a psychodynamic therapist, this is not a surprising evolutionary path for his theory.

The Parent state is the state of providing guidance and protection, as well as discipline and authority; it is concerned with controlling behavior and shaping others. Because sometimes the rules we learn from our parents are dysfunctional and can be generationally transmitted, it can become systemic in a multi-generational manner. The Child state – characterized by the feeling self – is the repository of all our feelings. Exploratory in nature, this ego state usually interacts with the Parent state, which serves to suppress or quell this exploration when things go badly, or when negative feelings are stored and may become irrational beliefs about the self, the world and/or others. The Adult state – whose role is similar to a corporate executive – is the decision-making state, akin to the "responsible person" in the situation, one perhaps less amusing who balances the messages and communication between the other two states. The Adult processes the feelings stored by the Child state and makes decisions as to their appropriateness for the current situation.

Having described Berne's three ego states, we can now look at the interpersonal transactions between individuals who may be occupying any one of these ego states at a given time. Transactions are said to be complimentary, crossed or ulterior in nature. *Complimentary transactions* occur between individuals when their behavior and messages are appropriate for the roles of the situation. Thus complimentary transactions refer to appropriate communication between ego states, e.g., Adult-to-Adult between spouses or Parent-to-Child between a mother and daughter. *Crossed transactions* are dysfunctional in that they do not correspond to the appropriate roles expected of each person. *Ulterior transactions* operate when people "play games" and hide communications within other communications; this includes sex-related behavior and sales manipulation.

TA is easily understood by clients and can be a powerful tool for demonstrating many types of common interactions between couples in a counseling session that may either be complementary, crossed or ulterior in nature. Moreover, transactional roles may be summarized as "I'm OK – You're OK" through "I'm not OK – You're not OK". The first one is healthy, whereas the rest are typical of domineering relationships, co-dependency or many of the relationship problems we shall describe later in this book.

TA remains an attractive modality for couples and marriage counseling. It is easy to grasp, and yet presents a powerful approach to understanding the ways in which members of a couple interact, both for better and for worse. It is also worth noting that many therapists who would label themselves as practicing "cognitive behavioral" or "family systems" therapies, also incorporate a good deal of Berne's techniques and assumptions into their toolkits, and in our opinion it remains a powerful and viable model for relationship analysis.

COGNITIVE-BEHAVIORAL THEORIES

Cognitive-Behavioral Therapy, or "CBT" as it is known, is currently the most widely practiced and generally accepted approach to both individual and group counseling in use today. CBT defines the practice standard for virtually all the affective disorders, works well with children as young as seven-years old and, combined with pharmacotherapy, is believed to define the most effective treatment for the largest subset of psychological diagnoses. As of this writing, the American Psychological Association reports that between 70% and 80% of therapists identify themselves as practitioners of one or another type of CBT (2007). This is hardly surprising, as most HMOs and other group health plans will not reimburse or pay for sessions unless they are described as meeting the criteria for CBT.

Although most textbooks attribute the origin of cognitive behavioral therapy to Aaron Beck (1976), it was in fact first practiced and taught by Albert Ellis starting in the 1950s under the name "Rational-Emotive Therapy" (Ellis, 1996). Beck was a student of Dr. Ellis, and Ellis claimed until the time of his death in 2007 that Beck had failed to cite his primacy and later contributions to CBT (it was Beck who coined the term "Cognitive-Behavioral

Therapy" and was ultimately credited with its inception). One of your authors (Dr. Lambos) studied under Dr. Ellis during his post-doctoral training and recalls Ellis's frustrations regarding the matter quite well. Regardless of the facts and realities, however, both of these therapist investigators made enormous contributions to the evolution of effective techniques of psychotherapy. Another advantage of their techniques is that they tend to achieve favorable results in terms of improvement in client symptomatology in fewer sessions than other therapeutic modalities.

Regardless of whether one uses the language of Beck, Ellis or others who claim to have defined the CBT model, the basic ideas remain the same. They may be summarized in the following points:

1) The most proximal cause of our feelings and actions is our system of *beliefs* or *cognitions* about the world. If we experience anger or depression, it is not that the world has mistreated us, but that we harbor irrational or illogical beliefs about the world. These beliefs or cognitions, and not the events that happen to us, are the true cause of psychological disturbance.
2) Beliefs and cognitions can take two forms: (1) rational and/or logical; and (2) irrational and/or illogical. The latter lead to undesirable feelings and behaviors, whereas the former do not lead to disturbance and problems.
3) Therapy involves identifying our irrational or illogical beliefs/cognitions, flagging them as such, and learning to *reframe* them so they become more logical and reality-based. Thus therapy is primarily psychoeducational and concerned with changing beliefs and cognitions. The past may explain where the illogical cognitions came from, but is of little help in correcting them. Therefore, therapy teaches clients to live in the present and constantly to examine the rationality of their beliefs.

The CBT model has also been the basis of the largest body of scientific research on the effectiveness of counseling and therapy, and research study after study supports the effectiveness of this approach to self-change and relief from mental suffering. Of course, it requires that a person be able to distinguish reality from perception, so it is not particularly well suited for severely disturbed individuals who are displaying floridly psychotic symptoms. But none of these therapies can make that claim. Such serious problems are the province not of the mental health counselor or even the clinical psychologist, but of the neuropsychologists and psychiatrists who specialize in neuropsychiatric disorders.

MAKING SENSE OF IT ALL: "THE MAGIC NUMBER THREE"

Two more subjects require our attention before we can conclude this chapter. The first is that students and/or faculty of Marriage and Family Therapy programs may complain that the preceding list ignores what are called "Systems Theories" of family counseling. These were described briefly in Chapter 1, and we shall indeed return to them later in this book. They did not receive their own section in the above list, because historically, they have played a major role in *family counseling* situations, which include individuals other than the couple. This book's focus is not the family, however, but on the couple, or *dyad,* which may exist as an isolated unit in a two-person household, may live in separate homes, or may be just one aspect of a larger family system that includes children and perhaps extended family. System-based approaches to counseling have many of their own excellent books available for the interested student or practitioner. We have repeatedly found, unfortunately, that they do not serve well as textbooks for those who wish to learn how to effectively work with *couples*. Since efficiently and effectively working with couples is the subject of *this* book, your authors feel that a book specializing on the dyad is long overdue.

The second subject we wish to address before closing the chapter is, we believe, a more interesting one. Given the seemingly vast differences between the six groups of theories described in this chapter, we expect our reader may be wondering how one is to reconcile them. Are they all *just* theories? If not, which one is the *correct* theory? If they all contain some amount of truth or even only a useful perspective, then how does one choose among them?

We, your daring authors, are going to be so bold as to offer something typically unheard of in a graduate level textbook: *an original idea!* As such, it is best to look at what follows as a working hypothesis, or a theoretical perspective of its own, rather than a statement of fact. We offer no empirical research to support our idea.

Here it is: What do all the six preceding theories have in common not only with one another, but with our current understanding of the brain at the highest level, as described in Chapter 1? The answer is:

> Every one of the six groups of theories, as well as our best overall view of the brain as a neural pattern-matching network driven to accomplishing a set of goals, all seem to have *three key components*.

For the brain, they are the three *neurofunctional areas:* (1) brainstem/limbic system (for arousal and motivation); (2) the posterior subcortex and cortex (the back-half of the brain) for parsing the world and identifying objects; and (3) the anterior portion of the brain (consisting of the basal ganglia, the median forebrain bundle and, the pre-frontal cortex) for executive functions and decision making. We have already described, how, for psychodynamic theories, these areas seem to overlap to an almost eerie degree with the id, ego and superego, respectively. Moving on to behavioral theories, they are also organized around *threesomes*: for Pavlovian approaches, they are the conditioned stimulus, the unconditioned stimulus and the response; for operant approaches, the three essential components are the signaling stimulus, the behavior and the consequence; and for ethological theories, we have the gene, the environment and the behavior resulting from their interaction.

This analogy continues: in TA, three ego states (Parent, Child and Adult), and three types of transaction (complimentary, crossed and ulterior) characterize the theory. In Gestalt therapy, we have three stages of therapy or "rules:" the rule of epoché, the rule of description and the rule of horizontalization (Spinelli, 2005). For Humanistic approaches, these correspond equally well to the *subjective*, the *objective* and the *outcome* (positive growth). Finally, in CBT, the overlap between any of these three ideas with Ellis's A-B-C model or Beck's "event-cognition-conclusion" description is too obvious to deny. We posit here that every one of these theories is organized around three distinct variables *because they correspond to the three basic elements of both neural and human reality: drive, identification and goal-appropriate action*. If nothing else, this schema will serve as a powerful organizational tool for classifying and remembering both the brain and the mind. We believe that so many coincidences cannot be the result of chance factors alone. What do you think?

THEORIES OF COUNSELING – A MULTI-DIMENSIONAL APPROACH

There is another dimension over which we should seek to evaluate the differences in these theories: *effectiveness*. The theories may all be based on three underlying components, but this is a far cry from asserting that they are equally effective in mitigating suffering or achieving change in clients. In order to compare the theories on a more pragmatic scale, it helps to concentrate on *differences among the theories* rather than their commonalities. To help organize the theories with respect to their relative effectiveness, we developed Figure 2.1. It is based on a system of organizing the various theories according to two other dimensions: (1) the degree to which the theory relies more on insight versus action in its orientation; and (2) the degree to which it posits that rational versus affective processes underlie basic motivation. In general, current evidence points to a "slope of efficacy" that is highest in the bottom left corner of Figure 2.1 and lowest in the upper right-hand corner. Thus techniques based on the cognitive behavioral approach are the most widely accepted and most widely used in real counseling situations, because the research data we have says that they work the best. To relieve mental suffering and decrease emotional turmoil, science today says, somewhat opposite to what might be expected based on "common sense," that our therapeutic interventions work best when they address *cognitions and behaviors* rather than *insights and emotions*.

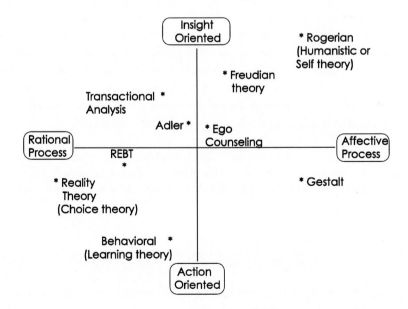

Figure 2.1. A Two Dimensional Organization of Counseling Theories.[*]

---

[*] The authors extend their appreciation to Dr. Theo Carroll at the University of South Florida for the original concept behind this Figure.

This organizational scheme captures many of the core relationships among counseling theories in an easy to categorize way. It also overlaps with our approach to functional areas of the brain. For example, those theories that emphasize the Rational Process over the Affective Process proffer that humans are more strongly dominated by the activity of the prefrontal cortex than by that of the limbic system.

Regardless of which theory the student of couples counseling finds most appealing, we hope that it remains evident that each approach captures something relevant and true – not only about why people are the way they are and do what they do – but also how best to help them change unwanted aspects of their self-perceptions, emotions and/or behaviors. We invite the student to use this model as a guide to understanding many of the topics related to couples counseling that we will be examining throughout this book.

One additional thing needs to be mentioned in any discourse on theoretical approaches to counseling, or to any area of the human experience. At the same time that the properly trained therapist is able to draw upon each of these theories (as they might be useful in a given circumstance), the effective counselor never allows any theoretical approach to come between his or her clients' problems and the solutions that will help resolve them. Theories are meant to be useful sets of organizing principles that work best when they lead to pragmatic outcomes. If a therapist's theoretical orientation stands between a client and his or her improvement, it is worse than useless in that context.

CHAPTER SUMMARY

Following a discussion of the importance of having a theoretical model and rationale for working with couples as a professional counselor, six broad, pertinent categories of theories of counseling were presented and discussed: (1) psychodynamic; (2) behavioral/ethological; (3) existential and humanistic; (4) gestalt and phenomenological; (5) interpersonal and transactional; and (6) cognitive-behavioral. Importantly, it is hoped that the reader not only understands each of the theoretical approaches but also appreciates how they can be utilized effectively and efficiently – prior to as well as during your counseling sessions. As Dr. Emener vividly recalls saying to a pilot as he was boarding an airplane:

> I'm not all that concerned about your ability to explain to me, two hours from now, what you did and how you got us safely back on the ground; I'm more concerned about the extent to which you can explain what you're going to do before we take off and while we are flying – at 40,000 feet.

CHAPTER 2 DISCUSSION QUESTIONS

Considering the six theoretical approaches to counseling discussed in this chapter (1) psychodynamic; (2) behavioral/ethological; (3) existential and humanistic; (4) gestalt and phenomenological; (5) interpersonal and transactional; and (6) cognitive/behavioral:

1) Why is it important for a counselor to have a theoretical approach to working with individual clients and couples?

2) In your opinion, what are some of the pros and cons of these six approaches?

3) What are some of the important aspects of your own theoretical approach to individual counseling and couples counseling?

4) To what extent is each of these six approaches an integral part of your own theory of counseling?

5) What are some aspects of you own background and/or personal beliefs that have a meaningful impact on you theory of individual and couples counseling?

LOVE, LOVING AND ROMANCE

Your authors lament that most books on the subject of *love* do not even attempt to define what it is their books are about. It has become more the standard of writing, and quite customary, to skip the definitions altogether, assume the reader knows what the author means ahead of time and launch into what is supposed to be an erudite discussion of the complexities of the subject matter. And why not – who needs definitions when we have television, the Internet and YouTube to synchronize our understanding of what everything means? (In case you missed it, this is your authors' way of being sarcastic about the new millennium approach to writing and thinking.)

Once upon a time, however – approximately when the renowned philosopher and mathematician Bertrand Russell was at the height of an extraordinary career that, according to some experts of intellectual history shaped nearly every aspect of our modern understanding of the world (circa 1913) – things were different. Scholars wouldn't dream of writing about a subject without first discussing its proper definition by "genus" and "species" (for example: a *skyscraper* [term to be defined] is a *building* [genus] characterized by *a height of at least 20 stories* [species]). To launch into a discussion of a topic without first defining it was just not done! It was a simple fact that people could not be expected to understand the subtleties of an important concept without first having the author explain what was meant by the very term under discussion. (Those seeking proof of this need only ask to see a copy of Dr. Lambos's first draft of his doctoral dissertation, a 240-page document that was returned by his Committee Advisor, unread, with a single note on the first page in bright red ink: "Why not start by telling the reader what the hell this mess is about exactly?")

Thankfully, such an approach to thinking and writing is still with us today, albeit as the exception rather than the rule for today's books – even graduate level textbooks. But you, dear reader, have the good fortune of having been assigned or chosen to read a book authored by two scholars whose students consider us among the ancients: wise beyond measure (or at least major pains in the rear) and uncorrupted by such losses of modern standards of discourse and teaching. We therefore begin this chapter by asking the single most important question a book on the subject of love can ask: *what is it?*

WHAT IS LOVE?

Long before the eminent William Shakespeare asked the same question – "What is Love?" – no one has succeeded in defining the term well. As of the date of this writing, Wikipedia offers: "Love [term to be defined] is any of a number of emotions and experiences [genus] related to a sense of strong affection [species]" (downloaded from http://en.wikipedia.org/wiki/Love on October 23, 2008). This may seem like a reasonable definition at first, but imagine trying to explain love using this definition to our hypothetical (and, recalling from Chapter 1, impossibly existing) *Mr. Data* on "Star Trek: The Next Generation." Would this definition convey *any* meaning to a person who had experienced neither human emotions nor affection? Of course not! It is, in fact, a completely circular definition, a tautology, defining love in terms of strong affection. Clearly, this is not helping us advance our cause to be succinct and logical in our definition of *love*.

Having struck out with the "definition by genus and species" approach, how else might we still achieve our objective of defining love before launching into an entire book on the subject? At this point, we return to our book's title for a suggestion: *Neuroscientific and Cognitive Aspects of Human Love*. Perhaps if we can describe what happens in both the brain and the mind when a person experiences love, we can get an independent idea of what the subject of this book is about. In fact, if we add some evolutionary biology to the mix to attempt to see how and why love might have evolved, and throw in a smattering of other findings from modern science and philosophy on the subject, we might just achieve our goal of defining it. Having done so, hopefully to everyone's satisfaction, we can then confidently proceed with the rest of the book (and without fear of having our publisher return the first draft to us in the same condition as the first draft of Dr. Lambos's doctoral thesis).

So, we ask the question again: *What is Love?* If you can hold out and be patient for just another page or two, we assure you will have the beginnings of an answer (although we do not guarantee you will like it). But before doing so, we very much want to qualify what we are attempting to do and, just as importantly, talk about the limitations of our approach.

This book is about the *science* of human love, and we promise to do a thorough and illuminating job discussing it. But to many people, wise and important as well as ordinary and work-a-day, love encompasses much more than any scientific treatment of it could offer. Having taught many courses over the years on love, marriage and family psychology, Dr. Emener and Dr. Lambos often have asked their students, both young and old, many newly graduated with their bachelor's degree and some who held doctorates in other subjects, what the term *love* meant to them. The following list of answers is just a small sample of the answers we have received. We want you to understand that while these suggestions from our students may not help us establish a scientific understanding of the subject, we consider every one an equally good answer from a different set of perspectives, and from a phenomenological perspective we would not disagree with any of the definitions on the following list:

- Love is caring more about another person than you care about yourself.
- Love is what you experience when someone else makes you feel incredibly *special*.
- Love is what makes getting out of bed in the morning possible.
- Love is the only thing that gives meaning to an otherwise meaningless existence.

- Love is God.
- Love is the best drug anybody ever came up with.
- Love is a brand new Lamborghini Countach.
- Love is misery and anguish, the source of a pain no torturer could ever equal.
- Love is the sweetest illusion (borrowed, we suspect, from the musical artist *Basia).*
- Love is the force that binds two individual people into a single being, with the synergy that makes the total greater than the sum of the parts.

One definition we will *not* abide by, however, is the definition offered by the book and movie *Love Story.* This wholly unoriginal tripe, actually written on a bet by a Harvard professor that all anybody would have to do to create a best selling romance novel would be to modernize Shakespeare's *Romeo and Juliet* (he obviously won the bet), offers what is unquestionably, in our humble opinion, the worst definition of Love ever offered: "Being in Love means never having to say you're sorry." Personally, your authors will go with the Lamborghini.

Figure 3.1. A 2008 Lamborghini Countach.

WHY WE LOVE: ANALYSES OF LOVE IN THREE DOMAINS

In Chapter 2, we concluded our look at theories of counseling by positing that all the theories seemed to hypothesize three important parts of the psyche that reflected, to a greater or lesser degree, the three primary neurofunctional areas of the human brain: (1) the "emotion and arousal center" (roughly comprised of the brainstem, ventral tegmental area and the limbic system); (2) "world parser and memory store" (consisting of the occipital, temporal and parietal lobes); and (3) the "executive brain" (the orbitofrontal and dorsolateral areas of the pre-frontal cortex).

Although this idea is at least somewhat original, and to us quite exciting, we suspect that our readers may have been asking "What in the world does that have to do with love?" Here we boldly venture onward to offer yet another example of the "magic number three" that follows the same pattern.

The question "Why We Love?" has been asked and quite possibly answered from a scientific perspective, by the Rutgers University anthropologist Helen Fisher (2004) in her eponymous book, *Why We Love: The Nature and Chemistry of Romantic Love*:

> Romantic love, I believe, is one of the three primordial brain networks that evolved to direct mating and reproduction. *Lust*, the craving for sexual gratification, emerged to motivate our ancestors to seek sexual union with almost any partner. *Romantic love*, the elation and obsession of "being in love," enabled them to focus their courtship on a single individual at a time, thereby conserving precious mating time and energy. And male-female *attachment*, the feeling of calm, peace and security one often has for a long term mate, evolved to motivate our ancestors to love this partner long enough to rear their young together.
>
> In short, romantic love is deeply embedded in the architecture and chemistry of the human brain. (2004, p. xiv, italics hers.)

In addition to collecting and examining an enormous body of cross-cultural evidence to validate her hypotheses about the evolutionary origins of human love, Dr. Fisher went a step further than most anthropologists – she observed the brain activity of individuals who had just fallen wildly in love using functional neuroimaging (in particular, fMRI imaging) while they thought either about their lover or about something else. Shortly we will see what her evidence revealed.

We expect by now you may be noticing two additional and very interesting aspects about Dr. Fisher's research: First, her three types of love surprisingly correspond with the three types of love espoused by the ancient Greeks and described in Chapter 1. *Eros* corresponds well with lust, *agape* is identical to what she calls romantic love, and *philio* is closely analogous to attachment.

Second and more importantly, the "primordial brain networks" to which Dr. Fisher referred seem to overlap with the three neurofunctional areas discussed in Chapter 2 and summarized above. From one perspective, all three of Fisher's types of love require interaction among the three neurofunctional areas – emotion and arousal, identification and memory, and judgment/goal orientation – are necessary to engage in lust, romantic love and attachment. But more to the point, the contribution of each area of the brain is not equal across these three types of love. For example, lust – erotic attraction and the associated drive for sexual contact – involves the hypothalamus, which is itself under the control of the limbic system. Lust can be said to be most associated with the arousal and emotional areas of the evolutionarily oldest a part of the brain. Romantic love involves two brain areas, both central to the operation of the pre-frontal cortex. Being "in love" and the accompanying feelings of obsession and soaring inner fulfillment is, to a far greater degree than other types of love, very much under the control of the frontal lobes (with some major help from the reward center, or *nucleus accumbens*, as we shall see in more detail in Chapter 4). Finally, attachment involves the comfort of stable pattern recognition and long term memories that are mediated by the world parser at the posterior of the brain. The brain centers that "light up" in this phase of love are located in the temporal and parietal lobes.

Thus, our "magic number three," when we understand its reference to being either the three types of love or the three neurofunctional areas, remains very much at the center of our understanding love, as well as broader aspects of human psychology). We hope a pattern is emerging for our readers at this point: Although modern science often forces us to discard certain old notions of the world (the Earth is not, after all, flat), it also confirms other notions as very likely having been "spot on," as the British might say. Just as the ancient Greeks recognized three types of love, and early psychologists devised their theories of mind around three central concepts, they did so because they detected deep underlying truths about the nature of things by simple observation and further analyses. Science confirmed what they figured out, and related it to other important aspects of being human (i.e., evolutionary forces and biological substrates), but they managed to figure these things out in complete ignorance of evolution or neurophysiology. The message here is that the human brain and its partner – the mind – are very powerful tools that recognize and characterize patterns by their very nature. High tech measurement instruments and methods (such as computers and neuroimaging machines), as well as advanced mathematics and the logic of the scientific method, really help us confirm hypotheses we already have more than they act to create new knowledge. (This is a central message of this book and we will return to this theme again in subsequent chapters.)

In any case, Dr. Fisher's book could be considered required reading for any person who seeks to understand how complex human behaviors and emotions can be shown to have evolved and selected without the need to refer to supernatural or transcendental sources. As stated previously, although we expect some readers to find such explanations personally unsatisfying, they do permit one to understand the depth and complexity of human love from a simple set of underlying principles. Again, to quote Helen Fisher (2004):

> The results [of imaging the brains of people in love] were startling. We found gender differences that may help explain why men respond to visual stimuli and why women can remember details of the relationship. We discovered ways in which the brain in love changes over time. We established some of the brain regions that become active when you feel romantic ecstasy, information that suggests new ways to sustain romance in long-term partnerships. I came to believe that animals feel a form of romantic attraction for one another. Our findings shed new light on stalking behavior and other crimes of passion. And I now understand more about why we feel so depressed and angry when we are rejected, and even some ways to stimulate the brain to soothe the anguish.
>
> Most important, our results changed my thinking about the very essence of romantic love. I came to see this passion as a fundamental human drive. Like the craving for food and water and the maternal instinct, it is a physiological *need,* a profound urge, an instinct to court and win a particular mating partner. (p.xv)

This portion of her introduction, nonetheless, leaves out something terribly important about love: the *felt* experience, the *urgency* of passion, the *inability* to describe in words alone, what it *means to experience* love. Can such feelings, motivations and passions actually be reduced to evolutionary selection or the way our brain is wired? Surely this cannot be our reality!

Fortunately, neither Dr. Fisher nor your authors believe it can. We are not transcendentalists, but explanations of love based on evolutionary biology, neural circuits and hormonal influences cannot account for perceived experience. *The brain does not explain the mind!* Your authors have examined, in nearly obsessive detail and with our minds open to every possibility, the neurology, psychology, philosophy and (especially) the physics applicable to this issue. Whether one chooses to rely on the mind-body problem as espoused by René Descartes (Lakoff & Johnson, 1999), recursive systems theory as explained by Douglass Hoffsteader (2007), the explanations of consciousness offered by philosophers such as John Searle (2004), the Heisenberg Uncertainty Principle of quantum physics as recently elaborated on by David Lindley (2007), the existence of zero point energy as explained by Lynn McTaggert (2003), or neuroscientist Beauregard and O'Leary's (2007) treatment of the spiritual brain, the weight of evidence is overwhelming: *material determinism cannot account for mental phenomena.* Moreover, as Jeffery Schwartz so eloquently argues in his treatise *The Mind and The Brain* (2002), *it is more likely that mental forces determine neural events than the reverse!*

Helen Fisher (2004) saw this as well. She concluded her introduction to *Why We Love* with:

> This drive to fall in love has produced humankind's most compelling operas, plays, and novels, our most touching poems and haunting melodies, the world's finest sculptures and paintings, and our most colorful festivals, myths, and legends. Romantic love has adorned the world and brought many of us tremendous joy. But when love is scorned, it can cause excruciating sorrow. Stalking, homicide, suicide, profound depression from romantic rejection and high divorce and adultery rates are prevalent in societies around the world. It's time to seriously consider Shakespeare's question: "What is love?" (p. xiii)

WHOM DO WE LOVE?

We conclude this chapter with what we believe is the next logical question following our "definition" of love as explained in the preceding section: If, as Dr. Fisher's studies suggest, we evolved the capacity to experience the three kinds of love in order to facilitate mating and the survival of our offspring, then *why do some potential partners appeal to us so much more than others*? After all, we don't fall in love with just anybody. In fact, some individuals will stay single for years or even a lifetime, if they don't meet the "right" person. If love boils down to finding a good mating partner, a female capable of delivering strong, healthy children, or a male capable of protecting and providing for the brood (in evolutionary terms), then how do we know when we have found a good candidate for this "right" person?

This is not a trivial question. There are, after all, "a lot of fish in the sea." Fortunately, a diverse and rapidly growing body of research exists to shed light on this question (or, perhaps as the discussion about science and mind in the previous section suggests, to help us choose which of our existing intuitions are more likely accurate, and in which circumstances they best apply).

There seem to be five major categorical bases for both attraction and mate selection (although these two do not always overlap, as we shall see). They are:

1) Scent, smell and taste (as determined from kissing).
2) Body proportions and symmetry (especially facial).
3) Voice tone.

4) Movement style and/or gait.
5) Similarity to oneself, both genetic and cultural.

We have found, when presenting this list to our couples counseling students, two very different and yet equally likely types of reactions. The first is: "Exactly! If someone doesn't smell good to me, I just can't be with them." Or "Man, the way she walks makes me NUTS!" Or, the ever popular "Men just want to marry their mother. Ugh!" And yet for other individuals, at first read the list seems *patently absurd*. Many of our students have expressed sentiments such as: "I care about this other person's inner qualities, not their physical characteristics!" Or perhaps "That can't be right…I just *love* foreign men!" Or, as one young fellow once told Dr. Lambos "I can fall in love with a girl from a rich family just as easily as I can with one who's broke. Rich is better."

So, what does the research tell us? The answer is, of course, both. *Initial* attraction seems to depend on the five categories in the list. Scientists are still conducting research to determine not only why these factors result in attraction but also to discover what particular parameters of these characteristics matter most. For example, only a few reasons are known about why a given person finds one scent attractive and another intolerable. Although virtually all non-human animals release and respond to powerful scents called *pheromones*, the human pheromone system is far subtler than that of our evolutionary ancestors and has proved very difficult to unravel. It appears to be related not only to an individual's characteristic scent, but also (at least in females) to the timing of the ovulation cycle (Haselton & Gangstad, 2006). Other research on scent and taste points to olfactory cues that may be related to how compatible two individuals' immune systems are, and therefore the likelihood that their offspring will be capable of fighting infection (Thornhill, et al., 2003). Although the research on the other factors listed above are better established, much remains to be learned about how and why these determine who makes us swoon and who makes us want to run the other way. Even so, they play their most important role in predicting or explaining the immediate reactions and sexual attraction people have with one another, as opposed to predicting the person with whom they actually decide to bond.

The latter issue – mate selection – is known to be more influenced by immediate family influence, cultural similarity, and indicators of social status such as education, income or wealth, and job position, even in our own open society. The fact is, people tend to marry or stay together for practical reasons more so than for emotional attraction. The previously popular television program *Dirty Sexy Money*, about the blatantly hypocritical and selfish behavior of America's wealthiest fictitious family ("The Darlings"), makes this point repeatedly to the apparent delight of viewers, who had given the show very high ratings. Marriage and partner selection are, indeed, more likely to be governed by family approval, power and wealth, whereas daily behavior and short-term liaisons, including infidelity, are driven more forcefully by sexual attraction.

And so we have embarked on our voyage to examine human love in all its grandeur and mystery. The remainder of this book will look at nearly every aspect of love as it has presented itself to us in the actual relationships of over three hundred couples. We shall see along the way that even though the "wisdom" of our first three chapters will show itself to be true over and again, there are always exceptions. Every human loving relationship is, like a snowflake, unique and without equal. The combinatorial explosion resulting from an infinite supply of unique individuals interacting in infinitely unique relationships is fascinating, sometimes staggering, to behold. At the same time, when all is said and done, snow is pretty much snow. Many patterns continually reappear, and it is these regularities on which we will focus. Ultimately, our society has evolved to a level of complexity that more and more people require – or can at least benefit from – professional help in managing their loving relationships. As a (or an aspiring) psychologist, counselor or marriage and family therapist, it is or will be your job to provide this assistance. We trust that this book will be of great help to you in doing so.

CHAPTER SUMMARY

Following a discussion of the importance of defining the central phenomenon of this book – love – the question "What is love?" is addressed. Appreciating how science would answer this question – essentially via neurology and cognitive psychology – is enhanced by a discussion of phenomenological and romantic consideration, along with our proposed conclusion: material determinism cannot account for mental phenomena. Every person's conceptualization and experience of love, who they love and why they love who they love, is individualized and unique. Thus, the challenge of assisting couples with their love and loving issues indeed is tremendously challenging – every person's answer to these questions is different and unique, and to some extent forever changing.

> *How do I love thee? Let me count the ways...*
> Elizabeth Barrett Browning

CHAPTER 3 DISCUSSION QUESTIONS

1) In your own words, what is love?
2) In the section on determinism and mental force, several approaches to the philosophical "mind-body" problem are mentioned. In your own words, what does Jeffery Schwartz mean when he says, "I*t is more likely that mental forces determine neural events than the reverse!*
3) Why do you love, or fall in love with, another person?
4) What attributes of a potential partner meaningfully contribute to your loving, or falling in love with him or her?
5) When you love, or are in love with someone else, how do you know it?
6) As a couples counselor, how will you assess the extent to which the two individuals love, or are in love with each other?

ANALYTICS: INDIVIDUAL ISSUES

The term *analysis* refers to one of two types of logical thinking (the other is *synthesis*). To analyze something is to break it down into its component or constituent parts and see how those parts interact to explain or describe the topic or subject of consideration. The analytical process is by its nature more descriptive than inferential and constitutes a helpful method or approach to understanding.

In this book, where a primary subject of inquiry is the nature of human love, the topic is so complex and multi-faceted that simple analysis is insufficient to provide in-depth understanding. Moreover, the component parts are themselves complex and have subcomponents and subsystems that must, in turn, be analyzed separately. A goal of this book is to unravel these layers within layers.

This chapter approaches individual issue analysis from three different perspectives: (1) analyzing the behavioral patterns and tendencies each person brings into their loving relationship and how they impact the interactions between the individuals (behavior analysis); (2) analyzing each individual's role in a loving relationship from his or her own point of view (self-analysis); and (3) analyzing how individuals can maintain focus on themselves for their own benefit and their relationship's benefit (self-identity). As is true for most of our discussions throughout the book, the perspective of importance is that of the counselor. We have found that to work effectively with couples and help them improve or make meaningful changes in their relationships, it is often necessary to help them look at their individual issues from each of these three perspectives.

BEHAVIOR ANALYSIS

"You talk the talk, but can you walk the walk?" It is amazing how often we hear people make that statement, and it is frequently expressed with emotion. What is being communicated, essentially, is a request (or demand) for another person to substitute statements about what they will or will not do with actual behavior. "I'll believe it when I see it!" is another, more sardonic verbalization of this phenomenon. One of our clients recently said that she bought a shirt that she wears around the house on Saturday mornings when she and her husband typically do their weekly house chores. It reads in big bold letters, "**JUST DO IT!**"

In this section we will embark on the first leg of our analytical journey by examining how a counselor can help couples analyze the importance of consistent behavior, as well as how perception relates to behavior, the difference between avoidance and escape behavior, and different modalities of compensatory behavior.

Importance of consistency. It is very helpful to people in a loving relationship that their partner's behavior be reasonably consistent. Consistency in behavior refers both to what he or she does, as well as what he or she does not do. The primary reason that consistency is so important is that it is pivotal to a relationship as being *predictable*. The importance of the ability to predict the actions of others cannot be overstated. When we accurately can predict and anticipate what a person will and will not do, we tend to be less nervous, less anxious and more at ease. Simply stated, *excessive unpredictability is a stressor that damages relationships.*

When we consider the importance of consistency of behavior in relationships, we are referring to two different types of behavior: (1) actions; and (2) expressed intentions. The latter type of "behavior" is what we usually refer to as language, but it is behavior nonetheless (in fact, the famous behavioral psychologist B.F. Skinner referred to all human language as verbal behavior and wrote a book named just that, *Verbal Behavior* [1991]). Thus, it is critical to address both types of consistency: (1) that people *act* towards each other in a consistent fashion across different times and situations; and (2) that people will act as they claim they will act – they "walk the walk" as well as "talk the talk."

For example, a client recently said, "I don't necessarily like everything that Ralph does and I wish that he would actually do some things differently. Nonetheless, he is very predictable! And I have to admit to you that it is somewhat comforting for me because I can always accurately predict Ralph's behavior. I know where he is and what he is doing." On the other hand, when a person's behavior is inconsistent, there is a tendency to find oneself "walking around on eggshells." Our years of experience teaches us that there can be little question – *in loving relationships, it is comforting and much less anxiety producing when one can accurately predict what another person will do or will not do, simply because their behavior is consistent.* Many couples have been able to greatly improve their relationship by learning this.

There is yet another type of consistency: *message consistency.* As noted above, people communicate their feelings and intentions toward one another through actions and language. Message consistency refers to the ongoing degree to which behaviors (actions) and language messages (verbal statements) are consistent with one another. When action and language messages do not communicate the same thing, people become suspicious of one another and trust breaks down. In such cases of so-called mixed messages, relationships become unstable and partners feel confused or worse.

Recently, Bill Lambos counseled an attractive couple in their mid-40s whose marriage of 25 years with three children was close to ending. (She was 17 and he 19 when they married.) There were a number of reasons for their presenting problems, but halfway through their first session it became clear that they were suffering from what is sometimes called the "empty nest" syndrome: their youngest child was preparing to go off to college and the parents had very different ideas as to how their lives should proceed. This is not an uncommon situation for couples counselors to encounter, and Bill was not overly concerned until he watched the two interact as the session continued.

Sitting together on the sofa, Gary spent much of the session affectionately stroking Sherry's arm and hair. Sherry seemed to like this very much and smiled frequently with each caress. At the same time, however, they spoke of each other with disdain and without regard to the other's feelings. For example, Gary said, "Dr. Lambos, she is shallow, and dresses provocatively at best and like a whore at worst. At the gym she parades around like some kind of spandex exercise-bunny, flirting and flaunting herself at any guy there. It's embarrassing!" All the while Gary was saying this he continued to stroke her hair and look at her lovingly. Sherry responded, "Gary is like a ball and chain – I have friends, he has none. I work at my massage therapy business and make as much or more as he does, and then I come home and clean and cook before he gets home. He waltzes in, eats, doesn't help with the dishes or laundry, and promptly lies down on the couch with his only friend – the remote control – and that's it for the night until bedtime. If I ask him to come out with me and meet some friends at a local hangout, he is uninterested and won't go. But if I change into my after-work clothes and go out by myself, he tells me I dress like a slut and am probably having an affair. I really want to leave him, but I know he loves me and it's very hard to do." Meanwhile, Sherry was holding Gary's hand throughout this description of their daily interaction, gladly accepting his caresses.

This was perhaps the largest discrepancy between verbal and nonverbal behavior Bill Lambos had ever witnessed. The level of message inconsistency was hard to reconcile even for an experienced counselor. Bill expects to be seeing this couple for quite some time, and although he believes they love one another and that the marriage can be saved, their communication patterns have to be addressed before any of their other issues can.

	What I Actually Do	What I Actually Do Not Do
What I Say I Will Do	"Consistent"	"Inconsistent"
What I Say I Will Not Do	"Inconsistent"	"Consistent"

Figure 4.1. Relationships among what I "Say" and "Don't Say," and what I "Do" and "Don't Do."

Bill Emener saw a couple that struggled with a different kind of inconsistency, yet equally as troubling to a relationship. When Roberto and Marta first came to see him, they appeared to be incredibly frustrated with each other – Marta especially so. In the first session she said to him, "Roberto, you drive me crazy! You tell me that you'll do something and then you never do it. And when you tell me you're not going to do something, most of the time you wind up doing it anyway. For instance, for the last month you kept telling me that you would take me to the movies so that I could see that movie I wanted to see, yet you never did.

For the last two months, you told me that you would stop going by the pool room so often and that you would come right home instead. But there you go, Roberto, you say you're not gonna to do it but you continue do it anyway!"

As illustrated in Figure 4.1 that Bill diagramed for them during the session, it was clear what Marta was saying to Roberto – that she would prefer him to be more consistent in what he says he will or will not do and what he actually does or doesn't do.

To reiterate, issues of predictability, comfort and trust tend to be highly associated with consistency. Generally speaking, our experiences suggest six recommendations that we openly give to our couples in the form of a handout (see Figure 4.2). As Marta shouted at Roberto, "You sure can talk the talk, but someday I would like to see you walk the walk!"

---

1. Think about, and give careful consideration to, the extent to which your loved one believes you, trusts you, and is invested in you and what you say when you tell him or her what you will and will not do;
2. Be sensitive to when you say you "will do" something versus when you say you "will try to do" something;
3. Remain appreciative to the extent to which your loved one becomes emotionally invested in your commitments and statements of what you will do and what you will not do;
4. Anchor your commitments and statements with specificity. For example, if you truly plan to take someone to the movies and you know that he or she will be genuinely excited and looking forward to it, if at all possible do not say "I will take you to the movies next week," but rather "I will take you to the movies next Saturday night;"
5. Be consistent at the *micro level*. That is, do what you say you're going to do and don't do what you say you will not do. At the *macro level*, try your best to keep your behavior consistent throughout your relationship; and
6. Be conscious of the nonverbal messages you are sending, and try to ensure that your body language is consistent with your verbal messages. If you are frowning while saying "everything's fine," you are inviting confusion and doubt (and may even be accused of being deceitful or lying).

Figure 4.2. Recommendations for Being More Consistent in a Relationship.

Behavior and Perception. One principle of human behavior that is pertinent to loving relationships that our experiences have shown to be true is: People tend to behave in ways consistent with (their perception of) other people's expectations of them.

This principle became vividly clear when Bill Emener was talking with Paula. During one of their sessions, Paula was sharing that her husband, Leonard, would repeatedly say to her things such as, "I'll be back in an hour – trust me," "I won't do that anymore – trust me," and, "I'll stop by the store and get that for you someday this week – trust me." Despite his assurances, however, she continually felt the need to check up on him, remind him and pester him. She felt that she could not trust Leonard. Bill said to her, "Paula, I wonder if it is possible that he behaves in untrustworthy ways because he figures that you won't trust him anyway?" She calmly asked, "What are you trying to tell me, Dr. Emener?" "What I am suggesting to you, Paula," Bill replied, "is that maybe if you want Leonard to behave in more trustworthy ways, it would be helpful if you could begin to act toward him in more trusting kinds of ways."

Paula pondered Bill's thought and said that quite frequently when she would talk with Leonard, he would say to her, "It really doesn't matter what I do, Paula, you never trust me anyway." It was very difficult for Paula to begin to treat Leonard as if he were trustworthy.

Yet, following Bill's advice, when Paula substituted her reminders and pestering with an occasional "OK, Leonard, I trust you to do what you say," their relationship dynamic distinctly changed for the better. In a subsequent session Leonard declared, "Of course I'm being more trustworthy and responsible to Paula. I have consciously tried to change my ways. However, I also know that she is beginning to trust me and believe me, and that feels good to me. I don't want to spoil it!"

Perceptions and Difficulties. It repeatedly has been our experience that it is helpful to assist people in relationships in understanding and appreciating that when it comes to predicting and planning their behavior and its outcomes, it also is important for them *to keep their goals and expectations realistic.* For example, when a person – in a relationship or otherwise – anticipates the amount of time it will take to do something, it is important that his or her perceptions and expectations be based on some realistic considerations. Bill Emener has frequently and kiddingly referred to what his graduate students affectionately call "The Emener Formula: When I am planning to do something and I try to estimate how long it will take me to do it, I multiply my expected time by 2.75." Therefore, when people are doing things with, on behalf of, or for a loved one, it is important to temper their perceptions of setbacks with some reality. For example, a client of ours was getting very upset because he had promised his wife that he would finish painting the house by Sunday evening, and when he ran out of paint with only one wall to go, he panicked. Nonetheless, once he realized that it wasn't the end of the world and that he could pick up some more paint on his way home from work the next day, he felt much less frantic and was able to feel good about what he had accomplished. It is amazing how many times people will encounter a small setback and perceive it to be a disaster. The tendency to immediately go into a panicked frenzy over such misperceptions is what Albert Ellis (1996) referred to as "catastrophizing."

Avoidant and Escape Behavior. Larry and Pat had been married for about 10 years, and it appeared that for the majority of their marriage, especially over the last three to four years, Larry would somehow avoid any confrontational conversations with Pat. "Whenever we have something heavy or messy to discuss, Larry never seems to have time to talk about it," she once said. A very important consideration that emerged in subsequent counseling sessions was that Larry was reared in a dysfunctional family. Any form of confrontation in the family was extremely painful for him. "It seems," he said, "that now whenever I anticipate having a confrontational conversation with Pat, I simply do anything and everything to avoid it." Pat was very frustrated by this.

To help the two of them understand what Larry had *learned* from his childhood, Bill Emener drew two little figures similar to the ones in Figure 4.3 and described the difference between learned escape and learned avoidance behaviors. He told them the following: "One of the very interesting pieces of research on behavior conducted behavior conducted in the field of psychology was related to how rats could learn not to get shocked.

In Experiment A, when the rat was in the box eating some food, a light would come on and, one second later, a shock would be delivered. Immediately, the rat would run away. After some learning, at which time the rat associated the light with a shock, once the light came on the rat would run. Eventually, when the experiment was changed – by continuing to turn the light on *without the shock* – the rat soon learned, 'Hey, now they're just turning the light on without the shock. I can stay here and eat even when the light's on.' Thus, it was demonstrated that the rat could not only learn to run away when the light and the shock came on simultaneously, and learn to run away even when just the light came on, but the rat could also eventually learn that when the shock was *not* associated with the light, it could stay there and eat. Learning psychologists refer to this process as *extinction of behavior in the absence of reinforcement*. In Experiment B, however, the light would come on and the shock would not come on until ten seconds later. The rat soon learned that when the light would come on it could stay there and continue to eat for eight or nine seconds, and then it could run away and not get shocked. Once the rat had learned this, the experimental conditions were reversed – the light would come on but the shock would never come on. Basically, the procedure was made the same as for Experiment A. Yet in Experiment B, no matter how many times the light came without the shock, in eight or nine seconds the rat would always run away – it never learned that the shock wouldn't come on as the rat eventually learned in Experiment A. In Experiment A the rat learned *escape behavior* – that is, how to get away from the shock after it received the shock. In Experiment B, however, the rat learned how to avoid the shock – a*voidant behavior*. The important thing to note from these two experiments is that learned escape behavior can be extinguished (or unlearned) whereas learned avoidant behavior cannot be extinguished or is extremely difficult to unlearn."

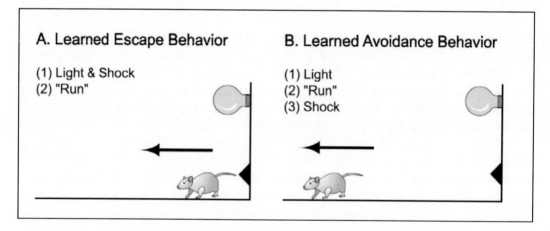

Figure 4.3. Learned Escape Behavior and Learned Avoidant Behavior.

What Larry learned as a child was *learned avoidant behavior*. What he specifically learned was: I don't have to participate in confrontational conversations with loved ones as long as I can figure out some way of avoiding them. Bill explained, "Pat, it's not that Larry doesn't love you or that he doesn't want to talk with you, maybe he is just doing what he has learned to do – avoid confrontation."

As time went on, and with some therapeutic intervention during subsequent sessions focusing on himself, Larry eventually learned how to overcome his learned avoidant behavior with Pat. And now that the two of them can participate in confrontational conversations, a multitude of other difficulties are avoided and their relationship is more pleasant and meaningful.

Negative and Positive Compensatory Behavior. It is not uncommon for people to compensate for their inadequacies and inabilities with alternative behaviors. The important thing is that the compensatory behavior be positive – not negative. For example, Robert was separated from his fiancé for six months because his company sent him to Florida to work on a special project. About every three weeks he would fly back to Dallas to spend a long weekend with Susie. When he came to see Bill Emener, he said, "About three nights a week, when I am really feeling down and missing her, I go out and eat a big dinner. Then I go to a sports bar and drink a lot of beer. Look at me. I've gained almost 40 pounds in the last six weeks!" Bill responded, "Robert, that's a negative compensation. Is there anything you could do on those three nights a week, or possibly on a regularly scheduled basis, that would help you feel less lonely, feel better about yourself, and not have a negative outcome?" Subsequently, Robert joined a local gymnasium. Three nights a week he goes there to work out, and then he goes to a different sports bar where he eats a big salad and drinks low calorie soda. The last time Bill spoke with him, Robert told him that he had already lost 18 pounds, was not missing Susie as much as he had been, and was feeling much better about himself. He also added that when Susie would see him next, he expected that she also would be pleased with his new way of dealing with missing her.

There is nothing wrong with compensatory behavior, provided it is not destructive; the important thing is that we help clients remain aware of how their compensatory behavior is affecting them, their loved ones and their relationships so they may adjust it when necessary. In this case, Robert and Susie were joyously happy with Robert's new compensatory behavior.

Perceptions of Behavioral Analysis. For some people, the idea of analyzing their individual behavior and their relationship-related behavior is a noxious thought. "It's not very romantic... that's not love," Ben said to Bill Emener. This is a fallacy that permeates our culture and has, in our opinion, been a great disservice to both individuals and couples alike. Consider the following:

- counseling and psychotherapy continue to be associated with stigma and shame by a significant proportion of our population;
- the only ways in which people learn relationship skills are by modeling their parents and other couples behavior, which, as the greater than 50% divorce rate suggests, is dysfunctional at least half the time;
- one cannot legally operate a motor vehicle without taking a proficiency test, but society imposes no such requirements for entering into marital relationships or for bearing children and responsibly parenting them; and, finally,
- Age-appropriate television for adolescents, and family viewing television, which remain an important source of learned relationship behavior, present in many cases what can only be described as "a fairy tale view of love" in which people live happily ever after without effort (of course the actual "ever after" is presumed but typically not shown).

Admittedly, the situation is improving. The unspoken cultural ethos of "rugged individualism" as exemplified by the "cowboy mystique" is fading away in the face of a society that grows ever more complex and rapidly changing by the day. In our opinion, it is not a moment too soon. Successful relationships are based on effective learned behavior and interaction patterns. The only way to change these patterns when they cease to be functional is to analyze and correct them. Clients who believe this sensible act of self-regulation is equivalent to weakness or is unromantic are doing exactly what it takes to assure their relationship will continue to deteriorate.

If you are counseling clients who seem to buy into any of the above dysfunctional and irrational beliefs, we recommend you disabuse them of these notions early in the counseling or therapy process rather than later.

SELF ANALYSIS

Most people in loving relationships tend to focus on the other person and/or the relationship, and they spend a relative paucity of time focusing on themselves. Working through the following nine sets of issues with our couples usually resulted in real progress within their relationships. Because each of these issues arose repeatedly, we feel it is likely they will come up in your future couples counseling sessions, if they have not already. To wit, our advice is to look for these issues in counseling sessions with your own clients. Doing so will assist you in helping your client to develop a clearer, richer and more accurate understanding of him- or herself – especially as that understanding relates to their involvement in a loving relationship.

The Importance of Me. It is our contention that there are three things that people pay attention to when they are involved in a loving relationship: (1) themselves; (2) the other person; and (3) the relationship they create and maintain. While we will be discussing the latter two in greater detail later, we begin with the importance of teaching the client to pay attention to him or herself. This is critical. Of course we are not suggesting that clients be narcissistically involved in themselves to the extent that they become unaware of the other person or their relationship, but simply that relationship skills begin with understanding one's own role in the interaction.

A counseling approach combining a metaphorical comparison and Aristotelian logic á la Aaron Beck (1976) that we frequently use to assist clients in appreciating the "remember to take care of your self" corollary to this overall axiom, is to ask them if they have ever been in an airplane. We then remind them that what typically occurs is that while the plane is taxiing out to the runway the flight attendant stands up front and gives specific instructions regarding what to do in case of an emergency: "Should an unexpected reduction in oxygen occur in the cabin, oxygen masks will come down from the ceiling. And if you are traveling with a small child, put your own mask on first." There are many reasons for this– primarily: we must make sure that we are able to take care of the child. In the loving relationships in which our clients have been involved, we many times have wondered: if the client is not able to take care of him- or herself, how could he or she possibly take care of or attend to their significant other or their relationship?

In a loving relationship, *the most important thing a person has to offer to his or her partner is him- or herself.* We assume that if a person loves their partner, they would want to give him or her things that are good, things that are the best they could be. If the most important thing each person offers the other person is him or herself, it intuitively would make sense that everyone would want to be the best they could be. The bottom line is that when you are guiding clients through the process of attending to various, important aspects and considerations of their love relationships, it is important to remind them always to be aware of themselves.

"What I am" versus "Who I am." Throughout our lives, we play many roles and engage in numerous activities that contribute to "what" we are. For example, people frequently tell us that they are a police officer, a school teacher, mechanic, receptionist and a variety of other occupational "whats." Sociologists have a special term for this – "master status." We also are mommies and daddies, aunts and uncles, brothers and sisters, golfers, tennis players, friends, and a variety of other non-occupational types of "whats" – that is, people also hold several other statuses through which they additionally define themselves.

It is not uncommon to hear people describe their loved ones with "what" pronouns. For example, "I am married to an accountant." "My fiancé is a librarian." "My boyfriend (or girlfriend) is an excellent tennis player." The famous psychologist Albert Ellis (1996) has stated as a central part of his theory (called "Rational Emotive Behavior Therapy") that it is a mistake to define oneself in these ways. According to Dr. Ellis, people mistakenly equate one or more of these statuses (instead of how they act, especially toward other people) with *who* they are. It is more accurate to define ourselves less upon the basis of our various statuses and more on the basis of how we behave. This is simply a different way of stating that *we frequently do not accurately attend to the "who" we are or the "who" other people are.* "*Who*" questions are those that refer to intention and behavior. As such, "Who a person is," is always subject to change, something from which clients in counseling can greatly benefit when reminded. For example, while recently addressing these phenomena with the members of a counseling group he was running, Bill Emener said, "Okay Jerry, we clearly know *what* you are. Nonetheless, *who* are you?" Jerry paused, stared out the window, turned and replied, "You mean since my divorce last year?" Bill said, "Yes." Jerry looked down at the floor then back out the window, and with a sullen voice said, "I think what is contributing so much to my depression is that *I am a family man without a family.*" In a similar fashion, Bill remembers Linda recently saying, "Yes Dr. Emener, I know *what* I am. I am a very, very successful *what!* What is sad for me, however, is that *I am a loving woman with no one to love.*"

Another one of our clients, Anna, recently asked if she should divorce Phil, her husband of 25 years. She then added emphatically, "Dr. Lambos, Phil isn't the same man I married. He used to be motivated and energetic, but now he just lies around and watches television every night. That's not the type of person I want to spend the rest of my life with." Anna was focusing on her husband's habits of recent years and defining *what* Phil had become rather than *why* he was behaving as he had been.

The bottom line here is that as long as clients are reminded that (a) what matters is their intention and behavior, and (b) they can make adjustments to these in order to improve or save their relationship, and thus they remain empowered to solve their issues (with assistance as necessary). Their first step toward helping them remember this is to teach them to change their focus from a "what" question to a "who" question, putting the emphasis back on their behaviors and intentions, which they are free to change if they desire.

Physiological and Emotional Considerations. Neuroscientists and psychologists now know an enormous amount about how the human brain and body interact to create the felt experience of emotion. The upper brainstem and limbic system are one of the three primary neurofunctional areas of the brain and largely responsible for the experience of emotion. Perhaps more importantly, scientists have learned that the human experience cannot be understood without appreciating the role feelings and emotions play in our ability to navigate even the simplest tasks of daily living. Thus, as we have seen, the popular idea offered in many science fiction shows and novels that people-like entities, supposedly devoid of emotion such as "Mr. Spock" or the cybernetic "Mr. Data," could not exist at all and behave as they do. Emotions play a central role in every human decision and behavior, no matter how trivial. There is simply no such thing as behavior or thoughts that do not contain an emotional component.

Furthermore, emotions overlap with another central component of the human experience: our level of *arousal*. It is often hard for psychologists and counselors – who undergo training in theories of personality and human behavior and in techniques of clinical intervention – to appreciate the role played by the ability to appropriately modulate one's level of arousal in efficiently navigating through daily life. It is not an exaggeration to state that the majority of clients' presenting problems, whether in couples counseling, individual or group counseling contexts, are directly related to difficulties associated with the inefficient modulation of arousal. For example, anxiety and depression may both be characterized as arousal-related problems (over- and under-arousal, respectively). Similarly, panic disorder, post-traumatic stress syndrome, attention deficit/hyperactivity disorder, obsessive-compulsive disorder, Tourette's syndrome and many varieties of executive dysfunction share a central if not defining feature – the inability to efficiently modulate an individual's level of arousal that is appropriate to one's circumstances. Stress may, in fact, be defined simply as consistent hyper-arousal and its (usually negative) consequences on the mind, brain, body and family system.

Your authors contend that the future of psychotherapy and mental health counseling will increasingly be interwoven with training clients to effectively modulate and regulate their level of physiological arousal so that it is appropriate to the situation at hand. The ability to do so is one of the most important skills taught at Dr. Lambos' Tampa practice, often using techniques based on breathing regulation, heart rate variability training, progressive relaxation training, biofeedback and EEG brainwave feedback. One must never forget that although our brains comprise only 2% to 3% of our total body mass, they consume up to 30% of the calories we ingest! The brain and the body continually and mutually interact to determine one's ongoing level of physiological arousal.

You may be wondering how this applies to relationships. This is where things really get interesting. It turns out that when two people are first getting to know one another, they each assess the other person's level of arousal and compare it to their own. If the other person's arousal is within a certain distance of their own, they continue to interact and show interest in the other person. If, on the other hand, they find the other person has either insufficient or excessive arousal relative to their own, they will often break off the interaction (Fisher, 2004). Based on judgments of relative levels of arousal, it seems that people are attracted to those whom they judge to have an interest in us that is roughly equal to their interest in them. It is an important aspect of the "dance" two people undergo during the early phase of establishing a relationship. This explains, for example, the importance of "playing it cool" after meeting someone in whom you may be intensely interested: if they judge you to be more aroused about the prospect of further interaction than they are, it could be a deal breaker.

Self-Inflation. Our self-concept, self-esteem and overall sense of self-worth are very important aspects of our lives. It also is important that we temper our self-concept and sense of self-worth with some reality. When Bill Emener was talking with Julia, who was sharing some aspects of her relationship with her fiancé Frank, she frequently used the expressions, "When I did this, he did that," "I know he did that because I did this," and "If I could only do this, then he would do that." After hearing a number of these types of statements, Bill chose to use some paradoxical intention and humor in his response to her. He said, "I have the feeling that everything Frank does, in fact everything that everyone around you does, is a function of you. That makes sense. What the hell – you're the center of the universe!" Being a very intelligent and quick-witted young woman, she instantaneously looked at him and said, "Of course, Dr. Emener, that's the effect of your modeling!" They both enjoyed a hearty laugh.

In teaching our clients to better understand themselves, their significant others and their relationships, it is important they learn to be careful of those times when people fall into the trap of believing that everything others around them do is a function of them. In reality, it is typically the case for all of us that the people around us do things independently of us. Our brief digression into emotion reminds us that people are motivated primarily to meet their own needs. Knowing that others do not base their realities on us is among the select aspects of mature and healthy functioning that we call *wisdom*.

Physical Attributes and Attractiveness. We have known many individuals who felt that if they had strong feelings with regard to any preferred or necessary physical attributes of a current or future significant other, then it defined them as being shallow. This is one of the great hypocrisies perpetuated by modern cultures. As anyone who has ever gone on a blind date or met someone on the Internet knows – looks matter. A lot.

"How is this being shallow?" we ask our clients. In the ideal world, when you love another individual, you love the whole person – not just one part of them. Nonetheless, it has also been our observation that prior to the development of a loving relationship between two individuals, in many cases they will not even begin the bonding process unless they find one another physically attractive. There is a large and growing scientific literature on physical attractiveness, some of which we reviewed in Chapter 3. We need not revisit this research to state what should be common sense: attraction towards another person is largely biological and subconscious. If a client does not acknowledge importance in it, they will have more variety in finding an appropriate partner. For the majority of individuals, however, physical attractiveness is prerequisite to forming a loving relationship, and there is nothing wrong with that – something that we need to assist our clients in appreciating and accepting.

During a therapy session, one of our clients prepared a chart similar to the one in Figure 4.4. She was suggesting that there are some men whom she dislikes or finds distasteful, in terms of their physical attributes and appearance; she tends to have negative feelings toward them and avoids them. Moving up her continuum, at the other extreme there is total physical intimacy – where she would feel joy and ecstasy. She also said this describes someone with whom she would enjoy snuggling and someone with whom she would enjoy making love. It is interesting to note how she separated love-making from sex. We specifically chose this area, physical attributes and attractiveness, as an important consideration for two reasons: (1) it is critical for a person to be clearly aware of how they feel about the physical attributes and physical attractiveness of another person with whom they may be contemplating having a loving relationship; and (2) it is also important to be realistic in terms of the extent to which we may want or expect a person to modify or to change their physical attributes and appearance. For example, it may be unrealistic to expect a 50-year old woman, even with cosmetic surgery, to look like a 30-year old, or for a longtime couch potato to look like a marathon runner, even if he jogs regularly.

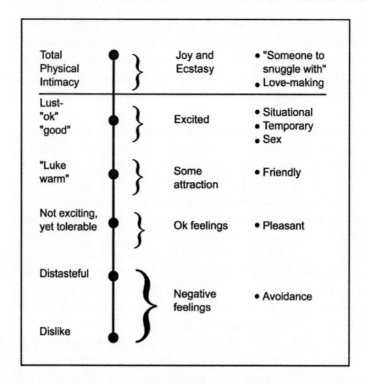

Figure 4.4. Physical Attributes and Attractiveness Issues.

Multi-trackers and Uni-trackers. As we have suggested earlier in this chapter, some people are tall and some people are short, some people have black hair and some people have brown hair, and some people tend to be heavy-set while others are slender. People are different. Likewise, some people tend to be multi-trackers and some people tend to be uni-trackers. As displayed in Figure 4.5, multi-trackers have the ability to attend to multiple tasks simultaneously, while uni-trackers can only attend to one at a time. Scientists know that these differences are due to how our brains are wired, typically from birth, and they also play a large role in certain conditions such as AD/HD and Obsessive-Compulsive disorder. From the viewpoint of the brain, they reflect tendencies or preferences toward what is called *sustained* versus *divided* attention styles. It also is important to remember that for most people, being a multi-tracker or a uni-tracker, or having divided or sustained attention is frequently task-specific. For example, a person may be able to watch a football game, send and receive text messages, and hold a conversation with his or her partner; nonetheless, when writing a detailed recommendation for a multi-million dollar buyout or a book chapter, that same person may have to be more uni-tracking and engage in more sustained focus.

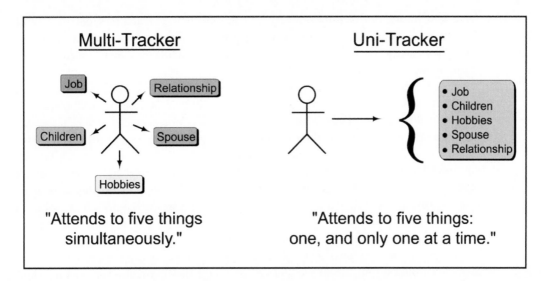

Figure 4.5. Uni-Trackers and Multi-Trackers.

Dialogue 4.1 shows a good example of how helping a couple when one partner is a multi-tracker and the other a uni-tracker can play out in the therapy room.

Dialogue 4.1 Multi-Trackers and Uni-Trackers

As displayed in Figure 4.5 and with the following scenario with Jane (J), an attorney who came with her husband, Alex (A), to see Bill Emener (B), the concepts of uni-tracker and multi-tracker and of sustained versus divided styles of attending to the world should become clear to you.

J: On almost a daily basis, Dr. Emener, I simultaneously pay attention to my job, my three beautiful children, and my hobby, which is playing tennis. My husband Alex and I also pay attention to our relationship. I can attend to all five of these things simultaneously. For example, while driving the children to little league practice, I can also be thinking about my job, and on the way back, I can think of stopping at a store to pick up a special treat for Alex. Alex, on the other hand, drives me crazy. Whatever he does, he does it incredibly well. The only problem is that he can only do one thing at a time. For example, if he is trying to negotiate a new contract at work, where he is a construction supervisor, it seems like that's the only thing he can do until the contract has been finalized. If the children or I talk to him, or if I want to go to dinner with him, he is preoccupied. It's like he's somewhere else, out in space.

B: I assuredly can see, Jane, that this is very upsetting for you. My first suggestion is that you might want to talk about this with Alex at you earliest opportunity. My sense is that you are continuing to become more and more frustrated with him, and it is because you are interpreting his uni-tracking lifestyle as an indication that he does not care about you or your children. Not only that, you are feeling alone with an increased sense of responsibility to take care of everything.

A: Jane, you lifestyle strikes me as very chaotic, shallow and at times out of control. Sometimes it seems that you just focus on getting things done rather than on getting things done right or with any attention to quality. Sometimes this... well it really frustrates me.

B: It's clear to me that in a fundamental, lifestyle way, each of you is different. While some people are tall, others are short; some people have brown hair, others have black hair. People are different. And with regard to the two of you, Jane, you tend to be what we call a multi-tracker – you can attend to and do many things simultaneously; Alex, you tend to be what we call a uni-tracker – you can do just about anything extremely well but you only attend to and do one thing at a time. And please try to remember, neither is right or wrong, good or bad – just different. I would suggest that in order to keep your differences from destroying your relationship, instead of trying to change each other – try to focus on what each of you can do so that you can love each other, live together and enjoy a wonderful relationship in spite of your differences.

J: (After a pause and then looking at Bill) You mean like if we could agree on certain things that Alex would do instead of me and certain things that I would do instead of Alex? That's assuming of course that there are some things uni-trackers can do very well and there are some things that multi-trackers can do very well.

B: That would be an excellent place to start... 'cause, for openers, that way both of you would be respecting and appreciating each other for what you are doing and not for how each of you are doing them.

In a general sense, we are suggesting that it is important for you to help your clients remain aware of the extent to which they and their loved ones may be a multi-tracker or a uni-tracker. Furthermore, try to help them understand and appreciate the extent to which any differences between them and their loved one might have an impact on their relationships. As Bill Emener humorously says in his lecture on this topic, "Multi-trackers think their uni-tracker partners are lazy, and uni-trackers think their multi-tracker partners are crazy." Neither style is necessarily better than the other, but understanding one's partner's style and that it may differ from one's own, can help greatly to reduce relationship problems.

High-Maintenance and Low-Maintenance People. We use the terms *high-maintenance people* and *low-maintenance people* to represent the extent to which a person needs attention from, or needs to be in contact with, their loved one. A couple Bill Lambos recently saw, Peter and Anita, were in trouble and Peter was ready to call off their engagement. He knew that if he did not call Anita every day, two or three days would go by without him hearing from her. To Peter, this was a sign that Anita was not committed to their relationship. Anita was stunned when she heard this: "Peter, I think about you all the time! I just assume you'll call me if you need something until our next scheduled time together."

In a similar example, Victor and Carla came to see Bill Emener because they were beginning to get very frustrated with each other. Although their wedding date was only seven months away, they felt that this was a good time for them to figure out what was going wrong. An illustrative portrayal of how Victor and Carla were able to modify their maintenance needs and establish a "comfort zone" is in Figure 4.6. How they addressed this in their counseling session with Bill is shown in Dialogue 4.2.

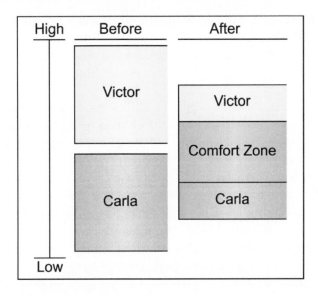

Figure 4.6. High Maintenance and Low-Maintenance People.

Dialogue 4.2 High Maintenance and Low Maintenance People

When one partner in a relationship is a "low maintenance" person and the other is a "high maintenance" person, many frustrations can be experienced by both individuals and numerous relationship problems can develop. The following scenario regarding Carla (C) and her fiancé Victor (V), who were seeing Bill Lambos (B), demonstrates how a counselor can assist individuals in a situation such as this. Most importantly, as you will see, the two of them were able to identify a more comfortable relationship lifestyle. As indicated in Figure 4.6, Victor was able to lower his maintenance needs and Carla was able to increase her maintenance responses. Thus, they were able to identify a comfort zone for themselves.

V: (Speaking to Bill) I don't understand Carla at all. Sometimes we can go for two or three days without having any contact with each other. She doesn't leave messages for me on my answering machine, and she won't give me a call at work just to say hello. And even though I know that sometimes she works late into the evening, she will not return my phone messages until the following afternoon.

B: Victor, it sounds like sometimes you wonder if she really loves you… you almost sound as if you are feeling abandoned.

V: That's exactly it. Sometimes I feel lost and lonely without contact from her.

C: (Speaking to Bill) I don't know what's wrong with Victor. He has to realize that I work two jobs. I have a day job and then I do some typing in the evenings. I'm also caught up in the arrangements for our wedding and I try to work out at the gym three nights a week. It seems like if I don't see him or talk to him everyday, he goes ballistic!

B: Carla, it sounds like sometimes you feel smothered by Victor. Maybe you also are wondering if he is just a little insecure about your relationship when he acts this way.

C: Sometimes it's just too much!

As their session continued, they both developed clearer understandings of each other and with Bill's urging established some helpful boundaries and limits. For example, they agreed that before ending a telephone conversation or departing from seeing each other they would always try to indicate when they would call or see each other again.

It is important for people to be cognizant of their maintenance needs, the maintenance needs of their loved ones, and the extent to which their relationships attend to their needs, desires and wants in these areas. As Carla and Victor experienced, by talking about it and working out agreed upon arrangements and agreements, getting into a comfort zone also helps avoid other, possibly bigger troubles.

Pursuers and Distancers. A pursuer, also known as a chaser, is a person who in a relationship tends to be the one always making things happen, initiating contact with the other person and assuming responsibility for making plans for everything they may or may not be doing. On the other hand, a *distancer*, also known as a runner, is a person who tends to sit back and wait for the other person to make things happen, to wait for the other person to contact him or her and to wait for the other person to suggest plans for what they may or may not do. Basically, it is important for people to remain aware of the extent to which they are a pursuer or a distancer and the extent to which their loved one is a pursuer or a distancer. Furthermore, it is critical for them to be aware of the "interaction effect" of their and their partner's individual styles. For example, if George is a pursuer and Mary is a distancer and they both feel comfortable with that, chances are that they will not experience any difficulties in this area of their relationship. However, if they are both pursuers, they may be tripping over each other all the time, and if they are both distancers they may eventually not have a relationship because neither of them will contact each other frequently enough. Sometimes it is very helpful for couples to talk openly about their pursuing and distancing. For example, a pursuer can easily feel hurt and ignored by a distancer, and a distancer can easily feel smothered and trapped by a pursuer. When discussing this phenomenon with one of our colleagues, she suggested a poignant phrase: "Don't lunge after a gerbil." Basically, she was suggesting that if you have ever tried to catch a gerbil you quickly discovered that the more you chase it the more it runs away. Sometimes the best way to catch a gerbil is to sit down quietly and turn your thoughts to other things, and eventually the gerbil will find you.

Me and You – Self and You. In your client's process of self-analysis, he or she may be wondering, "Why am I paying so much attention to me?" We often find it helpful to suggest to clients that *their ability to trust their significant other is ultimately an indication of the extent to which they can trust themselves.* The further we discuss this, the clearer it becomes that this is true. As a continuance of this perspective, we also have wondered: *Is my ability to love you an indication of the extent to which I can love myself?* If this were carried further, other postulates also could be considered: *Is my ability to understand you an indication of my ability to understand myself? Is my ability to take care of you an indication of the extent to which I can take care of myself?* Each of these questions may not necessarily be valid questions for all people. Overall, however, it is not uncommon for us to say to a client, "Whenever we ask ourselves any questions regarding what we can or cannot do with, for, or on behalf of a loved one, it might be important for us to ask ourselves to what extent are we able to do such things with, for and/or on behalf of ourselves."

SELF IDENTITY

The essence of the following – for an individual to not lose his or her identity in the process of attending to their partner and their relationship – is captured in the title of an excellent self-help book by Paul and Paul (2002): *Do I Have to Give Up Me to be Loved by You?* When assisting clients with their relationship issues and not mortgaging or sacrificing themselves and their own identities, it behooves counselors to facilitate their clients' attention to: (1) their "little child" within; (2) their individual and unique need for someone in their lives; (3) their individual and unique need to be fought for; (4) their need to feel special; (5) the importance of feeling appreciated, admired and adored; and (6) how they meaningfully can attend to their partner and their relationship without giving up or losing themselves.

The Little Child Within. Sometimes there is nothing more beautiful to behold than a young child at play. Watching a young child feeling and acting totally free, with undaunted and unbridled curiosity and inquisitiveness, with total open expressions of feelings and an untainted and uncontrolled appreciation and love of people and things, is refreshing for most adults. We trust that most of us can recall those wonderful days in our childhood when on a hot summer day we could stuff our face with ice-cold watermelon and not worry about it dribbling down our chin. Those wonderful days when our biggest worry in the world was whether or not our mother would allow us to have seconds of ice cream. It has been suggested by many psychologists that even though in our process of becoming an adult we learned how to control our childhood openness and sense of total freedom with the world, our "little child" continues to live within us.

If you have ever observed a middle-aged man building drip castles in the sand, a middle-aged woman frolicking in a pile of fall leaves with her children, or grown-ups having a water pistol fight at a company picnic, you know what we are talking about. We readily agree with the theory that "each of us has a little child continuing to live within us – a child who always is eager to find a way out, eager to come out and play." This phenomenon will be further illustrated in Chapter 9 and in the following example.

Bill Emener readily recalls the way in which Anna, a 38-eight-year-old married woman and mother of three children, described her reason for enjoying and continuing a two-year affair with a slightly older lover. "It wasn't the sex," she said. "It was that I could feel totally free to run on the beach, say whatever I wanted to say, drop a scoop of ice cream in his hair or throw a glass of cold water on him while he was in the shower. Yes, I will admit that when we made love it certainly was good. But that's not why I continued the affair. The major reason was that our relationship allowed the little boy within him and the little girl within me to come out and play together."

As couples counselors, it is important for us to remain alert to the strong possibility that within every adult there is a little boy or girl who likes to come out and play. It is equally important to remember that one of the major characteristics and attributes of a "good" loving relationship is that the two individuals can provide opportunities for the little children within them to come out, have fun and play – especially with each other.

A Need for Someone in One's Life. In the process of facilitating clients' analyses, it is important for you to help each of them glean some estimation of their individual need to have someone in their life. For example, Bill Emener vividly remembers Jack, a man who had been divorced three years prior to his seeing him and who recently had ended a six-month relationship with a woman with whom he was very much in love. Bill very quickly realized that Jack was the type of person who felt much better about life when he had someone with whom to share it. Bill sketched a diagram similar to the one in Figure 4.7. Jack clearly was able to see what parts of his life were devoted to his friends, sleep, play, and work, and that there was a "missing piece of pie" that he referred to as "a missing companion." Jack also shared with Bill that the one thing he was hoping for at the age of 55 was "someone special to grow old with." This realization was somewhat comforting for Jack – he said to Bill, "If this is my life, one in which I would simply desire to have someone to share it with even though I don't, then at least I know that I can still go on living well without that special someone."

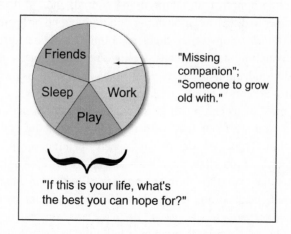

Figure 4.7. Living an Unbalanced Life without a Special Someone.

If a person's philosophy is that their life is more meaningful when they share it with someone, then in the absence of such an individual he or she occasionally may feel a little off balance, unfulfilled and incomplete. There is nothing necessarily wrong with this. However, we think Jack offered a good suggestion when in such a situation: "If that's the way it is, then I better make sure that all of the other pieces of my life are the best that they can be. If all I have are lemons, then I better do all I can do to make the best lemonade I can." Unfortunately, many people don't follow Jack's advice. Instead, they imagine that whenever they are unable to get what they are looking for *right now*, it defines a catastrophe. The results of such *irrational beliefs* (á la Albert Ellis' Rational Emotive Behavior Therapy, 1996) typically result in some combination of anxiety or depression, which then causes them even more problems in managing relationships.

An interesting issue we have noticed with many of our clients is their inability to enjoy their own company. Although it is true that *homo sapiens* are fundamentally social animals and that a shared sunset is often better than a sunset seen alone, we have also noticed the increasing difficulty that many of our clients have with being alone even for short periods. This tendency is, in our opinion, unhealthy. We find ourselves frequently reminding our clients that the ability to enjoy one's own company is not only necessary and psychologically healthy, but *it also fosters relationship health.* The inability to enjoy one's own company, on the other hand, is one of the bases for relationship dependency and/or co-dependency. Once people discover this connection and learn how to enjoy time spent absent the company of others, and specifically without the need for the constant companionship of their significant other, their relationships usually improve markedly.

A Need to be Fought For. Over the years, we have observed that some people have a high need to feel fought for. To some extent, in a loving relationship this is an indication of a need for validation of his or her loved one's feelings for them and their own perceived sense of worth.

Each of us has listened to clients explain why they ended a relationship, had an affair or simply gave up caring (and lead what we call living "parallel lives") because they were convinced – sometimes correctly so – that if their partner or former partner cared about them, they would have done something to fix the relationship, but chose not to. And, if at times this has resulted from misperceptions or feelings of insecurity, it nonetheless turned into a relationship ending event. As one of Bill Emener's clients said to him after filing for divorce, "Okay, it's true that I was the one who filed for divorce. But I actually felt that she had emotionally divorced me 10 years prior. If I ignored her, she would act hurt and the kids would feel sorry for her. I had affairs, which I honestly felt she knew about, but again she just acted hurt and the kids felt sorry for her. When I told her I wanted a divorce, she said, 'If that's what you want, Henry, there's nothing I can do about it.' I figured that she didn't care enough about me and our relationship to do anything about it."

In the absence of overriding psychopathological issues, such as a serious psychological disturbance or mental health problem, there is nothing wrong with a need or desire to be fought for. It might be helpful to suggest to such clients the following. One, a "need to feel fought for" is often an indication of unresolved personal insecurity. If so, the client is advised to examine and work through the insecurity before looking to fix any aspect of the relationship. Second, if the client sees this desire to be fought for as an unalterable aspect of their self, then it may be a good idea for him or her to select a partner who is compatible with the condition. The most important thing is for people to be aware of their need or desire in this area and how it impacts their relationships with those they love.

A Need to Feel Special. One of the things we often see in couples in therapy is: when they feel loved and in love, it is because their partner and their relationship make them feel special. The importance of this should not be underestimated. A family therapist with whom Bill Lambos has shared an office for some time remarked that the standard wedding vows should be rewritten for the modern age as follows: "To have and to hold, in sickness and in health, until death do us part, or until it sucks." In our experience, the last condition comes to be true when one no longer is able to feel special about, or by one's partner.

You may recall that in Chapter 3 we discussed the forces that bond individuals together in romantic relationships. Regardless of the underlying selection pressures, our brains evolved in such a way that we normally experience all of lust, romance and attachment in the course of a loving relationship. The question now arises: "Which of these is related to the need to feel special?" Perhaps unsurprisingly, in our experience, romantic love is most often associated with feeling special.

To a large extent, the term "special" is synonymous with "unique" or "like no one else." Thus to "feel special" is to feel better – at least in the eyes of one's lover – than anyone else. We have undoubtedly all met someone at a party or other social situation, found them to be stunning or gorgeous and experienced immediate lust for this person. Yet only the most naïve among us would confuse this with feeling special – we recognize lust for what it is: intense but superficial physical attraction. On the other end of the spectrum, when we comfortably have settled into a very long-term relationship such as a 20-year marriage, we no longer expect to feel special, at least not all the time. In fact, in such relationships most people very much look forward to special occasions such as anniversaries or vacations when the feelings of romance are rekindled. Thus feeling special is closely associated with romantic love, which in turn is associated with the old cliché "Two's company, three's a crowd." The need to feel special in a relationship is the need to experience (or re-experience) romance in that relationship. Helping clients appreciate what their loved one does with them and for them, knowing how such things are associated with their feeling special, and knowing what they do with and for their loved one that are associated with his or her feeling special, indeed are paramount in any loving relationship and frequently need to be addressed in counseling sessions.

A Triple-A Rating. Bill Emener only met with Sandy for one session. "I just want to have an opportunity to talk with you about my relationship with my boyfriend, George," she said as they began. Sandy, a 34-year-old single parent with sole custody of her two children, had divorced her husband about 10 years before coming in. She further reported that she had had a number of difficulties trying to establish relationships with "good men" over the past few years. Sandy then added, "And now I have almost gotten to the point where I don't even know what I'm looking for anymore!"

Following some discussion regarding loving relationships, her feelings about herself and her thoughts and attitudes regarding loving relationships with men, Sandy was asked, "What would be three important characteristics of a 'good' loving relationship with George that would have to be there in order for you to feel loved by him?" After pondering the question for a few minutes and jotting down some notes, with a cute little smile, she said, "A Triple-A Rating."

Bill asked her to explain what she meant. While pointing to the three capital A's on her piece of paper, Sandy said, "Well, first of all, he must *Appreciate* me – for my accomplishments, for my hard work, and most importantly for who I am not what I am. Secondly, he must *Admire* me – for my accomplishments, my hard work, and, most importantly, for who I am not what I am. And thirdly, he must *Adore* me – not only for what I am, but for who I am."

"It sounds to me, Sandy," Bill replied, "that in view of the fact that you are a well-known attorney in this city, you want to be assured that George loves you not for your stature, your status, your visibility, your accomplishments or your income. You want to be assured that he loves you for being Sandy. And among other things, you want to feel genuinely appreciated, admired and adored by George."

As she folded her notes, she professionally added, "Yes, those are my minimum expectations, and I cannot accept, nor will I accept, anything less." When Bill asked Sandy whether she thought about the extent to which George might have the capacity and the ability to communicate and demonstrate those three A's, she said, "I don't know. Only time will tell. But at least now I have a clearer idea of what I am looking for."

About six weeks later, Bill received a postcard from a beautiful Mexican beach resort with the following inscription: "Dear Bill, Having a wonderful time! It rained most of the day today, so I would grade the weather as a 'B.' The important thing, however, is that my traveling companion, whose name starts with 'G,' has clearly earned a Triple-A Rating! With love, Sandy."

When you help a couple with the establishment or maintenance of a loving relationship, it is important that you help them know and appreciate: (1) *what they are looking for*; (2) *what they need;* and (3) *what they minimally need to have from each other* in order to have and enjoy a "good" loving relationship. Likewise, it is important for each of them to have an accurate understanding and appreciation for what their partner is wanting, is looking for, and minimally needs from them and their relationship.

Don't Give Up You. In Chapter 5 we examine the concepts of *independence, dependence, codependence* and *interdependence* in detail. For this section, we feel our list of topics under the heading of "self identity" would be incomplete without at least mentioning these terms.

Successful and enduring relationships are those in which each person's needs, wants and desires are more or less balanced with those of their partner. In our experience, many relationships have failed because one of the two partners decided that maintaining the relationship was more important than continuing to be the person they were when the relationship started and continuing to grow and be the person they could be.

CHAPTER SUMMARY

Sigmund Freud theorized that two-thirds of our lives reside in our subconscious. Without the functionality of our defense mechanisms, such as repression and denial, most of us couldn't make it through the day. Nonetheless, a major challenge in life, à la Socrates, is to "know thyself." Pertinent to loving relationships, it very well may be that *one's ability to understand his or her relationship is highly contingent upon that person's ability to understand him or her self.*

In this chapter, we examined three critical areas of analysis pertinent to the establishment and sustenance of an individual's self while attending to their loved one and their relationship: (1) behavior analysis; (2) self-analysis; and (3) self-identity. Facilitating clients' analytical journeys down each of these roads constitutes an important, pivotal part of professional couples counseling. By helping clients calmly analyze their own troublesome issues and then helping them accepting responsibility for ameliorating or fixing their problem areas, a healthier and happier individual will result and his or her loving relationship will be facilitated and strengthened immeasurably.

> This above all: to thine own self be true,
> And it must follow, as the night the day,
> Thou canst not be false to any man.
> *Hamlet*, Act 1, Scene 3

CHAPTER 4 DISCUSSION QUESTIONS

1) Assuming that "love is a matter of the heart," why is it important for people in loving relationships to analyze their behavior?
2) As a couples counselor, what are some things you can do to assist couples analyze their own and each other's behavior so that their analyses eventually translate into improving their relationships?

3) Why is it important for an individual to engage in self-analysis if he or she is having a relationship problem?

4) As a couples counselor, what are some things you can do to help clients analyze themselves so that their self analysis eventually translates into improving their relationships?

5) Why is it important for individuals in loving relationships to be careful not to lose their self-identity in the process of attending to their partners and their relationships?

6) As a counselor working with couples, what are some things you can do to assist the individuals in the relationships to "take care of themselves and not have to give up who they are" in order to maintain their loving relationships?

Chapter 5

ANALYTICS: RELATIONSHIP ANALYSIS

Whereas Chapter 4 addressed analytical aspects of the individual's issues pertinent to a loving relationship, this chapter focuses on analytical aspects of the relationship – as an entity unto itself. We urge our readers to keep two important things in mind regarding relationship analysis: (1) as you assist clients in analyzing and ameliorating their individual issues (e.g., those in Chapter 4), you also will be indirectly analyzing and ameliorating their relationship issues; and (2) most of our discussions are from your perspective – the perspective of the counselor.

During our first session with a new couple, we may explain that neither person alone is considered our client. Rather (as we discuss in detail in Chapter 14), our client may be considered as both the two individuals *and* their relationship. Although this may sound unusual, we have found it to be a highly effective approach to helping couples.

Why does this approach work? Even though there are many angles to the issue, the simplest answer is that when two people decide to come together as a couple, they must do so in the context of a set of shared assumptions and rules (often tacit, implicit and even unrecognized) that define their relationship. When they seek relationship counseling, couples counseling or marriage counseling, they are looking for professional help in fixing or improving their relationship. If either person thought that their relationship did not need help and/or that they had an individual issue that needed to be addressed, they probably would not have come as a couple. Thus, by the very fact that they came together, the counselor is justified in assuming the issue to be with their relationship.

Treating the relationship as "the identified client" (to use counseling terminology) has many benefits and cuts to the core of the matter. It also helps counselors from being viewed as biased toward one or the other of the two individuals. On the other hand, if "the identified client" is the relationship, then the counselor better have a solid understanding of relationships, including when, how and why they work effectively or become dysfunctional. Clients also must be offered goal-specific strategies and techniques, or interventions, for making their relationships healthier. To wit, one of the two primary goals of this chapter is to help you understand and appreciate what constitutes both healthy and unhealthy or poorly functioning relationships; the other is to offer some of the techniques for helping couples improve their relationships that we have found helpful and effective over the years.

By looking back over years of session notes with couples, we derived a list of relationship issues. The resulting relationship-issue questions that seemed to arise when working with couples repeatedly comprise the following 11:

1) Is the relationship "a house built on one stilt or many stilts?"
2) In what ways is the relationship based on "dependence and/or independence?"
3) How does each partner view their need and desire for "public space, private space and together space?"
4) Is each partner aware of "the loving roles they play" and how they impact their relationship?
5) Do the partners do "big little things" with and for each other that mean a lot to them and their relationship?
6) Do they love each other and "feel loved by" each other?
7) Can the couple honestly assess their "relationship's pros and cons?"
8) To what extent is "intimacy, passion and commitment" a meaningful part of their relationship?
9) Does the love they have for, and feel from each other "unconditional?"
10) When bad things happen, do they "forget and/or do they forgive each other?" and,
11) Does the couple do things that would promote "relationship happiness?"

Once again, our advice to you is: look for these issues when working with a couple.

A HOUSE BUILT ON ONE STILT OR MANY STILTS

In our experience, the degree to which each member of a couple places the relationship at the center of his or her world often differs dramatically with respect to the two people. As displayed in Figure 5.1, for some individuals, the relationship approaches the *raison d'être* of their existence, while for their partner it may be important but not the center of their universe. When individuals place differing degrees of importance on the role of the dyad in their lives and when these differences are unspoken or tacit, problems can ensue. Dialogue 5.1 emphasizes how such an issue was resolved by Bill Emener in a counseling session with Chuck and Nancy, and illustrates the importance of this principle.

Dialogue 5.1 A House Built on One or Many Stilts

Chuck (C) and Nancy (N) had been married for almost a year and were living in a very nice apartment not far from Chuck's family in Tampa. Nancy's family was in Minneapolis. She had moved to Tampa shortly before their wedding. When they first came to see Bill Emener (B), it was clear that Nancy was incredibly frustrated with Chuck. It was her contention that Chuck did not value her or their relationship as much as he should. Indeed there were numerous aspects of Nancy and Chuck's relationship that were addressed in their sessions.

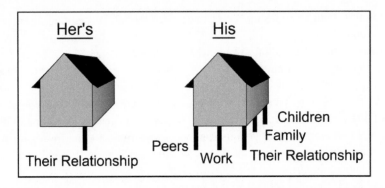

Figure 5.1. A "House" Built on one Stilt Compared to a "House" Built on Many Stilts.

N: If he would only pay half as much attention to our marriage as I do, everything would be okay.

B: I would like the two of you to describe your average day, weekday and weekend, including the typical pattern of each of your days. Nancy, you go first.

N: I wake up first and start breakfast and coffee – Chuck is awful before he gets his first cup. I lay out breakfast while he showers and dresses, and then joins me and we eat together. Shortly thereafter, he takes off for work to beat the traffic and I clean up the dishes and get myself ready for work.

C: If I miss the traffic window, the commute is pure hell!

N: Then I dress and I'm off to attend to the daily chores. I clean, shop, cook, but the truth is most of the time I think about what Chuck and I are going to do that evening. The rest of everything I do is just there and I do it, but it doesn't mean much to me. Chuck also works long hours, so before he gets home I make dinner, make sure his beer is cold, and everything is ready for him when he walks in the door. He is often a bit grumpy from work and traffic, so I try to give him some time to settle in. That's when the problems usually start.

B: What do you mean *problems*?

C: She assumes I've spent my entire day thinking about nothing but walking in and attending to her. I love her, Doc, but honestly, I'm stressed as hell by the time I get home. I have my entire department's problems to think about on the way home, and half the time I've been on the cell phone putting out some fire, or setting up for the next day or the rest of the week. So I'm looking forward to that beer and then seeing what's on TV, or maybe hitting the gym for a workout. If I tell her I'm not hungry or I have other plans, she looks as if her world is about to collapse. That's just more stress on top of it.

B: OK, you two, time out. It seems like you do both love each other very much, but your individual lifestyles are very different in important ways. Let me draw a diagram for you to show you what I mean. [Bill then drew for them a sketch that is in Figure 5.1].

B: Nancy, you are devoting almost one-hundred percent of your energy to your relationship with Chuck. You are enjoying your opportunity to stay at home during the day, exercise on a regular basis, and prepare some of the most scrumptious meals any man could hope for. There is nothing wrong with your life, except for the fact that you are practically living in a house that is built on one stilt – your relationship with Chuck. When you were in Minneapolis, you had numerous friends who you went out with, your family was nearby, you had a job with several co-workers whom you enjoyed, and yet you paid attention to your relationship with Chuck even though it was long distance. But look at what you have now.

N: [Looking at the diagram]. Yes, I see what you mean.

B: [Pointing to "Chuck's house"] Chuck, if I understand your life, it appears that you have a house built on five stilts. You have your peers, your fellow attorneys with whom you enjoy spending time, you enjoy your work and its various job tasks, you obviously pay a lot of attention to your relationship with Nancy, you spend a lot of time with your mom, dad, and two brothers, and you also attend to your two children from your first marriage. You basically have a variety of things to which you devote not only physical time, but psychological time.

C: I understand. Yes, that's the way it is for me.

N: Wow – I guess I've been paying so much attention to Chuck that I've forgotten about *me*. I used to do so much more, but since we moved, I just fell into taking care of Chuck.

C: Nancy, as much as I love you, I feel a tremendous amount of responsibility for you. You are devoting so much energy to our relationship, that when we have a minor argument, your whole world is threatened, and you go into a tailspin and become very upset.

N: Yes, I can understand that. When something seems to be going wrong with Chuck and me, I flip-out. I go crazy. It seems that what I might need to do is to develop some friendships, look for a job so I can go back to work and broaden my interests.

C: [Looking lovingly at Nancy] Nancy, I would really like to encourage you to do that. Not only would that be more helpful for us and our relationship, but it would be so much better for you. I want you to be happy. I love you, Nancy.

After that session, Nancy applied for a job and joined a women's tennis league; Chuck set a timer on his Blackberry three or four days a week and called Nancy just to say hi. With those kinds of changes, as well as modifications in their attitudes toward each other, Nancy and Chuck indeed were enjoying a happier and more meaningful relationship.

DEPENDENCE AND INDEPENDENCE

It repeatedly has been clear to us that partners can be confused regarding acts of *dependence* as opposed to acts of independence. At first blush, this seems relatively obvious: if I want something for me or do something for myself, I am being independent; if I want something from you or want you to do something for me, I am being dependent.

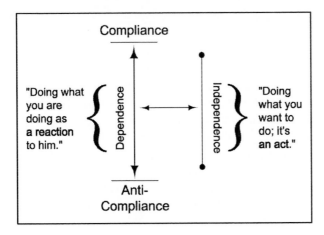

Figure 5.2. Relationships among Compliance and
Anti-Compliance, and Dependance and Independence.

As displayed in Figure 5.2, however, it is not that simple – if I do what I want to do, no matter what it is, in most instances it is an act of *independence*; nonetheless, if I do something that is a reaction, be it compliance or anti-compliance, in most instances it is an act of dependence. How this was pertinent to Marie and Nate's relationship, and how it played out in their counseling session with Bill Emener is in Dialogue 5.2.

Dialogue 5.2 Dependence and Independence

Bill Emener (B) was counseling a couple, Marie (M) and Nate (N), in which Marie described numerous instances in which the two of them did what Nate wanted them to do, and she was upset because she felt that she was constantly complying with what he wanted to do. Furthermore, Nate shared a number of instances in which one of them would purposely go just the opposite way.

N: Marie, the other night when we were watching television, did you put that movie on because you wanted to watch the movie, or did you put the movie on simply because you knew I wanted to watch the basketball game?

M: I wanted to watch that movie.

B: Before we go any further, I'd like both of you to look at the picture I have just drawn. [See Figure 5.2] When we comply with another person or, when we do something just to spite them and anti-comply with them, it is an act of dependency because our decision to comply or anti-comply is still dependent upon what the other person wanted, said or did. At the other end of the continuum is independence, where we do what we do because that's what we want to do, not as a compliant or anti-compliant reaction to the other person.

N: Dr. Emener, can you make it clear what the difference is between my doing things for me, doing things for Marie, and doing things for our relationship?

B: Depending upon an individual's motivations, intentions and verbalizations, the differences among these three can be obvious. Using you as an example, Nate, let me offer the following three illustrations:

- *When Doing Things for Nate* you might say something like, "Marie, if it's alright with you, tomorrow I am going to call a travel agent and see if we can get a weekend special at the beach somewhere down south. We can leave here Friday night and come back Sunday night. As you know, I have had to work the last two weekends and at least two or three nights each week. I really feel worn-out. I need to get away. If it's all right with you, it would be great if we could do this. I simply need to get a break. As I said, I need to get away."

- *When Doing Things for Marie* you might say something like, "Marie, I know that for the last two weeks you have been taking care of your mom almost every evening and spending most of the weekends with her. I think you need an opportunity to get away. If it's all right with you, I'm going to call a travel agent tomorrow to see if we can get a weekend special at the beach down south. I think you just need to get out of town for a few days."

- *When Doing Things for Your Relationship* you might say something like, "Marie, I know for the past couple of weeks the two of us have been running hectically almost twenty-four hours a day. Given my work, your work and your mother's illness, you and I have been like two ships passing in the night. If it's all right with you, I am going to make reservations for us to go to the beach for the weekend somewhere down south. I feel like the two of us just need the opportunity to get reconnected and back together again."

When couples learn to address their needs and desires in these ways, Nate, instead of either assuming the other person knows what they want or, worse, outright manipulation, relationships tend to remain healthy and stable. When they don't, well, couples end up here, just like you two did.

Neuropsychologists call this "need to know the motivation of others" *theory of mind* and it is considered among the most important of the aspects of frontal lobe brain function, which as we now know is called executive function; it is, more than anything else, what makes human beings different from other species.

This helps to explain why, when two individuals are able to understand not only *what* their partner wants, but *why* they want it (i.e., for them, for their partner and/or for their relationship), thoughts of defiance and feelings of manipulation are significantly reduced. Most importantly, with such understandings relationship transactions proceed more smoothly.

PUBLIC SPACE AND PRIVATE SPACE

It is very important for people in loving relationships to remain cognizant of their need, desire or preference for spending time in what we refer to as public space, private space and together space. As depicted in Figure 5.3, public space is representative of where (and when) people are doing things with other people. Private space is where (and when) they are doing things alone, and (usually) by choice. Togetherness space is where (and when) they are doing things exclusively with the person with whom they are having a loving relationship. When the amount of time, the percentage of time, and the when of the time we spend in these spaces (e.g., on a daily basis, weekly basis, monthly basis, etc.) are commensurate with their needs, preferences and desires, they tend to be happy (or at least happier).

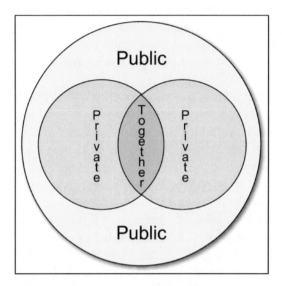

Figure 5.3. Public Space, Private Space and Together Space.

Difficulties occur when the *way*, *how*, *when*, *where* and *with whom* time is spent is less consistent with what they prefer, need or want. For example, consider the following illustrative statements that we occasionally hear people make – statements you may often hear from your clients:

- "Sometimes I just wish that Alice and I could spend more time doing things with other people, like going to concerts, picnics and dinners."
- "I really love John very much, but sometimes I just like to have some private time for myself. I wish he could understand that!"
- "Monica and I really get along well. We give each other time to have privacy and spend some time alone, and we also spend time with other people. However, it really would be helpful if sometimes we could do things, just the two of us. The truth is that sometimes I just need to have Monica all to myself."
- "Alex and I seem to have everything worked out pretty neatly. We have a lot of good friends with whom we spend time. We give each other time for ourselves, like when I just enjoy curling up on the couch to read a book or like when he enjoys going to the driving range to hit golf balls by himself. And yet, we also make time to do things together, just the two of us – we stay connected."

From an overall perspective and when pertinent, it is important for you to help your clients to: (1) remain aware of his or her own needs, desires and preferences for *public space*, *private space* and *together space*; (2) remain aware of their loved one's needs, desires and preferences in these three areas; (3) remember that from time to time one's needs, desires and preferences in these three areas may change (or have to change due to external causes); and (4) actively assure that their relationship sufficiently accommodates all three of them.

LOVING ROLES WE PLAY

In a *New York Times* article on Dr. Humphrey Osmond, clinical professor of psychiatry at the University of Alabama in Birmingham and an expert on the roles people play in life, Dr. Osmond was quoted as saying, "Roles are marvelous human inventions that enable people to get on with one another… We cannot live without roles. But we cannot allow ourselves to be oppressed by them, either" (Collins, 2008).

Sociologists have long emphasized the centrality of social roles in maintaining social functioning (Maconis, 2007). A role may be defined as a set of behaviors that is customary and usual for a given social position. These positions are called *social statuses*, as we saw in Chapter 4. We also noted that every individual has more than one social status – a woman may be an attorney, a mother and a wife all at the same time. Each of these different statuses is associated with different roles, and the average person gives little conscious thought to the process by which they and others constantly juggle different roles.

Sociologists also study the problems that ensue when a given individual's different roles are incompatible with one another – situations labeled as *role conflict* and *role strain*. From the perspective of counseling couples, we have seen many situations in which relationship issues arose because of role conflicts that developed over time. Figure 5.4 shows an illustration that Bill Emener used to explain to one of his client couples how the roles of man, husband and father *and* of wife, mother and woman, came into conflict over the course of a long-term marriage. The dialogue from his sessions is shown in Dialogue 5.3.

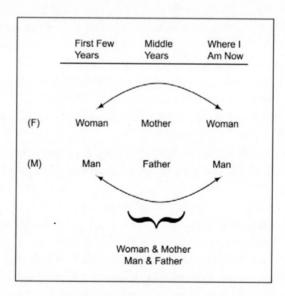

Figure 5.4. Loving Roles We Play.

Dialogue 5.3 Loving Role We Play

After 21 years of marriage, Donna (D) and Jimmy's (J) marital problems "had finally gotten the best of them." About a month before coming to see Bill Emener (B), Jimmy had moved out of the house and began living in his own apartment. A 43-year-old supervisor of a road construction crew, he told Bill it was extremely frustrating for him to continue to live with Donna "because it felt more like I was living with my mother than living with the woman I married."

Donna, a 44-year-old legal secretary, was equally frustrated with Jimmy because, as she said, "For years he had been giving more love, attention and affection to our two sons than to me." The conversation during the first session began to focus on the various loving roles that the two of them had played in the course of their marriage.

B: [While sketching a diagram for D and J similar to the one in Figure 5.4] From what you have been telling me, Donna, it appears that for the first few years of your marriage, your predominant gender identity was that of a "woman." However, as your sons became more demanding of your time, your gender identity became more of that of a "mother." And now that your two sons are off at college, you are trying to reduce your mothering role and increase your being a "woman." Nonetheless, it appears that you are struggling to some extent with your transition and that Jimmy is very frustrated with you. [Then turning to J] For the first few years of your marriage, your gender identity was primarily that of a "man." However, as your two sons grew older and were more demanding of your time, your gender identity turned to more of one of a "father." And, like Donna, you are trying to increase your primary gender identity, that of a "man,' and you appear to be struggling with your transition. At the same time, Donna appears to be very frustrated with you as well.

D: [After staring at the diagram for a few moments] It is only too bad, I guess, that during those middle years I was not able to be both – woman and mother!

J: [First looking at Bill and then turning to Donna] I guess I could say the same for me.

As the session continued, it was clear to Donna and Jimmy that during their middle years they *replaced* their gender identities instead of *adding* the gender identities that were pertinent to their respective loving roles in their family. Prior to their next session (below), both Donna and Jimmy carefully read some self-help materials that had been suggested to them.

B: Well now, where do we go from here?

J: How about if we start off with some dating? It is clear to me that although I indeed have learned how to be a loving daddy, I have forgotten how to be a loving man. There is no doubt I will be clumsy at it. [Then turning to Donna] So... would you like to go out with me this Saturday night?

D: [Leaning back in her chair, turning red from blushing] Jeez, Bill I feel like I am back in junior high school. But I have to admit, it does feel good! [Then turning to Jimmy with a coy smile] I don't know, Jimmy, I'll have to check my schedule. [Following a few moments of silence...] Yes, Jimmy, I believe I am free Saturday night. Did you have anything in mind?

J: Well, my dear – not that I have given it any thought, you understand – but I was thinking if I could pick you up at around five, we could get something to eat and then go to a movie I know you would enjoy seeing – one you've been talking about for over a month now!

D: I think I know what movie you are talking about. But don't tell me. I'd rather be surprised.

J: Great. It's a date.

D: I have to admit, Jimmy, I am really looking forward to going out with you Saturday night. But let's go slow; I need to keep things simple so I can feel comfortable.

Jimmy's manner and nodding in agreement clearly indicated that he too had read the recommended materials on "boundary setting" and was communicating to Donna that he felt respect for, and a sense of commitment to, honoring her boundaries. They did not schedule another session. Both of them said they were comfortable with continuing on their own. Bill told them he agreed with their assessment, but also told them he would appreciate some follow-up communication from them just to know how they were doing.

About two months later, Donna left a message on Bill's answering machine. It was short and sweet, yet in its own way very complete: "Hi Dr. Emener, this is Donna Johnson. I just wanted you to know that everything is going extremely well. If it doesn't rain this weekend, we will be able to move all of Jimmy's furniture in my brother's pickup truck. And if all of our plans come through, by Sunday night I will be doing something that I haven't done in years – I will be living with a man! A wonderful, loving man... his name is Jimmy."

Role conflict that develops slowly over time as each partner undergoes changes in their so-called gender identity – their *master status* with respect to their relationship – can have an insidious impact on the health of loving relationships. Sometimes, as in the case of Donna and Jimmy (see Dialogue 5.3), all that is necessary to get the relationship back on track is to point out the role conflicts and advise the partners how to readjust them. It should go without saying that the earlier this happens after role conflicts become an issue, the easier it is to correct.

LITTLE THINGS MEAN A LOT

When working with couples on their loving relationships, we occasionally ask them to tell us *what they consider to be the most loving thing their loved ones ever did for them*. After we have shared the following two examples, we shall discuss the principle illustrated by them.

John said to Bill Emener, "One winter when we were living up north, I woke up at six a.m. only to find that because of a snowstorm during the night, the schools would be closed. Although I unfortunately had to go to work, I tried my best to be quiet and not disturb our three children or my wife, who was a school teacher. The first things I had to do were to dress, go out and shovel snow off the driveway and brush the snow off the car. By the time I got back inside, I felt frozen through and through. Before going into the bathroom to shave and shower, I peeked in at the children and my wife, and with great envy noticed they were nice and warm and continuing to enjoy their sleep. Being a dutiful family man, I quietly went about washing up. Furthermore, I knew I would have to hustle because I was running late. When I finished toweling off, I opened the door of the shower stall and there on the counter top was a cup of piping hot, fresh coffee. As I thought to myself, *What a loving thing for her to do for me*, a tear rolled down my cheek. I thought, *What a lucky man I am!*"

Jennifer said, "About three years ago when our youngest child began going to school all day, I decided to return to work. I started a good job with a local marketing company. About a month later, my boss told me that on the last Wednesday of the month I would have to go directly from work to the airport, fly to Atlanta, and attend a meeting the following morning. I was so scared! It was going to be the first time that I ever flew in an airplane by myself, caught a cab to a hotel by myself, checked into a hotel by myself, and spent a night alone away from my family. I remember saying to my husband, who was a frequent traveler, 'I just wish I could be like you – confidently checking into a hotel and before retiring for the evening going to the lounge to unwind a little bit. But I think that I would be too scared to do that, and I am sure you would prefer I go directly to my room and call you as soon as I get there.' That Wednesday morning, as luck would have it, we all overslept. My husband was wonderfully helpful in assisting my getting the children ready for school and packing my small suitcase. At the end of my workday, I went directly to the airport, flew to Atlanta, checked into the hotel and went directly to my room. But before calling home, I figured that it might be a good idea to unpack. When I opened it, there on top was a $10 bill with an inscription in red ink that read 'Have a drink or two on me. Love, Tommy.' I took him up on his suggestion, but only had one drink because I wanted to hurry back to my room so I could call him and tell him how much I felt loved by him and how much I loved him."

The commonality in these two examples is clear. What John's wife did for him and what Jennifer's husband did for her were not big things. They were little things. However, it is not the size, the cost or the lavishness associated with the things that people do for each other that mean so much to them. Rather, it is the other person's empathic thoughtfulness and the anticipation that it would bring them relief and pleasure that really counts. The diamond ring at Christmas, the anniversary cruise and the new car as a birthday present are expensive and lavish. But things like the unexpected cup of coffee on the countertop and the unexpected love note fall into the category of "the big little things." It seems reasonable to conclude that for individuals in loving relationships, *the big little things that they do for each other everyday* are the primary things that contribute to their feeling special and deeply loved.

BEING LOVED AND FEELING LOVED

"I can't believe you do not appreciate how much I love you," Carolyn said to Ross during a counseling session. "I steam-press your shirts, I fix you a snack when you come home late from work, I fix you breakfast early on Saturday mornings before you go to play golf, and I always do my best to look my best whenever I go anywhere with you!" Ross replied, "Yes Carolyn, I believe you feel a tremendous amount of love for me. As far as you are concerned, I am being loved by you everyday of the week. The problem, however, is that in many ways I don't feel loved by you."

Ross and Carolyn had been married for almost 12 years, but for the past 10 years they apparently were not feeling loved by each other. "When the frustration and loneliness finally caught up with us," Ross said, "we decided it was time to come and get some help."

Bill Emener invited them to accept a homework assignment that involved two things. "I would like to suggest that each of you make two lists:

1)   a list of those things the other person does that results in your feeling loved by him or her; and

2)   a list of those things you wish the other person would do because in doing so you
     would feel loved by him or her."

When they returned for their next session, the three of them reviewed the two lists. Ross
and Carolyn also discussed their feelings regarding what they were hoping the other might do
to contribute to feeling loved by each other. Importantly, at the end of the session, they both
left with subtle senses of commitment to actually do some of the things on each other's lists.
When they returned for their third session – their last – Ross said, "Not only is Carolyn
actually doing some of the things that I had indicated would contribute to my feeling loved by
her, but she is actually doing them better than I had ever anticipated or hoped for! Have I felt
more loved by her over the last three weeks? Hell yeah!"

While caressing Ross' hand, Carolyn added, "And I never realized, my dear, what a
loving little teddy bear you could be!"

As they were leaving the office, hand-in-hand, Ross turned and said, "You know, Dr.
Emener, over the past few weeks I have felt incredibly loved by this woman. And it just hit
me: part of the reason is simply that *she is trying so hard to help me feel loved by her*. I can't
begin to tell how good that feels."

"I am happy for the two of you," Bill Replied. "I think you are well on your way."

Knowing that you are being loved is the next best thing to feeling loved.

RELATIONSHIP PROS AND CONS

The following includes an excellent relationship-analysis exercise we have frequently
used with couples, often during the first session or as a homework assignment between the
first and second sessions. On a piece of unlined paper, we draw a chart similar to the one in
Figure 5.5, and then make a copy for each partner. We then ask each of them to make three
lists: "The first is a list of those things about your partner you like, love and cherish and
wouldn't want to change. The middle column is for things you wish were different about your
partner, yet you can live with them. The rightmost column is for those things you wish were
different *and* need to be fixed for the relationship to continue – some people call these
'relationship enders.' You may have nothing to list in the last column, but many couples who
seek the help of a professional counselor tend to have at least one item in that area."

Once your clients have filled in their charts, it is helpful to look them over with them and
weigh the pros and cons about their relationship. The more each person's chart is skewed to
the right, the higher the chances that their relationship has serious issues that should probably
be addressed. The more their items cluster to the left, the healthier their relationship probably
is, at least from each respective individual's point of view.

Of course, each person's chart gives only half of the story; his or her partner will have
their own lists in each column. To get the full picture of the relationship, both partners need to
fill in the worksheet. In addition to each partner gaining more empathy for each other, this
exercise also can surface other negative or harmful aspects of the couple's relationship that
need to be addressed.

With their understanding that the exchange of information is intended to strengthen their
relationship, you not only can help your couple gently, respectfully and compassionately

compare their individual lists, but also to identify specific things each of them can do to improve their relationship and ultimately make themselves and the other person happier.

Things About My Partner...		
I Like, Love and Cherish	I Wish Were Different and Are Okay	I Wish Were Different and Need Fixing

Figure 5.5. Three Lists to Assess Relationship Pros and Cons.

LOVE TRIANGLE

A relationship-analysis technique we frequently find helpful during a first session with a couple is to review what we call the "Love Triangle." This was first developed by a well-known psychologist, Dr. Robert J. Sternberg, in the late 1980s. Basically, we draw a diagram for them similar to the one Figure in 5.6 and say something like: "In all my years of working with couples, I have concluded that the three pillars of love are *intimacy*, *passion* and *commitment*. Starting on the top of the triangle, for example, I found that in 'good' loving relationships people tend to have a high level of *social intimacy* – like holding hands when you are in a restaurant, gently touching the other person on his or her earlobe as you walk past at a social gathering, or inviting her to sit on your lap for a few minutes while you are at a barbecue. *Personal intimacy* is when you wake up at seven o'clock on a Saturday morning and, knowing that you do not have to get up, you just lie there, watch each other breathe and cuddle and nuzzle, simply for the pleasure of being together.

"Another pillar of a loving relationship is passion. *Social passion* is demonstrated when you run up to me at the airport and throw your arms around me as soon as you see me coming down the gateway, or when I sneak up behind you in the kitchen and throw my arms around you and give you a big hug. *Personal passion* is what most people tend to think of as being associated with lovemaking.

"Last but not least is commitment. An example of how *social commitment* can be demonstrated is when I get a call from you telling me that your car has broken down and I immediately drive to meet you and help you. *Personal commitment* includes the connotation 'If there were only room for one person in my heart, it would be you!' Do you have an understanding and appreciation for these six critical aspects of love in a loving relationship? If not, I would be more than happy to discuss any of them further with you."

Figure 5.6. The Love Triangle.

After we have concluded that both individuals understand and appreciate these six critical considerations, we say, "For the moment, I am going to assume that if the two of you had high levels of these six aspects of your relationship, you wouldn't be here. If this assumption is accurate, then I would like for each of you to tell me, from your own individual points of view, where are the strengths and weaknesses in your relationship? Said another way, where is the good news and where is the bad news – or simply, 'What needs fixin'?'"

To illustrate the insight-producing power of the Love Triangle, we want to share with you Bill Lambos' work with a client named John, whom he had been seeing on and off for over a year. John was a successful 42-year-old night-club owner who had no difficulties with feeling passion and intimacy for the women with whom he had relationships. However, he was having difficulty with the third leg – commitment. As they explored John's blocks to forming feelings of commitment, Bill suggested, "John, every night when you work at one of your clubs, you see and talk to many attractive younger women. Knowing you are the owner and well off, and being a good-looking man, they flirt with you and try to get your interest. Yet you keep them at arm's length because you are involved with the girl you are seeing. Nevertheless, do you think the constant attention from the younger women might interfere with you wanting to make a commitment to your girlfriend?"

John thought about Bill's question and then said, "Yes, it's a factor, but not the whole story. I also think that my girlfriend has similar issues – after all, she is very attractive and works as a bartender at one of my clubs. Guys are hitting on her all the time, and even though she always tells them 'Sorry, I'm in a relationship,' it's obvious she likes the attention. It doesn't seem right that someone who is always asking me for a stronger commitment – like getting engaged – should act like that."

When Bill drew the Love Triangle for John, he suggested that he and his girlfriend each think about the difference between social intimacy and romantic intimacy, adding, "Maybe both of you are confusing the former for the latter?" Following a pause, John replied, "Dr. Lambos, you might just be right. Both of our jobs require a certain level of social intimacy, which involves no commitment at all, and if we can separate that from true romantic intimacy, which in a relationship should go along with commitment, maybe we can get over this stumbling block."

The last time John saw Bill, he showed him the engagement ring he was going to give his girlfriend. Bill smiled and said "John, I'm happy for you and think as long as you can keep the distinction clear, you'll do fine."

A couple counseled by Bill Emener also demonstrates the effectiveness of the Love Triangle. After having had the opportunity to work with Richard and Janice for approximately four months, he did not see them again until five years later when he met them in a mall. Janice immediately ran up to Bill in her typical excited way and, after requesting permission, threw her arms around him and gave him a big hug. Richard's long and hearty handshake clearly indicated he was glad to see his former therapist as well. Even though Bill sensed that he didn't have to ask, he did. "How are the two of you doing?"

Janice immediately responded "Ever since the last time we saw you, the intimacy, passion and commitment that we give and receive from each other has just been wonderful!" With some light laughter and a warm smile of happiness on his face, Bill responded with a quip, "Oh, so you remember all that stuff we talked about?" Richard replied, "We live it everyday. I can't begin to tell you how happy Janice and I are!"

After parting, Bill glanced back over his shoulder for one last look at them as they began to blend into the crowd. In that last glimpse, he saw not only two very happy adults, but also two people who looked like two little kids in early summer, frolicking along on a country road, on their way home from their last day of school.

Indeed, there are many important attributes, characteristics and aspects of a "good" loving relationship. Nonetheless, the meaningful differences between a relationship and a loving relationship are primarily vested in three important relationship attributes – *intimacy*, *passion* and *commitment*.

UNCONDITIONAL LOVE

Toward the end of one of Bill Emener's sessions with Jack and Irene, the three of them realized they were his last appointment for that evening. Since none of them was in any rush to get home, they enjoyed the unexpected opportunity to simply sit and chat for a while. The conversation drifted to a question many people have struggled with over the years: Is there such a thing as unconditional love? Bill really felt on the spot when Jack directed that question to him and added, "Come on, Dr. Emener, commit yourself! What is your personal and professional opinion regarding this question – do you really think there is such a thing as unconditional love?"

Bill looked at the two of them, smiled with some sense of trepidation and said, "Yes and no." While falling back in her chair, Irene quipped, "Typical college professor!" The three of them laughed.

Bill then went on to explain himself. "I do believe that one person can feel and experience unconditional love *from another person*. So in that sense, my answer would be yes, there is such a thing. On the other hand, if the nature of our love is 'unconditional love,' then we feel intimacy, passion and commitment to and from each other; each of us is committed to being the best person that we individually can be; we are committed to helping each other to be the best person that each of us can be; and each of us is committed to making our relationship the best that it can be. But what if you change and no longer feel those types of commitments? Will I continue to be able to feel the love for you that I feel now? And because I tend to believe that most people's answers to those last two questions would be 'no,' then my current unconditional love for you may have some conditions: you will continue to be committed to being the best person that you can be, you will continue to be committed to helping me be the best person that I can be, and you will continue to be committed to working with me so we can make our relationship the best it can be. Thus, in view of these latter considerations, I feel that my answer to your question is, 'no' – in the purest sense, there is no such thing as unconditional love."

After pondering Bill's statements, Irene said, "So what you are suggesting, Dr. Emener, is that, philosophically speaking, *a person can feel unconditional love from another person, but can only give conditional love in return?"*

"Yes," Bill replied, "at least at this point, Irene" those are my thoughts about those particular issues."

Jack, while looking at both Bill and Irene, said, "But those may be two entirely different phenomena – the feeling and *receiving* of unconditional love and the feeling and *giving* of unconditional love." The three of them, then feeling comfortable with the reality that they had actually raised and discovered more questions than answers, looked at their watches and unanimously decided they "had done enough thinking for one night."

The *feeling and receiving of unconditional love*, and the *feeling and giving of unconditional love*, are two related yet separate phenomena. Thus, when working with a couple it indeed may be helpful to assist your clients in analyzing the extent to which each of them is *feeling and giving* conditional and/or unconditional love to each other, and the extent to which they are *feeling and receiving* conditional and/or unconditional love from each other.

FORGETTING AND FORGIVING

When Bill Lambos was undergoing his post-doctoral internship, he once asked Dr. Vince Parr, his supervising psychologist, "What is the single most important kernel of truth or wisdom you have gleaned from your 30 years of clinical counseling? Put another way, Vince, if you could only teach me one thing about being an effective therapist, what would it be?"

Vince thought for a moment and replied "Bill, that's an easy one. Health and happiness, whether individually or in relationships, comes from learning how to remain firmly in the present – regardless of what the past has dealt you or what you think the future may hold. If you can teach your clients that, they will always leave your office healthier and happier than when they came to see you."

Bill has never forgotten that conversation, in or outside of the therapy room. Although it is true we must learn from our past mistakes and experiences, as well as prepare for future contingencies, we nonetheless always exist only in 'the now' – the present moment.

The wisdom of this simple proposition was made abundantly clear when Bill Emener counseled Alex and Tammy about the subject of holding on to grudges versus forgiving and forgetting. "Alex and I never forget anything either of us ever does with, for, or to each other. Not only do we never forget, but we always remember the good things and the bad things as well," Tammy once said. "Remembering or forgetting is really not all that important to us anyway," she added. "It is our ability to genuinely and authentically forgive ourselves and forgive each other for what we do and don't do that is the most important thing."

The processes involved in overcoming addiction, anger and grief, as well as numerous other difficult realities of life, is not predicated on people's ability to forget – they are predicated on people's abilities to forgive. "When something bad happens between Alex and me," Tammy continued, "one of the first things we work on is trying to forgive ourselves. Once I can forgive myself, I can forgive Alex. And once Alex can forgive himself, he can forgive me. Then, the two of us are able to get on with our lives and our wonderful relationship."

Analyzing the extent to which your clients can forgive themselves and each other can be very important:

➤ Love and loving are, in many ways, about *giving*.
➤ Love and loving are also about *forgiving*.

Promoting Relationship Happiness

Just as the previous example shows the pitfalls of living in the past, neither is it uncommon for couples to obsess about and question the future of their relationship. Some turn to astrology charts, tarot cards, palm readings and psychics; and while these options very well may work for some individuals, such avenues of inquiry are outside the scope of this book. Regardless, neither the past nor the future is a good place to spend all of one's time.

As is commonly experienced, the excitement, joy and happiness people experience in the beginning of a relationship is wonderful – it's exciting. As time ensues, however, there understandably is less of that kind of fun. The beginning segment of a loving relationship contains a lot of idealistic perceptions and illusions; while projecting their light onto their new partner and their new relationship, people see what they want to see. Once they begin to see each other's humanness, insecurities and flaws, however, the idealism begins to fade and reality enters the picture. Seeing each other's weaknesses is perhaps not as exciting, but isn't it deeply profound that people can love each other, not only in spite of, but even *because* of each other's flaws? And as they feel safer and more secure with their partner, they can be open to greater depths of intimacy. Nonetheless, new found intimacy and its resulting excitement, joy and happiness can only evolve if the individuals are paying attention to their relationship and nurturing it rather than allowing all the other demands of life suck the life out of it.

There are many things that couples can do to counteract the tendency to fall into a relationship rut and not experience relationship happiness. In many ways, it's about taking responsibility for creating passion and desire rather than expecting it to just be there. In our experiences, frequently during our first session with a couple, we have found it helpful to ask them the following 10 analytical "Promoting Relationship Happiness Questions," and when appropriate discussing the respective surrounding issues (as briefly discussed below) with them.

1) *Do you take time each week to go on a date with each other, to be romantic and sexy?* This includes making time to make love. The more couples do it, the more they want it. The less they do it, the less they want it.

2) *Do you take time each month or so to experience something totally new with each other, whether attending an interesting lecture, kayaking or going to a new town?* Experiencing new things adds a level of excitement to a loving relationship and adds to the couples "history."

3) *Do you spend time regularly thinking about all the things you love about each other and share your thoughts with each other?* When partners get stressed, it's easy for them to focus on what they find irritating. It's important for partners to make a conscious effort to shift their thinking to the positive and look for the best in each other.

4) *When discussing money issues, do you set a time, go to the kitchen table, discuss it, and then let it go?* If a money issue – which is cited as the number one cause of divorce – hasn't been resolved, it's helpful for the couple to set another time to discuss it in that way. Moreover, it's important for the couple to avoid letting it become a discussion in the bedroom or over dinner and avoid any tendency to discuss it on and off throughout the day.

5) *Do you promote intimacy by making time to share your feelings, needs and desires, as well as remaining open to hearing about each other's?* Having deep level empathy for each other is an essential aspect of a healthy and meaningful loving relationship; keeping each other's dreams and fears confidential and not using them against each other is equally crucial.

6) *Do you dream with each other and set goals that you work on together to reach them?* Listening to and talking about a partner's dreams is one thing – helping them set and work towards achieving them is another.

7) *Do you deal with upsets at the time they happen or soon after so that they don't fester and become resentments?* Not attending to upsetting issues in a timely manner matters – not doing so makes them worse.

8) *Do you take time at least once a day to say thank you to each other for loving you and for sharing life's journey with you?* Making time for such intimate interactions is like the unseen epoxy under the hull of a good boat – it holds a lot of important things together.

9) *Do you do "Big Little Things" for each other?* The diamond earrings for her birthday and the expensive new set of golf clubs for his are much appreciated. The unexpected "I Love You" sticky note on the bathroom mirror and the unexpected hot cup of coffee waiting on the counter after an early morning shower when running late are equally appreciated (and sometimes even more).

10) *Do you always speak to each other in loving and respectful ways?* Speaking to each other with disrespect, disdain and indifference communicates a powerful damaging message – one that frequently trumps the content of the statement. It is important for couples to remember: *love* is not just a noun – it's also a verb.

Ultimately, using these 10 analytical questions indeed can help couples make commitments to each other to do these relatively simple things on a regular basis – things that can meaningfully help them from falling into a relationship rut and feeling that they're not in love anymore. As one of our happily-in-love clients poignantly said, "We both have taken responsibility to keep the sparks flying and enjoy a lasting love. We're recommitted to making time to nurture our relationship everyday so that like a beautiful garden that is well tended, it will continue grow and grow, and continue to bring both of us happiness and joy, year after blissful year."

You may be wondering, "Do my clients really have to learn to memorize 10 things to worry about to keep their relationships healthy?" Of course not. What these 10 questions have in common, however, is that they involve ways of keeping a relationship healthy and happy *now* – in the present… in the moment. We cannot think of better examples that demonstrate the simple yet profound truth that to live in the present moment – to "stay now" – will help every couple you counsel stay committed to maintaining a happy and healthy loving relationship.

CHAPTER SUMMARY

In this chapter we examined 11 critical areas of relationship analysis pertinent to the establishment and sustenance of a functional, meaningful and happy loving relationship: (1) a house built on one stilt or many stilts; (2) dependence and/or independence; (3) public space, private space and together space; (4) loving roles partners play; (5) big little things partners do in relationships; (6) being loved and feeling loved; (7) relationship pros and cons; (8) the importance of intimacy, passion and commitment; (9) unconditional love; (10) forgetting and forgiving; and, (11) relationship happiness. Facilitating clients' analytical journeys down each of these roads constitutes an important, pivotal part of professional couples counseling. By helping clients calmly analyze the troublesome issues in their relationships and then helping each of them accepting responsibility for their part in the problem areas, a loving relationship can be strengthened immeasurably.

Socrates said,
    "The unexamined life is not worth living."
Emener and Lambos say,
    "The unexamined relationship is not worth being in."

CHAPTER 5 DISCUSSION QUESTIONS

1) Generally speaking, why is it better for a relationship to be built on many stilts?
2) In what ways is a relationship based on dependence and/or independence?

3) How could you help a couple address their individual needs and desires for public space, private space and together space?

4) Why is it important for both partners in a relationship to be aware of the loving roles they play and how they impact their relationship?

5) Do you believe it is important that partners in a loving relationship do big little things with and for each other?

6) In a loving relationship, what is more important – to be loved or to feel loved?

7) Can any couple honestly assess their relationship's pros and cons?

8) To what extent is intimacy, passion and commitment a meaningful part of a loving relationship?

9) Have you ever experienced unconditional love?

10) When bad things happen in a loving relationship, can partners ever truly forgive each other?

11) As a couples counselor, what can you do to help a couple promote their relationship happiness?

THE PAST

Few issues in modern psychology have been the topic of as much debate as the impact one's past has on the present person, how one functions today, and how well adjusted one may be in the future. Equally open to debate is the separate yet related question of whether one must revisit the past in order to address current issues and move beyond them. Although many theories of counseling assume this at their core, other schools of thought propose that it is better to "just let go" of one's past and focus on learning how to effectively deal with the present and future. Of course, such questions are particularly salient when dealing with loving relationships. Do we advise clients that they are destined to carry the baggage of past relationships into every new one? If not, how can we assist them in learning from their mistakes and profiting from them, achieving ever better relationships as they grow from experience?

As discussed in Chapter 2, various schools of thought answer such questions very differently and, in most instances, definitive answers are elusive. For example, the psychodynamic psychologist who looks to the theories of Sigmund Freud and his contemporaries sees our pasts, and particularly our early childhood years, as constituting the single greatest influence on who we are today. By their account, people *must* resolve any issues of significance in their past before they can overcome the lingering effects on them. The behavioral psychologist also recognizes the impact of our past, but very differently. From his or her perspective, people have been conditioned through associations, rewards and punishments to behave in certain ways, but new contingencies of reinforcement can replace older learning and, as such, the past is less important. From another point along the spectrum, we are told by those who adhere to the cognitive-behavioral school of thought that too much is made of dwelling on our past and we should advise our clients not to allow it to distract them from going forward. This is particularly true of the therapist who adheres to the rational emotive behavior theory of Albert Ellis (1996). Bill Lambos still fondly remembers meeting Dr. Ellis during his certification training at the Albert Ellis Institute in New York City where he personally advised Bill that "In therapy, sports and relationships, the best advice is 'never look backwards' – in all three cases, what is behind you no longer matters!"

Your authors' position on the subject of the past lies somewhere between the two extremes proffered by Freud and Ellis. Few practicing counselors can realistically deny that certain past experiences have shaped who we are today. This is especially true of highly emotionally-charged experiences such as trauma. Neuroscience now has shown that trauma can permanently change the brain in significant ways and may result in problems ranging from mild generalized anxiety to specific phobias and, among the most severe cases, non-epileptic seizures and even multiple personalities, now called Dissociative Identity Disorder (Cozolino, 2002). Post-Traumatic Stress Disorder (PTSD) also lies on this continuum. On the other hand, achieving mental stability and healthy functioning, especially in loving relationships, relies on escaping the pull of earlier experiences and learning to choose new, more effective behavior patterns and making wise choices, based not on the comfort of familiarity but on what one knows, in one's heart and head, to be the right thing to do. People who blame their inability to function on their past and think they can never overcome it, will live a life of self-fulfilling prophecies in which their beliefs come true only because they insist on believing them. One of the great traps people tend to fall into is seeking out partners whose behavior is familiar and predictable, *even if it's unhealthy and the last thing they might consciously choose had they been aware of their underlying motivations.*

Whenever discussing adult loving relationships, we operationally define an adult as "anyone over 20 years of age." Our reasons are threefold: (1) individuals over the age of 20 tend to have accumulated sufficient life experience such that they now enjoy some sense of independence; (2) they have had some experiences with relationships (experientially as well as by observation); and (3) any adult loving relationship that one enters into also includes some leftover baggage from previous relationships. We trust that the meaning and importance of this last assumption regarding leftover baggage will be clearer to you by the end of this chapter. This chapter will describe and discuss some of the critical ways by which our past loving relationships, our past observations of other peoples' loving relationships and our present conceptualizations of loving relationships (which are highly affected by our past) can significantly affect our present and future loving relationships.

We thus begin our exploration of the role of one's past in defining and managing loving relationships with two assumptions in hand: first, that past experience does leave a footprint on the brain and, in so doing, on the heart and the mind. We therefore cannot ignore the role of the past in counseling others with respect to their loving relationships. Second, that despite these "footprints on the soul," people are not prisoners of their pasts. As most of Bill Emener's students and many of his clients can recall him rhetorically saying, "At what point do our past explanations become our excuses not to change?" As couples therapists, our role is to teach clients to benefit from their past experience without carrying the residue of that experience as baggage into the future. With this in mind, we begin this leg of our journey.

A RELATIONSHIP'S PAST, PRESENT AND FUTURE

Long-term relationships may develop patterns that act as a kind of inertia that constrain the dynamics of an otherwise healthy ongoing relationship. In all probability, all of us have listened to a discussion between two partners that went something like this:

➢ "Why do we always have to go to the movies on Saturday night?"
➢ "Well, we've been doing it for three years. I thought you liked it."
➢ "No, I just agree to go because I assumed you were so gung ho about it."
➢ "And you never thought to mention this before?"

➢   "Well, I didn't want to rock the boat."

In such cases, a pattern becomes established – one which then becomes the basis for maintaining behavior for no other reason than "that's what we've always done." We have found it important for couples in long-term loving relationships to (1) examine their repetitive patterns that may have developed and (2) discuss them from time to time.

Another time at which relationships can be influenced by an individual's own history arises at points of significant, meaningful change – when a child is born, someone goes back to work after raising children, or the family moves into a new house, perhaps in a different area of the country. Patterns of behavior and interaction that have become comfortable and predictable over time indeed may be greatly disrupted by such changes. As we have noted in the previous chapter, too much unpredictability is a relationship stressor – in general, *people value predictability and find it comforting*. To wit, we know of many cases in which couples have sought help and advice when their patterns of interaction changed. Moreover, it is usually the case that one of the two partners is more troubled than the other by the change.

Bill Lambos recalls first meeting with Trudy and Manny after the birth of their first child, which came during the sixth year of their marriage. Trudy was very happy about having become a mother, but Manny was not all that happy about the changes brought about by the birth of their daughter. When Bill asked Manny what the problem was, he replied, "Dr. Lambos, I am as thrilled as Trudy to have this beautiful child in our lives, but our marriage is suffering from it. I feel totally unattended to, except on payday when I become 'the family ATM.' I do my best to help with the baby and don't expect to be the center of Trudy's attention all the time, but quite frankly I'm feeling like a third wheel, and I can't say I like it." Trudy calmly yet immediately responded, "Oh come on, Manny, nothing much has changed for you: you get up, go to work, come home, and your supper is waiting. I have to catch my sleep when the baby is napping because I never get to sleep through the night. And when I am up, I have to do everything in between the baby's schedule. How can you be so selfish?"

Bill Lambos interrupted at that point: "Both of you have had your well-established routines turned upside down by the changes of parenthood. From my years of counseling couples after the birth of a child, I urge you to find time during the week when you can be together comfortably, just by yourselves. During that time treat one another to a healthy dose of TLC. Make a date of it. Trudy, your baby is old enough to be watched for an evening by a sitter. Find one and make it a priority. And Manny, don't confuse Trudy's love and attention for your daughter with the loss or lessening of her love for you. Things will never be as they were, but they can become even better. All it usually takes is: (1) to try and see things from the other person's point of view; and (2) to become part of the solution instead of continuing to be part of the problem."

The important point is that change disrupts patterns of familiarity, and with that often comes relationship stress. By addressing the underlying areas of concern with your clients earlier rather than later following such a change, issues can often be defused before they lead to more serious consequences.

THE INTERACTION EFFECT OF YOUR PASTS

To appreciate the meaning of the term "interaction effect," think about the following. As all of us know, hydrogen, H, is a gas. Oxygen, O, also is a gas. If you put them together, in a special combination and in a special way – such as H_2O – you have water. A loving relationship involves the unique and special pasts of two people. While each person's past, in and of itself, indeed may be unique and special, it may in no way be troublesome. However, when two members of a couple carry incompatible behaviors developed from some portion of their pasts, the result may sometimes be troublesome. This is illustrated in Dialogue 6.1.

Dialogue 6.1 The Interaction Effect of Your Pasts

Vick (V), a 32-year-old manager at a local car dealership, on behalf of himself and his girlfriend, Melissa (M), a 28-year-old legal secretary, scheduled an initial session with Bill Emener (B). When Bill noticed that it was five minutes past the scheduled appointment time and Melissa was in the waiting room by herself, he invited her into his office and introduced himself. Following some cordial pleasantries, the following ensued:

M: Vick just called me on his cell. He's stuck in traffic and will be a few minutes late. [Following some small talk...] While we're waiting for Vick, let me at least tell you what's bothering me about our relationship. Vick is a wonderful man and I love him dearly. And I know he loves me. But there are times when he's just too controlling. Sometimes he'll just announce what we'll be doing the following day or where we're going for dinner.

B: What I hear you saying is that you love each other very much, yet Vick is doing things that are very frustrating and annoying to you. [At that moment, Vick arrived and he and Bill exchanged cordialities, briefly discussing the horrible traffic.]

V: Maybe it would be helpful if I told you what's bothering me about our relationship. Melissa is a wonderful woman and I love her dearly. And I know she loves me. But there are times when she's just so controlling. Sometimes she'll just announce what we'll be doing for the evening or where we're going on vacation.

B: [Bill glanced at Melissa and struggled to hide a smile.] It sounds like you believe you both love each other very much but are frustrated by what you see is her trying to control you and aspects of your relationship. However, Vick, I'd like to ask you about your previous loving relationships.

V: After two serious relationships, I was married for five years. My divorce was finalized about two years ago. We never had any children. Mary, my ex, is a good person and we got along... most of the time. She was the director of a small-town library and very good at what she did. The problem was that she treated me like one of her staff – and in some ways like my mother – telling me what to do all the time. Once my divorce was finalized, I promised myself that I'd never allow myself to be bossed around again.

B: So based on what you've experienced in past relationships, you've promised yourself that you would never again be in a relationship where your partner would control and boss you around.

V: You bet.

B: Okay, thanks Vick. That's helpful for me to understand... and we'll get back to that. [Bill turned and faced Melissa.] Melissa, I'd like for you to tell me about your previous relationships.

M: Sure. I've lived just about all over the world, I was an army brat. And since moving to Tampa nine years ago, I was in two serious relationships – engaged once, never married. Both of the guys were good guys – one was a sergeant and the other a lieutenant in the army. [Then with a furrowed brow, she added...] They were good guys – a little too structured and controlling for me though. Sometimes even when they said "Good morning," it sounded like an order. [Toward the end of the session, Bill invited them to read a self-help book on communication styles and offered a possible explanation for what he saw as a critical issue in their relationship.]

B: It seems to me that at times both of you are interpreting each other's statements and actions based on your past experiences. [Then, looking at Melissa...] For example, going back to your previous examples, by giving Vick the benefit of the doubt it could have been that he simply knew that that restaurant was having live music that evening and thought it would be a nice surprise for you and that after dinner the two of you could have danced a bit. And it possibly could have been that your harsh memories of being controlled by demanding men made you interpret his saying, "I made reservations for us at David's," – a potentially very loving gesture – as an indication of his trying to control you. [Then turning to face Vick...] In a similar fashion, Melissa indeed may simply have wanted to surprise you with the room on the beach for the weekend so you could do some surfing. But based on your past experiences with controlling and demanding women, you interpreted her initiative – which very well could have been a very loving gesture on her part – as an indication of her trying to control you and demanding that she get her own way.

Two weeks later when Vick and Melissa returned, they said that the self-help book was very beneficial to them, and they were trying to be more careful when speaking to and listening to each other. Importantly, with their renewed understandings of each other's pasts, they were being more appreciative of each other's initiatives.

V: And please remember, Melissa, I'm not one of the men from your past; I'm the man in your present.

M: [Cuddling into Vick, with a wry smile on her face and through a gentle laugh...] Ditto, my boy... ditto.

What the dialogue demonstrates is that to the extent your clients' past relationship experiences guide their expectations for, and interpretations of new relationships, they may be committing an error of inductive logic. As couples counselors, it is important to identify such problems with *mistaken forward reasoning* and point them out to your clients. In many cases, simply identifying the tendency is all that is needed to correct it.

MOM AND DADS – OUR PRIMARY TEACHERS

Our parents have taught us and may even continue to teach us, directly and indirectly, many important aspects of loving relationships. Possibly because we believe this so much, it is not uncommon for us to say the following to our clients, students and friends:

- Daddies teach their little girls how to deal with men – they teach them many things about loving a member of the opposite sex. Daddies also teach their little boys how to deal with men – they teach them about male bonding.
- Mommies teach their little boys how to deal with women – they teach them many things about loving a member of the opposite sex. Mommies also teach their little girls how to deal with women – they teach them about female bonding.
- Together, mommies and daddies teach their children how to deal with loving relationships – they teach them many things about how two members of the opposite sex can love each other, be in love with each other, and be loving toward one another.

In terms of what we know about loving relationships, we consider mothers and fathers to be our primary teachers. Typically, our parents were the ones from whom we first learned our beliefs, attitudes, values and behaviors regarding what it means to be loving, what it means to be loved, what it means to be loveable, and what it means to be in a loving relationship. Family therapists and relationship counselors such as ourselves have a phrase we use to describe this tendency: "the impact of family of origin issues." Let's look at some more examples of this based on our counseling sessions.

Bill Lambos was seeing a couple, Jackie-Ann and Phillip, who generally got along but occasionally would come to quarrel so vehemently that one or the other would threaten to end their relationship. In retrospect, they told Bill, the issues were not major ones, but the problem kept recurring because both of them would get to a point where they would "dig their heels in and insist on getting their way." After a threat of breaking-it-off was made, sometimes by Phillip, sometimes by Jackie-Ann, one would back down and the issue would be settled – until the next time. Said Jackie-Ann, "Dr. Lambos, what's so frustrating about these arguments is that they tend to be about things that aren't all that important to us. We just get this idea that we have to get our own way, and then come the explosions."

Bill Lambos then asked each of them about their relationships with their parents when they were children. Phillip explained that he was from a British family and that whenever family decisions were discussed, his father had the final say – and that was the end of the discussion. Jackie-Ann related that she was "reared by a strong woman who was the ruler of the roost." When it came to matters at home, her mother made the final decisions. It occurred to Bill that each of them was carrying the expectations learned from their family of origin into their current relationship. Phillip unconsciously expected that final decisions should be his to make, and Jackie-Ann felt they were hers. When Bill pointed this out, it was an "Aha" moment for them. Once they could see the reasons for their expectations, a plan was hatched. Bill helped them divide the areas of their home and affairs into two groups – his domain and her domain. Each ceded final say of one of the two areas and agreed not to challenge the other's final decision in their respective domains. The negotiations were tense at times, but a breakthrough occurred when Phillip allowed Jackie-Ann to have final say in matters of home décor, in exchange for Phillip having final say on the use of frequent flyer miles for vacation planning. To Bill's knowledge, this couple is still together and doing quite well, having been able to change the expectations they had learned from unconsciously adopting the relationship patterns present in their respective families of origin.

In a similar example, Jonathan, a 32-year old welder who told Bill Emener that he was "totally confused about many aspects of his relationships with women," came to see him because he "could not figure out why he was having so much trouble developing and maintaining meaningful relationships with women." During their first session, they briefly discussed Jonathan's childhood, his relationship with his mom and dad and what it was like when he was younger and living at home. Their conversation ended with a mutual agreement that it would be helpful for them to spend some time focusing on Jonathan's relationships with his parents and the modeling effect of his parents' relationship on him. Bill suggested a homework assignment to Jonathan. He asked him to give some serious thought to, and write out his answers to, the three following questions:

1) What did you learn about loving relationships from your father?
2) What did you learn about loving relationships from your mother?
3) What did you learn about loving relationships from observing your parents' relationship?

Jonathan's experience of thinking seriously about these three questions and writing out his answers to them was extremely helpful.

We suggest that you, the counselor, may want to ask your clients these three questions. The process of doing so can be very enlightening and helpful. Take care to prepare your clients that they are doing this to discover more about themselves. That is, they should not consider this to be a fault-finding mission! We truly believe that whatever parents do (and don't do) with, for and on behalf of their children, at the time they are doing what they are doing because: (1) they are doing the best they can; and (2) they are not necessarily doing it with any intent of malice. When a person holds their parents responsible for their issues and/or blames them for what and who they are, they are not achieving the purpose of the inquiry. In fact, doing so will in all likelihood cause them more problems than any they perceive to be the "fault" of their parents. Á la "When does the explanation become the excuse?" Clients must be helped to learn and appreciate that it is healthier and much more productive to remember that they are responsible and accountable for themselves.

Finally, clients should be reminded that since we believe our parents were our primary teachers, it also is important to remember that if or when they have children of their own, they also become primary teachers. The recording artist John Mayer delightfully put this to music in the song "Daughters" with the lyrics:

> Fathers, be good to your daughters
> Daughters will love like you do
> Girls become lovers who turn into mothers
> So mothers, be good to your daughters too

LEARNED INTERPERSONAL NEEDS

In the context of loving relationships, the phrase "interpersonal needs" refers to the degree to which people prefer dependent versus independent styles of interacting with their significant other. Some individuals prefer to rely upon their partner for guidance and decision-making much of the time, whiles others are more comfortable being relatively independent. Other people feel comfortable in a relationship only when they are "in the driver's seat," or take on a leadership roll.

Sometimes people misidentify their partner's interpersonal needs because of behavior they have experienced in a past relationship. Your authors have seen this arise repeatedly in couples counseling situations. When such misidentification is causing a couple difficulty, it can be very helpful to assist them in exploring the basis for their "irrational" belief. This is demonstrated in Dialogue 6.2, taken from Bill Emener's case files.

Dialogue 6.2 Learned Interpersonal Needs

It is not uncommon for counselors to assist their clients in understanding and appreciating how their relationships with their parents can subconsciously set the stage for how they deal with other people throughout their lives. Ginger (G), a co-owner of a dry cleaning business, told Bill Emener (B) that she had been married twice, divorced twice, and currently "was fed up with her boyfriend, Jack, whom she had to take care of all the time."

B: It would be helpful for us to begin by your telling me about the men in your life and what your relationships with them were like.

G: Hank, my first husband, was an alcoholic and after two years of putting up with his crap I just couldn't take it anymore. I married him right after high school. Maybe I just needed to get away from home... My second husband, Russ, was a real mommy's boy. He thought he was the center of the universe. He was so in love with himself. There was no room in his life to be loving toward anyone else. I was like a slave to him – took care of him probably better than his mother did. He used to say to me, "You're just lucky that I married you." Can you believe that? Then along came Jack about three years ago. He's the one I'm dumping. Jack's a workaholic. He devotes all of his time to his business – works day and night. But when he's not working, he just expects me to wait on him hand and foot. He also expects me to be emotionally responsive to him all the time. When he comes home, the first thing I have to do is to see what kind of mood he's in. Then I know how I can be and how I can deal with him. But I've had it. I told him I want him out of my house by the end of the week!

B: As I was listening to you, I was impressed with your ability to control your anger – some of which is toward the men in your life and some toward yourself. This is something we will talk about. Not only that, we probably will also talk about some of the deep sadness and sorrow you may be feeling. But for now, let me tell you – it surely does seem that the men in your life were emotionally expensive. [Ginger began to cry. After she dried her eyes and got refocused, Bill continued.] What about the other man in your life – your father?"

G: I loved my daddy. And he drank too. Probably that's what killed him. He died about six years ago. All in all, however, I had a real good relationship with my dad. I even think he felt closer to me than he felt toward my mother. She used to holler at him all the time, especially when he was drinking or mad about something. I just would attend to him. When he didn't feel good, Mom would yell at him; I would fix something for him to eat or tell him to lie down on the couch and take a rest.

At the end of their session, in addition to suggesting some reading materials to her, Bill asked Ginger to continue to think about her relationships with the men in her life.

G: [At the start of their next session.] Between reading this book on co-dependency and talking with my sister about what you and I were talking about, I think I figured out why I have continued to pick losers! What I learned from Daddy was that if I wanted a man to be nice to me and love me, I had to take care of him. Simple, isn't it. I even became good at finding men who were looking for someone to take care of them – like Hank, Russ and Jack.

Subsequently, Ginger and Bill talked at length about her learned needs and her feeling responsible, especially emotionally responsible, for the men in her life.

G: Looking back on all of this, one of the best things I did to help myself was when I wrote that letter to my dad, which you asked me to write. It sounded silly at first when you asked me to write him a letter and mail it to you. He's dead. But my writing that letter allowed me to remember my loving thoughts about him, to no longer feel guilty about how I acted in order to get his love, and to choose not to be that way with men any longer. Like I told you when we reviewed the letter, I never want a man, or anyone for that matter, to be dependent on me. Nor do I want to be dependent on him. I want an interdependent relationship.

The last time Bill spoke with Ginger, she was doing very well – she was able to grow beyond the "bondage" (as she called it) that she learned when she was a child. She also told Bill, with a smile, she "was dating a man who was so different. He's healthy!"

PAST PEOPLE, CHARACTERISTICS AND RELATIONSHIPS: THE "SELF-FULFILLING PROPHECY"

A "self-fulfilling prophecy" may be defined as a prediction that comes true because of the behavior it – the prediction itself – creates. A recurring theme of this chapter is that people will replicate the kinds of loving relationships they have had earlier throughout their lives, and often do so unconsciously. Thus people tend to attract, be attracted to and have relationships with, similar kinds of people, *even when it is not in their best interest to do so*. Fortunately, as we saw in the case of Ginger in Dialogue 6.2, this does not mean people are destined to recreate their relationships from early life, only that people tend to do so and will benefit from being aware of the tendency. This is the most problematic in self-replicating abusive relationships, which we examine at the end of this chapter. But even in relationships free from the threat of violence or physical abuse, the *self-fulfilling relationship prophecy* can limit what people allow themselves to experience in new relationships and is a central issue for couples and relationship counselors to address.

Robert was a client being seen by Bill Emener. "When I was 16 years old," Robert said, "I fell in love with Julie and went steady with her for over two years. When I got to college, only about two months after breaking up with Julie, I met and eventually married Barbara. Last May, Barbara and I were divorced, and since last June I have been going with Sherry. But now that relationship seems to be going sour. I don't know, but there's got to be something wrong with me. The same thing seems to happen over and over." To some extent, Robert was right. Bill suggested to him: "Robert, rather than assuming there is something wrong with you, I prefer we assume that based on your life's experiences and what you have learned as a result of living, you are the way you are. And being the way you are and living your life the way you do, it just doesn't seem to work out the way you would like it to. So instead of trying to fix something that is broken or wrong, let's just agree that we are going to try to understand how you deal with people in your life and see if there are any changes that you would like to make." Robert agreed with this approach (and seemed to like it better too).

Toward the end of their session, Bill drew a diagram for Robert similar to the one in Figure 6.1. As they looked at the diagram, Bill said, "Based on what you have been telling me, there seems to have been a pattern in your life. When you were 16, you felt alone in the world and felt scared of being alone. Then came Julie for the next two years. When you got to college, you again felt alone and scared. Then came Barbara. When you were 23, you got your divorce from Barbara and then you again felt scared and alone. Then came Sherry. Now this one is going sour. How were you feeling toward the end of your relationships with Julie and Barbara, and how are you feeling now that you seem to be toward the end of this relationship with Sherry?" Robert pondered these questions for a few minutes and then said, "Angry... I feel angry and trapped. I also feel lost. I don't know who I am anymore. And I sort of had the same feelings with Julie and Barbara." Then he added, "But if I end this relationship with Sherry, then I know I'll probably just feel scared and alone again. I can't win!"

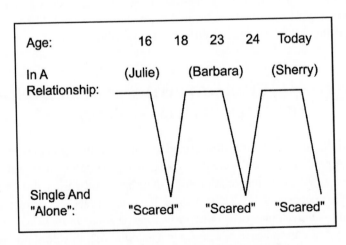

Figure 6.1. In a Relationship for Fear of Being Alone.

Bill invited Robert to work with him and try to work through his fears of being alone in the world. For years, his strategy of dealing with his aloneness was to run into another relationship. Fortunately, Robert said, "Okay, let's give it a try. I can't just keep doing this for the rest of my life."

A few months and a few sessions later, Robert shared, "I now see how my old pattern used to work. I would establish a relationship. I would enjoy the relationship, possibly even more than the person, but I was enjoying the relationship -- not necessarily because the relationship was so great but because it was better than feeling scared and alone. Then I would feel like I was losing me, feeling lost and like I was going nowhere! I would sabotage or actively end the relationship, feel scared and alone again, and find someone else to start the cycle with all over again. However, now that I have been reading some of these books, attending an Adult Adjustment Group and working with you, I recognize my fear of abandonment issues from my past. For the first time in years I can feel good about me, good about being in the world as me. I feel comfortable alone in my own skin. Most important, I don't have to have someone in my life to be able to feel good about me. That, in and of itself, simply feels wonderful!" Robert later added, "And the next time I am in a relationship, it will be because I want to, not because I have to!"

By analyzing himself and the people as well as relationships in his past, Robert was able to identify and understand his "self-defeating relationship pattern." And from that monumental first step, along with feeling much better about himself as a person, he was able to explore and find new ways of establishing and maintaining more meaningful interpersonal relationships. Occasionally taking time to process similar types of phenomena in your clients' lives can be extremely enlightening and helpful to them.

DYSFUNCTIONAL RELATIONSHIPS AND LIVING PARALLEL LIVES

A difficult case of a persistent maladaptive relationship pattern comes from Bill Lambos' practice. He was seeing Vickie, a 39-year old homemaker with two children, 8 and 12. During their third session, it became apparent that Vickie was holding back something important. Fittingly, Bill challenged her: "Vickie, it's become obvious you have a secret you haven't shared. If it's what I suspect it is, you need to let it out, or there's not much point of continuing with these sessions."

Vickie teared up as she replied, "It's true, Dr. Lambos, I'm in love with another man. We met on a long plane trip two years ago, and from the moment we started talking, the intense attraction we both felt was obvious. After that we started e-mailing and phoning one another to try and decide what to do about our mutual feelings. But we're both married with children, and neither of us wants to break up our families. We're stuck in this sort of limbo, seeing each other every six months or so. When we are together, I feel like this was how it was always meant to be, and I know he does too. But every time we start making plans for leaving our spouses and being together, something happens with one of our kids. What am I supposed to do? Be miserable for the sake of the children, or drag them through a divorce and a move across the country?"

Bill warmly said, "Well, at least now it's out for us to address. Let me ask you something, Vickie. If I was able to guess you were having an affair after three one-hour sessions, don't you think your husband has figured something out after living with you over the past two years?" She replied, "I never go there. I don't know what my husband thinks or knows. It's obvious to both of us that our marriage is dead, but neither of us will address it. We're both just going through the motions for the sake of the children." Bill continued,

"Vickie, divorce doesn't hurt children, but conflict does. In the long run, living in a loveless relationship is teaching them something that may affect them even more negatively. You need to take a stand and decide to break off the affair for good and forget about it and try to reinvigorate your marriage, *or* you need to take your lumps and move out of the house so you can begin building your future. Your children will be upset, especially at first, but so long as you and your husband do not expose them to open conflict, put them in the middle or use them as pawns, they will get over it in time. And then, when they are able to see their mother express true love to another person, they will learn something far more valuable than what they are learning now, which is how to live a parallel life with someone you don't love – not to mention how to lie about it to everyone else. You are not doing them, or yourself, any favors."

That was Vickie's last visit, and Bill has not heard from her since. We hope she took the advice offered, both for her sake and that of her family. When your client's relationship issues and decisions significantly affect others – such as the couple's children – it is important to remember your responsibilities to them as well as to your clients.

SECRETS AND THE PAST

We understand and respect the philosophical position of many people who assume that secrets in loving relationships are bad. They tend to believe that "there is no place for secrets in a loving relationship." However, we prefer an alternative conceptualization – that is, not to consider secrets as being either good or bad. Our experience tells us that it is preferable to allow individuals to decide for themselves what place their secrets have in their lives and relationships. Thus, rather than telling your clients whether having a secret is good or bad, we suggest that you have them ask themselves the following six questions:

1) What kind of secret is it?
2) Why do I feel a need to keep it a secret?
3) How do I feel about keeping it a secret?
4) From whom am I keeping it a secret?
5) What effect is my secret having on my loving relationship?
6) What would happen if I no longer kept my secret?

It should be apparent from an ethics perspective that a counselor or therapist should take great care when advising clients what to do with their secrets. The consequences of revealing their secret is theirs to face, and the decision to do so (or not) should therefore be their own. Their answers to questions above, nonetheless, will be helpful to them in making a decision and recognizing the consequences of that decision.

In loving relationships, there are different kinds of secrets, which can, from a tongue-in-check perspective be categorized as: (1) secret-secrets; and (2) not-so-secret secrets. A secret-secret is a piece of information (for example: a fact, a feeling or an idea) that is known to only one partner and not to their significant other. Moreover the person holding the secret expends considerable care to consciously keep their partner from knowing it. Sometimes it translates into lying by omission (i.e. by not telling something) or lying by commission (i.e. by denying it or telling a falsehood).

This type of secret can have a high cost. If the other member of the couple learns the truth, it can be a relationship ender. This is especially true of secrets about activities or behaviors that are on-going. If a married person is having an affair and knows it would result in an unwanted divorce, then he or she has a secret-secret with a high potential cost.

A not-so-secret secret is a piece of information that both individuals know (or think they know) but do not recognize their knowledge of or talk about (i.e., we both know something, we both know or strongly suspect that we both know what it is, but we never openly recognize it or talk about it). Sometimes these are called *taboos*. They are not so much secret as tacit, or unspoken.

You may be wondering why we are addressing the topic of secrets in a chapter about the past. There is a good reason: Secrets about the past, or about past behaviors that are not ongoing, are usually safer than secrets about things in the present. If a client is troubled by guilt related to something they did in the past that they have kept secret from their significant other, a counselor must help them weigh whether it is better to help them "let go" of the past, and thereby the guilt, than to clear their conscience by revealing their secret in order to clear their conscience. Again, this is a decision that can only be made by the client. The therapist's job is to help them make the best and most informed decision.

On the other hand, secrets about the present are dangerous. If a secret about a present situation is causing problems and you are seeing the couple, then there is little choice but to advise the couple that the truth should come out before real progress can be made.

We have taken the position that when a counselor is working with a couple, he or she must decide early on whether they agree to see each partner separately as well as together as a couple. Some counselors' stated position is that if one member of the couple reveals a secret they cannot reveal to the other partner, then they will not continue to see the couple together. Other counselors do not feel this is a problem as long as the rule for secrets is stated at the outset of counseling the couple. Bill Lambos, who is also certified as a family mediator, is used to dealing with secrets under the rules of confidentiality for individual sessions, and allows this over the course of couples counseling. Bill Emener, who prefers to work with couples only when they are together, lets the couple know that he will not keep a secret from either member. As long as the rules are known beforehand, both approaches are acceptable, and each has its advantages and disadvantages.

The two types of secrets – secret-secrets and not-so-secret secrets – can have different functional outcomes in a loving relationship. As your client answers questions five and six, you may prompt them to consider what kind of secret theirs is. The following are illustrative examples of functional differences between a secret-secret and a not-so-secret secret, as well as how different people can handle their secrets.

A Secret-Secret. Donna was terribly troubled by an important aspect of her marriage to Arnie. "There is something about my life that I have never shared with Arnie. It scares me to think about it!" she said. Donna and Arnie had been married for 12 years, they had one child, and "all things considered, we have a good marriage," she added. "However, we always have prided ourselves on our honesty. We have an open and honest relationship. With one exception. Last year I went to a four-day conference in Chicago. One of my old co-workers – who was transferred two years ago to Houston – was at the conference. We had a great time going out to eat with the group, dancing at a nearby club and attending the meetings all day.

However, I spent the last two nights of the conference in his room. Basically, we had a two-day affair. I feel so bad about having done that! Even though I have worked through my guilt about what I did, I have never done anything like it again, nor ever will. I feel just as in love with Arnie as I ever did, possibly even more. What is tearing me apart, however, is that I just can't look Arnie straight in the face. Continuing to keep this a secret from him is killing me!"

In addition to offering some suggestions to Donna, Bill Lambos asked her to think about and write out her answers to the six questions listed earlier. At their next session, Donna shared her answers to the six questions. It obviously had become clear to Donna: "For me to continue to live with this secret would be worse than what Arnie might say or ever do if I were to tell him." Thus, she decided to tell him. It was very difficult for Donna. It was very difficult for Arnie. The important thing, however, is that Donna had decided what was best for her. Moreover, she determined that what she did also was best for their relationship. "Arnie told me that he thought there was something wrong for a long time, but figured I would eventually tell him." Donna further added, "I told Arnie that the best way of showing my love for him was by not keeping the secret from him any longer. Importantly, he felt my love for him."

A Not-So-Secret Secret. For a personal, illustrative example of a not-so-secret secret, we will share with you what occurred with Bill Emener's maternal grandparents. For spring break vacation in 1966, he went home for a visit with his family, especially to spend some time with his Grandma and Grandpa, who lived next door. Unfortunately, however, it turned out to be a very difficult visit. When his grandfather had been in the hospital, the doctors told him that his cancer was spreading uncontrollably throughout his body. They basically sent him home to die. By the time Bill got home to see him, he was bedridden. Grandpa was more than just an avid baseball fan; he probably was the biggest fan the Brooklyn Dodgers ever had. As soon as Bill got home, he went next door to see Grandma and Grandpa. Big smiles and big hugs, as usual. However, when Grandpa and Bill were talking alone, he said, "Willie, promise me you'll take me to Ebbets Field this summer. I want to see the Dodgers play." With a sad face, not only because he knew the Dodgers had moved to Los Angeles in 1958 but also because of the gravity of Grandpa's condition, Bill then said, "But Grandpa, you're not well and you're not going to get any better because..." At that moment Grandma came running into the room, pulled Bill aside, and with tears in her eyes whispered, "Please go along with it. Don't tell him. It would break his heart." "Okay," Bill replied. He then turned to his Grandpa and said, "I'll take you to Ebbets Field, Grandpa." Instantly, he smiled and said, "Thanks Willie, we'll have a good time!"

That evening, Bill walked back over to talk with Grandpa. Bill's stomach was in knots. Finally, he couldn't help himself. "Grandpa," he said, "I was talking with my Mom and she said..." At that moment, as Grandma was walking into the room, Grandpa held his finger up to his mouth and said softly, "Shush. We're going to Ebbets Field and that's that. You hear me? And whatever you do, don't tell her. It would break her heart." The truth was that Grandpa knew the Dodgers weren't in Brooklyn anymore and that he was dying. Grandma knew it too. But because they loved each other so much, they did not want to see each other hurt. Out of their love for one another, they kept a not-so-secret secret from each other. Bill realized that it was not his place to interfere with that! Bill never went to Ebbets Field that summer. Every day, however, Grandpa and he talked about going. On July 9, 1966, Grandpa died. And for the next eight years, Grandma lived on with a warm glow and the comforting thought that in Grandpa's final hours she loved him with all her heart, by keeping a secret. Importantly, he felt her love.

ONLY-CHILD ISSUES

We have suggested many times that in a multi-child family, as soon as the second child is born the battle begins: the first child fights for what he or she has lost – to be the one and only; and the second child fights for what he or she will never have – to be the one and only. In a multi-child family, the children not only have to learn how to develop and maintain relationships with mom and dad, but with sisters and/or brothers as well. In a one-child family, another consideration may also exist. "Since I am the only game in town (the only kid mom and dad have), it's me or nothing. So if I don't get what I want, I can withhold my attention and affection from them, they'll feel bad, have no one else to turn to, and I'll eventually get my way." We have explored this type of subconscious thinking with a number of our clients, and many of them have sheepishly smiled and said, "Makes sense, doesn't it." We are not suggesting that this is true for all only-child people. Please do not hear that. Parent-child relationships and the types of interpersonal-relationship learning that takes place in one-child families, however, tend to be different from multi-child families.

A very famous early psychologist named Alfred Adler, a student and later a colleague of Sigmund Freud, built a theory of personality development around the importance of the being an only child versus having siblings. In the latter case, Adler also examined how birth order and one's position contributed to one's sense of identity. This, Adler claimed, is especially true regarding how one interacts with other people as an adult. It also has consequences for one's own feelings of inferiority versus superiority. Although for many years Adler's ideas were almost forgotten, today they are witnessing a major resurgence. Neither one of us is surprised by this. The following case of Bill Emener's is an excellent example of why this is so.

When they first met, Gus told Bill that he was fearful that his marriage was slowly falling apart. Gus and Loraine had been married for slightly less than nine years. They had three children. Gus said, "Loraine keeps telling me that I always want to get my own way. And when I don't get my own way, I emotionally shut her out and give all of my affection to our children. She said that for years it was just easier to let me get my own way because she didn't like being shut out. But the other night she said, 'I've finally come to the point where I just can't take anymore of your self-centered, get-my-own-way bullshit.' Basically, I think she's right. I guess I never realized how I was manipulating her, by withholding affection from her, to get my own way." When Loraine came to one of their sessions, she identified numerous situations in their marriage when Gus would do this. Fortunately, some of her frustration and anger had subsided by that time, she was more understanding of Gus, and even though it was not easy for her to be as understanding as she was, she offered to help in any way she could. It was helpful for Loraine to understand that for Gus it was a matter of a learned behavior pattern: "If I don't get what I want, I pout, I withhold affection, and eventually I get what I want." Her complying with his manipulative behavior for nine years also reinforced his learning. It was not easy for either of them. With some additional counseling, however, Gus was able to better understand the only-child, manipulative way of life he had learned to use successfully with his parents (as well as with others in his life). Loraine also realized that some of his withholding of affection was not necessarily an indication of how much he loved or didn't love her. It was a learned behavior pattern. She also was learning some effective strategies for dealing with Gus when he wouldn't get what he wanted. The last time they spoke, Gus told Bill that he and Loraine were even starting to humorously refer to his having been an only child as a gentle way of keeping things in perspective. Gus has made excellent progress in his "challenge of growing up," as he called it, and he and Loraine have made excellent progress in improving their relationship.

Not every adult who was an only child learned to manipulate people as Gus had. But if you or your adult loved one was an only child, you simply may want to remain sensitive to the possibility that there may have been some unique aspects of your or your loved one's childhood that may be influencing your relationship.

RECYCLING ONE'S ABUSIVE RELATIONSHIP HISTORY

It is well known to psychologists, mental health counselors and social workers that individuals sometimes repeatedly find themselves in abusive, alcoholic or other dysfunctional relationships. Many of us have known people who, having finally "escaped" from a relationship marked by domestic violence, go on to become involved with another abusive person. Although at first this seems incredible – "You thought she would have learned from that last jerk!" – it is nonetheless a well-documented phenomenon. As one of our clients poignantly said, "I defeat myself because I repeat myself."

How can it be that such a counterintuitive tendency persists? The answer reveals several fascinating aspects of relationship dynamics. We alluded to part of the cause above when we addressed the topic of *the comfort of predictability*: the traps that people tend to fall into – the seeking out of partners whose behavior is familiar and predictable, *even if it's unhealthy and the last thing they might consciously choose*. The second part of the cause and effect cycle of abusive relationships arises out of the changes that occur to people who are exposed to, and remain in, abusive relationships: *personality traits develop as a result of exposure to abuse that reinforce the tendency to remain in such relationships*. Let's look at some of these in detail:

- A background involving physical, emotional or sexual abuse.
- ACOA issues (Adult Children of Alcoholics/Addicts).
- A codependent personality disorder.
- An inability to set and enforce interpersonal boundaries.
- A strong need for a relationship to validate themselves.
- Belief that, "It will change if I just try harder."
- Clinical depression, self-medication.
- Difficulty expressing anger, internalizing it, or acting it out in other ways.
- Drug or alcohol dependence.
- Enforced isolation creating resentment.
- Intense need for love and affection (sometimes called "Love Addiction").

- Low self-esteem or self-efficacy. (Belief that they can't have/don't deserve better treatment.)
- Repeated attempts to leave the relationship, followed by an inability to follow through, with leaving-returning to the abuser again and again.
- Suicidal ideation or attempts.
- The sense of worth gained by care-taking the abuser.

Abusiveness is a family dysfunction that repeats not only through generations but also within the same individual over a series of relationships. Just as addictions can pass down through generations, abusers often leave their families of origin for a family of choice – then repeat the abusive cycle from the other side. The abused becomes the abuser and so continues the cycle – you may be familiar with the adage: "Hurt people hurt people." It also is important to remember that abusers and addicts are not to blame for their behavior, but they are responsible for it. Accountability is a concept that addicts, co-dependents and abusers have trouble grasping until they are well into recovery.

In healthy, functional, "good" loving relationships, both individuals empathically know about and understand each other – including their pasts. Trust is a key component of this process. Every couple that wants to stay together must eventually learn that they agree to accept their partner's past, which cannot be changed. Moreover, if their partner is going to openly share their past with them, including the truth about past relationships, the other member must learn to trust that they will be respected by their counterpart for their honesty: "They are communicating in order to help me heal wounds from the past." The worst thing their lover can do is use the information against them in such a way as to hurt them further with it.

To a large extent, the members of every couple are the culminations of their pasts, and the better they know each other's pasts the better they will know and appreciate each other as they are in the present. Most importantly, by knowing each other's pasts the better they will be able to know and appreciate each other in their relationship. Indeed, all of this must be carefully considered and used when counseling individuals and couples that are struggling with loving relationship issues.

CHAPTER SUMMARY

This chapter's numerous examples of the extent to which people's past loving relationship experiences – beginning with their mothers and fathers – impact and influence their current and future loving relationships are very compelling. As counselors work with individuals and couples, it indeed behooves us, when pertinent, to assist clients with their learned interpersonal needs, potentials for "self-fulfilling prophesies," the extent to which their dysfunctional relationships are related to their secrets, only-child issues and history of abuse. Helping clients understand their past loving relationship experiences and how they may be impacting their present and future loving relationships is important; equally so, nonetheless, is the facilitation of their accepting responsibility to change whatever needs to be changed so that their pasts are not inadvertently repeated and replicated in their present and future loving relationships.

Watch your charts and keep an eye on your bow –
make sure you know where you are going.
Look over the stern occasionally too,
appreciate your wake –
it can tell you a lot about you and your boat,
as well as where you're heading.

CHAPTER 6 DISCUSSION QUESTIONS

1) How and in what ways may your personal past and current loving relationships influence you in your work as a counselor working with individuals and couples who have relationship issues (i.e., what are your potential counter-transference issues)?

2) What techniques do you see yourself using as a counselor to assist individuals and couples in addressing (a) their learned interpersonal needs and (b) their potentials for self-fulfilling prophesies?

3) What philosophical and ethical issues may be involved when assisting an individual client or a couple attend to their dysfunctional relationship and consider living parallel lives?

4) What techniques do you see yourself using as a counselor to assist individuals and couples in addressing (a) their secrets and (b) when pertinent, their only-child issues?

5) What would be your procedural approach to assisting an individual client or a couple stop recycling their abusive relationship history?

THE INDIVIDUAL AND THE COUPLE

In this chapter we continue our journey through human loving relationships by moving away from analytics, including the effects of the past on the present, and moving squarely into the present, or "the now." We have grouped the topics in this chapter together by including those aspects of individual beliefs, feelings and behavior (1) that are most closely associated with what each individual partner brings into the relationship, and (2) how these impact the couple.

We begin by looking at a number of ideas that cross many of the theoretical approaches reviewed in Chapter 2. From the humanistic school of thought, we examine the role of congruence and balance of each partner's concept of *self*, and from the cognitive-behavioral theories we examine how each member's *beliefs*, in particular how these may be seen as being rational vs. irrational, contribute to relationship health and stability. We then go on to look at how needs, wants and expectations can either contribute to or conversely negatively impact relationship functioning. Finally, we examine how each partner's sense of, and comfort level with independence vs. dependence regarding their partner affects the relationship.

Whereas analysis involves breaking down a complex subject into its component parts, the material in this and the next four chapters is not intended to further the counselor's ability to *understand* the relationship as much as to assist the counselor in *intervening*, or helping the couple to ameliorate or repair relationship problems. Therefore, this leg of our journey is less theoretical and more synthetic in nature – we offer the couples counselor specific approaches and suggestions that in our experience have proven useful in assisting our client couples with moving forward with their relationships or, when necessary, to help clients leave them behind and move on with their lives.

CONGRUENCE AND BALANCE

"I wonder if people describe me that way?" How many times have we heard clients ask themselves that question when we hear people say things like:

> "What you see is what you get!" "One of the things I love about Bob is that there is nothing phony, plastic or put-on about him. He always seems so natural." "There's nothing

pretentious about Mary, she's so easy to talk to, so easy to be around, and everything about her just seems to be so consistent."

Individuals who are described in these kinds of ways also are individuals with whom it is comfortable to have a loving relationship. It also is important to note that these quotations are descriptors of individuals who are *congruent* and have a sense of *balance* in their lives.

The A, B, C's of Loving Relationships – Version One. We like mnemonic devices – especially straightforward ones that help us remember large sets of complex facts and ideas easily. Needless to say, mnemonic devices based on the first three letters of the alphabet are popular, and we'll make use of two of them in this chapter. In the first version of A-B-C's, we use them to organize three important aspects of our lives: (1) our **A**ffect – our feelings and emotions; (2) our **B**ehavior – our actions and activities; and (3) our **C**ognitions – our thoughts and beliefs (in the next section of this chapter, we will explain Albert Ellis's A-B-C model; this, however, is a different set of A-B-C's). When something happens to us in our lives, or when we encounter a new experience, it is important for us to be aware of *our feelings* about whatever it was that occurred, *how we acted* as a result of the experience, and what our *thoughts, ideas and beliefs* are about it. It is important for our emotions, our behavior and our beliefs to be congruent – to overlap and co-vary. For example, a less congruent person is someone who may be acting as if they are very happy, but who actually is feeling the opposite: down and depressed. As Figure 7.1 suggests, the individual who is less congruent is a person who's *Affect* (feelings), *Behavior* (actions), and *Cognitions* (thoughts and beliefs) are somewhat disjointed and their feelings are not in synchrony. On the other hand, a person who feels good about him- or her self, who spends a lot of time acting happy with and around others, and who simultaneously thinks, or not together. Quite often, an incongruent or less congruent person expends a tremendous amount of energy simply because their thoughts about themselves, their behavior of him- or her self as being a liked, loved and happy individual, is more congruent and more balanced. The core of our idea is that it is important for people to remain cognizant of the extent to which their thoughts, behavior and feelings are consistent or inconsistent, which is what we mean by *congruence*.

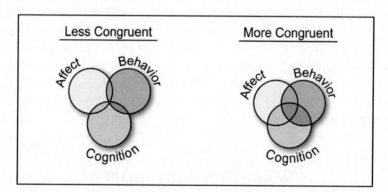

Figure 7.1. How we relate to each other. Affectively, Behaviorally and Cognitively.

These three phenomena – our affect, our behavior and our cognitions – also can represent the modes by which people interact and relate with one another. For example, we have known some couples to deal with each other primarily on an affective, or feelings, level. Other couples have shown themselves to be more physical with each other on a behavioral level. Finally, we have known couples that interact and relate to one another primarily with thoughts and words, on a cognitive level. Occasionally, however, couples will get into trouble when they only rely mainly on one of these three modes of relating. This is especially true if one person is frustrated because he or she is feeling uncomfortable as a result of the predominance or exclusiveness of one mode.

You may be wondering what types of circumstances lead a person to lose congruence. There are, unfortunately, too many answers to this question to make sweeping generalizations. Every theory of personality or human psychology offers its own approach to congruence, and although these answers often overlap, they also may be very different in philosophy and approach. For example, a psychodynamically-oriented analyst may claim that such dissociations among feelings, thoughts and behaviors are the result of defense mechanisms that protect the ego from noxious aspects of reality. The Freudian or Jungian psychologist will look to powerful subconscious motivations. On the other hand, a cognitive-behavioral therapist, as we shall see in the following section, will look to irrational or illogical beliefs. Such beliefs, which go unchallenged for various reasons, are themselves the source of incongruence. By definition, an irrational belief will lead to both emotions and behaviors that are inconsistent with reality and thus produce incongruence. Other approaches to human psychology posit different explanations. This book is not about theories of psychology; thus we are not going to examine other explanations in detail.[1]

Finally, sometimes people choose as their relationship partners others who differ from themselves in terms of their primary mode of being. For example, affect-oriented persons may find themselves attracted to others who tend to operate on the cognitive level.

Linkages: Feelings, Thoughts and Actions. Herewith we are proposing two different types of incongruence. The first type is inconsistency among a person's *own* A-B-C's. The second concerns incongruence between two individuals in a relationship. The following example from our practices highlights these.

Bill Emener's first session with Diana is offered in Dialogue 7.1.

Dialogue 7.1 Linkages: Feelings, Thoughts and Actions.

As a result of having had numerous relationship problems for a long period of time, Diana (D) started seeing Bill Emener (B) for counseling. During their first session, Diana shared her primary concern.

B: So, Diana, is there anything in particular that brought you here today?
D: Yes there is, and I've been thinking about it for quite awhile. In a nutshell, sometimes what I do, what I feel, and what I'm thinking seem to be totally unrelated to one another. For example, last weekend I went out on two dates – Friday night and Saturday night –

---

[1] We do believe that there is at least one idea that all of the theories share: *incongruence arises in part as a result of what people experienced while growing up in their family of origin.* Few therapists would deny that dysfunctional family dynamics result in incongruence and, therefore, in dysfunction and unstable relationships as adults. This is not to say that all examples of incongruence result from family issues. Indeed, stressful situations encountered as adults also can destabilize us, which may persist after the stressor is removed or resolved.

and spent Sunday afternoon at the mall with my girlfriend and acted real happy. Yet in spite of all that, I felt depressed all weekend and was constantly thinking or wondering whether anyone in the world really cared about me or loved me.

B: You went out on two dates, and I assume you had a good time on them, and had a good time at the mall with your girlfriend, but felt down all weekend. That certainly is something worth talking about.

D: It's not the first time either.

B: Firstly, Diana, let's take a closer look at your feelings, your behaviors and your thoughts, and see whether we can find some reasons as to why they seem to be so fragmented.

D: *Fragmented*... yes that's a good word for it. I've occasionally used that word when I talk to myself.

B: What kinds of things do you say to yourself?

D: Things like that – I'm fragmented, I'm not together... basically that there's something wrong with me and no matter what I do I'll always be depressed and unhappy.

B: [While softly smiling] Well at least at the end of the weekend you can feel good about something.

D: [While noting Bill's upbeat smile] Feel good about something? What would there be for me to feel good about?

B: That you were right. You entered the weekend with a presumptive prediction – "There's something wrong with me and I'll always be depressed and unhappy." So at the end of the weekend when you were still feeling depressed and unhappy, in spite of doing things that were fun, you then could say to yourself – and it very well could be subconscious – aha, Grasshopper: "I was right – I'll always be depressed and unhappy."

D: [After a reflective pause] Jeez... you know, Dr. Emener, that makes sense to me. It's almost funny in a way. Is that why you were smiling?

B: Yes. But remember, Diana, I wasn't smiling or laughing at you...

D: I know. No problem. But what do I do about that?

B: Well for openers, there are two things we need to talk about. Firstly, we need talk about your self-fulfilling prophesying self-talk. Second, it might be helpful for us to discuss your decision-making – instead of looking at the data and making a decision, you make a decision based on how you *should be* or *should feel.*

Their ensuing therapy sessions were very helpful to Diana. In addition to reading two self-help books (*Letting Go of Shame: Understanding How Shame Affects Your Life* by Potter-Efron and Potter-Efron [1989] and *How to Stubbornly Refuse to Make Yourself Miserable About Anything: Yes, Anything* by Albert Ellis [2000]), Bill used three approaches with Diana that were effective: (1) addressing her negative self-talk (á la Donald Meichenbaum, 1977); (2) her decision-making process (á la Aaron Beck, 1976); and pertinent aspects of rational motive behavior therapy (á la Albert Ellis, 1996). Subsequently, she told Bill during a telephone conversation that she was feeling so much better about her life. "I feel like I'm one again, or to put it in your words, I'm more congruent. The important thing, however, is that my overall life is so much happier now."

During one of their later sessions, Bill and Diana also discussed her relationship with Roy, a young man with whom she was enjoying a relatively good relationship, yet about which she also had some serious concerns. Bill took out a piece of paper and drew a figure for her (Figure 7.2) and suggested that she attempt to answer a number of questions.

B: Diana, think about and eventually let's talk about the three following sets of questions:

What do you *think* about yourself? What do you think about Roy? And what are your thoughts regarding your relationship with Roy?

How do you *act* toward yourself? What do you do for yourself? How do you act and what do you do with Roy? How do you act when you are around Roy?

How do you *feel* about yourself? What are some feeling words that describe how you feel about yourself? How do you feel toward Roy? How do you feel about Roy? How do you feel about your relationship with Roy? What feelings do you feel when you are spending time with him?

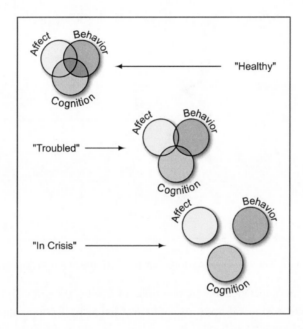

Figure 7.2. Linkages Among Feelings, Thoughts and Actions.

Bill and Diana eventually not only discussed her answers to Bill's three questions, but also focused on discrepancies or inconsistencies among them. For example, Diana noted that she thought of Roy as being a very warm and caring person who loved her. However, she said she tended to "act differently" when she was around him as compared to when she was alone. Even though she thought she had a loving relationship with him, she did not feel comfortable in his presence. In follow-up sessions they were able to identify specific things about Roy and her relationship with him that tended to contribute to her uncomfortable feelings when she was with him. (For example, Diana was still struggling with her toxic shame – "fearing that Roy would eventually see what I see when I look at myself in the mirror – a woman who has something wrong with her.") They also discussed what she could do to reduce the identified discrepancies and live a life in which her affect (feelings), actions (behavior) and thoughts (cognitions) were more consistent. During that discussion, he drew a diagram for her that is depicted in Figure 7.2.

Basically, he was trying to explain to her the importance of having a congruent relationship among feelings, actions and thoughts. Bill also shared with her that happier and healthier people, who try to be more congruent than individuals whose feelings, actions and thoughts are fragmented, disjointed and inconsistent with each other, tend to be less troubled and spend less time in crisis, as displayed in Figure 7.3. Bill eventually met with Diana and Roy (See Dialogue 7.1), and when they were processing Roy's responses to the diagrams and the questions they raised, he discovered that Roy was having some experiences similar to Diana's. By minimizing their discrepancies in these areas, their relationship was improved in many meaningful ways.

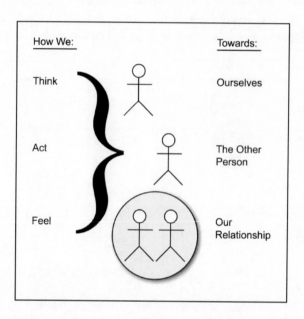

Figure 7.3. Our Feelings, Thoughts and Actions Toward Self, the Other Person and our Relationship.

Balance. When incongruence among a couple's feelings, thoughts and behaviors persists, relationships experience what we refer to as a loss of balance. A couple that was experiencing this ended up in Bill Emener's office.

When Carl and Theresa came to see him, they said, "It's not that our relationship is bad… it is just unfulfilling." They began living together approximately one year prior to coming to see Bill and said that as time went on their relationship was getting worse and worse, less and less enjoyable, less and less fun, and they were afraid they were "going to lose it." It did not take them long to identify that their lifestyles had simply gotten out of balance. Carl, a high-energy workaholic, was an engineer who worked approximately 10 to 12 hours per day. Theresa, who owned her own flower shop, worked approximately 8 to 10 hours per day in the shop and then brought an attaché case full of work home with her. When they looked at a sketch similar to the one in Figure 7.4, it was clear that once they diagrammed the amount of time in their lives they devoted to work, sleep, themselves and others, there was very little "fun time" left for themselves.

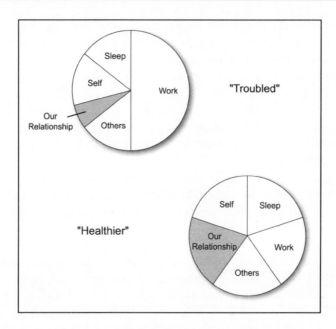

Figure 7.4. A Need for Balance in our Lives.

Basically, they had little time, if any, to do things together and to enjoy their relationship. They decided very quickly that they would make some decisions so their individual lives, as well as their life together, would be more like the "healthier" diagram in Figure 7.4. When they came back for their next session, they shared the following: "We have agreed that it is okay if Carl does not win an award as Engineer-of-the-Year and if Theresa does not open six more flower shops by Christmas. We may not retire by the age of forty, and some folks may consider us as having become less productive. But we don't care – we are now simply spending more time together, and enjoying each other more. Our relationship has become so much fun for us. This is the way we want our collective life to be from now on."

Importantly, Carl and Theresa genuinely appreciated that they were the ones who realized their relationship, as it interfaced with their individual lives, had simply gotten out of balance. They discovered that they had choices they could make in their lives. They were the ones who made it more balanced and more consistent with their values and what they wanted in their lives. Carl and Theresa now have a much healthier relationship.

New Experiences – Old Feelings. In our discussion of the causes of incongruence earlier in this chapter, we noted the impact of family-of-origin experiences on self-perception and congruence of feelings, thoughts and behaviors. A good illustration of this comes from Bill Emener's experience with Cathy and Keith, which is recorded in Dialogue 7.2.

Dialogue 7.2 New Experiences – Old Feelings.

When Cathy (**C**) first came to see Bill Emener (**B**), he could not help but notice her winning smile, very attractive physical features and very exciting and upbeat attitude. Unfortunately, it was not very far into their first session that her real issues surfaced.

C: I don't know what's wrong with me. For the last few years I would go out with someone maybe two or three times and then it simply would not work out.

B: For the last few years… that's a long period of time.

C: I don't know what to do… where to start.

B: I don't have a crystal ball, Cathy, but can see a few possibilities worthy of consideration – it may be helpful to talk about your thoughts regarding the extent to which you truly are thinking that there's something wrong with you, the possibility that the men you've been going out with simply are not right for you, and if that's true – then why are you choosing to go out with them?

While they talked about all three of these possibilities, including relevant specifics and details, toward the end of the session Bill drew a little diagram for Cathy similar to the one in Figure 7.5.

B: From what you've been telling me, Cathy, when you were a child, and let's say up until the age of 18 or 19, you had a number of experiences with your parents and with young men that led you to believe that people didn't like you because you were not a good person. This is what you truly believed. As I recall, one story you told me was about the high school football star that refused to go to the beach with you and said, "You're not the kind of person I should waste my time with." And when you would think about things like that, you would feel rejected, abandoned, down and depressed. As a result, you would withdraw, stay away from people and hide. You would not avail yourself of opportunities to meet people. It seems that now, at the age of 26, when you meet someone for the first time and you go out with him two or three times, everything seems to be going fine until you feel that you might be rejected. Unfortunately, you then immediately experience the old thoughts, "Here it goes again… he doesn't like me because I'm not a good person."

C: [Smiling and nodding in agreement] I'm with you so far…

B: The old feelings you associate with rejection – feeling down, hurt and depressed – immediately flood back and you revert to the old learned behaviors – withdrawal, running away and hiding. For example, let's look at the situation you just told me about regarding your new boyfriend, Keith. All week long you were thinking about inviting him to go to the Tampa Boat Show with you on Sunday afternoon. When you called and invited him, he said, "No. I'm sorry. I don't feel like doing that this Sunday." You immediately thought, "Here we go again – he must not like me because I'm not a good person." You got a knot in your stomach and felt terrible. You quickly got off the telephone and have not called him back. Furthermore, you're screening his calls with your answering machine. You're avoiding talking to him. Same old pattern, isn't it?

C: [She started crying, yet non-verbally indicated that she agreed with Bill's analysis.]

B: It would really be good if you could find out from Keith why he turned you down. Somewhere along the line, Cathy, you're going to have to remember that Keith is not the high school football star who turned you down years ago.

In their next session, Cathy came bounding into the office and jumped into the chair she usually would sit in.

C: You'll never guess what happened! Keith said he already had made arrangements to play in a golf tournament with his father that particular Sunday afternoon and had been planning to invite me to join him as his guest at a post-tournament gathering. Not only that, he told me that after listening to me tell him how exciting it would be to go to the boat show, he felt bad, didn't know what to say, felt incredibly disappointed, and unfortunately just said, "No. I'm sorry."

While it is true that Keith could have done a better job in handling his end of that particular conversation, Cathy quickly realized how she took his "No" as a personal rejection and allowed the old pattern to take over. She is now learning how not to associate new experiences with old ones and how to respond differently. As she was leaving Bill's office, Cathy looked up with a big smile and said, "Oh, and by the way, Dr. Emener, next Saturday morning Keith and I are getting up really early because we're driving all the way to Miami for the day – we're going to the Miami Boat Show!"

Bill also used Figure 7.5 in helping this couple understand how Cathy's family of origin issues was impacting her current relationship with her new boyfriend, Keith.

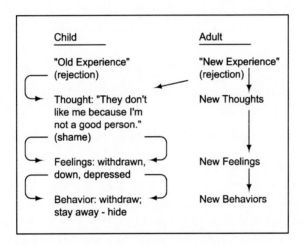

Figure 7.5. Relationships Among Old Experiences and Responses to New Experiences.

What I Want You to See. It is not uncommon for people to want others to always see them at their best. This tends to be a very natural phenomenon and is probably one of the primary reasons why we spend so much time fixing our hair, selecting the "right" clothes to wear, and repeatedly looking at ourselves in the mirror before going out.

For example, one of the things troublesome for a client of Bill Emener named Yvette was that ever since her divorce she had a number of repeated short-term, yet very intense, relationships with men. Pointedly, she said to Bill during their first session, "Men seem to fall head over heels for me right away, and everything seems to be going great. Then all of a sudden they start to get very cautious around me. Then they disappear. I don't know what's going on!" As the conversation continued, Bill drew a diagram for her like the one in Figure 7.6. Bill shared with her that most people have three selves: (1) a *Social Self* – the self or the "me" who I want you and others to see; (2) an *Ideal Self* – the person I would like to be; and (3) a *Real Self* – the person I really am. Over time, however, our Ideal Self tends to fade, and as people get to know us, our Real Self and our Social Self become more apparent and they come closer to being the same thing. Bill knew that Yvette knew what he was talking about when she said, "In other words, it's like when after we go out together a few times and we get to feel comfortable with each other, it might be okay if my hair isn't perfect and my blouse isn't one-hundred percent wrinkle free?" "Exactly," Bill replied.

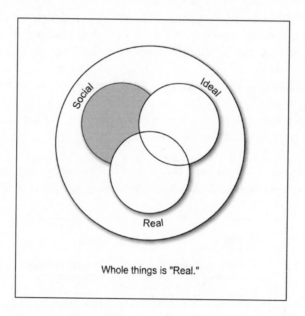

Figure 7.6. My Social Self, My Ideal Self and My Real Self.

What eventually surfaced for Yvette was the realization that her relatively recent divorce from her verbally abusive former husband had left some real deep scars on her self-concept and sense of self-worth. Unconsciously, she had come to believe that she was not a good person. Thus, she felt that in order for any man to find her attractive and a person with whom he would want to spend some time, she had to "act as if she was someone other than herself – Ms. Perfect!"

In a subsequent session she told Bill that when she talked with her new boyfriend, George, about this aspect of her life, he admitted to her that he was wondering when he was ever going to meet the real Yvette. Although George, as well as others, suggested to her that the "social Yvette" was a lot of fun and very charming, many times she simply did not seem very real. In fact, Yvette added, "George told me that it was my phoniness that was starting to turn him off. And that really stung!"

Bill said to her, pointing to Figure 7.6, "In other words for George, the 'whole thing' is actually the real thing. He was simply starting to think of you and see you as being a phony."

"Yes," she said, "and from now on I'm simply going to be the real me, and if they don't like it, tough!"

As they were heading toward the front desk she whispered, "When I go out with George tomorrow night I am going to wear one of my new dresses and make sure that my hair looks very nice. But if I feel like ordering clams on the half shell, I'll do it. If he doesn't want to go out with a clam eater, that's his problem." The smile on her face, her sense of pride and self-worth, her confident body posture, and the twinkle in her eye said almost out loud that she was feeling better about herself, and much less obsessed, worried and depressed. Bill walked back to his office with a feeling of goodness about Yvette and her life. For Yvette, this was an excellent beginning.

RATIONAL VERSUS IRRATIONAL THINKING I:
THE A-B-C'S OF HAPPINESS

Few individuals have had as much influence on modern clinical psychology as Albert Ellis (Ellis, 1996, 2000). Trained first in philosophy and semantics, Ellis applied his ideas to individual functioning – first to his own, we might add – and went on to found a school of thought whose offshoots remain the dominant approach to counseling and psychotherapy today. The core of Ellis' approach was described in Chapter 2 and yet important enough to warrant revisiting.

One of the first ideas Bill Lambos, who studied under Dr. Ellis, tries to impart to his clients regarding *happiness* is that every person is largely responsible for his or her own sense of happiness, misery or whatever else might fall in between. This is not the same as blaming the victim of a tragedy or situation out of their control. Rather, it is a philosophy and a theory of personality or counseling that focuses on the central roles played by one's *beliefs* about oneself, others and the world. This model, diagrammed in Figure 7.7, is based on the approach of Albert Ellis and his model of Rational Emotive Behavior Therapy (1996).

A	B	C
Activating events Past, present (or possible future) adversities or aggravations	Beliefs Thoughts, attitudes, and assumptions	Consequences Emotions Actions/behaviors

Figure 7.7. The "A-B-Cs" of Happiness.

Most people automatically assume that when some action or event happens to us (the "A" in the Figure), it causes us to respond to it – that is, it generates a "consequence," either feelings, behavior, or both (the "C" in the Figure). Ellis' insight was that the connection between "A" and "C" is mediated by, or is a function of, our beliefs. When these beliefs are irrational in nature – when they are unrealistic or illogical – we may experience unwarranted feelings or engage in inappropriate behaviors because of them. It is much healthier to recognize that:

1) the activating event – what happens to us (the "A") – does not automatically cause "C," but rather "A" activates a belief in us about how the world (or we, or other people) should be; and

2)   it is the combination of the event and the belief that causes the resulting feelings and behaviors. Furthermore, since each of us has the power to alter our beliefs, we are ultimately in control of how we react to the things that affect us.

Road rage is one of the best examples of this paradigm. When some inconsiderate driver cuts us off, we often immediately become furious. But if we realize that the world is full of inconsiderate motorists and that to believe otherwise is unwarranted by reality, we will not experience the rage. We are more likely to sigh and say to ourselves, "So what else is new?"

The point of this discussion is that people have much more control of their day-to-day happiness than they typically realize. To the extent that we make irrational and selfish demands about the way our partners *should* or *must* treat us, we allow ourselves to experience anger or deep disappointment when they fail to live up to these expectations. On the other hand, when we focus on our role in responding to them and to the beliefs we harbor about them, positive strategies for managing our loving relationships naturally present themselves. This is a very powerful and effective philosophy of being, and we advise you to think about this the next time you are about to blame your significant other for something he or she did or did not do, and then inappropriately act out to the detriment of the relationship.

The ELF versus DR BOLL. When counseling a couple about rational and irrational beliefs, Bill Lambos is frequently asked: "How do you know if a given belief we harbor is rational or irrational?" Although it may sound like a trivial question, it is not. The power and elegance of Albert Ellis's theory is, in fact, based on the assumption that people do *not* generally know, without some amount of training or psycho-education, what makes one given belief rational and another irrational.

We mentioned when discussing the two A-B-C models above that we liked mnemonic devices and here is a case where they could not be more helpful. Bill uses the Table in Figure 7.8 to help his clients easily remember whether a given belief is either rational or irrational.

These acronyms – ELF and DR BOLL – have proven very useful for clients in situations in and outside of relationships. They are the bases of the *Four Blocks to Happiness* for both couples and individuals alike: (1) anger; (2) anxiety; (3) guilt; and (4) depression. It is safe to say that if a person or either partner in a couple is experiencing any of these four destructive emotions, it is because they are holding a belief about themselves, other people, or the world, that cannot be characterized as (E)mpirical, (L)ogical and (F)unctional but is, instead, (D)emanding, (R)ating the self or others, (B)laming, (O)vergeneralizing, and/or characterized by (L)ow frustration tolerance and (L)iving elsewhere.

A Belief is Rational if it Meets *All* of the Following Conditions:	A Belief is Irrational if it Meets *Any* of the Following Conditions
The Belief is:	The Belief is:
Empirical: It is true about the world	Demanding: It is seen as a *Must* instead of a *Preference*
Logical: It follows from its premises	Rating a person or thing: Rational beliefs rate *Behaviors*, not people or things
Functional: It works and has positive consequences	Blaming: Rational beliefs hold oneself *Accountable* for one's emotions rather than blaming others
	Overgeneralizing: Rational beliefs are specific and situational
	Low in frustration tolerance
	Living elsewhere: As in the past, future or other place than the here and now

Figure 7.8. Differences Between Rational and Irrational Beliefs.

RATIONAL VERSUS IRRATIONAL THINKING II: NEEDS, WANTS AND EXPECTATIONS

In the spring of 1970, Bill Emener had an opportunity to go to a round of the Masters Golf Tournament in Augusta, Georgia. One of his more memorable experiences that day occurred while watching the players practice their putting. One of the veteran pros, who had recently recovered from major surgery and was playing again for the first time in months, dropped three balls onto the green and was getting ready to putt. A nearby spectator called out, "Come on, Chi Chi, you need to win this one. Then you'll feel real good about yourself." Without batting an eye, the pro gently turned to the spectator and respectfully said, "No my friend, you are wrong. First of all, I am here. I am alive. I am healthy. I have a beautiful wife and beautiful children. I *want* to win, yes, but I do not *need* to win to feel good about myself or about my life." Bill will never forget that exchange. Clearly, Chi Chi Rodriquez knew the difference between his *needs* and his *wants*. In this chapter, we will focus on how our needs and our wants can interface with our loved one's needs and wants and how they can affect and influence our loving relationships.

Differences Between Needs and Wants. One of Ellis's major posits was that people are not disturbed by things that happen to them (i.e., the As in his A-B-C model), but that people *disturb themselves* due to harboring irrational beliefs (the Bs). Many irrational beliefs, as we saw in the previous section, arise from the confusion of one's *needs* with one's *wants*.

Human beings are said to have four basic needs: oxygen, water, food and shelter. In this book, nonetheless, we would suggest that for the vast majority of us, some amount of the company of other people certainly could be added to this list. Although some people do live as hermits, it is rare for a person to live and enjoy life without interacting with others. Therefore, we take some exception to other theorists and propose that most human beings do, in fact, *need* to associate with other people. This exception withstanding, there remains a fundamental difference between (1) recognizing that something is a desirable preference or *want*, and (2) harboring the belief that what one would like to have or want to have is the something that one *needs* or *must* have.

A relatively easy way to determine the difference is to ask ourselves: *"What is the worst that would happen if I did not get what I need or want?"* For example, we need air because if we did not get air in approximately three to four minutes, we would die. The same can be said for water, food and shelter from the elements. On the other hand, if we want a new car because the old one has bad shock absorbers, we would consider this a "want" because if we do not get a new car, the worst thing that would happen is that we would continue to ride around in an uncomfortable car. Although it is true that we need food, going to a very expensive restaurant also would fall under the rubric of being a preference or a want. When we do not gratify or satisfy a true need, the outcome can well be catastrophic in the sense that it is life-threatening. Nonetheless, when we do not satisfy or gratify a want, even though the outcome might *appear* to be catastrophic, it actually is not. To wit, it is important for both individuals involved in a loving relationship to remain sensitive to the extent to which they are attending to their needs versus their wants. If we confuse the two, we quickly assume, consciously or otherwise, that we *must* get what we want *or else* it will be a disaster. Taking such a stand is almost guaranteed to result in our becoming unhappy – none of us can ever get everything we want.

From the point of view of relationships, needs and wants take on a slightly different meaning. Loving relationships typically are entered into on a voluntary basis, and can just as easily be terminated in most cases. Therefore, the definition of *need* with respect to a relationship is less dramatic than a biological need – it is, by definition: anything that affects a person's decision as to whether or not to remain in the relationship. Therefore, if a failure to meet a desire or want in a relationship is strong enough to warrant ending the relationship, then from this perspective it qualifies as a need. We call such relationship-centric needs *deal breakers*.

Meeting Relationship Needs and Wants. We suggest that when counseling individuals in loving relationships, you urge each of them to ask themselves three questions:

1) What are my *needs* from this relationship? Stated another way, what has to happen in order for me not to terminate this relationship unilaterally?
2) What are my *wants* with respect to this relationship? In other words, what would make the relationship better, but is not a deal breaker? and,
3) How and with whom do I get what I *need and want*?

Most individuals meet and gratify their interpersonal needs and wants in a variety of ways. Having a clear understanding of each other's answers to questions such as these can be very helpful. A married man, for example, may feel a strong need to continue to play softball one or two evenings per week because of his need for male bonding. Likewise, a married woman may feel a strong need to continue to play tennis with her girlfriends one or two evenings per week because of her need for female bonding. It is important to remember, nonetheless, that it may be impossible for a wife to meet her husband's need for male bonding, and it equally might be impossible for a husband to meet his wife's need for female bonding. Thus, while a husband and wife may want to play softball and/or tennis one or two evenings per week, we must remember that through such activities they may be meeting very important interpersonal needs. When two individuals in a loving relationship have a mutual understanding of issues such as these, there is also a greater chance that they may not feel threatened by each other's outside activities (such as softball and tennis). It also may be important for a wife to know that her husband is playing softball to meet his male bonding needs and not to avoid spending time with her; likewise, it might be important for a husband to know that his wife is playing tennis one or two evenings per week because of her need for female bonding, not because she wants to avoid spending time with him.

Matching Our Roles with Our Needs. In Chapter 5 we examined the subject of roles and noted that every person must manage multiple roles both in and outside of relationships. Figure 7.9 shows that relationship-centered needs and wants must be in synchrony with relationship statuses and roles.

Our "Roles"	Needs and Wants
Man/Woman	
Lover	
Husband/Wife	
Son/Daughter	(e.g. Our needs and wants such as friendship, companionship, belongingness, love, etc.)
Dad/Mom	
Accountant/Teacher	
House-Fixer	
"Others"	

Figure 7.9. Understanding Our "Our Roles" and How We Meet Our Needs and Wants.

Similar Wants and Needs. Doris and Buddy, both in their late 20s, had been married for about five years and wanted to start a family. However, they were very hesitant because of their "marital problems." It did not take long during the first session to realize that although they both loved each other very much, both of them were hurting and very angry. These feelings had been surfacing in forms of anger toward each other for a long time. Bill Emener handed each of them a sheet of paper and asked them to write down their answers to the two following questions:

1) What is the number one thing that you are wanting from your relationship and are not getting?
2) How have you been feeling as a result of not getting what you want from your relationship?

When Bill asked each of them to share their answers with each other, interestingly, they both came up with very similar statements. Except for some minor differences in their expressions and vocabulary, they both basically said: (1) I want him/her *to reach out to me and love me*; and (2) I am feeling *ignored, hurt* and *lonely*.

Bill shared with them that in his clinical practice it is not uncommon to find two individuals in a long-term loving relationship having similar types of feelings because their needs and wants of the relationship were not being met or gratified. Bill looked at each of them and said, "In many ways, this is sad. Each of you loves each other very much, but you are not feeling loved by each other. Not feeling loved by someone whom you love very much can be very painful – both of you are hurting. Simultaneously, because each of you also tends to feel helpless in not knowing what to do about it, you are both feeling frustrated and angry."

At that point, Buddy looked at Bill and said, "Yes, that is very true – at least it certainly is for me. But there's another thought I want to share with you. I can recall numerous situations over the last few months when I have wanted to reach out to Doris and express my love for her, but I think my own pain and sorrow were simply getting in my way."

After a few minutes of silence, Doris turned to Buddy and said, "Buddy, honey, maybe we just need to get away from each other for a little while?"

Buddy, while drying his eyes, looked at Doris and said, "The two of us being away from each other scares me a little. However, I think maybe you're right."

A few minutes later, Bill looked at each of them and said, "It sounds to me like there are four considerations we need to recognize: (1) each of you loves the other very much; (2) each of you wants to be loved and wants to feel loved by the other; (3) each of you wants to love and wants to be loving toward the other; and (4) what you seem to be identifying as a need, at this point in time, is for each of you to have an opportunity to stay away from each other for a while so that you can attend to your own hurts and sorrows."

The couple, with Bill's help, identified some important boundaries and agreements that would make a brief separation possible and relatively comfortable for them. For example, Buddy took some clothes and moved in with his brother who lived about 15 miles from their apartment. During their two weeks apart, they agreed to speak on the telephone each night, to see each other one evening for dinner, and to go out together sometime during each weekend. Bill also recommended some materials for both of them to read and discuss. We are happy to share with you that they eventually were able to resolve many of their marital difficulties, and their "new found relationship" (their words) has been working out extremely well.

Doris and Buddy helped us truly appreciate and realize how frequently individuals in long-term loving relationships can have very similar needs and wants. Although they both *wanted* to be loved and feel loved by each other, what they *needed* was an opportunity to heal some of their own emotional wounds before trying to reach out to, and be loving toward, each other. As demonstrated in this case example, when working with a couple such as Doris and Buddy it is very important for you to help your clients express to each other what they want. It is equally important, however, to help them identify and clearly articulate what they might need in order to be able to get to a position to help each other get what they want.

In or Outside the Relationship. During the three months when Bill Emener was working with Fred and Gina, they focused on numerous aspects of their relationship – especially the needs and wants aspects. Fred was a 32-year-old professor at a nearby junior college, and Gina was a 33-year-old account rep at a local bank. Both of them worked very hard and enjoyed their careers. Fred also enjoyed his hobby of fishing, and Gina very much enjoyed hers of playing bridge. An identified source of frustration for each of them, however, was their jealousy and resentment of each other's relationships with co-workers and friends. For example, Fred said, "Gina, sometimes you seem to enjoy doing things with your friends at the bank and your bridge club friends more than you enjoy doing things with me." Gina replied, "You sure do seem to enjoy your friends at the college as well as your fishing buddies!"

Bill drew a chart for them similar to the one in Figure 7.10 and invited them to complete a homework assignment. He said, "I would like each of you to take a copy of this chart home with you. Gina, I would like you to write in this box what you need and want from Fred.

| Needs & Wants | From And/Or With | | | |
	My Significant Other	My Adult Loving Relation-ship	My Work (Career)	My Hobbies (Interests)
Needs				
Wants				

Figure 7.10. Specifying How and with Whom we Meet our Needs and Wants.

Likewise, write in what you need from your relationship with Fred, what you want from your relationship with Fred, what you need from your work, what you want from your work, and what you need and want from your bridge club activities. Similarly, Fred, I would like you to fill in your eight boxes with regard to your needs and wants in each of these four areas." They both understood the instructions and agreed to bring their completed charts with them to their next session.

At their next session, Fred and Gina shared with each other what they needed and wanted in each of these four areas of their lives. One of the first things that they noticed was that each of them tended to need and want similar kinds of things in their life areas. For example, both of them needed and wanted to be loved by each other, both of them wanted to feel special, valued and cherished in their relationship, both of them needed and wanted to feel a sense of worth and accomplishment in their careers, and both of them wanted companionship and same-sex bonding from their hobbies and interests.

There are three important aspects of loving relationships and couples counseling that can be learned from Fred and Gina. *First*, most people have a variety of interpersonal needs and wants that are best met by having a variety of interpersonal relationships. *Second*, it is important for those in loving relationships to realize that they cannot meet all of each other's interpersonal needs and wants – for example, our needs for companionship, camaraderie and same-sex bonding cannot be totally met by our significant other. *Third*, it is important for individuals in loving relationships to communicate and respect each other's alternative ways of meeting their interpersonal needs and wants. That is, it is very helpful if we can avoid feeling jealous of, resentful of, or threatened by the other important people in each other's lives.

Over-Estimating Our Expectations of Each Other. Bill Lambos only had two marital counseling sessions with Wally and Marian. They were able to ameliorate and resolve their relationship issues rather easily. Part of their difficulties had to do with the fact that they needed and wanted too much from one another. Both Wally and Marian were very high energy, highly productive and highly goal-oriented, especially in their professional lives. Understandably, they had very high expectations of themselves. Unfortunately, however, they also had extremely high expectations of each other. For example, Bill remembers Wally saying to Marian,

> "Sometimes I get very frustrated with you because I have the feeling that I can never meet your expectations of me. I'm always feeling like I am letting you down. I think that if you actually looked at all of the things I do for you, for our relationship and for myself, you would see I am a very productive person. Now that I'm in my late 40s, I am getting older, I don't have as much energy as I used to have, and I simply think some of your expectations of me are a little unrealistic."

Interestingly, Marian expressed very similar types of frustrations with regard to her perception of Wally's expectations of her. What the two of them realized, nevertheless, was that each of them was overestimating the other's capabilities. They were being *over-expecting* of one other. As Marian said to Wally, "Ten years ago, I was able to get up early, get the kids up and ready for school, put in a full day's work, come home and fix dinner for the children, change clothes, and meet you at a restaurant to accompany you at a dinner meeting. I now find that sometimes by eight-thirty or nine o'clock at night, I am just too tired." By tempering their expectations of each other, Wally and Marian were able to develop more realistic expectations of each other, reduce their frustrations and better enjoy their relationship.

It is important for individuals in loving relationships to communicate with each other so that their expectations can be realistic and comfortable. As Wally said, "Before Marian and I were able to modify our expectations of each other, our marriage felt like work – it was like a job. Now I feel that our marriage is so much more comfortable and enjoyable."

Limited Assumptions. When Bill Emener was talking with Millie, a 24-year-old schoolteacher, she told him that she sometimes felt a little nervous about marrying Paul, her fiancé, "because I had always hoped I could go on to complete my master's degree." Bill said to her, "What does your marriage to Paul have to do with your completing your master's degree?"

"Paul and I have been living together for a little over one year now," she replied, "and every night when he comes home from work I have dinner ready for him. We always enjoy eating together, and then he and I enjoy the evening together. If I were to go back to school for my master's, I probably would be taking classes one or two evenings a week and occasionally going to the library on the weekends to work on term papers. I even have wondered if I should delay our marriage and wait until I complete my degree before marrying Paul."

Bill suggested to Millie that it would be very helpful for her to talk with Paul about her desire to go back to school. He also asked her, "If you do not go on for your master's degree because you are marrying Paul, will you ever feel resentful?" Millie pondered the question for a few minutes and then said, "Yes, I think I would. But I don't know whether I would resent Paul or if I would resent myself. Maybe both?"

At their next counseling session, Millie offered she mentioned to Paul that she had been thinking about going back to school. "I couldn't believe it! Paul's response to me was 'What can I do to help you?'"

As they processed Millie's thoughts and feelings regarding this aspect of her relationship with Paul, Millie's discovery about herself was: "I was so in love with Paul, I wanted to marry him so much and was so afraid that I would mess things up, I underestimated him. I actually was going to limit my own life without even talking to him about school. That would have been a tragedy."

When we are in a loving relationship and want to do something for ourselves, it is a good idea to share our desires, wants, wishes and needs with our significant other, at least to get responses and input. *"What would I do with my life if he or she were **not** in my life?"* is a good question to ask ourselves on occasion. The bottom line is that we have to be careful to not limit ourselves or "make sacrifices" based on our assumptions. It is better to discuss our needs and wants before imposing any restrictions or limitations on ourselves. As Millie said, "Paul told me that one of the key ingredients of our relationship is trust. He is an incredibly wonderful man! Basically, he invited me to trust him and trust our relationship enough to always feel comfortable in telling him what I needed and wanted. He said to me, 'I can't promise you that I will always respond to your needs and wants the way you would like me to, but I will promise you that I will always try my best to understand and respect what you tell me you need and want.' Isn't he wonderful?"

Bill smiled. She got the message.

Logical Consequences. Sometimes when people in loving relationships think about their needs and wants, they think of their individual needs and wants as either being "good or bad" or "right or wrong." Based on the "ELF" characterization of rational beliefs presented earlier in the chapter, we have found it more useful to examine and determine whether wants and/or needs meet the criteria of being based upon rational beliefs. For example, when working with a couple attending to these issues, we always have found it to be quite helpful to ask each of them to ask themselves three questions:

1) What are the logical consequences of your getting what you need or want from him (or her) or your relationship?
2) What are the logical consequences of your not getting what you need and/or want from him (or her) or your relationship? and

3) Do your needs or wants logically flow from your beliefs about the other person's ability to meet them?

For example, when talking to Sandra about her wanting to take a two-week cruise with her husband for their 10th wedding anniversary, she told Bill Emener that the two of them had been struggling with making the arrangements for the cruise "because it felt *wrong* for us to spend that much money at this point in our marriage."

Bill asked her, "What are the logical consequences of the two of you taking the two-week cruise?" Sandra answered, "We would be spending approximately $2,700. But at the same time we were hoping to be able to buy all new living room furniture."

What Sandra eventually realized, however, as a result of Bill's helping her reframe her questions and concerns, was that there was nothing *wrong* with wanting to take a two-week cruise to celebrate their anniversary *and* wanting new furniture. Nonetheless, the logical consequences of wanting both things, was that it would cost approximately $5,400 and they only had $2,700 in their budget. They simply had a decision to make – a decision based on their values. What ultimately was helpful for them was that once they were able to identify the logical consequences of their decision, they were able to free themselves from thinking of the alternatives (i.e., what they wanted) as either being right or wrong. As Sandra poignantly observed regarding her and her husband's relationship, "Maybe the most important thing my husband and I need is to learn that we cannot always get everything that we want." It is not uncommon for our clients to say to themselves things like, "This would be right, that would be wrong. This would be good, that would be bad." It is more helpful, however, if we can facilitate their asking themselves, "This is what I need and that is what I want. What are the logical consequences of getting what I need and getting what I want *and* of not getting what I need and not getting what I want?"

Frequently, the premature value-labeling of our needs and wants can: (1) preclude us from identifying the logical consequences of our alternatives; and (2) block us from exploring additional alternatives. For example, Sandra and her husband identified a third alternative: they decided to go on a less expensive, one-week cruise and purchase *some* new furniture. The important thing is that they were able to make a decision *together* and feel good about it.

The third question above is perhaps even more critical: can I rationally expect my partner to live up to my expectations, to fulfill my every need and want? We are frequently surprised how often in the counseling office we hear clients say things such as "If only George would do this" or "Things would be fine if she could just stop doing that!" Our response is usually the same: "Is it logical for you to expect your partner not to behave in a way that he or she has since the day you met one other?" We have found that once a person looks at the issue this way, many tensions related to needs, wants and expectations are diffused. Not only has a specific want or relationship need been identified, but the consequences of *demanding* that the other person's behavior change magically are seen for what they are: unreasonable. People can and often will change even long established and ingrained patterns of behavior to make a valuable relationship work, but they cannot be expected to do so all at once. That is an irrational belief that only adds more problems to those caused by the unwanted behavior.

RATIONAL VERSUS IRRATIONAL THINKING III:
DICHOTOMOUS THINKING

People have a tendency to oversimplify reality by taking shades of gray and making them either black or white. This tendency is hard-wired at the lowest levels of the perceptual system, and is found at nearly every level of the brain. It reduces the amount of information an organism must process in order to negotiate the world, and can therefore be a very useful strategy. On the other hand, the world is not a binary place. Little or none of reality is of an "either/or" nature – the world *is* defined by shades of gray.

Nonetheless, it is often helpful to point this out to clients, especially as it relates to their feelings and emotions. For example, every experienced couples counselor has undoubtedly heard statements similar to the following ones during sessions:

> "During Christmas break, we were together every day. It was wonderful. If we can't have it that way all the time, I don't want a relationship with him at all."
> "If I can't spend every day of every week with her, it just seems never to be enough for her. It's either all or nothing. Forget it!"
> "There's no way that I'm going to meet him for coffee. If I do, I know what will happen – we'll wind up in bed. No way!"

"Dichotomous thinking" is representative of the aforementioned cognitive process by which we mistakenly conceptualize aspects of life that typically vary along a range or a continuum as being binary, or all-or-none, in nature. For a dichotomous thinker, there are no midpoints. Quite frequently, we also tend to have equally extreme feelings associated with the phenomena at the extremes of continuums. Dichotomous thinking is a type of what the well-known psychologist Aaron Beck (who, with Albert Ellis, led the Cognitive Behavioral Psychology movement), calls a "cognitive distortion." It is a way of looking at a world made up of shades of gray and distorting it so that we see it only as being all black or all white at any given time.

For example, when Terry and Arlene came to see Bill Emener because they "were trying to rekindle, renew and work on their relationship," it became very clear that both of them were engaged in dichotomous thinking. At one point, Bill drew a sketch for them similar to the one in Figure 7.11 and said, "It appears to me, Terry, that you see life either with Arlene or without Arlene. You tend to vacillate between these two extremes. You are either with her all the time and you feel very good and happy, or you are without her and you feel very sad and sorrowful." Bill then looked at Arlene, and said, "Arlene, you tend to be the same way." With a sigh, she replied, "Yes, Dr. Emener, that's true." Turning back to Terry, Bill continued, "Might it be possible that rather than either being with her all the time and feeling very good and very happy, or being without her and not seeing her all the time and feeling very sad and sorrowful, that there might be some mid-range alternatives that we could talk about? For example, Terry, could you see her occasionally – for example, maybe once or twice during the week when the two of you are very busy with your work and other personal activities?" Both of them, looking at each other and then looking at Bill said, "Yes, that's possible. It makes sense too. Let's try to see if we can work something out." Subsequent sessions revealed that both Arlene and Terry also had been individually struggling with other critical aspects of themselves as well as their relationship (e.g., abandonment, feeling smothered, etc.). Importantly, however, the two of them were able to identify some middle-range kinds of activities, interactions and ways "to be with each other" without having to have an all-or-nothing relationship and experiencing either horrendous sadness or incredible joy.

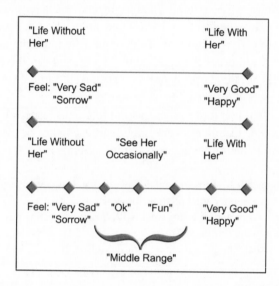

Figure 7.11. Dichotomous Thinking and the Development of a "Middle Range."

It is not only people in loving relationships who fall into the tendency to make this error. Some of the brightest minds in science, politics and business have made the same mistake. In science, we refer to this as "binary" thinking: someone is either an alcoholic or not, a success or failure in their career, a Republican or a Democrat or, in the words of a politician, "with us or against us." The truth of such assertions, however, is rarely so simple. Nature and human experience are typically more accurately described as varying along ranges of values rather than oscillating between the end points of these ranges. Of course, there are exceptions (for example, pregnancy comes to mind – you either are or you aren't), but for the most part, dichotomous thinking is an error in judgment and sometimes a costly oversimplification.

How We Spend Our Time. Bill Lambos was counseling a couple, Sally and David, for whom Sally's career was becoming more and more of a "deal killer" for David. Having never finished college, Sally took a job at an advertising agency as an assistant to an account executive. The executive soon realized that Sally's talents went beyond clerical and filing tasks, however, and after 18 months arranged a promotion and raise for her to the position of junior account manager. Sally was thrilled that someone else valued her abilities and she threw herself into the job with gusto. At first David was happy; it meant more income and new things for them. However, David, a foreman at a warehouse, soon became dissatisfied: "Dr. Lambos, Sal has to realize that she's either my wife or she isn't – she can't have it both ways," he exclaimed with authority. Bill asked them to describe their normal work week. Each put in about nine hours a day, including commute-time, except that Sally stayed late on the average of two nights a week to finalize a proposal or finish a project. On many of those nights, she would make sure David's dinner was in the refrigerator before she left the house in the morning and always called David if she had to stay late. Nonetheless, David was not satisfied; he felt if she could not get home every night by six, she "was not there for him anymore." Even after calculating the number of hours per week that Sally worked late and showing David that it amounted to less than 10% of their total time together before the promotion, it did not change David's outlook. David had fallen into the trap of dichotomous thinking and would not budge. Sadly, they divorced within six months. David still blames Sally "for choosing her job over him," and Sally has moved on and is seeing someone else. When people are unable or unwilling to give up their "all or nothing" outlook on their relationships, those relationships often end.

Bill Emener recalls a similar case with a better outcome. Susan and Nelson had been living together for approximately six months, were planning to eventually get married, but as they said, they "were living an extremely hectic and frustrating life together." Susan was working part-time in a restaurant. She also was a full-time law student at a nearby law school. Nelson was working part-time as a real estate agent and attending advanced real estate classes in night school. During two weeks of the Christmas holiday season, when both of them were on Christmas break and not in school, their relationship was exceptionally good. They felt "very together" and "very happy." After both of them went back to school and to work, however, they both began feeling down, lonely and abandoned. Both of them were constantly wondering, "Why can't he (why can't she) make time to spend with me?" The verbalizations that really got Bill's attention were: "If he really loved me, he would find more time for me during the week," and "I know she's busy, but sometimes I hardly ever see her during the week, and if she really loved me she'd make time for me!" While they looked at a figure that Bill drew for them, like the one in Figure 7.12, he suggested that their relationship could be thought of as a bell-shaped, or normal distribution curve, in which over a year's period of time there were limited instances – like when both of them were on Christmas break and could spend a large amount of time together; or at the other extreme, instances when both of them were studying for exams and hardly had time to breathe, much less find time for each other. What they quickly realized was that the two weeks during Christmas break and the two weeks of exam time were not typical of their relationship time. Bill suggested to them that if the normal curve distribution were representative of their relationship, as they were describing it, approximately 86% of their time was somewhere other than these two extremes. Then he said to them, while pointing to Figure 7.12, "What can you do during this 68% of the time?"

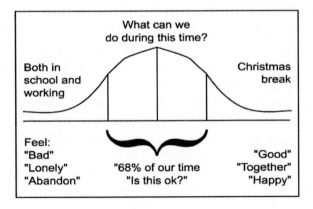

Figure 7.12. How We Spend Our Time.

With some modifications in their class and work schedules, they were able to identify one night a week when the two of them could go out to dinner and two evenings during the week when they could devote some time specifically to themselves and their relationship. Bill is happy to share that when they came back for their last session, Susan told him, "We have come to realize a number of things. While the two of us are in school and working, it is not very easy. The two weeks of exam time are typically the pits around our house! At the other extreme we certainly enjoy our Christmas breaks and are looking forward to our week together during spring break. However, during this middle-range time we now are enjoying those precious opportunities when we can spend time together, realizing that the relatively small amount of time we have together is by choice. It has nothing to do with our love for each other; it has to do with our career developments." Terry looked at Bill, smiled and added, "It seemed that once we were able to stop ourselves from blaming each other for our scheduling constraints and stop seeing the limitations of our time together as indications of our love for each other, we were able to take control of our schedules and ultimately take control of our lives. Now we are truly enjoying each other so much more."

People Are Either "Good" or "Bad." In addition to having "lived through a stormy lifestyle for the past fifteen years," Kate, a 38-year-old single parent with two children, also told Bill Emener in their first session that she "wanted to be able to sustain a meaningful, loving relationship for a change." Kate, who was from a rather typical dysfunctional family, also said, "Over the past 15 years I have been in a number of relationships with men, most of whom were good, decent human beings. But after about six months, when we would really start to get to know each other, the relationship would get very rocky and turbulent. Then within two weeks of arguing daily, we would separate and poof, the relationship would be over. Maybe there's something about me that brings this 'here-we-go-again outcome' all the time? How can I stop this pattern?" After confirming what she specifically wanted to change about herself and her life, they clarified Kate's therapy goals. In addition to reading some pertinent self-help books, Kate also began journaling (writing down perceptions, thoughts and feelings on a daily basis).

During a subsequent session, Bill drew a diagram for Kate similar to the one in Figure 7.13 as he was explaining to her what he saw as being a critical component of her difficulties in relationships with men. "By and large, Kate," he suggested, "most of us learn to conceptualize people as being Good and Bad. That would mean that if I saw you as Good and Bad, I (1) would see you as being one person, and (2) would accept you and love you for both your good qualities, which I liked, and your bad qualities, which I didn't like. If we were in a loving relationship, I hopefully would work toward minimizing those qualities about myself that you didn't like, and you hopefully would try to be tolerant and accepting of my qualities that you didn't like. Unfortunately for you, Kate, you see men as being Good *or* Bad. And that would mean, for example, that (1) you would see men as being two people, and (2) you would accept them and 'love them dearly with all you've got when they were good' and 'run like hell when they were bad'." As tears streamed down her face, Kate said, "Yes, that's exactly how it is for me. When Joe was Good, I talked to him every day and spent evenings and weekends at his house. But when he was Bad, I would go to my apartment, not talk with him and simply avoid him for four or five days. Finally, he just got fed up with the craziness."

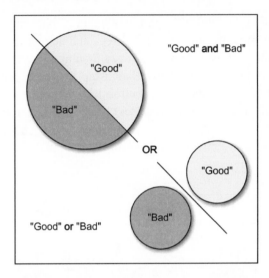

Figure 7.13. People Are either "Good" or "Bad."

Over the next 10 months, Kate continued to journal, selectively read self-help books and worked on her "conceptualizations of men and how she dealt with them." About six months after their last session, Bill by chance saw Kate in a shopping mall. As they briefly chatted, he felt a warm closeness for her when she said, "I was lucky, Dr. Emener, Joe was understanding and willing to try to work things out. And even though he really pisses me off sometimes and it's hard for me to hang in there and work through my negative feelings with him, I do love him dearly. Both of him!"

All or Nothing Relationships. The following example is instructive of another type of binary, or dichotomous thinking – the All or Nothing relationship fallacy. This story comes from Bill Emener's files: "Ever since Norman got out of the Army and we became engaged, our relationship is either everything or nothing." That was the way Betty described her relationship with Norman when the two of them came to see Bill. It appeared that for weeks at a time they would spend almost all of their time together, except when they were at work, or they wouldn't see each other at all for a three or four day period. He sketched a diagram for them similar to the one in Figure 7.14 and suggested that their relationship was extremely dichotomous: "It is either an all relationship, or it is a nothing relationship." Since Norman mustered out of the Army, the only thing he did was take a job, move into a new apartment and spend time with Betty.

Likewise, Betty would go to work every day, be home alone in her apartment, or do something with Norman. Pointing to the middle of the diagram in Figure 7.14, Bill said to them, "We already have identified the midpoint where the two of you enjoy time together. This is the shaded area. However Norman, you could renew your enjoyment of some wind surfing on the weekends and maybe some softball in the evenings during the week; and Betty, you could get back to playing tennis and spending more time with your sisters whom you said live nearby." What Norman and Betty needed to do was to take some time to develop a relationship that did not have the characteristics of either extreme – All or Nothing.

In the process of identifying a midpoint for their relationship, Betty was able to realize that she could go out for an evening with her sisters or play tennis on a Saturday afternoon and not be any less in love with Norman. Nor would Norman feel any less loved by her.

Similarly, Norman could spend the better part of a Saturday wind surfing with some of his old buddies or playing in a softball game during the week and neither feel any less loving toward Betty nor worry that she was feeling any less loved by him. Once the two of them were able to realize the dichotomous nature of their relationship and appreciate the benefits of their midpoint, they were able to exercise some control, use their creativity and imagination, and develop a relationship lifestyle that was less dichotomous. Furthermore, their "new relationship" was more enjoyable to them, more manageable, and more characteristic and supportive of the kind of overall life that the two of them wanted to live – individually as well as collectively.

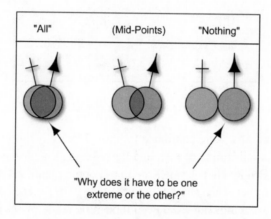

Figure 7.14. All or Nothing Relationships.

FEELINGS AND EMOTIONS

"I know that we love each other, and I know that we have a good relationship. But sometimes, and I don't know why, I just don't feel good about us."

Hundreds of people have said that to us. You may have said something like it to yourself or heard one of your clients say it. We have said it to ourselves. And on such occasions, we think, "There's a message here. Could this be a signal to take some action?"

Action that can be very helpful, as well as preventative, is to address some important questions such as: How do I feel about us? How do I feel about me in this relationship? How are my feelings related to my actions? I know that I occasionally get angry, but is my anger related to any other feelings? What do I do with my feelings? Where do my anxiety and jealousy come from? Why do I sometimes just not feel anything? How can I get some resolution to my feelings and have a sense of serenity with this relationship? The following is specifically designed to assist you in helping your clients address questions such as these, especially in terms of how they may relate to them and their loving relationships.

Emotional Intelligence. The role of emotions in understanding human behavior has a long and diverse history. Various schools of thought have taken very different positions on the role that emotions play in determining human behavior. Such approaches have varied from placing emotions at the epicenter of the self and as the root determinant of all other behavior (e.g., the phenomenological approach of Carl Rogers), to the opposite extreme of denying the role of emotion as a proper subject of the study of human psychology (e.g., radical behaviorism à la B.F. Skinner). Common sense tells us, however, that whenever an issue seems to have only two sides, in reality a continuum of values exists about the subject, and truth is typically somewhere in the middle. Remember what we learned in the last chapter about dichotomous thinking? The subject of emotion is no exception.

Since the 1980s and the emergence of the Cognitive Behavioral Movement, the debate over the importance of emotion versus cognition in guiding one's life had been leaning toward the role of thoughts as the primary determinants of behavior. Eminent psychologists such as Albert Ellis and Aaron Beck stated loudly and with near certainty, that our emotions are the result of our cognitions and our beliefs, rather than the other way around. But just when it looked like the brain was about to assume prominence over the heart forever, the debate was rekindled dramatically. In 1995, a now equally famous psychologist named Daniel Goldman published the best-selling book, *Emotional Intelligence: How it Can Matter More than IQ*. Since then, the heart has made a strong comeback and psychologists have relearned the importance, if not the primacy, of emotion.

As described in Chapters 1 and 4, it is now recognized that there can be no such thing as pure intellect in the absence of emotion. Emotion and intellect are bound at the hip and will forever be so intertwined. Shortly we will describe in detail how emotions impact loving relationships and the importance of emotional management in healthy couples. But as long as we are on this short detour, let's reexamine why this is so from the point of view of 21st century neuroscience. It won't take long, and we trust our readers may avoid falling into several of the common pitfalls of emotional mismanagement if they understand why the heart and the mind must always walk side by side.

Consider the following two questions: (1) What is the capital of France? and (2) Where should I go on vacation this summer? What is the most important difference between these two questions? After a little thought, you will probably figure out that the first question can be answered definitively: Paris is the capital of France, and no other answer is correct. On the other hand, where you should spend your summer vacation has no right or wrong answer: it depends on your values, what you want, and what pleases you (and perhaps your partner and family). As we also noted in Chapter 1, the brain is divided into different areas to deal with these two aspects of reality: knowledge about the world, and knowledge about our needs and wants. The latter issues, which are called *Issues of Agency*, turn out to be just as important as the former and perhaps even more so. In the last 15 years, psychologists and neuroscientists have learned that a sense of agency – seeing the world as emotionally pleasing or not – is inseparable not only from intelligence, but from consciousness itself. The bottom line is that *emotions determine how we see the world and how we react to every aspect of it*. Anyone who tells you differently is simply wrong (and, in all likelihood, is emotionally attached to their belief). If people wish to learn how to intelligently manage their relationships, they had better start by learning how to intelligently manage (or at least meaningfully influence) their emotions – something to always remember when working with clients.

The Importance of Feeling "Safe." Of all the emotions produced by our brains, fear is certainly the strongest, at least in terms of immediacy. A small but very important part of the brain, called the "amygdala," is dedicated to producing the felt emotion of fear. The brain is wired in such a way that the amygdala can override almost any other impulse or choice a person might otherwise make. It is the seat of the "fight or flight" response and can cause intense changes in the mind and body nearly instantaneously. Anecdotes of superhuman strength in times of emergency (e.g., a mother lifting a car off her baby after an accident) probably reflect a massive release of adrenaline and other hormones and transmitters at the time the amygdala is activated. Interestingly, it has also been shown that the amygdala stores memories. Many are learned over generations throughout our evolutionary history (e.g., fear of spiders and snakes), but the amygdala can also encode new memories. Psychological trauma, including dissociative disorders such as multiple personalities, have been shown to rely on excessive and ongoing activity of this primitive, sub cortical part of the brain in functional imaging studies.

But the reverse is also true. When the amygdala is quiet, we feel safe. This, too, is associated with other important emotions, and though they may be felt as less intense, they are no less important. Think of the changes our society underwent as a result of 9/11. First came fear, and Americans were willing to allow restrictions on our freedoms and even a war that were unthinkable just weeks before. After some years, as people felt safe again, the political atmosphere reversed (along with it the popularity of our elected leaders). Fear can be a powerful motivator, but it is ultimately a negative one that normally can last for only so long. Feelings of safety, on the other hand, never seem to lose their appeal.

Many loving relationships are based on maintaining the feeling of safety. This is one of the true joys of coupledom. Problems can arise, however, when the need to feel safe pushes us to stay in an otherwise unhealthy relationship. For example, Peter and Debra came to see Bill Lambos because of Debra finally insisting that after years of putting up with it, "something had to be done about Peter's drinking problem." Peter, however, said, "I really don't know what the big deal is. I work all day at my lousy job, and when I get home all I ask is to have some dinner and grab a few beers while the game is on. And lately she's getting all bent out of shape about it!" Debra replied, "Peter, a few beers is two or maybe three – you're up to a 12-pack a night, every night. Half the nights you pass out on the sofa and I can't even wake you up to come to bed. Two weeks ago, after I went to the bedroom alone, again, I heard noises in the house and got scared out of my wits. I thought someone had broken in and I ran out to the living room to tell you. But you were out cold and couldn't be woken up. I'm sorry, but I won't stay in this marriage if I can't feel safe in my own home."

Peter first looked as if he was about to get very angry, but then took a deep breath and sighed, "I'm so sorry, honey. I didn't realize how bad it's gotten. Maybe we should find me some help. I can't feel like a man if you don't feel safe around me because I'm in love with my beer. And truth be told, I still love you more than my beer." Bill arranged for Peter to enroll in an outpatient program for substance abuse. Peter hated it but stuck it out, and to his credit he drinks very infrequently these days – a single glass of wine with dinner on Saturdays, and no alcohol during the week. Debra feels safe now, and their romance has blossomed once again. Peter sent Bill an e-mail not too long ago saying he had quit his job and started over at a new company. Although he took a salary reduction, he said it was the best money he ever spent. "Ever since the new job, I don't even think about beer after work. It was the stress of that lousy job that was making me nuts."

Peter's drinking had begun to resemble an alcoholic pattern, but he was able to change the pattern in time. More importantly, his drinking was fueled not by the desire to get drunk (although that clearly was beginning to play a role), but by the need to reduce the anxiety he experienced at his former job. In counseling, we call such behavior "self-medication" and it is usually a poor solution to control stress. Like many prescription medications, it controls symptoms without addressing the underlying problem or imbalance.

Anxiety Reduction. Jerry explained to Bill Emener one of the difficulties in his and Norma's relationship for which they wanted assistance: "All of our married life, and even before we were married, at least once a week we get into a big fight, get all upset with each other, and then, as they say, 'kiss and make up.'"

"It's just not fun anymore," Norma added, "we can't continue with this pattern, even though when we kiss and make up, we do have the best sex." Jerry smiled in agreement. "But why do we do this all the time?" they wondered. As they were exploring this aspect of their relationship, Bill reminded them of a basic principle in psychology – the reduction of anxiety can be very reinforcing (Dollard & Miller, 1979). "For example," Bill said, "ever wonder why we wait until the very last minute to go to the bathroom when we actually knew ten minutes ago that we had to go?" Jerry chuckled before saying, "Sometimes for me it's almost like a challenge, like 'How long can I hold it?' But it is true – when I finally go, for some crazy reason, it does feel good." After returning to some serious discussion of this pattern in their relationship, Jerry and Norma agreed on two things: (1) they subconsciously had been creating anxiety in their relationship because it felt so good when they would reduce it by kissing and making up, and (2) they would try to recognize the pattern as it was developing, talk about it and try to short-circuit it. They worked on this aspect of their relationship, experienced success with their new approach, and found their relationship to be much more enjoyable without their weekly fights. With a wry smile, Norma added, "And now we don't have to wait until Saturday night when we kiss and make up to have great sex."

The reduction of anxiety can be very reinforcing and feel good to us (Dollard & Miller, 1979), and sometimes we may subconsciously create anxiety because of the eventual and anticipated reinforcement that comes with its reduction. However, if a client's pattern of anxiety enhancement followed by anxiety reduction becomes a pattern that creates serious problems and difficulties, it very well may be a good idea to help them work on changing the pattern.

Jealousy. For the three months prior to coming to see Bill Emener, Tonya had been feverishly busy with all of the running around involved with her upcoming wedding. Time was very precious for her. "Nonetheless," she said, "I simply have to talk with someone. I have a number of feelings about Les and our relationship that I need to sort out." The number one troublesome feeling that she identified was her insatiable jealously. "If he goes out for the evening without me, or if he gets home from work later than he said he would, I go nuts. I right away think that he has run into an old girlfriend or something." As they processed this, they discovered that she also had strong fears that Les would eventually call the wedding off "because maybe I am not worthy of his love." As Tonya and Bill therapeutically worked on her fear of abandonment as well as her overall feelings of insecurity, she found herself becoming less jealous. "Now that I'm feeling better about myself, I'm finding myself feeling better about Les and our upcoming wedding," she said in a follow-up session. About three months later, Bill received an envelope in the mail with an after-the-fact wedding announcement in it. On the bottom was written, "Thanks, Mrs. Tonya Johnson."

When a client in a loving relationship is experiencing feelings of jealousy, it is recommended that you help them explore their other feelings, such as their feelings of insecurity and fear of abandonment. Quite frequently, feelings such as these are related to each other. Moreover, feelings such as jealousy also can be early warning signs of other, more serious difficulties.

Emotional Shutdown. Sometimes in loving relationships, it is not uncommon for people to experience intense feelings of joy and happiness at one moment and intense feelings of sadness and aloneness a moment later. Rob said to Bill Emener, "At times like this, it's like being on an emotional yo-yo." After feeling like this for some time, Rob became emotionally exhausted and "stopped feeling." When he first came to see Bill, Rob said, "I know I love her. In my head I know I love her. But I just don't feel anymore." As they talked, it became quite clear that Rob had been experiencing numerous difficulties with Rhonda and their relationship for a long time. Interestingly, he added, "It seems like I have been on this emotional yo-yo forever!" After a while, it appeared, Rob's defense mechanisms kicked in and he just shut down his emotional system. As he had said, "I just don't feel anymore." Moreover, Rhonda apparently was sensing Rob's emotional shut down. Understandably, yet counterproductively, she was pressuring him to be more emotional with her. "She keeps saying to me, 'For God's sake, Rob, tell me what you are feeling. You're like a robot!'"

As the therapy continued, Rob eventually was able to feel more comfortable with being in touch with his emotions. He began to be more aware of his feelings and started to trust his ability to deal with them again. He also asked Rhonda to be patient with him and to assist him in making some adjustments in their relationship. For example, he shared with her that at times he felt she was trying to move too fast with their relationship and he was feeling smothered. From what Rob shared with Bill, she apparently was comfortable with and actually appreciative of Rob's requests and suggestions. As time progressed, they were able to more openly discuss their feelings and be more lovingly responsive to each other. For example, Rob said to Bill in a subsequent session, "The other day when Rhonda and I were talking, it was clear that she understood what I was saying to her when she said, 'In other words, Rob, you'd like for me to slow down the movie.' I said to her in return, 'Yes Rhonda, and if you try to put your high speed film in my slow speed camera it will underexpose.' We got a good laugh out of that analogy." The important thing is that in their counseling sessions Rob and Rhonda were able to attend to their individual feelings and be respectful and responsive to them.

If people do not attend to their intense feelings, especially if they are of the yo-yo variety and left unattended over too long a period, it would make sense for them to shut down emotionally. As Rob said to Bill, "Burn your hand on the stove too many times and eventually you just start staying away from the kitchen."

A Need for Resolution and Serenity. Sometimes people will shut down emotionally when over a long period of time they feel flooded with a multitude of intense feelings regarding numerous people. At other times, people will experience great emotional upheaval and feel intense levels of anxiety. Furthermore, in such instances, it can be very difficult for them to focus and identify toward whom and for what reasons they are experiencing specific feelings. For example, when Kim first came to see Bill Emener to talk about her feelings toward Chris, her fiancé, she was "emotionally bouncing off the walls."

During their first session, they were able to identify four people in her life, not just one, toward whom she was having some intense feelings. Bill drew a diagram for her similar to the one in Figure 7.15. Then they discussed it. For example, Bill said, "If I understand you correctly, Kim, you:

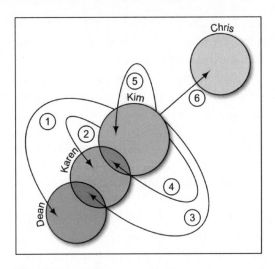

Figure 7.15. Areas in Need for Resolution and Serenity.

1) have strong feelings of anger and resentment toward Dean, your ex-husband, and you get nervous when your daughter spends the weekend with him because you do not like the way he treats her;

2) are angry at your daughter, Karen, because she manipulates you and Dean to get her own way, and you especially feel angry when she acts like her father;

3) resent Dean and Karen's relationship, especially when she tells you what fun they have together;

4) don't like some aspects of your relationship with Karen because you don't have the control over her that you think you should have because you are her mother;

5) have some feelings of anger toward yourself because you allowed your bad relationship with Dean to go on for so long; and,

6) have a tremendous amount of love for Chris, yet you struggle with telling him all of your feelings for fear that he may get angry at you and leave you."

Kim nervously replied, "Yep, that's it alright. Now you know why I am an emotional basket-case!"

As Kim was able to further parcel out her feelings about herself, as well as toward whom she had all of her feelings, she was in a much better position to understand what was going on within herself. Understandably, she felt more in-control, her anxiety started to diminish, and her self-help skills began working for her again. "All I want is a sense of serenity in my life," she said to Bill. "I think I need to deal with things one at a time," she added. Bill agreed, and as time ensued, Kim was able to attend to the significant people in her life – one at a time – and move more toward resolution of her feelings toward them.

When at times we feel flooded with a variety of emotions toward and regarding other people, it can very helpful if we can: (1) parcel out and specify our feelings, and (2) target or identify them with the specific individuals toward whom we have such feelings. Getting away and sorting things out can be extremely helpful. Not only does this process assist us in moving toward resolution and serenity, but it avoids adding to our difficulties as well. For example, when our feelings and the people toward whom we feel them are confusing to us, we can inadvertently compound our problems. As Kim said to Bill, "One Saturday night Chris said to me, 'Why are you so angry at me? Karen's with Dean this weekend. And for whatever it's worth, Kim, I'm Chris – I'm not Dean!'"

Among other things, a good sailing ship needs good sails and a good rudder. Think of the brain as the hand on the tiller controlling the rudder. Likewise, think of feelings and emotions as the energy-generating sails that propel us. As illustrated in this metaphor – one we occasionally share with our clients – keeping a close watch on our sails is important: an unattended small tear can quickly turn into a big rip, an unnoticed small hole can quickly send it flapping in the wind. The majority of the time, we can find a good wind. And with a watchful eye on the sails and an occasional checking of the mast, there's nothing more beautiful than a full sail.

Confronting the Fear and Pain. It repeatedly has been our experience that underneath the surface feelings of anger, resentment and passive-aggressiveness are the deeper feelings of fear and pain. The following examples from our practices show this.

Bill Lambos, who also works as a Florida Supreme Court Certified Family Mediator, was hired to negotiate a prenuptial agreement for two physicians, Grete and Carlos, who had been dating for three years but were having trouble making the commitment to get engaged. (Later in this book we will look at mediation as an alternative to family court battles in cases of divorce.) Bill's work with Grete and Carlos was simply supposed to be a non-confrontational forum for negotiating how money would be handled in the event they married and later divorced or one of them died suddenly. Each had children from a previous marriage, each owned a home and each earned roughly the same income – Bill anticipated a single two-hour session without complications. However, it turned out to be not so simple. As they discussed the various arrangements that would meet their needs (trusts for the children, equitable distribution of joint assets into the trusts upon unexpected death, etc.), Bill noticed the tenor of the discussion changing in a rather negative way. When he probed what was behind their questions, Grete blurted out, "He hates my children and will steal everything from them!" Carlos stood up and proffered his own accusation: "It's funny how upset you get when I pay for my son's tuition bills, Grete. Who hates whose children here?"

Bill tried to explain that by allocating the assets to trusts, the children would be protected should Grete and Carlos divorce or if one passed away. It quickly became clear, however, that money issues were not the problem at all. Both of these highly educated physicians were really expressing fear that the other person loved their children more than their partner. And as soon as that started to become apparent, their fears translated into anger. The mediation continued for three sessions, but no agreement was reached because of the negative feelings that arose at each session. Neither of these two intelligent professionals had the slightest ability to control his or her own emotions.

Ethical standards preclude a professional from assuming the roles of both mediator and therapist with any person or couple. This constraint exists because a certified mediator must be, above all, both impartial to the parties and neutral with respect to outcome. It is assumed for the sake of protecting the integrity of both professions that one individual cannot guarantee to be both neutral and impartial in the context of counseling. Because Dr. Lambos was acting in the role of mediator, he could not provide counseling services; thus, he referred them to another professional counselor. The last Bill heard, Grete and Carlos were still together, still living in their own homes, but marriage was off the table. Once again, unless one can learn to intelligently manage or meaningfully influence one's emotions, that person cannot fully succeed in a loving relationship.

Bill Emener's files contain a similar story, but one with a slightly different twist. From the moment that Wendy and Douglas entered his office, even before they sat down, they were throwing daggers of anger at each other, looking at each other with harsh resentful eyes, and reminding each other of how they were repeatedly being hurt by each other's passive-aggressiveness. After exchanging the typical cordialities and routine kinds of information exchanges, Bill looked at Wendy and said, "It is very clear to me that you are feeling a tremendous amount of anger toward Douglas." She immediately replied, with a hostile and sarcastic voice, "You're the psychologist!" After a few moments of silence, however, and after she turned back to look at Bill, in a soft and gentle voice he asked her, "Wendy, what are you afraid of? What is the 'little girl' inside of you scared of?" Tears instantly began welling up in Wendy's eyes, and with a quivering chin she softly said, "My Daddy left us... I remember the day he pulled away... my first husband left me... and when Doug doesn't come right home from work, doesn't call and then wanders in at about eleven o'clock at night, it tears me up." Bill replied gently, "It sounds as if when that happens, Wendy, you feel abandoned." "I just can't take it anymore," she said to Douglas, "it just hurts too much. And I try not to let the kids see me worry and cry, but the hurt is just too much now." As she wept, Douglas reached out to her, held her hands and said softly, "Come on now, Punkin, you know I love you... I wouldn't leave you... I love you." After Wendy's crying subsided, they discussed what Douglas could do to be more responsive and attentive to her fears and her hurting, especially with regard to his not coming home when she expects him.

Bill later looked at Douglas, intuitively sensing what Douglas said to him: "I can't stand being told, 'You hurt me' by anyone... especially Wendy." Bill just looked at him with an understanding look. "For years, when I was younger," Douglas continued, "my mother would take any little thing I would do wrong and cry and tell me how much I hurt her... it was horribly painful. I remember those times very well." "So when Wendy..." Bill began to respond but was cut off. "When I know Wendy is hurting, I guess I just holler at her so that she won't have a chance to tell me how much she is hurting." They proceeded to process Douglas' mechanism of using anger to avoid feeling hurt. Their ensuing discussions were very helpful to both Wendy and Douglas – they were able to discover that underneath each other's intense anger was equally intense fear and pain.

As with Wendy and Douglas, people frequently respond to another person's intense surface feelings with similar levels of intensity. In a loving relationship, however, and as illustrated in Figure 7.16, it is very helpful if we can look beyond the surface feelings and see and respond to the deeper feelings. We submit that when you look beneath surface feelings of anger, you frequently will find feelings of fear and pain.

What to Do with Your Feelings. From Bill Emener's experiences comes another pertinent story about managing one's feelings. "I came to see you, Doc, because I am afraid that if I don't get some help, someday I am going to lose it and hit Nancy, my wife." Andy continued. "When she is pushing my buttons, I feel the anger building up in me. But I'm good. I'm okay. I just stand there and don't do anything. But she just keeps going on, hollerin' and pickin'. Then she yells, 'How can you just stand there and not say anything?' That's when I almost lose it. And up to now, I just walk out of the house or I go for a ride. But I'm scared, Doc. What if someday..." Bill could see that Andy was genuinely scared. As they processed his feelings and reactions in situations such as the one he described, Bill suggested to Andy that when he felt his anger building up he had choices. He said, "When you feel anger building up within you, Andy, you can:

1) deny it... Say to yourself, 'She's not all that angry or upset with me. She'll get over it in a minute or two;'
2) act on it... Strike out and possibly hit her; or
3) express it... Say to her, 'Nancy, I am really beginning to feel angry at you.'"

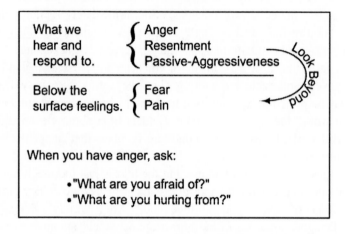

Figure 7.16. Confronting the Fear and Pain.

As time went on, Andy discovered that because of his fear of not being able to control himself if he were to express his anger toward Nancy, he would first deny his anger. If she persisted and his feelings got too intense, he would run away from the situation. With some role-playing and other therapeutic interventions, Andy eventually began to learn how to express his feelings and trust his ability to express them. Indeed, this was very helpful for Andy as well as his relationship with Nancy.

It is important for us to try to remember that when we have feelings building up inside of us and we are aware of what we are feeling, we have choices as to what to do with them. Learning new responses and new ways of dealing with our feelings is very important, especially if our current response patterns don't work for us and at times create additional difficulties. Not learning how to effectively attend to one's feelings, such as anger, can lead to other, more serious problems, such as violence – which should be avoided at all costs.

CHAPTER SUMMARY

In this chapter we moved away from analytics, squarely into the present, or "the now," and focused on aspects of individual beliefs, feelings and behavior that are most closely associated with what each individual partner brings into the relationship and how these impact the couple. Specifically, pertinent to loving relationships we examined the role of congruence and balance of each partner's concept of *self* and how each partner's *beliefs* contribute to relationship health and stability. We then examined how needs, wants and expectations can either contribute to, or conversely negatively impact, relationship functioning. Next we put the phenomenon of dichotomous thinking under the microscope, focusing on how people spend their time, their perceptions of "good" and/or "bad" people, and all-or-nothing relationships. Lastly, we examined human emotions and how they impact individuals, as well as their partners and loving relationships. In a synthetic way, specific approaches and suggestions for counselors were discussed and demonstrated – ones that can meaningfully assist client couples in moving forward with their relationships or, when necessary, help clients leave them behind and move on with their lives.

CHAPTER 7 DISCUSSION QUESTIONS

1) Why are congruence and balance important attributes of loving relationships?
2) In what ways are the interaction effects among a person's Affect (feelings), Behavior (actions) and Cognitions (thoughts) critical for the sustenance of happiness?
3) What counseling techniques could you use in assisting a couple having difficulties because their needs, wants and/or expectations were negatively impacting their relationship?
4) Why and in what ways is "dichotomous thinking" troublesome for (a) individuals and (b) loving relationships?
5) What are some of the ways by which you could assist a couple whose individual feelings and emotions are harmful to their relationship?

CHAPTER REVIEW QUESTIONS

Chapter 8

THE COUPLE AND THE INDIVIDUAL

In this chapter we continue our examination of the factors that impact the stability of loving relationships. Perhaps more importantly from the viewpoint of the couples or marriage counselor, we deepen our look at interventions that have proved helpful in assisting clients to repair and improve their relationships. The three topic areas of this chapter's focus are on those that impact the couple as a result of the impact they exert on either of the individual partners. Although some of these sources of difficulty may impact both members of the dyad, for the most part they are destabilizing to the relationship because of the particular influence they wield on one or the other partner.

The first of these, *outside factors,* refers to family of origin issues, blended families, boundary issues, a disability of either partner, and the disruptive force of geographical separations. These may seem like they have little in common, and from one perspective they are very disparate phenomena. What they share, nonetheless, is their common point of origin: the world outside the microcosm of the couple's universe.

This leads naturally into the second area of such factors – the impact of *other people.* The relationship between the former and the latter should seem obvious, and the overlap is a natural one. When other people impact one or the other member of the dyad unequally, congruence and balance must be restored to right the relationship dynamic. As we shall see, however, achieving this is easier said than done.

Effective techniques for relationship repair caused by the influence of third parties do exist, which brings us to the remaining topic to be addressed in this chapter – the *boundary conditions* the couple imposes, first between the two partners in their ongoing "dance" of interactions and secondly between the couple itself and the rest of humanity (broadly speaking).

We urge the student or professional counselor to consider the following. A couple meets and both parties have a sufficient level of attraction for them to continue seeing one another. Over a period of time, they decide they are sufficiently compatible to commit to an exclusive relationship. Trust is established and grows until at some point during this process they fall in love with each other (however each of them defines it). Just as things start looking good, some part of the outside world or another person intrudes and disrupts their happy circumstances. They come to you, the counselor, to seek help and sage advice to protect, repair or otherwise save their relationship. You help them by analyzing the situation, determining the blocks to their ability to function as a couple, and conclude by examining and establishing appropriate boundary conditions, returning stability to the relationship.

With this in mind, to help you succeed in this hypothetical scenario, we now turn to these three important areas that impact the couple and the individual (outside factors, other people and boundaries).

OUTSIDE FACTORS

There are numerous factors, realities, extenuating circumstances and conditions outside of (or surrounding) a loving relationship that can have a significant impact on one or both of the two individuals in the relationship and, therefore, on the relationship itself. For example, we occasionally hear people say things such as:

"I know that when he was a child his family always spent every Sunday together – big dinner, everybody hanging around the house together and all that stuff. But this is our family. Why do we always have to do what his family used to do?"

"Sometimes it can be very trying around our house. We just about get things squared away for Saturday and Sunday with her kids, and then my kids will come over for the weekend. Then the whole chaos starts all over again. My ex-wife isn't any help either."

Trust me, we love the kids dearly. But by the time we finish running them all over town to their ballgames, their friends' houses, the mall, and then there's always something coming up that we didn't expect, we never seem to have any time for ourselves."

"Julie and I were doing just great until I was transferred. It might be a year before we can be working in the same city again. She's got a terrific job. So do I. But just seeing each other on weekends really is tough – on both of us."

"Our lives haven't been the same since Sam had his heart attack last year. It's not just that we aren't as active as we used to be, it's more than that. I've come to feel more like a nurse than a wife. And he's so into himself and afraid he'll have another heart attack, he's just not the same old Sam anymore."

In each of these five statements we have examples of outside factors that pose distractions to individuals' loving relationships. The phenomena of interest are thus: (1) primary family versus immediate family issues; (2) blended family issues; (3) child-rearing issues; (4) distance issues; and (5) disability issues. It is important to remember, however, that not all outside factors are distracters – at times they can be enhancers (as discussed later in the chapter). As we also shall see in this chapter, it is important for individuals in loving relationships whose relationship is being affected, influenced or impacted by outside factors such as these to be: (1) aware of what the outside factors are; (2) cognizant of any temporal considerations (e.g., knowing how long the condition or situation will last); (3) understanding of each others' thoughts, feelings and values regarding the outside factors (e.g., to talk openly with them); (4) aware of possible alternative courses of action they can take regarding the factors; and (5) aware of the extent to which they can take more control of the factors (i.e., to change what they are willing to, and can, change).

Primary-Immediate Family. We and other counselors often joke that the annual holiday season from Thanksgiving through New Years Day is like the approach of the annual harvest for farmers – when the most work will be required of us. The holidays, which are of course intended to be a time of joy and celebration, can actually be very stressful on relationships (as well as a major source of depression for those who live alone and have no family).

For example, Bill Emener spent several sessions at this time of year with Jim, a divorced, 41-year-old school administrator. Jim came to see Bill the Monday morning immediately following a Thanksgiving weekend. In addition to being extremely nervous, highly stressed, very tense and expressing guilt, he was worried because, as he said, "I am an assistant principal of a high school and I should be at the school doing my job and not here seeing you." He then added, "The problem is that I have been under so much stress lately that I am having trouble functioning at work." When questioned, Jim explained that a significant source of pressure and stress in his life was his multifaceted sense of family responsibilities. As many people in our society today very well know, sometimes it is extremely difficult for them to continue to be an active member of their family of origin as well as of their immediate family. The tongue-in-cheek use of the term "outlaws" when referring to one's in-laws is a frequent reflection of this issue.

Bill sketched a diagram similar to the one in Figure 8.1 and said to Jim, "It sounds like you were a very active and involved member of your primary family – you did many things with your mom, dad, and brothers and sisters. Then while you were married, you were actively involved in many activities with your wife and your two children. You have been dating your girlfriend, Lynn, for quite some time now and you are beginning to be actively involved not only with her but with her two children as well. I imagine that sometimes you wonder when you can ever get a chance to rest."

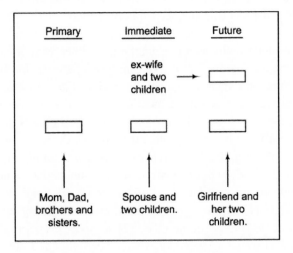

Figure 8.1. Primary, Immediate and Future Families.

Jim sat back on the couch, looked up and said, "You have no idea what it is like! Just getting through Thanksgiving was a chore in and of itself. I am dreading Christmas! I certainly want to be involved in my family's traditional Christmas festivities – mom, dad, and my brothers and sisters and I all have our annual, holiday activities. Obviously, I also want to do many things with my two children. And even though I am divorced, I do want to spend some time with my ex-wife. However, I also know that Lynn is trying to plan activities that would include her two children and me. I just don't know how I will be able to fit it all in. Sometimes I wish that I could go to sleep on December 15th and wake up on January 15th."

Over the next two minutes of silence, Jim sat there staring at the Figure. He then turned to Bill and said, "I just can't do it all anymore!"

Bill responded by saying "Jim, you have some alternatives. One option is that you could continue to try to play superman and respond to all of the expectations of your primary family, your current immediate family and your possible future family. But from what you are saying, that would not be a very enjoyable Christmas vacation for you."

Jim replied, "If I don't spend time with my mom, my dad and my brothers and sisters, I will feel guilty as hell. If I do not spend time with my two children and somehow spend some time with my ex-wife, I also will feel guilty as hell. And, I certainly want to continue working on my relationship with Lynn – there may be a future for us. So, I'm feeling a strong need and desire to spend time with Lynn and her kids. It seems to me that somewhere along the line I'm going to have to set some priorities and learn to live with them. I guess that's what you're telling me, isn't it?"

As time went on, Jim realized that he was not a member of just one family. He was a member of three: his primary family, his immediate family, and his possible future family. It was very helpful for him to understand what, for him, was a "three-family configuration." He eventually gave himself permission to modify his expectations of himself, especially with regard to all of the people in his life whom he loved so dearly. Once he was able to do so, he was able to explain his priorities to his loved ones and thereby have an impact on their expectations of him.

One aspect of Jim's dilemmas that deserves a closer look is his feelings of anticipated guilt, which led to considerable anxiety. You may recall that in Bill Lambos' practice, clients are taught that guilt and its cousin, anxiety, qualify as two of the "four primary blocks to happiness" (the other two being anger and depression). Guilt differs from other sources of disturbance in that it alone includes a presumption, whether warranted or not, that "I have done (or will do) something wrong." It is amazing how often we find that clients internalize this sense of wrongdoing and, in as such, deny themselves the chance to function in a healthy fashion. This is what we mean when we use the phrase "giving oneself permission" to do what one wants. It behooves the couples counselor to remind clients that they simply cannot function well if their only yardstick as to what they *should* do is what others *expect* of them. This is especially true of family members, regardless of *which* family they belong to.

We make it a habit to gently but firmly remind our clients that as people grow older and find themselves involved in multifamily configurations, relationships and activities, it is important for them to: (1) *remain cognizant of the realities of time and the realistic limitations* of what one person can do in a day; (2) *set some priorities*; (3) *recognize that no matter how hard they try, they often cannot please everybody;* and then, (4) *spend their time accordingly.* Most importantly, they must not deny themselves permission to, or better yet, recognize the irrationality of believing that one *must* attempt to please all of the people in their extended family system all of the time.

Blended Families. In a society like ours, where the divorce rate is over 50% and the remarriage rate is even higher (almost 70%), blended families have become more of a norm than the exception they once were. As a result, in the last decade or so, social scientists have devoted an increasing amount of time and effort to study such families (Frisbie & Frisbie, 2005). This research has revealed a variety of interesting findings, some of which are surprising. Among them:

1) Today, between one-third and one-half of all children in the U.S. are expected to live in a blended family before they reach age 18.
2) The stepparent has the hardest role in a blended family.
3) The need for the couple to build and sustain a strong marital relationship is often at direct odds with the need to care for children from previous marriages.
4) Relationships between stepparents and stepchildren tend to involve more conflict than those of biological kin, especially in the first four to seven years.
5) Adolescent children aged 10 to 14 may have the most difficult time adjusting to a blended family. Younger children adapt more readily, and older children spend most of their free time away from the home, tending to separate from the new family and potential conflict as they develop independent identities.
6) An individual who had a secure attachment relationship with a parent or caregiver when he or she was very young has a better chance of relating well in his or her new family than one who did not. This is true whether the individual is the biological parent, stepparent or stepchild.

On the other hand, myths and misconceptions about blended families abound. Some of the more common fallacies include the following italicized statements.

1) *Love occurs instantly between a stepchild and stepparent.* It takes four to seven years for a blended family to establish its own stable patterns and become adjusted. There is often a tacit or unstated expectation that because you love your new partner, you will automatically love his or her children, or that the children will automatically love you because you are a nice person. The reality is that establishing relationships takes time and does not happen magically or overnight.
2) *As long as you truly want a relationship with your stepchild, he or she will want one with you.* Despite your best efforts, your new spouse's children often resent having to form a relationship with you. Such rejection hurts, and when people feel hurt, they may in turn become resentful and angry. Stepfamily adjustment will be easier if you begin your relationships with your stepchildren with minimal, realistic expectations about how those relationships will develop. Then you will be pleased when respect and friendship blossom and less disappointed if it takes longer than you anticipated.
3) *Children of divorce and remarriage are damaged forever.* No evidence supports this claim. Research has demonstrated that in time most children recover their emotional equilibrium. Five to 10 years after the formation of a blended family, most young people are no different from children in first-marriage families.
4) *Stepmothers or stepfathers are wicked.* This myth is based on the fairy tales children hear. Because these stories tell about stepparents who are not kind, nice or fair, people who accept this position may be confused about their roles. You may be a wonderful person who wants to do a good job, but much of the world seems to have another idea about stepparents. There is no harder job in the world than step-

parenting. It often seems like a lose-lose proposition. Be aware that the negative model of the stepparent can impact you in a very personal way, making you self-conscious about your new role.

5) *Adjustment to stepfamily life occurs quickly.* Couples are optimistic when they remarry. They want life to settle down and to get on with being happy. If your hope is that once the wedding is over life will return to normal (whatever that is), you will be disappointed. Because stepfamilies are so complicated, it takes a long time, often four to seven years or longer, for people to get to know each other, to create positive relationships and to develop a family history.

6) *Children adjust to divorce and remarriage more easily if biological parents withdraw.* Children will always have two biological parents. However, they will adjust better if they have access to both. They need to be able to see their nonresidential parent and to think well of him or her. Sometimes visitation is painful for the nonresidential parent, but it is important to the child's adjustment and emotional health (except in instances of parental abuse or neglect). It helps if the residential parent and stepparent work toward a parenting partnership with all the adults involved. Sometimes this can't happen right away, but it can be something to work toward.

7) *Part-time stepfamilies are easier.* When the stepchildren visit only occasionally, perhaps only every other weekend, there may not be enough one-on-one time to work on stepchild/stepparent relationships. And there is less opportunity for family activities. Since stepfamilies follow an adjustment process, the part-time stepfamily may take longer to move through the process.

8) *There is only one kind of family.* The stepfamily will not be just like a biological family. It doesn't have to be and probably shouldn't be. Today, there are lots of kinds of families: first-marriage, second-marriage, single-parent, foster and stepfamily. Each type is different; each is valuable.

Such misconceptions and misplaced expectations that people bring with them when entering a blended family contribute to the difficulty of the adjustment process. The example below shows this principle in practice.

Ira, a 38-eight-year-old auto mechanic, and Carrie, a 34-year-old customer service representative with an airline, had been married for about one year when they came for marriage counseling with Bill Emener. Both of them had been married before, and each of them had joint custody of three children from their previous marriages. Before their marriage they had dated and had been engaged for a period of two years. During that time, while they had limited time together, they "truly enjoyed every moment they had spent together." Since their marriage, however, with anywhere from one to six children in the house at one time, their relationship "had deteriorated significantly!" As the counselor and couple continued to talk about their premarital relationship compared to their marital relationship, Bill sketched a diagram for them similar to the one in Figure 8.2. He also suggested that it would be helpful for them to try to identify what had changed in their relationship. What became clear was that prior to their marriage, whenever the two of them would do anything together, they were able to focus all of their attention and energies on each other *and* their relationship. Now that they were married, however, living in the same house, sleeping in the same bed and being intimately involved in each other's multiple other-person issues, they were feeling as if their own relationship constantly had to take a back seat to other people, other relationships and other issues. For example, they identified some critical time variables that related to their: (1) marital life; (2) individual ex-spouse issues; and (3) child-time constraints and demands.

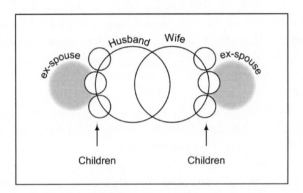

Figure 8.2. Illustration of a Blended Family.

Bill heard a clear danger signal when Carrie said, "Sometimes I almost wish we had never married. Our relationship was so much more fun and so much easier to manage when we were just dating and engaged." As Ira and Carrie's analysis of their life continued, it became clear to them that the one thing they had not done was to take control of their family – their blended family. Ira was continuing to try to be "superdad" to his three children and Carrie's three children as well. Likewise, Carrie was trying to continue to be "supermom" to her three children as well as to Ira's three children. As they discussed the realities of the extent to which they were involved with their six children, Ira said, "It's becoming clearer and clearer to me, Carrie, that the kids have simply taken over our life!"

Bill discussed some of the misconceptions and lack of awareness that impacts newly blended families and told them it would be very helpful for them to read some literature on the subject. As time went on, Ira and Carrie were able to modify effectively their six children's expectations of them. Furthermore, they established some priorities as to how and with whom they would spend their time. It also had become clear to them that they would have to continue to pay attention to their blended family issues. The most important thing was that they had recognized that their new blended family was out of control and their marital relationship did not have the high priority it once had. The two of them were beginning to work as a team to reconfigure their family life so that it also would provide quality time and nourishment for their own relationship.

It is not uncommon for two individuals to enjoy a pleasant, meaningful and stress-free relationship. However, when two individuals, such as Ira and Carrie, then marry and bring children and extended family members from previous marriages into their own marriage, what emerges is a blended family situation. In such situations, it is extremely important that both individuals be sure to attend to their own relationship and not allow their relationship to be caught up in the disquietude of others' demands, expectations and time-consuming activities.

We also see in the above situation what is a recurring theme in this chapter: that the relationship was able to be repaired only after appropriate *boundary conditions* were established that were suitable to the couple's new circumstances.

Children. As every couples counselor learns with experience, the importance, the impact and the influence of children on a loving relationship are difficult to overstate; hence the attention this topic receives throughout this book. Many of the myths listed earlier, as well as the realities concerning them, address the child-stepparent issue in detail. Unquestionably, children are significant "outside factors" of a loving relationship. Children understandably can be very demanding of a couple's time, resources, attention and love. It is important that a couple learn not to ignore these demands. As we have many times said to our students, clients and friends, the most important thing parents (biological or otherwise) can give to their children is *unconditional love,* and the worst thing children can experience from their parents is *fear of abandonment.* Even so, as parents communicate and demonstrate their unconditional love to their children, it is important that they continue their sensitivity and attention to: (1) themselves; (2) each other; and, (3) their relationship.

Á la the wisdom of Kahlil Gilbran (1965) in *The Prophet,* one's children do not belong to them; they pass through and, eventually, get on with lives of their own. While it is extremely critical for us as parents to attend to our children's needs and wants it, also is important that couples be careful not to mortgage their own loving relationship in the process. As one of our clients articulated, "I am proud to share with you that we have four beautiful, successful, loving and extremely healthy adult children. Unfortunately, we paid a very high price for that – our divorce was finalized about six months ago. And I continue to wonder how much all of our wonderful accomplishments with our children may have been tarnished by the fact that their parents are now divorced. It is ironic in the long run that we have taught them not only what love, loving and loving relationships are all about, we also have taught them what can happen if you don't do it right."

Distance. Any person who has attempted to weather a "long distance relationship" knows that such arrangements are inherently unstable, that geographical separation can be a significant negative factor in a loving relationship. When two individuals are separated by significant distance, *they will not*: (1) have as many opportunities to be together; (2) understand all of the things that are going on in each other's lives; (3) have a genuine appreciation for the impact of what is going on in each other's day-to-day lives; and (4) have opportunities to assist each other in attending to their daily issues, difficulties and frustrations. As one of our clients told us, "It seems like since we have been living apart during the week, we have so much less appreciation for what is really going on in each other's lives. And in that sense, I feel very lonely. I guess the bottom line is that sometimes a long-distance relationship can simply be hell!"

A long-distance loving relationship can be extremely difficult for any two individuals. In counseling either or both partners in such relationships, it is helpful to assist the client couple to address the following questions:

1) What is the reason for our being geographically apart? (e.g., an employment/career move, a school/educational opportunity, a family illness);
2) How long will this situation last? (e.g., for a fixed or uncertain period of time);
3) How is our being apart affecting us personally? (e.g., feeling sad, lonely and/or depressed, feeling relieved and/or pleased);
4) How is our being apart affecting our relationship? (e.g., not at all; we're drifting away from each other; we're arguing and fighting with each other);

5) Are there any things we could do to make the situation better? (e.g., talk on the telephone more frequently and/or on a regular schedule); and

6) What would happen if we decided to stop being apart and one or both of us moved so we could be together (or closer to each other)? Said another way, what would be the logical consequences of our changing the situation?

There may be additional questions pertinent to a geographically-separated situation. These six, however, provide a good starting place. Also keep in mind that loving relationships are voluntary and therefore can persist only to the extent they satisfy the desires of the couple. In most cases, this requires regular personal and face-to-face interaction, including intimacy, which is disrupted by geographical distance. It is simply unreasonable to expect a long-distance relationship to last indefinitely, and we advise against allowing your clients to harbor any such belief.

Disability. Your authors, in addition to being licensed psychologists, were professionally trained as rehabilitation counselors. We often wish that more therapists received such training, because the nature of physical or other kinds of disability is among the most overlooked aspects of interpersonal functioning.

Mildred and Chris came to see Bill Emener primarily because of a recommendation from Mildred's physical therapist. Six months before coming to his office, Mildred, at the age of 47, had suffered a stroke. Needless to say, it changed her life dramatically. Her husband, Chris, a 48-year-old owner of a limousine service, was a very caring, loving and compassionate man. They had been married for 25 years and had three daughters and one son. When Bill asked them if there was any specific reason why the two of them had come in, Chris said, "It's our marriage. Ever since Mildred's stroke our relationship seems to have been falling apart." Life had become very difficult for the two of them. One of the factors complicating their relationship was their inability to communicate with each other – as a result of Mildred's stroke, she had expressive aphasia.

The term "aphasia" refers to language deficits. Expressive aphasia refers to "outbound" language, or what we communicate to others. Receptive aphasia refers to the inability to understand "inbound" language. For many years neuroscientists have associated these two types of language deficits to damage to particular and separate areas of the brain. Expressive aphasia has been associated with a brain region known as Broca's area, near the front left side of the brain (in right handed people), whereas receptive aphasia was assumed to relate to two areas closer to the back left side of the brain, which are Wernicke's area and the angular gyrus. Today, however, we know that while damage to these brain areas usually does cause aphasia, so does damage to other areas of the brain. Complicating our understanding further, in many cases damage to these specific areas may leave language abilities unaffected. The situation is considerably more complicated than previously believed.

Basically, Mildred could hear and understand what another person was saying to her and she could conceptually formulate a response. The difficulty was that it was extremely cumbersome, time-consuming and difficult for her to express herself verbally. This was very frustrating because she knew what she wanted to say but could not get the words out. In addition to identifying some ways to help Mildred express herself, as well as to help Chris learn to be patient and give her the time she needed to say what she wanted to say, they also discovered what were the more salient factors contributing to the difficulties in their relationship.

Bill sketched a diagram for them similar to the one in Figure 8.3. While pointing to the figure, he said, "It appears to me that before Mildred's stroke, this is what your relationship, as it interfaced with your family, looked like. The two of you enjoyed a very meaningful and loving marriage. Your sister and your four grown adult children also were getting on with their own lives. But since Mildred's stroke, you have had a new type of family configuration that looks like this: the four children and Mildred's sister have rallied around her to provide her all kinds of love and support, and Chris is sort of feeling like he is out here by himself watching Mildred getting everybody else's attention." Mildred began crying. When her tears subsided, she began to speak slowly and with painstaking duress. What she eventually expressed was, "I am not stupid. I know what is going on. Everyone is showering me with all kinds of attention and no one pays any attention to Chris. I know he is angry with me because of my stroke and he is resentful of me for having had the stroke. I want so much to be loving toward him and want to make love to him. But I am scared. I'm afraid that if I attend to him the way I would like to, I might have another stroke. At the same time, I'm afraid that if I don't attend to him, I will lose him."

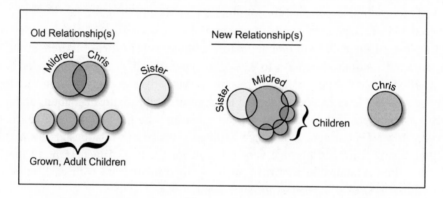

Figure 8.3. Impact of a Disability on Chris and Mildred's Relationship.

Chris was shocked and amazed at the extent to which Mildred understood him. And yet, in his very compassionate and loving way, he told her that he did not resent her for having had a stroke. That was something that she had no control over. He very beautifully said to her, "Millie, I do not resent you or your stroke. What I do resent is the way it has changed our relationship." With tears in his eyes, he continued, "Millie, Honey, I love you more than ever. And at this moment I am feeling closer to you than I have in the past six months." They held each other's hands for the rest of that session.

Mildred received assurance from her medical doctors that if she did not rush in where angels fear to tread, she and Chris could again begin to enjoy an active sex life. To wit, the two of them "joined forces" and slowly, yet delicately, explained to their children and Mildred's sister that Mildred did not need as much attention as she had been receiving. Interestingly, one of the things that Mildred did to help herself with her ability to communicate was to purchase a laptop. During the day, she was able to type out things that she wanted to communicate to Chris and her family, which, she told Bill, was really helpful for her. She even began to use the laptop during her sessions with Bill. Mildred learned to take advantage of what, in the rehabilitation world, is called an "assistive technology."

The last time Mildred came in, she brought a piece of paper that included the following:

For the past six months, everyone in the world has been paying attention to my disability. I understood that. However, it lasted too long. The worst thing that happened was that Chris and I forgot to pay attention to each other and our relationship. But we've changed all that! Now that we are back together again, I'm feeling more like Mildred, people are responding to me as Mildred, and sometimes it is even as if people forgot I had a stroke.

When one person in a loving relationship acquires a disability, it is understandable that the other person, as well as family members and friends, will pay exclusive attention to the disability rather than the person. As time goes on, however, if everyone's attention continues to be focused on the disability, the nature of the person's loving relationship will begin to change and possibly disintegrate. Mildred and Chris learned this the hard way. However, they were able to turn things around and once again enjoy their relationship. Bill felt very good inside when he received a note from Millie in which she said, "At this time, the only three differences between our relationship today and our relationship the way it was over the past 25 years is that: (1) we have to do things more slowly and more carefully; (2) there are some things we cannot do as well as we once could; and, (3) I talk funny. But, Chris and I are so in love. At times I feel like our marriage is better than it ever was."

Because of laws such as the American's with Disabilities Act and the development of assistive technologies (e.g., Mildred's laptop computer), today individuals with disabilities have options undreamt of only five to 10 years ago. The number of cases in which a disability can be substantially overcome is far greater than it ever was. Couples need only realize that an entire world of rehabilitative assistance is available to assist such individuals and their loved ones to cope with disability-related changes.

Other Outside Factors. There are numerous other factors, realities, extenuating circumstances and conditions outside of (or surrounding) a loving relationship, in addition to the five just discussed, that can have a significant impact on two individuals and their relationship. For each of the following five additional outside factors, edited quotes from our clients or friends are included to illustrate some of the salient features of each factor and its impacts.

1) *Socio-economic factors.* "Willis and I have been engaged since Christmas. He has many excellent qualities – he's handsome, intelligent, a good dancer and has a good job. However, he also is extremely self-centered. I sometimes fear I would feel lonely if I were married to him. Then again, he has a big house, a membership in the country club, we go skiing in Colorado every winter and scuba diving in the Bahamas every spring, and we attend those fancy balls and the symphony. He promised me a new car as a wedding present too. I guess if it doesn't work out at least I'd be suffering in comfort."

2) *Relatives.* "Most married people have in-laws and outlaws. We were married last year and we live in the same town as her parents. They're constantly trapping us into doing things with them. They just assume when they call and say, 'We're barbecuing Sunday,' that we're supposed to just be there! They're good folks – I like them. But how can I get them to realize that we have a life of our own?"

3) *Cross-cultural Factors.* "I know that in his country the role of the husband and the role of the wife are different. But this is the United States. He and his family seem to think I should be the kind of wife they have back in their native country. It's like

when his brother and his wife came over for dinner last Sunday afternoon. When we finished eating, she and I cleaned up and did the dishes. But then she and I had to sit in the kitchen, while the men talked in the living room and wait until they said it was okay for us to join them. Well, no more. This crap is going to come to a screeching halt!"

4) *Inter-racial Factors.* "Jane and I have been going together for about six months. We see each other almost every evening and spend most weekends together. When it's just the two of us alone somewhere, it's wonderful. As you can see, I'm Black and she's Caucasian. I know her family really struggles with my color. I've even overheard her brothers telling 'nigger jokes.' Her sister thinks it's her way of protesting and declaring her independence. My relatives and friends give me heat too – the sisters in the neighborhood are always telling me that I'm selling out. Like, 'They're not good enough for me.' It's really tough – for both of us!"

5) *Social Status.* "My husband's a popular, well-known, elected public official in our city. I also have some popularity by association – I have name and face recognition wherever I go. We're known as 'the most popular couple in town.' Not only that, but my job and his job thrive, to some extent, because we have this 'Mr. and Mrs. America' reputation. All I want, however, is to be happy. But not him. He thrives on that stuff. I think of us as 'Ken and Barbie with the most empty relationship on earth.' I'm so lonely – even when we're at the Governor's Ball, surrounded by the city's finest! If I stay with him, I'll always command respect and dignity for what I am. Who I am, though, is a woman who's dying inside."

6) *Extended Family Issues.* Rhonda and her siblings were very concerned when their 65-year-old mother called and said, "I just want you to know that I cashed in half of my 401K to purchase a used Winnebago so my 35-year-old boyfriend and I can tour the country for three months." For numerous reasons, the Baby Boomers are not only living longer – they're living more actively. Occasionally, the "Viagra generation" has been said to be out of control (financially, sexually, etc.). There is nothing wrong with older people enjoying the wonders of a loving relationship, but when there are legitimate concerns about "acts of desperation," financial risks, and less-than-desirable attention to existing family, among others, the individuals involved would be wise to carefully review the gerontological issues special to each of them.

OTHER PEOPLE

When one of us begins to work with a couple who has come to see us because of difficulties in their relationship, it is not uncommon for us to ask them a number of specific questions such as "How long have you been together and/or married?" "Do you have any children?" We also typically ask, "Are there any other people involved?" With this question we are seeking to know if there are one or more people who serve or have served as distracters to, or enhancers of, their relationship. Consider, for example, the responses to this question we have heard from the five following individuals:

Ted: "Ever since Dad came to live with us two months ago, which I can understand because he broke his hip and can't manage for himself, we never seem to be able to do anything. He's always either needing us to do something for him or butting into our conversations. The only time we ever get any time together is late at night when he's asleep!"

Sonya: "Since last June when your brother and his wife moved back, our life has been so different. Now that they're only 10 minutes away we can do a lot of things with them. And they're always getting something going. Before they moved back, we just sat around all the time. We're having so much more fun nowadays."

Ryan: "Let's face it, our youngest son is 23 years old, he has a college degree, and even though he is still looking for a better job and is only making minimum wage now, he's been back living with us for over a year now. His lifestyle and our lifestyle are about as close as June and January. Either he goes or I go!"

Paula: "I know you have broken it off with her. I believe you when you say the affair is over. But you still see her once in a while during the week while at work. I know you talk with her, you see her and she sees you. I just don't like it. Why can't one of you be transferred to another office or something?"

Jewel: "Now that Mom's been staying with us, it's been really nice. We can go out if we want to. She's always offering to watch the kids. Before she came, it seemed that we were in the same geographical location but never 'together.' By the time we got the kids in bed and got the place straightened up, we were too tired to do anything."

We trust that you can readily see that three of these people are referring to "the other person" as a *relationship distracter*: an individual who interferes with or has a detrimental impact on the relationship – e.g., Ted's father, Ryan's son, and in Paula's case, the woman with whom her husband had had an affair. On the other hand, two of these people were referring to "the other person" as a *relationship enhancer*: an individual who adds to or enriches your relationship – e.g., Sonya's brother-in-law and sister-in-law, and Jewel's mother. And sometimes, "the other person" is not a distracter to or an enhancer of a loving relationship, but is intricately connected to one's past, current or future loving relationship. This may occur for instance when "the other person" is directly or indirectly providing *transition assistance* or *maintenance assistance* before, during or after a loving relationship. The critical nature of these kinds of "other persons" will become clearer to you as we look at them in more detail.

A Third Person in a "Two-Seater." Even though Stan and Lois were both in their mid-40s, they had only been married for five years. They had lived together three years before getting married, and both said that when they had their daughter they "both were very ready to have a child." They came to see Bill Emener primarily because they were having "serious difficulties in their marital relationship." From what they shared, it was apparent that the two of them constantly were devoting large amounts of their time and energy to their four-year-old daughter. In his typical humorous way, Stan said, "I love my daughter dearly. I know Lois loves her just as much. The three of us are very close – too close! I hope you can understand, Dr. Emener, but in spite of the fact that I love my little girl so much, there are moments when I wish I could get away from her." What Stan was actually saying was that his daughter was what he called, "a third person in a two-seater." Stan and Lois wanted very much to have a close marital relationship – a relationship similar to what they had before being married and having a child. However, their daughter became such an integral part of their marital relationship that the two of them were beginning to grow apart.

Bill sketched a little diagram for them similar to the one in Figure 8.4. He suggested to them, "It would seem to me that this is the type of relationship you have now. The two of you, mom and dad, are basically growing apart and are focusing more and more of your attention on your daughter." Stan, asking if he could borrow a pencil, drew the other part of Figure 8.4 and said, "And this is what I want to have – a relationship in which the two of us are very close, where we would have a very loving monogamous relationship, where each of us could enjoy a special relationship with our daughter, and where the three of us could enjoy a relationship as a family." In addition to some marital counseling sessions with Bill, Stan, Lois and their daughter also met with a child psychologist so that, as a family, they could move toward a marital and family relationship that would be more in keeping with what they wanted.

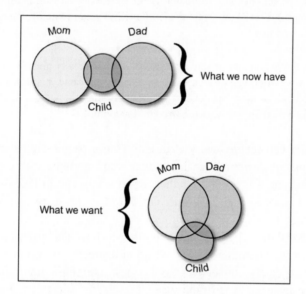

Figure 8.4. A Third Person in a Two-Seater.

It is not uncommon for a visiting or ill parent, a child, an old high school or college friend, an AA sponsor, or even the memory of an old relationship to come between two loving individuals. When another person starts to become the third person in your client couple's "two-seater" relationship, it is important for you to attend to it.

The Transition Person. The beginnings and endings of loving relationships are often times of great upheaval in the lives of those involved. Early on, new patterns of behavior must be established and other people involved (e.g., close friends of each member of the couple, particularly if they are single) must make adjustments. At the end of a loving relationship, a similar upheaval typically occurs. Often one or both of the parties may experience bereavement, the feelings of loss associated with the death of the relationship. A transition person is an individual who helps one member of a loving relationship get from one place to another. For example, we have known of numerous situations in which the person with whom a spouse or significant other was having an affair was, in effect, a transition person. If we look, for example, at Figure 8.5, we can see a descriptive depiction of how a man may be married, unhappy and wanting a divorce, but may not have the ego-strength, self-confidence and courage to negotiate one. A transition person can enhance those qualities in him. After the divorce, he may be happier and still maintain a close relationship with his transition person. However, it is important to remember that a transition person helps someone get from one place to another. Thus, it is not uncommon for such a scenario to eventually work out whereby the ex-wife and ex-husband are separated (or divorced), and the ex-husband also drifts away from and is eventually separated from the transition person. For example, Bill Emener recalls the time when one of his clients, Tracy, said to him, "I had wanted to get a divorce from my wife for years. However, I guess I never felt good enough about myself, I never felt strong enough, to pull it off. Then I met Rita. She and I were very close, and even though we never talked about a future, long-term relationship, I guess the thought of our getting together someday was always there. To be honest with you, without Rita I probably would not have been able to go through with filing for my divorce. But once it was finalized, I guess I just didn't need her anymore. I don't have to tell you how angry she was when I started drifting away from her!"

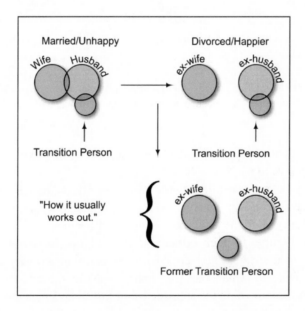

Figure 8.5. Example of a "Transition Person".

Sometimes a transition person will help an individual, like Rita helped Tracy, get from being married to being divorced. At other times, a transition person can help an individual overcome a divorce, or change jobs or move to another city. Whatever the individual case may be, it is important to remember that a transition person typically is just that – a person in a transition – and *it is not his or her transition*. It is understandable that a transition-person relationship is typically time-limited, intertwined with the transitioning of *one* individual, and commonly "over" once the person has transitioned to where he or she wants to be.

The Affair Person. We are well aware of the fact that there are numerous religious, philosophical and legal considerations of an extra-marital affair. We do not address such issues in this book, but urge you to consider them to whatever extent they are relevant, pertinent and important to the couple you are counseling. Herein, we shall focus primarily on the functional, pragmatic and psychological aspects of an affair, specifically in terms of how they affect individuals involved in loving relationships. It also must be remembered that an individual may have different kinds of affairs. An affair can be primarily sexual in nature, as well as psychological and/or emotional in nature. As one of our clients recently said, "Alex and I have not even held hands. But we talk almost every day, we feel very close to each other, and I guess I could say that Alex and I are heavily involved in a psychological affair."

Throughout our clinical experiences, we repeatedly have observed that when an individual is involved in an extra-marital affair, the most meaningful aspect, which also tends to be the longest lasting aspect, is not the sex – it's the intimacy, the human connection felt by the individuals involved. This is one of the most overlooked aspects of counseling couples in which one (or both) of the partners has had an affair person involved. When men and women have told us about affairs they have had, they frequently include the following types of statements:

"The most important thing I learned from my affair with Henry was that I am a lovable person."

"During the six months I was having an affair with Alice, I had a taste of what the good life was like." And,

"After being treated like a princess and feeling so special during my affair with George, I developed the self-confidence I needed to finally take action and do something about my horrible marriage."

How many experienced counselors have heard something like "My husband has sex with me; my lover makes love to me"?

Affairs typically do not last forever. The reason is rather simple: people who are in a relationship and have an affair usually claim they came out of the affair as stronger individuals, even if they wish the affair never happened for other reasons (see below). Most of the time, they then either fix their primary relationship, perhaps with the help of you or another counselor, or one or both partners chooses to end their primary relationship. If you are counseling a couple in which one (or, again, both) members of the relationship are involved in an affair, keep in mind the amazing set of mixed and even incompatible emotions your client(s) can be experiencing: feelings of elation, self-confidence, personal renewal, and increased self-worth, coupled with strong confusion, sorrow and guilt. Nonetheless, we advise you to ask your clients three questions (in addition to others):

1) What was missing in your primary relationship that led you to have the affair?
2) What did you learn about yourself and your existing relationship needs as a result of the affair? and,
3) With this new knowledge, what do you now want to do with regard to your primary relationship?

On the other hand, there is the partner who was cheated on. If you are counseling a client that is currently in a relationship with someone who is having or has had an affair, they likely may be struggling with feelings of confusion, betrayal and anger. Nonetheless, in the long run it may be important for you to ask this person the following two questions (among others):

1)   What was there about your relationship that contributed to his or her having an affair? and,
2)   What does this mean for the two of you in terms of what he or she and you need to do about the future of your relationship?

As we have suggested throughout this book, fault finding, blaming, shaming and trying to figure out who is "right" and who is "wrong" tend to represent strategies that do not resolve difficulties or solve anything – in fact, they often create more problems than the one started with. Although it may be very critical for one person to ask, "What did I do, what did I not do, and what was going on in my life that may have contributed to my having an affair?", the other person may ask, "What did I do, or what I did not do, and what was going on in our relationship that may have contributed to my loved one having an affair?" It has been our experience that in the majority of cases, an affair is not only an indication of a problem on behalf of one person; it also is an indication of a problem in the relationship.

A fair amount of research has been conducted on the reasons people have affairs, and although they vary across individuals and situations, a single thread ties most of them together: *People have affairs because they meet someone who they say makes them feel special in a way their current partner does not.* Studies have time and again shown that while wonderful sex is very often reported as a benefit of an affair, it is rarely ever the reason people begin one. More often, people have affairs because they are lonely, are living unsatisfactory parallel lives, or are just unable or unwilling to recognize that their current relationship does not meet their needs and desires. When counseling clients who are in an otherwise satisfactory relationship and meet someone with whom they express that they would consider entering into an affair, we strongly suggest you ask them to honestly answer the questions listed above *before* they enter into the affair. Research also reports that more people regret having affairs than say they were happy the affair happened. This is true even years after the affair, regardless of whether it led to the dissolution of their then-current relationship.

The Maintenance Person. A maintenance person is an individual in one's life who helps to fill a void, meet a need, give companionship and essentially provide a limited number of positive experiences with a limited amount of responsibility. Basically, a relationship with a maintenance person tends to be focused, time-limited and designed to meet a finite number of needs and wants.

A loving relationship does not necessarily have to be an exclusive, all or nothing, or "you're the only one for me for the rest of my life" kind of relationship. Men have male friends with whom they do limited things (e.g., they have fishing buddies, golfing buddies, etc.) and women have women friends (e.g., friends to go shopping with, friends to play tennis with, etc.). Why cannot men and women have such types of friends who happen to be members of the opposite sex? As Rachel said to one of us, "I know I am not ready for a long-term, emotional, loving relationship. But at this point, my life is not only very comfortable but it is also exciting. I go to dinner with Roman, I play tennis and go to the beach with Philip, and there's nothing more fun than dinner and dancing with Ronald." She and each of her male friends tend to truly enjoy what they do with each other. None of them is getting hurt, all of them agree to the boundaries of their relationships, and the nature of their relationships contributes to their overall enjoyment in life. When Bill Lambos was discussing the concept of a maintenance person with one of his friends, she said, "Jack and I have a wonderful relationship and we have agreed to keep it right where it is – why ruin a good thing?"

Note that in the previous two sections, problems with both outside factors and other people were, in some of the examples we used, resolved via setting or resetting *boundary conditions* – rules that limit behavior and create a clear line between what are and are not acceptable actions. We conclude this chapter by examining these conditions in somewhat greater detail. We have found over the years that just as "good fences make good neighbors," a well-managed set of boundary conditions – one that is neither overly restrictive nor unduly permissive – makes for sustainable and healthy loving relationships.

BOUNDARIES AND CONTROL

We have often heard one member of a client couple tell their partner something along the lines of "You do not have to give up *you* in order to be loved by *me*." What they were communicating was an application of an important philosophical approach to their relationship:

1)   each member will be responsible for taking care of *him- or herself;*
2)   each member will support the other as they respectively take care of themselves; and,
3)   both partners will share responsibility for taking care of their relationship.

By doing these three things couples can enjoy a loving, nurturing and meaningful relationship. In effect, this encompasses the importance of discussing, negotiating, establishing and honoring boundaries and controls in loving relationships.

Boundaries are the limits of how far it is permissible to go and remain comfortable. Boundaries define the "space" in which a given individual is not invited or welcomed at a given time.

Controls are those things people do to assure that they stay within their boundaries and assure that other people do not violate their comfort zone.

If, for example, a woman is invited out to dinner by a gentleman she does not know very well, she may not feel comfortable with him picking her up and knowing where she lives – at least not at the present time. Her boundaries, therefore, are that although she may feel comfortable joining him for dinner, she is currently uncomfortable with anything more. A reasonable control for her to impose would be to reply with, "Yes, I would enjoy joining you for dinner. Tell me what restaurant you have in mind and at what time, and I will meet you there." If he is an understanding gentleman, he would recognize and respect her control, honor it and not violate her boundaries.

It is very difficult to enjoy a relationship while feeling uncomfortable with, or about, one self. As we said earlier, we advise our clients that *"The best indication of the nature of your relationship is how you feel about yourself in your partner's presence."* Remaining in touch with your feelings, knowing your boundaries (the limits of your comfort zone) and establishing functional controls that sustain your boundaries are necessary ingredients for each individual in a loving relationship.

In this final section of the chapter we will look at some of the experiences of individuals who have avoided their individual and/or each other's boundaries, failed to employ functional controls, and at times violated each other's boundaries and controls. We will also look at what we suggested they do to remedy or improve their situations.

Values: Foundations for Boundaries. Values are shared assumptions, often tacit and unspoken, of what is good or bad, positive or negative, acceptable or not. A given individual's or couple's values are the basis of their boundary conditions.

Practically speaking, everyone has had his or her boundaries breached at some time. The result is never without some consequence, and it is usually negative. What is odd about this fact is that, as noted above, the values that underlie boundary conditions are rarely openly discussed. Rather, two individuals entering a relationship typically discover through ongoing interactions what the other person's unstated or tacit values, and therefore boundaries, are. This type of interaction is often referred to as a "dance." Learning another's boundaries without being told what they are and without violating them too seriously, is an acquired social interaction skill set that in many ways is best described as an art form.

Bill Emener met with Glen and Jennifer, who had just celebrated their first wedding anniversary, because they were "constantly arguing and fighting over unimportant things." Moreover, they were becoming deeply concerned about their arguments because they were starting to harbor resentments toward each other. When Bill asked them to give an example or two of some of the things they were arguing about and beginning to feel resentful about, Glen said, "Last Friday night, when I was trying to do some work in the garage, I told Jennifer that I could not find my vacuum sander. She replied that a few days prior she lent it to one of our neighbors. Knowing how much that vacuum sander had cost, how important it is to me and that my neighbor is the kind of person who has no respect for tools, I went ballistic!" At that point, Jennifer said, "Well Glen, three weeks ago I came home only to find that you had lent my new blender to his wife – how do you think I felt about that!"

It did not take long to realize that Glen and Jennifer were not understanding, appreciating and respecting each other's values, specifically in these instances with regard to their tools. Moreover, as is so often the case, they had not discussed the establishment of boundaries and controls in order to avoid disrespecting and not honoring each other's values.

Toward the end of the session, Bill drew a chart for them similar to the one in Figure 8.6. He suggested that they could look at an individual's values from four different perspectives:

1) those that relate to *unacceptable* behaviors or considerations;
2) those that are *negotiable*;
3) those that are *acceptable*; and,
4) those that are *preferable*.

Bill then asked them to think about some of their basic values that would relate to the four categories. Glen looked at the chart and immediately said, "No drugs! That would be *unacceptable*. As far as I am concerned, it would be totally wrong for either me or Jennifer to ever get involved with illegal drugs."

Unnacceptable	Negotiable	Acceptable	Preferrable
"No drugs."	"Our vacation plans."	"To spend up to $50 of our money."	"Discuss weekend plans and activities."

Figure 8.6. Establishing Values in a Loving Relationship.

Jennifer quickly agreed with Glen's value statement and therefore "no drugs" was added to the chart. Jennifer then said, "Based on my values, I would be pleased if Glen and I would *negotiate* our joint vacation plans. For example, I would be annoyed if he were to make vacation plans for us without discussing them with me first." Glen agreed. Therefore, "vacation plans" was added to the chart.

Glen, pointing to the third column, said, "It would be *acceptable* to me if either Jennifer or I could spend up to $50 of our money without our having discussed it or talked about it first." Jennifer agreed, so they added that value statement to the chart.

Jennifer pointed to the fourth column and said, "Each of us has a work schedule and tends to do his or her own thing in the evenings during the week. However, it is my *preference* that the two of us discuss any weekend plans and activities before agreeing to anything or making any specific plans." Noting Glen's agreement, Bill added that value statement to the chart.

Before they left his office, Bill invited them to accept a homework assignment of discussing more of their individual values and adding them to the chart in one of the four columns. Their enthusiasm for the assignment was captured in Glen's statement, "I think this is something that would be very important for us. I look forward to it!"

When they arrived for the next session, they brought six additional pages of the chart. As they reviewed and discussed their value statements, the couple shared that they were both tremendously surprised to realize the extent to which they had not been appreciative or understanding of, and basically had been violating, each other's values. As Jennifer said, "I simply never knew there were so many little things that I was doing that were so disturbing to Glen. But now that I know what his values are, I am in a better position not to upset him or hurt him."

In continuing work with Glen and Jennifer, the three identified some controls the two of them were able to agree upon that would protect their basic individual and collective values. These two processes were very valuable to them and their relationship. For example, Glen said, "The other night when I came home from work, one of my other neighbors walked over and told me he had asked Jennifer if he could borrow my lawnmower and she told him she would prefer that he discuss it with me. After putting gas in the mower and taking it over to him, I immediately went into the house and gave Jennifer a big hug. That was cool!"

Jennifer added, "One of the things I am realizing, Dr. Emener, is that I am able to demonstrate my love for Glen not only by the things I do, but also, and sometimes more importantly, by the things I don't do."

This example shows the importance of "the dance of boundary discovery." When it breaks down or is ignored, people feel violated and angry, and the partner often has no idea why. Taking the time to verbalize and lay out the rules and boundary conditions each member of a relationship desires to maintain as personal space, is a simple but very important step in fixing such issues before they cause irreparable damage to the relationship (and indeed can constitute a helpful intervention on behalf of a couples counselor).

Negotiating Boundaries and Limits. Abbie and Ken, who had been going steady for two months, said they "really liked each other a lot but were continuing to do things that tremendously annoyed each other." After some brief discussion during their first session, Ken said, "I have the feeling that we are going to have to do something about our relationship soon! I really like Abbie a lot, and I feel that she has strong feelings toward me as well. If we are going to have any kind of future, however, we are going to have to initiate some damage control mechanisms right away!"

In view of their goal of improving their relationship and making some necessary adjustments, Bill Emener suggested that they discuss three sets of boundaries and limits:

1) Do's;
2) O.K.'s; and,
3) Don'ts.

Utilizing examples from their expressed frustrations with each other, Bill offered them the three following examples of these categories of boundaries and limits: "*Do*, let me know if you'll be late when we are planning to go somewhere," "It is *O.K.* for you to go out with your buddies after work during the week without clearing it with me, as long as we have not made any previous plans," and, "During the week, *don't* call me after eleven o'clock at night."

As Dr. Emener continued to work with Abbie and Ken, on numerous occasions they shared with him that it was very helpful for them to discuss and negotiate their three areas of boundaries and limits. As Abbie poignantly stated, "When we first started seeing you, we were doing many things that were extremely annoying and bothersome to each other. The mere fact that we stopped doing such things was noticeably and appreciably helpful right from the beginning."

Only One "Should." As a result of their escalating marital problems, Joy and her husband decided to separate for some time. When she came to see Bill Emener, she said her husband had moved into a one-bedroom apartment and she was continuing to live in the house. She also mentioned that she and her husband were planning to come in together for some marital counseling, but he unexpectedly had to go out of town the day of their first appointment. She decided to come by herself, however, "just to have a chance to meet the therapist and for the two of us to have a chance to talk." Among some of the frustrations Joy expressed were, "Roger should call me before coming over to the house," and "He should tell me when he has an out-of-town trip planned."

Bill suggested to Joy that they take a moment or two to discuss the extent to which she utilizes the word *should*. "Joy, the word *should* indicates an obligation, a duty, a propriety, a necessity and/or an expectation. Thus, when you believe and say that Roger *should* do something, you are basically suggesting that you assume: first, that he knows your values, wants, desires, wishes and preferences; secondly, that he feels a sense of obligation, duty, propriety or charge to tell you what such things are; and thirdly, you assume he summarily agrees with your *should(s)*."

Joy pondered that consideration for quite some time, and then said, "In other words, Dr. Emener, you are suggesting that my *should* statements may not necessarily be universal – especially when it comes to Roger."

Bill replied, "Yes, Joy, that is exactly what I am suggesting. If, based on your values, you prefer that Roger call you before coming over, then maybe it would be important for you to tell him that instead of assuming he knows it, that he agrees to it and feels a sense of obligation to honor it."

Two weeks later, Bill had the pleasure of meeting with Joy and Roger as a couple for the first time. Joy had shared with Roger their conversation regarding *shoulds* and informed Bill that the two of them had had several discussions regarding their individual values, wants, desires, wishes and preferences with regard to how each of them behaved in their relationship. For example, Roger communicated that until Joy mentioned it to him, it had never crossed his mind to call her before going over to the house. This, interestingly, is typical for many couples. At that point, Joy said, "We have a suggestion for you to share with other couples: *In a loving relationship, there is only one should – there 'should be' no shoulds.*" From our point of view, even *that* should is better restated as "our relationship will be stronger and we will be happier if we agree not to make demands of each other, but to discuss our preferences whenever we feel the need."

The following provides a richer appreciation of why and how people disturb themselves. When working with couples, Bill Lambos nearly always explains that in Rational Emotive Behavior Therapy (REBT), the counseling approach developed by Albert Ellis, a *should* is considered just another type of demand – another pernicious "must" that underlies self-disturbance. Believing that one's partner "should" do or not do something is equivalent to *demanding* (as opposed to *preferring*) they behave a certain way, which is by definition an irrational belief (recall DR BOLL in Chapter 7). The problem with *shoulds* and other types of demands is that, when they are not met, people typically react by getting angry, or becoming anxious, feeling depressed, or experience guilt, instead of directing efforts to communicate their preferences. This takes one problem (the unmet desire, behavior, etc.) and instead of fixing it, adds a second problem: self-disturbance.

We, your authors, therefore have strong opinions about *shoulds*:

1) *Should* statements, whether tacit or stated, are by their very nature one-sided *demands*, and as such can be very troublesome in a loving relationship; and,
2) Discussing and negotiating individual values, wants, desires, wishes, preferences, boundaries and limits makes for a much more helpful and constructive approach to relationship management.

Functional and Dysfunctional Controls. It is important to remember: Controls are those things people do to assure that their own boundaries are maintained and that other people do not violate their values, boundaries and comfort zone. What is important to remind your clients, however, is that not all controls are equally effective or, for that matter, acceptable. And some can be downright damaging to a relationship. A control is functional when it maintains an important boundary without negative consequences. Conversely, controls that "upset the apple cart" or destabilize the relationship are best viewed as dysfunctional and therefore inappropriate – often causing more harm than good. It indeed appears to be important for you, as a counselor, to help your clients in loving relationships negotiate and set into place relationship controls that are functional – ones that enhance, enrich and contribute to the quality of their relationship. If, however, a relationship control is not discussed or negotiated, or if it is undesirable, uncomfortable or constrictive for either individual, chances are that it will be a dysfunctional control. The more functional controls that two individuals have in their relationship, the better, more meaningful and more loving their relationship will tend to be.

Active and Passive Control. Although the term "control" implies active behavior, this is not always the case. Many people find that they can exert control over the behavior of their significant other by *not* doing something otherwise expected of them, or by other acts of omission. The former of these is called an *active* control, and the latter a *passive* control. It is important to understand that the two approaches are not equal. Active controls are more obvious and, therefore, more likely to be negotiated and discussed. Passive controls can be misunderstood or worse, missed entirely. Resulting internalized resentments can have very negative effects on a relationship, as the next couple that came to see Bill Emener demonstrates.

Don and Shirley, who were engaged and planning to be married, had been living together for approximately two years prior to seeing Bill. From the outset, Shirley was very concerned with Don's controlling behaviors. For example, she said, "Don, you always have to get your own way and will do whatever you have to do in order to get your own way – you will argue with me, you will pout, or you will treat me overly special. Sometimes I just feel so controlled by you." As they continued to discuss various aspects of their relationship, however, they soon began to realize that both of them were controlling types of individuals.

Bill sketched a chart similar to the one in Figure 8.7 and suggested to them that in a relationship people can exert control both actively and passively – "We can control people actively by 'what we do,' and we can control people *passively by 'what we don't do.'*" Don said, "Yes, I agree that I tend to be an active controller in our relationship. I do what I have to do to get what I want. Nonetheless, if there's something that she wants, Shirley will, on occasion, withhold love from me, withdraw or give me her famous silent treatment. The trouble is, because we so strongly want to enjoy a good relationship, we tend to give in to each other's controls. And although it seems to work in the short run, in the long run we are beginning to resent each other for feeling so controlled by each other."

As time went on, Bill helped Don and Shirley identify more functional communication and negotiation styles in which they were able to more specifically, accurately and comfortably attend to each other in terms of what they wanted. They realized, moreover, that at times each of them would not always be able to get what he or she wanted. As their basic value sets were explored, they were able to put their "wants" in perspective and, on occasion, accept the fact that they might not always get what they want. For example, Don said, "My relationship with Shirley is more important than a weekend fishing trip. Arguing, pouting or manipulating, and thus messing up our relationship, is just not worth it."

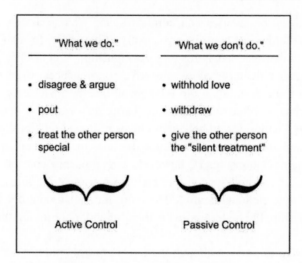

Figure 8.7. Active and Passive Control.

Another caveat to keep in mind regarding controls is: how controls are perceived by the other partner matters more than how they were intended. From a phenomenological perspective, we hope that by this point in the book our readers have come to appreciate the weight the authors place on people's *perceptions* of reality rather than the reality itself (if there is such a thing). To recall our Chapter 2 paraphrase of the famous football coach Vincent Lombardi, "Perception isn't everything, it's the *only* thing." Given the normally tacit or unspoken nature of boundaries and controls, it should come as no surprise that in many relationships each partner's perception of the other person's behavior as controlling or not may differ markedly. Without sharing and discussing such perceptions, couples and relationships can quickly get into trouble.

Internal and External Control. The term "locus of control" has a growing importance in modern psychology. First introduced over 40 years ago by Julian Rotter (1972), it has been the subject of much research related to education, social psychology, personality theory, clinical interventions and other important areas. It is said to be an *attribution style* that differs across individuals and even groups. Psychologists believe that those people who have a relatively stronger *internal* locus of control, who assume that they themselves play the greatest role in how their lives develop, are relatively healthier than those who believe they are controlled by outside forces. Indeed, the important concept of self-efficacy we examined in the previous chapter can be considered central to having a strong internal locus of control. With respect to boundaries and controls, the concept is very much apropos to loving relationships, as Figure 8.8 shows.

The reader, looking over Figure 8.8, will likely notice something about external controls we have discussed frequently in this chapter: External controls are more examples of *demands*, whereas internal controls are self-stated *preferences*. Again, the REBT framework makes clear that the latter are preferred over the former, for all the reasons stated throughout the chapter. Thus one's individual perceptions of the extent to which the controls in our life are within us (internal) or outside of us (external) are important considerations in our self-awareness, not only because an internal locus of control is healthier, but because self-regulation (homeostasis) is always preferred to being regulated by other people or agents. For those incapable of even basic self-regulation, our society has a system of imposing controls at the highest level: Prisons!

```
┌─────────────────────────────────────────────────┐
│                                                   │
│                 Loss of Control                   │
│                 ──────────────                    │
│                                                   │
│       External                  Internal          │
│       ────────                  ────────          │
│                                                   │
│      "I have to..."            "I want to..."      │
│                                                   │
│      "I must..."               "I chose to..."     │
│                                                   │
│      "I should..."             "I don't want to..."│
│                                                   │
│      "I can't..."              "I will not..."     │
│                                                   │
│       ─────────────────────────────────          │
│                                                   │
│      How we avoid responsibility with our language!│
│                                                   │
└─────────────────────────────────────────────────┘
```

Figure 8.8. Internal and External Control.

Our perceived locus of control and how it affects our language, our verbal and nonverbal expressions to others and our relationships with others, are indeed important aspects of loving relationships. This tenet was central to Bill Emener's counseling with Karen and is illustrated in Dialogue 8.1.

Dialogue 8.1 Internal and External Control.

Karen (K), a 46-year-old program manager with a computer company who was experiencing many frustrations in her relationships with men, came to see Bill Emener (B) for counseling. As the following dialogue reveals, many of her relationship issues had to do with aspects of internal and external control.

K: For some reason, many of the men who I have tried dating over the last year or so tend to have difficulties believing me and trusting me when I say things to them.

B: What I hear you saying is that when you say things to the men in your life, even when you are telling the truth, you can sense that they don't believe you.

K: Yes. And it's very frustrating.

B: Have you considered possible reasons as to why they're not believing you?

K: I'm not sure I know what you mean?

B: Well, it could be that you have chosen to date men who are non-trusting – non-beleivers if you will. It also could be related to the way in which you are saying things to them.

K: Good question... good possibilities. I don't know.

B: Well, let's start with this: give me an example of something you said to a date – something you knew was true yet he didn't believe you.

K: Okay. This last Saturday evening I received a call from Fred. He was calling from work – he's a manager in a store at the mall. He asked me if I would like to go out with him Sunday evening to a movie and maybe a drink or coffee and a snack afterwards. This past

Monday morning I had an early meeting with my boss and didn't think it would be a good idea to go out the night before, so I declined his invitation.

B: I see your reasoning. But let me ask you, Karen – what did you actually say to him when you were on the phone.

K: I told him I couldn't go out Sunday night. That I had an early meeting the following morning and, as a responsible professional, that's something I shouldn't do.

B: Okay, I hear you – you're a responsible person and you don't want to disappoint your boss or jeopardize your job. But let's take a closer look at it.

K: Okay. I'm listening.

B: There's a phenomenon we call "locus of control" – basically the thinking is: "Where is the control of whatever it is I am talking about?" For example, let's say I'm playing golf and I miss a putt to the left. If I am an "internal" – meaning that the cause of the miss was within me and/or my control, I might say something like, "I pulled the putt to the left" or "I didn't hit it hard enough." But if I am an "external" – meaning that the cause of the miss was not within me and/or my control, I might say something like, "These darn greens" or "That gust of wind made it go left."

K: [Smiling] Okay, I understand that. [Chuckling] As we say in my world, "There's only so much you can blame on the computer."

B: Good. You got it.

K: But now how does that relate to what I said to Fred?

B: [After drawing a chart similar to the one in Figure 8.8 and then while pointing to it] Karen, if I say things like *I have to*, *I must*, *I should*, or *I can't*, I am implying that I have no control over whatever it is that I am addressing. The control or freedom to choose is outside of me. On the other hand, if I say things to you like *I want to*, *I chose to*, *I don't want to*, or *I will not*, I am implying that the control of doing or not doing something is within me and I am assuming the responsibility of doing or not doing it.

K: And when Fred asked me out, I said "I can't" and "I shouldn't."

B: Yes.

K: In other words, Dr. Emener, the other evening when Fred invited me to go to a movie and then for a drink or coffee and a snack and I told him "I can't," he may have been hearing me say, "I don't want to go to dinner with you"? Or maybe he's just thinking I'm not being honest with him?

B: I don't know. But those are possibilities. You said that you have a fairly good relationship with Fred. Ask him.

The next time Bill met with Karen, she told him that she had a lengthy talk with Fred and he confirmed her suspicion as to why he had perceived her to be a deceptive rather than an up-front and honest person. "He said to me, 'You always seem to have some reason why you have to do something or why you can't do something – you seem to rarely ever say what you want or what you don't want.'"

As Bill continued to work with Karen, she was able to identify and understand more clearly why she was struggling with taking responsibility for her decisions. Moreover, her manner of expressing herself also changed. That is, she began using fewer "I have to" or "I can't" kinds of statements and more "I want to" and "I don't want to" kinds of statements.

CHAPTER SUMMARY

In this chapter, we examined (a) how *outside factors* (family of origin issues, blended families, boundary issues, a disability of either partner, and the disruptive force of geographical separation), *other people* (a transition person, an affair person and a maintenance person), and *boundary conditions and controls* impact the stability of loving relationships, and (b) how couples or marriage counselors can help couples repair and improve their relationships. When a couple comes to see you for couples or marriage counseling, they are seeking help and sage advice to protect, repair or otherwise save their relationship. And in addition to other possible counseling interventions, you can meaningfully help them by: (1) analyzing the situation; (2) determining the blocks to their ability to function as a couple; and (3) conclude by examining and establishing appropriate boundary conditions, returning stability to their relationship.

> When you are in a good loving relationship, you're not only in love with your partner you're in love with your relationship with him or her.

CHAPTER 8 DISCUSSION QUESTIONS

1) When a couple and their relationship are being troubled by an "outside factor," what are the similarities and differences as to whether the factor is short-term, long-term or permanent?

2) Some "outside factors" are by choice (e.g., a blended family) and some are not by choice (e.g., a disability). To what extent is a couples "choice" an important consideration as they address the disruptiveness of their outside factor?

3) To what extent are "other people" (a transition person, an affair person and a maintenance person) both functional and dysfunctional?

4) When working with a client who is in a relationship with an "other person" (a transition person, an affair person and/or a maintenance person), to what extent should there be any ethical and/or moral obligation to the "other person?"

5) What are the similarities and differences between an individual's "ego boundaries" and a loving relationship's "boundary conditions?"

6) As a couples counselor, what are some specific things you can do to assist a couple in identifying and establishing their boundary needs?

Chapter 9

THE COUPLE IN THE WORLD

The previous two chapters examined a myriad of ways by which factors arising in the outside world can exert a significant impact on a couple's relationship. In some cases, as we saw in Chapter 7, our focus was on the beliefs, feelings and behaviors that each partner brings into their relationship and how best to assist the couple when their individual "baggage" causes relationship problems. In Chapter 8, we turned the spotlight away from what each member of the dyad can bring from within themselves, examined how the outside world can impact the couple's relationship, and how a counselor can effectively intervene, especially in cases where and when that impact is felt more by one partner than the other.

In this chapter, we sharpen our focus on outside factors and look at three areas that impact the couple more or less equally – those that primarily affect the dyad itself. The first of these, *Monetary and Equity Issues*, examines the roles that economic forces can exert on the relationship. Because a couple often has less control over the fiscal resources available to them than they do over other aspects of their lives, this is a difficult area in which the professional counselor can intervene. For example, we may be able to advise the client to spend more quality time together, but we cannot sensibly advise a couple to "make more money." Our goal in addressing this quandary is to identify some effective strategies for assisting the client couple in such situations.

The preceding example is not intended to imply that time is of limitless supply, either. As we shall see, assisting client couples with matters of *time and timing* can pose vexing challenges for the counselor. Not only is time often in too short supply, but unlike money, it is *impossible* to create more of it, rather than just difficult to do so. Like money, when time is used, it is gone – we even use the same word for parting with both money and time: *spending* them. Couples with whom we have spent time (no pun intended) have found it deeply frustrating to balance their commitments to allocating their preciously limited time to others who require it. In addition, time by its very nature, has a *sequential* aspect to it that money does not: the order in which we choose to do things or attend to others can make a great difference in the quality and even the success or failure of a relationship. This is the all-important subject of *timing*.

Finally, the repetition of events or sequences over longer durations gives rise to *patterns and trends*, the final topic of this chapter. In this section we will look at some of the ways in which patterns and trends can have detrimental effects on loving relationships. Specifically, we will focus on: (1) how patterns and trends can emerge in relationships; (2) their effects on relationships; and (3) how we have counseled some individuals and couples to try to change their patterns or trends to avoid unhealthy relationship dynamics and create more positive and meaningful templates of interaction.

Money, time and trends – these are three of the most significant variables that determine the success versus failure of relationships. Assisting your clients in dealing with them ranks as among the couples counselor's most challenging jobs. We hope the insights we offer based on our experiences with these concerns will help make your job not only manageable, but also more efficient, more effective and ultimately more deeply rewarding.

MONETARY AND EQUITY ISSUES

A sign in the lobby of Bill Lambos' Tampa practice reads:

> Money cannot make you happy.
> It can, however,
> help you to suffer in much greater comfort.

The most common cause of disagreement between people in both new and established relationships and the cause of fundamental problems if not addressed is money. In part, this reflects the reality that, for most people, their relationship to money determines so much about their lives. The number of variables correlated with income level seems endless – from the average lifespan and most health-related measures, to years of education completed and even intelligence, to the chances for upward mobility, to the likelihood of criminality, and so on.

For better or worse, as one's income rises, often so does one's status and sense of self-worth. We live in a culture dominated by values linked to the ability to consume material goods and services (and to do so as conspicuously as possible), and consumerism requires income or wealth (accumulated money). Moreover, compared to other advanced societies, particularly European ones, the distribution of income and especially wealth in the United States is staggeringly uneven. Although the *average* income of Americans may be among the highest in the world, the disparity in incomes among individuals and socioeconomic strata is much greater than in most other countries, even compared with our somewhat similar neighbor to the north, Canada. This reflects the fact that America has a tiny stratum of superrich families whose combined income and wealth is so great that it is nearly inconceivable (Frank, 2007).

With respect to loving relationships, money is a factor from the outset. Today, most people enter into relationships with partners whose income level is similar to their own, whether or not it was a conscious decision. On the other hand, people have different attitudes toward money, often influenced by personal experiences and upbringing. When such attitudes differ significantly, problems often arise. Here are some of the most common signs that a couple you are counseling may face trouble ahead:

- *Do they talk about money?* The crux of money problems is often down to communication. Partners are unlikely to be able to deal with money problems unless they can both discuss finances and their feelings about them.

- *Does one member in particular want to, or insist on, being in control?* Money can be very powerful, and if either member of the dyad likes to be the controlling personality in the relationship, it is easy for them to use money as a tool to gain and stay in control. This can be a real issue when one party earns much more than the other. Money issues frequently mask deeper underlying issues of control and power in a relationship.

- *Is there a difference in levels of responsibility in their relationship?* If one partner is irresponsible by habit and the other is more sensible, this may be reflected in their attitudes toward finances and toward one another.

- *Do they have the same financial priorities?* If a couple does not have a spending or savings plan and have not agreed on how much both may spend after all the bills have been paid, ongoing conflict may result.

- *Has either of their attitudes towards money been colored by their upbringing or a previous relationship?* If one's upbringing was burdened by financial worries, that person may be afraid to spend money now. If either person previously had a partner who was very careless with money and caused financial problems, they may be overly cautious.

- *Are the issues really financial?* Their issues may be more about unspoken aspirations for the future, the financial planning that goes with it, or the subject of money may be just an outlet for other deeper issues that the couple does not know how to address.

Money. People are uniquely different in how they view money. By and large, this is because people process problems and opportunities from different vantage points. Compounding this phenomenon is the precept that in many ways "opposites attract." Thus, chances are that in a relationship, one of the two individuals is good at working numbers (the "nerd") and the other one isn't (the "free spirit"). But that isn't the real problem. The problem is when the party who adopts the role of money manager neglects the input of the less involved person, or when that other person avoids participating in the financial dealings altogether. It is at such times, that problems seem to become inevitable.

We have found it important to consistently remind our clients that *marriage or coupledom is a partnership*. Fittingly, both parties need to be involved in the finances. The choice option of "separating the finances and splitting the bills" is up to the couple. If they do, however, advise your "nerds" not to keep the finances all to him- or herself – don't use the "power of the purse" to abuse the other party. On the other hand, those who would prefer to avoid dealing with money matters should be reminded that they have not only a right to give input, but a *responsibility to do so*. We consistently advise our couples: "Work on the budget together!"

Values and Attitudes. Sometimes one or both members of a couple bring their attitudes toward money into their relationship from their past relationships. Although it sounds easy enough to remind them that what they did with money in the past often will not work for the present situation and the future, in practice it is often not an easy task.

Bill Lambos recently saw a couple in their mid-40s, Kelly and Jim, who told him they needed help with *trust issues*. Kelly began with, "My first marriage was to a man I knew for only six months; he was in the Navy. He seemed perfect for me. But within a year, I found out he ran up over $10,000 in debt on my credit cards without telling me and hid the bills from me, and by the time I filed for divorce, I also had to file for bankruptcy. It took me years to re-establish my good credit, and now I can't allow anyone else to have any control over my finances." Jim countered, "I've known about that since the beginning, Hon, and that's why I agreed to separate bank accounts and credit cards. But you don't trust me in many other ways either. If I stop at the store on the way home from work to pick up a few things without calling you first, you demand to know 'where the hell I've been.' If I have to work late, you call the office line every 45 minutes to make sure I'm still there. I know you aren't jealous of other women and you say that you believe I'm faithful to you, so what's the deal?" Kelly began to cry as she said, "I just can't let go of having been so *violated* by that man financially. And now I have trouble trusting everything else about men."

As Kelly and Jim's experience illustrates, people often carry a problem from the past that dictates behavior in the present. For example, if during one's childhood he or she suffered a large loss of money, this same individual today might be afraid to deal with money because of the fear they continue to harbor about re-experiencing the loss. Not urging clients to address the problem of their attitudes toward money (or the lack of it) makes for ineffective counseling. It is very important to assist your clients to differentiate and discover whether their attitudes toward money are based on facts or based on some feelings they carry from the past. The fact is, most of the time disagreements on how to spend money or the way a couple deals with not having enough money has little to do with their current situation. Sometimes, as with Kelly, it is based on some baggage carried from our past.

Worth and Meaning. Money can have symbolic meaning. For example, some people use monetary problems as an excuse for the reason that their relationships are not working. When in therapy, it is important to show clients, that a clear choice exists between the baggage they carry and the quality of their relationship, and most will choose relationship health over the former. Based on Bill Lambos' advice, Kelly and Jim entered into mediation to draft a postnuptial agreement that concerned not only money issues but behavioral and trust issues as well. The last time Bill saw them, they were doing much better.

It is natural and healthy for an established couple to have developed stable patterns and rules with respect to money issues. As long as control issues aren't mistaken for decisions about fiscal priorities, such arrangements become consistent and reduce ambiguity.

On the other hand, some couples, particularly younger ones, may be living paycheck to paycheck with very little in the way of savings or reserves. If family members or others are unavailable for help when an unexpected expense arises, it can add a great deal of stress to the relationship. Finally, if such stress continues over time, one of the partners can start identifying with the problem and then he or she can become, or perceived to be, the problem. It is important to counsel clients in such situations and help them develop a positive attitude toward money – a negative attitude just keeps the couple stuck in a cycle of disagreements and recriminations. Your goal as therapist is to promote your clients to develop a positive attitude – one of integrity – towards money.

Sometimes a negative attitude develops because one of the partners is critical and judgmental of the other. This attitude may be accompanied by significant aggression, or equally likely, by passive-aggressive behaviors. Active aggression is expressed by openly criticizing one's partner, and showing negativity. Alternatively, a money issue may express itself when a partner takes on the role of victim, yet couples it with an outwardly positive presentation. Every experienced counselor has seen this act many times. Acting positively while judging the other partner negatively, is mirroring one's own negativity with a lot of sugar coating. A positive attitude toward money can be negative if it is accompanied with making judgments or excessive rigidity.

The French philosopher Voltaire said that he spent 90% of his life worrying about problems and disasters that never materialized. People should be reminded that they are not going to change their partner; at best, they may bring about a change in behavior. In all probability, a partner who is a spender will continue to be a spender. Fittingly, couples should be advised to make a workable plan on how to manage their money.

It also is no secret that couples argue. Studies have reported that, on average, arguing occurs once every two weeks. Most of these spats are temporary conflicts that can often be solved with an apology and a bit of sustained effort. But the arguments that last – the ones couples find hardest to resolve – frequently revolve around monetary issues. Interestingly, 38% of men and women in a recent national Harris Interactive poll for *Men, Love & Sex* say that money is the number one cause of marital strife. (By the way, that's well ahead of either of the distant-second hot-button subjects that cause friction: the division of household chores and the amount of sex in the relationship.) Needless to say, it makes dollars – and (excuse the pun) "sense" – to counsel your client couples to address money matters as soon as possible after they arise. Otherwise, remind your clients that each can expect less sex, less affection and a lot more dirty dishes around the house…a strong motivator if ever there was one!

Equitable Equity. Many money problems stem from the fact that couples often have different financial goals. For example, she wants granite countertops; he wants a flat screen TV (or they may struggle from the lack of communication about what those goals are). If one partner is in charge of the bills and the two rarely talk about anything beyond the month-to-month expenses, then there is little opportunity to develop shared economic goals. At other times, problems arise out of the major and basic stresses associated with making sure there is enough money to pay the bills, provide for the children, have some fun and avoid living under a bridge upon retirement (or before).

As we have stated numerous times throughout this book, *perception* is a critical factor in loving relationships. Both partners view all situations differently, no matter how small such differences may be. Thus, as issues are discussed and negotiated, it is imperative that (1) both partners have an opportunity to express their perceptions of the issues; and (2) both partners' perceptions are respected and reflected in final decisions. When this is accomplished, *equitable equity* is attainable. An example of how this can be realized comes from one of Bill Emener's client couples and is the subject of Dialogue 9.1.

Dialogue 9.1 Equitable Equity.

Rob (R) and Teri (T), both in their mid-40s, had been married previously. Rob had a son from his previous marriage, and after dating for three years he and Teri got engaged. One month prior to coming in for their first session with Bill Emener (B), Rob had sold his business and was unemployed. He was seeking leadership opportunities with local companies, but at the time was living off the sale of his business. Teri was a long-term regional manager at a utilities company with a good salary – probably higher than what Rob would start for when he returned to work. At the time, they were living together, splitting the rent on their townhouse, but planning to buy a home of their own after the wedding.

Understandably, one of their rather daunting concerns involved their differential "current worth" and "potential earning power." While they both were committed to each other and very optimistic about their impending marriage, they also had some concern about assuring that their individual estates would be protected and honor their individual long-term wishes with regard to Rob's son and Teri's nieces and nephews.

B: [Toward the end of their first session] It seems clear to me that the two of you have some rather daunting concerns regarding your current differential worth and earning power. Even though you're currently unemployed, Rob, with the money you got from selling your business you are bringing more money into your marriage than Teri is. On the other hand, considering your continuing long-term employment in your company, Teri, your earning power and take-home pay will be larger than Rob's – at least for the next few years. Does that seem to capture the essence of your financial concerns at the moment?

R: Yes, that's exactly where we're at... or at least that's it as far as I am concerned. Plus, I am feeling concerned about making sure that should anything unfortunate happen to me, my financial wishes for my son are protected.

T: And I respect that, Rob. I know you trust me, as I trust you. But should something happen, you want to make sure your son gets what you want for him to get from your estate. Likewise, I want the same for my nieces and nephews.

R: And in view of what I've said to you, Sweetie, we're both on the same page with regard to your concerns about your younger family members.

B: Okay, so it seems that both of you agree and respect what each of you want for yourselves – individually at the moment, as well as long-term for yourselves as a married couple.

R: [Nodding] Yes.

T: [Nodding and reaching for Rob's hand] Yes.

B: Good. So what I would like to do is give you some reading material we have in the front office about estate planning. I know that ultimately you want to balance out your collective assets, but you also want to assure that between now and then your respective beneficiaries are protected. Thus, between now and our next session I also would like for both of you to talk with a professional estate planner.

R: [Looking at Teri] I know a guy at the country club who is supposedly an excellent estate planner. Maybe I could see if he'd be willing to work with us.

T: Sure. Give him a call. And while I tend to agree that that would be a good idea, Dr. Emener, actually what is estate planning anyway?

B: Estate planning is the process of accumulating and disposing of an estate to maximize the goals of the estate owner. The various goals of estate planning include making sure the greatest amount of the estate passes to the estate owner's intended beneficiaries, often including paying the least amount of taxes and avoiding or minimizing probate court, as well as providing for and designating guardians for minor children and planning for incapacity. Among the many benefits of having a good estate plan for you two are that it would provide a sense of peace of mind for both of you and it would facilitate your focused attention to your relationship in the here and now.

Three weeks later, Rob and Teri showed up for their next session – their last session – with an air of calm about them. They reported that they had read some excellent materials on financial planning and met with the estate planner who was assisting them with their wills and living wills, and setting up an irrevocable family trust.

T: That, in and of itself, has been very comforting.

R: [While opening up a chart he and Teri had developed] And, Dr. Emener, we worked out and totally agree on an amortization schedule that will equitably respect our individual assets and eventually translate into an equal partnership.

B: [Looked at both Rob and then Teri, and smiled back at them.]

R: We calculated our individual assets and agreed that of our present total assets mine are about four times as much as Teri's. However, when we estimated my and Teri's current and potential earning power, we agreed that over the next six years we'll get to a fifty-fifty ratio. As you can see on this chart, when we get married three months from now and all of our assets are combined, 80% of the total will be mine and 20% will be Teri's. But between now and our wedding, we both will be signing a prenuptial agreement that will amortize our assets as the percentages show: at the end of year one, it will be Rob 75% and Teri 25%; at the end of year two, it will be Rob 70% and Teri 30%; year three, Rob 65% and Teri 35%; year four, 60% and 40%, year five, 55% and 45%, and on our sixth wedding anniversary we will be totally equal – 50-50."

B: [Nodding and smiling wider.]

R: [Reaching for Teri's hand] Isn't this great?

T: [After kissing Rob's hand] It's wonderful.

B: I certainly can see your individual and collective excitement about feeling relieved regarding your previous financial concerns, and you are now able to focus more on each other and your relationship – not to mention your upcoming wedding.

T: Yes, Dr. Emener, that's certainly true. And it's also symbolic of the kind of marriage we want to have – one that is equitably equitable.

This dialogue raises another important point: it is often worthwhile to seek the involvement of an expert when it comes to financial matters. This may be a certified financial planner, an accountant, an attorney, or a certified mediator. It behooves the licensed therapist to keep in mind that managing money is very much an acquired skill, but also – much like counseling – providing professional advice in this area is subject to professional regulation. Very few therapists are crossed-trained as certified financial planners, and therapists must not practice outside the limits of their expertise or regulatory area. It can be well worth the time (and money!) to advise your clients to consult other experts for purposes of financial planning or to dispute resolution.

On the other side of the coin, counseling a client couple about generalities of a "common sense" nature with respect to money matters is well within ethical limits. *The key is to keep the advice general and avoid advising on the intricacies of specific financial decisions.* We, for example, advise our clients as follows with respect to monetary issues:

1) *"Understand your gift dichotomy differences.* One of you may go for the wow gift – the gift that impresses… the gift with the big monetary outlay. But as the 2007 New York Yankees taught us, a big monetary investment doesn't always produce the best results. The other may go for creativity and thoughtfulness, which can sometimes be lost on those masters of the short attention span. To avoid conflict over gifts, one of you may need to understand that the odd, quirky presents truly express one's heart; one of you may need to understand that some people deeply care, but their way of showing it might seem as though they're substituting money for forethought. For some people, their way of showing genuine care involves a discussion with the clerk

at the CVS pharmacy rather than the gem specialist at Tiffany's. At the same time, be aware that when either member of a married couple makes a credit card charge, he or she is obligating *both* members of the marriage to repay the debt. Your partner may not find it very generous if you "buy" an expensive gift for him or her that incurs an unwanted debt."

2) *"Don't let money become a control issue.* If one person in your relationship makes significantly more money than the other, one of two things typically happens. The person who makes the least is afraid to spend anything, because he or she feels like they don't have a right to any of the money. Or that person will spend like crazy as a way of regaining some of the control they feel they've lost. To avoid such conflicts, set a budget for the both of you, and make sure each of you has access to cash."

3) *"Don't equate your financial worth with self-worth.* Arguments about money can be irritating because some people tend to look at life like a stakes race – they ride a whole lot taller in the saddle when they're sitting on a nice fat wallet. In their minds they feel they either have what it takes to stuff the stocking or they don't. When a conflict arises, it helps if people express their appreciation of the value their partner already is bringing to the relationship, aside from dollars and cents. Since money problems are rarely about money – but rather fear, power, insecurity and the like – it pays to learn how to manage these bigger aspects first. In short, the money and value each person brings into a loving relationship are not the same. Don't make the mistake of confusing one with the other."

Monetary and Equity Issues in Long-Term Relationships. With respect to money issues, we frequently hear the phrase "I wish we had…" Moreover, many times people didn't address or manage a monetary matter because they didn't think of it or where unaware of its importance. Thus, we recommend that your clients and, if necessary, their financial advisor, review the following 23 issues that they may want to attend to now or plan to attend to at an appropriate time in the future:

1) *Asset Allocation.* The single most important thing a couple that wants to invest can do is to practice asset allocation. Again, common sense tells us never to place all of our eggs in one basket.

2) *Auto insurance.* This can be a nightmare. It's costly, confusing and unrewarding – until it is needed.

3) *Basics of Banking and Saving.* Both partners need to be knowledgeable of the basics of banking and saving.

4) *Basics of Investing.* Discussions, plans and action are highly recommended – someday, "tomorrow" will come.

5) *Buying a Car.* Buying a car is like no other shopping experience. The choices can seem endless, and the pitfalls and opportunities are many. Purchasing a car – together – is good practice for a couple in making joint decisions.

6) *Buying a Home.* Owning one's own home is part of the American Dream. But if unprepared, buying a home can not only be a nightmare, but a poor decision: there are times in the ups and downs of economic trends when it truly makes more sense to rent. Advise your clients to learn as much as they can about home ownership – before they decide to purchase one.

7) *Children and Money.* Up until they start earning a living, and sometimes well beyond that, children are apt to spend money like it grows on trees. It is important for parents to teach their children how to handle money responsibly – primarily by example.

8) *Controlling Debt.* Individually and collectively, people should learn when to hold debt…and when to avoid it. As of the date of this writing (the first quarter of 2009), the next wave of economic crises is projected to be uncollectible credit card debt (after the decline in home values and the near collapse of the banking system due to the depreciation of securities based on bundling the mortgages on those homes with inflated values).

9) *Employee Stock Options.* More companies are providing stock options for a much broader group of employees. Wisely taking advantage of this can be tremendously helpful. On the other hand, couples should not confuse stock options with tangible or fungible assets. They should be regarded as mid- to long-term investments, not liquid assets.

10) *Estate Planning.* Americans are in the midst of one of the greatest inter-generational transfers of wealth in history, yet few have done the planning required for it. Together, couples should learn how to do this…and get it done.

11) *Health insurance.* Whether your employer provides you with a group medical plan or you need to buy coverage on the individual market, understanding how health insurance works is the best way to get your money's worth. As of this writing, there is hope that a true national health care system will emerge from the current financial crisis which began in 2007. The United States is the only remaining modern economy not to have such a system in place.

12) *Hiring Financial Help.* By reading and studying, couples need to learn how best to find the appropriate professionals to assist them with matters of financial planning, stock trading, insurance coverage and tax returns.

13) *Investing in Bonds.* Bonds can provide a steady and reasonably secure income, while adding ballast to your portfolio. On the other hand, not all bonds are equal. Couples need to learn to differentiate safe bond investments from "junk."

14) *Home Insurance.* Homeowners' and renters' insurance can also be costly, confusing, and unrewarding – until it is needed. Couples and families need to be sure to have the coverage needed in cases of crisis.

15) *Investing in Mutual Funds.* Developing a simple and manageable portfolio is a recommended option to consider in your investment planning.

16) *Investing in Stocks.* The stock market can be a great place to turn savings into wealth – or, as we have seen in 2008 and 2009, one can just as easily lose one's shirt. The fundamentals needed to invest wisely must be learned.

17) *Life Insurance.* Life insurance is a critical part of financial planning and is a necessity for anyone with dependents who would be affected financially by the demise of their caregivers. Yet, life insurance is one of the hardest financial products to understand, and it is sold by agents who are sometimes more concerned with their commissions than their customers' needs. Be cautious and knowledgeable when purchasing it.

18) *Making a Budget.* Individually and collectively, couples need to be advised to keep spending under control so that they get the most out of every dollar.

19) *Planning for Retirement.* Achieving a comfortable retirement in the 21st century requires a new approach to retirement planning. Counsel your clients to learn about available retirement vehicles and their pitfalls (remember when 401Ks seemed like magic? Look again!). People need to carefully plan for their needs (and wants).

20) *Saving for College.* It is not rocket science… just common sense. By starting early and investing regularly, children may have a wider choice of colleges, and paying the bills won't hurt as much.

21) *Setting Priorities.* Unless they are independently wealthy, your clients will not be able to have everything they want. Advise them to set priorities carefully and honor them in their choices.

22) *Taxes.* Among the long list of necessary evils we must encounter throughout our lives, perhaps the most constant – taxes – is also typically the least understood. With some basic knowledge, however, people can learn what they need to know to avoid getting hurt.

23) *401(k)s.* By some, this is considered the most important tool you've got for retirement. Others have seen their entire nest eggs wiped out in six months through collapsing stock retirement plans. To make the most of it requires research and sage counsel.

Money and equity indeed can be the roots of many evils. Fittingly, it is critical for people in loving relationships to openly discuss, on a regular basis, the multitude of issues related to their money, equity, values and attitudes related to their money and equity, and senses of worth and meaning. At the end of the day, it is equally important for both partners to think about and discuss the money and equity aspects of their relationship and not stop until both of them see everything as being equitably equitable.

MATTERS OF TIME AND TIMING

"I still miss Richard so much. It's been over two years now since his death. But I still miss him so. I would give up the insurance money, his car, the house, everything – if I could just spend one more day with him."

"I know what life has been like being married to Alice for these past ten years and I have an appreciation for what it is like now. What it will be like to be with her in the future, however, is a big unknown for me."

"By the time we get home from work and attend to the children and the usual house things, we never seem to have any time left for each other – not to mention ourselves."

"As I think about our relationship over the past five years, the things that bring the biggest smiles to my face are not the rings, the expensive presents or the new house we had built. It's the wonderful times we spent together and the precious moments we shared."

All of these four statements have something in common. They illustrate the importance of *time* in loving relationships. In this section we will focus on the construct of time, its characteristics and attributes, and take a look at how time, if unattended, can have detrimental effects and influences on loving relationships. We also will address and take a look at how some people we counseled were able to attend to their time issues for the purposes of improving their own quality of life, their loved one's quality of life and their loving relationships.

Time: A Precious Commodity. There is an old cliché that suggests that the way an individual spends his or her time and money is the best indication of his or her values and what he or she considers important in life. We would argue that of these two, time and money, *time* is the more precious commodity. On numerous occasions we have suggested that time is the most precious commodity in a human being's life; we do not know how much of it we have left, we are constantly running out of it, we have no way of knowing when we will run out of it, and there is no way to get more of it. Fittingly, one of the first questions we frequently ask individuals who come to see us with a relationship problem or concern is: *How do you spend your time?*

It also would appear reasonable to assume that if a person loves another person and wants to give to them and share with them the one thing that is most precious, it would be his or her time. As we shall see in this part of the chapter, it is not only the *amount of time* that is given and shared – it is the *quality of that time* as well. We always have believed that one of the most helpful things two individuals in a loving relationship can do is to remain cognizant of (a) how each of them individually spends his or her time and (b) how they spend their time together.

Pursuant to the issue of *quality of time*, many individuals are unable to experience the passing of time without feeling either anxious or bored and, in fact, spend the majority of their time toggling back and forth between these two states. Others feel that time is wasted unless they are sufficiently stimulated or experiencing some thrill (e.g., the "adrenaline junkie"). Many such people eventually give up trying to feel any sense of quality of life, and give in to the mindless distraction of television or, in some cases, work. Others succumb to the lure of self-medication and often develop serious problems with alcohol and/or drugs. Yet it is quite difficult, if not impossible, to develop a healthy and sustainable loving relationship if one is unable to enjoy periods marked by the mere passage of time. Counselors often refer to this as learning to feel "comfortable in one's own skin."

It stands to reason that learning not only to manage one's time well, but also to learn how to make the most of it across a wide range of circumstances, is a core skill needed for loving relationships. Our case reports look at many of these issues in hopes of illuminating our readers about this important subject. Toward the end of this section we also suggest some ways of learning how to live well in the moment of the present, or "in the now," and how this can also enhance the quality of a relationship with one's significant other.

You Can't Create it – Just Allocate it. John and Mary, both of whom were single parents in their early 40s with four small children between them, "had been going steady for the past six months" before coming to see Bill Emener. Both of them expressed and demonstrated a tremendous amount of frustration: John was frustrated with Mary because she did not spend enough time with him, and Mary was frustrated with John because he did not understand why she was not able to spend more time with him. John, who lived in his house with his two children, owned his own lawn service and worked nine or ten hours a day, six days a week. Mary, who lived in her house with her two children, was a co-owner of an answering service, and not only put in long days during the week but also had to be on call every other weekend. "But why can't you just spend more time with me?" John repeatedly asked Mary.

Not to help Mary defend herself but to assist her in explaining herself and communicating her frustration to John, Bill drew a diagram similar to the one in Figure 9.1. He then said to Mary, "It appears that this circle on the left represents your life as it is now in terms of the relative amounts of time that you spend at work, at play, sleeping, with your two children, with John, and for yourself. And what I hear you saying Mary, is that although you would like to increase the amount of time that you spend with John, the 'You' in the diagram..." Mary interrupted Bill and looked at John and said, "That is exactly it, John. I do want to spend more time with you, but where do I take it from?"

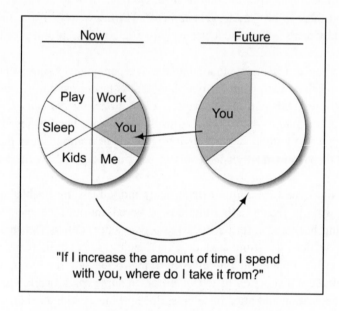

Figure 9.1. You Can't Create Time – Just Allocate it.

The important thing that John was able to understand was that Mary, like all human beings, could not create time, only try to reallocate it. Much pleasure was gained by the two of them when, over the next few weeks, they were able to reconfigure some of their work schedules, as well as their social activities, so that both of them were able to comfortably allocate more time to be with each other. There was no doubt that they were in love with each other. However, their intense emotions, specifically their frustrations, were preventing them from identifying ways to (re-)arrange their lives so that they could comfortably spend more time together. As John poignantly said at their last session, "I used to say to Mary, 'If you loved me you would spend more time with me,' but I eventually realized that given all of the things going on in her life it was not that easy and the amount of time she could allocate to me and to us was not necessarily an indication of how much she loved me. Once we were able to get over that hurdle, Dr. Emener, we were able to work things out and improve things rather quickly."

Priorities Change Over Time. Katie, a 29-year-old nurse, made an appointment to see Bill Lambos because, "For the last year or so I have been feeling empty and aimless. My marriage is okay by all the usual criteria, but my husband, Phil, an insurance salesman, is happy just to come home, have supper and watch TV or play on the computer. Then the day ends and it starts all over again. I mentioned I wanted to go back to school to work on my master's degree in nursing, and he couldn't believe it. He couldn't understand why what we already had wasn't enough. He even accused me of having an affair with the doctor I work for and asked if my employer wasn't behind it all!"

Bill asked Katie more details about their situation. She was unable to have children because of a medical condition; her husband accepted this when they married. Neither of them wanted to adopt a child, so they fell into a comfortable set of routines. But after a few years, Katie developed a need for becoming someone better and more accomplished – something psychologists and counselors refer to as the need to *self-actualize* – whereas Phil was fine with things as they were. Since their core relationship was the main issue, Bill suggested they come to sessions together. Bill explained to Phil that as some people move from one life stage to another, their priorities can change. Moreover, Bill suggested that Phil could choose to see Katie's need for growth and self-actualization as a positive and admirable quality, rather than to feel threatened by it. Phil looked down and said, barely loud enough to hear, "What happens if I'm not good enough for her after she gets her degree? I'm happy as a salesman and don't want to change."

Over the course of several sessions, Phil came to realize that it is unrealistic to expect a loved one to remain the exact same person as the years pass by. Although Phil remained nervous that Katie would not remain in love with him, when Bill last saw them Phil had accepted that Katie's need for self-growth was not about him at all – it was about her changing priorities. To our knowledge, they remain together.

In a similar vein, Donna, a 48-year-old computer programmer, came to see Bill Emener because she was experiencing "mild levels of anxiety and worrisome levels of depression." She tended to focus her conversation not only on her job but also on her 24-year marriage to Daryl, a 50-year-old life insurance salesman, and their "three almost-grown children." She also said, "I keep telling Daryl that I feel like I'm going through some kind of transition, but I don't know what it is. For reasons that I do not understand, I just feel off balance, off-center and not really focused on what's going on around me." As Donna and Bill continued to talk, the "transition" to which she had referred became evident.

Bill drew a chart for Donna similar to the one in Figure 9.2. He then said to her, "Donna, from what you have been telling me, it appears that you went through your *first lifestyle transition* in your late 20s to early 30s, and now you are going through your *second lifestyle transition*. When you and Daryl were first married and did not have any children, your priorities were relatively clear: first came you, then came your relationship with Daryl, and then came your work. By the time you were in your mid-30s, your priorities had shifted: first came your children, then came your work, then came you and Daryl, and then yourself. Now that you are getting older and your children are moving out on their own, you are transitioning into a new set of priorities: first it is you, then it is you and Daryl, then it is your children, and then it is your work. Does this make sense to you?"

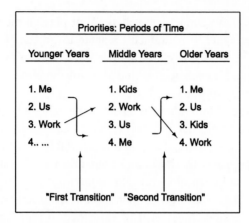

Figure 9.2. Priorities Change Over Time.

After pondering the diagram Donna replied, "Yes, it surely does. That's me!" She then added, "But this second transition seems to be a hell of a lot more difficult than the first one! If I continue to attend to and dote on the kids, they get frustrated with me and say, 'Leave me alone!' Then when I leave them alone, I feel guilty because I still have a sense of responsibility for them and don't know how to continue to be their mother." Bill could not help but smile as he looked at her and said, "Yes, Donna, that's very true they... they keep changing the rules on us. Just when we learn how to be parents of child-children, they become adult-children and we have to start all over again." She laughed and nodded in agreement.

Donna took the chart home with her and shared it with Daryl. "It's amazing," she said in their next session. "When I went over the chart with Daryl, he immediately told me that he had been experiencing the same thing, but was afraid to share it with me for fear that it would bring me down." Donna then went on to explain the many ways in which both she and Daryl had been struggling with how to allocate their time during their transition phase.

Toward the end of their last session, they were interrupted by a knock on the door – it was Daryl. Earlier, Donna had told Bill that Daryl was going to try to stop by to join them for a few minutes when he got out of work. That provided them with a very enjoyable opportunity to collectively review how the two of them were doing with the transitioning of the time priorities in their lives, and how they were doing in assisting each other in allocating their time. "Now that we have been helping each other with this," Donna said, "it has been so much easier."

"Timing is Everything." The phrase "timing is everything" captures an important aspect of reality: What works perfectly *now* may have been a disastrous choice earlier or later. We posit that this phenomenon is more salient and hard-wired (in terms of the brain) than most people realize.

Events occur not in isolation, but in a context, and it is the context *even more than the event itself* that determines how it will be received – as fortunate or problematic, lucky or a "Murphy's Law" moment, as reflecting wisdom or foolishness. Why? A short digression into network theory (including nerve networks) helps answer this. Essentially, the brain is a neural network, and that network changes states both from moment to moment and over longer periods of time. Inputs to the network (what happens to a person) are evaluated based, in part, on the level of *readiness* of the network to process them. When the network is optimally predisposed to handle an input, we perceive the event as positive (or lucky or perhaps "in the nick of time"). When, on the other hand, the network is ill suited to process the input, the event is perceived as disruptive and troublesome (a disaster or a case of "awful timing").

For example, experienced therapists know that much of what transpires in the early sessions of treatment is preparatory in nature. Early in therapy, the client's nerve network (his or her brain, and, thereby, mind) is being "nudged" out of a stuck or repetitive pattern and new ways of processing inputs are introduced (changes in perspective are considered, for example). Later in therapy, when the "network" is in a ready state, the client will experience a cathartic, or "Aha" moment, when the crucial input is received that transforms the system and restores balance. Brain scans of clients undergoing psychotherapy based on fMRI, PET and even EEG methods have captured these changes in real time (Cozzolino, 2002).

Relationships also may be considered networks, and dually so: they are social networks that are processed by the neural networks of their participants. Therefore, it is central to effective relationship counseling that the "system" of the relationship be prepared to accept the changes exerted from the outside, as the following example from Bill Emener's practice demonstrates.

Jack, a 34-year-old plumber, came to see Bill because he was feeling extremely frustrated with his relationship with Sharon, a woman he had been dating for about two and a half months. "A little over a year ago, I finalized my divorce. We had been married for nine years and had no children. A few months ago, I began dating occasionally. Then I met Sharon. She is really neat! Sharon is 28, divorced, is the head receptionist in a law firm in town and has the most adorable little three-year-old daughter that you would ever want to meet." It was clear, however, that Jack was also feeling some depression and anxiety regarding his life, as well as a growing level of frustration with his relationship with Sharon. Bill asked him whether there were one or two specific issues that he and she tended to have the most difficulty with. With a big sigh, Jack said, "There's only one. And, I don't know what to do about it."

As their discussion continued, the primary nature of Jack's difficulty with Sharon became relatively clear. Sharon had been divorced for approximately two and a half years, and as Jack said, "has her life together: she is comfortable with her divorce, she has worked out a comfortable and cordial relationship with her ex-husband, and basically she is ready to settle down. The problem for me," he continued, "is that I am still reeling a little bit from my divorce. I don't really feel like my feet are firmly on the ground yet. I have tried to tell Sharon that, but somehow she has difficulties hearing me. Just the other night, I said to her, 'Our timing is terrible!' Whenever I tell her that I'm not ready to see her as often as she would like or that I am not ready to consider living together, she right away thinks that either there is something about her that I do not like or that she has done something to upset me. I don't know why, but for some reason I cannot get through to her."

At Jack's invitation, Sharon came to their next session. After each of them had the opportunity to express some individual feelings and thoughts, Bill asked them to identify some boundaries for their relationship that would be comfortable for the two of them. When they left, they were planning to go to dinner together and to discuss what boundaries each of them needed in order to feel comfortable with and enjoy their relationship. Jack said, "Thanks a lot, Doc. I don't feel any need to schedule another appointment at this time, but I will get back to you. I really feel that the two of us are heading in the right direction." As Sharon threw her arm around Jack's waist, she looked at Bill with a smile of understanding and agreement. Bill had not heard from Jack and Sharon for about six months when he received an envelope at his office in which there was a photocopy of a newspaper clipping announcing their engagement. Across the bottom was written, "I finally felt ready – it feels good. Just wanted to share this with you. Thanks again, Jack."

In this case, the mere recognition that the two partners were not equally ready to "process" the new relationship was helpful in allowing the partners to give one another permission to achieve the readiness state. In other cases, the therapist may have to assist one or both partners in actively overcoming a psychological block in order to resolve a relationship issue. In every case, it goes without saying that timing is a very important consideration in any loving relationship. Moreover, most of the time it is futile to simply advise the client to hurry another individual's timing if he or she is not ready. Rather, it is wiser to devise an approach that helps "ready the network" for the change. As Sharon had said, "I guess for the time being, *patience* is going to have to be my middle name." And given what eventually happened, it apparently had been – and it worked.

A Long-Term Trade Off. This concept of timing as reflecting the readiness of a network to accept and adapt to change has broad explanatory value. For example, as the following example shows, time even over the long term is relative and it impacts every human being's life differently. *What* we ultimately decide to do when we are at a relationship crossroads, many times is influenced by *where* we are along our journey of life (again, the readiness of the network to accommodate change). To say the least, this indeed was an important and critical consideration for Betty.

A 48-year-old instructor at a junior college, Betty had been married to Henry for 25 years. Their two children were no longer at home – one was married and living in another city and the other was in graduate school. "It's just the two of us now," Betty said. Following a relatively lengthy discussion about her life, she finally said, "The truth of the matter, Dr. Emener, is that while I love Henry very much and truly believe he loves me very much, I simply do not feel *in love* with him. In fact, I haven't for a long time. I have come very close to having an affair or two, but up till now nothing like that has ever happened. It is not that I have a bad relationship with Henry; in fact, it's comfortable. But for me, the spark is gone, I no longer feel romantically involved with him. He is more like a friend than a lover or husband, and I guess from a romantic point of view our relationship is somewhat dull, meaningless and empty." Bill suggested a couple of self-help books for Betty to read and invited her to return for another session at which time they might take a serious look at some of her options. She agreed and scheduled another session.

Within two minutes of entering Bill's office, Betty said, "I read the two books you had recommended and have made a decision, at least for now, and I feel okay about it! I made a list of the pros and cons of either staying with Henry or leaving him. On one side of the ledger, I have a good friend. He is a good man and is very good to me. I live a very comfortable life. Considering that he is 50 years old, he is still in pretty good shape and we enjoy a relatively active life together. From a romantic point of view, however, our relationship is about as exciting as a dial tone. I guess that is a sadness I will have to live with because I have decided to stay with him." While wiping back some tears, Betty continued, "At this time in my life, I guess I simply just don't want to go through all of the hassles involved in separation and divorce. Furthermore, I don't want to screw up my relationship with my children or create any difficulties for my future grandchildren. If I was 28 and felt this way, there is a chance that I might be more inclined to end my relationship with Henry. But at 48, I am simply at a different place in time." Betty's body language and facial expressions, while communicating the sense of sadness that she was verbalizing, also communicated a sense of peace and tranquility with her decision. As she was leaving, she turned and said, "If I ever change my mind and/or need any further assistance from you, I will call you."

Betty's self-evaluation reflected her own perception that her "internal network" was not ready to accept any dramatic change of inputs, such as separation, divorce, and the processes and the lifestyle changes they would entail. She reasoned further that her family's social network would also be disrupted to its detriment by her making such a choice.

The preceding examples serve to demonstrate that matters of time and timing are best understood by considering the suitability, or readiness, of the system they will impact to accept and efficiently process the changes presented to them. In late 2008, President-elect Barack Obama's designated chief of staff Rahm Emmanuel quipped that "a crisis should never be wasted." What he meant was that, because of the dire economic situation of the day, the social and economic networks of the country were in a state of readiness to accept broad and transformative changes, once-in-a-generation programs to reform health care, education, and infrastructure. Timing, it seems, is indeed everything.

Staying in "The Now." This brings us to the final issue related to the topic of time and timing. How do we deal with issues during the majority of times when our networks, neural or social, are not in a state of readiness to accept change?

Many times clients complain of generalized feelings of *ennui* – low-level anxiety, or a pervasive sense of restlessness that leads to risk-taking, thrill-seeking or substance abuse. The same individuals are not willing to make large changes in their lifestyles or career choices (their networks are not ready), yet neither are they happy with their current circumstances. Invariably, such individuals also tend to experience difficulties in their loving relationships and may even blame such feelings on their significant other. In fact, we believe such experiences to be pervasive in our culture, which leads people to feel the need for continuous and ongoing stimulation, coupled with immediate gratification. As psychologists, we can advise our readers that this frequently is a common but serious trap of unrealistic expectations. Any given moment or period of time will either be positive, neutral or negative, and the degree to which a given period of time is judged as one or the other is as much determined by one's expectations as the quality of the moment or time period itself. We simply cannot be "up" all the time, if for no other reason than our "ups," "downs" and "neutrals" are experienced relative to themselves as well as our perceptions and commensurate expectations.

Many people dream day after day of winning the lottery as if it would make them happy forever. Research reveals, however, that most lottery winners turn out to be unhappy people – some even commit suicide. In order to have a fulfilling, loving relationship, we must first learn to achieve a level of contentment with the ebb and flow of time over the course of each day. Those who have difficulty with this many times look for help through meditation, yoga, spiritual fulfillment, or other methods of learning to be at peace – living in the current moment. Increasingly, several modalities of therapy offered in Bill Lambos' practice, including EEG-biofeedback (or neurofeedback), emotional freedom techniques, and other interventions based on energy psychology have helped many of his clients achieve the same result by helping clients change their brainwave patterns, their states of emotional balance, or both. As we have frequently said to our clients, "Regardless of how you get there, however, remember that you cannot be happy with another person for very long if you have never learned how to appreciate life and your situation as it is right now."

PATTERNS AND TRENDS

It is not uncommon to hear from a client, "Doctor, I just want to be happy all the time," or "Counselor, our relationship is mostly good, but not all the time. What's wrong?" Although extreme swings in one's level of happiness or satisfaction can indicate deeper problems, it is more likely that such clients are being unrealistic in assuming they can be happy or that a relationship can be good, "all the time." Life, as we experience it, is not static. It has its "ups" and "downs," and these patterns over time form trends. One's success or failure in a loving relationship has much to do with the ability to successfully adapt to change and is no exception to this common sense rule of thumb: *to deal with life means to deal with change*.

If we accept this premise that virtually all loving relationships have such patterns and/or trends, then it follows that we can learn much from studying them. Consider how frequently you have heard clients say things like, "Whenever he seems to be having a lot of stress at work, a pattern emerges in our relationship in which he typically..." and "It seems about every month or so the two of us need some time away from each other. So, about every four or five weeks I will take a fishing or golfing weekend with my buddies, or she will spend a weekend with her sister and her brother-in-law. That seems to work very well for us because..." It is important to remember that there is nothing wrong with patterns and trends in loving relationships. What is important is that people learn how to maintain a mutually satisfying relationship within the context of fluctuations in day-to-day quality and functioning.

There are five important considerations to address regarding patterns and trends: (1) How do they affect our client's lives? (2) How do they affect their relationships? (3) When should we advise clients to change them? (4) Is the couple's "network" ready to, or capable of, accepting the change? and, (5) If so, what effect will the changes we suggest have on their existing relationship?

Patterns and trends can emerge in loving relationships in a variety of ways: (1) *by natural circumstances*: for example, "As part of his job, he has to go to the coast for the last Thursday and Friday of each month. And because we both enjoy the beach, I meet him there on Friday evening. Therefore, we usually spend one weekend a month away from home;" (2) *by learning*: for example, "Ever since I was a teenager, whenever I had anyone in my life whom I considered to be an important person, I always expected that she would go with me to church on Sunday mornings and then join me for dinner with my family;" and (3) *by design*: for example, "Given the nature of her job and my job, we find ourselves getting on each other's nerves about every three or four weeks. We plan an opportunity to spend one or two nights away from home so that we can be by ourselves. When I look at my credit card bills, I can tell there is an obvious trend there. But that works for us, and we have no intentions of changing it." While a pattern or trend may occur as a result of a combination of the foregoing, it is important to remember that patterns and trends in loving relationships are neither good nor bad, per se. It furthermore is important for us to focus on the extent to which our patterns and trends affect our individual lives and our relationships, especially if they are harmful. On occasion, we remind a client engaged in harmful patterns of an old, tongue-in-cheek definition of neurosis: "Neurosis is the pattern of defeating yourself by repeating yourself."

Learned Response Patterns. The living experience of reality has embedded within it the properties of *time* and *change over time*. If some part of our experience becomes static or ceases to vary over time, our nervous system is strongly predisposed to learn to ignore it. Learning psychologists call this "stimulus habituation." You probably never notice the sound of your home's heating or air conditioning systems – you filter them out or ignore them. You may have known people who live near airports or train tracks and don't notice sounds that may startle you. Evolution has taught living organisms to selectively attend only to those aspects of the environment that have predictive value, and there are few aspects of our environment more important for us to predict than what will come next in a loving relationship.

To give a more concrete example, Bill Emener was seeing Marleen, a 31-year-old nurse, who was reared in a dysfunctional family. Both her parents were alcoholics. Due in part to the lack of healthy role models, Marleen never learned how to appropriately and functionally deal with anger. In fact, she told Bill that when she was younger and living at home, whenever anger would emerge she would get scared and, if at all possible, leave the house. She came to see Bill because she was realizing that over the past 11 years she had had a series of eight relationships with men, none of which ever lasted more than five or six months. As they processed and discussed Marleen's previous relationships, an understandable pattern became evident.

After Bill drew a chart for Marleen similar to the one in Figure 9.3, he said to her, "Marleen, these eight relationships seem to have followed a pattern. You would begin a relationship with a gentleman then, for understandable reasons, many of which may have had nothing to do with you, he would get angry or express anger. You would then get scared and withdraw, psychologically, and run away from him. He would then get angry with you for withdrawing from him. Then when he would express increased anger, you would get more scared. As this pattern continued, both of your emotions escalated further. Eventually, you would run away, leave and/or end the relationship. You would begin to feel lonely and look for someone new. Then the pattern would start all over again." With tears in her eyes, Marleen softly said, "Yes, and I have lost some beautiful relationships and have let some extremely wonderful men get away from me too."

For Marleen, this was a monumental challenge and a very difficult struggle. Learning how to deal appropriately and effectively with fear and anger is not easy. As Bill and Marleen therapeutically processed some of her earlier experiences with her mother and father and she learned that it was possible to receive and express anger without being devastatingly hurt, she began to learn how to deal with the emotion of anger in much more positive and functional ways. The last time Bill spoke with Marleen she said to him, "I am truly beginning to enjoy my relationship with George. He and I have been going together for about a month now. The important thing, however, is that we have had, and have survived, some good shouting matches and arguments. I'm learning! And that's cool. The most important thing I have learned is that I can be angry with George and he can be angry with me, and we can work through our angry feelings and still enjoy a wonderful relationship. I'm so happy!"

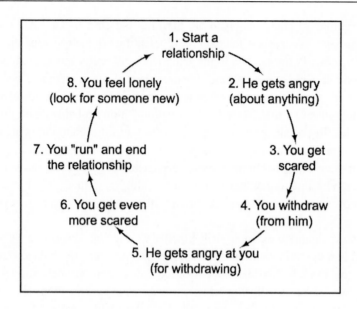

Figure 9.3. Learned Response Patterns.

The ultimate turning point for Marleen was when she was able to address her feelings of anger toward herself – for not having known how to deal with anger, and then for sabotaging and losing many good relationships in her life. Once she was able to forgive herself for having been that way, she was able to get on with her life and, as she said, "enjoy wholesome relationships – not only on the sunshiny days but on the rainy days as well."

There are two important lessons we can learn from Marleen. First, poorly managed emotional responses to immediate events can prevent us from seeing the forest for the trees. In order to learn how to be comfortable over the long run, we must learn to manage momentary emotional responses that seem threatening, lead to anger or lead to overreaction. Second, the reality of both life and relationships is that the days are mixed between the good, the neutral and the not so good (and maybe even outright bad ones). It is unreasonable – or as the late Albert Ellis (1996, 2000) would say, "Irrational" – not to expect fluctuations in the quality of interactions. Later in this section, we will offer some specific guidance as to when a trend or pattern can be said to signal true dysfunction or even personal danger. For now, however, the message is straightforward: patterns and trends will always exist to some degree in relationships and for the most part play many useful roles. What is important is that you assist your clients to learn how to manage them and not let past patterns and trends dictate their futures.

Role(s) of Sabotage. Like Marleen, Mick also had been reared in a dysfunctional family. For many reasons that he and Bill Emener discussed and explored, Mick, as an adult, had a tremendous fear of rejection. As Mick said, "Whenever I think a good friend or important person in my life might possibly tell me that he or she is angry with me or that he or she doesn't want to see me anymore, I go crazy!"

As they discussed the patterns and trends in Mick's relationships with women, it became clear that Mick's fear of rejection ultimately would lead to the unconscious sabotaging of his relationships with them. When he would meet a woman who he thought was "cool and interesting," he would work very hard to build a relationship with her. He would call her on the telephone, send her flowers, take her to nice restaurants and go for long walks on the beach together. However, once he would begin to realize that she had some positive feelings toward him, he would start to become nervous and scared. His ultimate fear was that: (1) she would fall in love with him; (2) he would fall in love with her and with their relationship; but (3) she then would reject him and he would experience what he said would be "gut-wrenching pain." Thus, to avoid gut-wrenching pain from being rejected, he would stop calling her, not treat her very nicely and basically drive her away. He initially came to see Bill because his most recent girlfriend said to him, "Mick, I cannot understand you. You worked so hard to build a relationship with me and now you're doing just the opposite. First you did everything you could to pull me in. Now you're doing everything you can to push me away. I do not think that I have done anything wrong or different. I think you're the one with the problem." Mick agreed with her and subsequently came for some assistance. Among other things, Bill helped Mick work on his fear of abandonment and issues associated with toxic shame (discussed in Chapter 10). Once Mick realized that if a loving relationship did not last and he would be able to survive the fear and the pain of losing it, he then would be able to risk having one.

Old Patterns with New People. A slightly different form of the same issue (when one's history determines one's present and future) was problematic for Bea, a 40-year-old woman who had been engaged three times and married twice. Bea came to see Bill Emener because she was having difficulties in her relationship with her new boyfriend, Hector. Unfortunately for Bea, all of the previous men in her life, including her father, were non-trustworthy and emotionally abusive. She once said, "The only way I could deal with my dad and the other men in my life was not to believe them or trust them when they would say anything to me, otherwise they would let me down and I would get hurt." The difficulty Bea was having was that Hector considered himself to be a very trustworthy individual. But Hector was growing very frustrated with Bea because she constantly acted as if she did not trust him. For example, she said, "The other night Hector said to me, 'Bea, no matter what I do, you do not seem to trust me or think of me as a trustworthy person. You never give me a chance. I always have been open and honest with you. I always have followed through on anything I said I would do. Yet for some reason I do not feel trusted by you.'" Obviously, Bea was scared. She liked and loved Hector very much. She wanted to continue her relationship with him. However, it became clear to her she was having difficulties with trust.

During their second session, Bill asked Bea, "Might it be that you are continuing to use your old patterns with new people?" She replied, "That is exactly what I said to Hector. I am so afraid of being disappointed and hurt by someone because he isn't trustworthy that I have trouble trusting anyone." Interestingly, Hector said, 'Please try to remember, Bea, I'm not anyone. I'm Hector!'"

As Bea was able to learn new ways of dealing with people, she was able to learn to take some risks and be more trusting. It is interesting to note, however, that one time when Hector told her he would come over by seven o'clock but did not show up until nine-thirty, she talked with him about it and realized that: (1) Hector was a human being who would occasionally forget what time he said he would arrive; and (2) it did not necessarily mean that he was an untrustworthy person – he was just human. She added, "That old cliché, 'to err is human,' is very appropriate for me. For once in my life I feel that I am in a relationship with a person who is basically trustworthy, and my sense is that as long as I continue to act trustingly toward him, things should be okay. Hector is being very patient with me, and that certainly has been very helpful." Treating each individual as an individual and not using old patterns from old relationships as the only way of dealing with new people, is occasionally a difficult thing to learn. For some people, it can seem like an insurmountable obstacle. However, by changing one's perspective and becoming willing to take some risks, almost anyone can free himself or herself from the trap of the past. As a counselor, it is critical for you to counsel clients to be aware of the basic nature of the person with whom they are having a current relationship, and to be sensitive to how they respond to a new person versus how that person learned to respond to people in his or her past.

Poor Communications Patterns. Patterns emerge not just in the ebb and flow of the day-to-day quality of relationships, but also in the ways people become used to communicating with one another. Pioneering research by the relationship psychologist John Gottman (Gottman & Silver, 1999) studied such communication patterns for many years and revealed some very informative findings (which have since been replicated by other research). You may have read about his work in the popular book *Blink: The Power of Thinking Without Thinking* (Gladwell, 2007) or saw it on several television series by the same name in which his work was featured.

By videotaping newlyweds (with their permission, of course) for as few as four hours in his "love lab," and then carefully scoring the tapes for instances of various types of signs, Dr. Gottman developed a system whereby he can predict, with 90% accuracy, whether or not a newly married couple will be divorced within four to six years. (In the behavioral sciences, that level of prediction is nothing short of astounding.) He found six types of interaction associated with arguments, each of which predicted eventual divorce. They are detailed in his books and writings for the interested reader. For our purposes in this chapter, however, we will focus on the signs Gottman calls "The Four Horsemen" – an allusion to the Biblical prophesy of doom in Revelations. These four patterns of interaction are: (1) criticism; (2) contempt; (3) defensiveness; and (4) stonewalling. Let's take a brief look at each to discern how patterns based on these types of communicating lead to downward spirals (trends) that in turn lead to divorce.

Criticism is essentially blaming one's partner for problems in the relationship, rather than taking accountability for one's own contribution to the problem and/or looking at the behaviors of both partners as the source of the problem. (Interestingly, blaming others is also one of the irrational behaviors often attacked in Rational Emotive Behavior Therapy.) We often recall our own parents telling us when we were children, "It's not what you say, it's how you say it that matters." This is the core of criticism: stating or implying that whatever is bothering you is caused by deficiencies in your partner. Even if true (for example, if your partner has a drinking problem), criticism never helps. By turning this style around and suggesting something positive, couples can avoid falling into this destructive pattern of interaction.

Contempt is the expression of hatred. As couples counselors, we cannot remember when it ever has played a positive role in managing a relationship. Yet this pattern can develop into a two-way street, leading to a relationship style that sociologists refer to as "conflict-habituated." If you have ever watched the film *Who's Afraid of Virginia Woolf?,* you will recognize this pattern immediately. Richard Burton and Elizabeth Taylor do a magnificent job in portraying such a disturbed pattern in a relationship between a university professor and his wife.

Most of us are very familiar with *defensiveness*. In a loving relationship, it is a feeling of anxiety fueled by a belief that our partner is blaming us for something. Often such anxiety is channeled into anger and unproductive "not-my-fault" declarations. Couples who fall into this type of interactive pattern are headed nowhere good.

Finally, *stonewalling* is a type of active avoidance in dealing with issues as they surface. Both of our experiences are replete with examples of how loving relationships have soured and ended because one of the partners refused to deal with issues brought up by the other person.

The Four Horsemen do not in and of themselves predict that a relationship will end or that a married couple will divorce. But in combination they can establish a style or pattern of interaction that in most cases indicates a negative trend and portends an unhappy future.

Gottman is not the only one to have studied patterns of interaction. An entirely different approach comes from the work of Eric Berne (1964) called "transactional analysis." Recall from Chapter 2 that, according to Berne, interaction patterns may be looked at as a series of transactions between people. During repeated interactions, each person comes to assume one of three so-called "ego-states" – the Adult, the Parent, or the Child. In a healthy loving relationship, both partners are advised to spend the majority of their time in the Adult role, which is considered the healthiest overall pattern of interaction. But there are times when the Parent-Child pattern may be more appropriate, perhaps when one of the partners is ill and requires tender loving care. Or the couple is on vacation and just needs time to "play" and de-stress. In this latter case, the Child-Child interaction pattern may be the best. Healthy loving relationships are characterized both by the preponderance of Adult-Adult transactions, and by the flexibility to switch transactional modes when appropriate.

Another important issue in communication patterns is that of "selective attention," also sometimes called "filtering." These basically are fancy terms for "not listening" or "hearing only what you want to hear." One does not need to have a post-graduate degree in counseling or clinical psychology to figure out that this is also very frustrating for the partners and unhealthy for relationships.

What is so interesting about selective attention from a psychological perspective is its paradoxical nature. By filtering out what they don't want to hear, people simultaneously all but eliminate their opportunity to communicate what they want the other person to hear. Communication is a two-way affair. As anyone who has had a bad cellular phone connection can verify, if even one side of the line is garbled, the conversation cannot proceed. We, your authors, are reminded of the central message of the recent film *Babel:* If You Want to be Heard – Listen. To wit, in Bill Emener's last session with Alice and Mark, a couple he had seen for four sessions, Alice looked deep into her husband's eyes and softly said, "Over the past two weeks, I have felt so loved by you, Mark. And the most powerful way you have told me you love me has been when you listened to me."

Patterns are Like Addictions. The brain's cortex – the part of the brain that learns to recognize all that we know – may be thought of as the greatest pattern recognition system in existence (Hawkins & Blakeslee, 2004). As the neurons of the cortex process the same inputs over and again, time after time, the brain efficiently groups these patters into "chunks" that are assigned to hierarchical cortical neural cell assemblies, and filed away as classes of objects or events (Goldberg, 2002, 2005). Each time the same object or pattern of events is encountered, it is then recognized as just another exemplar of the previously stored pattern. Since the cell assembly representing the pattern can be triggered as a whole, the pattern is recognized efficiently and without much effort. This uncanny ability, yet to be replicated even in the most "artificially intelligent" computing systems, nonetheless, has a downside. When we become accustomed to dealing with these easily recognized patterns, we get "lazy" about taking steps to change them, even when they are unhealthy. We are, in a sense, so facile at handling patterns with a minimum of energy or attention – that is, with so little *effort* – that we will become stuck in and with them. Bill Emener's sessions with Shelly and Rodney, the subject of dialogue 9.2, shows how this principle operates in an actual counseling session.

Dialogue 9.2 Patterns are like Addictions

Sherry (S), a 28-year-old single parent, initially came to see Bill Emener (B) by herself.

B: Okay, Sherry, now that we have gotten to know each other a little, maybe you can tell me what it is that brought you in to see me.

S: In many ways I am feeling incredibly depressed. I am feeling helpless. I have no feeling or sense of what is going on and now I'm almost starting to feel hopeless.

B: In your view, is there anything in particular you are feeling helpless or hopeless about.

S: [With tears welling up] It's Rodney.

B: Rodney.

S: Yes, Rod and I have been dating for a year and a half. And over this period of time…

B: [After listening to Sherry's description of what had been going on with her and Rodney] It seems to me Sherry that a relatively clear pattern has emerged in your relationship with Rodney. You and he would establish some very specific boundaries, guidelines and parameters with regard to your relationship, ones which would allow the two of you to enjoy a meaningful relationship, yet also allow each of you to enjoy individual lives of your own. As time would go on, however, your relationship would seem to become "more and more involved," as you said, and eventually Rodney would end your relationship. Then a week or so later, you would talk and get back together again.

S: Yes, that's what has been happening.

B: Okay. And just before the two of you would break up, did anything in particular happen or was there anything either of you would say that we need to consider?

S: Oh I'm sure there were. All I know is that typically Rodney would say something like, "Sherry, I can no longer go on this way."

Following Sherry discussing it with Bill and then via her invitation, Rodney (R) came with her to her next counseling session.

S: [Looking at Rodney] Whenever we break up, Rod, you say to me, "This is driving me crazy – I can no longer go on this way." Could you tell me specifically what it is that drives you crazy?

R: [After some introspection] Sure. You and I will agree as to what we will and will not do. For example, I will plan to play golf on Saturday mornings and play softball one or two nights a week. I also will plan to spend most of Sunday evenings preparing for my upcoming week at work. You not only will agree to this, but you also will plan to play tennis one night a week and go shopping during one of the days on the weekend with one of your girlfriends. But then, over the next four-to-five weeks, it will seem to me as though I had been spending almost every night and every day with you! Either you would tell me that you needed to talk to me because you were upset about something or you were catching a cold. It's always something! You would leave messages asking me to return a call immediately, or you would have already made plans for us to go away for the weekend even though you knew I enjoyed playing golf. Somehow, Sherry, I can never seem to give you enough time. I try to tell you that, but you don't listen to me. The only way I can get my own life back is to tell you I do not want to see you anymore.

S: [Beginning to cry and murmuring] I don't know why I do that.

R: [Toward the end of the session, gently speaking] Sherry, I love you very much. More than anything else in the world, I want to share my life with you. What you seem to need, however, is for me to give my life to you. And I will not do that.

Over the next two months, Sherry and Bill had a number of sessions during which they took in-depth looks at her fear of abandonment, her low self-esteem and her low sense of self-worth. As she was able to identify some of her own addictive needs for love and affection from Rodney, as well as her ill-founded fear of Rodney not loving her anymore, she was able to relate to Rodney without putting high demands on him for constant attention and affection.

S: [During her last session] Until I started working with you and identifying why I was the way I was, my love for Rodney was like an addiction. I never seemed to be able to get enough time with him. I am not out of the woods yet, but it sure as hell is getting better. He is such a wonderful man. And as I continue to become a stronger and healthier person, I will enjoy my relationship with him so much more. I feel so grateful!

B: You're very kind, Sherry – I appreciate your gracious comments. Nonetheless, remember: it was you who did the work – you read that self-help book I recommended to you and took the risk of looking at yourself – looking deep within yourself – and taking on the truth about yourself.

S: [Smiling, purposefully slurring her tongue-in-cheek words and raising her hand in Bill's direction] I'll drink to that.

B: [Smiling and raising his hand in return, they hi-fived.]

Nature is full of trade-offs. Having evolved the ability to recognize and process complex patterns without awareness, we can become trapped by them. As a relationship counselor, this example offers you a powerful strategy for breaking the logjams that can undermine a relationship even when both partners have the best intentions.

Paradigm Shifts: A Place to Start. Bill Emener made similar use of this wisdom when counseling Barry, a 45-year-old attorney who came to see him because he was having difficulties in his relationship with his girlfriend, Gladys. Part of the reason why he remembers this client so well is because Barry is a very engaging man who commands attention immediately – the fact that he is 6'10" and weighs close to 300 pounds certainly accounts for much of this. Barry had been married for 20 years and had three children. Since his divorce, approximately three years prior to coming to see Bill, he had not dated very much – until he met Gladys, a single parent with two children. Gladys had many of the same characteristics of his first wife, "Except that Gladys is so much more loving toward me," he said. When asked if there was anything that he was afraid of, Barry said, "I am afraid that if I eventually marry Gladys, I would fall back into the same old pattern and routine I had with my 20-year marriage."

It is important to note that Barry indicated that on a number of occasions, Gladys would say to him, "Barry, I just wish you would pay more attention to yourself." This was very perplexing for Barry. As time went on, however, Barry and Bill were able to discover his old paradigm – that is, his old pattern of dealing with the people in his life. His old pattern was: "First comes my wife, then come my children, then come my parents, and then comes me. After I take care of everyone else, then I will take care of me." As this pattern was explored, he actually did express some resentment and distaste for that way of dealing with people. Bill suggested to Barry that it might be helpful for him to consider a new paradigm – that is, a new hierarchy of importance in terms of what and whom he would pay attention to in his life.

Once Barry was able to overcome his codependent need to take care of everyone else in his life before attending to his own needs, he was able to form a new pattern of dealing with the people in his life. Nonetheless, it was not easy for Barry to operationalize or put into practice his new paradigm. For example, his children would become very frustrated and angry with him when he would say to them, "I'm sorry, but I have been planning to play in this golf tournament for over a month. I regret I will not be able to go to your ball games today, but I need to do this for me. I hope you understand." Over time, however, Barry mentioned that his children were beginning to understand and accept his taking care of himself as well as lovingly attending to all of the other important people in his life. To her credit, Gladys was not threatened by Barry's new paradigm either. The most important thing was that Barry was feeling much better about himself, his life, his children, his parents, and especially his relationship with Gladys.

Relationship Patterns. Given the combination of experimental data, theoretical approaches and real-life stories we have presented so far in this section, the professional couples counselor may be wondering if there is a way to summarize or condense all this information. How does one look for and recognize such pattern-related phenomena in their own clients?

To answer this very reasonable question, we return to the five questions addressed at the beginning of the section with regard to patterns and trends in loving relationships.

1) *How do they affect the couple's life?* Knowledge is power and, for many therapists, merely knowing that patterns and trends in life and relationships are not only natural and expected, but unavoidable and necessary, may be enough to help recognize them. Part of our job is to educate our clients as well as to help them "fix" their problems. Therefore, when thinking about the patterns of your client's life and relationships, have them ask: "Is there really a problem here, or am I making one up because it is unfamiliar and therefore scary?" A second question is about trend: "Is there a noticeable negative trend in my life or relationship that truly concerns me, or am I merely afraid of any type of change?" Most clients answer these questions just by giving them a little thought. If a person is relatively happy overall but fears the unknown, then he or she probably doesn't need to be too concerned. If one either can't answer the question or the answer is "Yes, this pattern or trend is a real problem," then it may be time to intervene and help the client break the maladaptive behavior that underlies the pattern or trend.

2) *How do they affect the relationship?* This is closely tied to the previous question, except that you may want your client to focus more on trends than on patterns. Our

advice is straightforward: If you sense a persistent negative trend or downward spiral in your client's relationship, you should strongly consider some type of intervention.

3) *Does either partner want to change anything about them?* Again, our advice is to ask them to think about change over long periods of time. Are the patterns just another annoyance they can live with or do the patterns cause disturbance to the point that action is warranted? Also, help them look for recurring self-defeating and self-destructive patterns that form trend lines. Reviewing Bill Emener's case examples in this chapter to see if any match your own circumstances may be a good place to start.

4) *Is the couple's "network" ready to, or capable of, accepting the change?* It is not hard to judge client resistance to change. Defensiveness, blaming, criticizing their partner, or otherwise stonewalling in therapy are all excellent sources of evidence that one or both of your clients are "addicted" to their pattern. Sometimes, merely pointing out the behavior is enough to break the logjam. At other times, clients may benefit from being told that the power to resolve their issues lies with them, but they must take responsibility for accepting the need to change and getting on with it. Finally, some clients are so attached to their dysfunction that there will be little that can be done at the present time, because "the network is simply not ready."

5) *If the couple is ready to, and does make changes, what differences would the changes make?* This is where your training as a therapist, and the advice we offer throughout this book, can help you. A good piece of advice is: keep reading! But do not forget the very first piece of advice offered in the section about staying in the now: No person can rationally expect to be happy 100% of the time. If that's what your clients want, then you need to remind them they just are not looking at life rationally.

The Relationship Paradox. We end the chapter with one final case from Bill Emener's practice. Allie, a 27-year-old high school math teacher, was increasingly frustrated with her relationships with men. "Why do they always try to control me?" she asked. As they discussed the men in her life, Allie shared with Bill that her father, a career military officer, was very controlling of everyone in her family. Furthermore, her high school boyfriend, her fiancé in college, her first husband and her current boyfriend, "all tended to be very controlling." Allie not only resented them for being so manipulative and controlling, but she also indicated that she resented them "because basically they were so insecure." After reading a self-help book that Bill had recommended to her, she said, "This is an interesting paradox, Dr. Emener. I resent the controlling men in my life not only because they're controlling, but also because they are so terribly insecure. The paradox, however, is that I am initially attracted to them because they are controlling and I am basically insecure. Maybe I just need to learn to be a controlling person?"

"Well Allie, that would be an option," said Bill. "However, maybe we ought to put that off for a while and begin by identifying some ways by which you can take more control of your own life." Over the next six-months, Allie engaged in some heightened, detailed planning of her day-to-day and week-to-week activities. She identified those things she enjoyed and wanted to do in her life and made sure she was able to do them. By doing so, she was exercising more control over her own life. Interestingly enough, her boyfriend didn't like that and eventually broke-off their relationship. Allie said with a smile, "Now that I am exercising more control over my own life, I seem to find myself less attracted to controlling men, and controlling men seem to be less attracted to me. That's wonderful!"

Bill had not seen or heard from Allie for about a year when he received a little note from her. The end of the note read, "Someday I would like you to meet my new boyfriend, Jonathan, if that would be possible. He doesn't try to control me and I do not try to control him. We each control our own lives and jointly engage in some controls so that we can enjoy our relationship together. I am so happy! Hugs, Allie."

Sometimes we exercise the most control over our own lives and those of our partners by consciously choosing not to control them. Sometimes it is necessary for all of us simply to get out of our own way and instead flow along with the patterns and trends that carry us through our lives.

CHAPTER SUMMARY

This chapter focused on three areas of outside factors that impact a couple more or less equally – those that primarily affect the dyad itself: (1) *Monetary and Equity Issues,* with a focus on the role that economic forces can exert on a loving relationship; (2) *Time and Timing* and how such matters can be sources of troubling issues for couples and pose vexing challenges for their counselors; and (3) *Patterns and Trends*, with a focus on some of the ways in which they can have detrimental effects on loving relationships. These three areas – money, time and trends – are three of the most significant variables that determine the success versus failure of relationships. Assisting your clients in dealing with them ranks as among your most challenging jobs as a couples counselor. We trust that the insights we offer based on our experiences with these concerns have helped make your job not only manageable, but as we posited: more efficient, more effective and ultimately more deeply rewarding.

> With money you can buy a house, but not a home.
> With money you can buy a clock, but not time.
> With money you can buy a bed, but not sleep.
> With money you can buy a book, but not knowledge.
> With money you can see a doctor, but not good health.
> With money you can buy a position, but not respect.
> With money you can buy blood, but not life.
> With money you can buy sex, but not love.
>   Chinese Proverb

CHAPTER 9 DISCUSSION QUESTIONS

1) In addition to what money can buy for a couple, in what other ways is money an important variable in a loving relationship?
2) How can inequity be a troubling phenomenon in a loving relationship – for the individual partners as well as their relationship?
3) Why is time such an important aspect of an individual's life as well as in a loving relationship?
4) What are some specific things you could do as a counselor to assist a couple with their timing issues?

5) When you see a pattern in a couple's relationship, what are some things you can do to help them not only see the pattern but also appreciate it?

6) As a counselor, why is it important for you to assist individuals and couples in learning how to recognize trends in their individual lives and in their loving relationships?

Chapter 10

WHEN THE INDIVIDUAL IMPACTS THE RELATIONSHIP

No one enters a relationship without bringing along his or her history. Even at the time of childbirth, the neonate has been shaped by the mother's uterine environment since the moment of conception. This history will impact how the newborn first reacts to the world in which it finds itself and will be an important determinant of how the baby bonds with its parents or caregivers.

In the case of adult loving relationships, the history of the individual is millions of times more complex. There have been innumerable interactions with others, ranging from the sublime to the terrifying, with most falling somewhere in between. By the time we are ready to consider ourselves adults, our social life and the history around which it has developed will have been shaped by thousands of other people. The number of associations a single individual will have formed between their responses to these interactions, the other individuals involved and the environments in which they occurred, is too large to imagine. Of course, these associations are brought forward into every new interaction and, more importantly, from the couples therapist's point of view, into each loving relationship. This history and all that comes with it is a part of both the "baggage" and the value people carry with them into each of their relationships.

As if this were not complicated enough, history is not the only determinant of either the so-called baggage or the person's perceived worth as a partner, there is also an entire human genome to consider. Social scientists have studied and confirmed what common sense and experience dictates must be true about people: we are all born as unique individuals, each as genetically different from one another as two snowflakes. Longitudinal studies have shown that certain aspects of personality, such as individual temperament or resilience in the face of adversity, seem to be less a product of our experience and carry a heavy weighting by our genetic endowment.[3]

---

[3] Even so, it seems that scientists have placed undue weight on genes. For example, monozygotic, or genetically identical, twins will have had different genes *expressed* by so-called *epigenetic* factors, both before and, especially after, birth that make these twins quite "un-identical." Recent reviews such as Bruce Lipton's delightful book *The Biology of Belief* (2005) show how genes must be viewed as elements of potential rather than determinants of biology, i.e. more as "blueprints for construction" than as inescapable forces of development.

Each and every individual brings with her or him, into every human relationship, a web of entanglements with both the past and his or her biology that make him or her truly unlike any other. This "singularity of personhood" will then interact with another human agent, equally as different from all others who ever have existed, to create a new loving relationship which, it goes without saying, will also be one-of-a-kind in the universe. Finally, when these people decide they require or might benefit from professional help in managing this relationship, their problems and issues become yours, the professional couples counselor, one hour at a time.

This chapter focuses on the issues we tend to associate with a given individual in a relationship, rather than with their joint interactions (their "dance") or with the context of the world in which their relationship unfolds. You, as a professional counselor, will be tasked with helping the couple to understand and manage their individual uniqueness as it contributes to their relationship difficulties. As Dr. Scott Johnson pointedly stated, "... all good family and couple therapists, whether working with individuals, partners or spouses, families or other constellations, organize their thinking around how clients' relationships impact their problems" (Johnson, 2009, p. 128). Thus in this chapter we look at the roles played by individual characteristics such as guilt and shame from past experiences or relationships, with fears, phobias and anxiety that block the relationship from progressing in its development, and other blocks to healthy functioning including depression, grief and anger. We conclude the chapter with a brief look at substance abuse, which we view as a symptom of other problems rather than a primary issue, including suggestions for referring individuals and couples with such problems to other qualified specialists who have the requisite training and experience to address such issues.

Now that we have set the scene, we trust you are ready to continue on in this part of the journey into couples counseling – namely, *what to do when the individual impacts the couple*.

GUILT AND SHAME

"In some crazy way I sort of feel guilty about the way she and I treated each other. We were forever putting each other down. In some respects, that was the only way I could keep her off my back. But you know, I would go to our national headquarters and present a proposal for a multimillion-dollar deal and be wined and dined by the brass for doing such an excellent job, but during the ride from the airport to the house I would feel it coming on. By the time I got home, I would feel small, inferior, incompetent and worthless. And usually her opening remarks would be reminders of what I hadn't done around the house before leaving for the business trip and what a hardship it caused her and the kids. 'What kind of man are you?' she would always ask me, and then add, 'What's wrong with you anyway?' I just couldn't take it anymore!"

What's being expressed here? Guilt? If so, what kind of guilt? Shame? If so, what kind of shame? Is this man feeling ashamed and sensing "Whatever I do, it's not good enough because there's probably something fundamentally wrong with me"? Yes, he is verbalizing the experience of toxic shame in a shame-based relationship. On top of that, he is also feeling guilt because of the way he treated his wife, even though he offers it as having been his only defense against her shaming.

If this scenario seems familiar when counseling couples, then we suggest you pay close attention to the material in this section. As we shall see, guilt and shame are truly powerful emotions that add little if any value to loving relationships. At best they represent unresolved feelings or experiences from a person's past, and at worst they are intentional (although in many cases subconscious) choices of behavior meant to get what one person wants in the relationship by preying on the weakness of their partner. The only difference in these two extremes is the degree to which the experience of the emotion is unhealthy and manipulative.

In the form of Rational Emotive Behavioral Therapy known as REBT, developed by Albert Ellis and practiced daily in Bill Lambos' professional practice, guilt is considered one of the "four blocks to happiness" (the other three being anger, anxiety and depression). According to the REBT approach, guilt is the result of two co-occurring beliefs, at least one of which is irrational. The first belief is: *I did something wrong.* The second belief – the one responsible for the guilt – is: *I shouldn't have done it.* Since, as Dr. Ellis was fond of pointing out, "We are all fallible human beings; we all make mistakes," it is entirely possible (but by no means assured) that a person who experiences guilt or shame did in fact do something he or she regrets. If the person actually made a mistake, this first belief may not be irrational. But the second belief – that they *should not* have done so – cannot be considered rational.

Why not? *Because they already did it!* Demanding that reality be different is not only irrational but also self-defeating and hence toxic. Harboring the impossible demand that what was done cannot, and indeed *must not*, have occurred, simply adds a second (and often worse) problem to the first one. And because such individuals are blaming themselves for being at fault, instead of taking responsibility for their mistake and looking at how to make it better and move forward, their guilt now has become shame, and hence the toxic shame. They have fallen into the self-defeating pattern of self-berating and self-blame and are in worse shape than they would otherwise be.

Guilt and Existential Guilt. It is not uncommon for people to find themselves between a rock and a hard place – simultaneously feeling that what they *have done, are doing*, or *will do*, will result in something that is or would be (1) harmful to someone else, *and* (2) harmful to themselves. Recognizing the situation that you are in and continuing to make progress toward resolution is very important.

What, then, is the advice for the "guilty?" Bill Lambos tells his clients about *unconditional self-acceptance*, the necessity of learning to accept oneself as a fallible human being, and reframing the irrational belief that a person is defined by their actions. Fittingly, it is important for you to counsel your clients: (1) to consider their options; (2) to make the best choices available about both their past and future decisions; and (3) to accept the situation that results from having done so.

Dialogue 10.1 demonstrates this in a compelling example from one of Bill Emener's files. And as Eli later said, "Resolving my conflict was extremely difficult. However, I will be the first to tell you that continuing to live in the conflict was even worse!"

Dialogue 10.1 Guilt and Existential Guilt.

The following dialogue is from the first two counseling sessions Bill Emener (**B**) had with Eli (**E**), an artist with a local graphics company who had been married to Donna for 12 years; they had three children, ages 6, 9 and 10.

During their first session:

E: I just can't seem to overcome my constant nervousness and depression. It seems like it's been this way for over a year. I think I really need help in taking a serious look at my life.

B: It sounds like you're really concerned about your nervousness and depression that's been going on for a long time.

E: Yes, it sure has.

B: Is there anything in particular you believe is associated with or pertinent to your nervousness and depression?

E: I'm sure it's my marriage.

B: (After putting his pen down and relaxing back into his chair) Okay. How about if you just tell me your story. What is it about your marriage that you would like me to know?

E: (With a thin smile) It's a long story.

B: I'm not going anywhere. Take your time – I'm listening.

E: (After a deep breath and relaxing sigh) For the first couple of years of our marriage, everything seemed to be really good for us. That's when we were living in Minnesota. However, we moved down here to Florida about seven years ago, and starting about five years ago our marriage just continued to get worse and worse. We just drifted further and further apart. Being very candid with you, I basically just do not love Donna anymore. Over the last two years, we have gone on numerous trips, cruises and weekend getaways. I have tried everything I could think of to rekindle my love for her – but none of it has worked. Donna is a nice person. She is one of the most wonderful people you would ever want to know. The problem is, I do not feel in love with her anymore. I know, however, that she is incredibly in love with me. She tells me she loves me and acts like she loves me every minute of every day. At the same time, I am very close to my three children. I love them dearly and certainly do enjoy spending time with them. *As a family unit*, the five of us are very, very happy. Every once in a while I think about leaving and divorcing her. I get a real warm glow with the thought of being free. The problem then is that I feel so terribly, terribly guilty! She has never done anything to hurt me, she has always loved me, and by every standard I know of, she has been and continues to be an excellent wife. The idea of leaving her and the children just terrifies me – the guilt is incredible. On the other hand, I also feel bad because I'm not doing what I need to do to take care of me. I am still a young man – I'm only 33 years old. The idea of spending the next 30 to 40 years in the same situation that I'm in now is very depressing. The bottom line, Dr. Emener, is that I feel like I am between a rock and a hard place. I don't know what to do.

B: It almost sounds like the proverbial prisoner's dilemma.

E: Yes, in many ways that's the way I feel – damned if I do and damned if I don't.

B: Like being pulled in both directions simultaneously. But let me give you something to think about. Guilt, rather simplistically defined, is when we feel bad because of something we have done, something we are doing, or something we are thinking about doing. And although you feel that you have a very functional and happy *family*, you are simultaneously experiencing a dysfunctional and very unhappy *marriage*. When you think about leaving Donna and the children, you know it would cause great emotional pain for them, and thus you feel horribly guilty. At the same time, however, you are also experiencing what I refer to as "existential guilt" – that is, the guilt we feel when we sense that we have hurt, are hurting, or might hurt *ourselves*. Essentially, guilt is when we feel we have caused a transgression against someone else – existential guilt is when we feel that we have caused a transgression against ourselves. In a nutshell, you're feeling guilty either way. Either you are feeling guilty because you are thinking about leaving Donna, or you are feeling guilty about staying with Donna.

E: (With tears welling up) Yes, that's exactly it.

B: (Light-heartedly and with a warm smile) When I lecture on this in my classes at the university, I tongue-in-cheek refer to it as "Guilt 22."

E: That's good – that's exactly what I am feeling. (He then started crying.)

During their second session:

E: I've been doing a lot of thinking over the past two weeks, and I think I've made a decision.

B: I sense that you feel good about having made a decision – a tentative one at least – yet I'd bet that it wasn't easy for you.

E: You got that right.

B: Okay. Talk to me – I'm listening.

E: Well, Doc, there's good news and bad news. The bad news is that I identified another source of guilt that was bothering me. The good news is that the same source of guilt motivated me to make a decision and take action. What I mean is that I was feeling guilty about allowing Donna to continue to be in love with me, to think that I was in love with her, and to think that our marriage would last. That simply was not true. Allowing her to continue to think what she was thinking felt dishonest and very uncomfortable for me. It just didn't seem fair. I also recognized that she is also a young person. She is only 32-years old. Part of my decision included the thought that the sooner I tell her the truth and get on with a divorce, the sooner she would be able to get on with a real life of her own.

Eli also shared with Bill that he had made arrangements for Donna to have an opportunity to talk with a psychologist or a counselor herself, just in case his telling her that he wanted a divorce would be overly disturbing to her. Interestingly, in a subsequent session Eli added, "She handled it much better than I ever anticipated."

The last time Bill spoke with him, Eli indicated that he was doing very well and that Donna was relatively on her road to recovery. "I hope that what I foresee is true – " Eli further said, "that Donna will not only get on with her life but possibly even be happier than when she was married to me."

Healthy Shame and Toxic Shame. As we repeatedly have stated: human beings are not perfect. At some point it becomes necessary to realize that people, as human beings, are not able to do everything to perfection – one cannot be all things to all people. People have limitations and are often forced to choose "the lesser of two evils." Healthy people accept their limitations and imperfections as parts of their natural make-up. When talking to a client who was a sports enthusiast, Bill Emener reminded him about Broadway Joe Namath, one of football's greatest quarterbacks, who told millions of listeners during an interview that he was quitting broadcasting football games because he simply was not good at it. His deep sense of disappointment came clearly through in his words and expressions. This, however, was *healthy shame* – he was totally accepting and appreciative of his many accomplishments (as a football player), yet also accepting and appreciative of his limitations (as a television broadcaster). More recently, Michael Jordan, one of the best basketball players in the history of the game, decided to quit professional basketball and play professional baseball. During an interview, Jordan said that if the day ever came when he would not only feel like a failure but that there was no more reason to expect improvement, he would quit playing baseball and get on with his life. Again, this is an example of healthy shame – an awareness and acceptance of one's limitations as a human being. In situations such as this, healthy shame is the emotion that signals our limitations.

Toxic shame, on the other hand, is an all-pervasive sense that "I am flawed and defective as a human being." It is a basic, core identity, and fundamentally irrational and damaging to the self. With toxic shame come feelings of worthlessness, failure as a person and a detachment of self from self: "I can't identify with myself because I am flawed, I am bad, and there's something fundamentally wrong with me." Thus, the person with healthy shame might say, "I lost the game" or "I got drunk last night;" and the person with toxic shame would say, "I am a loser" or "I am a drunk." This concept is illustrated in Figure 10.1.

Figure 10.1. Guilt versus Toxic Shame.

There is a quick and foolproof test of whether any shame your client may be reporting to you is healthy or toxic. It was alluded to earlier in the chapter. Because toxic shame always involves *blame* of oneself or others, we recommend that whenever you sense any type of regret on behalf of a client (which is, after all, a form of shame), immediately look to see if he or she is blaming himself, herself or another person for his or her feelings. If he or she is, then it's a good bet that their shame is toxic. If, on the other hand, your client is unconcerned with who is to blame and is focused on how to make the situation better – including acknowledging his or her own role in it – chances are that your client's shame is healthy. Simply stated, *blame of self or others is a root cause of toxic shame*. It does not accomplish anything positive for anybody. The better able people are to avoid the "blame game," the more psychologically healthy they will be.

To see how quickly toxic shame can erode a relationship, we refer you to a case from Bill Lambos practice during his Internship at the Rational Living Foundation in Tampa. This is presented in Dialogue 10.2.

Dialogue 10.2 Healthy Shame and Toxic Shame.

Guilt and toxic shame can erode a loving relationship very quickly. Jerome (**J**) and Lindsey (**L**) came to see Bill Lambos (**B**) because they were experiencing increasing conflict in their marital relationship. Having just returned from New York City on vacation, they described a Friday evening they spent at the Albert Ellis Institute where they sat in on one of Dr. Ellis's famous Friday night seminars on REBT – complete with a demonstration involving audience members with real problems. Impressed that REBT might offer a solution to their own relationship difficulties, they came to the Rational Living Foundation in Tampa for counseling.

Jerome, an accomplished jazz-rock guitarist with lots of studio work on his résumé and a band that had regular bookings but had yet to make a breakthrough, began.

J: Dr. Lambos, I love Lindsey and I love my work. Unfortunately, I haven't made it yet in the music business because when I proposed to Lindsey she said she didn't want to move away from Tampa. I promised Lindsey that this was where we would live, and so we married. The problem is, in the music business, there are very few opportunities in Tampa for anything but local gigs in bars. As you might imagine, I don't make much money from the band, even working other day jobs and giving lessons.

L: We've been married three years and we've been happy, but I feel strongly that it's time to start a family. We can't do that on what Jerome makes, and even if I keep working afterwards, it will be tough. I know Jerome loves his music, but he's also great with computers and he's been offered a job with a media company in town. If he took it, it would solve everything! But he doesn't want to take it because he would have to start on evening shifts and that would mean giving up the band. I am getting less and less patient, yet every time I bring it up, he says all it does is make him feel inadequate. Then he tells me I'm being selfish; then *I* start to feel guilty. We agreed when we married that we both wanted children, and now is the time. It seems like all we do now is accuse each other of who is at fault for our recurring arguments, and I can't live like this much longer.

B: As a former failed musician myself, I feel for you both. Let me start by advising you that you have two separate problems, and I can only help you with one of them. (Jerome and Lindsey looked up quizzically.) You have a marriage that is itself healthy, but you have developed conflicting goals, or at least goals that can't both be met at the same time. I am happy to help you work through the possibilities and come to some type of compromise or agreement, but as your therapist I am more concerned about your *other* problem: the blame, shame and guilt you both are experiencing. I can tell you that until you fix this second problem, the first will never be successfully addressed. No matter what you decide, one of you will feel like they gave up something near and dear and blame the other for it. My bet is that then the other party will feel guilty about it. This blaming and guilt very well may destroy your marriage. On the other hand, if we can fix these emotional issues, the solution to the first problem may be much easier to figure out.

Over the next six sessions, Jerome and Lindsey learned about irrational beliefs, about the danger and uselessness of blaming, and about how much of the problem they thought they had actually was based on their irrational beliefs. By *re-framing* their perspectives, giving up blame, and focusing on a solution that met both their needs, they were able to work out their issues. Jerome gave up the band and took the computer job. Lindsey was soon pregnant and delighted. With some of the extra income from Jerome's job, he was able to purchase a digital music studio and continue to compose and play. Bill ran across Jerome at an Apple Store a few months ago. He has several "indie" singles available on the Internet, is gaining recognition as a guitarist and songwriter, and even likes his computer job. Finally, he beamed with pride when he introduced Bill to his new son, Sean. "Life is good when you let it be" was Jerome's parting comment.

Guilt-Based and Shame-Based Relationships. As mentioned previously, guilt and shame become especially pernicious to relationships when they are used – consciously or otherwise – as manipulative strategies to get one's way at the expense of the other party. For example, when Bill Emener was talking with a client, Eduardo, about his relationship with his wife, he said that she "continually got away with doing whatever she wanted to do and that he simply would never argue with her or deny her anything she wanted." Not surprisingly, he came to resent this manipulation and her "always getting her own way."

Moreover, the combination of his and her interpersonal dynamics was starting to seriously interfere with their relationship and their family. Further exploration of their relationship revealed a skeleton in their closet that explained how their interaction got to this point. Some years prior, as it turned out, Eduardo had made a poor decision and had a brief sexual encounter with another woman. Try as he might, he could not live with the guilt of his action and admitted what happened to his wife, who, as he explained, "…went berserk." Although he swore it would never happen again (and it had not), his wife learned to use his guilt over the incident as a club to get what she wanted. In fact, she felt justified in doing so. Their entire relationship had become based on guilt. Such relationships are inherently unhealthy and doomed to fail if not corrected.

It is important for individuals in loving relationships to understand the difference between guilt and shame, and the critical role played by the destructive act of blaming oneself or one's partner. Thus, when counseling a couple that has developed a guilt-based relationship, it is vital for the counselor to remember that there are two critical dimensions of guilt and shame: (1) *rational versus irrational guilt* (based on blaming versus accepting and fixing); and (2) *healthy versus toxic shame* (based on mistaking our actions or behaviors for who we are at our cores). Learning to manage each of these "semantic errors," people can solve many of their worst problems by self-monitoring and catching themselves when they fall into these traps. In healthy relationships where blaming is seen as unacceptable, both individuals tend to feel highly respected, valued and honored by themselves as well as each other. As we frequently have said to our clients:

> *Guilt* is basically when we feel bad because of *failure of doing*. We feel bad because of something we did. When we are feeling guilty, we tend to focus on our transgressions – things we did that were wrong. Moreover, when we are experiencing guilt we tend to fear punishment. On the other hand, when we are experiencing *shame*, we feel bad because of a *failure of being* – like, "There's something wrong with me as a human being." When we are experiencing shame, we tend to *focus on our shortcomings and fear of abandonment.*

FEARS AND PHOBIAS

"I have wanted to leave Harold for a long time. I thought about divorcing him seven or eight years ago. I know what to do and probably could do it rather easily. I'd probably be good at it too. I know it would be the best thing for me. Probably would be the best thing for him too. I have even spoken to an attorney once. But I've been a married woman for the past 23 years, now I'm 44 years old and the thought of being single scares the hell out of me."

"For a long time now, I have known that I want to ask Jennifer to marry me. I love her so much. I know she loves me. I'm convinced that we would make a great couple. We have a super relationship. It's simply been great these past three years! I know we would have a tremendous marriage. Children, family, the whole nine yards. Of course I know what to do. I know how to ask her to marry me, how to plan a wedding and all that stuff. I guess I'm just scared. About six years ago I had the same experience with Diane, and four years ago I had the same experience with Lynn."

It is not unusual to hear clients make statements like these. In the course of your own life, you may have felt or expressed similar statements yourself. Many individuals experience having personal fears and phobias associated with difficulties in their loving relationships.

Fear is a painful emotion, a deep sense of fright and an overall feeling of anxiousness associated with *a specific event*, current or anticipated. A *phobia* is an irrational, persistent and recurring fear associated with *a particular type of event* or set of events. This would suggest that the woman making the first italicized statement is expressing a fear (a fear of being alone after a divorce), and the man making the second one is expressing a phobia (a fear of committing himself to another person).

As we discussed in earlier chapters, fear is among the most powerful and primitive emotions. Fear is present in some form or another at nearly every level of the evolutionary ladder in the animal kingdom, from the simplest to the most complex of species. For eons, fear has served individual animals and people greatly to enhance their survival, and no individual creature could be expected to live very long without the capacity to experience fear. On the other hand, fear is somewhat of a blunt instrument. When fears become disconnected from reality, they can dominate behavior and lead to making poor choices and decisions, even when the rational mind "knows better." Finally, when fears generalize to entire situations or sets of events – and become phobias – they are quite counterproductive. In such cases fear may greatly interfere with one's life and especially one's relationships with others.

The following identifies, discusses and illustrates some of the common ways by which peoples' fears and phobias can be critical aspects of their loving relationships. Specifically, we will look at the relationship between fear and anxiety, and review cases from our files in which the clients' issues concerned fear of change (or the unknown), growing up, abandonment and intimacy, as well as commitment issues.

Fear and Anxiety. Fear is closely related to anxiety, which, as mentioned previously, we consider to be one of the four central "blocks to happiness." (The other three are *anger*, *depression* and *guilt*.) Like guilt, fear and its less salient cousin, anxiety, are based on two beliefs, only one of which may be rational or real. The first belief is that "I am in danger," or "Something bad is going to happen." This belief may or may not be realistic depending on the individual's circumstances. The second belief, which is nearly always irrational, is along the line of, "I *couldn't stand it* if that happened." We call this second belief "catastrophizing" – elevating one's fear to the level of impending and certain doom. To catastrophize is to harbor an irrational belief because, in all likelihood, you *could* in fact stand it if it happened. While you might not like it very much and in all probability greatly prefer that things be different, you could sensibly plan ways to avoid or fix the situation. But unless it led to death, it would not be the end of your client (or you).

When people catastrophize, they act as if the consequences of seeing their fears realized are unthinkable, that it would be disastrous if this or that outcome occurred. In this case, *the fear of the anticipated event becomes worse than the actuality of the event itself*, and in most instances our client's lives become unmanageable. It is therefore not surprising that clients become unable to manage their personal lives, and especially their loving relationships, when fear rears its ugly head.

Fear of Change or the Unknown. Among many other things, the possibility of change can cause fear in and of itself. The phrase "living within one's comfort zone" has made its way into the popular literature to describe the feelings of security and safety associated with that which is familiar and routine (Lerner, 1995). In Chapter 9, we described the brain's propensity for "routinization," or linking complex experiences or activities into single neural templates and, in so doing, making them automatic and largely unconscious for recognition or action (Hawkins, 2004). We did not, however, mention a side benefit of such so-called automaticity: in addition to freeing up scarce and valuable neocortical resources and thus allowing them to be used in dealing with novel situations or to attend to complex new stimuli, routinization also allows the brain to bypass the amygdala – its fear center – when dealing with the familiar. Therefore, the nervous system is predisposed to *dissociate* the familiar with the fearful. Thus our brains, and those of our clients, are mostly free from fear when dealing with the familiar, and this makes sense. This does not, however, imply the converse to be true: There is no *a priori* reason for that which is novel to be associated with fear. Nevertheless, people often adopt this logical fallacy and, in so doing, it becomes a cognitive distortion or irrational belief (Beck, 1976; Ellis, 2000).

Many times in our clinical experience, we have observed that when people fear change they will subconsciously sabotage progress on behalf of themselves or their loved ones simply to avoid the fear associated with imminent or anticipated change. For example, Bill Emener recalls working with Louis and Althea for the original purpose of helping Louis, who was in early recovery from alcoholism. As time went on, it became evident that on a subconscious level, Althea was actually trying to sabotage Louis' recovery "because she knew how to deal with Louis when he was drinking, but was afraid of what might happen if he ever continued to be sober."

Likewise, Bill Lambos worked with Christina, a lady who had embarked on a regimen of regular exercise to reduce her high blood pressure. One of the consequences of her exercise program was that she lost weight and toned up to the point where she began to look at herself differently. Nonetheless, she expressed concern that her boyfriend, Donald, started buying high-calorie desserts on a regular basis, for which Christina had a considerable weakness. "It's like Donald wants me not to get better. How could he be so inconsiderate?" Bill suggested that Donald possibly was fearful that if she became more attractive, she would lose her interest in him. As it turned out, Donald had been in a comfort zone with respect to their relationship and had grave, groundless fears that Christina's feelings for him would change along with the change in her body. After several sessions, seeing both of them together, Donald was able to overcome his anxiety, and their relationship once again became stable.

Many of our clients have said to us, in effect, "I do not necessarily like my loved one the way he or she is, but at least I can trust and predict what will happen." Fear of change, and of the unknown that it implies, indeed can be a controlling, manipulative and destructive aspect of a loving relationship.

Fear of Growing Up (and Out). Dan Kiley (1983) wrote a best-selling pop psychology book, *The Peter Pan Syndrome: Men Who Never Grow Up*. Although it is not a diagnostic category listed in the DSM, such fears can be real and can indeed cause problems in client relationships. An example of this phenomenon can be seen in the following case from Bill Emener's files.

Danny and Pat came to see Bill because they were having many difficulties with their 15-year-old daughter, Kristin. For approximately two years, Kristin had been continuously acting-out in school, getting into trouble and, as Danny and Pat said, "...has been driving us crazy all the time." Bill suggested that the three of them come in for a family counseling session.

During their first session, two very important sets of fears emerged. First, Kristin was struggling with many of the typical types of fears that teenagers struggle with as they are maturing into young adulthood. Nonetheless, she was also fearful that when she would eventually leave home "mom and dad wouldn't make it." Very succinctly and eloquently, Kristin articulated several marital problems that Danny and Pat had been having for a number of years. Secondly, Danny and Pat were fearful of Kristin's emancipation from the family because, as Pat said, "We are not sure we would make it when it is just the two of us." Thus, while Kristin genuinely feared that growing up would translate into marital problems for her mother and father, Danny and Pat were also having similar types of fears. Kristin was afraid of growing up (and out), and her parents were equally fearful of it.

As time went on, it became clear that although Danny and Pat came for help because their daughter was having problems, it was primarily Danny and Pat who were having the problems in the family. Few nonprofessionals realize how common this situation is in family counseling. Often, the family member initially identified as the one with the problem is actually the person *least* in need of assistance! Fittingly, it is not surprising that as Bill continued to work with Danny and Pat on their marital relationship, Kristin was acting-out less, getting into trouble less and enjoying her life so much more. Needless to say, it was extremely difficult for Kristin to be going through life feeling as if she were responsible for "holding mom and dad together."

Fear of Abandonment. Fear of abandonment by a significant other can make the establishment of a meaningful and intimate relationship extremely difficult. Developmental psychologists have studied this phenomenon in great detail for many years under the rubric of "attachment theory" (Bowen, 1988; Bowlby, 1983, 1990). Most of this work was focused on the bond that develops between infants and their caregivers early in life. However, attachment theory was extended to adult loving relationships in the late 1980s, by Cindy Hazan and Phillip Shaver (1987). Their work focused on four styles of attachment they identified in adult relationships: secure, anxious-preoccupied, dismissive-avoidant, and fearful-avoidant. All but the first style are believed to interfere with establishing and maintaining healthy loving relationships.

For example, Angie was a 32-year-old hostess at a local restaurant. During their first session, Angie said to Bill Emener, "For some reason I have always had difficulties really feeling close to, and getting close to, the men in my life. In the last five years, I have had over a dozen boyfriends and was engaged twice." As time went on, some of Angie's fears of abandonment became more evident to her. For example, she said, "I really felt close to my father when I was a freshman in college. Then he divorced my mother and within six months remarried. He moved to California and my contact with him became less and less. During that same period of time, my boyfriend, whom I was hoping to marry, graduated and joined the military. I never saw him again. And, as I have already told you, three years ago my mother died."

Angie's experiences in life "taught her" that "every time I have a close and intimate relationship with someone, they leave me. I am left behind. Alone." This is a nearly perfect example of the type of cognitive distortion to which we referred above. Bill responded, "Given your experiences, Angie, what you are telling me makes sense. And you fear the risk of having another intimate relationship with someone because you know how painful it can be if it doesn't last." As they continued to work on her fear of abandonment, Angie found herself becoming more comfortable with other people – especially those with whom she wanted to enjoy an intimate relationship. Toward the end of one of their sessions, Bill said to Angie, "Isn't it interesting how many times in life those things that we want the most are simultaneously those things that we fear the most." She replied, "That certainly has been true for me. Once you get the thing in life you want the most, you have to constantly live with the fear of losing it."

An individual's fear of abandonment can appear to be very real and gut-wrenching at times. Unfortunately, fear of abandonment can limit or even preclude an individual from having and enjoying loving relationships. Everyone has some level of fear of abandonment – it makes sense to assume that there is always a possibility that our loved one could leave us or die. Nonetheless, when our client's fear of abandonment becomes a dysfunctional aspect of his or her life – that is, it prevents him or her from establishing and maintaining loving relationships – that is when the fear of abandonment has become significantly problematic and should be addressed in therapy.

Fear of Intimacy. Closely related to the fear of abandonment is fear of intimacy. Bill's client Helen demonstrates a good example of this. With tears streaming down her face, she said, "Yes, Dr. Emener, it is true that I have many friends, and many of my friends are men. However, I never can seem to have more than a friendship with a man. I guess maybe it's just my weight?" At that time, Helen was five-foot-four and weighed 230 pounds. As Helen's story unfolded, it was clear that a number of significant events in her lifetime had had continuing effects on her. For example, she had been sexually abused as a child and had been abandoned by a number of men in her life. And, she said, "For a multitude of reasons that I know you understand, I am incredibly afraid of sex and intimacy with a man." Bill told her that her fears were understandable. What Helen discovered, however, was that her weight problem was significantly related to her fear of intimacy. "In many ways, I think I just use my weight as a shield. It's my protection," she concluded. "And I guess as long as I'm this much overweight, I don't have to worry about a man wanting to have sex with me or to have an intimate relationship with me. I guess in some ways this is very comforting. But I don't want to continue to be this way. I have tried numerous diet programs over the last couple of years, but none of them seem to work. I guess that before I try another diet program, it would be a good idea to spend some time focusing on my fear of intimacy."

Fear of intimacy is not easy to overcome; it can be a very dysfunctional component of a client's life and very restrictive and destructive to a loving relationship. As counselors, we need to understand the roles that fear of abandonment and intimacy play in sabotaging relationships. Quite often, such fears are largely imaginary and most individuals are able to quickly benefit from therapy addressing them. Because all people have more control over themselves than they do over others, it is easier to address those problems that people create for themselves. This is an important piece of wisdom we encourage counselors to remind their clients: *When you are your own worst problem, the solution is usually easier than when the problem is out of your control and in the hands of another person.*

Shame-Based Fear. In our discussion of toxic shame in the previous section, we suggested that it is an "all-pervasive sense that I am flawed and defective as a human being," and reflects a fundamental error in confusing one's past choices and behavior with one's continuing sense of self – confusing *what one did* with *who one is.* People who go through life with such toxic shame not only live with many internal struggles, daily discomforts and other assorted problems, but they also tend to experience many difficulties in establishing and maintaining loving relationships.

The subconscious scenario the client experiences goes something like this:

1) I truly believe there is basically something wrong with me, my character and my make-up as a human being;
2) If anyone ever were to know "there is something wrong with me," they would leave me and not want to be close to me; thus,
3) I better be careful and not allow anyone too close because if they find out that I am basically flawed they would back away and leave me.

Simply harboring the irrational belief that one is a rotten or worthless person – the very definition of toxic shame – often will lead one to subconsciously assume others believe the same. It is simply another irrational fear or cognitive distortion. In anticipating further rejection based on this delusion (a fixed false belief), a client may then go on to sabotage any relationship that comes to bring her or him pleasure without conscious awareness of these actions.

Shame-based fear – fear of one's existential or underlying nature – can prevent the establishment and maintenance of a loving relationship. This can be especially true if the other person is healthy and sensitive to the outcome effects of toxic shame-based fears. If your client expresses a need to hide something from his or her loved one, especially if that something is the client themselves the client is likely struggling with toxic shame. And if this is the case, it should go without saying that you should help your client attend to it.

Fear of Ending a Relationship. It is not uncommon for individuals in a loving relationship to find themselves wanting to end the relationship, knowing how to end the relationship, but having tremendous fear of ending it. Earlier in this chapter (in Dialogue 10.1) we saw how Eli was struggling with many fears with respect to ending his marriage. When he contemplated divorce, he would struggle with his fear of guilt – feeling that he was betraying his wife and children. However, it was not until Eli was able to feel comfortable with his wife and children's abilities to survive a divorce that he was able to overcome his own fear. This reminds us of a client of Bill Emener's named Nellie, who struggled for over two years before she was able to end her relationship with Mitch. For Nellie, it was a "fear of what my life would be like, alone in the world and without Mitch!" Thus, while Eli was struggling with ending his relationship with his wife for fear of what might happen to her and his children, Nellie was struggling with ending her relationship with Mitch for fear of what might happen to her.

When the fear that the ending of a relationship will bring about suffering on behalf of loved ones or ourselves, that fear can grippingly prevent our clients from not only doing what they think is best but also from doing what they want to do. We have learned from clients like Eli, Nellie and many others that when we feel a need to end a loving relationship, it is helpful to identify the fears we have associated with such an act. Then, it is important to explore, discuss and try to understand more deeply our fears of ending the relationship so that people can get on with their lives and do what they need and want to do.

Fear of Losing Individuality and Commitment Phobia. We have counseled many individuals who were reluctant to enter into a loving relationship because they feared they would be asked to give up important aspects of themselves in order to make the relationship work. Similarly, we have met with clients whose fear of taking their current relationship "to the next level" was largely irrational, and better described as a phobia of commitment in general. While not exactly the same, these two fears are closely related. In the first case, the client, Millie, was saying, "I am an intelligent, well-educated and goal-oriented woman. I want to complete my master's degree and enjoy an exciting, productive and successful career. Why do I have to be anything less than that in order to marry Paul?" One of the many things Bill said to her was, "Millie, I think it is safe for us to assume that one of the reasons Paul loves you and wants to marry you is because of *who* you are and *what* you are. If you were to discontinue to be who you are and what you are, not only would that hurt you, but it also might disappoint Paul." We suggest that there is a message in this for all of us:

> When someone is in love with us and wants to share their life with us, it is reasonable to assume they are doing so because of who we are *and* what we are. Continuing to be who we are *and* what we are is not only important for us to do for ourselves, but it is also important for us to continue to be who we are and what we are for the benefit of our loved one as well as for our relationship.

Although Millie's fear of losing herself was defensible, if not wholly warranted by the facts of her situation, another of Bill's clients, whom we shall refer to as Mary, was not. While talking about how she could not commit to a deeper relationship with Ronald, Mary drew a figure similar to the one in Figure 10.2 and said, "Ronald and I are currently friends and lovers. I consider us to have an 'I-thou' relationship. Part of my concern, however, is that if we start to have a committed relationship or eventually get married, it would be more of a 'we' relationship. And my concern, Dr. Emener, is that while I feel I can be me in our 'I-thou' relationship, I am fearful that I would not be able to continue to be me if we had a 'we' relationship." Mary quickly realized that (1) this was a very important issue with regard to herself, and (2) if she wanted to seriously explore further potentials for her relationship with Ronald, it would be equally important for her to discuss it with him.

Commitment phobia can be a very daunting, emotionally-draining and relationship-troubling phenomenon. When Michelle first came to see Bill Emener, her story, in a nutshell, went like this: "I am 48-years old, I am a successful attorney, I own my own home, and I am head over heels in love with Ben, a 54-year-old single attorney who lives near me. We have been going together for over a year now. I love him very much, but for some reason we have reached a plateau, a stalemate.

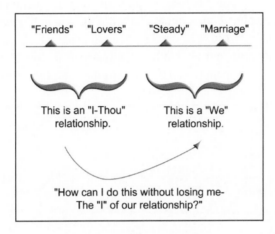

Figure 10.2. Fear of Losing Me.

Every time we talk about getting married, getting engaged or living together, I tell him, 'Ben, let's talk about that next week.' I don't know what's wrong with me, Dr. Emener; he surely does seem to be the perfect man for me in every way. Recently, however, he suggested that there might be something wrong within me and it may not necessarily be him. In summation, if you will pardon my attorney talk, that's why I am here to see you. I need to find out what's wrong with me!" At the very outset, Bill told Michelle that he would prefer not to begin working with her under the assumption that there was something wrong with her. What he told her, however, was that he would be more than willing to help her find out why she is the way she is. And as her life story began to unfold, she increasingly became more aware of herself and why she was responding to Ben the way she was.

When Michelle was a sophomore in high school, her parents divorced. Her father quickly remarried and "got totally involved with his new family." Michelle then lived in a three-bedroom apartment with her mother. She said, "My mother was a wonderful mother to me. Almost too good – I felt she was smothering me all the time. Yes, we were very close, but I'm glad I eventually went away to college because I think I needed to get away from her." When Michelle was 28, she fell madly in love with José, a very successful, 35-year-old businessman from Spain. José was in the United States for one year to help with the establishment of an American-based satellite company. After knowing each other for approximately six months, Michelle moved in with him. "It was wonderful!" However, when José's year was up, he returned to Spain not only to continue his work in the corporate office of the company, but also "to see if he could renew his relationship with his ex-girlfriend." With tears in her eyes, Michelle said, "I was devastated. Fortunately, my firm gave me a three-week paid vacation so I could try to get my life together. I was a basket case!" Over the next decade, Michelle never dated or had any more than a friendship relationship with any other man.

During their second session, Michelle said, "After reading the book you suggested, I think I understand myself more clearly – I have commitment phobia. When I was in high school, I loved my father very, very much. He left me. I loved my mother very, very much. She smothered me. I guess I subconsciously concluded that if you commit yourself to someone they will either leave you or smother you. Then about 10 years later, I took a risk and made a lifelong commitment to José. What happened? I was abandoned again! I guess maybe that's why I'm having difficulties making any kind of commitment to Ben." She then went to her portfolio and pulled out a figure similar to the one in Figure 10.3 that diagrammed these experiences. As Bill looked at Michelle's diagram, she said, "I guess because of my fear of abandonment, my commitment phobia became really locked-in. But I love Ben so much! Maybe if I just continue to be patient and share all of this with Ben, it might get easier."

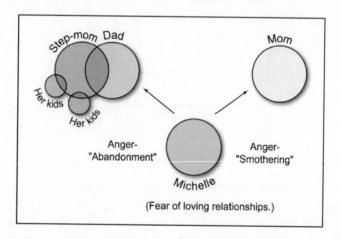

Figure 10.3. Michelle's Commitment Phobia.

Not only was it very helpful for Michelle to share her commitment phobia with Ben, it was also very helpful that they decided to establish a "living together relationship" on a gradual, approximation basis. Michelle moved some of her clothes and other belongings into Ben's house and spent three nights a week there. After approximately one month, she spent four nights a week at his house. After six-months, she was living almost exclusively with Ben and going by her house once a week to water her plants. Eventually, she became more trusting of Ben and more trusting of herself. She then put her house up for sale. With a somewhat "let's celebrate" attitude, she came into Bill's office and said, "If you want a good deal on a house, I've got one for you!" That was her way of telling Bill hat she had overcome her commitment phobia and had made a commitment to Ben. Commitment phobia can be a very dysfunctional and destructive aspect of life. As Michelle observed, "It can rob us of the most exciting joy and sense of meaningfulness that life can behold." When you are working with a client who is skeptical of making a commitment to another individual, in addition to asking the client what is wrong with him or her, what is wrong with the other person and what is wrong with his or her relationship, also ask your client if possibly he or she is experiencing a phobic response to commitment.

The core ideas of this section can be summarized rather succinctly. First, fear is a powerful and necessary emotion, but it too easily can become divorced from the realities of people's lives. When this happens and fear becomes generalized or otherwise without basis, it affects them adversely. We have seen many examples in which the *fear of a perceived reality* (e.g., "There is something wrong with me.") that is not shared with others can make it difficult or impossible to manage – especially if the individual is in a loving relationship. And remember, such fears typically do not go away by themselves. Thus, helping your clients attend to them can be incredibly liberating for them and ultimately contribute to their living a healthier, more meaningful and happier life.

DEPRESSION AND ANXIETY

"Ever since his girlfriend broke up with him and moved out about a month ago, he has been feeling utterly dejected. He sounds helpless and hopeless when he talks about anything. He seems to have lost interest in *everything, especially people, and he talks about himself as if he is totally worthless.*"

"Ever since he divorced me, everything I do requires effort. People tell me I will answer their questions but will not initiate anything. I just feel blue, down and lonely all the time. It bothers me that people won't talk with me, but then again, I don't want to talk to anyone anyway. And even if I did, it wouldn't make any difference. I have nothing to say or add. Why would anyone want to be around me? I'm a loser. I wish people would just leave me alone."

These two scenarios are not uncommon. When a person has painful emotional experiences within or as a result of a loving relationship, one of the emotions commonly felt is depression. The first scenario is an illustration of a person's description of a friend who is feeling depressed because his girlfriend ended their relationship. The second is an illustration of what a person who is feeling depressed as a result of a divorce may say. We suspect there is a high probability you may have heard statements like these from your clients and possibly may have experienced such feelings yourself.

Feeling depressed and behaving like the individuals in these two illustrations, can result from biochemical and/or psychopathological etiologies (e.g., a person may have an illness called "depression" for many years) or from situational conditions (e.g., when a person is divorced and feels abandoned by an individual with whom they were, and still are, very much in love). The first of these two conditions is known as "endogenous depression" (coming from within), while the latter is referred to as "reactive depression" (due to causes outside the body). Sometimes a person can suffer from both types of depression at the same time. For example, a middle-aged woman recently said, "I have had bouts with depression ever since I was a teenager. However, with some occasional visits to my psychologist and by sometimes taking medicine prescribed by my doctor, I have been able to live a good life. But this recent breakup with Jerry just brought me down. I emotionally hit bottom."

There also are several different components to depression. Feelings of sadness are part of what we call the *affective* component, whereas difficulty initiating behavior (i.e., just wanting to lie around all day) reflects the *motor* component. Finally, there is a *cognitive* component of depression, in which a person experiences difficulty solving problems, remembering, or being able to think clearly about things. Neuroscientists now know from brain imaging and mapping studies that these components reflect dysfunctions in different parts of the brain. Cognitive depression, for example, is closely associated with lower than normal neural activation of the left frontal lobe (in a right-handed person), affective depression includes this part of the brain and the limbic system, while motor depression stems from brain disregulation in deep sub-cortical areas, particularly the brainstem and ventral tegmental area.

We include this information to make sure our readers understand that depression is an illness, not some type of character flaw.

Although endogenous and persistent depression are among the most serious and widely diagnosed mental illnesses in our society, in this chapter we focus on the reactive depression that many times results from relationship issues. We will look at some of the ways by which feelings associated with depression may be related to loving relationships and what some people have done to help themselves. We also will look at depression as one of the "four blocks to happiness" we frequently address in counseling, where our focus is not on underlying biochemical factors, but on one's beliefs about themselves, their significant others and/or the world around them. Finally, we want to help the professional couples counselor learn new and often effective interventions for treating reactive depression in clients, which, after all, is our primary purpose.

Ultimately, we want to help our clients understand that the experience of depression that results from relationship issues is shared by nearly everyone at some point or other. Reactive depression is quite normal and even expected at times; for example, it is a mistake to believe that one is somehow inferior or to blame if he or she should suffer from it after a loving relationship ends. The fact that our culture tends to characterize such reactions as evidence of weakness or shortcomings of character is in fact more of a shortcoming of our culture. The often unspoken but widely assumed philosophy of "rugged individualism" that permeates our society can greatly harm people because it equates seeking help with weakness. If ever there were a better example of "blaming the victim," we are unaware of it. Depression in all its forms is a treatable illness. If you wouldn't feel right about labeling someone with a broken leg a loser because he or she can't walk without crutches, then we urge you never to make the mistake of allowing a client to blame him- or herself, or another person (i.e., their significant other) who is suffering from depression.

I Don't Know How to Act. Wayne, a 38-year-old construction worker, not only told Bill Emener that he was feeling blue and depressed for a long period of time, but his behaviors and mannerisms tended to indicate it as well. When Bill asked Wayne to tell him what his life was like, Wayne said, "Ever since my divorce about a year ago, I go to work, sleep and every other weekend I see my two children. Sometimes it seems like the walls in my one-bedroom apartment are closing in on me. I basically live a very boring and sterile life. Part of the problem is that I just don't know how to act. I don't know what to do. And let me assure you, that bar scene, that single life scene, and that running around trying to meet someone basically sucks!" In almost a humorous fashion, Wayne added, "It's almost funny – on the weekends I really find myself not wanting to talk to anyone. I screen my telephone calls with my answering machine. Quite frequently when someone calls, I listen to them talk to me and ask me to call them back, but then I just sit there and stare at the walls. I guess I just don't feel like talking to anyone. By Sunday evening I start feeling sorry for myself because I haven't talked with anyone all weekend. Sometimes I just don't know what to say, I don't know what to do and I don't know how to act."

One of the first things Bill did to help Wayne was to identify some ways that he could continue to keep himself active. Prior to his divorce, he was a very active man; he played on a softball team, he and his wife went out together at least one evening a week and he was very actively involved in the lives of his two children. Wayne agreed that it would be important for him to try to continue to be active. He felt that he could do this successfully by surrounding himself with active friends, buying tickets ahead for plays and ballgames, and joining a softball team. "Basically," he said, "I need to take control of my life and plan things so that my depression doesn't get the best of me."

There is an important message here. Although depression often leads to a loss of motivation, committing oneself to staying active is one of the more effective ways to combat its symptoms. As paradoxical as this may seem, as counselors we have experienced this time and again. In the case of Wayne, for example, the last time Bill saw him he reported that he was doing much better. When asked specifically what was going on in his life, Wayne said, "First of all, I took your advice and I have been making sure that before I go to bed on Wednesday nights, I have at least one planned activity for the upcoming weekend. You were right, waiting until Saturday morning or Saturday afternoon to call people to see if they want to go out was simply too late – everyone already has plans by then. In fact, last night I called some friends of mine and we are going to meet at the beach this coming Saturday night to have some dinner and listen to some reggae music. I'm looking forward to that! I've been playing softball one or two nights a week and I have tickets for four – for a buddy of mine, his girlfriend, her roommate and me – to go to a concert the last Saturday night of this month. By being careful, going slowly and planning things, I'm gradually learning how to act. Having been a married man with children for the last 14 years, it's hard to learn again how to be a single person. But I'm getting there!"

As is illustrated by Wayne's experiences, it is easy to understand that when a significant change occurs in one's life – especially if it has to do with changes in loving relationships – it is quite common for people simply to not know how to act. The alternative of doing nothing may seem like a sensible choice, but it usually only makes one's condition worse. On the other hand, by planning activities and committing oneself to them, surrounding ourselves with good role models, spending time with friends who understand and are helpful to us, and not putting pressure on ourselves to live up to everyone else's expectations in addition to our own, it indeed is possible to stop the perpetuation of what can feel like a meaningless and sterile life and overcome depression. Wayne's experience shows that as time goes on a depressed person can learn or relearn how to once again get involved with other people.

Alone – Lonesome – Lonely In the introduction to this section we looked at how tacit or unspoken assumptions of our culture can lead to making poor choices and to inaccurate ways of understanding our issues. Another one of these tacit cultural values is gregariousness – the belief that it is always better to be with others than to spend time alone. As counselors in private practice, we have been surprised at how often this is expressed by our clients. Learning how to enjoy one's own company for varying periods of time is both healthy and undervalued. Teenagers seem to understand this naturally, as anyone who has had to spend time while their 16-year-old child spends hour after hour in his or her bedroom with the door closed can readily attest. Time spent alone allows one to *process*, or think through, many aspects of their recent past and to better understand their world and the role they play in it. As we grow older, however, we somehow seem to lose this affinity for soulful reflection and assume that if we are not in the company of at least one other person, something is wrong with us. There is no doubt that human beings are highly social animals, and that most people cannot survive or prosper if they go for long periods of time without quality company and interactions with significant others. But in the short run, time spent alone is much underrated, as clarified by the following example.

When talking with Paula, a 28-year-old stenographer, it became clear to Bill Emener that she was confusing the phenomena, or conditions, of being alone, being lonesome and being lonely. *Being alone*, in simplistic terms, is just that – being by oneself, spending time without others around and not being in a significant or meaningful relationship. *Being lonesome* is an experience we typically think of as pining over or painfully missing a special, significant, identifiable individual. *Being lonely*, on the other hand, is the missing, pining and feeling down because there simply is no one else in one's life at that time. "So in other words," Paula said, "when I stay in my apartment by myself or go to a movie by myself, I am simply being alone. When I am feeling down and depressed because I miss Harold, I'm being lonesome. And when I am feeling down, depressed and sad because I do not have a significant other in my life to share things with, I am feeling lonely." Bill nodded and replied, "Yes, that's right. In many ways these three conditions are mutually exclusive and independent. Being alone, feeling lonesome and feeling lonely can be three entirely separate kinds of experiences. It might be helpful, however, if we could identify some things you could do to try to reduce your feelings of depression resulting from each of these three conditions."

The next time Bill saw Paula, she shared with him that she had gone back to the spa where she had been a member for years and began working out and attending aerobic classes. She renewed some of the friendships she used to enjoy with the other women whom she knew from the spa. Furthermore, she began doing some of the things that Wayne (from the previous example) had found to be helpful, such as planning for future activities with people she knew, felt comfortable around and could trust. Interestingly, Paula said, "I think there is a reason why I have been feeling less depressed. By not being alone all the time, as I used to be, I'm now finding that I'm not feeling as lonesome or as lonely as I used to feel either!"

When a client is experiencing feelings of depression as a result of significant changes in, or the loss of, a loving relationship, it is understandable that the person may feel lonesome and/or lonely. If, however, clients simultaneously allow themselves to spend all of their time alone, they can: (a) magnify the intensity of their lonesome and lonely feelings; and (b) find it difficult to work their way out of the depression and find a way to enjoy life again. There is nothing wrong with being alone; as we have said, sometimes it is very important for people to spend time with and enjoy their own company. However, when spending too much time alone contributes to feeling lonely, lonesome and depressed, it is frequently helpful to do some things, as Wayne and Paula did, to reduce the amount of time we are alone.

Loneliness: It Could be Worse. Bill Lambos was counseling Mike, a 31-year-old restaurant manager who had recently given up drinking after a DUI arrest. "Doc, the restaurant business is like this: first you spend an hour or more prepping tables and the kitchen before the crowd arrives. Then you spend five or six hours running around like mad serving customers and making sure they are happy with their food and the service. Finally, you spend the last hour cleaning up and decompressing from the stress of the evening. That's when all the staff starts drinking – I mean, the bar is right there, and everybody feels like they need one or two just to calm down. *Then,* since they feel so much better, they all go out and party half the night until they are plastered, crash – in bed if they're lucky, or into a pole like I did – and the next day they do it all over again." After taking a sip of water, Mike continued, "The problem is, now that I've decided to clean up my act, I can't spend time with any of my former friends. If I do, I'll just end up drinking again and I'm not going to let that happen." Mike's new problem, however, was loneliness. "I end up spending night after night in front of the TV by myself and it only makes me depressed. I'm starting to wonder if this is any better than drinking myself to death."

Bill and Mike spent the next few sessions doing what we like to call "advocational counseling." They created a list of things Mike enjoyed doing besides watching television, which included racquetball and hiking. Mike also expressed an interest in learning to practice yoga. A brief time on the Internet revealed a local fitness club that offered opportunities for doing all three, and Mike reluctantly joined. (One of Mike's issues was that he was shy; meeting new people socially was hard for him.) With a little prodding, however, he forced himself to start by getting a free day pass to the club where he took a lesson from the racquetball pro and was introduced to several other players at his level. He also joined a yoga class.

After more than a year of not hearing from him, Mike recently dropped by Bill's office early one evening to say hello. "Life is good, no complaints at all," he said. "I switched to the lunch shift, which is just as busy, but now I get off at four. Three nights a week I head to the club for regular games and classes, and on weekends there is a group that goes hiking. I thought things couldn't be better until my regular racquetball partner pointed out that a certain young lady was paying a lot of attention to me, and I was clueless." He laughed. "We've been going out for seven months now, and I'm starting to think she's the one. I just came by to say thank you."

The preceding case histories offer some good advice for clients who are experiencing reactive depression ("force yourself to get out and stay busy and engaged; don't sit around by oneself and ruminate about one's sad state of affairs"). However, as good as the advice may be, these cases don't shed much light on the psychological make-up of depression. This is the purpose of the following section.

Helplessness and Hopelessness. We have mentioned that depression is one of the "four blocks to happiness" that is routinely addressed in Bill Lambos' Tampa practice, along with anger, anxiety and guilt. Like these others, we believe that depression is often sustained by the irrational beliefs we come to harbor. As with the other blocks, in the case of depression, there are two sets of beliefs people hold – one realistic and the other usually not. The realistic belief goes something like, "I am sad and I want to feel better." This is entirely expected from someone who is depressed, regardless of the reason. The irrational belief that can accompany it, however, is "My situation is hopeless and I am helpless to change it." Once again, this is irrational. It is almost never true, it is illogical in that it doesn't follow from any premises, and it is dysfunctional – it won't help you get better. From our years of professional practice, we have learned that the faster we can help clients realize the irrational nature of this belief, the sooner they will begin to recover. This is not to say one can snap one's fingers and overcome such dysfunctional beliefs and the feelings that accompany them. It takes effort, a commitment to change, and a sincere desire to climb out of the hole. Hopelessness is a self-fulfilling prophecy – a prediction that comes true because of the behavior it evokes in those who believe it.

Each of your authors has many times said to clients and friends, "The only thing worse than a feeling of helplessness is a feeling of hopelessness." This postulate became eminently clear when Bill Emener was talking with Lonnie, a 30-year-old schoolteacher who had been living with her boyfriend for two years prior to coming to see him. How this can evolve in the therapy room is illustrated in Dialogue 10.3.

Dialogue 10.3 Helplessness and Hopelessness.

After Lonnie (**L**) and her boyfriend agreed to end their relationship, she moved into her own apartment and soon began feeling very depressed. Thus, she came to see Bill (**B**) Emener for counseling.

Toward the end of their first session:

B: (While writing on a blank piece of paper) What I am writing down, Lonnie, are three statements you have made to me in the past few minutes: (1) "I don't like what happened between Reggie and me;" (b) "I am feeling very down and depressed about it;" and, (c) "There's nothing that I can do about it." Now take a look at what you said. (After a pause) It looks to me like you went from feelings of disappointment, to feelings of depression, to feelings of despair. First, you were disappointed because of what happened, then you began feeling very down and sad about what had happened, and then you began feeling that no matter what you did it would not make any difference.

L: (After nodding in agreement, she began sobbing. A minute later, she composed herself) I'm sorry Dr. Emener. But when you put it that way... well, that's exactly what happened.

B: It's tough isn't it?

L: Yes, it is. But I don't want to do this anymore. I want to fix this.

B: *Fixing* is a strong term Lonnie. But I would like to invite you to accept a homework assignment – there's something I'd like you to do between now and our next session.

L: Sure... whatever it is.

B: I'd like you to pretend that I – yes, me, Bill Emener, your counselor – am a good friend of yours and I tell you that I just ended a three-year relationship with my girlfriend. I also tell you that ever since my girlfriend and I ended our relationship I've been feeling a lot of disappointment, sadness, depression and despair. With me so far... ?

L: Yes. Go ahead.

B: Okay. I then say to you, "Lonnie, my good friend, what do you think I should do?"

L: Okay...

B: I'd like you to write a letter to me, Lonnie, and put it in the mail by the end of this week. And in your letter, give me a list of suggestions and recommendations – things I could do, to help myself.

L: You will have my letter by next Monday.

B: Good. I'll look forward to receiving it.

Second session – two weeks later:

L: I hope you received my letter.

B: Yes, I did. It arrived last week. (Handing Lonnie the letter she had written) Here's your letter. Only you'll notice that wherever you wrote "Bill" I crossed it out and replaced it with "Lonnie," and wherever you wrote "Lonnie" I crossed it out and wrote in "Bill."

L: Yeah... I see that.

B: Okay. Now let's assume for the moment that you had been telling a good friend of yours, a friend who lives somewhere else, about your breakup with Reggie and she sent you this letter. Now, read it aloud.

L: Okay. "Dear Lonnie, I am sorry to hear about your ending your relationship. And per your request, here are a few suggestions I'd like to give you. First, I think it would be helpful for you to…" (After reading the letter, she started smiling.)

B: (Smiled in return).

L: You know, Dr. Emener, for whatever it is worth, these 10 suggestions really are very good recommendations!

B: Yes they are, Lonnie, whoever wrote that letter really knows what she's talking about. (They both laughed.) There is only one question remaining, Lonnie. If these are such good recommendations and if they come from such an intelligent person, then why can't *you* listen to them and try to do what is being suggested?

L: Hmmm. Well, the truth is that the last time I was here in your office, I was so emotionally caught up in my feelings that I totally shut off my brain. Not only did I think that nothing would work, but I didn't even think I was capable of coming up with any halfway decent ideas or recommendations of what to do about my situation.

B: I understand. Your emotions were so frazzled they got in your way.

At their next session, Lonnie spoke about all of the exciting and helpful things she had been doing to help herself. Many of these were similar to the kinds of things that Wayne, Paula and Mike had been doing – things we discussed earlier in this chapter. The fact that Lonnie was not only doing helpful things but doing *things that were her own ideas*, also contributed to her self-efficacy and sense of self-worth. That was the last time that Lonnie ever came in. A few months later, however, when the weather had turned colder, Bill received a postcard from the island of Nassau. On the back was an inscription that said, "I am helplessly and hopelessly in love with this place! Having a wonderful time! Your good friend, Lonnie."

Mixed Depression and Secondary Depression. Throughout this chapter, we have been looking at situational depression as it relates to loving relationships. The essential experiences illustrate what is termed *primary reactive depression* – the depression that one experiences as a result of a specific situation and/or other related considerations. In our clinical work, as well as in our personal lives, we also have experienced and observed *secondary depression* – the experience of feeling depressed because one recognizes and realizes that one is, and has been, depressed. As Bill Emener recently said in a lecture, tongue-in-cheek, "Depression can be very depressing." Closely related to secondary depression are anxiety-related depression and its cousin, depression-related anxiety, both forms of *mixed depression*. These arise when one experiences depression or anxiety *as a consequence* of feeling the other. One of our favorite acronyms from the DSM, the *Diagnostic and Statistical Manual of Mental Disorders* (the diagnostic bible of our profession) is MAD, which stands for "Mixed Anxiety and Depression." Rarely will you hear of anything better described by its own acronym!

Secondary depression can affect couples. For example, Mark and Ginger had been trying very hard to reconcile their engagement and improve their relationship. They lived in their own apartments; but since their apartments were in the same complex, they were able to spend large amounts of time together. During their second counseling session, Ginger said, "Yes, Dr. Emener, our relationship does seem to be improving. We talk more than ever. But sometimes I think we talk too much. It seems that the only thing we do nowadays is sit around each other's apartment and talk about our relationship." Bill looked at both of them and suggested, "You may be experiencing what I think of as *the paralysis of analysis.* Collectively analyzing your relationship and working on it is very important. However, sometimes it also is important for people to enjoy doing things together. For example, when is the last time the two of you went away for a day and did nothing but have fun together?" They looked at each other with saddened expressions. Mark said, "I can't remember. I think Ginger is right, all we do now is sit around and talk about our relationship!"

The following weekend, the two of them went away to the beach for the day. They left their watches and cell phones locked in the trunk of the car. They also went with the agreement that they would not talk about their relationship or each other; they would just try to enjoy having fun. When Bill saw them the following Tuesday, it was clear that they had been to the beach – their sunburns were quite revealing. The two of them had had a wonderful day together and, to a large extent, they felt they had reduced their "paralysis of analysis." With a chuckle in his voice, Mark said, "You can only sit in front of a scrumptious meal for so long without finally shutting up and eating! Sometimes the only way to enjoy good food is to eat it, not talk about it. And I am coming to understand the best way for Ginger and me to enjoy our relationship is to live it!"

Living the life of a couch potato is easy – you just keep doing the same thing. Living the life of a runner is easy – you just keep doing the same thing. However, the transition from couch potato to runner can be very difficult. Simply said it's really tough sometimes to get running again, getting the muscles accustomed to being used and getting into a routine of running. But the transition from couch potato to runner can be made a little easier. If a person has a plan of attack, a schedule of incremental increases in running, and a genuine sense of patience with this incremental progress. With regard to Bill Emener's couch potato-runner analogy, Ginger said, "We are not ready for a 5K or a 10K race yet. However, we are up to one mile per day, three times per week, and that feels good!" Mark added, "And within that analogy, Bill, we've also quit bitching about what bad shape we're in!"

At one time or another, depression will become a challenge for almost everyone. To the degree that a person is able to accept periods of reactive or situational depression as part of life, he or she normally will be able to cope with it, sometimes alone, other times with the help of friends, family or a professional counselor. When the fear of depression prevents an individual from engaging in the things once enjoyed, however, it typically becomes very dysfunctional and self-defeating. This is especially true of moving on to the next loving relationship. Similarly, when a person becomes depressed over a situation that he or she has the control to change, depression becomes a self-fulfilling prophecy. Finally, when an individual reacts to depression with more depression and/or with other negative emotions, a downward spiral has begun. We trust that after reading this chapter, you, our reader, will keep these things in mind when depression rears its ugly head in your clients' lives, and respond accordingly. If you do that, and you teach your client to identify, dispute and reframe the irrational beliefs that underlie the depressed emotions and the loss of volition (the will to act purposively), the chances are that your clients will experience it no longer than necessary.

GRIEVING

"I can't believe it. I came home from work today and found a note on the kitchen table next to her engagement ring. All of her clothes and her portable TV were gone. I just can't believe it!"

"I know our divorce was finalized a few months ago, and now he's living with her. But he still loves me. He'll be back. As soon as he gets this thing out of his system, he'll be back. He loves me. He'll eventually want me back."

"She deprived me of my dream of growing old together with the mother of my children. I still love her, but what she did to me is unforgivable. And now she's playing the children against me. What a manipulator she is – and always has been. Well, wait until she needs something. She better not come crying on my doorstep!"

"I took all of his fishing equipment and roller blades to his mother's house today. There's no need to punish him. It's time to bring closure to our relationship so I can get on with my life."

"We went together for four years and lived together for the past year or so. In many ways it was wonderful. But in many ways it wasn't so wonderful either. I'm sad that it's over, but that's behind me now. I'm making new friends, going out some and beginning to enjoy life again."

These are examples of statements people may make during the process of *grieving* – the process of dealing with loss. As we will see in this section, there are different kinds of loss that can be experienced within, and as a result of, a loving relationship. How people experience loss, the effects of loss on people and their lives, and what people may do as a result of their feelings of loss, are different and unique for all people. *Grieving is not an event, it is a process* – a process that typically evolves in stages. The individuals expressing the five statements above are illustrating shock, denial, anger, restitution and adjustment, which respectively, are common stages of grieving. It is helpful for people to understand their grieving process, to be aware of the loss for which they are grieving, and to appreciate that there may be some things they can do to help themselves with their grieving.

There are different ways in which the grieving process can impact your clients' loving relationships. Most books such as this one typically focus on the grief that follows the client's loss of a significant other in a break-up initiated by the other party. But the subject of grief and its impact on relationships also must consider another type of grief, known to counselors (and funeral directors) as *bereavement* – the grief that follows the loss of life of a loved one. To wit, there is a large body of research that has reported the death of a spouse, a child or a close family member to constitute three of the top major, life-changing events in people's lives (Kessing, et al., 2003). Bereavement stemming from the loss of a family member other than one's spouse or significant other indeed can have a significant impact on current and/or future loving relationships. The loss of a child, however, is probably the most difficult thing a couple can experience and occasionally is responsible for ending many otherwise well-functioning relationships.

In the following, we will focus on the grief associated with breaking up. However, we also will examine these other sources of loss and the impact they may have on your clients and their relationships. In so doing, we hope to help you more efficiently and effectively assist your clients to deal with each of these sources of loss and to better understand the process of making the transition through them. We trust that you then can teach those you counsel to benefit from some helpful advice, designed to help them (a) manage their sense of grief that results from these various sources of loss, (b) be of more assistance to their significant others, and (c) caringly aid those outside their dyadic relationships (e.g., children and family).

Grieving: A Process. It is not uncommon for people to experience the evolution of their grieving process through identifiable stages, such as: (a) shock; (b) denial; (c) anger; (d) restitution; and (e) adjustment. Elizabeth Kübler-Ross, a Swiss-born psychiatrist and author of the groundbreaking 1969 book, *On Death and Dying*, first described these stages systematically. The stages constitute what is now known as "the Kübler-Ross model." Her work originally focused on how one prepares for one's own death, rather than on bereavement or loss due to the end of a loving relationship. Psychologists and counselors soon came to realize, nonetheless, that her work, with minor adjustments, generalized well to these latter areas.

It is important to remember that every individual's grieving process is different and unique. A person can experience various aspects of grieving at almost any time during a day, an evening, a week, a month or a year. Furthermore, an individual may experience the process of grieving as a sense of loss while in a relationship as well as after a relationship may have ended. The most important thing to remember, however, is that *grieving is not an event – it is a process*. And if an individual is experiencing a sense of loss and going through various stages of the grieving process, it also is critical for that person to remember that these stages tend to be fluid. For example, while an individual may experience denial on Monday, he or she may experience intense anger on Tuesday and Wednesday, and by the end of the week be back to experiencing various aspects of denial. Teaching clients to be patient and allowing themselves to experience these facets of their grieving process are paramount.

Among many things you can do to help clients when they are grieving over a sense of "loss" within, or upon the ending of, a relationship, are: (a) teach the person to recognize and accept the process that he or she is experiencing; (b) help them give themselves permission to experience whatever they are experiencing (e.g., "if you feel like crying, cry; if you feel very angry, go out and chop some wood or punch a pillow"); and, (c) allow themselves to obtain and accept some assistance (e.g., having a close network of helpful friends, continue seeing you or another psychotherapist and/or reading self-help books).

We begin our case reviews by looking at the loss associated with one's loving relationship caused by break-up or divorce. Then we will look at bereavement due to the death of a partner or spouse, and finally we will look at how the loss of a child or partner's loved one may be expected to impact an intact relationship.

What Are You Grieving? Bill Emener recalls the first time he met Wilma, a 31-year-old legal secretary who had recently gone through an emotionally embattled, draining divorce. "I came to see you because I feel so depressed all the time, and I don't know what to do about it," she said. As they talked about her five-year marriage to John and some of the details of her divorce, they quickly realized that Wilma was experiencing many aspects of grieving. For example, at one point she softly said, "I have a very intense feeling of loss."

Later in their first session, Bill said, "It might be helpful, Wilma, if you could somehow identify your feelings of loss as well as the *objects* of your grieving. That is, what are your feelings of loss associated with? Are you grieving over the loss of John, *the person*? Are you grieving over the loss of *the relationship* that you had with John? Are you grieving over the loss of *a relationship*, in general? And/or are you grieving over the loss of *your dream* of having a future with John?" As tears welled up in her eyes and she stared out the window, she slowly and softly managed, "All of the above. There are many things about John that I loved so much. And I guess I still miss them incredibly. At the same time I miss our relationship; we had many good times together. I also miss having a person to have a relationship with – hugging my pillow as I fall asleep at night is no fun. Likewise, I think that my dream of having a little 'John Jr.,' who would have the same cute little ears that John had, is gone." For Wilma, this was a very good beginning of her journey toward overcoming her grieving over (a) the loss of John, (b) the loss of her relationship with John, (c) the loss of being in a relationship, and (d) the loss of her dream of the growing-old-with, and raising-a-family-with, John. As time went on, it also was helpful for Wilma to understand how her sadness, denial and anger were associated with each of these various objects of her grieving.

As was discussed earlier in the chapter, it is important to know the difference between being *alone*, being *lonesome* and being *lonely*. For Wilma, knowing specifically what aspects of John and her relationship with him that she was grieving over was very helpful. The last time Bill spoke with Wilma she said to him, "I think that there will always be a place for John in my heart. And I hope I never will forget the wonderful memories of the times we enjoyed together. But now that I am able to have a place for John and my relationship with him as a part of my past, I can get on with my life. What you said during our last session is true: it is very difficult to start to write a new chapter in your book of life until you have started to bring closure to the previous chapter."

Grieving Can Sneak Back on Occasions. Chuck, a 28-year-old videographer, was trying very hard to improve his current relationship with Irene. Chuck and Irene had been "going together" for about six months and had even begun discussing the possibility of a long-term relationship, including engagement and marriage. "Even though I truly believe that I have overcome the ending of my relationship with Linda, to whom I was almost engaged two years ago, I sometimes have the feeling that all of my issues with Linda are not totally gone," he said. Bill Emener suggested to Chuck that there was a definite possibility that he was still emotionally involved in some aspects of his process of grieving over the loss of Linda and their relationship. "That could very well be true," Chuck replied, "because just the other day when I was driving home from work, a song came on the radio that reminded me of the time Linda and I took a two-week vacation together. Visions of Linda and visions of the two of us playing together on the beach flashed through my head as I was listening to the song. Tears began rolling down my face. A couple of months ago I was going through some boxes in my storage bin and ran across a Christmas ornament Linda had given me. A lump in my throat, a knot in my stomach and a strong feeling of sadness quickly engulfed me. I just stood there holding the ornament in my hand, speechless."

Bill sketched a little diagram for Chuck similar to the one in Figure 10.4. He then suggested to Chuck that although he currently was very much in love with Irene and enjoying his relationship with her, he was still experiencing some grieving over the loss of Linda and his former relationship with her. Chuck took the diagram with him and shared it with Irene. When he first said that he shared it with Irene, Bill got a little nervous. Sharing with a current loved one that you may still be grieving the loss of a previous loved one and/or a previous loving relationship indeed could be explosive and/or destructive to a current relationship! He felt relieved, however, when Chuck said, "That was a very helpful thing for me to do. First of all, I recognized that my grieving had nothing to do with Irene, my love for Irene or my love of my relationship with Irene. Luckily for me, Irene responded in a very compassionate manner and did not feel intimidated or threatened by the fact that I was still experiencing some grieving over the loss of Linda. In fact, she very lovingly told me she would be patient and allow me to experience whatever I had to experience in order for all of that part of my past to finally stop interfering with my relationship with her. And since we had that conversation, I find myself not grieving half as much as I used to."

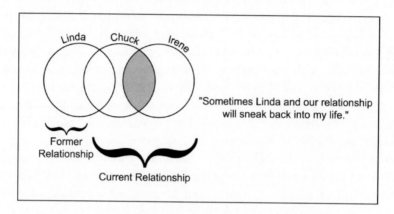

Figure 10.4. Grieving Can Sneak Back on You on Occasions.

It was clear to Chuck that his grieving over the loss of Linda and his former relationship with her was a process – a process that was taking time and could not be rushed. He also recognized that while he was writing a new chapter in his book of life – the chapter with Irene – he simultaneously was writing the ending of the former chapter of his life – the chapter of his life with Linda. It is also interesting to note that while it was helpful for Chuck to talk with Irene about his occasional grieving, it also allowed Irene to talk with him about some of her occasional remembrances of her former relationship with Tom, a gentleman to whom she had almost become engaged about three years prior to meeting Chuck. By allowing each other the freedom to experience their residual grieving over previous relationships and to share their grieving experiences with each other, Chuck and Irene further enriched and strengthened their relationship with each other. During his last session with Bill, Chuck said, "The more I am able to find a place for Linda in my past and the more Irene feels free to find a place for Tom in her past, the better we seem to feel about our present relationship and our future."

The Stalls in Your Barn. Bill Emener counseled Lynn, a 33-year-old elementary school teacher. Her divorce from Rob had been finalized six months previously and she had primary custody of her five-year-old son, Jason. However, she was having trouble sleeping, staying focused and basically getting on with her life. Her primary care physician gave her a 30-day prescription for antidepressants, but told her to see a therapist to work on her post-divorce issues.

During their first session, Lynn not only appeared depressed but fidgety and somewhat anxious as well. About halfway through that session, Lynn pointedly said, "Sometimes I feel like my head has a hundred ping pong balls bouncing all around in it. No matter what I am trying to do, I just seem to be thinking about a hundred other things and a thousand other people all the time. I'm managing, but I can't get on with my life! For example, my neighbors invited me to join their Friday night co-ed bowling team. It's a lot of fun – it's me, my two neighbors, Jerry and Sally, and Sally's father, Roy. And not only do they have to remind me when it's my turn a lot, but... Well, last Friday night Sally told me that this real nice guy on another team, Scott, was asking about me. I could tell he was looking at me a lot. Sally said she thought he might ask me out. But every time I would look at Scott, I would think about Rob. I left and went home as soon as I finished my last frame. Jeez, I can't get Rob out of my head! I know I have to see him two or three times a week – we have shared custody of Jason. But… I just wish I did not have to 'see him' when he's not around."

After talking more about Lynn's experiences, Bill asked, "Didn't you tell me that you grew up on a farm in Wisconsin?" Lynn smiled and replied, "Yes." While starting to draw a diagram similar to the one in Figure 10.5, Bill said, "Lynn, I want you to think about what it would be like to be a farmer up there in Wisconsin, in the wintertime, with a barn full of animals with no stalls or pens in the barn. What would that be like?"

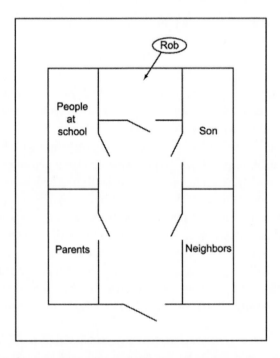

Figure 10.5. The Stalls in Your Barn.

"Crazy… on a good day," Lynn said through a chuckle. "With all of the animals free to go wherever they wanted to go in the barn, it would be 24/7 chaos." Bill continued to draw the diagram and said, "So you would have all of the animals in their respective stalls or pens, and when you wanted to milk the cow you would bring it out of its stall into the middle of the barn and milk it and then put it back in its stall, and then when you wanted to groom the horse you would bring it out of its stall into the middle of the barn and brush it and then put it back, and so forth." Lynn knowingly smiled and said, "Of course. Can you imagine…?"

"Well," continued Bill, showing Lynn the Figure, "the good news is that if we were to think of this as your current barn, you have stalls or pens for your parents, the people at your school, your son and your neighbors. And based on what you have told me, you may have to reinforce and mend some of the walls on those stalls and pens. *However, you don't have a stall for Rob.* And if this is true, no matter what you do in the barn, he just wanders in and around you, whatever you're doing whenever he feels like it."

A thin smile slowly splayed across Lynn's face. "Jeez, that makes so much sense," she softly said. "So what you're saying is that I need to make all the existing stalls in my head more secure and build a stall for Rob so that he only comes out when I want him to – like on Wednesday nights and every other weekend?" Bill smiled and replied, "Well, that's up to you, Lynn – it's your barn."

Two weeks later when Lynn came for her next appointment – her last appointment – she introduced herself as "Farmer Lynn." In addition to saying that she had been feeling less depressed and less anxious, she told Bill that the self-help book he had recommended had been very helpful to her. "I also have rebuilt some of the stalls and made one for Rob," she proudly stated, and then through a smile added, "That one has a lock on it, and I have the key."

At the end of the session, Lynn happily said that she was much better and would call to make an appointment if she needed to come back. "Oh and by the way," she added with a grin, "I may need to build another stall – this Saturday night Scott's taking me out to dinner and a movie."

Sometimes it simply is important to make sure that you have control over those parts of your life – especially the people in your life – that you can have control over. As Lynn aptly said, "If you don't, your life will be crazy… on a good day."

Have Something to Take Care Of. A large part of struggling with loss is the consumption with, and hyper-vigilance of, one's self. When we are hurting and in pain, paying attention to ourselves is understandable. Nonetheless, being self-absorbed and self-focused, all or a majority of the time, unconsciously or otherwise, mitigates against healing and getting on with one's life. Thus, from a logical perspective, it makes sense to identify ways of making yourself focus on and pay attention to some things outside of yourself. One of Bill Lambos' case files provides an excellent example of this suggestion.

Alex came to see Bill because, as he had said, "I'm still so caught up in Sherry, I can't relax or enjoy myself anymore. Okay, our divorce was finalized three months ago and we have agreed not to have any contact with each other. But I think about her all the time… I miss her so much!"

Toward the end of their first session, Bill suggested a self-help book for Alex and said, "Alex, a while ago you said that you like dogs… you said something about Sherry having taken your collie with her. Well, I would like to suggest that you think about getting a puppy." Alex thought about it for a moment and with a small smile said, "My sister's terrier just had a litter a few weeks ago. I'll see."

Two weeks later when Alex came in for his next appointment, he had a terrier puppy with him. After an exchange of greetings and comments about Alex's new friend, Blackie, he said to Bill, "When I told my sister that I felt like a family man without a family, she handed me this little guy and said, 'Here, he needs a good home.' And ever since I got him, I've slowly been feeling better. I take him with me wherever I go." Then as he petted Blackie and set him down on the rug, Alex said, "You're my buddy, aren't you."

In addition to Blackie giving him something to attend to outside of himself, Alex also was enjoying the unconditional love people tend to receive from a puppy. Alex was feeling special again. That was Bill's last session with Alex, and Bill believes that Alex is progressing, feeling better every day and getting on with his life. When appropriate and if you enjoy animals, getting a pet indeed can facilitate your working through the grieving process.

(It is not recommended, however, that your clients take their pets with them to their doctors' appointments – especially if they're not housebroken yet!)

When a Loved One Dies. The death of a significant other, especially when unexpected, can be a devastating experience. Most people are not well prepared for it, and such losses can be especially difficult for people in long-term or life-long relationships. The probability of a person dying within two years following the death of a spouse is statistically quite high after 25 years or more of marriage. This is true even if the individual was healthy at the time of the loved one's passing.

The well-known Viennese psychiatrist, Victor Frankl, proffered one reason for this. A survivor of nearly four years in Nazi concentration camps where the odds of making it out were estimated at only 1 in 25, he witnessed his parents, brother and pregnant wife perish. Based on his experiences, Frankl went on to develop both a theory of human motivation and a form of psychotherapy based on the human need to ascribe *meaning* to one's existence. In his famous book, *Man's Search for Meaning*, first published in 1959, Frankl stated that his survival depended on his focusing on the one thing his tormentors could not take away from him: *his choice of how to view his situation.*

In one of the more poignant recollections from his book, Frankl describes an elderly man, a retired medical doctor, who came to see him because he was suffering greatly over the loss of his wife of 40 years. Frankl asked the man a simple question: What would life have been like for her if you had died first? Upon reflection, the man realized that his suffering had spared his beloved partner of having to experience the same terrible fate. This gave such a profound sense of meaning to the man's situation that he shook Dr. Frankl's hand, thanked him and left the office.

As counselors, your authors tend to be eclectic in their choice of theoretical perspectives, looking for explanations and treatment approaches from many theories of personality, motivation and change. For example, one of us (Bill Lambos) is quite heavily involved with the neuroscientific origins of psychological phenomena and also has an extensive background in Rational Emotive Behavioral Therapy. The other (Bill Emener) originally was trained within the Rogerian model, but since then also has made use of many other approaches, including behavioral, cognitive and solution-focused models. Nevertheless, neither of us is prone to underestimate the importance of one's perspective in matters of mental life – a perception-based orientation sometimes called *phenomenology*. No matter what else life throws one's way, as long as one is conscious, one retains the choice to adopt one or another perspective for their situation. This is among the more important messages we convey in this book.

The Loss of a Child or Another Loved One. Many a marriage or relationship is put at risk when parents lose a child. This is especially troubling – an ensuing breakup often becomes a second source of grief and can make an already difficult situation seem unbearable. There are several signs to look for in one's relationship when a family member or other loved one dies.

The first is *isolation*. Although a person may need to spend time alone for a period following the death of a loved one to process the change it involves in their life, extended isolation is associated with depression and mental instability. It can be difficult to judge the balance between needing to process a loss privately and the need to remain in social contact with others. Should an individual's partner react to such a loss by separating from him or her and others for an extended period, it is very helpful if the grieving individual can be patient (while monitoring for depression along with the need to remain functional at some level).

Another warning sign to look for is extended *denial*, which counselors sometimes refer to as "stuffing it." The grieving process must be allowed to unfold, and this cannot happen when one cannot or will not face the reality of a loss. Again, there is a fine line to be walked here, like Somerset Maugham's rhetorical "razor's edge." If you are helping a client and/or his or her partner cope with the loss of a loved one, (1) try to engage them in conversation about their feelings, and (2) encourage them to recount the previous joys they experienced when they had the deceased person in their life. If they refuse to deal with it for a prolonged period, gently suggest that the sooner they move away from denial and toward the other stages of bereavement, the sooner they can begin to get on with their lives.

Sometimes a person will find it convenient or even necessary to *blame her or his partner* for the loss. As irrational as this may seem it is very common and it may be helpful, when pertinent, to encourage your client to remind their former partner that it is a part of their grieving process and should not be taken personally. Once again, sometimes gently pointing out what is happening is enough to stop it from continuing.

Another warning sign to look for in clients is *self-destructive behavior*. Abusing alcohol or other substances – means of self-medicating – is never a healthy response to loss. In addition to substance abuse, look for behaviors such as excessive risk-taking, self-cutting or other compulsive, self-destructive behaviors. If discussing them with your clients does not resolve such behavior patterns, immediately suggest or arrange for professional intervention as the case warrants.

Among the most important things you can do to assist a client or their loved one who is grieving, is simply to be there for them and to accept them and their situation – within the limits discussed above. Pressuring them to "get over it" will do little other than to generate resentment and put your professional relationship at risk.

Loss and the grief that accompanies it are ultimately a part of life. To move beyond it, one must allow oneself to undergo the grieving process, to search for and find meaning in the loss, and ultimately move on. This is, like so many of the issues we address in this book, more often easier said than done. Nevertheless, one of the wonderful benefits of loving relationships is that they can lead people to grow and become more than they were before. In the ideal world, everyone can find some solace in the "meaning" their former partner brought to and added to their life.

ANGER

"All this time, I've been thinking 'Wow, Susan is such a great catch.' Then, six months into our so-called committed relationship, I not only find out she's been sleeping with another guy, but that half the people I thought were my friends knew about it! I am so damn mad I could choke someone. I want to make all of these people pay for making me out to be such a fool!"

Anger is the fourth and last of our "blocks to happiness" – examples of self-induced disturbances in feelings and behaviors that clients normally attribute to the actions of other people or to events that happen in the world. In fact, as with anxiety, guilt and depression, such reactions are caused not by others or events, but by our own beliefs or perceptions about other people or what happens in the world.

Like the other three disturbances, anger is the result of two separate beliefs that must occur together in order to experience it. And as with the others, at least one of these beliefs will always be irrational. First, however, it needs to be pointed out that anger differs from the other forms of emotional disturbance in that it is extremely energizing and associated with harmful and often irreversible behavior. For example, the vast majority of murders in our society are committed not for monetary gain or by serial killers, but by people who know one another (including family members), and occur during a period when the murderer is experiencing rage. Very often, alcohol or other illicit substances and firearms (typically hand guns) are involved as well.

Anger is also closely associated with domestic violence that falls short of murder but includes physical harm such as punching, kicking, choking, blows to the head and other forms of physical assault that often result in bruising and/or broken bones and other serious injuries. Unfortunately, children are also often victims. The World Health Organization estimates that the total cost to American society of domestic violence, including gun violence, while hard to estimate accurately because so many incidents are unreported, runs between $165 and $200 billion dollars annually (Waters, et al., 2004). This is more than the United States spent on the war in Iraq in any single year of that conflict! Of course, in addition to the economic cost, there is the cost in human suffering and in the mental health of both the victims and perpetrators.

Given the staggering cost of expressed anger both to our society and to our individual clients, we need to ask two salient questions about this ugly emotion: first, *where does it come from*, and second, *how can it be controlled*?

As alluded to above, anger is the result of two co-occurring beliefs about some aspect of the other person's behavior or some event that took place in the world. The first belief involves egocentric thinking – such as: "I don't deserve this," or "People don't treat *me* like that!" At times these beliefs are quite rational (one may, indeed, not deserve to be struck by the car of a drunken driver) and at other times they are less so (as in assuming that one is special and above certain types of treatment). But in neither case is the first belief by and of itself the cause of anger. Rather, anger results when the first belief ("Why me?" or "Not me!") is combined with a second belief, which is always irrational: *It should not have happened!* This belief is, by definition irrational, for the simple reason that *it did happen*. Demanding that something be different than it already is, is simply magical thinking without basis in reality. Perhaps the following example will help make this seem more obvious.

Bill Lambos was meeting with Dexter, a recovering alcoholic, who came into his session clearly embarrassed. When asked about it, Dexter related the following story. "I was riding the elevator up to your office when I felt a sharp poke in my ribs. I had noticed when I got on that a smug-looking 'lawyer type' with a $3,000 watch got on and was standing next to me, talking on his cell phone. I figured he wasn't paying attention and his briefcase hit me in the ribs. I was all set to let him have it, but when I turned to face him I realized I had not seen a very short woman with a red-tipped cane standing between him and me. It was her purse that had poked me – I hadn't even noticed her there. All of a sudden I felt so embarrassed!"

What happened? The "anger stimulus" (an unexpected poke in the ribs) had not changed, nor did Dexter's belief that such events are unpleasant. What *did* change, however, was Dexter's discovery of who accidentally poked him. In his belief system, arrogant lawyer-types *should not* be so self-absorbed that they accidentally poke others, whereas a blind woman *may* rightly be excused of such a behavior. Notice that Dexter's anger evaporated nearly instantly, yet all that changed was his belief about the offending party. Clearly, Dexter's anger was *caused* by his demand that arrogant people *must not* act the way they sometimes do – which is an irrational belief about others and the world.

Anger management programs that teach people to be accountable for the unacceptable behaviors associated with their tempers by focusing on their beliefs, have been shown to be very effective. But what about anger in couple relationships? Counseling a couple in which anger is a problem is a sensitive and challenging area for the professional couples therapist. Laws in many states now require reporting of credible evidence of harm to an individual from domestic violence, even when it violates confidentiality. Ethical standards require that the informed consent agreement that the client couple signs prior to entering into counseling (or mediation) state this clearly. In our opinion, if a counselor suspects that either member of a couple is at serious risk from their partner, the counselor should ask to see each of the parties alone and question them about it. If either states that he or she is fearful of bodily harm, it is the counselor's responsibility to alert the authorities – there and then if necessary.

Fortunately, much of the anger that plagues relationships does not involve physical violence. Instead, it takes the form of ongoing and low intensity bickering that characterizes certain interactional styles that, while not associated with physical risk, are nonetheless psychologically unhealthy over the longer term. Sociologists sometimes refer to such relationships characterized as "conflict habituated." We recommend when counseling a couple that has fallen into this pattern that the following steps be taken:

1) Use biblio- or videotherapy to help clients understand the nature and unhealthy aspects of such relationships.
2) Help clients understand that (a) they are responsible and accountable for their emotions and (b) they can learn to have a great deal of control over them.
3) Point out the role(s) that irrational beliefs or cognitive distortions play in creating emotional distress. In therapy, attempt to isolate the specific beliefs, including the unspoken *demands*, that are the true cause of anger. Then help the client to *reframe* such beliefs – to change or restate them in ways that do not lead to their upsetting themselves about their partner or to taking out their frustrations about other things on their partner.
4) Remind your clients that legally, ethically and morally, *people never own other people*. We do not own our partners, spouses, parents or children. We therefore cannot *force* others to do anything they do not want to do.
5) If alcohol or substances play a role in episodes of anger, or especially violence, refer the couple to treatment for substance abuse or dependency (remember: AA and NA are support groups, *not* treatment programs).
6) Teach clients strategies for cooling down and avoiding harm when tempers rise. Suggest time-out periods, breathing exercises and other strategies for dispelling anger before it gets to a level when parties lose control.
7) Assure that when domestic violence is deemed a risk, the potential victim has a "safe" strategy for getting out of harm's way. This can include calling 911, getting out of the home and going to a friend or relative's, or if necessary to a shelter.

Anger can be frightening, but nearly everyone can learn to control it. The sooner people learn that it is they, themselves, who are responsible for their emotions, the faster anger will cease to be a problematic factor in their lives.

ADDICTIONS, OBSESSIONS AND COMPULSIONS

This is a textbook about counseling couples in loving relationships. In this chapter, we have looked at a number of issues that *impact* such relationships but are not the bases of the presenting reason. For example, when counseling couples to deal with anger or depression as it affects their relationships, we hope you have found the information herein about these subjects to be helpful in better assisting such couples. But, and we trust we have made clear, we do not intend for this book to be a substitute for professional training in these areas. Indeed, one of the bedrock ethical principles by which professional, licensed therapists live, is not to practice outside or beyond the scope of their expertise.

This channel-marker advice particularly applies to this final section of the chapter. Clients suffering from addictions, particularly issues involving substance abuse and dependence, should be referred to counselors or therapists with specific training, certification and expertise in this area. Serious cases of substance-related problems may require residential treatment, possibly for prolonged periods. Such treatment options may not be available to your clients for economic or insurance-related reasons, in which case community-based programs are the only alternatives.

Therefore, this section is included not to offer advice on treating client couples, or one of the partners of a client couple, with serious cases of these issues. Rather, it is to enrich the couples counselor's understanding and appreciation of how addictions, obsessions and compulsions tend to impact relationships, why we consider them in the same section of this chapter, and to get a better feeling for when the time has come to refer the afflicted individual or couple for additional professional help.

The current version of the DSM (DSM-IV-TR) considers substance abuse and dependence to be categorically separate from obsessions and compulsions. Simply stated, they are considered different illnesses, and we cannot predict how the DSM-V, due to be published in 2012, will categorize them. What we *can* state is that a growing number of treatment approaches to *both* substance-related mental health issues and repetitive and/or ritualistic behaviors characterized as obsessions and compulsions *do* characterize these conditions along the same continuum of disturbances: the *obsessive-compulsive spectrum disorders, or OCSDs* (Arden & Linford, 2009). We know of many approaches to therapy for this class of self-destructive behaviors that include substance dependence, "addictions" to gambling, sexual behavior and/or pornography, video games, and abusing the Internet. Eating disorders are believed by some to fall under this spectrum as well. Also included are a variety of impulse control disorders such as pulling one's own hair out to the point of bald spots (known as trichotillomania), and more classical forms of obsessive-compulsive disorder such as repetitive hand washing, checking for locked doors, and others.

Converging evidence on this class of disorders from neuroscience and psychotherapy provide compelling evidence that these disorders share a brain-based etiology. The subject is made more complex when substance abuse and dependence are included because the substance introduces other causative elements into the picture. Nevertheless, all these disorders have two things in common: *(1) the inability to stop engaging in a behavior that has become unwelcomed and intrusive; and (2) the interferences with one's life in substantial ways.*

Needless to say, one of these "substantial ways" is in interfering with interpersonal relationships, including loving relationships. When counseling a couple for whom the inability to control intrusive behavior has become an issue, we offer the following advice to the professional couples counselor:

1) *Try to determine whether the behavior co-varies with the quality of the relationship.* For example, if relationship problems precede periods in which the intensity of the OCSD behavior intensifies, make the couple aware of this connection. It may give the couple added incentive to resolve their relationship issues quickly and also can help mitigate the compulsion.
2) *Remember that the loving relationship can play a major role in assisting the afflicted individual.* We know of no better support system than a healthy loving relationship, especially one free from enabling and codependence. Therefore, if possible, continue to assist the couple in managing their relationship issues while the afflicted individual is being treated (while remaining sensitive to evidence of codependence).
3) *Remember that the unafflicted partner also may require support.* Groups such as Alanon may be quite helpful in this regard.
4) *Assist the couple to avoid blaming one another for the situation.* Help both the afflicted individual and his or her partner attribute the problem to a brain-based problem. Remind them that (a) the condition that afflicts one of them is *not* them, and (b) most such conditions are treatable.

We believe these strategies can not only help couples to overcome such disruptive influences on the part of the afflicted individual, but can ultimately serve to strengthen their loving relationship.

CHAPTER SUMMARY

The commonality of the concepts addressed in this chapter is that they focused on issues we tend to associate with a given individual in a relationship, rather than on their joint interactions (their "dance") or the context of the world in which their relationship unfolds. Specifically, the six areas of "individual issues" were: (1) Guilt and Shame; (2) Fears and Phobias; (3) Depression and Anxiety; (4) Grieving; (5) Anger; and (6) Addictions, Obsessions and Compulsions. One of the ultimate challenges individual issues such as these can pose for the couples counselor is helping the partners understand and manage their individual uniqueness as it contributes to their relationship difficulties.

I am not perfect, nor ever hope to be,
    and you are not perfect, nor ever hope to be.
What we hope, however,
    is that we can be perfect for each other.

CHAPTER 10 DISCUSSION QUESTIONS

1) When working with a couple, what can you do to help one of the partners understand his or her guilt and shame and how it affects his or her relationship… without feeling guilty and shameful in the eyes of his or her partner?

2) What is the difference between a fear and a phobia, and how might such differences differentiate how you might address them with a couple?

3) In what ways can being in a loving relationship with a depressed and/or anxious partner be challenging to the other non-depressed and non-anxious partner (and their relationship)?

4) How and in what ways is grieving an inevitable part of life, and how can grieving constitute a serious challenge for a couple?

5) What distinguishes healthy/functional anger from unhealthy/dysfunctional anger, and how can you help a client understand and appreciate such differences?

6) How might an individual be addicted to and/or obsessed with his or her partner (and/or their relationship)?

WHEN THE RELATIONSHIP IMPACTS THE INDIVIDUAL

In Chapter 10 we began by establishing how loving relationships are influenced by the unique and individual characteristics each of the two partners bring to the table. We noted how these elements include each partner's developmental history and their genetic predispositions. Most importantly, it is the interactions among these factors that resulted in two one-of-a-kind persons.

Your authors have little doubt that the depth and complexity of the material in Chapter 10 surprised many of our readers, especially those students for whom this text is their first introduction to working with couples. Looking back, there seems to be a nearly infinite variety of ways in which each individual can impact the relationship dynamic. We hope our attempt to organize and structure the material was helpful in preventing the topics from being perceived as overwhelming.

Among the reasons why working with couples is so fascinating is the fact that causes and effects run in two directions at the same time. Relationships are not simply a function or the sum of two individuals' behaviors; rather, they are *emergent* phenomena (Hoffsteader, 2007; Johnson, 2001). A phenomenon is said to be emergent when an interconnected system of relatively simple elements self-organizes to form higher-level behavior or properties that could not be predicted beforehand. Loving relationships certainly meet this definition. Other examples of so-called emergent phenomena are insect colonies, cities and (you guessed it) – the brain. Emergence and related aspects of complexity theory pose daunting challenges for any philosophy that seeks to rely on unidirectional cause and effect explanations, such as material determinism.

Before we get lost in such philosophical conundrums, however, let us return to our subject matter. From the point of view of this chapter, the salient aspect of such emergence is that loving relationships are both affected by and, in turn, impact their individual constituents – the partners. To some, this seems like no more than simple common sense. But to the scientist lurking inside each of you, our readers, it should send a tingle through you. This, ultimately, is the reason that relationships must be viewed as dynamic processes, a *dance* as it were, and never merely as things.

In this present chapter we look at three broad areas in which the relationships turn around to impact each of its member partners. We first look at people's lifestyle choices and how they are impacted by loving relationships. The term *lifestyle* includes more than just the type of work people choose to do and how they spend their leisure time. It also refers to (a) how they communicate their wants and needs, (b) how they choose to compromise so that both partners can be happy, and (c) how some patterns of interaction can be considered more functional than others, which are often labeled dysfunctional.

The second area in which the relationship impacts the individual is when one or both partners experience problems relating to one another. Of course, much of the content of this book is about relationship problems. Here, however, the focus is on *managing* problems in general, regardless of their nature. As we shall see, a relationship characterized by a healthy interactional style can weather many problems – even severe ones – without losing its moorings. Helping your clients develop functional and healthy patterns of interaction can be a powerful general-purpose remedy for many of the relationship issues that are bound to arise along the way in any and every relationship.

Finally, we spend a considerable portion of the chapter addressing the issues of separation and divorce, and how they impact each of the partners in the ever-changing dance of a loving relationship. Needless to say, the professional couples counselor will spend a good deal of his or her time helping couples to navigate and understand the consequences of decisions in these very serious areas.

With this introduction behind us, let us embark on the next leg of our journey through the maze that is, each day, navigated by the professional counselor when the relationship impacts the individual.

LIFESTYLE CHOICES AND RELATIONSHIPS

By now it is obvious that loving relationships never exist in a vacuum. Like dynamic overlapping circles, each person maintains a significant degree of individuality, including their other family members and friends, their jobs or careers, and some portion of their interests and hobbies. Where and when the two partners' circles overlap, time is spent together, attention is directed toward one another and the relationship is the primary focus of being. To understand and appreciate the role played by lifestyles in your clients' loving relationships, it is helpful to consider each partner's "outer circle" as well as the couple's shared "inner circle."

Most people work hard at developing and maintaining loving relationships because of the value and meaning that the "inner circle" adds to their lives. Thus, among the reasons typically given by individuals who are in "good" relationships is that "Our relationship meaningfully adds to my quality of life." However, healthy relationships also add value to each partner's "outer circle" – another commonly offered reason being "Our relationship is a significant, integral factor in my own, individual lifestyle."

It should be apparent by now why we have included a section on lifestyles. Quality loving relationships impact and enhance both aspects of the partners' lifestyles – the shared portion and the individual portion. To the degree that the relationship enhances both the individual's and the couple's shared lifestyle, the relationship will remain valued and desired by both parties. On the other hand, when there is a meaningful discrepancy between a couple's inner and outer circles, it usually spells trouble for the relationship.

Considering that the notion of "lifestyle" includes one's work, leisure activities, and family of origin issues, there are, unfortunately, many opportunities for such discrepancies to arise. The following case points several of these areas out quite succinctly.

A number of years ago, Bill Emener was facilitating a marital enhancement group in which there were two couples associated with a professional athletic team. Both couples were in their first year of marriage, the two wives were not originally from the geographic area where they were living, and their husbands were in their rookie seasons. When asked the question, "How has your marriage affected your lifestyle?" the two wives offered responses indicating two distinctly different experiences:

- Jan: "Since my marriage to Charles, I've been able to travel a lot, see new places and things, meet new people and develop new friendships, and enjoy an opportunity to see different parts of the United States. And there's always something going on: if it's not an important upcoming ballgame, it's participating in a celebrity golf tournament. I just love it!"
- Sandy: "Since my marriage to Rob, I've been on the phone a lot talking to my family and friends back home. And if Rob's not out of town, he's either in the gym or on the practice field. The apartment complex we live in is nice, but it's lonely. I love Rob – that's for sure. But being married to a professional ballplayer stinks – and that's for sure too!"

Thus we see two women, similar ages, both from small, Midwestern towns and now living in a big city, recently married to and very much in love with their husbands, and both with similar lifestyle opportunities, yet both with extremely different experiences, perceptions and feelings regarding the effects of their marriages on their lifestyles.

This example demonstrates two issues of importance regarding the connection between relationships and individual lifestyles. The first was already discussed in several previous chapters: *relationships are healthier to the extent that the partners have similar levels of satisfaction with their individual and shared lifestyles.* The other equally important issue however, is that *satisfaction with one's lifestyle may have little to do with the specific nature of that lifestyle.* Lifestyle needs and wants are unique and vary greatly across individuals. Maintaining a healthy loving relationship requires that the couple be aware of, and make adjustments to, the lifestyle issues of their partners.

With this in mind, the reader should easily see the purposes of this section – to help you, the couples counselor, assist your clients to focus on: (1) "individual lifestyles" in relation to, and compared with, "relationship lifestyles;" (2) "functional" versus "dysfunctional" lifestyles; (3) ways of influencing and controlling relationship lifestyles; (4) how communication styles can affect relationship lifestyles; and (5) how dishonesty, or "living a lie," is pertinent to and affects individuals' relationship lifestyles. Before going further, however, let's take a look at a more meaningful definition to the concept of "lifestyle."

From an overall perspective, a lifestyle is primarily a consistent and integrated way of life of an individual, typified by one's activities, manners, attitudes, possessions, and senses of meaning and worth. As is illustrated by the examples in this section, a loving relationship directly and indirectly affects a person's lifestyle, and vice versa.

An advertisement for the Florida Lottery says, "Winning the Lottery will not change your life, just the way you live it." We beg to differ. Like winning the lottery, a loving relationship will normally change both your client's life or lives *and* the way he, she or they choose to live it (i.e., the lifestyle).

Individual Lifestyles and Relationship Lifestyles. As we discussed, in the best relationships there is high congruence (or compatibility) between the lifestyle choices of each individual and of the couple as a unit. Moreover, as we stated, when this congruence breaks down, it often bodes relationship problems. The example from Bill Emener's case files, presented in Dialogue 11.1, provides an excellent illustration.

Dialogue 11.1 Individual Lifestyles and Relationship Lifestyles.

Dutch (**D**) and Olivia (**O**) came to see Bill Emener (**B**) to discuss problems they were having with their relationship. He will never forget how funny they were. When they expressed frustrations to each other, they would say things that were at times "cold and cruel," yet at the same time extremely humorous.

Dutch, a 28-year-old, rough and tough, Paul Bunyan-type outdoorsman and co-owner of a small trucking company would jump at any opportunity to go fishing or hunting, or simply to be outdoors. As he many times said, "There's nothing more fun than to spend a whole day with my buddies on a good trout stream, with a six pack of beer iced down and a good chaw of tobacco!" Olivia, on the other hand, a 26-year-old claims accountant for a local insurance company, sang in the church choir, taught Sunday school and was chairwoman of the church's bake sales. She once quipped, "I don't smoke, I don't drink alcoholic beverages and I don't curse – not like some people I know!"

Dutch once described Olivia by saying, "She is so conservative that she could make Rush Limbaugh look ludicrously liberal. If she gains any more weight, she'll have to have her clothes custom tailored by Omar Khayyam [the tentmaker]. Her idea of an erotic experience is to eat two Fig Newtons at the same time!"

Olivia quickly quipped, "Oh sure, and here we have Macho Mike, the walking Skoal commercial, who, if he had his own way, would buy all of his clothes out of an L.L. Bean catalog! If we were sitting in the living room with the screen door open and I said, 'Honey, would you please get that fly out for me,' he would go to the garage for his tackle box!"

Although they had been married for slightly more than a year, their verbalizations of their frustrations already had become a traditional comedy routine for them and their friends. They said that at times they "could entertain friends for hours by cutting each other down." They came to see Bill, however, because while their comedy routine was still funny to their friends, as far as they were concerned "it wasn't funny anymore."

Toward the end of their first session:

B: (While diagramming Figure 11.1 on a blank piece of paper) It appears to me that the two of you live rather uniquely different individual lifestyles, which tend to be inconsistent with each of your individual values. And understandably, another part of your difficulty is that you are having trouble developing a collective lifestyle in which you can enjoy doing things together. Olivia, you probably would not enjoy joining Dutch on a beer-drinking, tobacco-chewing fishing trip; and Dutch, you probably would not enjoy going with Olivia to a church picnic.

D & O: [After looking at each other] Yes, that's right.

In addition to suggesting a self-help book for them to consider reading, Bill invited them to try to identify some activities both of them could do together and enjoy. When they left his office, they expressed a sense of excitement and felt optimistic about their ability to identify some mutually enjoyable activities.

During their second session, three weeks later:

B: So, how have things been going for the two of you?

O: Well, there's good news and there's bad news. The good news is that we were able to identify some activities we could enjoy doing together, and we actually did some of them. For example, last Saturday we went to a company picnic with all of the folks Dutch works with. By and large, it was fun. Then, this past Friday evening, we went out to dinner and to an early movie with two other couples. That wasn't too bad either.

D: Yes, those particular things were okay. But I think our problems go deeper than that. When I am out in public or in a social situation with Olivia, I really feel I cannot be myself. I always have the feeling that she's watching every move I make and is thinking critical thoughts. I don't know, but I just can't be myself around her!

O: Well, it's the same for me Dutch, because I feel you are watching me with a critical eye all the time as well.

B: So what I hear both of you saying is that when you are out together you feel like you're constantly watching each other with critical eyes and therefore not able to enjoy yourselves.

O: Yes.

D: Indeed.

B: With regard to your very different individual lifestyles, I'd like to ask you this – what was it like when the two of you first met and were dating?

D: Speaking for myself – I lied... in effect... Before we were married, when we were dating, I'd go to her events with her and made believe it was okay... I made believe I was having a good time. But the truth is, I hated those fancy-dancy dinners and that play she dragged me to.

O: Well, while you were enjoying the bites you were getting from the fish when you dragged me along on that fishing trip, I was just trying to survive the bites I was getting from all those damned mosquitoes!

D: [Looking at Bill] Do you think we will ever be able to enjoy a collective lifestyle as husband and wife – doing things together and truly enjoying ourselves?

B: I really don't know, Dutch, that's a good question. And while I'm here to help you in any way I can, that is something the two of you will have to work on and find out for yourselves.

Dutch and Olivia canceled their next scheduled appointment and never returned. Bill left a message on their answering machine inviting them to call him and let him know how things were going, but never heard back from them. We wish we could share with you what eventually happened with them. But we can't – because we don't know. The only thing we do know is that they probably would have been better off if they had been honest with each other at the outset.

In the case of Dutch and Olivia, there was a strong initial attraction that served as the basis of their courtship and decision to marry. But, they never thought through the wider implications of their very different lifestyle preferences.

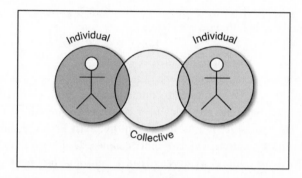

Figure 11.1. Individual and Collective Lifestyles.

As couples counselors, whenever either of your authors meets two individuals who are contemplating the establishment of a long-term, committed loving relationship, we invite them to critically analyze the extent to which the two of them can enjoy a collective, relationship lifestyle. We also suggest to them that if they are unable to enjoy a collective, relationship lifestyle together, it indeed may be very difficult for them to enjoy a long-term loving relationship. How people spend their individual time in life is important. And when they are in a loving relationship, how they spend their collective-, together-, relationship-time is equally important.

Functional and Dysfunctional Lifestyles. In the introduction to this section, we discussed the importance of maintaining compatibility between a couple's shared lifestyle and each partner's individual lifestyle – a concept we referred to as *lifestyle congruence*. It is hard to overestimate the importance of this aspect of relationships. When the demands of one or both partners' separate lifestyles negatively impact the couple's ability to enjoy a shared lifestyle, the relationship will suffer. For example, Bill Emener recalls a couple, both of whose friends were envious of their relationship. The problem was that they were very unhappy!

After Bill invited them to talk more about this discontinuity, they began to explore the couple's day-to-day lifestyle. One of the two thought about it for a moment and said, "I think the problem is that we give our best to everyone else! All day long, I am being friendly and warm to everyone I meet; I have to – I'm a salesman. At the same time, my wife, the administrative secretary for a head honcho at the college, has to be warm and friendly to everyone she sees all day long too. Then when we get home, we're focused on being good parents to our boys. The problems arise during the times we are alone together, either very early in the morning or very late in the evening. That's when we are both either very tired or worn out from the day. Again, it just seems to me that *we are giving our best to everyone else.*"

With Bill's guidance, the couple engaged in some reconfiguring and overhauling of their individual lifestyles so that they could spend more time "giving our best to each other." What we can learn from them is somewhat simplistic, but very important:

In the process of maintaining a loving relationship, it is very important for the two individuals to remain aware of their individual lifestyles so that their relationship lifestyle is functional – that it enhances their lives, is pleasant and enjoyable, and when they are together they are giving each other their best.

This is the essence of "lifestyle congruence."Controlling the Relationship Lifestyle: Putting Partners First. Similar to the example above are cases in which the overlapping "inner circle" – the shared part we call the "relationship lifestyle" – not only becomes incongruent with the lifestyle of each individual but actually ceases to exist. When this happens, the relationship exists in name only. Although this may sound obvious to the point of triviality, we have counseled many couples that, over the years, had let the shared portion of their lifestyle dwindle away to almost nothing. This too is a recipe for potentially serious relationship problems, including dissolution, if it is not properly attended to.

When two individuals are actively involved in their careers and in the rearing of their children, it is very easy for them to allow their relationship lifestyle to get out of control whereby they "never have any time for each other." Each of us has many times heard, "We married each other years ago because we enjoyed spending time together. Over the last two years, however, we simply allowed other things to get in our way and we haven't been spending time together. It's no wonder that we felt we were drifting apart!"

Bill Lambos has a general rule of thumb for couples – he states early in the counseling process: *to the extent possible and after careful thought and consideration, put your significant other first*. Obviously, this does not mean neglecting the primary needs of children, ignoring other family members and/or failing to meet one's work and career demands when they require attention. What it *does* mean, however, is that each partner in a long-term relationship should place meeting the needs and desires of their significant other as high as possible on the daily list of priorities. And, of equal importance, it must be a two-way street!

Bill has kept a running log not only of his own clients, but also of many of his friends and colleagues' serious relationships and their outcomes. Bill has yet to see an exception to the rule. When both members of a loving couple put their partner's happiness first whenever possible, then the relationship endures year after year. When a child comes along, for example, if the parents take care to make time for one another, to get away when possible and, when the child wants something, say something like "Let's help Mom first, then we'll take care of that afterwards," the marriage lasts. On the other hand, when the needs and/or desires of one's spouse are relegated to the bottom of the priority list, the marriage typically will last no more than five years. Relationships are like living things: they need to be cared for or they will wither and die. And the lifestyle choice a couple adopts in this regard is often what makes the difference one way or the other.

Communication Styles. Shared lifestyles include not only shared activities, but shared values and norms of behavior as well. One critical area in which we have seen couples slide into problems is in their communication styles – the manner by which the two individuals jointly express themselves and interpret the messages expressed by the other person. Not surprisingly, people differ with respect to communication style, and this can negatively impact relationship lifestyles.

Counselors and psychologists often talk about *The A-B-C's of Communication*. We can communicate with each other through our *Affect* (or feelings), our *Behaviors* (or actions) and/or our *Cognitions* (or thoughts). For example, if you and your spouse were worried about one of your sons who was supposed to have been home an hour ago, you might begin shaking, getting fidgety and snapping back as a way of communicating your fear and concern. That would be an affective way of communicating. On the other hand, your spouse could simply pick up the telephone and call his friend and find out whether your son had left yet to return home. That would be a behavioral response. And lastly, one of you could look at the other, and from a cognitive or thought-processing perspective, say, "I wonder why he has not returned yet? I don't understand this!" The following example shows how this can impact – and improve – a couple's shared or relationship lifestyle.

As Leonard and Theresa were talking with Bill Emener, they eventually began discussing their communication styles. "It seems that we just can't communicate with each other anymore," said Leonard.

Bill invited Leonard and Theresa to bear with him while he gave them a brief lecture on communication styles that included considerations pertinent to their specific relationship – basically the A-B-C's. Bill sketched a diagram similar to the one in Figure 11.2. Then, pointing to the diagram, he said to them, "One of the things the two of you might want to do is to analyze the extent to which each of you individually expresses yourself, or communicates – in a cognitive style, an affective style and/or a behavioral style."

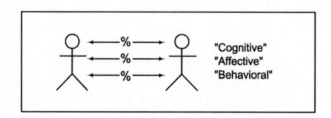

Figure 11.2. Communication Styles.

Almost immediately, Leonard said, "I'm clearly a C-B-A." Although Bill understood him, he asked him to explain specifically what he meant. "It makes sense," he replied. "I'm an attorney. My primary way of dealing with the world is through thoughts and words. I am very cognitively oriented. My next way would probably be the behavioral style, and last but not least, I deal with feelings."

While looking at the Figure, Theresa said, "Oh that's great, Len, I'm just the opposite! I'm an A-B-C person. My first thing is to deal with feelings. Then I deal with behavior, and if all else fails, I guess, I will talk from an intellectual or cognitive perspective." Based on his observations of their interactions during the session, Bill suggested to them that their individual analyses were accurate.

What was additionally difficult for Leonard and Theresa was that whenever they would discuss something that entailed disagreement, Len would try to overpower Theresa with his cognitive style (and by the way, he was a very intelligent and highly educated individual), and whenever Theresa wanted to neutralize Len, she would start crying or throw a temper tantrum, knowing he had difficulties dealing with feelings.

Over the next two sessions with Leonard and Theresa, Bill assisted them in developing more functional communication styles that would help to prevent each of them from overemphasizing the communication style that was most comfortable and productive for each of them. For example, when Theresa would feel that Leonard was overwhelming her with his *thoughts*, she would say, "Okay, Len there you go again by bullying me with your brightness." Likewise, if Theresa were to throw a temper tantrum or begin to cry, Len would say, "There you go again, Theresa, playing with my feelings to get your own way." Obviously, these were not necessarily the best, verbalized communication signals for them to use for "calling" each other on an overuse of an individual communication style, but as time went on they were able to communicate much more effectively.

Some people communicate to us that they love us by giving us a big hug and putting their head on our shoulder. Others communicate to us that they love us by saying, "I love you." Others communicate to us that they love us by bringing over a stool so we can put our feet up and/or fixing a cup of tea for us when we are tired. There is nothing wrong with us using any of these three styles, as long as: (1) they are functional; (2) they communicate what we are feeling; and (3) the other person accurately hears and understands what we are feeling and trying to communicate. When an overemphasis on, or an over-utilization of, one of these three styles becomes dysfunctional and/or prevents accurate communication, we get in trouble (for excellent discourse on this, consult Chapman, 2008).

Living a Lie. One of Eleanor's primary difficulties in processing her plans to divorce her husband was that her "three children and parents were shocked." At the age of 48, after 26 years of marriage to Russell and about two months after their last child went off to college, Eleanor moved out and filed for divorce. From what she told Bill, Russell "was not fighting her" and it appeared that the divorce itself was going to be a rather amicable one. "The biggest thing for me to handle right now," she said, "is that my children don't believe me. They think I'm crazy. The other night, however, I had a conversation with Russell, and we decided that both of us would talk with our three children the next time there is an opportunity for the five of us to get together. The truth of the matter, Dr. Emener, is that for the last 15 to 20 years, Russell and I lived a lie. About 15 to 20 years ago we fell out of love but continued to act lovingly toward each other, continued to play our mommy and daddy roles, and continued to tell everyone that we were 'doing wonderfully' anytime anyone would ask how we were doing. As Russell admitted to me the other night, 'We have enjoyed a beautiful, functional family, but for most of the time we have had an empty, meaningless and dysfunctional marriage'."

By and large, *people tend to believe what they see and experience.* Eleanor and Russell's children, parents, family and friends saw and experienced Eleanor and Russell having a functional, loving relationship. The problem was, obviously, that their lifestyle – their shared social relationship lifestyle that they allowed everyone to see – was simply a lie. After having had the opportunity to learn from Eleanor and Russell's experiences, we now will occasionally say to couples, "Okay, I believe I understand your relationship lifestyle. However, *is the relationship lifestyle that you just described the one that everyone else sees? And is it true or is it a lie?"*

As Eleanor rather poignantly said, "When it comes to an individual's relationship lifestyle, there is nothing wrong with living a lie as long as living a lie doesn't bother you. For me, it eventually did. And as painful as it was to change things, I decided to be honest – with myself, with Russell and with my family."

As you help your clients analyze their individual and their relationship lifestyles, help them to remain aware of the extent to which they are fabricated, falsified or "for show," *and/or* authentic, genuine and "for real." Then, you may want them to ask themselves: *"Is this what I want?"* And if it isn't, *"What am I ready, willing and able to do about it?"*

PROBLEMS RELATING TO ONE'S SIGNIFICANT OTHER

"The problem with our relationship is that we have relationship problems."

This is not an uncommon statement. And while it may appear trite and flip, it is anything but. In fact, as we noted in the introduction to this chapter, you may be wondering why a book like this would contain a separate section on "relationship problems." After all, isn't every single chapter in this book devoted to some important aspect of relationships that can be a potential source of problems? Our answer, as stated above, is that this section is about the subject and management of relationship problems *per se*, rather than any specific type or source of problem.

Our approach herein falls under the rubric of "meta-analysis" – the stem "meta" being derived from the Greek word for "after." In epistemology, however, the stem "meta-" means "about." Today it is common for philosophy texts to have sections on "meta-logic" (logic *about* logic) and for psychology books to include a discussion of *meta-cognition* (thinking *about* thinking). Commensurately, this book includes this chapter on the subject of meta-problems (problems *about* problems). To wit, we will take a look at relationships that is one step further removed from individual issues and concerns (money, jealousy, trust, etc.) and address the general issue of relationship problems (regardless of the specific cause).

For the couples counselor, the ability to engage in meta-relationship problem analysis is a core skill. The couples counselor will hear stories about every imaginable topic, namely, all those addressed in the previous chapters of this book. For this reason, counseling cannot be driven by the nature of specific problems (although they must always be considered), but must be guided by a framework based on the counselor's theoretical approach and an understandably limited set of interventions. For each case and/or client, the approach is adapted to the specifics of the case as guided by the client's presenting problem. Furthermore, given the absence of a coherent and consistent framework from which to operate, the counselor is forced to "reinvent the wheel" for each new client. And given that a couples counselor has three clients (each partner and their relationship), this clearly can be unmanageable.

Therefore, from an overall perspective, we propose that (a) relationship problems (again, irrespective of their proximate or immediate causes) can be grouped into various categories, (b) these categories have something in common that other types of problems do not, and (c) understanding this is helpful in formulating a strategy to address relationship problems more effectively. In this regard, we classify relationship problems into the following three "meta-classes:" (1) solvable problems; (2) unsolvable problems; and (3) dangerous problems.

Solvable Problems. Considering that slightly more than half of all marriages in the United States end in divorce, one might be tempted to assume that half of all relationship problems are solvable (i.e., those that don't lead to divorce) and the other half are not amenable to solution (and therefore lead to divorce). Although this sounds like common sense logic at first pass, in fact a small amount of meta-analysis shows it to be quite false – the majority of relationship problems are solvable.

Every couple has many problems to work through, often several per month. Thus, if half were unsolvable, then probability theory would suggest that eventually every marriage would end in divorce. But almost half never do. Moreover, even unsolvable problems may not be serious enough to warrant giving up on an entire relationship that is otherwise a source of comfort, meaning and worth to the partners. People can agree to disagree on certain issues without throwing out the baby with the bathwater (figuratively speaking!). Even the healthiest of long-term relationships have at least one or two rough spots or problem areas that never get solved, but instead are ignored for the purposes of "the greater good." In fact, as we shall see below, people sometimes choose to remain in relationships where their very health and safety is at risk due to abuse. Thus, the overarching question: what makes one type of problem solvable and another type unsolvable? The following examples from our case files illustrate and help clarify the distinction.

Sam and Liz came to see Bill Emener for marriage counseling because they had a number of issues that were troubling them, many of which had to do with parenting their adult children. While addressing these issues, they also discussed another problematic concern in their marriage. When Sam and Liz's three children were still at home and they were living in a large, four-bedroom, three-bath house, Sam went to work everyday and took care of the yard; Liz was a stay-at-home homemaker. The year before, however, when their last child went off to college, they sold the big house, bought a three-bedroom, two-bath condo on water and a boat, and Liz went back to work. "One of our big issues – *problems* actually," said Liz, "is that Sam always has insisted on living in a neat and clean home. But he hates to do housework! So now that we're both working and living in our condo and he doesn't have any yard to take care of, he still expects me to do all the housecleaning. Trust me – it's a very big condo! It just isn't fair."

Toward the end of his first session with Sam and Liz, Bill suggested a self-help book for them (one that discussed the parenting of adult children) as well as a homework assignment. "Between now and our next session," Bill said, "I would like for the two of you to identify as many possible solutions to this 'clean house' problem as you can. Try to think outside the box and don't worry about the negatives – at least not while you're identifying the possible solutions. We'll get to the 'downsides' later."

Two weeks later when they arrived for their next session, they said the recommended self-help book had been helpful and they already had addressed half of their parenting concerns with their children. Then as Liz opened her pocketbook and started removing a folded piece of paper, she and Sam started laughing. Their laughter was contagious – Bill began laughing as well, then he asked, "What's so funny?"

"For the past year and a half," Liz began, "on Tuesday nights Sam has been on a men's bowling team and on Thursday nights we both have bowled in a couples-league." Then as she handed their "Outside the Box Solutions to Our Housecleaning Problem" to Bill, with a grin she continued. "One of Sam's solutions was for him to drop out of the Thursday night league, and with the saved money we would hire a 20-year-old Swedish maid – he of course would be willing to stay home to supervise." Sam then laughingly interjected, "Yeah, and one of Liz's suggestions was for her to drop out of the Thursday night league, and with the saved money we would hire a 20-year-old Chippendale Houseboy – she of course would be willing to stay home to supervise." Liz wadded up the list and playfully threw it at Sam, saying, "We're a trip!"

When the cajoling subsided, they told Bill what they had decided to do about their housecleaning problem: Sam agreed to drop out of his Tuesday night league and with the money they would save they would hire a housecleaner to come in every other week. "Hey," Sam concluded, "it's a win-win: Liz and I still have our Thursday night bowling, we'll still have our evening and weekend boating, I'll be living in a clean house without having to clean, and Liz won't have any cleaning to do either." "There's another win," Liz said with a warm smile. "We're not arguing anymore!"

As Sam and Liz experienced – when a counselor can nudge a couple to get beyond roadblocks such as *I want to get my own way* and the *power and control issues* associated with relationship problems *and* to "think outside the box" – many relationship problems can be solved.

The question, "What can make some problems solvable and others not?" also may amount to issues beyond the specific problem such as: perceptions, rigidity, access to professional help in dispute resolution, and the strength of the wider relationship. These all play significant roles in making problems solvable. Ultimately, all but a narrow range of relationship problems are solvable as long as: (1) both partners place a higher priority on keeping the relationship intact than on other factors, such as *having to win*; and (2) the couple does not hesitate too long to look for outside help when it becomes necessary.

Unsolvable Problems. As just discussed, an unsolvable problem does not necessarily lead to the end of a relationship. People can and do choose to accept less than optimal arrangements all the time, and often there is nothing wrong with this. Common examples of this type of "unsolvable problem" are in-law issues, career-relationship conflicts, lingering resentments over past behaviors, and so forth.

There are two types of problems, however, which are unsolvable and will lead to the ending of any relationship, later if not sooner. The first is the end of emotional gratification in the relationship. The second is the accumulated damage done through emotional and/or physical abuse that is not addressed immediately in a relationship. Let's examine these in order.

Yvonne originally came to see Bill Lambos because of her nine-year-old son's academic issues in school. She wanted Seth, a third-grader, evaluated for attention deficit disorder (ADD) because he was falling further and further behind his classmates. After interviewing Seth and administering a battery of neuropsychological scales and tests, Bill concluded that the boy did not meet the criteria for ADD or the criteria of a learning disability. Rather, Seth seemed to be distracted at school (and elsewhere) because he was highly anxious over his parents' relationship. During further interviews, Yvonne admitted that she had been having an affair with a married man she met at a school function and "felt no love at all anymore for her husband." Her husband, Peter, traveled four days a week out of state for his company, and when he was home the marriage was carried on only for the sake of the children. Bill asked Yvonne, "Do you think you are protecting your children by continuing your pretend relationship with Peter?" Yvonne's eyes swelled with tears as she answered, "Yes, my children would be devastated if their parents were to divorce. In addition, my lover is a respected businessman with a wife and two small children of his own, and his conservative colleagues and parents would be mortified if he left his wife for another woman. Furthermore, he feels the same way I do about exposing his children to divorce."

"Yvonne," Bill replied, "your son is having problems at school and is not getting along with other children because he senses something is very wrong at home. How much of a favor do you think you are doing him by carrying on the charade of the 'happy family'?" While dabbing her eyes, Yvonne said, "I really have made a mess of things. My lover is not ready to break up his family, so I'm not going to break up mine. And if this is impacting my son, then I'm just going to have to pretend harder that I still love Peter."

Bill referred Seth to a child counselor with expertise in marriage and family therapy and continues to see Yvonne as his client. As Seth's anxiety was addressed in therapy, his school performance improved markedly. As for Yvonne, she continues to live for the time secreted away with her lover and has resigned herself to living with an unsolvable problem, at least for the time being. Her anxiety level has also been reduced through her sessions. The last time she saw Bill, she said, "I would rather have what I have with this man, however difficult it is to be away from him most of the time, than to go back to where I was not able to feel anything at all. Since I resigned myself to my situation and stopped 'wanting it all,' I've actually been less stressed and happier."

As we have said numerous times, loving relationships are entered into on a voluntary basis because they offer something of value to the partners that they did not have prior to the relationship. Typically, the value is the emotional gratification gained by satisfying the need to connect to and with another human being and to "feel special." When this gratification ceases to occur – when one is no longer capable of feeling special with the significant other – the relationship has an unsolvable problem and will usually end, later if not sooner.

The other type of unsolvable problem comes from the buildup of what we like to refer to as *emotional scar tissue*, due to repeated hurtful interactions. Although such interactions may or may not qualify as legally abusive, any interaction that leaves a permanent mark, emotional or otherwise, often does lasting damage to that relationship. One of the banes of being a couples therapist is that couples sometimes wait too long to seek outside help. By the time they do, so much emotional scarring may have occurred that it is too late to heal. In such cases, the only solution left is dissolution of the relationship in a manner that does the least possible further harm.

Making Clients' Problems Less Problematic. As Victor Frankl (1946, 1984) convincingly proffered, people often do not realize the amount of control they have in choosing how to look at, understand, find meaning in, or otherwise think about their problems. One's perception of the problem is a key factor in determining its severity, and we counselors and therapists spend much of our time in helping clients to alter their perceptions of their problems. Thus, one of the most effective approaches a couples counselor has at her or his disposal is to help clients adopt strategies and habits that serve to lessen their perceived severity of their problems.

There are a number of strategies you can employ to help clients reduce the severity of their relationship problems, even though they may not involve solving the problem. Our list of "sage advice" to clients includes the following suggestions, repeated as often as necessary during sessions:

1) *"Don't react impulsively.* Think before you act or speak in a way you might later regret. The emotional scar tissue discussed earlier is lasting and builds up bit by bit. Every time you do or say something that hurts your partner, you have become a part of the problem rather than a part of the solution. Keep your cool."

2) *"What you say is less important than how you say it.* This grade school truism is still good advice for adults dealing with relationship problems. It is nearly always possible to frame a complaint or a demand as a *request*, and to explain why you are requesting that something change. Frame such requests using 'I' rather than 'you' as the subject (i.e. 'I would feel better if we lowered our voices' rather than 'You should stop yelling at me.'). Diplomacy can work wonders in minimizing relationship problems."

3) *"Pick the time and place to address the problem.* Timing is everything, it is said, and especially so when dealing with relationship problems. If necessary, schedule a time and place to have problem-focused discussions, so your partner does not feel like they have been subject to a surprise attack. It is also a good idea to choose a 'neutral' territory for such discussions, for example while out for a walk."

4) *"Look at the big picture.* Don't sweat the small stuff. If you know you really don't care about something, don't let yourself get hung up on it for the sake of pride or selfish reasons. Chances are, you have chosen to be in your relationship because it offers something very important to you. Keep that perspective in the front of your thinking."

5) *"Offer concessions when appropriate or feasible.* If you are requesting your partner to change his or her behavior, or give up something of value, offer something in return. Ask your partner what he or she would like in the way of a concession – you don't have to agree to it – and it might be something trivial you are happy to offer."

6) *"Relationships are not a zero-sum game.* When trying to resolve or reduce the scope of a problem, keep in mind there is not a prize of a fixed size that must be split up, so that the more your partner gets, the less you do. Think of ways of enlarging the pie rather than cutting it up."

7) *"Focus on issues, not on 'positions.'* A position is a stance you take on an issue, often on a matter of principle. An interest is something you would like or something you would like changed. Avoid the temptation to focus on your position when trying to resolve a relationship problem (i.e., what you demand of your partner, what is 'right' or 'fair') and instead think about what will satisfy your interests or meet your general desires. Always try to think in terms of win-win instead of 'you vs. me'."

None of the above means that you can teach clients to snap their fingers and make relationship problems disappear. If that were so, this chapter would not be necessary. Rather, the point is that when client problems present themselves, the clients can learn, with your guidance, to handle them either so as to reduce their probable impact on the relationship, or alternatively, so as to breed more conflict, lead to contempt and scar the relationship. In our experience, people in relationships tend to under-appreciate the role they play in dealing with problems effectively. Reminding your clients of this simple reality can save many a break-up.

Gridlock Gridlock is a term describing an inability to move within a space or network, usually in regard to traffic. In relationships, gridlock is used to describe a situation in which competing interests prevent progress toward some goal. Relationship problems that remain unresolved because neither party is willing to make a concession or accommodation are often described as in a state of gridlock.

A state of gridlock represents a warning sign when a couple is trying to deal with a relationship problem. It means that the relationship problem causing the gridlock is in danger of escalating to the point where the relationship itself is threatened or at risk of permanent scarring. We recommend learning to recognize gridlock for what it is – mutual stubbornness and unwillingness to compromise – and to seek ways to resolve or reduce the gridlock quickly. For example, having each partner suggest two or three solutions and then facilitating a discussion of the pros and cons of each can be very helpful. Failing to do so puts the relationship at risk and often causes minor, solvable problems to become major, unsolvable ones. Many failed relationships are characterized by a pattern or state of unresolved gridlock in their later stages.

Abuse. Earlier in this chapter we described relationships problems as being of three types: solvable, unsolvable and dangerous. We now will look at *dangerous relationship problems* and the damage they cause to the individuals and family members involved in them – and, at times, to our society as a whole.

In general, dangerous relationships are characterized by one of two characteristics: enabling and abusive. We will look at enabling in the next chapter under the heading of codependence. Herein, however, we address the other factor that can make a relationship dangerous – *abuse* (which is synonymous with domestic violence). In the previous chapter, we briefly looked at the staggering costs associated with domestic violence and physical abuse. Here we look at it from a different perspective – that of a type of relationship problem that requires outside intervention.

Abuse refers to the use or treatment of something, be it a person, an item, a substance or something else, in a manner that is seen as harmful. In the context of relationships, abuse normally refers to the severe maltreatment of a person. Abuse may come in any of several varieties. These include: *physical abuse*, in which one person inflicts physical violence or pain on another; *verbal abuse*, such as when a person uses insulting or profane language, demeaning talk or threatening statements; and *emotional or psychological abuse,* such as coercion, humiliation, intimidation, relational aggression and/or alienation, in which one person uses emotional or psychological coercion to compel another to do something they do not want or is not in their best interests. In some cases, one person manipulates another's emotional or psychological state for their own or commits psychological aggression using ostensibly nonviolent methods to inflict mental or emotional violence or pain on another.

Physical and even some forms of emotional abuse are considered sufficiently serious and damaging to society that psychologists and mental health counselors are required to violate confidentiality and alert authorities in many cases when a credible report of abuse is made. This is particularly true if the abuse involves minors or elderly persons. As a licensed professional, you may have a legal obligation to report to the police a case in which there exists, in your professional opinion, credible evidence of physical abuse. Laws vary by state and jurisdiction, so you must be aware of your legal obligations in this area.

Most municipalities have hotlines for reporting abuse, and we strongly encourage any person who is experiencing an abusive relationship to place the well being and safety of themselves and their dependents first, and to immediately take any steps necessary to remove themselves from the dangerous situation. This is especially true when there is no requirement mandating that the therapist report it, due to local statutes that place the importance of confidentiality higher than that of the requirement to report. When in doubt what to do in a specific case, seek professional guidance from a colleague, supervisor or the ethical advisory board of your professional association.

Separation. When relationships involve serious unsolvable problems, or whenever any relationship is abusive, separation is the next step. Although in many cases separation is a precursor to divorce or dissolution of the relationship, it need not be. A temporary separation has led many couples to realize the value of their relationship and to take serious steps to resolve their problems. Separation also allows people to test the water, as it were, and to try living independently before committing to permanently ending a significant relationship.

Separation should, if possible, be discussed and the new terms of the relationship stated openly and agreed upon. The partners should, with your assistance as necessary, openly discuss and agree to what they both consider important for the future of their relationship. This may include rules agreed to such as "no dating other people while separated"; "neither will do anything 'stupid' (such as excessive gambling or drinking)"; "neither will go over to the other's residence without calling first"; "there will be daily contact (either in person or by phone)"; "neither will call the other after ten o'clock in the evening"; "neither of them will 'create a scene' in social situations"; "both will notify the other person should an emergency arise"; and, "both will remain available to the other" (i.e., neither of them will "disappear" or purposefully avoid the other). The couple should be reminded that an added benefit to such rules is that in honoring these agreements, they will not add to their problems and issues, and thus when they "talk" they can stay focused on the important issues in their relationship.

The term separation means different things in different places in the context of marital relationships. For example, some states do not recognize legal separation in the absence of a separation agreement filed with the family court system, particularly if children are involved. An informal separation not involving a written agreement is referred to as an *estrangement*. Whether a couple is separated or estranged, however, it is important for them to openly discuss, identify and honor agreements such as the examples above.

Fighting Well. As couples in healthy and happy relationships address and live with their day-to-day and overarching problems, they occasionally fight. There is nothing wrong with fighting – as long as each person fights fair. According to Dr. John Gottman's research (Gottman & Silver, 1999), the way a couple fights is one of the most accurate indicators of whether they'll stay together. Couples who are good at de-escalating arguments with humor and compliments are in good shape. Those who shut each other out or jab each other with sarcasm and insults are headed for trouble. Fortunately, any couple can learn the tools of relationship-friendly fights. We try to teach our clients for whom fighting is an issue the following "Ten Recommendations for Fighting Well." We lightly advise our clients that these rules offer excellent insight and advice on how to "argue happily ever after."

1) *"Surrender the need to be right.* People tend to fight because they believe that they're right, and they want the other person to understand that. However, it is important for them to ask themselves: Would I rather be right or happy? When you fight, if at all possible, focus on a solution that would be right for everyone, rather than worry about who's right and who's wrong."

2) *"Stay on topic.* If you're fighting about the fact that he or she drank too much at your sister's wedding, then stick to that grievance. This is not a good time to throw in that he or she was late picking you up last week and never puts the empty bottles in the recycling bin. Bringing up all the past hurts and reading your list of 'done-wrongs' will put your partner on the defensive; sticking to your point will keep your partner from getting confused, impatient and possibly even more angry."

3) *"Focus on your partner's point, rather than yours.* Your significant other will be more likely to hear your perspective if you let him or her know that you're genuinely listening to his or her perspective. Instead of just trying to ram your point of view across, spend at least as much time listening to your partner's point of view. Asking questions like, 'Could you say more about that?' can be very helpful."

4) *"Give the other person an out, when necessary.* Many people get frustrated when a partner changes the subject or makes a joke during a heated argument. However, this is not necessarily a bad thing, as it can be an effective way to break the tension and give each partner some breathing space. By allowing your partner to change the subject and stop talking about the problem, you're giving him or her an out. That can be helpful if emotions are running high or he or she is starting to feel defensive or trapped. You can also do this by doing what is done many times in athletic contests: when you feel things are getting out of hand, call 'time out' and agree to finish the discussion when both of you have cooled off. Just remember, of course, to resume the conversation at a later date."

5) *"Pick your battles.* Sometimes you just have to accept that he or she will always be 15 minutes late and will never learn to see the black stuff dripping under the car or the green stuff that grows between the bathroom tiles. If you're always picking a fight about little things, it will be hard to get your partner to listen to the big things. So before you start to fight or argue about something, ask yourself, 'Is this really important to our relationship?' and 'Do I really want to spend my time and energy bickering about this stuff?' Choose your battles wisely."

6) *"Avoid personal attacks.* Say for example that a wife is mad at her husband for leaving her stranded at his office barbecue. Fine, she has a right to be angry about that. But telling him what an inconsiderate jerk he is probably won't make him correct his behavior for the next office function. Instead, it would be better for her to explain how she felt 'when he left her stranded for 45 minutes with that tedious dweeb from HR.'"

7) *"Offer positive feedback.* John Gottman's research (Gottman & Silver, 1999) found that happy couples make at least five positive statements or actions for every negative one. Positive feedback includes anything from saying, 'Good point. I hadn't thought about it that way,' to a warm smile or nod. Validating your partner's position does not mean that you agree with him or her, and it may even disarm him or her and keep things from escalating."

8) *"Watch your body language.* We trust that you've seen negative and at times hostile body language; head-shaking, eye rolling, clenched jaws and derisive snorts can be just as damaging as verbal insults. If your partner looks hurt or has closed body posture, such as folded arms, crossed legs and sagging shoulders, you indeed may be broadcasting more hostility than you realize or intend."

9) *"Pick the right time and place.* If you've had a brutal day at the office, if your precious children have been perfect monsters or if the outdoor temperature is above 95 degrees, it might be a good idea to try to avoid a major conflict with your partner. These are called 'vulnerable times' and thus it may be more helpful to say something like, 'I truly want to work this out, but I'm not at my best right now. Let's set a time for later this evening or tomorrow.'"

10) *"Take the high road.* Okay, say you've done everything you could to address your relationship problems and your partner continues to criticize or stonewall. Indeed, that's frustrating. However, it might suggest that you consider couples counseling. But whatever you do, try not to sink to his or her level. Treat your partner with respect even if you're not getting it in return. Nobody wins when you both start behaving with bitterness and derision."

SEPARATION AND DIVORCE

As they sat in the parents' pew watching their son and new daughter- in-law exchanging marriage vows, they glanced into each other's eyes with a silent, understanding exchange of their shared bewilderment:

"That was us 30 years ago. What happened?"

Divorce, the dissolution, separation and disunion of a marriage is a major life event. Commensurate with the high and steady rate of divorce in the United States over the past decade, the multifaceted aspects of divorce indeed can be appreciated in the fact that some human service professionals (e.g., lawyers, family mediators and counselors) specialize in it, and books have been written with focus on specific aspects of it (e.g., the legal and psychological aspects). Marriage, separation and divorce represent three distinctly different kinds and aspects of loving relationships. It is not uncommon to hear individuals, such as those in the parents' pew above, say things such as:

"The day we got our divorce, I felt convinced we still loved each other very much. We just couldn't live together anymore."

"We've been separated for almost two years, and I still love him. But I don't know if it would ever work for us."

"I still love her so much, and probably always will. But there's been so much pain and hurt between us that even if she ever asked me to consider trying to get back together again, I don't know if I could – or would even want to try."

"That marriage was the nightmare from hell! What in God's name ever possessed me to marry that lunatic? How could I have been so blind? All I ask for is never to have to see his face again for the rest of my life!"

Unquestionably, it is appropriate that a book on learning how to counsel those in loving relationships also address divorce and separation.

This section certainly is not designed to address all of the legal, financial, occupational, familial, economic, physical and emotional considerations of divorce and separation. Nor are you, the professional couples counselor, expected to be an expert or to offer advice in most of these areas. As in the preceding two sections, we instead offer a set of what we believe are pearls of wisdom attained in our experiences over the past many combined years that you can share with your clients. Between us, we have counseled and/or mediated every conceivable type of relationship issue related to marriage, separation and divorce, and/or helped those undergoing divorce and separation to negotiate nearly every type of settlement agreement one could imagine. Given our combined experience in the field, your authors feel it is fair to assume you are unlikely to be exposed to a client or couple in a situation we have not already experienced. We therefore trust our experiences will translate into overarching and meaningful insights for you, and that our advice will assist you in helping your clients.

We have found that the following questions pertinent to divorce and separation can be expected from clients because they depict many of the recurring issues for people:

1) What might I expect to experience? That is, what are some of the typical stages of divorce?
2) What do I need to consider doing to protect myself so that I can minimize my pain and sorrow?
3) What are some do's and don't-do's as I go through this?
4) In terms of what I may experience, what might be some of the effects of time?
5) I think I know what I will need to do as time goes on, but at what pace should I move ahead?
6) How can I deal with my anger after the divorce is over so that I can get on with my life?
7) How can we protect our children from psychological trauma?
8) How can we finalize this divorce without having an unfair arrangement forced on us by the family court system?
9) How can we retain our rights to see and care for our children after the divorce?

These questions are not by any means all-inclusive. Moreover, you may notice they fall into somewhat different categories. For example, the first six concern personal issues related to personal adjustment and functioning throughout separation and divorce. Question 7 pertains to the psychological welfare of children in the context of a divorce. The last two questions address matters of control over economic and child visitation issues – the very important "who gets what?" questions.

Despite the wide range of issues brought out by these questions, they are all representative of the primary concerns of adults who are contemplating or experiencing separation and/or divorce. Within selected question areas, we shall discuss pertinent issues, share some relevant experiences of our clients, and offer some suggestions and recommendations that may be of assistance to you as you assist your clients. (Those areas not addressed in the following are covered in other areas of this book.)

Stages of Divorce. Although we have read several theories by other specialists regarding the stages of divorce, the entire subject area remains murky at best. In many cases, the research is confounded by multiple sources of variance and/or has not been replicated. In fact, we feel it is fair to state that the stage approaches to divorce may not be appropriate as a general model. We do not know of any commonly specific stages of divorce that apply to all people. All of the individuals whom we have known in our personal lives, as well as those with whom we have worked as a psychologist or mediator, have experienced stages or identifiable processes of their divorces that were individualized. Thus, we recommend that you advise your clients that there are no specific identifiable stages of separation and/or divorce for all people – like everyone else's, *their experiences are unique unto themselves.*

Our personal and professional experiences and observations have revealed five identifiable aspects of divorce that tend to be critical. Because they are typically experienced in order, you may consider them stages, though bear in mind our thoughts on the uniqueness of each individual's experience. The following will briefly discuss each of these five critical aspects and will include some discussion pertinent to the generalized considerations within them.

I. The Decision

It is not uncommon for people to come to see us because they are having difficulties trying to decide whether or not to file for a divorce. Similarly, individuals will at times come to us and say, "My husband (or wife) has asked me for a divorce. I do not know what to do. Should I say, okay let's get a divorce or should I suggest that we try to fix our marriage?" Counseling such clients may be easier for you if you advise them to give focused attention to two areas of concern: (1) From a cognitive perspective, ask them to *think* about and make a list of: (a) the pros and cons of trying to fix the marriage, and (b) the pros and cons of filing for divorce. Their thinking it through is always highly recommended. And, (2) from an affective perspective, remind them to remain cognizant of how they *feel* about it. As one of our clients poignantly said, "I have thought it through and considered the pros and cons of trying to fix our marriage as well as filing for divorce. However, it just does not feel right at this point! We've been married for over 10 years, so why am I in such a hurry? I think I am just going to take some time to think about it and let it settle in – when it feels right, I'll do it; if it doesn't feel right, I won't do it." We frequently have said to our friends and clients, "Slow down the movie!" – our tongue-in-cheek way of suggesting that they may be in too much of a hurry and may need to slow down. Most of the pressure to make a decision regarding a divorce tends to come from within the person. You therefore may also want to have the client ask him- or herself another question: "Why am I in such a hurry and where is the pressure coming from?" When the client is confident that their decision is correct (i.e., the client thinks it is in her or his best interest) and when it feels right, she or he will usually be ready to act on it.

We have a colleague, a couples counselor herself, who thinks that the wedding vows should be changed to end with the phrase "to have and to hold forever, or at least until you truly can't stand it any longer." While we offer this anecdote in part because it is amusing, there is more than a grain of truth to it. In our experience, most people who undergo a divorce before thinking and feeling it through long enough to be sure it's the right decision, or who do so without trying to fix the relationship first, come to regret their haste. It is very easy to underestimate the emotional and economic trauma of divorce. Likewise, it is hard to overestimate the difficulty in finding a new partner that will truly be an improvement over your most recent one. In many cases, it is worth pointing out to your clients that effective couples or marriage counseling is a truly worthwhile alternative to divorce. (We, as both authors and people, make this statement both from the experiences of our clients and based on our own previous marriages.)

We therefore recommend a person confronted with a decision regarding separation or divorce to focus on *"Why should I..."* kinds of questions. Examples of these include: *Why should I* separate from my wife (or husband)? *Why should I* file for a divorce from my husband (or wife)? *Why should I* suggest that we see a psychologist or a marriage counselor? Nonetheless, it also can be helpful to consider what we call the *contra- question.* Examples of contra-questions may include: *Why shouldn't I* separate from my wife (or husband)? *Why shouldn't I* file for a divorce from my husband (or wife)? *Why shouldn't I* suggest that we see a psychologist or a marriage counselor? During a recent marriage counseling session, John said to his wife, "Can we afford to take that two-week vacation together?" She gently, yet firmly, replied, "Can we afford not to?" It has been our experience that attending to contra-questions facilitates our having a deeper and richer understanding and appreciation of the issues and consequences of our decisions. And in the overall decision-making process, this is very important.

Finally, ask the client to consider the concept of reciprocity: "What does my partner or spouse think about the relationship?" "How would *I* feel if he or she were to suggest we separate or divorce?" Our society, for better or worse, reinforces self-centeredness. It is easy for people to forget what they have shared with their partner, how that person may have been of great solace to them in the past. The fastest pathway from civility to anger and even hatred is insensitivity to the feelings of one's significant other.

"Why should I divorce my wife?" was a question that Ralph exclusively addressed while he proceeded to separate and move out into his own apartment and see an attorney. When he came to see Bill Emener, "Just to see if you could be of any help to me," Bill asked him to consider a contra-question: "Why shouldn't I divorce my wife?" He called Bill three weeks later and said, "I had had a really long list of answers to my original question, 'Why should I divorce my wife?' but over the past few weeks I found myself developing an almost equally long list of answers to the contra-question, 'Why shouldn't I divorce my wife?' Last night Shirley and I were talking and we decided to explore the possibilities of reconciliation. Could you recommend a good marriage counselor for us?" Not only did Ralph help Bill appreciate the value of the contra-question, but he also reminded him that when we make important decisions such as those pertaining to separation and/or divorce, it also is a good idea to remain open to the possibility that if for some reason it doesn't seem right, you may want to revisit your original question(s) and possibly even change your mind.

A decision regarding a separation and/or a divorce is a process, not an event. While your client is focusing on his or her thoughts and feelings regarding the decision, remind them also to try to remain aware of the decision-making process.

II. Communicating the Decision

After your client has made a decision, the next question is: "How do I communicate my decision?" Always keep in mind that *how* one communicates the decision is as important as the decision itself. The following series of questions tends to capture the majority of concerns that individuals have with regard to the communication of their decision, and we recommend you encourage your clients who must communicate their decision to ask questions such as those that follow. (Please note that although the following questions use male and female pronouns, they are not gender-specific and are equally applicable to both men and women).

"*How* do I tell her?" "*How* can I tell her in such a way that she doesn't get hurt?" "*What* should I actually say to him?" "*How* will he react when I tell him?" "*Where* should I tell him – over the telephone or in a public place such as a restaurant, in case he gets violent?" "*When* should I tell her?"

We suspect that your client will find most of his or her questions regarding how to communicate the decision will begin with: *How... What... Where...* and *When...* words. As they think through these questions, however, they also may find it helpful to ask some *Why...?* questions. In most cases the communication of a decision regarding divorce is never easy, painless or comfortable for either party. Making the communication of the decision *easier, as painless as possible* and *as comfortable as possible*, may indeed be more realistic goals to consider.

III. Negotiation Areas

Should your client decide to separate from or divorce his or her loved one, it is understandable that she or he would be attending to settlement issues. Alimony and child support agreements are important considerations, as are issues pertaining to the distribution of assets (i.e., "who will get what?"). It also is helpful if the couple can still negotiate some relationship issues. For example, during the separation or after divorce, can they set some boundaries, limitations and guidelines regarding the relationship? Here are some examples to illustrate this consideration:

> "I appreciate your allowing me to leave all my tools in the garage, but I will never come over without calling first."

> "When I bring the children back on Sunday evenings, I will call you first."

> "While we are separated, I would be open to talk with you at anytime. However, I would appreciate it if you would not call me after ten o'clock in the evenings."

> "If you would like to get together so we can talk about things, that would be fine with me. However, I prefer that we meet at a public place, like a restaurant, a beach or a mall, and I will drive my own car and meet you there."

> "When your mail comes to the house, I will leave it in the mailbox with a rubber band around it. That way you can come by and pick it up at anytime."

Again, setting some boundaries and honoring them can be very helpful.

If your client tells you they find emotional issues such as feelings of deep hurt or abandonment make boundary-setting discussions impossible, then by all means think about referring the couple to another professional counselor, a family mediator or both.

IV. Divorce

What is a divorce? We frequently have said to our clients that there is a difference between a *legal divorce*, a *physical divorce* and a *psychological divorce*. When thinking of a divorce from a legal perspective, try to remember that this is a legally sanctioned, adjudicated and finite declaration of each individual's continuing responsibilities and culpabilities regarding each other (as well as children if there are any involved). A physical divorce is when the partners no longer see each other, make love together, go to dinner together or live together. In essence, they are physically apart and intend to remain so. A psychological divorce is one in which the former spouse is no longer central to one's psychological and spiritual being; he or she no longer has a significant place in your client's heart. As one of his clients said to Bill Emener, "I got my physical divorce in 2001 when she moved out and began living with someone else. I got my legal divorce in 2002. But it wasn't until 2004 that I felt I had finally gotten my psychological divorce; it took me two years to get her out of my mind, my spirit and my heart. I just could not stop myself from being in love with her."

It is important to remember that everyone's experiences are not the same. It is also true that individuals will differ as to whom they hold responsible for the situation. For example, in 2006 a client, Linda, once said to Bill Lambos, "I am convinced that I psychologically divorced Robert in 2004 but didn't get the courage to physically divorce him and move out until 2005. We've basically been gone and out of each other's lives for two years now. Can you recommend a good divorce attorney? It's about time for me to make it legal." Again, in terms of timing, *when a person is physically, psychologically and/or legally separated and/or divorced from someone, is unique to, and for, that person.*

V. Post-Divorce Processes

After a divorce is legally and physically finalized, it is not uncommon for individuals to go through two processes: (1) the grieving process; and (2) the forgiving process. The experience of going through a grieving process following the death of a loved one, as discussed in detail in Chapter 10, is unique to all individuals. Grieving a divorce is in many ways a similar process; it is fair to say, however, that bereavement associated with death may better be understood as consisting of discrete stages than is the grief which follows divorce. The person's experiences of anger, denial, bargaining, depression, and acceptance can be very difficult if and when they occur. Nonetheless, remember: a divorce entails loss – the loss of the person, the loss of the relationship, the loss of a dream, and possibly the loss of many other things (e.g., the house that was lived in, pets, daily contact with children, etc.). The acceptance and forgiving processes, which people sometimes think of as being part of the latter stages of the grieving process, is where one person not only forgives their "Ex" for what he or she has done, but they also forgive themselves for having allowed it to happen. As we have said many times throughout this book, recovery (not only from an addiction but from the loss of a relationship) is not contingent upon forgetting; it is continent upon forgiving. Assisting a client with charting, plotting and understanding the unique aspects of his or her separation and divorce can be very helpful to them. And try to remind them, a separation and/or a divorce is not an event – it is a process.

Self-Protection. When clients come to us and say they are separated and/or filing for divorce, one of the first questions we ask is, "What are you doing to take care of yourself?" It is very easy to be hurt as a result of ignorance and self-neglect. Protecting oneself and others in the family is important, whether legally, occupationally, financially, physically and/or emotionally. If your client has been emotionally connected and/or married to another person, it is understandable that he or she may still have feelings of love, care, concern and possibly wanting to be helpful to that person. Once he or she is separated and/or divorced, however, in addition to being caring and concerned for the other person, it is also important that the client be reminded of the need to pay special attention to him- or herself – they will likely be vulnerable. They may feel secure physically and financially, but that does not mean they are secure emotionally and legally. It is understandable for a person in such a situation to be vulnerable. Thus, we highly recommend that they understand and accept that possibility and take protective steps.

In your client's self-protection mode, it is fitting that they consider their needs and desires, and him- herself in general, to be their first concern – "I am Number One!" As discussed previously, however, your client must balance this with trying to remain sensitive, yet at the same time *not* be punitive, harmful and destructive to others in the process. For example, your client may indeed be able to attend to him- or herself without emotionally beating up, physically abusing, economically destroying and/or hurting in any way his or her (ex-)loved one. As Bill Emener recently said to a friend, "I truly understand your need to consider yourself Number One at this time in your life. However, is there any room in your life for anyone to be Number Two? Can you take care of yourself *and* be a little sensitive to John, who is economically destitute and hurting like hell because he still loves you so much?" She must have heard Bill because she began to talk with John on the telephone when he called. She told John that she realized his economic situation and was sorry that he was hurting financially. Interestingly, John later shared with Bill that her responding to him with compassion was very helpful: "Okay, I know she's not in love with me anymore and that still hurts. But at least she's not emotionally beating me up anymore. For a while it felt like she was grinding me into the ground with her heels every time she got the chance."

Some Do's and Don't-Do's. Under the rubric of self-protection, we frequently offer clients what we refer to as the *Three Don't-Do's* and *Six Do's*. When an individual first tells one of us that he or she is separated and/or going through a divorce, we review with them the following *three- and six- lists* to remind them of things they can be aware of and sensitive to in the process of protecting themselves. (And as you will see, we discuss them similarly to how we actually may say them to clients.)

Three Don't-Do's:

1) *"Don't do anything stupid."* We unfortunately have known many men and women to do things immediately following a separation or a divorce that in the final analysis, as they admitted, "were stupid!" For example, one gentleman said, "For the last two months, I would screw anything walking. I guess I had to prove to myself that it wasn't me." And a young woman said, "For the last three weeks I have been the easiest punch in the city. It was like I had to prove to myself that I was still attractive." Selling your house for half of what it is worth, giving away valuable belongings and quitting a good job are also examples of doing things that you may later look back on as stupid.

2) *"Don't do anything to excess."* During a separation and/or a divorce, try to avoid doing things in excess, especially if they are harmful things such as excessive gambling, drinking or anything that in the long run is detrimental to you.

3) *"Don't avoid reality."* As we discussed in Chapter 10, denial is one of the first stages of the grieving process. However, if for example your husband has set up his own bank account, transferred the credit cards into his name only, has not come home from work before eleven o'clock at night for the last three weeks and has applied for a transfer to another city, there indeed may be a message there! Although it may be emotionally very difficult to accept and tolerate reality, try not to deny it.

Six Do's:

1) *"See an attorney."* Talking with a divorce lawyer in your local community who knows the laws of your state is one of the first things we recommend. We also suggest it is a good idea not only to tell the attorney everything that is going on, but also to ask, "Is there anything I need to know, or is there anything I need to do, to protect myself?"

2) *"See a counselor, mediator, or both."* Discussing your issues and concerns with a professional counselor, psychologist or mediator not only can be very helpful, but talking with a professional also can be preventative, (e.g., he or she can help you prevent further harm later on). It also may be helpful for you to know that the professional with whom you already have met and hopefully feel comfortable will be there for you should you need to talk to him or her later.

3) *"Be aware of your own vulnerability."* In the process of being separated and/or going through a divorce, you may not be able to take care of yourself as well as you would be able to under other circumstances. This does not mean you are a weak, insecure or a less-than-normal human being! All this means is that for this brief period of time you may not understand everything that is going on, you may not be able to foresee and anticipate things that are going to occur, and you may not have the self-discipline and self-control you typically have. Accept the possibility that you may be vulnerable.

4) *"Develop a support network."* Surround yourself with good friends who not only understand what you are going through, but who also will be supportive and helpful (and not take advantage of you). As one of our clients said, "To some extent, I am only as strong as the people around me. Fortunately, while I am emotionally hurting very much, I'm not scared. I have good friends standing by me."

5) *"Try to get into a good routine."* Establishing a good and nourishing diet, a restful sleeping pattern, a comfortable work schedule, and an enjoyable and relaxing recreational life are important. Many times in situations such as separation and/or divorce, people do not eat properly, they consume alcohol to excess, they do not have good sleeping patterns, and they find their lives in total chaos. Having a routine in your life not only will help you minimize, and perhaps prevent, many harmful and possibly dangerous side effects of separation and divorce, but also will contribute to your sense of security and well-being.

6) *"Stay active."* Feelings of embarrassment, depression, sadness, guilt and shame easily can put us into a behavior pattern of withdrawal. "All I want to do is lie on the

couch; I don't want to see people," is a statement we frequently hear. It is a hallmark of impending or experienced clinical depression. It is, therefore, very important to try to stay active, even if it means asking your friends to help you to stay active. During a last session with Norma, who had "successfully gone through a very difficult divorce," she said, "You're right, Dr. Emener, it was helpful for me to always remember your three don't's and six do's. I kept them on a 3x5 card on my refrigerator door as a constant reminder. Last week I took the card off of the door and it felt great! But I'm going to keep the card – in case any friends of mine ever need it."

Effects of Time. "Time is my best ally," is a statement that is frequently made when someone says, in effect, "I will get over my divorce; it is just a matter of time." Two of the many critical aspects of time that are relevant to separation and divorce involve (1) the concern that Kim had with "When is it a good time for me to file for divorce?" and (2) Kevin's experience with "When I finally got my psychological divorce."

When talking with Kim, a 43-year-old tax accountant, she shared what turned out to be a rather humorous yet poignant experience with her 20-year old son. "A few weeks ago, my son asked me why I filed for a divorce from his father in March. 'That messed up my college spring break!' he said. I told him I was truly sorry that that had happened to him. I had considered waiting until April, but since I am a tax accountant that would not be a very good time for me. I also thought of waiting until May, but that is when he and his sister would be getting out of school for the summer. I thought of waiting until June, but June was our wedding anniversary month. I thought of waiting until July, but since our family had always had our annual Fourth of July Bash, symbolically that would not have worked very well either. I thought of waiting until August, but that's when he and his sister would be going back to college. I thought of waiting until September, but that would have messed up my birthday. I thought of waiting until October, but that would have messed up his father's birthday. I thought of waiting until November, but that would have messed up Thanksgiving. I thought of waiting until December – oh sure, Merry Christmas! I thought of waiting until January, but here we go again – Happy New Year. I thought of waiting until February, and thought, 'Wouldn't that make a nice Valentine's Day present!' By that time, he and I were laughing, and I finally said to him, 'I'm sorry, son, but there is never a good time to file for a divorce.'"

Kevin, a 36-year-old computer programmer, shared that it took him approximately three years to overcome his divorce. He brought to one of our sessions a sketch similar to the one in Figure 11.3. As he was describing it, he said, "This is what my relationship with Maria was like when we were married. We each had our own lives yet we were connected.

In the second stage, we still each had our own lives but our life together was definitely starting to fade. Once we were legally divorced, we each had our own lives and there was nothing between us except mountains of unexpressed anger. In addition to my anger, I also was heavily grieving the loss of her and our relationship – I still loved her. To complicate matters, as we began at least to be friendly during our post-divorce times, I did not have a place for her – was she my former wife, my friend, my children's mother? I simply did not know how to deal with her because I did not have a place for her. Over time, however, I was able to forgive her and forgive myself for all of the many transgressions that had occurred in our lives. In my stage four, I feel that I am now psychologically divorced in that Maria and I have our own lives yet can still enjoy the memories of the wonderful times we had together. We now can be caring and loving toward each other and not struggle with all of the crap surrounding whether or not we will ever get back together again."

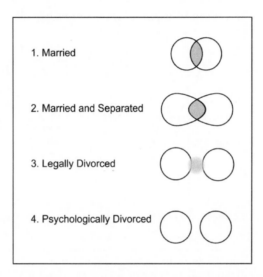

Figure 11.3. Stages of Kevin's Divorce and the Effects of Time.

Time indeed can be our client's best ally, and it is important to remind them, "Don't rush it."

Rocking in the Comfort Zone. Jill and her husband had been married for 14 years before their divorce. She originally came in because she was struggling with her decision as to whether or not she should file for a divorce. Approximately three months after her last visit, she scheduled an appointment with Bill Emener and came in "Because I am feeling guilty that I have not done anything about my divorce." At that point she had seen an attorney, had all of the legal papers filled out and was separated from her husband (he had voluntary moved out). "For the last three months I have just been doing things that are comfortable. I have not formally and legally filed for my divorce yet. What's wrong?" Bill replied, "Jill, maybe you are just rocking in the comfort zone." She looked up with surprising eyes and said, "What are you talking about?"

Bill drew a diagram similar to the one in Figure 11.4. He then said to her, "For the last two years of your marriage, Jill, your quality of life had continued to spiral down. At that point, however, you made a decision to legally separate and file for a divorce. The process of telling your husband that you wanted to separate and file for divorce, and for him to find an apartment and move out, took approximately six months. Nonetheless, even though that was a difficult time for you, your quality of life did improve somewhat. By the end of those six months, the two of you had set some boundaries and agreed upon some rules of your separation, and your life had become relatively comfortable. However, you knew that the process of filing for divorce was going to be difficult for you. Understandably, you were not in a big hurry to rush out and do it. For the first time in two and one-half years, you were feeling comfortable. Wanting to stay there in that comfort zone and, in effect, enjoy life for a little while makes total sense to me. The question is: why is it bothering you?" With a sense of relief, Jill said, "I guess it's because I have always been a believer in the philosophy that says if there's something that needs to be done, do it."

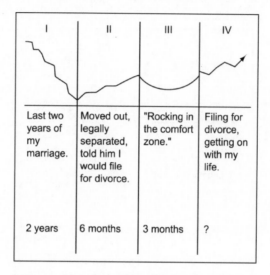

Figure 11.4. Jill's Divorce Process Over Time.

Bill reminded Jill that the separation and divorce process is a process, not an event. Furthermore, he suggested to her that there is nothing wrong with occasionally taking some time out to catch your breath, enjoy life a little and give yourself an opportunity to recharge your batteries before moving on to the next stage. She nodded her head in understanding and said, "I see what you mean. It is sort of like calling a timeout in the middle of the fourth quarter of a football game." Bill smiled and nodded in agreement.

As a person thinks through and remains in touch with his or her feelings about an impending or in-process separation and/or divorce, having an awareness of *time* and *timing* issues is important. If we were to look at Kim's and Kevin's experiences and Jill's experiences, it would be reasonable to conclude that: (1) there is never a good time to separate and/or file for divorce; (2) the time at which we are legally divorced, physically divorced and psychologically divorced may not be the same for each partner; and (3) in the overall, long-term process of separation and divorce, there's nothing wrong with occasionally calling a timeout, especially when it may be needed.

Post-Divorce Anger. Anger is a very strong emotion that a person can experience during the processes of separation and divorce. "Post-divorce anger," however, is a long-term pervasive emotion that we have observed people struggle with for years following a divorce. Walter's and Sonya's experiences may illustrate this phenomenon.

When talking about how he was feeling about being divorced, Walter said, "For the last 20 of the 25 years I was married to Sonya, she deprived me of feeling loved and being loved. It was very painful for me to see her be so loving toward our children, yet so aloof and cold toward me. I resent her for that! It wasn't until after my divorce and I started dating other women that I realized I was lovable. I am also angry because in the process of her not being loving toward me while we were married, and maybe in return I was not loving toward her, my children thought of me as a non-loving man. To this day, my daughters will not openly show affection to me or unsolicitedly tell me they love me. Sometimes I feel incredible anger toward Sonya and my daughters, as well as toward myself. And until I am able to let go of this anger, I will not consider myself emotionally available for any other kind of loving relationship. And I am angry about that too!"

While talking to Bill Lambos about her divorce from Henry after 28 years of marriage, Becky said, "I am so enraged with Henry! By divorcing me, he deprived me of having a lifelong, loving relationship with the same person. I always had the dream of growing old together, not only with the husband of my children, but also with the grandpa of my grandchildren. And even if I were to someday find someone else with whom to fall in love, it would not be the same. Henry and I share a family root system together, and I simply do not know if I will ever be able to feel toward another man the way I have always felt toward him. Whenever I go to the beach and see an old couple hobbling along, holding hands with their gnarly little fingers, tears roll down my cheeks. Henry robbed me of my dream!"

Post-divorce anger is a strong negative emotion people can experience when they consider their marriage and their divorce from a lifelong, long-term perspective. As a friend of ours who is very depressed and angry recently said, "Whenever I see a family come into a restaurant, I think to myself, 'That used to be me. That could be me. That *should* be me. But it will never be me again.'" And in this sense, post-divorce anger puts people in a position of not only coming to terms with their divorce, but coming to terms with what they have experienced over their entire life span.

Sometimes, when our clients are dealing with strong, deep feelings of anger, it is helpful to encourage them to engage in physical exercise, read self-help books on anger, talk with close friends about their anger, and surround themselves with understanding, compassionate people. Nonetheless, remember that strong, deep feelings of anger also are, at times, best dealt with through the assistance of a professional counselor or therapist. You may need to remind your client that "toughing it out alone" may be a poor choice, and thus be sure to remain available to them if they need you.

CHAPTER SUMMARY

In this chapter we presented and discussed three broad areas in which a loving relationship can impact each of its member partners. First we looked at people's lifestyle choices and how loving relationships can impact them. Secondly, we addressed how a loving relationship can impact the individual when one or both partners experience problems relating to one another. Lastly we focused on pertinent issues of separation and divorce and how they impact each of the partners in the ever-changing dance of a loving relationship.

It is not uncommon for partners in a troubled or less-than-fulfilling loving relationship to see, and focus on, each other as the sources of their relationship concerns and issues. However, as a professional providing counseling to couples, it is imperative that you understand and appreciate that couples can have relationship issues not necessarily because of themselves and/or the world around them – sometimes couples simply can have "relationship issues" in need of attention.

A good dog can live a wonderful, happy life relating to the world around him or her. A good cat can live a wonderful, happy life relating to the world around him or her. But put them in the same room and they may have challenges relating to each other.

CHAPTER 11 DISCUSSION QUESTIONS

1) How and in what ways can an individual's lifestyle choices affect his or her loving relationships?

2) What are some things you can do to assist a couple that wants to enjoy their individual lifestyle choices and have a functional relationship lifestyle?

3) What can you do to help a couple (a) with their "solvable problems" and their "unsolvable problems" and (b) know the differences between them?

4) When working with a couple that fights, what can you do (a) to help them fight less, and (b) to help them fight fair?

5) Why might it be a good idea for a couple (a) to separate, and (b) to get a divorce?

6) What are some specific things you can do to assist a couple that decides (a) to separate and (b) to get a divorce?

Chapter 12

RELATIONSHIP SKILLS

We have often remarked to our clients and students what we, as therapists and professors, have found to be a glaring inconsistency in the way in which the western world manages the skills requirements it enforces on its citizens. In many areas of discourse and commerce, states regulate and license behaviors. For example, people are not allowed to drive an automobile without demonstrating knowledge of the rules and laws of the road (by passing a written test), and demonstrating that they possess the behavioral skills deemed necessary to proficiently and safely drive an automobile (as demonstrated by passing an actual driving test). Similarly, one may not legally engage in an ever-widening variety of occupational skills without meeting educational and proficiency requirements, as well as certifications and licensure. From finance to teaching, through legal matters and construction, in most of the so-called trades (plumber, electrician, auto mechanic, etc.), and in hundreds of other areas, engaging in an occupation requires demonstrated skills and government permission. State (or provincial) and federal departments of professional regulation and consumer affairs require of many occupations that in order to legally work in them the respective professionals demonstrate proficiency and undergo continuing education to ensure their ability to competently practice their skills, as well as hold an appropriate license or certification.

At the same time, there are no mandated preparatory requirements for two other sets of skills that can, and do, profoundly impact both other individuals and society as a whole: (1) managing loving relationships; and (2) raising children. Despite the obvious damage that can be done to people – individually and collectively – when people mismanage their relationships with their significant others and/or their children, the states require no training, certifications or licensure for engaging in these activities.

It is not our intent to suggest that people be required to be licensed to engage in loving relationships, which admittedly sounds ridiculous. Nor do we argue for the necessity of government approval to bear children[4]. But the fact remains that like driving a car or

---

[4] Although this *is* the case in some countries with strong anti-natal policies, such as China, where the threat of overpopulation has been deemed such a danger to society that couples may legally only bear a single child. With regard to the United States, we *do* believe we would benefit from holding a national discussion over the benefits versus the costs of requiring education for first time parents that addresses such issues as necessary pre-and postnatal medical care, dealing with psychological issues related to child birth (such as managing post-partum depression), and dealing with family counseling issues that are known to be associated with serious adjustment issues and behaviors. Two that come to mind immediately are managing blended families and, even more pressing, preventing the types of domestic violence associated with having and raising

preparing a tax return, entering into and managing a loving relationship requires a set of skills that ever fewer people seem to acquire through formal education and/or routine socialization. It is difficult to argue against this in the face of a divorce rate of 51+% and rising, and an overburdened juvenile and criminal justice system.

Looking at the title of this chapter – *Relationship Skills* – you, as a current or future couples counselor, may be wondering that since this is a book about helping couples manage their relationships, isn't the entire book about relationships skills? And if so, why is a separate chapter necessary to address the topic? The answer should by now sound familiar: as with the previous chapter about "problems," this is a chapter devoted to *meta-skills*. Whereas previous chapters have addressed the skills necessary to deal with particular issues that may arise in interacting with one's partner, this chapter specifically addresses *relationship skills per se,* independent of specific areas or topics of interaction.

We have three areas to address herein, all of which are quite important in assisting your client couples to (a) enjoy healthier and more functional relationships, and (b) be able to overcome the stubborn obstacles or blocks that bring them to you in the first place. The first of these areas is *empathy and listening skills*. It is our experience that many couples wind up in trouble due to persistent and ineffective intercommunication. In particular, if either or (especially) both partners feel that their significant other doesn't *understand* their feelings or perspective, the relationship is often headed for trouble.

Next on the list of meta-skills are *coping skills*. As a therapist or therapist in training, we expect that by this point you will have learned that although it remains a "trade secret" of which the public seems to remain forever unaware – people summarily do not become upset, nor are disturbed by, other people or events. Rather, people disturb themselves due to their beliefs (including expectations and demands) about themselves, others and the world, and particularly their *perceptions* of such things. This is the foundational basis of cognitive behavioral therapy and it not only makes sense philosophically, but has been shown in a myriad of research studies to be the most effective approach to reducing psychological disturbance in both individuals and couples (Butler, Chapman, Forman & Beck, 2006; Dobson, 1989; Gloaguen, Cottraux, Cucherat & Blackburn, 1998).

We then go on to look at how the different stages of relationships over the course of their "lifespan" require different relationship skills, each appropriate to the current relationship stage. By *stage*, we mean not only early middle and later with respect to the time a couple has been together, but what is happening with respect to the relationship's future. For example, are they still in the bonding stage or have they settled into a long-term rhythm of stability and comfort? Finally, they may be, consciously or otherwise, in the process of terminating the relationship, for which yet another and entirely different set of skills is required.

The chapter concludes with a discussion of relationship skills related to the contrast between the individual and the couple. Here we look at the important issues of Co-, In-, and Inter-Dependence. We shall see that as with so many areas in understanding and managing relationships, *healthy relationships are those that strike a balance between the two less healthy end points of a continuum*, in this case the middle of the range between parallel independency and codependency, a healthy state known as *interdependence*.

---

children. Such violence not only permanently scars children and adults, both physically and emotionally but, as we have seen in earlier chapters, also imposes enormous economic costs on society.

Finally, we want to remind you that throughout this book we have emphasized our position that in order for two individuals to enjoy a "good" loving relationship, both partners have to effectively attend to:

1) themselves (e.g., their own needs, wants, wishes and desires);
2) each other (e.g., their loved one's needs, wants, wishes and desires); and,
3) their relationship (e.g., agreements, compromises and/or expectations, whether tacit or openly acknowledged, that promote and sustain the couple's happiness together).

It therefore makes perfect sense (at least to us) that for people to succeed in these three areas, they must develop or have developed effective, high-level *skills* in these three areas – abilities we call relationship skills.

The professional couples counselor spends a considerable portion of his or her sessions assisting clients with the development and management of their relationship skills. Although at first blush this may strike some you as unusual, in fact much of professional counseling is devoted to skill development and behavior management, whether in the area of loving relationships or any of the other areas of adult functioning. As mentioned at the beginning of this chapter, life has become too complex to assume that all the skills needed to navigate loving relationships can be learned through routine socialization. That this fact has been recognized at the highest levels of our society is most dramatically evidenced by the recent federal requirement that health care insurers must, by law, offer parity for coverage of both physical and mental health (Pear, 2008). Most of us can recall with clarity the "learning curve" we had to endure in order to function well in new jobs and in new neighborhoods or adapting to the addition of children to our families, as well as in many other areas of life change. Thus, in the "dance" we call loving relationships, it should come as no surprise that we devote an entire chapter to the important subject of counseling clients with respect to their *relationship skills*.

EMPATHY AND LISTENING SKILLS

"The best way you tell me you love me is when you listen to me," Sharon said to her husband. She then added, "When you demonstrate to me that you understand, respect and appreciate how I see things and how I feel about things, I really feel that you care about me. I figure that in order for you to understand me the way you do, you cannot always be focused on yourself, your way of seeing things and your feelings about things. My first husband was so enamored with *his* way of seeing things and so caught up in his own feelings that he never was able to see things through my eyes – to appreciate how I saw things and how I felt about things. I felt so alone. But with you it's different. You consider me important; you validate my perceptions and feelings. And I figure that for you to be able to do that, you must love me. That's one of the reasons why I love you and feel so loved by you."

As Sharon's story very well illustrates, empathy requires the ability to see things from another person's point of view. Neuropsychologists call this ability "theory of mind," and it is considered one of the six essential *executive functions* of the brain. People who lack the capacity for theory of mind are considered either very impaired or very evil, depending on how the impairment manifests itself (e.g., as in Asperger's disorder vs. sociopathic behavior, both of which reflect serious deficiencies in theory of mind). Terms used to describe such people include self-centered, uncompassionate, schizoid, narcissistic and psychopathic – terms with which few people would care to be labeled.

Empathy is not the same as theory of mind, but depends upon it – one cannot imagine how another person feels unless they are able to "put themselves in that person's shoes" or see the world from their perspective. Empathy, therefore, requires the willingness and ability to see the world from the point of view of another *and* the ability (or at least the willingness) to feel the way we imagine they do. Moreover, empathy is experienced internally. Evidence of empathy requires behaviors that demonstrate one has or is experiencing it, and there's the crux of the matter: *if one's partner does not see evidence of empathy he or she will naturally assume it is absent.* Thus, it is not uncommon for someone to love and be in love with someone else very much and yet not be able to, or fail to, *communicate* and *demonstrate* that he or she has empathy for that person. Most people, nonetheless, tend to agree that having, communicating and demonstrating genuine empathic understanding to a loved one is a very loving thing to do. "It feels so good when I can tell that she understands me," Edward said. "It certainly helps in our relationship too." Fittingly, our advice to clients with respect to relationship skills is, "If you are feeling empathy for your significant other, *take steps to show it.* It can make a very big difference in keeping the relationship healthy."

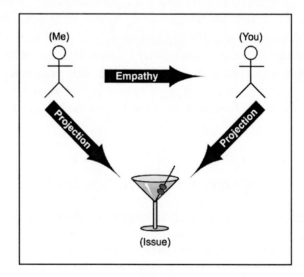

Figure 12.1. Empathic Understanding.

Sometimes people will confuse sympathy for empathy. Sympathy is feeling *for* another person, as in "I feel sorry for you." Empathy is feeling *with* another person, as in "I understand you; I see you are scared and can almost feel your fear." What Sharon was saying to her husband illustrates the differential effects of a loved one being locked into his (or her) own "projections" versus having the capacity for being "empathic." As is illustrated in the diagram in Figure 12.1, when we look at an object or an issue, we do not see the object or the issue, *per se*, rather, we see our perception of it. Somewhere between the retinal wall in the eye and what is registered in the brain, the object or the issue is filtered by one's own personal experiences, philosophies, values and beliefs. And when a person projects his or her experiences, philosophies, values and beliefs onto the object or issue, what is registered in their brain is their perception of the object or issue. We call this "projection." On the other hand, when your client is able to look at the object or issue through *their partner's* eyes, his or her experiences, philosophies, values and beliefs, then he or she can see it "through their partner's eyes." This is what we call "empathy." To return to the language of neuropsychology for a moment, empathy requires both a valid theory of mind and an emotional response to it, whereas sympathy requires the former but not any such shared emotion. Or as the Joe South song *Walk a Mile in My Shoes* suggests, "Don't judge me until you can see life through my eyes."

Whenever lecturing on the concepts of empathy and empathic listening, we, your authors, frequently use an example from our personal lives in which the differences between projection and empathy are clearly distinguishable and appreciable. Such a particular, personal experience on behalf of Bill Emener is presented in Dialogue 12.1.

Dialogue 12.1 Empathy and Listening Skills

The following is an example of how Bill Emener experienced and witnessed the value of empathy and listening skills. It did not occur in his counseling office, but rather one evening when meeting an old friend for dinner. To wit, it does not follow the counselor-client interaction format of the other dialogues in this book. Nonetheless, let's remember the old cliché, "Being empathic and understanding is more than a counseling skill set – it's also a way of life."

Bill had not seen his old buddy, Rob, for a long time. When they lived in the same town, they frequently played tennis and golf together, and their families would get together on weekends. In many ways, they were very close. Job changes on both of their behalves, however, geographically separated the two. And although Bill and Rob kept in touch by phone and by mail and e-mail, they had not seen each other for about eight years. Then one day Bill received a call at his office from Rob. He did not identify himself to Bill's receptionist or to Bill. After Bill picked up his phone and said, "This is Bill Emener," Rob simply said, "Lynn, my new wife, and I are on vacation and will be in St. Petersburg tomorrow night in a hotel on the beach. We'll only be there for the one night. Any chance of our getting together – flip you for the drinks!" The somewhat familiar voice suddenly became very familiar when he heard their old, typical, traditional, "Flip you" line.

As vivid, warm, wonderful memories shot through his mind, Bill immediately knew it was Rob and replied, "Two out of three!" They simultaneously laughed and shared their enthusiasm and genuine excitement about getting together the following evening.

As Bill entered the hotel lounge, he spotted them immediately. Rob still had his muscular build and his broad, winning smile… hair a bit gray, but distinctively the same old Rob. Lynn exemplified Rob's every description of her – long brown hair, warm smile, bright blue eyes, and soft, small hands. Following a few big hugs, the coins immediately came out – "Two out of three!" Rob won.

A few minutes later, the waitress brought the three drinks: an iced tea for Lynn and two martinis, *"dry, on the rocks, three olives, and with a smile"* – the way they always ordered them, of course. As Rob and Bill relished their memories brought back by the two martinis, "the way they are supposed to be," Bill noticed that although Lynn truly enjoyed their "remember when" stories, her body posture and facial expressions suggested a possible, mild concern about the martinis. Although he noticed her somewhat less than positive attitude regarding their drinks, Bill didn't say anything. About thirty minutes later when their table was ready, they moved into the dining room.

When the waiter asked them if they would like to order a drink while looking over the menus, Rob and Bill immediately looked at each other. "Two out of three!" they both chuckled. This time, Bill won. Rob said, "One iced tea for this beautiful woman here, and two martinis, *dry, on the rocks, three olives, and with a smile.*" Again the memories and old war stories flowed. Lynn even shared some of her and Rob's from the past two years of their marriage. It was great. When the waiter brought their drinks and said, "With a smile," everyone did – except Lynn. This time she was noticeably put off by the sight of the martinis.

Bill again declined to say anything. However, when Lynn excused herself to go to the ladies room, Bill softly said to Rob, "It's really none of my business, Rob, and I don't want to pry. But I could not help but notice that Lynn seemed to be irked a little with the martinis. Is there anything going on that I should know about? She's a real neat lady and I surely do not want to offend her."

Rob quietly stared at his glass for a moment and then said, "No Bill, neither you nor I did anything wrong. She's okay. She's just a little sensitive still. About five years ago her mother, father and younger brother were killed by a drunk driver." Chills immediately swept through Bill's body – with that information he clearly understood where Lynn was coming from. While the sight and smell of the martinis were wonderful reminders of joy, excitement, happiness and fun for Bill and Rob, they were horrible reminders of tragedy, sorrow, loss and suffering for Lynn. During and after dinner, Bill felt a special closeness to Lynn. While the three of them were sipping their after-dinner coffees, Lynn unsolicitedly and apologetically shared her reactions and her reasons for her reactions to the martinis. Bill's heart went out to her. He then reached for her hand and softly said, "Lynn, I am truly sorry that happened. Even after five years it's still painful for you. You certainly don't need to apologize. If that had happened to me, I cannot assure you that I would be reacting any differently than you are."

As they were leaving the restaurant, big hugs abounded, with threats and promises of when and where they would get together again. It had been a wonderful evening. When Bill was heading toward the parking lot and his friends were heading to the hotel elevator, he said, "Next time dinner's on me." Both Rob and Lynn, smiling from ear to ear, replied, "Two out of three!"

Demonstrating empathic, active listening skills indeed is not just a skill set used in a counselor's office with clients – it is a way of life.

As illustrated in the diagram in Figure 12.1 and demonstrated in Dialogue 12.1, when Rob and Bill were looking at the martinis they were projecting their personal experiences, philosophies, values and beliefs onto the objects and perceived not just martinis, but martinis associated with joy, excitement, happiness and fun. When Lynn was looking at the martinis, she was projecting her personal experiences, philosophies, values and beliefs onto the objects and not only was seeing martinis, but martinis she associated with tragedy, sorrow, loss and suffering. And when Rob helped Bill understand Lynn's projections and perceptions by providing him with information regarding her experience, he then was able to have empathy for her. He felt her pain. It is important to note that none of them had any real fears regarding Rob and Bill having two martinis. They knew that a period of four hours would have transpired and a large meal would have been consumed between the time Bill would have finished his second martini and the time he would leave to drive home. Nonetheless, not only did Rob and Lynn have deep empathy for each other, they did not impose their values on each other. Rob truly understood Lynn's struggles with her family members' deaths and he did not shame her or tell her what to do. He did not become upset when she ordered iced tea or emotionally reacted to the martinis. Likewise, Lynn understood Rob's enjoyment of his martinis and did not shame him or tell him not to have and enjoy them. Clearly, both Rob and Lynn have the abilities and the skills: to (1) have and demonstrate genuine empathy for each other; and (2) not impose their values and "shoulds" on each other or others. Among many other things they respect each other. These indeed are big reasons why they have and enjoy the great loving relationship they have.

When counseling a couple who make statements like "No matter how many times I repeat it, *she just doesn't get it*" or "He should try going to my office five days a week and see how he feels when he gets home!" the problem will often lie with deficits in one or both partners' empathy and listen skills. Interventions in these areas can be among the most effective in assisting clients improve their relationships. We have found that some targeted psycho-education in this area can be invaluable. In fact, we often teach our clients the same skills we teach our students in a typical first year graduate course in clinical psychology and/or mental health counseling: *Active Listening*.

We trust that if you are reading this textbook as a graduate student or professional counselor, it is not necessary to revisit the subject of active listening in great detail. What we tell our clients is that active listening is a way of listening and responding to another person that focuses attention on *them*. Suspending one's own frame of reference and suspending judgment are important in order to be an effective active listener. So is giving the other person all the time they want to express themselves, and avoid interrupting or responding to each and every point they are making. As Bill Lambos often reminds clients, the tag line from the 2008 film *Bable* states, "*If you want to be heard, listen*." When one person in a troubled relationship begins to feel that their partner is *finally* listening to what they are saying, the relationship almost always improves immediately.

Remind your clients that in a healthy loving relationship both individuals remain aware of their own projections and perceptions of themselves, each other and their relationship, and respectfully and lovingly of each other:

- they are empathic with and toward each other;
- each takes the time and makes the effort to carefully listen to their partner; and
- they skillfully communicate to and demonstrate their empathic understanding of one another.

COPING SKILLS

Coping skills are another set of skills often found to be lacking when a couple seeks help from a therapist. Broadly speaking, coping skills reflect the ability to self-regulate or absorb stressors without experiencing a loss of the ability to function effectively. We should also point out that the term tends to refer to those abilities that are seen as both positive and effective. Contrast this with the phenomenon *defense mechanism*, which usually (but not always) connotes self-regulating strategies deemed either or both unhealthy and negative in nature. Thus *denial*– a defense mechanism – is usually considered an ineffective approach to dealing with a problem, whereas *prioritizing* (recognizing that a problem exists but putting it on hold for the moment because of other, more pressing needs) tends to be viewed as a healthy coping skill. Helping your clients maintain a healthy relationship can sometimes be achieved by assisting them in developing healthy and effective positive coping skills.

Every involvement in a loving relationship entails risk-taking. For example, *fear of getting hurt* is one of the most frequent responses we hear when we ask people what they struggle with the most in managing their loving relationships. When people invest themselves in a loving relationship, they offer the other person and the relationship their time, effort and energy, as well as their sense of being, sense of worth, sense of what they are and sense of who they are. It is understandable for them to want to protect and preserve their sense of value with respect to *what they have* (e.g., a formidable bank account, a new car or a nice house), *what they do* (e.g., being a successful legal secretary with a good job at a good law firm), and *who they are* (e.g., a happy, fun-loving, warm and friendly human being). And in a loving relationship, people risk these things. More specifically, people in a relationship take the risk of having the other person *reject* the value of *what they have* and *who they are* and, in the process, feel as if they are *being rejected as human beings*. Of course, this is the very basis of an individual's irrational belief system, but clients who maintain rational beliefs aren't often those who seek our assistance. Thus we may wish to look at coping skills as a collective term representing the variety of thoughts, feelings and behaviors that can be engaged and utilized to *protect* what one has, the worth of what one does, and who one is at their core.

For example, Jim, a 29-year-old schoolteacher who recently ended a five-year relationship and was feeling very lonely and lonesome, said to Bill Emener, "I can feel my coping skills kicking in and that's good. I'm not ready for another serious relationship. I couldn't handle it right now. The other night when Beth, a lady whom I've been dating lately, invited me to go with her to the beach for the weekend, I respectfully declined. She may be ready for that, but I'm not. I would probably have fun and enjoy myself, but I guess I'm not ready. I feel relieved." Basically, Jim was engaging some effective coping skills to protect himself from jeopardizing his emotional health while trying to work through some relationship issues and difficulties.

Similarly, Janice, who had been married for seven years, was divorced by her husband "for another woman" and was not going out at all (other than to go to work and do her shopping), started therapy with Bill Lambos. "Between my fear of men and my anger toward them," she said, "I was afraid to go out anywhere where a man might talk to me. I became a shut-in. But with the books I've been reading and seeing you to work through some of my feelings, now I'm occasionally going out with my girlfriends and learning some very helpful coping skills. Sitting in a lounge and politely saying, 'No thank you' to a man if he asks you to dance, is easier said than done! I've got a long way to go yet with my recovery from what happened with my divorce. But now at least I am getting on with my life, and that certainly feels good!"

Just as coping skills can be viewed as positive or negative, a person's need to invoke them may also arise when they are experiencing both negative and positive stressors. Although today people are accustomed to viewing all stressors as negative in nature, resulting in *distress*, it was not always viewed this way. Stress can be positive as well, a term known as *eustress* (Sylye, 1956). For example, Bill Emener remembers when one of his graduate assistants got engaged a few years ago. She was so excited and so caught up in the delirium of her engagement, she was not able to function around the office – she would sit and stare at the walls. Her performance in her classes also suffered. "We are going to have to teach Allyson some coping skills," Bill overheard one of the other graduate assistants say, "and I'm getting tired of doing her work for her too!"

One of the most difficult challenges we, your authors, always felt as parents was that of helping our children learn how to be open, loving and trusting of others while simultaneously knowing how to protect themselves from being devastatingly, emotionally hurt. Not being open, loving and trusting of others is akin to living under a rock. But without good coping skills, one is quintessentially vulnerable and fair game for all of the harmful people and the punishing vicissitudes of the world.

SKILLS FOR DIFFERENT RELATIONSHIP STAGES

Our clinical and personal experiences have repeatedly indicated that there are three distinct stages of loving relationships: (1) *the Establishment Stage* – when two individuals are initiating, beginning and starting their relationship; (2) *the Maintenance Stage* – when they are continuing, developing, enriching, strengthening and extending their relationship; and (3) *the Ending Stage* – when they are reducing, diminishing, transforming and bringing closure to their relationship. We also have found that most people have "good" skills in *establishing and beginning* loving relationships, "mediocre" skills in *maintaining and continuing* loving relationships, and "poor" skills in *ending and bringing closure to* loving relationships. Part of the reason for this is that during the beginning stage, most people will invest large amounts of time and energy into what they are doing. Furthermore, during the beginning stage most people's feelings tend to be positive and typically there are numerous rewarding experiences associated with what they are doing. The truism "love is blind" refers primarily to the beginning stage of relationships, when people can convince themselves that their new flame has no flaws (that matter), and overlook evidence of future problems that seem painfully obvious to their friends and families. Conversely, during the ending and closure stage, people's feelings tend to be far less positive (and sometimes painful), and many of the outcomes of what they are doing are felt as punishing. It also is important to note that throughout these three stages, most people's motivations, intentions, needs, wants, desires and wishes also tend to change markedly from stage to stage.

During these three stages, the extent to which people attend to themselves, their loved ones and their relationship, are discernibly different, as are the skills that are necessary for each stage. For example, as is illustrated in Figure 12.2, differential considerations of (1) *"whom" and "what" people pay attention to*, and (2) the *corresponding specific relationship skills* within these categories may include the following:

Focus On:	Relationship Stage		
	Establishing	Maintaining	Ending
Self -	(2) 20%	(E) 33%	(1) 60%
Loved One -	(1) 70%	(E) 33%	(3) 10%
Relationship -	(3) 10%	(E) 33%	(2) 30%

Percentages fluctuate and vary for most people - they're not "fixed."

Figure 12.2. Areas of Focus During Three Loving Relationship Stages.

During the Establishing Stage:

- peoples' primary focus is on the other person (e.g., "Most of my energy is focused on making him or her happy, such as preparing his favorite meal or sending her flowers;" and,
- typical attitudes during this stage are "as long as I can make him or her happy and get some rewards out of it for myself, our relationship will take care of itself."

During the Maintenance Stage:

- most peoples' focus tends to be distributed somewhat evenly among these three categories: themselves, their loved ones and their relationships. Examples of this include:
  - *Self*: "Next weekend I would appreciate our going away to the beach for a few days. I need to get away so I can rest and forget about my pressures and worries."
  - *Loved-One*: "Maybe we could go away to the beach for the weekend. You look like you need to get away from your pressures and worries for a few days."
  - *Relationship*: "We've been so busy lately it seems that we have drifted apart. I'd like for us to go away to the beach for the weekend so we can 'get reacquainted.' I feel our relationship needs some attention."

During the Ending Stage:

- people's focus tends primarily to be on themselves (e.g., "I may need to attend to my own needs for freedom and/or my feelings of sadness and loss."); and
- attending to and negotiating "new" relationship boundaries is very important (e.g., "I suggest that we feel free to call each other on the telephone but not see each other for a few days").

Despite the fact that during each stage the primary focus of attention normally changes, it is important to remember that people continue to attend to all three categorical targets: *themselves, their loved ones* and *their relationships*. Moreover, the extent to which they are relatively attending to each of these is comprehendible, logical and functional. For example, "When we first met and during our courtship, we paid a lot of attention to each other," Alice said. "Then for the first few years of our marriage we paid a lot of attention to ourselves. Jimmy continued to practice and work on his golf game and I continued with my pottery. We also paid attention to each other. For example, one time I surprised him with a new pair of golf shoes, and one night he surprised me by bringing home a new, bigger kiln for me. We also paid a lot of attention to our relationship. We made sure we went out together, just the two of us, one night a week and spent at least one weekend a month away together. But now that we are separated and negotiating our divorce, we're attending primarily to ourselves and our relationship. We also have two small children and we want to make things as easy as possible for them. I know that Jimmy will be okay – he can take care of himself. And I know that I will be okay – I am learning how to take care of myself. It really pleases me, though, that we are able to have such a relatively friendly and amicable relationship through all of this. It makes things easier and less painful. Furthermore, it helps us do a better job of taking care of our two children."

Of course, Alice and Jimmy may not be typical. Professionals such as couples counselors and family mediators spend much of their working day helping people reduce the conflict and vitriol that is, unfortunately, more typical of the ending stage of relationships. Nevertheless, we advise our readers to help their clients take whatever steps are needed for them to continue to attend to all three areas – self, other and relationship – at every stage of their loving relationships. Learning to do so is among the most important relationship skills one can learn because it maintains the balance of healthy functioning at every stage. Specifically, we advise our clients – and suggest you do likewise with yours – in every stage of their relationships to:

- *Lovingly attend to yourself.* This necessitates the activation of self-help, self-nourishing skills. If you haven't learned such skills, then it certainly would be in your best interest to learn them (whether you are in a relationship or not). The key advice here is: *don't lose sight of yourself or your desires in any stage of a relationship.*
- *Lovingly attend to your loved one.* And without being manipulative, controlling, smothering or codependent; this also requires that you have high-level, identifiable interpersonal skills. For this, the central wisdom is simply a dual modification of an age-old rule: (1) *do unto your significant other as you would have him or her do unto you;* and (2) *do unto others as they would want done unto them.*

- *Lovingly attend to your loving relationship.* This also necessitates the implementation of identifiable, high-level interpersonal skills. The important advice here is: *don't burn any bridges, and keep them well maintained for as long as possible.*

It is important to remember that helping clients learn and develop effective skills in these three areas is critical and beneficial – for themselves, for their loved ones, and for their relationships.

These situations also illustrate three categories of relationship coping skills addressed in the previous section: (1) *Pre-relationship Coping Skills* (2) *During/Within a Relationship Coping Skills* and (3) *Post-relationship Coping Skills.* The relationship skills needed in the three main stages of the relationship "lifespan" often require different types of coping skills.

CO-, IN-, AND INTER-DEPENDENCE

Melody Beattie (1992), an author who spent much of her career associated with the famous Hazelden Clinic (the same place where James Frey spent his time in the controversial bestseller, *A Million Little Pieces*), is most closely associated with the concept of "codependence." To be codependent is to be unable to maintain a stable and healthy sense of independence and to exhibit excessive and usually inappropriate caring for those who depend on you. According to Beattie, the codependent is one side of a relationship between mutually needy people. The dependent – the needy person on the other side of this relationship – may have emotional, physical, financial difficulties or addictions they seemingly are unable to surmount. It is understandably noble to want to help others in need. But the codependent person is not trying to help the dependent other person become self sufficient or healthy (even though he or she may be doing it at a subconscious or preconscious level). Rather, he or she exhibits behavior that *perpetuates* the dependent person's condition by controlling, pitying, making excuses for, or taking other actions to ensure that the needy person remains dependent on them. This pattern of interaction is rooted in the codependent person's own need to feel needed and the fear of doing anything that would change the relationship dynamic of continuing dependency.

One of the major themes of this book is that in healthy loving relationships both individuals experience an enhanced sense of *self* and an enriched sense of *self-efficacy*. We advise both prospective and current professional therapists *never* to allow themselves or their clients to confuse self-efficacy with self-esteem. Self-efficacy, as defined by Albert Bandura and colleagues (Bandura, 1997) refers to the enduring belief that one can be successful and independent. Self-efficacy is an unconditional self-rating that does not depend on the views of others, nor is dependent on specific instances of success or failure. Self-esteem, on the other hand, is a concept that seems to have outlived its usefulness in both the mental health and educational fields (cf. Ellis, 2007). In unhealthy loving relationships either one or both individuals' senses of self and self-worth are contingent upon the other person and/or the relationship. In other words, the critical question to ask your client in such situations is: "*To what extent is your sense of you and your self-worth a function of him (or her) and/or your relationship?*" If the answer is a "very much so" kind of answer, there is a good chance your client couple may have an unhealthy relationship that could be considered a dependent or codependent one. In such a relationship, one or both partners' sense of self worth is dependent on the other person's support, which could of course vanish in a heartbeat.

On the other hand, if your client's answer is a "not necessarily" kind of answer, there is a good chance that they may have a healthy relationship that could be considered to be an interdependent relationship. In such a situation, conditional self-esteem is replaced with an inner, independent and persisting sense of self-efficacy. Therefore, if you want to know *"What the difference between an unhealthy dependent or codependent relationship and a healthy interdependent relationship is?"* the answer is: "It is the extent to which one's sense of self and self-worth is contingent upon the other person and/or the relationship."

Another way to say this is that it is a relationship in which each partner's sense of self is characterized by enduring and independent self-efficacy rather than a sense of self-esteem that depends on their partner's acceptance of them at any given moment.

This distinction is a very important one and deserves further exploration. For example, one of Bill Emener's clients, Evelyn, said, "Without Tommy and without my marriage to him, I would be nothing. I *am* Tommy's wife, Mrs. Thompson. That's all that matters." Bill leaned toward her and in a soft voice said, "Okay. I hear you. But where's Evelyn?" She stared out the window in silence. When the tears began rolling down her cheeks, he knew their work had begun. The six-month psychological voyage that followed indeed was difficult for Mrs. Thompson. Fortunately, for her, it was a journey she risked taking. She didn't know exactly where she was going or where she or she and Tommy eventually would wind up. The important thing for her, however, was that she found Evelyn along the way.

Common to the differences between unhealthy dependent and codependent relationships and healthy interdependent relationships, are the respectively unique considerations of *control, awareness, extent of invasion of the other person's life, associated feelings* and *types of one's actions*. In the following, we briefly explore these five considerations within the two categories of (1) unhealthy dependent and codependent relationships *and* (2) healthy interdependent loving relationships. The discussions highlight how each of these five considerations is differentially pertinent within each of the two types of relationships.

Unhealthy Dependent and Codependent Loving Relationships.

1) *Control.* The purpose of control is to manipulate the other person and/or the relationship exclusively for one's own benefit – for one's own sense of self and self-worth. This means that this sense of self-worth is contingent on the other person's behavior and therefore conditional. It is *not* self-efficacious.
2) *Awareness.* There is very little awareness of one's own real self because the primary goal tends to be the avoidance of self. Awareness is focused on the extent to which one is succeeding at avoiding one's sense of self.
3) *Invasion.* The dependent or codependent individual continually is directly and indirectly invading the other person's life (e.g., by being evasive or dominating).
4) *Associated Feelings.* In dependent and codependent relationships, one or both individuals tend to struggle frequently with feelings of fear, shame, anger, guilt and exhaustion.
5) *Types of Actions.* One or both individuals tend to engage in aggressive, relationship-threatening, and codependent or enabling types of behaviors.

Healthy Interdependent Loving Relationships.

1) *Control.* The healthy setting of negotiated boundaries, designed simply to protect one's sense of self, are established to enhance one's sense of self and *not* to be destructive to the other person and/or the relationship.

2) *Awareness.* The individual is keenly aware of his or her sense of self, the other person's sense of self, and the nature of their relationship and how it interfaces with their senses of self and self-worth.

3) *Invasion.* There is no sense of invasion of the other person; both individuals and the relationship complement each person's life.

4) *Associated Feelings.* Although there may be some occasional discomfort, each individual typically is comfortable with himself or herself as well as with their relationship.

5) *Types of Actions.* Each individual tends to be appropriately assertive with the other, dependence tends to be healthy (e.g., "I will do the grocery shopping this week since your ankle is sprained so badly" versus "I will do the grocery shopping this week [because I need you to feel guilty and therefore remain bonded to and loving toward me])," and the loving is experienced to be unconditional loving.

It is fitting for us to assume that couples counselors need to know how to differentiate healthy interdependent and unhealthy dependent or codependent relationships. It could be argued that most relationships, from time to time, experience some aspects of unhealthy dependency or codependency. In many instances when these types of issues or difficulties develop, healthy couples will make accommodations and adjustments in order to ameliorate and/or remedy the problems associated with them. Some readers may wonder, nonetheless, *"What is an interdependent loving relationship?"*

The following will address important aspects of an interdependent loving relationship. First, it is a safe assumption that most people have their own quirks and idiosyncrasies. We all seem to have our own little uniquenesses and peculiarities. Secondly, if this is in fact true, then "How can two people, who are not perfect, who are peculiar in their own ways and who in many meaningful ways simply are different, maintain a loving relationship?" To answer this, we will share the experiences of Bob and Arlene with you.

Bob and Arlene married "later in life." Bob was 46 years old and Arlene was 44. For both of them it was their second marriage, and they each had two grown children from their first marriages. Bob, a stockbroker, typically was at his office by 7:15 each morning and usually left for home around 4:00 every afternoon. Bob liked to get up early, jog a mile or two, have his coffee while reading *The Wall Street Journal*, and then set off for his 15-minute drive to work. When he got home, he liked to go to the golf course or tinker around the yard, have a relatively early dinner, and be in bed by around 10:00. Arlene was an attorney who sometimes had to meet with clients into the early evening, she preferred eating dinner late, "did her best work on the computer at home late into the night," and slept in until around 8:00 each morning. As long as she was at her desk by 9:30 she was able to get her work accomplished and not get into trouble with her boss. Pretty clear, isn't it? During the week, Bob and Arlene had two different lifestyles.

They bought a small lot and had a house built "the way they wanted it." The front foyer, living room, kitchen, dining area and screened porch in the back were rather standard.

However, to the right was a master bedroom suite complete with a sitting area, a computer, built-in bookshelves, a TV and recliner chair, a large walk-in closet and a full bathroom. To the left was another master bedroom suite – a replica of the other one. One was Bob's and one was Arlene's. One time Bob said to Bill Emener, "Our weekends are ours – we spend our weekends together and they're usually great! During the week, however, we probably only sleep together one or two nights. Our preferred occupational lifestyles are so different. We always feel *connected*, that's not an issue for us. We just value and respect each other's differences. She's a professional woman who needs her space and the opportunity to do her thing her own way. I have my space. It's really comfortable for us. We love it. We love each other."

Arlene added, "Yeah, sometimes we even leave little love notes on each other's answering machines during the day."

To have an interdependent loving relationship, a couple does not have to have a custom-built home. An interdependent loving relationship is not a relationship of the rich. It transcends age, education and socio-economic status. It is a mindset. What people in an interdependent loving relationship minimally need, however, are: (1) an operationalized genuine respect for, and sincere valuing of, each other's individual differences and preferences; (2) a level of comfortableness with allowing each other the freedom they each value and want; and (3) a high level of trust in themselves, each other and their relationship so that they do not feel threatened by each other's independence. We know Bob and Arlene well, and can assure you that there is nothing dependent or codependent about them or their relationship.

As you work with couples and help them explore the differences among these five considerations (control, awareness, invasion, associated feelings, and types of actions) as they tend to be associated with dependent, codependent and interdependent relationships, it is important to remind them that the critical, operative variable is *how their relationship with each other interfaces with their individual senses of self and self-worth*. As Evelyn, once said to Bill Emener, "I have been so focused on Tommy and our relationship that I have forgotten who I am." If we are offering any suggestion here, it is: "Try not to let that happen to your clients."

CHAPTER SUMMARY

Unlike many areas of occupational and personal skills where the government requires demonstrated competence in the ability to perform a task or job, there are neither training courses nor permitting requirements for managing relationships with significant others (or one's children). Although we do not argue that people should be "licensed" to have loving relationships, we do point out that the skills necessary to do so successfully are highly complex and not easily acquired. Thus, the overall goals of this chapter are to assist you in improving and enhancing your ability to help your client couples (a) enjoy healthier and more functional relationships, and (b) overcome the stubborn obstacles or blocks that brought them to you in the first place. Specifically, we focused on the meta-skills your clients need in order to have functional, meaningful and healthy loving relationships: (1) empathy and listening skills; (2) coping skills; and; (3) specific skill sets pertinent to particular loving relationship stages (the Establishment Stage, the Maintenance Stage, and the Ending Stage). The chapter then concluded with a review and discussion of co-dependent, independent and interdependent relationships, and the value, importance and skills necessary to establish and maintain the most functional and healthiest of all – the interdependent loving relationship.

As directly and indirectly addressed throughout this book, in order for two individuals to enjoy a "good" loving relationship, both partners have to effectively attend to: (1) *themselves* (e.g., their own needs, wants, wishes and desires); (2) *each other* (e.g., their loved one's needs, wants, wishes and desires); and, (3) *their relationship* (e.g., agreements, compromises and/or expectations, whether tacit or openly acknowledged, that promote and sustain the couple's happiness together). In the process of assisting couples establish and maintain good loving relationships, it behooves you, as a professional couples counselor, to effectively attend to these specified and delineated understandings, appreciations and relationship skills.

With tears in her eyes, she said to her husband:

> Sometimes the best way of telling me you love me is just by listening to me.

CHAPTER 12 DISCUSSION QUESTIONS

1) How can "modeling" be a meaningful factor when a counselor is assisting a couple in developing and improving their empathy and active listening skills?

2) How and in what ways can a counselor use a psycho-educational approach in helping a couple in developing and improving their empathy and active listening skills?

3) What are the similarities and differences between a couple's coping skills and their defense mechanisms?

4) Why might it be important for a counselor to assist a couple in developing and improving their coping skills?

5) What specific skills might a counselor have to teach a couple during different stages of their relationship – specifically, during the: (1) Establishment Stage; (2) Maintenance Stage; and (3) Ending Stage?

6) Why and when might clients be resistant to the idea of learning specific relationship skills during different stages of their relationship – specifically, during the: (1) Establishment Stage; (2) Maintenance Stage; and (3) Ending Stage?

7) What are the primary similarities and differences among: (1) a codependent relationship; (2) an independent relationship; and (3) an interdependent relationship?

8) How and in what ways is an interdependent relationship typically the most functional and healthy kind of loving relationship?

RELATIONSHIPS IN THE NEW MILLENNIUM

"In the three short decades between now and the twenty-first century, millions of ordinary, psychologically normal people will face an abrupt collision with the future."
Sociologist and Futurist Alvin Toffler, from his 1970 book, *Future Shock.* (p.9)

Forty years later, as we approach the end of the first decade of the 21st century, Toffler's words seem eerily prescient. In fact, the future continues to arrive at such an increasing rate that today, in 2010, it seems almost inappropriate to refer to the present day as a part of the "new" millennium. Granted, a millennium is 1000 years, and 10 years is but 1% of the next 1000. On the other hand, so much seems to have transpired and society has changed so dramatically in these last 10 years, that the "new" millennium just doesn't seem so new these days.

To drive this point home, let's think about some of the ways life differed at the turn of the century from how we live today:

- Facebook, MySpace and other on-line social networking sites did not yet exist. No one had personal web pages or "blogs."
- No one communicated by texting, not to mention Twittering. Cell phones were nearly all restricted to voice calling.
- Internet dating, where it existed at all, was a fringe activity considered at best appropriate only for desperate singles, and at worst for con artists and child molesters.
- Email was used primarily by businesses; junk email messages ("spam") had appeared, but it represented only a tiny fraction of email traffic.
- Identity theft was an almost unknown crime and had nothing to do with on-line commerce.
- There were no iPods or iPhones, and virtually all music was available only on commercial CDs. Music has just made it onto the Internet, via an illegal sharing site called "Napster;" there was no "iTunes Store" or similar legal on-line distribution systems, and movies and TV shows were unavailable on-line.

The point is that, in retrospect, the "new millennium" doesn't seem so new any longer.

This brings us to the essence of this chapter: *the pace of change in modern life is accelerating exponentially*, and not just with respect to technology. People work longer hours to support more extravagant lifestyles or, more recently, just to keep up financially. It has become routine to change jobs every couple of years and mid-life *career* changes, complete with re-education and extensive new training requirements, have gone from being exceptions to falling well within the norm. Many more people work from home, either as telecommuters, or for themselves as entrepreneurs in home-based businesses, than has ever been the case before. Finally, as of this writing, health care has become a hot-button issue, and, as mentioned in the previous chapter, insurers are now mandated under the Wellstone Mental Health and Addiction Equity Act of 2008 (Pear, 2008) to provide mental health care benefits on parity with physical or medical care benefits. This may be good news to professional mental health counselors, clinical psychologists and others who practice psychotherapy, but it shows that the increasing complexity of life in the "not-so-new-anymore" millennium has had an enormous and profound impact on social functioning. Needless to say, this includes how people manage their loving relationships and how couples counselors must adapt to assisting people with them.

Fittingly, we deem it unacceptable not to include a chapter designed to assist you, the aspiring and/or practicing relationship counselor, in navigating these "new new things" and how they affect the practice of doing couples therapy for a living. We address the impact of the Internet on relationships, both new and existing. In our look at this medium, we see how it is evolving into a powerful vehicle for fostering social interaction among individuals and groups, and how to assist clients when they ask your advice on how the Internet can impact their relationships.

Next, we look at the topic of counseling couples whose relationships have been impacted by "compression of time" so characteristic of modern living. Closely related to this is what we refer to as the "24-hour work cycle" and how it can lead to serious relationship problems if not managed properly.

Finally, during the period this book was completed, a global financial crisis was impacting the world and people were once again using the word "depression" for the first time in 80 years. Financial insecurity has become a major factor impacting loving relationships. We therefore conclude the chapter with a look at the age-old relationship between "money and love."

By way of closing our introductory remarks, we offer a much more recent quote and set of predictions than those cited at the opening of this chapter. They are by another futurist, Ray Kurzweil, from his 2006 book *The Singularity is Near*. We find his remarks both deeply fascinating and potentially disturbing:

> At the onset of the twenty-first century, humanity stands on the verge of the most transforming and thrilling period in its history. It will be an era in which the very nature of what it means to be human will be both enriched and challenged, as our species breaks the shackles of its genetic legacy and achieves inconceivable heights of intelligence, material progress, and longevity...he examines the next step in this inexorable evolutionary process: the union of human and machine, in which the knowledge and skills embedded in our brains will be combined with the vastly greater capacity, speed and knowledge-sharing ability of our own creations.
>
> That merging is the essence of the Singularity, an era in which our intelligence will become increasingly non-biological and trillions of times more powerful than it

is today – the dawning of a new civilization that will enable us to transcend our biological limitations and amplify our creativity. In this new world, there will be no clear distinction between human and machine, real reality and virtual reality. We will be able to assume different bodies and take on a range of personae at will. In practical terms, human aging and illness will be reversed; pollution will be stopped; world hunger and poverty will be solved. Nanotechnology will make it possible to create virtually any physical product using inexpensive information processes and will ultimately turn even death into a soluble problem. (Inside of the book cover)

Whether or not, and when, any of these predictions or extrapolations (which, in our opinion, can only be called astonishing) will come to pass is anybody's guess. But Kurzweil's (2006) point cannot be ignored: the rate of change of nearly every measurable variable of progress, for better or worse, is increasing exponentially, and to ignore such a trend is to stick one's head in the sand like the proverbial ostrich and deny the reality of a future that in all probability will be unrecognizable to us in 20 to 30 years' time. Change of such magnitude, like a tidal wave, alters everything in its path, including, of course, the conduct and nature of human loving relationships. To wit, we therefore begin our final chapter of topical subject matter in the book, namely, *relationships in the new millennium.*

THE INTERNET: THE GOOD, THE BAD AND THE UGLY

On Saturday, September 15, 2007, the following headline and first four paragraphs were on the front page of *The New York Times*:

Tell-All PCs and Phones Transforming Divorce (by Brad Stone)

The age-old business of breaking up has taken a decidedly Orwellian turn, with digital evidence like e-mail messages, traces of Web site visits and mobile telephone records now permeating many contentious divorce cases.

Spurned lovers steal each other's BlackBerrys. Suspicious spouses hack into each other's e-mail accounts. They load surveillance software onto the family PC, sometimes discovering shocking infidelities.

Divorce lawyers routinely set out to find every bit of private data about their clients' adversaries, often hiring investigators with sophisticated digital forensic tools to snoop into household computers.

"In just about every case now, to some extent, there is some electronic evidence," said Gaetano Ferro, president of the American Academy of Matrimonial Lawyers, who also runs seminars on gathering electronic evidence. "It has completely changed our field."

There can be little question that the management of loving relationships has been affected in important ways by our society's transformation in the digital, information-based age. As is made glaringly clear in Ferro's (2007) above statement in the *New York Times*, privacy has become far more difficult to maintain. Virtually all of our electronic transactions and communications leave a record of what we wrote and did. An entire industry has been created to collect and analyze such data – the electronic trail of our daily behavior and the consequences for loving relationships are sweeping beyond imagination. For example, we have found it useful at times to remind certain of our clients – usually in confidence – that anyone who cheats on a spouse or significant other using a cell phone, PDA or computer had better realize that the evidence of his or her tryst is permanent and mounts with each communication.

On the other hand, millions of people, including dozens of our own clients, have met and been able to enter into loving relationships because of the Internet and the advent of new phenomena such as so-called digital dating and social networking sites. These exist only because modern technology, and in particular Internet-based communication, has brought to our world new possibilities for forming relationships. Undeniably, the Internet and its related technologies have facilitated relationships that otherwise never could have happened. Many of these relationships are seen as a blessing for those involved in them and welcomed alternatives to their otherwise lonely and isolated daily existence. Moreover, the nature of digital dating and/or social networking allows people to get to know one another in a relatively safe context; however, as news stories of murders in 2009 showed all too graphically, precautions still need to be taken. The multibillion-dollar industry made up of Internet dating services such as eHarmony and Match.com has grown seemingly out of nowhere to meet the needs of people who wish to meet others with whom they can have a meaningful relationship. In 2002, *Wired* magazine predicted that:

> Twenty years from now, the idea that someone looking for love without looking for it on-line will be silly, akin to skipping the card catalog to instead wander the stacks because "the right books are found only by accident." Serendipity is the hallmark of inefficient markets, and the marketplace of love, like it or not, is becoming more efficient.

These two aspects of the Internet – *new opportunities* for meeting people and *digital espionage* – may be considered examples of "the Good" and "the Bad" of how the Internet has changed loving relationships in very profound ways. But there is also "the Ugly" – ways in which the Internet has acted as a fertile growth medium for some of the worst examples of human behavior. Child pornography, the electronic advancement of prostitution and the sex-slave industry, and violent sex offenders gaining access to unsuspecting victims are examples of this terrifying aspect of our modern technological age.

A Brief History of the Internet, Electronic Communications and Social Networking. As you might imagine, millions of people worldwide use both social networking and various on-line "love sites" daily, and as such there are now some statistics that reveal an interesting picture of Internet dating. Here are but a few pertinent factoids:

- Up to 30% of American singles have used matchmaking sites.
- U.S. residents spent $469.5 million on on-line dating and personals in 2004, and over $500 million in 2005, the second largest segment of "paid content" on the web.
- Women, on average, receive over 5 dating-related emails daily.
- Men, on average, receive 1 or 2 emails daily.
- Around 40% of men say they don't feel confident meeting women the first time.
- The overall cost of personal sites has dropped over the last 3 years.
- On the first date many women think men aren't truthful.
- Generally, men prefer women younger than themselves.

- 60% of women prefer men older than themselves.
- Most people would prefer to be in a relationship than not.
- Over a third of women don't like men being clingy.
- Most women say personality is much more important than looks.

Statistics such as these may reveal only individual facets of very complex, interrelated phenomena, but they do help us think in a richer and more in-depth way about the subject matter at hand. When thinking about a subject with as many different aspects as the Internet and loving relationships, facts such as these remind us that it is wise to look for a broader, unifying perspective. One way to accomplish this is to step back and look at the development of electronic communications and communities over the last 20 or so years; among other things, this would give us a handle on where these new media came from and why they have been adopted so readily and by so many people.

It is not our purpose to describe in detail the history of the Internet, email, blogging, social networking sites or other forms of digital interaction. This is, after all, a book about counseling those in loving relationships. Nonetheless, the following takes a brief look at how the new media arose, if only because it greatly helps to understand the purpose it serves and provides an important perspective pertinent to loving relationships.

First, let's look at the traditional telephone system – a highly centralized system built around a "hub and spoke" architecture. The line connecting you and all of your neighbors' landline telephones to the rest of the world travels more or less directly to a telephone company network switching station, called a "network operations center" or NOC. From there, calls are routed to other NOCs, each of which handles either a single area code or a single prefix (the three digits after the area code) and eventually finds its way to the receiving telephone line. The process is reversed for incoming calls. In major population centers such as Washington, DC and other large cities, the destruction of a single NOC could wipe out telephone use for long periods of time during a crisis. In the 1970s, the United States government, in particular the Defense Department, feared that a nuclear strike on a major population center would so disrupt the ability of military and government leaders to communicate that the country might be unable to respond rapidly and effectively to a surprise attack. They wanted a decentralized alternative means of communication that could withstand a nuclear assault and still allow leaders to communicate and respond as needed.

To achieve this, in the early 1980s, the Defense Advanced Research Projects Agency, or DARPA, envisioned a non-centralized alternative to the telephone system that could absorb localized nuclear strikes and continue to function. The idea was to use a distributed architecture instead of a hub and spoke system. If information trying to get from computer "A" to computer "B" couldn't make it via one relay station (which later came to be called "servers"), the system allowed for the information to automatically find an alternative route via a different server. Therefore, the destruction of one or more servers wouldn't prevent communication.

"DARPANET," as the Internet was first called, was limited to include only key government offices, military installations and some universities. Commercial traffic was prohibited. But the system proved to include the seeds of its own undoing – it was very efficient and easy to add servers and the associated hardware (like routers and switches), and the increased connectivity was so useful that the "Net" started to grow exponentially.

Graphics and a naming system to replace the numerical addresses were added to text messaging, which evolved into the World Wide Web – the "www" at the start of most of today's web sites.

Once the genie got out of the bottle, there was no getting it back in. The distributed nature of the Internet meant that ultimately, no one person or agency could control it. Early attempts to stop commercial traffic (as well as content related to sex, gambling, and everything else, good or bad) proved useless. The truth of the matter is, even if the same government that created the Internet wanted to shut it down, it could not. Repressive regimes around the world fear the Internet, and while they try to limit its use, they can only be so successful (as of this writing, mainland China comes to mind as the most prominent example).

So, for better or worse, the Internet, email, social networking sites like MySpace and Facebook, dating sites such as eHarmony.com and the rest of the world of digital relationships are here to stay. They have had an enormous and growing impact on loving relationships and will continue to do so. With the foregoing perspective on how all this came to be, it's now time to look at what the Internet has to offer those seeking loving relationships. We like the analogy of the "Wild West" when thinking about the Internet and relationships – a new frontier only partially explored, one like the Clint Eastwood movie of the same name, that offers some aspects of "The Good," "The Bad" and "The Ugly" to those intrepid enough to explore it.

The Good

What does the Internet have to offer those looking for a loving relationship that the older alternatives such as singles bars and clubs don't? Here are a few of the "good" aspects of the Internet and relationships you can share with clients who may be reluctant to try this approach:

- The variety is almost limitless.
- On-line dating is safe and secure, when used with common sense.
- People of any interests or backgrounds are almost guaranteed to find a match; you can meet people based on career, qualifications, looks or any other criteria.
- It can be fun?
- In most cases it's affordable and low cost. Options on many sites allow you to join for just a few days, a week, a month, quarterly or even a year.
- It's very easy to do: simply create a profile, place it on the on-line dating site and start emailing other members.
- Many sites cater to people with disabilities.
- Many dating sites include instant messaging, flirting, photo exchanging, etc.
- If you don't connect with the first person you meet, there are always plenty more fish in the on-line dating sea.

Is it possible to find love on the Internet? There is no question that it is. In fact, eHarmony.com claims that 90 of its members get married every day! Though many other dating sites won't give out specific information about nuptials among their paid membership, we personally know of many happily-married couples who admit they met on the Internet. Indeed, you can advise clients with confidence that provided some care and common sense is adopted, it is possible to find one's soul mate in cyberspace.

Many of our clients who have ended a previous relationship seek our opinion on using the Internet in order to meet someone new. There are several different avenues for meeting others on-line. To wit, we offer the following advice:

- The most direct approach is to sign up with one of the reputable services (again, such as eHarmony.com or Match.com) that specialize in loving relationships. These sites offer significant assistance with profile development that is designed to filter out the thousands of others that do not fit your wants, needs and desires. They therefore offer to maximize the possibility that each person one might meet on-line will be of interest to them, and vice versa.
- Other avenues include joining social networking sites such as MySpace and Facebook. Although these are not intended primarily for meeting other people for the purpose of loving relationships, they are free and filled with millions of profiles. And, of course, people typically have the option of limiting their search to their own geographical area.

Regardless of the avenue one chooses, we advise our clients, and suggest you do likewise, that the best strategy for finding love in the on-line world includes the following core recommendations:

- *Be honest* when developing your profile or answering the on-line interview form questions. If you are a male looking for a younger female companion, say so. If you are a female looking for someone who is financially secure, state it up front. It is also a "must" to include a recent, un-retouched photo of yourself. Honesty is truly the best policy in relationships, on-line or otherwise.
- *Keep an open mind* and "meet" as many potential partners as possible. All too often, love happens when we least expect it. Sometimes, the harder you look, the more elusive it may become (the metaphoric "butterfly").
- *Hone your on-line profile* continually and keep searching for the right chemistry. For each person you have met, tailor your profile to reflect the experience gained, both for the better and for the worse.
- If you want a partner for life, *look for a friend first*. No matter how strong the initial chemistry between two people or how good the sex seems at first, relationships that last are based on mutual compatibility and not on puppy love or physical aerobics. The pleasure derived from these cannot be other than fleeting in nature.
- *Don't give up.* You may have to kiss a lot of cyber-frogs before you find your real-life prince or princess.

It should be apparent by this point that the Internet represents a powerful tool – perhaps the most powerful that has ever existed – for meeting potential partners. Just remember the old adage: "There is no such thing as a free lunch." Remind your individual clients that they may have to work at finding their significant other and not to expect instant results. But if they follow the recommendations above, they have a good chance of being successful sooner or later.

The Bad

What are the downsides to the world of Internet romance? Here are a few – mentioned by various people with experience – that we share with those who seek our advice:

- You normally can't see the person with whom you are communicating (video chatting, if both parties have a web cam, is an exception).
- The person you meet may live quite far away. You may therefore have to deal with a long-distance relationship, or one of the two of you may have to relocate in order to be together full time.
- It's easy to pretend to be someone else, as identity is not verified. Approach new acquaintances with a healthy dose of skepticism. Because of the anonymous nature of the web, it can and does attract some undesirable characters.
- On some sites you have to pay a fee; there are some free ones but most free ones are not that sophisticated or overall helpful.
- You very well might be nervous meeting someone from the Internet you have never seen before.
- It can be time-consuming.
- If you're a female, you can usually expect a deluge of emails.
- If you are a male looking for an attractive partner, expect to compete for the most attractive females.

Other than these caveats and the material in the next section, there are not too many additional drawbacks to looking for a meaningful relationship, or even just a friend, in the on-line world.

The Ugly

The anonymity of Internet dating has afforded con artists a new playground for scams and allowed people to be anyone they think you want them to be because they are engaging you primarily through the written word. This is not meant to bring forth the message that it is impossible to find love through Internet dating, but to inform people of the dangers that are out there. The Internet dating scene is one of the easiest places for someone to cheat on their spouse or significant other, or to use the Internet dating venue as a source for promiscuity.

Internet dating is still a relatively new way of people connecting with people from all over the globe, and people need to understand the dangers so they can make their search a safe one. Interestingly, movies and T.V. have focused on the lighter side of Internet dating as opposed to the darker side. What's tricky here is that people want to believe they are going to find what they are looking for (nothing wrong with that) and don't want to believe someone may be lying to them or playing games. People easily can think they are "too smart to fall for B.S.," and it is that attitude that leaves them wide open to be proven wrong. Moreover, in view of the age-old adage "You get what you pay for," those who have adopted the attitude that "everything available on the Internet should be free" are likewise sadly mistaken.

Bill Emener recalls the first time he met with Marion, an attractive, 31-year-old owner of a successful lawn service company, who came to him for help with her relationship issues. During their first session, she shared with Bill her less-than-successful attempt at Internet dating, presented in Dialogue 13.1.

Dialogue 13.1 Internet Dating… The Ugly

During Marion's (M) first counseling session with Bill Emener (B), before telling him why she was there to see him (her feelings about renewing her relationship with her alcoholic mother who had been abstinent for over a year) she shared the following experience she had with Internet dating.

M: Yes, I wish I were in a relationship. But finding a good man… well that's the challenge. And trust me – I've been trying. My "Mr. Right" is out there somewhere. Hah… (with a widening smile) I've even tried the Internet.

B: I have a sense there's a story somewhere there…

M: Story? Let me tell you!

B: Okay.

M: One evening I was fooling around on my computer, sending emails back and forth to some of my girlfriends. One friend kept pressuring me to try Internet dating since my dating life seemed to be going nowhere fast. She sent me a dating site and we started going through the profiles; then she helped me to make one of my own. We decided to leave it to fate and go through the ones that contacted me first.

B: So you had a plan and some help from a friend

M: Yes, and I also had read some good stuff – recommendations and cautions – about Internet dating. Anyways, that's how I met Greg, who lived in another state, but said he put an ad in mine because his job was relocating him: "So I may as well look for love where I am going to be living," he said. This sounded reasonable at the time, but now, looking back on it, this was red flag Number 1.

B: Yes, I see that.

M: He and I exchanged emails with more and more frequency and seemed to have a lot in common. He asked for my phone number, but I asked for his instead. He said that since he was moving he had disconnected his home phone number and only used his cell in preparation for his move. Again, this sounded like no problem,

B: But…

M: But I should have seen it – red flag Number 2. We chatted on the phone, and he seemed anxious to meet me, adding that he would be in my area in a few weeks because he would be house-hunting. So, we kept talking on the phone. However, I began to notice that he didn't answer my calls during evenings and weekends. He said that since work was paying for it, he had to limit his evening and weekend calls. Once again, this guy had an excuse for everything.

B: Another flag…?

M: Yes – I should have seen this as red flag Number 3. When I went back on the dating site, I saw his profile was still active, even though we spoke every day and planned to meet the following month! This red flag...

B: Number 4...?

M: Greg! Actually, he was in several different states, with several different handles, but the one thing he did was keep the same photo. Yikes! So, I asked my friend to help me set up a phony profile on the site to try and find out what he was up to. I wrote to him pretending to be a woman from a different state, far away from where I actually live. We wrote back and forth and I got an email from him saying how he was going to be moving to that state in a few months! I was fuming. I realized this was all a bunch of lies, this man was never moving to my town or any other, he was just using this site as a way to make false promises to women looking for something long term, and it was obvious he had no plans to deliver!

B: But I have a clear sense that you learned from this.

M: Oh yeah! Now when I go on dating sites, I only choose people that live in my area, now. And I recommend to people looking for a long-term relationship to start in their own geographical area!

Needless to say, Marion was lucky; she easily could have gotten hurt. If your clients are planning to surf the web with high hopes and expectations, advise them to arm themselves with the knowledge of what to avoid and what to watch out for, so they have the best possible chance of a positive outcome.

Recommendations. The day has come when Internet dating is considered a legitimate way of meeting new people in the endless search for the "right" person. Chat rooms have replaced bar rooms, and dating sites and personal ads no longer have the stigma they once had. People may still get a raised eyebrow when telling others they are using the Internet to search for their perfect mate, but far from the negative reaction they would have gotten only a few years ago. While Internet dating has gained popularity by leaps and bounds, so have the dangers and horror stories some have encountered with it.

There are many hidden dangers in the world of Internet dating, and it is up to the individual to recognize the red flags so that his or her attempts stand the best chance of success, rather than leaving a bad taste in their mouth. Additional recommendations we offer, for protection of privacy as well as personal safety, include: obtain and use an anonymous email address; create a persona; use a cell phone (and, if necessary, a P.O. Box). Many times, before someone can verify what they've been told over the Internet, they are already emotionally invested and don't want to hear the truth or get hurt by hearing the truth. Your clients will be safer if they realize the Internet dating scene can be dangerous for those who don't approach it carefully, as well as for those too trusting in nature. To arm oneself with the knowledge needed to Internet-date safely, watch out for the signs of danger, and as Marion's experience in Dialogue 13.1 demonstrated – *remind people to pay attention to every red flag!*

For those who have educated themselves as to the pitfalls of Internet relationships and still wish to pursue this avenue, we offer some quick Internet dating tips to share with clients. As always, advise people to take them with a pinch of salt and try to enjoy using the net to meet like-minded people:

- Decide on want you want from on-line dating sites: marriage, long-term partner, quick fling, friends, and/or some fun?
- Read reviews of any sites you consider. They're out there; just search for them.
- Decide if a particular site is within your budget. Don't be fooled by 'Join for a buck for three days!' Believe us: you can't do much in three days.
- If you can afford it, we would recommend joining at least two Internet dating sites. That way you're more likely to meet more people and as a consequence achieve your goals quicker.
- Never give out any personal information whatsoever until you are completely satisfied the person you are in contact with is trustworthy. Before meeting someone, tell your friends and relatives of your intentions, and tell them where you are going.

RELATIONSHIPS AND THE TWENTY-FOUR HOUR WORK CYCLE

We recently have counseled couples and individuals whose relationships suffered because there were no clear boundaries between "time on the job" and "time off." One of the advantages of modern technologies is that people can communicate in more ways and more conveniently than ever before. For those, such as Bill Lambos' teenage daughter, who find being in near-constant touch with friends and family members a source of unending solace (other than her father, it seems, unless she requires gas money), the modern communications revolution has been a boon – so much so that Bill's children have learned that if they send or receive text messages on their phones during family meals, they will lose their phones for the next 24 hours, a fate tantamount to a near-death experience, or so Bill's children insist. With respect to work-related issues, the combination of cell phones, email, text messaging and twittering has allowed unparalleled gains in business productivity. On the other hand, such gains come with costs.

We know of many clients who refer to their data-capable cell phones as "electronic dog collars," turning what used to be periods of welcome down time (e.g., time driving to meetings or a half hour spent quietly reading in a doctors waiting room) into yet another opportunity to work. Even Bill Lambos, a self-admitted gadget freak, actually looks forward to airplane flights that are otherwise despised so he can turn off his iPhone for a few hours and read or converse with a fellow passenger without interruption. It has gotten to the point where it is now not uncommon for clients to ask if they can take cell calls during therapy sessions!

As stressful as this has become for the individual, the impact of such non-stop communications on many loving relationships has been yet more negative. Many people work outside of traditional office settings, including in their homes and while driving. If people do not take care or otherwise insist on segregating work time from family time, or from time that is otherwise expected to be dedicated to their significant other, the quality of such relationships can drop significantly. Such situations may be manageable for those whose employers conduct business only during regular office hours. But many business entities conduct commerce around the clock, or nearly so, and many of those who work at such companies feel as if they are always at work. The line between work and leisure time has blurred to the point it simply ceases to exist.

Bill Lambos has been counseling a couple for whom this situation has become a serious problem. A recent example of how this can play out in the therapy room is presented in Dialogue 13.2.

Dialogue 13.2 Relationships and the Twenty-Four Hour Work Cycle.

Tim (T) and Robin (R) were referred to Bill Lambos (B) for help with their relationship. They were engaged, yet had not set a wedding date. After meeting with them for two sessions to find out about their situation and listen to their issues, the following conversation took place in Bill's (B) office.

B: So, how did things go the previous week for you two?

R: (sarcastically) Fine, Dr. Lambos. Tim seems to listen to you as well as he listens to me, which is pretty much not at all!

T: Hey, that's not fair – I did my best to respect our "quality time" together, and the week was going along really well, until Robin "flipped out."

B: Robin, I take it something happened that you reacted strongly to?

R: I'll say! We planned to go boating on Sunday up the river, just the two of us, and have a picnic. I was really looking forward to it. But what ended up happening? The owners of the company and two other salespeople ended up joining us, that's what happened. I had to play "hostess" to these people on our day together – and worse, Tim had a great time while I felt like a servant!

T: Hey, that's not fair. The owners flew in from Colorado unexpectedly on Friday to look over the new offices and decided to stay for the weekend. What was I supposed to do, tell them "Sorry, I'm busy on Sunday because it's 'quality-time day'?" I'm the regional manager! They pay me a very hefty salary to run the entire state-wide operation. I'm not going to risk putting them off and looking like I'm not totally committed to the business. C'mon, Robin, be reasonable.

R: And you had to invite them to stay at our *home* for the weekend? Tim, these people can afford to *buy* a hotel, no less stay in one!

T: OK, but you seem to forget, without them and that job, we wouldn't have the house *or* the boat – besides… it was an exception.

R: No, it wasn't, Tim, it was just the "excuse du jour." The week before, the computer system crashed at the office and you also worked all day *that* Sunday, remember? And what about your cell phone? It starts at 9:00 am and keeps going until midnight most nights – think that's "quality time" too?

B: All right, Robin, I hear what you're saying – the job always seems to come first. Tim, can you see where she's coming from?

T: Yes and no. Yesterday, when I had to drive between offices and we met for lunch, I turned off the phone for the whole hour. But that doesn't count, I guess?

R: Wow, I got a whole hour! I feel so *special!*

T: See what I mean, Doctor. Nothing is ever enough. And forget about our love life – it's nonexistent!

B: Let me interject something here. Tim, you said last week that this job was your first major success story in your life. You earn a high income and can buy "anything" you two want. You also said it's more than the money – the job and your rise through the ranks has been very meaningful to you and you treat it as if it were of great value, which I am sure it is. But from Robin's point of view, you are more in love with the job than you are with her.

R: Let me be clear about that – I'm proud of Tim and I enjoy the lifestyle as well as anybody. But there has to be a time when the workday is *over* and it's time for *us*, no exceptions. If we can't have that, he should ask for his ring back – because he'll be getting it back soon enough!

B: Ok, time out, you two. The problem is clear. Now let's start working on some solutions...

As time ensued, the two most difficult things for Tim were: (1) telling his boss that he needed to modify his expectations of him; and (2) his felt need to agree that if his boss would not allow him to modify his work life, he would be willing to risk his high-income job for the sake of his and Robin's relationship. The most challenging thing for Robin was to be patient with Tim and allow him the time he needed to make his goals come true. Interestingly, while they discussed Tim's need to modify his boss' expectations of him, they also discussed their need to modify and manage their expectations of each other and their relationship.

As noted in Dialogue 13.2, Robin and Tim are making progress in learning to prioritize the demands made on their time, but Tim in particular finds it very difficult. However, as Bill has made it clear, if he wants to spend his life with Robin, as he claims, he has to find a way to juggle the demands of his business so she doesn't feel ignored and unimportant to him. For her part, Robin will benefit from accepting that Tim's success comes with a cost and learning not to overly disturb herself when exceptions occur that intrude into their "quality time."

Loving relationships should be treated, in our opinion, like the living things they are. Like gardens, they must be tended to and require effort to maintain. To the extent that a person affords them value, loving relationships sometimes – even frequently – need to come first. More to the point, and invoking the garden analogy once more, loving relationships sometimes require one's *full and undivided* attention for more than a few minutes at one time in order to thrive. To assume that one's significant other will always be there in between calls or meetings is to invite trouble. In an age in which sustained personal attention has become an ever rarer commodity, this is something about which we frequently remind our busy professional clients.

MANAGING RELATIONSHIPS WHEN TIME IS COMPRESSED

What do we mean by the phrase "compression of time"? One way to understand this phenomenon is to think about the density of events per unit of time that people find normal or expected. As more events occur in less time, time becomes relatively compressed.[5] It is this aspect of time compression that we focused on in the previous section regarding the 24-hour workday.

---

[5] Although it seems impossible that time itself could be compressed (i.e., while one may *perceive* time is compressed, most people assume that time itself just passes at the same rate for everybody). But in fact, the passage of time is not constant. Einstein's theory of special relativity tells us that time does indeed pass at different rates for different people (or even clocks) depending on their speed and acceleration relative to other observers. Here, however, we refer only to the perception of time.

There is another way to look at the compression of time, however. This refers to the *rate at which things change* per unit of time, rather than the number of events that occur during each period. For example, it took over 50 years for the telephone to develop from a novel invention into a device found in virtually every home in the United States. It took 20 years – less than half that time – for the desktop computer to turn from a toy and a curiosity into a necessary tool found in every business. It took only a decade for the cell phone to evolve from a new invention to a communications system with 200 million U.S. subscribers (and growing). And it took only five years for Google to grow from an unknown search engine company to the most dominant technology company in the United States, changing the entire architecture of information processing as it did (Kurzweil, 2006). Thanks to companies like Google, a majority of business data for all but the largest companies will soon have moved from being stored on in-house servers to being stored on "the cloud" and accessed over the Web – that is, in managed data centers operated by software-as-a-service companies like Google, Apple and Microsoft. Finally, by the time you are reading this, there will no longer be any analog television broadcasts in the United States, and high definition television sets will have found their way into a majority of U.S. homes. The switch from analog to digital broadcast television took place over a span of less than three years!

If you, the professional therapist, believe you can choose to ignore this exponentially increasing rate of change, think again. If the Obama administration succeeds in mandating electronic record keeping systems, even single practitioner offices will be required to share patient data and medical information with insurance companies and other health care providers electronically (subject of course to privacy rules). This will require you, the therapist, to maintain an electronic medical records system in order to retain licensure (fortunately, it will all be stored on and hosted over the Internet and the transition will be made relatively painlessly).

Our point is that not only is life changing faster with each passing week, but that the *rate of change* is itself accelerating. For managing loving relationships, this adds an ever-increasing dimension of stress as expectations and norms of behavior change faster than people can adjust to them. For example, just a few years ago the phrase "friends with privileges" – connoting relationships in which sexual intimacy is permitted but no commitments are expected – would in all likelihood have been associated with a sense of moral depravity, even in the more liberal areas of the country (the difference is not that such encounters didn't occur before – they certainly did – but that now such relationships are considered acceptable and normal).

Other changes that have swept our social order and impacted loving relationships in profound ways include:

- the need for ever-longer educations, often including post-graduate degrees, to obtain what were once considered entry-level positions;
- an increasingly mobile and transitory work environment, where it is not unusual to be transferred from one city to another by one's employer;
- the increasing tendency for individuals not only to switch jobs several times during one's working years, but to change entire *careers* two or three times (and the requisite need for re-education in order to do so);

- medical advances allowing couples to choose the sex of their children, and even their eye color and other traits deemed preferable; and,
- the concentration of wealth outside of the middle class and into an ever smaller cohort of the super-rich.

Needless to say, each of these circumstances can pose challenges to the professional counselor that require a level of sophistication beyond that normally included in the professional preparation of a Master's level or even doctoral level therapist.

We offer several suggestions to new or practicing relationship counselors to guide them in assisting their clients in managing their relationships in the face of constantly accelerating social, educational and economic change:

- Develop a network of professional contacts in a variety of fields other than counseling. For example, a well-prepared couples counselor is one who can confidently refer his or her clients to an experienced family mediator, a certified financial planner of high integrity, an experienced certified public accountant, a good set of attorneys who practice family, business and even criminal law, specialists in learning disabilities and educational assessment, and other specialties as needed.
- Make the most of the continuing education requirements set by the state or jurisdiction in which you are licensed. Learn proficiencies outside of your "comfort zone" that you can use to provide services that meet a wider range of client needs. Time compression creates stress on client relationships from a wide variety of sources. The more knowledge you have on recent trends and the relationship issues they engender, the better able you will be to assist a client couple when they seek your counsel on how to cope with questions like "Richard spends every minute of his free time playing *World of Warcraft*! How do I get him to pay attention to *us*?"
- If you are less than two years from retirement, begin planning to adopt an electronic medical records and patient management system immediately. Such systems offer more than just convenience and increased productivity – they can help improve the quality of treatment you can offer your clients. For example, when a client in Bill Lambos' office replies to an automated telephone call or email message confirming their next appointment, his office's patient management system automatically searches several Internet databases for the latest articles and changes to the standards of care for their diagnosis and treatment codes, and prints a summary to include in their paper chart prior to their appointment time (the paper charts are just a metaphorical convenience at this point – the *actual* chart consists of electronic data records stored in "the cloud" on highly secured servers whose physical locations are unknown).

None of these changes to the social order or enhancements to technology systems can make a well-trained clinician with good therapeutic intuition and skills obsolete. There is no substitute (at least not yet) for a caring human being with a strong client-therapist alliance for helping clients overcome their difficulties. Nonetheless, the range of electronic technology issues that present in therapy sessions has increased geometrically along with the rest of changes in the world, and as the rate of change continues to accelerate, psychological stressors will continue to multiply and have ever greater impact on loving relationships.

MANAGING RELATIONSHIPS DURING ECONOMIC DURESS

Paralleling the changes addressed in the previous section and the stressors that accompany them is the evolution of modern economies in an increasingly globalized world. An entire spate of new material about the making sense of 21st Century economics has recently appeared not only in the news media, but also in a series of fascinating books by economists, journalists, Wall Street-traders and others who should be in a position to know about such things. For the counselor looking to educate him- or herself about the subject, we recommend recent volumes that are both erudite and yet highly readable such as *The Return of Depression Economics and the Crisis of 2008* (Krugman, 2008), *The World is Flat* (2006) and *Hot Flat and Crowded* (2008), both by Thomas L. Friedman, and the "it-would-be-hysterical-if-it-weren't-so-sad" book *Panic: The Story of Modern Financial Insanity* (2008), by Michael Lewis. Our pick for the best of these goes to *The Black Swan: The Impact of the Highly Improbable* (2007), by Nassim Nicholas Taleb of The University of Pennsylvania's Wharton School of Business, who predicted the entire collapse at the very height of the boom years (and who by short-selling the markets at their peaks has become a very rich man). These authors all help to make clear – at least in retrospect – how the "Great Recession" of 2008 and beyond arose (it is still going "strong" at the time of this writing). Among the causes the authors cite are hubris, unpredictable social and economic trends, and lapses in government regulations with respect to banking that have been in effect since the 1930s. Also given credit is the development of a national philosophy (under the presidential administrations of both parties) that promoted short-term gain at the expense of long-term security and even unfettered human greed as "admirable" attributes, occurring between 1980 and 2009.

Regardless of how it happened, between 2007 and the time of this writing the world economy teetered on the brink of global collapse. The news media did better than their average job of continuously reminding citizens how vulnerable they were, and the unemployment rate approached 10%, with over 600,000 jobs per month being lost. In short, an aura of fear and doom resulted from the confluence of events, and many couples counselors found foremost that among their clients' most pressing relationship issues were problems related to economic insecurity.

Having an in-depth understanding of how the United States' current economic situation and commensurate conditions got to where they are (as discussed above), is very helpful in appreciating "how real the current realities are" – for everyone: us, you, and especially... your clients! To wit, we deemed it important to share with you our insights and suggestions on how to help such couples.

As we discussed in Chapter 9, the one issue couples fight about the most is money. Rather than duplicating that and the other related material already presented, we refer the reader looking for specific guidelines and advice on counseling couples with issues related to money matters back to the first section of Chapter 9. What we wish to offer in the current section are couples counseling approaches and techniques specific to current economic realities.

First, we are finding it helpful to advise client couples that the current recession is, in all likelihood, different from all those that preceded it in our lifetimes. Although there is yet much to be optimistic about, we urge you to remember that it would be a serious mistake to consider – and passively allow your clients to consider – the current climate merely another "bust" in the past series of boom-and-bust cycles going back to the 1960s. The underlying changes in the global and American economies over the past 10 years have left us with an economy that is fundamentally different than it was, and all indications are that it will remain so. As can be read in any of the books listed above, especially in Krugman's (2008) and Friedman's (2006, 2008) volumes, the majority of the hard work that will result in economic recovery in the United States has yet to be done. As of this writing, much of it has not even been started. We deem it quite probable that things will seem uncertain (at best) for at least another few years, and in all likelihood it will take another 5 to 10 years before the economy has adjusted to the "future." Therefore, if a couple is harboring the belief that things will soon change back to a time when that new home or boat they so desperately "need" – "to make everything all better" – is just around the corner, they are in for a rude awakening. The couple that is able to seek rewards in facets of life other than shared material success will have the easiest time making a go of it for the foreseeable future.

Second and closely related, is the underlying truth that "the economy" is essentially a construct and does not reflect anything tangible. It is a statistical amalgamation of individual transactions among people that has become divorced from anything to which even a Newtonian physicist would attach the label "real" or "existing." It cannot be touched or sensed, and money has no value other than that which we are willing to ascribe to it. What changed about the millions of homes that "lost value" during the housing "crisis" of 2006-2008? In most cases, nothing other than what people were willing to pay for them.

This is worth considering for more than the sake of philosophical curiosity. Two realities arise from the realization that the economy is a statistical illusion: First, it is especially subject to changes in people's beliefs of what things are worth. Thus it is a largely self-fulfilling prophecy and subject to wild swings related only to peoples' perceptions of it. The upshot is that it is healthier than not to expect fluctuations in economic circumstances – circumstances that lie far beyond one's control. Second and indeed pertinent to the couples counselor, is: how a couple's relationship is impacted by the economy is largely determined by *expectations, perceptions,* and (often irrational) *beliefs* about what they "deserve" or "must have" in order to be content. Given this, many relationships can be strengthened by assisting one or both partners to change their expectations, perceptions and beliefs. Often, no changes in behavior are needed to help the couple whose relationship has been impacted by economic duress.

This is not to deny that losing one's home, for example, is often deeply traumatic. And in cases of a dire change in circumstances, where true life necessities such as food, clothing and shelter are lost, appropriate action is warranted. Fortunately, the United States remains a relatively wealthy society and much social assistance is available to the truly needy. But we are also a society of the spoiled and demanding, and we have counseled many a couple whose relationship has suffered because they felt unable to "keep up with the Joneses." Therefore, our advice on counseling the couple that presents with issues related to economic insecurity is to assist them in maintaining a realistic perspective. It is not a "crisis" if one has to drive a seven-year-old automobile for another year or two (or three). Tongue-in-cheek, á la Albert Ellis (2000) you might ask, "Is your belief that you *should* or *must* get a new car every two or three years the 11th Commandment?" and á la Victor Frankl (1984) you might ask, "Specifically how does a new car or a new boat truly add to your personal sense of meaning and worth?"

CHAPTER SUMMARY

Today, many people in the United States and around the world are experiencing what Avlin Toffler (1970) referred to – 40 years ago – as "Future Shock." For many, today it is "Present Shock." So much seems to have transpired and society has changed so dramatically in these last 10 years, that the "new" millennium just doesn't seem so new these days. Thus, as we delineated and discussed, we find the underlying essence of this chapter – *the pace of change in modern life is accelerating exponentially*, and not just with respect to technology.

Pertinent to these spiraling rates of changes in our society, we took an in-depth look at how people are trying to manage their loving relationships and how couples counselors must adapt in assisting their clients with such change. Moreover, we addressed the impact of the Internet on relationships, both new and existing, and saw how the Internet is evolving into a powerful vehicle for fostering social interaction among individuals and groups. Next, we looked at the topic of counseling couples whose relationships have been impacted by "compression of time," so characteristic of modern living. And as we saw, the "24-hour work cycle" can lead to serious relationship problems if not managed properly. Finally, we examined how the current global financial crisis is impacting the world and how financial insecurity has become a major factor impacting loving relationships. Therefore, we concluded with a look at helping couples with the age-old relationship between "money and love."

In closing, we would like to remind our readers of the value of keeping things simple, and in counseling their client couples to do likewise. A quote Bill Lambos enjoys sharing with his clients is the following, by Antoine de Saint Exupéry, a French writer and aviator who lived in the first half of the 20th century:

> Perfection is achieved, not when there is nothing more to add,
> but when there is nothing left to take away.

CHAPTER 13 DISCUSSION QUESTIONS

1) How and in what specific ways are the spiraling rates of changes in our society affecting you: (a) personally; and (b) professionally?
2) What are some things you can do to assist your couples so that modern electronic technology can enhance rather than harm their relationships?
3) What are some of the "good" and "bad" ways the Internet is affecting loving relationships?
4) How is the current "24-hour work cycle" affecting couples and their relationships?
5) What are some things you can do to keep the current "24-hour work cycle" from having a negative affect on: (a) you; (b) your loving relationships; and (c) your work as a professional counselor?
6) What does it mean to say, "In our society, time is compressed," and how is it affecting loving relationships?

7) Specifically, how can you assist couples that are having relationship problems because of "time compression?

8) What are some of the ways the current economic duress in our society is impacting people's loving relationships?

9) How can Ellis' and Frankl's theoretical approaches assist you in helping couples appreciate how their (a) *beliefs,* and (b) *sense of meaning and purpose* can help them enjoy a healthy and happy loving relationship in spite of the current economic realities impacting them?

WHEN YOUR CLIENT SEEKS YOUR HELP

This is a good time and place to step away a bit from the text and look at our journey thus far from an aerial perspective – let's get up above the trees and look at the forest. In the previous 13 chapters we: (1) discussed some of the critical foundations and basic concepts of couples counseling; (2) reviewed pertinent counseling theories and related them to the underlying neural organization of the brain; (3) examined the phenomena of love, loving and romance, also with respect to their neuroscience underpinnings; (4) analyzed individual and relationship issues germane to loving; (5) reviewed how an individual's past can intricately interface with their loving relationships; (6) discussed the systemic interrelatedness among the individual, the couple and the world; (7) examined how an individual can impact his or her relationship, and vice versa; (8) reviewed relationship skills minimally necessary for healthy loving relationships; and (9) discussed relationship issues specifically within the new millennium. Combining your knowledge and appreciation of these nine sets of concepts with your already acquired knowledge, skills and expertise in counseling, you're now ready to work with a couple (or individual) with a loving relationship problem. "Okay," as the coach may say, "suit up – it's game time." But before leaving the locker room, it indeed may be helpful to take a serious look at some important considerations regarding when a couple or client first comes to see you for assistance with a loving relationship problem. This is the primary purpose of this chapter. As our journey approaches our destination, we feel it is the appropriate time to take a last look at some "nuts and bolts" issues such as those that follow.

"We read some self-help books over the past year or so while we tried to fix things in our relationship. Sometimes things would get better, but then after a while we'd be right back where we started. I guess that's why we're here. In their own way, our friends and relatives try to be helpful. They offer advice and suggestions. But that hasn't made any difference either. We need some help – professional help."

"She doesn't know I'm here. I just thought I'd come in to see you by myself first. I've been trying to get her to understand that I still need to see my first wife on occasions, like every other week when I get the kids for the weekend or when we both go to one of their school functions. She's so jealous. She just doesn't understand. I can't take it anymore."

"You are the fourth therapist we have seen in the last three months. All the rest didn't 'get it.' We've heard you're really good, so we expect you will understand what it is we are trying to say when we say it."

"As soon as I can get back to working day shifts, everything will be fine. We really don't need to be here! She just blows things out of proportion all the time. This is unnecessary. That's all I have to say!"

"Now that Luke has agreed to come to counseling, I can finally take a deep breath, a sigh of relief. I am convinced our problems are almost behind us just because we're here."

"This is embarrassing. We live in a real nice neighborhood. We both have professional jobs. Our families know we're doing just fine. Our two kids know we're okay – the four of us do a lot of things together all the time and have a lot of fun. Alright, so we have a few arguments once in awhile, but to have to come here to see a psychologist... I don't know."

"He agreed to meet me here today, but this afternoon he called me from his office and said that some honcho from the regional office was flying in and that he had to pick him up at the airport and take him to his hotel. 'Otherwise I'd be there,' he told me. But I don't know. He wasn't all that excited when I scheduled this appointment for the two of us. So I thought I'd come anyway, so at least I could fill you in on what's been going on."

"Being here, seeing you... I know this is the end. I'm so scared..."

"I can't believe we're seeing a counselor! We've been living together for over two years now and everything is really going great. We used to have our problems, but we worked them out. But now, because I just have a few beers when it's hot, she thinks I have a drinking problem. I don't have a drinking problem. She's the one with the problem."

"We've made appointments to see counselors in the past, but then she would cancel them. She would say, 'Look, I bought this new book on communications,' or something like that. I know we have problems and we need help. I'm just glad that the two of us are finally here."

"Yeah, we argue sometimes. It's usually because she gets on my case. She really knows how to push my buttons. Then when I get mad, she won't leave me alone. She just keeps pickin' and pickin'. Yeah, I may push her or slap her on rare occasions, but I don't mean anything by it. She just needs to learn to leave me alone when I'm mad. She just needs to learn how to let me cool off."

"We really wouldn't have to be here if he would just listen to me. I've been telling him for years that everything would be okay if he would just..."

"I came ready to negotiate and settle our differences. Lord only knows what you'll hear from her!"

When one or two individuals first come to see either of us for assistance with their loving relationship, it is not uncommon to hear them say things similar to the preceding statements. Seeing a professional counselor, therapist or mediator, especially for the first time, as is revealed in the following illustrative statements, understandably can be:

- *depressing* ("Reality has hit me. We really do have problems.");
- *saddening* ("I've tried so hard, but it hasn't helped.");
- *demanding-unrealistic* ("We're paying you good money, so 'fix us' and be done with it!");
- *threatening* ("My denial has worked so far. Who wants to look at the truth.");
- *optimistic-unrealistic* ("Now that we're in therapy, we have no more to worry about.");
- *embarrassing* ("I have my pride, you know. And what will others think of me when they know we're seeing a therapist?");
- *self-focusing* ("If he doesn't want to do anything about our situation, that's up to him. But I've had it! I'm going to do this for me if that's the way it has to be.");
- *scary* ("I know we have some very serious problems, and I'm afraid that if we ever look at ourselves as we really are, it may be over.");
- *relieving* ("We've talked about getting help in the past, but something always came up. Now maybe we'll get some help and actually improve our relationship. At least now there's some hope.");
- *denial inducing* ("I'm not the one with the problem. If only she would just...");
- *anger producing* ("I've been telling him what's wrong for years and he just won't listen to me... he never has!");
- *utterly unrealistic* ("I can agree to *anything*, as long as it is *reasonable*.")

If there is a common thread or theme to these expectations of, and reactions to, professional help, it is this: going for, receiving and benefiting from professional assistance with a loving relationship, is frequently easier said than done. Thus, in view of the real possibility that this may be true for your clients when they think about seeing you (a professional counselor), therapist or mediator, we will share with you some of our experiences, reflections, thoughts and suggestions that will be helpful to remember.

First, don't be surprised if your client uses the terms "counselor," "therapist" and "(family) mediator" more or less interchangeably. There indeed are differences among such professionals (even though the boundaries between them are fuzzy and getting yet fuzzier with time). Nonetheless, in numerous ways the terms *couples* or *marriage counselor*, *therapist* or *relationship therapist*, or *mediator* or *family mediator*, imply or mean the same:

> A person with at least a master's degree in mental health counseling, marriage and family therapy, clinical social work, or a doctorate in psychology from a regionally accredited university who is licensed by his or her state to practice as such, or a person who meets these educational requirements and is certified by the Supreme Court of their state as a family mediator.

Second, if your client and/or his or her partner never talked with a helping professional before, then one of the biggest hurdles they face may simply be not knowing what to expect. One reasonable prediction, however, is that their first several sessions with a helping professional are more likely than not to be *different* from their expectations. The only experience most people have is their recollection of "therapy" scenes from television shows and movies. For reasons we have assumed to be due to dramatic necessities and ratings, screenwriters rarely if ever manage to create a realistic impression of therapy. The therapy process is either depicted as unstructured and trivial chit-chat, or as complete emotional breakdown and catharsis, but seldom anything in between. We trust the case studies and dialogues from our files and counseling sessions interposed throughout this book have helped you gain a more realistic understanding and appreciation of what actually transpires. Nonetheless, it is critical that you remain sensitive to your clients' possible fears and apprehensions regarding their seeing you – especially if it's the first time they've ever seen a professional counselor.

CLIENTS' QUESTIONS AND PRESENTING PROBLEMS

The following addresses five questions are often asked by people who are (1) struggling with problems or issues in their loving relationships and (2) thinking about seeing a professional counselor.

1)   "Why would a person go to see a professional counselor?"

It has been our experience that most people go to see a professional counselor for one (or a combination) of the following reasons:

- *Anxiety and Stress*. "I spend every minute of my free time worrying about what will happen next. I can barely sleep or function anymore."
- *Danger associated with Anger*. "Lately when we have been arguing a lot, there's been some violence. I'm afraid that if this goes any further, one of us or possibly even one of our children may get hurt."
- *Pain, Hurting and Exhaustion*. "I've been living with a lot of emotional pain for a long time. I'm just hurting too much. I can't take it any longer."
- *Guilt*. "Because of what I did, I just can't look at myself in the mirror any longer. This has to be dealt with, and now."
- *Helplessness*. "I know that some things need to be done. We need to make some changes in our relationship. But we don't know what to do."
- *Hopelessness*. "The both of us have been trying to make some changes and do some things differently, but none of it seems to have made any difference. So before calling it quits, we thought maybe you could help us."
- *Ignorance*. "We want to make things better and improve our relationship, but we just don't know what to do."
- *Mandated*. "The last time we got into an argument we started hitting each other. So the judge said that if we want to be able to have the kids with us we have to see a professional."
- *Improvement*. "I wouldn't say that our relationship is bad. It's okay. But that's the problem – it's just okay. We love each other and have a great, fun-loving family. However, we need to try to improve our relationship because someday the kids will be grown up and out, and then it will just be the two of us."

2) "How would I go about finding a helping professional?"

Sometimes people know friends or coworkers who have seen a helping professional. Counselors, frequently hear "A friend recommended you to me." If an individual's employer has an employee assistance program, they may talk with their supervisor or call their human relations office to see whether their employee benefits program can provide any assistance. *The Yellow Pages* can provide the names of licensed psychologists, mental health counselors, marriage and family therapists, and clinical social workers that have expertise in assisting people with adult loving relationship issues and problems. Today, a majority of professional counselors have web sites and are listed in most or all of the commonly used Internet search engines. Alternatively, if a person has health insurance, he or she can call their primary care physician or insurance carrier and request a referral for professionals in their area. Also, many people have received helpful assistance from their ministers, rabbis or priests.

3) "What are the costs involved?"

If people see someone via a community agency or a religious affiliation, costs may be nothing at all, a voluntary donation, or set on a sliding scale or a minimal rate. If they see someone through the auspices of their employer's Employee Assistance Program, the first few visits may be free or at a very low cost. Private counseling and therapy, on the other hand, can be expensive – and in today's economy scary – ranging from $75 to $150 per session. If a person has health insurance and sees someone who is "in network," his or her only costs may be a pre-established "co-pay" fee. And as an aside, we occasionally tell people concerned about the costs of seeing a counselor that when they ask themselves the question, *"Can I (or we) afford to see a professional counselor?"* they also may want to ask themselves, *"Can I (or we) afford not to?"*

4) "How confidential will all of this be?"

As we discuss in Chapter 15, licensed helping professionals in every state are required under federal law to maintain strict confidentiality (with only a few exceptions as discussed in the next paragraph). Title II of The Health Insurance Portability and Accountability Act (HIPAA), enacted by the U.S. Congress in 1996, includes a set of Administrative Simplification (AS) provisions that addresses, among other things, the security and privacy of health data. Even self-pay-only professionals who do not accept insurance are subject to the law's security and privacy provisions. Very serious sanctions, including forfeiture of the license to practice and even imprisonment, can result. Remember this (even if you client doesn't ask about it).

Beyond requirements by law, helping professionals are very understanding of their clients' desire and need to keep their information and situation confidential. The only times when a helping professional may breach confidentiality are: (a) *if the client is a clear and imminent danger to them self* ("If I know you are planning to jump off a bridge, I will make efforts to stop you."); (b) *if the client is a clear and imminent danger to society* ("If I know you are planning to harm someone else, I will take measures to prevent it."); or (c) *if subpoenaed to court by a judge*. (In most states, the only three categories of individuals who have statutory confidentiality are attorneys, spouses and ordained clergy.) In the latter case, however, because judges understand and respect the importance of confidentiality in the client-therapist relationship, very rarely will they require a helping professional to testify. As we tell our clients, "If your husband, wife, family member or best friend were to call me genuinely with your best interest at heart, without your permission, I would not even acknowledge that you have been in to see me." Furthermore, in all cases where confidentiality is breached for the above reasons, the helping professional is required to disclose this breach of confidentiality to the client (unless it is an emergency situation or involving abuse of a child).

5)   "What do I need to tell my counselor before or during my first appointment?"

Be prepared to ask your clients the following kinds of questions and ready for their somewhat typical kinds of answers:

- *"What is the problem or concern?"* (e.g., "My wife told me about two weeks ago that she wants a divorce. I've been very upset ever since. I don't know what to do. I need to talk to someone as soon as possible.")
- *"Who will be coming in for the appointment?"* (e.g., "Both my fiancé and I.")
- *"Are there any special considerations that you would like us to know about?"* (e.g., "My husband doesn't know that I will be coming to see a counselor. If he found out, I know he'd get really mad. He gets violent some times. It's important that he not know.")
- *"When will you be able to come in for an appointment?"* (e.g., "I get out of work at about four thirty and my husband is self-employed. I'd say we could get to your office by five o'clock any night but Monday night, when he has to close the store by himself.")
- *"How can I contact you if I need to?"* (e.g., "My mother is living with me right now and I don't want her to know that I'm coming to see you. Please don't call me at home. If you need to contact me, please call me on my cell phone."
- *"Do you know where my office is?"* (e.g., "I'm pretty sure I know where your building is. Could you please confirm the address?")
- *"Will you be able to get here about 30 minutes before your first appointment to complete some paperwork?"* (e.g., "Yes, I will be able to do that. And my friend said that sometimes therapists may run a little behind schedule. So just in case that happens, I'll tell my supervisor that I won't be back to work until around three o'clock.")

There is no way to be prepared for every question you may have to ask a prospective new client – or for every answer you may receive. But being ready for these will surely be helpful.

INTAKE INFORMATION

Typically, clients are expected to complete intake forms prior to coming to their first session with a counselor that garners valuable information about them and their presenting problem(s). Although standardized intake forms may be useful and save the therapist and client time, we urge you to be use caution when drawing conclusions or forming opinions merely from the information on the form. Many agencies, facilities, companies and counseling centers also have an additional intake form specifically for couples; if you are in private practice, you may use a form of your own. In either case, Figure 14.1 contains an example of a *Couples and Marriage Counseling Intake Form* that you can modify or use as is (or use to improve or expand the form you currently use).

Having such information about the couple can certainly be helpful. A word of caution, however – there may be additional information not obtained by the form or extenuating circumstances and your potential conclusion may be wrong and ill-warranted. Should you see information of concern, it is advisable to review it with your client(s). For example, just because an individual may have been out of work for the past six months, it doesn't mean he or she is lazy (he or she may have acquired an injury or a disability or may be in an occupation where very few job opportunities exist, etc.).

There is another caveat regarding the use of intake forms, particularly with certain client populations, of which couples is a good example (neuropsychology patients, whose cognitive status is presumed to be questionable, comprise another such population). If a couple is asked to fill out the form together, or even if each of the partners fills out individual forms, *do not assume the information is accurate.* Couples are often seeking assistance because they *cannot* be honest with their partner about sensitive issues, or because past attempts to do so resulted in negative outcomes – including, for example, substance abuse and domestic violence. It may be more prudent to arrange for each member of the couple to individually fill out a detailed intake form (such as the one in Figure 14.1) in a separate room (from their partner), and hand it directly to the receptionist before returning to the waiting room. In Bill Lambos' experience, the client's experience of entering into counseling is diminished (sometimes significantly so) by the requirement to begin the process by filling out detailed forms that request deeply personal information with a high emotional valence. Therefore, the intake form used in Bill's practice is very cursory, listing only demographic information – name(s), address(es), contact information, referral source, payment information, current medications and a single line for "reason for visit." Whatever else Bill wishes to learn about his new clients, he will ask them, either together, separately or both. In Bill's experience, much more of value is learned in this way than via a detailed form requesting deeply personal and sensitive information of indeterminate accuracy – the old adage applies: "misinformation is worse than no information."

Name(s) of Agency, Practice or Therapist
Street Address
City, State, Zip
Telephone & Fax Numbers
Email Address(s)

Date: _____

Name: _____	Name: _____
Date of Birth: _____	Date of Birth: _____
S.S.N.: _____	S.S.N.: _____
Address: _____	Address: _____
_____	_____
_____	_____
Home Phone: _____	Home Phone: _____
Cell Phone: _____	Cell Phone: _____
Email: _____	Email: _____
Education: _____	Education: _____
Occupation: _____	Occupation: _____

Current Employment:
- □ Full-time
- □ Part-time
- □ Unemployed
- □ Full-time student
- □ Part-time student
- □ Retired

Current Employment:
- □ Full-time
- □ Part-time
- □ Unemployed
- □ Full-time student
- □ Part-time student
- □ Retired

Annual Income:
- □ $0-9999
- □ $10,000-24,999
- □ $25,000-49,000
- □ $50,000-74,999
- □ $75,000+

Annual Income:
- □ $0-9999
- □ $10,000-24,999
- □ $25,000-49,000
- □ $50,000-74,999
- □ $75,000+

Figure 14.1. Couples and Marriage Counseling Intake Form, Page 1.

Reasons listed below that resulted in your request for counseling (check all that apply):
  □ Depression or anxiety
  □ Alcohol/drug abuse
  □ Marital/Relationship problems
  □ Communication difficulties
  □ Psychological evaluation
  □ Improve sexual relations
  □ Child/parent conflict
  □ Divorce counseling
  □ Sexual orientation questions
  □ Thinking of harming self or others
  □ Learning difficulties
  □ School problems
  □ Family counseling
  □ Individual counseling
  □ Difficulty with loss or death
  □ Relationship enhancement
  □ Abuse (physical/mental)
  □ Pre-marital counseling
  □ Other (please explain):

Relationship Status (check all that apply)
  □ Married
  □ Separated
  □ Divorced
  □ Dating
  □ Cohabitating
  □ Living together
  □ Living apart

Length of time in current relationship: _____

Children (including, biological, adopted, foster, step) List under type:

Name	Gender	Age	Type	Custody (Y/N)

Figure 14.1. Couples and Marriage Counseling Intake Form, Page 2.

Have you ever been to counseling as a result of problems with this relationship prior to today? _____ If so, what was the outcome of that counseling?

_____

_____

_____

Have either you or your partner been in individual counseling before? _____
If so, give a brief summary:

_____

_____

_____

Were you referred to this center/agency? _____ To me? _____
If yes, by whom? _____

Do either you or your partner drink alcohol or take drugs to intoxication? _____
If yes for either, who, how often and what drugs or alcohol?

_____

_____

_____

Have either you or your partner struck, physically restrained, used violence against or injured the other person? _____ If yes for either, who, when, how often and what happened?

_____

_____

_____

Has either of you threatened to separate or divorce as a result of the current relationship/marital problems? If so, please explain:

_____

_____

_____

Figure 14.1. Couples and Marriage Counseling Intake Form, Page 3.

Has either you or your partner consulted with a lawyer about divorce? _____
If yes, who? _____

_____

Do you perceive that either you or your partner has withdrawn from the marriage? _____
If yes, which of you has withdrawn? _____

How frequently have you had sexual relations during the last month? _____ times

How enjoyable is your sexual relationship? (Circle one)

Terrible	More unpleasant than pleasant	Not pleasant, not unpleasant	More pleasant than unpleasant	Great

How satisfied are you with the frequency of your sexual relations? (Circle one)

Way too often to suit me	A bit too often to suit me	About right	A bit too seldom to suit me	Way too seldom to suit me

What is your current level of stress? (Circle one)

Extremely High	Very high	High	Moderate	Low	Very Low	Extremely Low

To what degree do you have family or friends that support you as a couple? (Circle one)

Extremely High	Very high	High	Moderate	Low	Very Low	Extremely Low

To what degree do the two of you share a similar basic outlook on life? (Circle one)

Extremely High	Very high	High	Moderate	Low	Very Low	Extremely Low

In your own words, what is the primary reason that brought you here?

_____

_____

Figure 14.1. Couples and Marriage Counseling Intake Form, Page 4.

As you think about the primary reason that brings you here, how would you rate its frequency and your overall level of concern at this point in time?

Concern:
    □ No concern
    □ Little concern
    □ Moderate concern

Frequency:
    □ No occurrence
    □ Occurs rarely
    □ Occurs sometimes
    □ Occurs frequently
    □ Occurs nearly always

What do you hope to accomplish through counseling?

_____

_____

_____

What have you already done to deal with the difficulties?

_____

_____

_____

What are your biggest strengths as a couple?

_____

_____

_____

Please offer at least one suggestion as to something you could personally do to improve your relationship/marriage regardless of what your partner does:

_____

_____

_____

_____

_____

Figure 14.1. Couples and Marriage Counseling Intake Form, Page 5.

OBSERVATION

Valuable information about a new couple also can be gleaned simply by observation. For example, when they are in the waiting room, are they sitting together, holding hands or is one sitting on the sofa smiling and excitedly looking around and the other sitting across the room appearing bored, annoyed and angry? In any case, we repeat our caution: be careful not to draw conclusions, opinions, beliefs and/or attitudes merely from what you see – there may be additional, non-observable information or extenuating circumstances and your conclusion may be wrong and ill-warranted. For example, Bill Emener observed a married couple in his waiting room (who came in because "We're trying to decide whether or not to adopt a child") and immediately took notice of the 6'4" muscular husband and the 5'1" wife who had one arm in a sling and two black eyes peaking out from behind large dark sunglasses. A few minutes later, however, he breathed a small sigh of relief when he found out that they just returned from a week of skiing in Colorado and on their last day, as Jane said, "I hit more than just the slopes – how about a full-grown Aspen tree."

As you make such kinds of observations, note them but don't take them to the bank. And unless additional information naturally surfaces, consider them as good discussion items during the session.

GOALS OF COUPLES AND MARITAL COUNSELING

At some point during the first session, most counselors or therapists will address with their clients what might be reasonable goals for them to work toward. Goal-setting is an integral part of counseling and therapy. "What do you hope to accomplish from our sessions?" is a rather frequent question. In our work with individuals and couples, we have found the following issues pertinent to goal-setting to be critical:

1) *"Are you sick or are you sorry?"* What we mean here is, "Do you have a deep-seated personality or biological problem that is causing your problems or difficulties? If so, we may need to consider including some psychiatric interventions in our treatment plan. *Or*, is it because of situational issues – such as, 'It sounds as if your life is just messed up a little right now.' If so, then our focus should possibly be on identifying ways to improve your life and your lifestyle. *Or*, is it a combination of the two?" There's a big difference, for example, between being depressed because you have a biochemical predisposition for endogenous depression, on the one hand, and on the other being depressed because your mother died last month and last week your husband (or wife) asked you for a divorce! The answers to these questions are typically quite useful in setting the stage to determine whether the problems and difficulties are relationship-specific or related to one or the other of the individuals. Only after this information has been determined can we move toward the next question.

2) *"Is it you, the other person or the relationship?"* Having "set the stage" (per the above), the next logical question is: "Are you having relationship problems or difficulties because of something within *you* (e.g., maybe you have a commitment-

phobia?), something with *the other person* (e.g., maybe your partner has a commitment phobia?), or is it *your relationship* (e.g., the two of you have difficulties communicating with each other because you remind each other of your previous spouses?) Usually, it is because of some combination of these three possibilities. Nonetheless, it is important to identify where we should focus our attention – on you, on the other person, on aspects of your relationship, or on a combination of these alternatives.

3) *"Do you want to end it, fix it, or just rest for a while?"* Another important question is, "If you have any outcome expectation, would it be: (1) to end your relationship; (2) to improve or fix your relationship; or (3) to rest for awhile and decide what you want to do at a later time?" In terms of this last alternative, sometimes people simply like to get away from each other for a while, stop the arguing and fighting (e.g., 'Stop the bleeding and allow each other to heal a little.'), and at a later time revisit this question and then try to decide what to do. Hopefully their answer will be an honest one! We say "Hopefully" because, as every experienced couples counselor has learned, it is not uncommon for people to come to see us with "hidden agendas." For example, one of us recently met with a couple, both of whom said that they wanted to improve their marriage. Upon further probing and questioning the two individuals, however, it became obvious that the wife wanted a divorce but was "going through the motions" so that no one could say she didn't try to "save the marriage".

4) *"No, I will not help you get back to where you used to be."* People will frequently say to us, "We would like to get our marriage back to where it used to be – when we were happy and not fighting all the time." It is a real shock to them, however, when we reply, "No, I will not help you do that." Then, after drawing a sketch for them similar to the one in Figure 14.2 (and while they stare at each other, aghast at our statement), we point to the sketch and say, "If your relationship was all that 'good' in the past, you wouldn't be here now. No, I will not help you go back. But I would be happy to help you move forward with establishing a loving relationship consistent with your wants and desires."

Usually when this happens, they look at each other and at us with (1) a genuine appreciation for what we are saying to them and (2) an agreement that "upward and onward" is ultimately where they want to go.

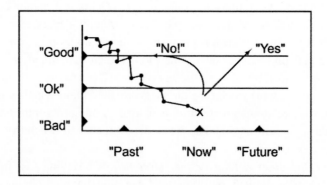

Figure 14.2. Going Ahead – Not Back to Where You Were.

It generally takes more than one session to identify specifically where an individual or a couple wants to go. Regardless of the time needed, it is important to have some general idea of where the client(s) would like to go before you start heading anywhere.

RULES OF ENGAGEMENT: CONJOINT VERSUS INDIVIDUAL SESSIONS

It is not uncommon to work with individual clients who could meaningfully address their relationship-related difficulties if they also could see a counselor together with their partner. Likewise, it is not uncommon to work with couples that could meaningfully address their relationship-related difficulties if one or both of them also could see a counselor individually. For example, think about a couple in which one of the partners has early-childhood-related fear of abandonment issues. The best-case scenario might be for the troubled individual to see a counselor alone and for the couple to see a counselor together. The question, nonetheless, is: should the troubled individual *and* the couple see the same counselor or should the individual see one counselor and the couple see a different counselor? The following will address this relatively large issue in couples work:

Scenario 1: One Therapist, One Client. When a client asks Bill Emener, "In addition to seeing me, would you also work with me and my husband (or wife)?" or when a couple asks him, "Would you see us individually as well as work with us as a couple?" he typically will respond with, "No." He follows with, "I can only have one client." When he tells his students this and they ask "Why?", he then proceeds to explain his position.

> "When I first began working as a therapist," Bill begins, "toward the end of my first session with a married couple they asked if I would see them separately. I said, 'Yes.' The following week I met with Richard. During our session, he said to me, 'About a year ago my receptionist was on maternity leave for six weeks. I hired a replacement receptionist from an employment agency. She was very good and did an excellent job. On her last day at work, I took everyone in the office out for drinks to celebrate her good work and, in effect, to thank her. As the evening wore on, it eventually came down to the two of us in the lounge by ourselves. To make a long story short, we wound up back at her apartment and made love for the rest of the night. It was wonderful. But I have never seen her again.' We briefly processed that experience and it was rather clear to me that it was not a significant issue for Richard nor was it particularly pertinent to his marital problems at the present time. The following week, however, when I was meeting with both Richard and his wife, Sally, she said to me, without being asked, 'One of the things I have always admired about Richie is that he has never cheated on me.' Richard immediately looked at me and inhaled for about four minutes! Needless to say, I also was extremely uncomfortable. If I had said anything to Sally about what Richard had told me, I would have betrayed Richard's trust and confidence. And by not saying anything to Sally, I felt that I was somehow betraying her trust and confidence as well. So, since that time, except for very rare occasions, I will only work with one client: *him, her,* or *him and her.*"

Scenario 2: One Therapist, One Identified Client, with both individual and conjoint sessions. Some professional counselors and therapists do not subscribe to Bill Emener's position on this and are very effective in their work. For example, there are occasions in which Bill Lambos will agree to see a couple both separately and conjointly, as long as the identified client remains the couple. In such cases, rules for confidentiality are carefully discussed with his clients prior to seeing either person separately. Thus when Bill sees a client couple, he explains at the beginning of the first session that he will very likely ask to see one or the other individually at times. In the majority of cases, this involves asking one or both of the partners to alternatively spend some time in the waiting room during a session when both partners have come together while Bill sees the other member of the couple one-on-one. Why? Because experience has taught Bill Lambos that by the time they have reached the point where counseling is deemed necessary and agreed to come, they have reached a point where they are, at a minimum, uncomfortable with being honest with the counselor in the presence of their partner. This is especially true early in counseling. If an affair, domestic violence, a substance-related problem or other emotionally sensitive issue characterizes the relationship, Bill wants to know about it as early as possible. Perhaps because he was trained as a family mediator prior to becoming a therapist, Bill is comfortable with holding secrets, as long as the rules are explained up front.

Thus, the decision as to which of the two scenarios above you, the counselor, adopt as your "practice standard," depends on your personal ideology and individual comfort level. Nevertheless, in our roles as psychologists, counselors and therapists, we will agree to treat *one identified client and only one client in a given family or relationship (even if the "client" is, in fact, the couple).* As long as such rules are explained clearly at the outset of the counseling relationship, there is much room for improvisation. For example, occasionally one of our clients will invite his or her spouse or loved one to a session or two, but on such occurrences it is very quickly established that: (1) he or she is our client; (2) there are specific reasons and goals for which the other person is being invited; and, (3) the other person is meeting with us by his or her (our client's) invitation. If we are working with one person and it is clear that he or she *and* their loved one or spouse need to see a marriage counselor or marital therapist, we recommend them to another helping professional specifically for that reason. The same applies if we are working with a couple and one of them needs to work at length on some individual, personal issues: we will recommend that he or she see a helping professional individually and specifically for that reason. Our experience has been that this approach works very well for us and for the people with whom we work. As we said earlier, however, some professional counselors, psychologists and social workers reportedly are very effective seeing both an individual partner and the couple conjointly. Thus, while we know what works well for us, we nonetheless encourage you to talk with such professionals to learn specifically how they do it and see if it may work for you.

CLIENTS' WANTS AND WILLINGNESS TO WORK

We begin our address of this subject by sharing with you an old joke in the counseling lore. Question: "How many counselors does it take to change a light bulb?" Answer: "One – but the bulb has to be willing to change."

It is not all that difficult for most people to identify what they want in or from their relationship. Moreover, such typical relationship wants and needs most often could be obtained quickly if the other person would do what he or she is convinced the other person easily could do if he or she only wanted to. As Charlotte said to Henry, "You know, my dear, these things that you want in our marriage are also things I want in our marriage. However, every time I listen to you, I'm the one who has to change, work harder or make sacrifices in order for us to have these things that we both want. What are *you* willing to do?"

As you have seen throughout this book, one of the couples counseling techniques we occasionally employ is to ask both partners to accept a homework assignment. With respect to "wants and willingness," we ask each of them to individually, and without consulting the other, bring the following two lists to our next session:

1) *Things You Want In, or From, Your Relationship*; and for each of the things on list 1., a corollary listing or indication of:
2) *What You Are Willing To Do To Get and Have Them.*

Then at our next session we discuss both lists and try to identify common Wants and Willingnesses. This process is designed not only to help them improve their relationship by getting more of what each wants and by sharing the responsibilities for getting them, but also to help them learn: (1) how to work together cooperatively to identify their wants; and (2) how to cooperatively share responsibilities.

Willingness to Work. Also as suggested in this book, there are differences between (a) a desire, capacity and willingness to love you, and (b) having a good loving relationship with you. An example of the *desire* to love you and having a good loving relationship with you is in the simple statement, "I would like such things to happen." An example of the *capacity* for such things is, "I would like such things if I am able to do what it may take to have them." An example of the *willingness* for such things, however, is, "I would like such things to happen and I am willing to work, sacrifice and do whatever it takes for us to have them." As Karen, one of our clients bluntly said to her fiancé, Ralph:

> "You say you love me with all your heart and that you love me with as much love as you have to offer. There are some things in our relationship that you and I both want, but you are not willing to do anything, make any changes or inconvenience yourself in any way in order for us to have them. And that, Ralph, is what I struggle with the most! I believe that if you really wanted some of these things you say you want, then you would be willing to do something or at least try to do something about them. You would *like* to have many things in our relationship, but you don't really *want* them. If you did, you'd do something about them, but those things would take time, effort and energy. You talk the talk, but you don't walk the walk!"

If it is true that our willingness to work for things is an indication of how much we value them, then we would suggest that Karen is expressing an important aspect of a loving relationship – one worthy of your client's consideration as they (and their loved one) think about, analyze and attempt to improve their relationship. This is why we typically directly or indirectly will ask our clients: "Are you willing to invest some time, effort and energy into getting what you want?"

CLIENTS' EXPECTATIONS

In order to effectively help clients and couples address their relationship problems, it is important to assess and monitor their expectations – of you, their counseling experience and ultimately their progress. To wit, the following is designed to arm you with some of the critical philosophical and functional aspects of clients' expectations that you can use in your counseling with them.

We Help You Help Yourself. It is not uncommon for an individual to come to one of us and say, "I would like you to tell me what to do about my relationship with my loved one." Nor is it uncommon for a couple to come to one of us and say, "We would like you to fix our relationship for us." For philosophical and professional reasons, our responses to these two statements tend to fall into the category of routine.

First of all, neither we nor other qualified and competent helping professionals tell people what to do in or with their lives. As Bill Emener has been known to say, tongue-in-cheek, "I have a Ph.D., not a G.O.D. – I don't tell people how to live their lives." Typically, helping professionals offer analysis and the opportunity for exploration and reflection in order for *their clients* to determine where they want to go and what they want to do with their lives. "Your life is your life – you must be the individual making the decision," is a line Bill Lambos frequently uses with clients.

Second, when necessary, we tell our clients that we choose not to fix, nor could we fix them or their relationship for them. An individual may be able to go to his or her dentist, lie back in the chair, be put to sleep, and with minimal cooperation allow the dentist to fix his or her teeth. But as professional counselors, we can no more help people than we can climb inside their heads or take their place in the relationship. *Our goal is to help individuals help themselves.* The somewhat familiar analogy that we also occasionally use is, "Give a person a fish, and you have taken care of their hunger today. Teach a person how to fish, and you have taken care of their hunger forever."

With regard to these two philosophical issues, we have been known to say to our clients things such as, "I will be your limo driver for this short period of your journey. But you will need to tell me where you want to go – remember, I'm only the driver," and "I prefer to think of myself as the coach and cheerleader on the sidelines; you are the player who will go out onto the field and do the work to win the game."

Stages of Change Efforts. The well-known psychologist Dr. James O. Prochaska and his colleagues developed a widely accepted and much studied model of the stages of individual change called the *transtheoretical model of change* (Prochaska & Velicer, 1997). Although this model is now applied and taught in many areas of health psychology (in particular, in substance abuse recovery programs), few remember that it was originally developed to address the stages of change a couple undergoes when seeking to improve their relationship or prepare for divorce. Prochaska's model posits the following six stages of change:

1) *Pre-contemplation* – lack of awareness that life (in particular, one's relationship) can be improved by a change in behavior;
2) *Contemplation* – recognition of the problem, initial consideration of behavior change and information gathering about possible solutions and actions;

3) *Preparation* – introspection about the decision, reaffirmation of the need and desire to change behavior, and completion of final pre-action steps;

4) *Action* – implementation of the practices needed for successful behavior change (e.g., regular sessions with a helping professional);

5) *Maintenance* – consolidation of the behaviors initiated during the action stage;

6) *Termination* – former problem behaviors are no longer perceived as desirable (e.g., when skipping a planned walk on the beach in order to have time to watch football results in frustration rather than pleasure).

When working with couples, it is not uncommon for us to recognize some of these stages of their efforts toward improving their relationship. Depending on the background of our client, we may simplify the six stages down to four and draw a diagram similar to the one in Figure 14.3. Since the couple is already in our office seeking change, we skip the pre-contemplation phase and note that the first stage involves *awareness* – when we are trying to heighten our understanding of, and appreciation for, what is going on within ourselves, the other person, and within our relationship. The second stage is *agreement* – when we tend to agree on what our problem areas are and what aspects of our relationship on which we need to focus our attention. Then, in stage three, we individually and collectively make *commitments* – when individuals begin to say things like, "From now on I will… and from now on we will…" The most difficult stage, however, is stage four when our awarenesses, agreements and commitments are translated into *behavior change*. As a client astutely said, "Stages one, two and three are when we talk the talk. That's easy. The fourth stage, however, is when we have to walk the walk. In this stage, we focus on behavior change. Indeed, this is the most difficult stage." And as another person recently noted, "Stage four is where the rubber meets the road."

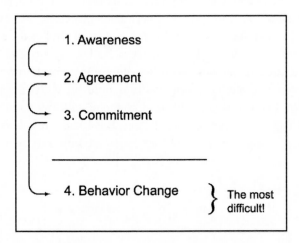

Figure 14.3. Stages of Change Efforts.

Regardless of how many stages one wishes to identify, the point remains that achieving the lasting and positive changes associated with increased happiness and/or decreased suffering involve a process of change that evolves through stages. And please remember: this is true whether or not a couple seeks professional assistance or is able to achieve such change on their own. Moreover, the progression through stages implies the passage of time – the topic addressed next.

Progress May be Slow and Gradual. In Chapter 13, we saw how our society has been forced to adapt to the compression of time, with rapid and accelerating change and constant motion being the norm rather than the exception. One unfortunate consequence of this is that some people have also grown more used to immediate (if not instant) gratification. Fittingly, we occasionally remind our clients that there is no such thing when working with a professional counselor on relationship issues. Achieving personal change or improvement in loving relationships involves adjusting long-held perceptions, thoughts and beliefs, and changing long-established behaviors. This in turn involves, as we have seen, a progression through stages that takes both time and effort. When clients ask us, "How long will it take to fix this?" we typically respond with, "I can't say, but my bet is – longer than you were hoping. You had better ask yourselves right up front, is fixing this relationship worth the investment it will require?" Most of our clients, having made it as far as getting to their first appointment, respond in the affirmative.

Rita, for example, an account executive with a large corporation, had recently been transferred from Dallas to the Tampa Bay area when she first came to see Bill Emener. She told him that she had been seeing a therapist in Dallas for over a year and had been making excellent progress. "I do not want to fall back just because I moved to Tampa," she said, "and I hope and trust you will be able to assist me in continuing to improve my life." The process of trying to understand what Rita had experienced prior to coming to see him culminated in Bill's sketching a diagram similar to one in Figure 14.4. They had identified three alternating states of her life: *happy, uncomfortable* and *troubled*. In a nutshell, this is how she described her experience: "Up until the end of 1991, I was relatively happy with my life and happily married to Walter. We had just celebrated our fifth wedding anniversary. But for reasons I do not understand, he started being absent from the house more and more, and I believe he began seeing other women. By 1992, my life was very uncomfortable, and by October of 1993 I knew I was in trouble. By the time our divorce had been finalized, my life was simply a wreck. That is when I began to see Dr. Johnson in Dallas. By November of 1993, with the help of some short-term medication, I was able to cope and go back to work. I had a relatively comfortable Christmas and started to enjoy life a little bit when I was transferred to the Tampa Bay area. Dr. Johnson suggested that I continue with my antidepressant medication until you and I feel that I no longer need to take it. But I know it is going to take some time before I can get my life back together and start to go out with men again. All I want to do is live a happy life."

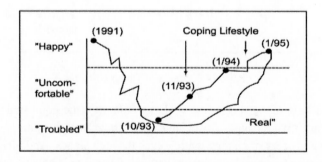

Figure 14.4. Progress May Be Slow and Gradual.

Basically what Rita was saying was that with the help of some short-term medication and the psychotherapy she had been receiving from Dr. Johnson, she had developed some effective coping skills and was able to live a relatively meaningful and enjoyable life. At the same time, however, her psychological and spiritual, or "real" happiness in life was still below what her "coping," "as if," or "socially appealing" lifestyle would have suggested. At the end of that first session, they agreed she would continue to work with Bill with the goal of continuing to have a "coping lifestyle" so she could continue to function occupationally and socially, and eventually her "real happiness" would catch up with her every day, "real" lifestyle behaviors.

Bill saw Rita for a total of six sessions. As she was leaving his office after their last session she told him she was enjoying her dates with Fred and was probably going to continue to see him on a regular basis. She also said to him, "I was a little nervous when I discontinued taking my medication and later started going out with Fred. But every day, every week, my life seems to be getting easier and much better. My happiness in life, indeed, seems to be coming around. When you and Dr. Johnson told me that my progress may be slow and gradual, I was not sure what you were trying to tell me. Now I do."

Some "good self-help work" on behalf of an individual or a couple working with you as their counselor indeed can reduce, ameliorate and possibly even eliminate their troublesome relationship issues, difficulties and problems. You may have to remind them that slow and gradual progress is, nevertheless, still progress. As Rita said, "Recovering from and bouncing back from a dirty deal in life sometimes simply takes time. I've done a lot of hard work over the last year and a half to help myself get to where I am today, and it surely has been worth it!"

Realistic Expectations: Behavior and Emotions. As noted above, the stages of change experienced by those seeking to improve a loving relationship are similar in some ways to the stages of recovery from substance dependence. One of the ways in which the two processes overlap is as follows: *each and every additional day of experiencing and working on the change process, results in an incremental (and sometimes small) movement towards positive change.* Of course, there are often temporary setbacks, and most assuredly, some days are better than others, but overall, the longer the behavioral changes are maintained (e.g., sobriety or being more considerate of one's partner), the more such change feels comfortable and natural.

When Matt and Rosa came to see Bill Emener, they told him that they had been married for five years and that for the past two years they had been having some serious problems in their relationship. For example, Rosa said, "I just don't feel special anymore. I feel more like one of Matt's possessions."

Bill believed Matt and Rosa when they told him they loved each other very much and wanted to improve their relationship. "One of my problems," Matt said, "is that I am from a very large family in which the men 'owned their women.' I do not want to be a chauvinistic person, but without a doubt I come from a chauvinistic background." Bill also believed Matt when he said, "I want to be a loving man and I want to be loving toward Rosa with all my heart. But sometimes I just don't know how."

A related difficulty was that when Matt would do something to try to be loving toward Rosa, she would have difficulty believing his authenticity. For example, she said, "Sometimes I don't know if he really means what he does."

Bill sketched a diagram for them similar to the one in Figure 14.5. As the couple looked at the diagram, Bill said to them, "One potential difficulty that you might try to avoid is the way in which each of you struggles with accepting each other's loving actions and behaviors. For example, Rosa, when you explained to me what happened when Matt brought you some roses, you had difficulty being excited because some of your long-term, angry feelings had caught hold of you. And when you did not respond to Matt with the level of appreciation and joy that he was expecting, he also was disappointed. The end result was that both of you felt bad about a very nice thing."

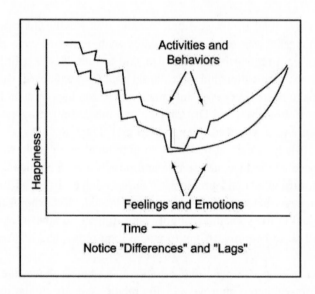

Figure 14.5. Realistic Expectations: Behaviors and Emotions.

Matt looked at Rosa and said, "Sometimes when I try to do loving things for you and with you, you still become upset and angry with me. It would be helpful if sometimes you could just appreciate what I do for you. If I bring you flowers, enjoy the flowers. If I take you to a movie, enjoy the movie."

"Okay Matt," Rosa replied, "I will try to do that. I will try to respond to what you do for me, and maybe as time goes on some of my deeper feelings and emotions will change and I will genuinely feel happier about my life and being married to you." As Matt held her in his arms, the two of them began to cry.

In loving relationships, changes in long-term *feelings* will sometimes follow changes in long-term *behaviors*. When working with a couple, try to remember: even if partners change their behavior toward each other today, it doesn't mean that their feelings and emotions will immediately change. But if we can assist them in continuing to act lovingly toward each other, chances are that as time goes on they may (again) begin to feel loved by each other.

Don't Expect Immediate Results. As Matt and Rosa experienced, when two individuals have been experiencing long-term difficulties, their feelings about themselves, each other and their relationship tend to be very deep and entrenched. For example, Rosa said to Matt, "You have been shitting on me for the past two years, and just because you have begun to be nice and loving towards me for the past two weeks doesn't mean that I can quickly overcome all of the hurt I have been experiencing."

On occasion you may have to remind your clients that as they begin to engage in "new behaviors and activities" with, for, and on behalf of each other, they should not expect their feelings toward each other and their relationship to change overnight. Likewise, as they begin to do loving things for each other and they both appreciate what each other is doing, they still may have some deeper level, less than positive feelings about each other and their relationship; thus, it will be very important for them to try to be patient with themselves and each other. *Behavior change does not necessarily guarantee emotional change* (thus, for example, the term "dry drunk"). To wit, it will be very helpful for them if you are encouraging and you help them try to remember that as they engage in long-term behavior change, their feelings and emotions will gradually and slowly come around.

The Downside of an Upswing. Helping your clients put things into perspective and look at their progress over a long period of time can help them (1) appreciate the progress they are making and (2) avoid overreacting to what they may have been experiencing in the last day or two. Like the stock market, long-term trends include up and down days. One thing we ask our clients to keep in mind when they reach a plateau or feel stuck in their progress is to consider that they may be in a slump that is part of an overall pattern of progress – the downside of an upswing.

Valerie, a 34-year-old-high school Spanish teacher, had been living with Ricardo for over two years and had been talking about getting married, "When suddenly he up and left me!" Over the next five months, Valerie and Bill Emener had six therapy sessions together. At their last session, when discussing her progress during that five month period, Bill sketched a diagram similar to the one in Figure 14.6. "Yes, that's it, Dr. Emener. That's what my recovery from Ricardo's leaving me looks like – a saw-toothed line that continues to go up."

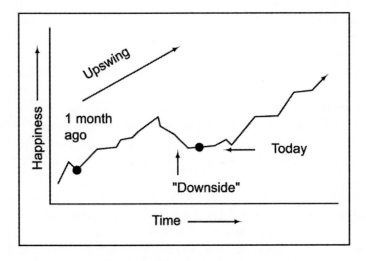

Figure 14.6. The Downside of an Upswing.

As they looked at the diagram, however, Bill said to her, "I suggest that you try to continue to remind yourself, Val, that as long as the line continues going up, you know that you are making progress."

Valerie looked up, smiled and said, "Yes, it has been that way and it is continuing to be that way. As time continues to march onward, my happiness continues to improve, and even though sometimes it appears to be gradual, it is definitely improving. My mother asked me how I was doing. I told her that for the past two days I have been a little down. She instantly began to worry. But I immediately told her not to worry because I was simply on *the downside of an upswing*. I told her that my worst day of this week, today, is still better than my best day a month ago. And as far as I am concerned, that's progress!" When relevant for your clients, facilitating their doing what Valerie was doing can be very helpful for them.

In general, we repeatedly find that it helps clients to focus on the overall trend rather than on the short-term. In such situations, we encourage you to remind your clients to stop dwelling on bad things from their past and focus on the good things in their present.

COUNSELING INTERVENTION STRATEGIES

"Sometimes it takes more than one chef to prepare a meal," is a quip Bill Emener uses when telling his students that no matter how good one is at working with an individual client or a couple, additional assistance may sometimes be needed. In this section, we will present and discuss five out-of-session options that may help your work with clients: (1) homework; (2) journaling; (3) bibliotherapy and videotherapy; (4) mediation; and (5) support groups.

Homework. An inaccurate *a priori assumption* about counseling is that the most important things that happen are in the sessions. In reality, however, clients frequently have meaningful epiphanies or "ah-ha" awakenings and related growth experiences outside or between sessions. Thus, as you have witnessed throughout this book, we frequently use "homework" with many of our individual clients and couples. Not only can such activities benefit clients in and of themselves, they also can reinforce what the clients experience in their sessions. In addition to the three out-of-session activities that follow, other homework that can be helpful to clients includes making lists (e.g., three things I could do that would be appreciated by my partner), writing letters (sometimes actually mailed and sometimes brought to the client's next session for review and discussion), a planned activity (e.g., a couple going away for a few days, leaving their laptops, cell phones and watches in a drawer; attending an open AA, NA or GA meeting), and a variety of other such activities. It is important to remember that when your client or couple agrees to your recommended homework task or activity, make a note of such in your client's file – should you forget about it at your next session, it can be very embarrassing for you and indeed threatening to your relationship with your client.

Journaling. As you may have experienced yourself or vicariously though your work with clients, journaling is and has long been a helpful tool to achieving better emotional and mental health. The need to express oneself in a safe and controlled manner is a powerful means to improving self-esteem and personal relationships. Couples also can use this tool to increase their communication effectiveness, respect and appreciation of each other. Here are 10 ways we tell couples that journaling can be helpful to them:

1) *Telling your relationship story.* What better way to immortalize your relationship than to write about it in a journal? The couple can create a memoir of their evolving lives, describe the many branches on their biological and spiritual family tree, or just make a scrapbook of their collective life together.

2) *Share yourself with each other*. Most people keep their journals private but choosing to share a journal with a loved one can close the gap on distant relationships or bring "close ones" even closer. Three options thus can be seen here: (a) each partner maintains their own journal, allowing the other to read it; or (b) maintaining a collective journal in which both partners enter entries; or (c) the partners each maintain an individual "private" journal *and* the couple keeps a collective journal. Option (c) may be the only way for couples with "secret-secrets," or for individuals who do not wish to share everything they think or feel with their partner, to attain the benefits of journaling.

3) *Share your wisdom (life experiences) with each other*. As we have heard individuals say to their partners (per #2 above), "I may not be an expert on life but I have had my share of successes and failures. So have you. Together we can learn and grow more than either of us could have done alone. And by writing it down, we can always go back to it should we forget."

4) *See the world through the eyes of your partner*. Again, further to #2 above, journaling can allow you to see life from the perspective of your partner's culture, geography, beliefs, age and gender. Take a trip around the world or through time simply by reading a family journal. If partners want to enhance and enrich their empathic understanding of each other, collective journaling can be exceptionally helpful.

5) *Organize yourself...emotionally and spiritually*. As Bill Emener says, "Whenever I go to the store, I usually make a list. If I don't, I am sure to forget something. Probably a few 'somethings.' Writing things down helps me recall what I need to buy." Journaling, individually or collectively, can help couples remember the emotional and spiritual items they need or want – in their individual lives as well as in their relationship life. "Journaling," as Bill has been known to add, " is the first step in your emotional and spiritual grocery store shopping."

6) *Track your emotions, moods, and experiences over time*. (If you recommend journaling to a client or couple, remind them to enter the day of the week and date of each entry.) As one of our clients recently said, "Monday was a high-energy day. Tuesday, I felt depressed and lethargic. Wednesday, I started to climb out of it. Thursday, I felt better but had difficulty focusing. You get the picture, right?"

7) *Unburden yourself and let go of old hurts*. Many people have carried old emotional baggage for many years. Isn't it time for them to let it go and move forward feeling a little lighter on the emotional load? For example, it may be important for clients to let go of the hurts and fears they inherited from childhood that have clung to them through adulthood and affected all of their important relationships. Releasing them into a journal and really living life to the fullest may be what they want. Because journaling can be anonymous (see #2. above), this is their opportunity to say it all and unburden themselves so that they can have freer, more productive relationships with their loved ones instead of venting it all at them.

8) *Clarify and achieve your dreams, goals and aspirations*. As any successful life planner, motivational speaker or therapist will tell you – in order to achieve a goal or dream you must write it down. Journals are a great way to realizing that goal or dream. While the path of life and relationships seems confusing and chaotic, a look

back into your journal will reveal some very clear patterns that will help you in your future journeying.

9) *Respectfully challenge each other's beliefs and enrich your lives.* Master therapists tell us that in order to change your life you must change your thoughts or beliefs. Doing this on your own is difficult if not impossible. Journaling is a great way to analyze thoughts and beliefs that get in the way of good mental health and better loving relationships.

10) *Realize you are not alone.* Have you had a loved one pass away? Suffered a financial loss? Had a prodigal child leave home? Anyone who has suffered a loss or felt the weight of depression knows how lonely that can be. It feels like no one could possibly understand the pain you feel. Collective journaling can remind you that you are not alone.

During a recent counseling session, Denise, one of our clients who had been collectively journaling with her husband for approximately three months, said to her husband, "Jerry, I really appreciated you stepping up and telling that guy at the party the other night to stop asking me about my father." Through a thin smile, Jerry replied, "I know how your father treated you when you were a child, and that still is a sensitive issue for you." When Jerry saw the somewhat surprised look on Denise's face, he continued, "I may not have said anything to you, but remember... I have been reading what you've been writing in our journal." Denise warmly smiled at Jerry and reached for his hand.

Bibliotherapy and Videotherapy. When people read self-help books or watch movies, they can invest themselves so that they come away from the book or movie with a better understanding of their thoughts, feelings and behavior (as well as the thoughts, feelings and behavior of others in their lives). Moreover, such experiences can challenge their ideas, thoughts, conceptualizations and overall considerations of themselves as well as their past, present and future loving relationships. Such experiences also can occur and sometimes even more so when partners engage in reading and movie-watching together.

For the reasons noted above, counselors often recommend self-help books to their individual clients. When counseling a couple, similar helpful outcomes also can be facilitated. When we recommend a self-help book to a couple, it may be a specific book we have used with other clients successfully. Alternatively, we may suggest they go to a bookstore, peruse the "Self-Help" or "Relationships" sections and select one they deem would be most helpful for them. In either case, Bill Emener suggests they read the book in a specific way. The easiest way to illustrate this is by example. Last week while talking with George and Betty, it was recommended that they read a specific book on relationships. Bill also suggested that George get a blue highlighter, Betty a yellow one. Then the following took place as he spoke to them:

"George, I would like you to read chapter one of the book. Read it slowly as if it were talking to you, not like you're studying to take a test on it." George smiled. Bill then continued, "And while you're reading it, when something jumps out at you like 'Yep, that's me!' take your marker and highlight it. When you have finished reading chapter one, give the book to Betty." Betty was then told, "I would like you to read chapters one and two and highlight in yellow those things that jump out at you. As a matter of fact, you may highlight some of the same things that George already highlighted. There's nothing wrong with that.

When you have finished, give the book back to George." Finally, Bill turned and said, "George, you then read chapters two and three the same way that you and Betty read one and two."

A very important aspect of this above described *dovetail reading* procedure, also called "integrative reading," is the need to establish a few ground rules:

> "First," Bill said to George and Betty, "while you are reading a given chapter and you notice that either of you has highlighted something and you're curious about it, turn to the other person and point to the highlighted materials and say, 'Would you please share with me what you were thinking about when you highlighted this?' The second ground rule to which it is crucial that the two of you agree is: whatever he or she says to you or you say to him or her, you just listen, and when they have finished you say, 'Thank you.' Period. Remember, the objective of this endeavor is to learn, not to win or prove something. This is not the time to start World War III when you look at the other person and say, 'See, for years I've been telling you that your parents have always...'"

We also have found that when we discuss this approach with our clients, both members of the couple usually smile and laugh comfortably. We then share with them that just because something is published in a book, it does not necessarily mean it is true for everyone who reads it. The contents of a book should not be used exclusively, as a verification or validation that one person in a relationship is "right" and the other person "wrong."

Usually, when contemplating the use of bibliotherapy with a couple, the first thing we do is ask, "Do you like to read?" If the answer is "No," then for them the potential benefits of bibliotherapy are considered minimal. There is, however, another option: videotherapy. In such situations we recommend a specific movie for them to watch together, including the basic bibliotherapy caveats and ground rules discussed earlier, with modifications.

Recently, Bill Lambos recommended a movie for a couple, Roberta and Ryan, to watch together and said the following to them:

> "First," Bill said to Roberta and Ryan, "pick a time to watch the movie when there is nothing else going on – the children are asleep, cell phones are turned off, etcetera – and put the remote between you. Then while you are watching the movie if either of you sees something that jumps out at you – such as, 'That reminds me of...' – pick up the remote and pause the movie. Share what you were thinking about. And after one of you has shared his or her thoughts, the other of you responds by simply saying, 'Thank you.' Period. Remember, the objective of this endeavor is to learn, not to win or prove something. This is not the time to start an international scene by looking back and saying something like, 'See, for years I've been telling you that your parents have always...'"

Basically, we are suggesting to the couple that when they read a self-help book or watch a specific movie that they *empathize with the issues, the people described and especially themselves and each other*. When we suggest that they invest themselves, we are suggesting that if they can feel the pain and sorrow of a given individual in the book or character in the movie, they should try not to hesitate to cry; if they feel a knot in their stomach, they should try to allow themselves to experience that frustration or anger; and if they can truly feel the joy and ecstasy of some of the individuals in the book, they should try to allow themselves to smile and feel the uplift that may naturally come with it.

To assist you in your use of bibliotherapy and videotherapy with your individual clients and couples, at the end of this book there are two lists:

APPENDIX A. A CATEGORICAL/ANNOTATED LIST OF BIBLIOTHERAPEUTIC SELF-HELP BOOKS

Ten categorical listings of a total of 86 self-help books, published since 2000, that can be very helpful for individuals and couples struggling with specific issues interfering and/or troublesome in their loving relationships.

APPENDIX B. A CATEGORICAL/ANNOTATED LIST OF VIDEOTHERAPEUTIC MOVIES

Ten categorical listings of a total of 61movies (except for some "classics," most of the movies are relatively new) that can be very helpful for individuals and couples struggling with specific issues interfering and/or troublesome in their loving relationships.

We also suggest that if you recommend self-help books and specific movies to your clients, read and watch them yourself as much as you are comfortably able to do so.

Mediation as an Alternative to Counseling and Therapy. Family or couples mediation was once reserved for the couple undergoing divorce. Of course, mediation remains a valuable alternative to the family court system. Succinctly defined, mediation is:

> ...one of many methods, or approaches, parties may choose to use when they have a disagreement, problem or issue to solve. Specifically, mediation involves the hiring of a specially trained person – the mediator – to help the parties communicate and negotiate, and hopefully achieve a resolution of their problem or dispute." (Lambos, 2009, p. 142)

In deference to the historical hold-in-reserve attitude toward mediation, today it is increasingly common for couples to seek the help of a family mediator to strengthen a marriage or relationship rather than just to help dissolve it. This is sometimes referred to as "therapeutic mediation." Inherently, this term is a bit confusing; to wit, your authors prefer to simply recognize that mediation is a technique for resolving disputes that can and do involve keeping a love relationship intact and/or strengthening it, as opposed to only helping to dissolve it.

What is the difference between a family or couples mediator and a family or couples therapist? Less than one might think. In fact, many family mediators are also licensed therapists and vice versa. (Bill Lambos is an example.) A mediator is a specialist in *alternative dispute resolution*. Other-professional mediators include attorneys, the family court system, nonprofessionals, and other helping professionals. The biggest difference between a family mediator and a family therapist is in focus: *whereas a family therapist is more often than not focused on improving a relationship by helping individuals change their perceptions, feelings and behaviors related to the relationship, a mediator places the emphasis on the nature of a dispute.* Think of a mediator as part King Solomon – a neutral and impartial third party whose job is to help find a solution. But unlike King Solomon, mediation is not binding unless the parties sign some type of agreement upon its conclusion; the mediator may never impose a solution. Important for you to remember is: mediation is an excellent alternative to counseling or therapy for situations when the couple's difficulties revolve around external factors as opposed to internal psychological ones.

What kinds of disputes can be mediated? In fact, there is almost nothing that cannot in principle be mediated. Within the context of existing relationships, Bill Lambos has mediated prenuptial agreements, disputes over how money is allocated, childrearing guidelines, behavioral contracts for couples in recovery from substance and even Internet addiction, rules and boundaries regarding in-laws and blended family issues, and other disagreements too numerous to list. Understandably, some couples that don't feel they need therapy or counseling will readily agree to see a mediator. Thus, if you see such a couple it indeed may be in the best interest of the couple for you to recommend that they seek assistance from a professional mediator.

There is one important difference between mediation and therapy, however – one that commands additional discussion. By ethical and legal standards, one individual cannot be both a therapist and a mediator to the same individual or couple. The hallmarks of mediation are the mediator's impartiality and neutrality. The focus is always on the disputed issue and how to achieve a solution amenable to both parties. A therapist, on the other hand, may well advise one member of the couple that he or she is the person with the problem and needs to change. Simply put: *therapists are trained to help people change, whereas mediators are trained to help people agree.* This leads to a simple rule of thumb when deciding which type of helping professional might best serve the needs of your client couple:

> If they are seeking help to overcome personal issues that negatively impact the relationship, then it is usually best to seek counseling or therapy.

However,

> If they have a disagreement about a thing or a situation and both parties have dug in their heels, so to speak, then mediation is usually advised.

In neither case does seeking one type of assistance over the other necessarily depend on whether the goal is to dissolve or repair the relationship. Therapists can be vital resources for couples ending a relationship or undergoing divorce, and mediators can keep a couple together by helping resolve an ongoing and intractable dispute. Thus, when you work with couples don't assume if they are seeing you that they could not benefit from seeing a mediator; likewise, if they go to see a mediator, don't assume that they no longer need your assistance. All couples are different – some could be best served by simultaneously seeing you *and* a mediator.

Benefits of Support Groups. During her first visit to Bill Emener, Elaine said, "After six years of marriage, Ed told me he wanted a divorce. I still believe he was in love with another woman. I don't really know. I just think so. Our divorce was finalized about a month ago. I just feel so lonely, scared and depressed."

In addition to talking at length about Elaine's feelings, lifestyle and future plans, Bill suggested a self-help book for her and also that she join a support group at a women's center not far from where she lived. When she came for their next session, she told him that she had called the center and found out there was a divorce-support group that met every Thursday evening for two hours. She went for an initial screening interview and then had gone to two of the meetings.

> "The book you recommended to me was very helpful," Elaine said at their next session, then adding, "It helped me understand some things better. Furthermore, many of the things you and I talked about at our first session have helped me understand why I am experiencing some things. However, I cannot thank you enough for recommending that support group to me – it really has been helpful. Seeing some of the anger in others, I can identify and relate to some of the anger within myself. There also are some women in the group who are further along than I am, and it is encouraging to see that this kind of thing can be survived. I also have befriended a couple of the women in the group. We occasionally talk on the phone during the week, and this coming weekend one of the ladies and I are going out to dinner together. All of this has just been terrific for me."

Not everyone needs or benefits from participation in a support group. On the other hand, however, support groups, especially those that are led and facilitated by a professional counselor or therapist, can be extremely beneficial and helpful to many people who are experiencing difficulties, problems and lifestyle-adjustment concerns related to previous, current and/or future loving relationships. Thus, if when you are working with a couple and it is clear to you that one or both of the partners and their relationship would benefit from a support group, translate your clinical observation into a recommendation for them.

ADVISING YOUR COUPLE: WHEN TO COME, WHEN TO STOP AND WHEN TO COME BACK

When clients start working with you, they may not have any idea as to how often they should see you (e.g., weekly, bi-weekly, monthly), for how long they will need to be seeing you (e.g., three sessions, five, ten), and by when and how they will know they are making progress. Once they understand and appreciate their real issues and what their options are, they then may have concerns about what you may expect them to do "to fix things." Issues and concerns such as these can be very daunting to first-time-in-counseling individuals and couples. The following is designed to assist you in facilitating your client's and couples' working with you – in helpful and less than daunting ways.

When to Come

Toward the end of our first sessions with clients, we have repeatedly found two things to be helpful. First, suggest to the client or couple when you think it would be good for them to come in for their next session (and if appropriate, even consider suggesting a tentative schedule, such as weekly or bi-weekly). Second, gently solicit their thoughts and feelings regarding your "when to come" suggestion; you may hear, "That sounds good to me," or you may hear, "No, I think I'd like to see you again sooner than that." But whatever the case may be, we suggest that "when to come" should be discussed and mutually agreed upon.

When to Come Back

Couples with whom we have been working frequently ask us, "We have agreed that there is no need for us to schedule another session. But how will we know if or when we need to come back to see you?" In response, it is not uncommon for us to sketch a diagram similar to the one in Figure 14.7 and say to them:

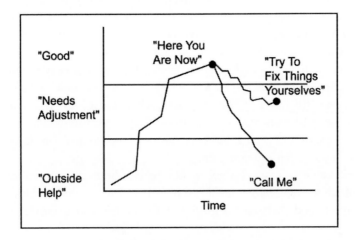

Figure 14.7. When to Come Back.

"We have met for enough sessions and I think you will agree that when you first came, you definitely needed some outside help. Over the last several sessions, the two of you were working on your relationship on a daily basis. Nonetheless, it continued to need adjustments and improvements. From what you have been saying today, however, your relationship is now up into the 'good' level and you are deriving much pleasure and joy from your own lives, each other's lives and your relationship. Here is where you are now. Therefore, the first recommendation is that you continue doing what you are doing – it indeed appears to be good for you. If in the future, however, you find your individual lives and/or your relationship aren't living up to your expectations, try to improve things yourselves. As a result of our sessions together you not only improved your relationship, but you also learned how to improve your relationship. Thus, try to help yourselves first! But should your attempts to help yourselves not meet with success, then call me and we'll schedule an appointment. In a nutshell, let's say, 'We're closing the door, yet keeping it slightly ajar – not shutting it all the way'."

From an overall perspective, we, as therapists, attempt to do two things when working with an individual or a couple: (1) we try to help them improve their individual lives and their relationship; (2) we try to help them learn to help themselves so that as time goes on if they run into a difficulty they do not have to call us right away (again, we want to teach them to fish for themselves). We try to help them learn self-help strategies and skills that will help them carry on and continue to improve their lives on their own. "So in other words, Dr.

Emener," Todd recently said, "if we start to run into some troubles, we can go back through some of our notes from our sessions, go back through some of the self-help books that you have recommended to us and try to fix things ourselves. However, I also hear you saying that we shouldn't wait to come back to see you as we are on our way to divorce court!" On that note, Todd, his wife and Bill, all enjoyed a hearty laugh.

Real versus Social Recovery. The summer season had finally come into full swing when Bill Emener first met Gloria, a 29-year-old dental assistant, who said, "I love the beach. I used to go all the time, but I have yet to put a toe in the water." Approximately six months before seeing Bill, her husband had filed for divorce. He said to her, "I'm sorry, Gloria, but I have fallen in love with another woman." Gloria went into a severe depression. She became socially dysfunctional, missed many days of work, and "basically became a shut-in who never went out except to go to work, go to the store or take out the garbage." When Bill asked her why she came to see him, she said, "I am tired of just existing. I want to start living again."

As they were discussing some goals to consider working toward, they agreed to begin by focusing on some relatively "simple" things such as going to a movie with her mother, to dinner with a girlfriend and, possibly, a walk on the beach with a coworker. It is important to remember that when Bill first met Gloria, goals such as these were not "simple." Pointedly, she said, "I will have to work up to them. Remember, I've been a shut-in for the past six months!" We are pleased to report that over the next six months, Gloria became more and more successful in going out and doing things.

When Gloria came to a session six months later, about a week before Christmas, she entered Bill's office feeling really good about herself and said, "On Saturday afternoon I went shopping by myself and then met a girlfriend for dinner and a movie. I'm so proud of myself!"

During their first session that January, they began talking about her deep feelings of anger and rejection. Further along, they discussed the fears of abandonment that Gloria had lived with since she was a child who "went from foster home to foster home." That March, she began going out on some dates with men whom she had known and "felt safe with." When she came to their first session in June, she said, "Roy and I joined a sailing club together. He's really cool. We have been enjoying some great times together lately. It was a year ago yesterday, Dr. Emener, that I saw you for the first time. I sure have come a long way. I'm really proud of myself!" Gloria then pulled a piece of paper out of her purse. It had a diagram on it like the one in Figure 14.8. It was the diagram that Bill had sketched for her in March. As she developed better coping skills, slowly taking some risks, such as going out with her girlfriends and then occasionally going out with men, her coping skills continued to improve and her "As If – Social Recovery" was steadily improving. Her inner, personal, psychological improvement and recovery, however, lagged behind a little, and that certainly was understandable. The more she went out and acted as if she were adjusted, the better she felt about herself; and the better she felt about herself, the more she felt comfortable going out and acting as if she had adjusted. "In other words," she said to Bill, "as I continued to accomplish my social recovery goals, the easier it was for me to accomplish my psychological recovery goals." Interestingly, she had carried the sketch around in her purse, "just as a reminder of my progress whenever I needed a pick-me-up."

If when you are working with individuals concerning their difficulties or problems in loving relationships, especially if they are down and out from a painful breakup, don't be surprised if you begin by establishing "Social Recovery" goals and then focusing on their

"Psychological Recovery" goals at a later, more comfortable time. Or as you may hear at AA meetings, "Fake it 'til you make it." When Gloria and Bill discussed and processed her progress over the year during which he had been working with her, she said, "The goals we started out with were reasonable and realistic. I was really down when I first came to see you! When we later worked on my heavier, psychological issues, I was ready. It's like the old cliché, 'It's hard to contemplate draining the lake when you're up to your ass in alligators'."

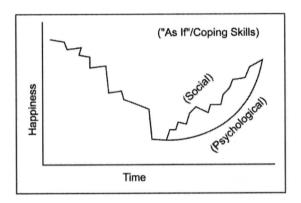

Figure 14.8. Real (Psychological) Versus Social ("As If") Recovery.

Respect Your Client's Options. In addition to discussing goals with your client, such as "Social Recovery" goals and "Psychological Recovery" goals, you also may discuss realistic "Options" that may be reasonable and attainable. For example, during Bill Emener's first session with Abby, a 41-year-old stockbroker, they discussed her 16 year marriage to Joe, a claims adjuster for an insurance company. They had two teenaged children. She added, however, that she had been feeling "totally unloved by Joe for the past eight years." Toward the end of their session, after telling Bill all of the things she had done to try to improve her relationship with Joe, she said, "Well, what are my options?"

Bill responded with, "What options do you see?" After pondering that question for a few moments, she said, "Well, let's see. *One*, I could stay married to Joe and meet my needs for love and affection from my children and my relatives. *Two*, I could stay married to Joe and have affairs. *Three*, I could try to negotiate a separation. *Four*, I could file for divorce. Or *Five*, I could see if Joe would be willing to come in with me for marriage counseling."

As a homework assignment, Bill suggested to Abby that it might be helpful to write out her five options and generate a list of the pros and cons for each option. She agreed that that would be a helpful thing for her to do and that she would bring her lists to their next session.

About two weeks later, Bill received a short note in the mail from Abby. It read, "I wrote out my lists. That was helpful for me. However, I cancelled my next appointment with you – Joe and I are seeing a marriage counselor next week. I truly am hoping for the best. If it doesn't work out, I'll get back in touch with you. Thanks for your help, Abby." We do not know what happened with Abby and Joe. Bill never heard from her again.

Occasionally, there are times in our lives when we get caught up in our emotions and feelings, times when we cannot think clearly in terms of where we are, what our options are, and ultimately what we want. And as simple as it sounds, sometimes just verbalizing our feelings and thinking through our options can be extremely helpful. Thus, when you are seeing an individual client or a couple, remember that you can be very helpful to them by asking, "What are your options?" We remain optimistic and truly believe it was a good question for Abby to have addressed, as well as many couples we have seen and helped address that very same question.

"They're here!" Before concluding this chapter, we thought it helpful to offer the new couples counselor a few last minute reminders – pearls of wisdom, as it were – for when you meet with your first couple (if you already have not done so).

At the end of Bill Emener's next-to-last class in his graduate course on Couples and Marriage counseling, after the students have presented and discussed their reports from their required three interviews with a couple, he typically says, "Assume for a minute that a friend or colleague is going to meet with a couple for the first time and the receptionist tells him or her, 'Mr. and Mrs. Troubled Relationship are here.' And when your colleague peaks into the waiting room and sees *him* with an angry scowl on his face and *her* with teary, hopeful eyes, immediately the computer screen in his or her head lights up in red, 16-font letters: *They're here!* In spite of having had a course in couples and marriage counseling and read an excellent textbook on couples counseling, an immediate emotionally-charged thought follows: *nothing short of a valium drip will get my heart rate down.* When a quick stop in the break room for a drink of water includes running into you, he or she asks, 'Before I see this couple waiting for me, do you have any last minute pearls of wisdom for me?' My question for you is: what pearl of wisdom would you offer your nervous colleague?"

Below are the typical "pearls" offered by Bill's former students (who vividly remember being in a break room, dry-mouth, sipping water, convinced that a valium drip would be an early Christmas present):

1) Relax (take a few deep breaths);
2) Stay focused on him, her and their relationship;
3) Pay attention and listen to them (in spite of the loud, scared voice in your head);
4) When in doubt, paraphrase with summary clarification responses (a.k.a. what Dr. Emener tongue-in-cheek calls "The Rogerian Bailout");
5) Remember, they came to you – they're coming looking for something; find out what they think they need;
6) Be pleasant and warm – be nice;
7) Be aware of counter-transference (regarding him, her and their relationship);
8) Remember that it's your office – stay in control… especially of yourself;
9) Honor their need to feel in control;
10) Award them permission to be open and honest – with each other as well as with you;
11) Notice non-verbal signals (but hold onto your observations until validated… they could be false-positives or false-negatives);
12) Stay in the present – stay with them in the room… don't let your mind wonder;
13) Work on building a therapeutic relationship/alliance with each of them.
14) Keep in mind that many seemingly intractable relationship problems can be "fixed" by assisting your clients to alter their expectations or perceptions – their belief system – instead of their behaviors. In the language of Ellis's (1996) REBT, sometimes it's easier to fix the "B"s than the "A"s; and finally,
15) Remind both yourself and your clients that Victor Frankl (1946) survived nearly four years in a Nazi concentration camp (in which the survival rate was less than 4%) by understanding that the one thing they could not deprive him of was his choice on

how to view his situation – how to find *meaning* in his circumstances. In the absence of all other interventions, this one "pearl" of wisdom stands above all others: if your client couple can be helped to find meaning in their issues and why they are experiencing them, they can overcome them.

CHAPTER SUMMARY

As we said at the outset of this chapter, the combination of your knowledge and appreciation of the concepts addressed in the previous 13 chapters and your ingestion of those in this chapter, you're now ready to work with a couple (or individual) with a loving relationship problem. Assuming you have appropriate supervision available to you… "Suit up – it's game time."

If there is any one thing to keep on your radar screen when working with a couple it is to ask each of the partners: "What are you doing to take care of yourself?" Two assumptions underlie this query: (1) in a "good" loving relationship, I take care of me, you take care of you, both of us are attentive to and supportive of each other, and both of us are attentive to and supportive of our relationship; and (2) if I don't take care of me or you don't take care of you, then both of us and our relationship are in trouble. As is suggested throughout this book, remind your couple:

> The most important thing you offer your loved one is yourself.

Thus, if one of your couple's goals is to have a "good" loving relationship, then it makes sense for each of them to offer each other something that's highly valuable and worthwhile – *each of them at their best*. As one of our clients said to her husband, "Be the best you can be for your own benefit, and I will also benefit from your being your best!"

> Seeing a helping professional can be very scary.
> He or she will probably be honest with us.
> My loved one also may be honest with me.
> I may be honest in return.
> We may even be honest… with ourselves.
> Not only that, we may be sharing my truths with someone else.
> I trust, however, that our counselor will help us deal with the pain of our discovery
> and grow from it.

CHAPTER 14 DISCUSSION QUESTIONS

1) What can you do to assess and address "unasked questions" on behalf of a couple who has never seen a counselor before and has just arrived for their first session with you?

2) Why might it be important for you (a) *to see* a couple's intake information before meeting with them, and (b) *not to see* a couple's intake information before meeting with them?

3) When you are seeing a couple for the first time, how can your clinical observations (a) confirm and disconfirm information about them, and (b) raise a need for additional information about them?

4) What would you do when (a) the two partners of a couple state similar and/or different goals for seeing you, and (b) when for some reason you don't believe that one or both of them are being truthful?

5) When one or both partners of a couple ask if they can see you individually as well as, as a couple, (a) what would you do, and (b) why?

6) What are some things you can do to assist a couple in maintaining realistic expectations of: (a) themselves; (b) each other; (c) their relationship; and (d) their counseling with you?

7) When you are seeing a couple and they say, "The group we are working with is more helpful to us then our counseling with you," (a) what would you say in response, and (b) why?

8) What are some specific things you could do to address with a couple regarding: (a) when and how often they should be seeing you; (b) when they no longer need to see you; and (c) what they should and shouldn't do if in the future they may need to see you again?

Chapter 15

ETHICS AND PROFESSIONALISM

"Ethics is knowing the difference between what you have a right to do and what is right to do."
    Potter Stewart (1915-1985)

"I recently went to a new doctor and noticed he was located in something called the Professional Building. I felt better right away."
    George Carlin (1937-2008)

We trust that anyone using this book already is a professionally trained therapist or a student enrolled in a human service professional preparation program and, as such, is well aware of ethics and professionalism. We also hope and believe that you richly appreciate Potter Stewart's wisdom regarding *ethics* from his years of experience as an Associate Justice of the United States Supreme Court, as well as the humor in George Carlin's tongue-in-cheek comment about *professionalism*. Given the seriousness and gravity of ethics and professionalism, we herein address these topics in order to: (1) enrich and strengthen your knowledgeable and appreciation of what a profession is; (2) remind you of the critical role of ethics in professionalism; and (3) assist you in always remembering the difference between what you have a right to do and what is right to do.

As addressed throughout this book, couples and marriage counseling typically are provided by a variety of human service professionals (counselors, marriage and family therapists, psychologists, social workers, etc.). Thus, while including a discussion of topics pertinent to the provision of couples and marriage counseling by human service professionals, this chapter will also address the broader issues related to: (1) professionalism in human services; (2) human service regulatory bodies; (3) autonomy and professional behavior; (4) professional codes of ethics; (5) the role(s) of knowledge in decision-making; and (6) the importance of a professional's professional self-concept.

PROFESSIONALISM IN HUMAN SERVICES

The continuing assurance of consumer protection is critical to the provision of human services and is all human service professions' first and foremost concern. Two generic attributes of human service consumers (our clients) are that they most often are: (1) hurting, in trouble and/or vulnerable; and (2) ignorant, unknowing and/or unable to help themselves. With the exception of routine check-ups, few people see a medical doctor because they are feeling good and not worried about some aspect of their health. In the mental health area, where "annual check-ups" are not customary, it may be assumed that people who seek professional services are hurting or worried about some condition or situation – as well as one they may not understand.[6] In addition, they tend to be ignorant regarding the choice of treatment interventions – they do not know what to do about their conditions or situations (otherwise, they would fix it themselves). Interestingly, it has been suggested that the two most powerful professions in American society are medicine and law (Emener, 1987). Most people who go to see a doctor or a lawyer are either hurting and/or in trouble and don't know what to do. Also, many people do not even know what knowledge and skills are minimally necessary for the professional assisting them to have.

Most definitions of "true professionals" include specific criteria such as (1) academic qualifications (e.g., a graduate degree earned from an accredited institution of higher education); (2) demonstrated specialized knowledge and expertise in the specific field in which they are practicing; (3) demonstrated adherence to a code of ethics and standards of professional practice; (4) certified and/or licensed by a pertinent regulatory or legislative body; and (5) demonstrated public confidence in the services provided by the individual and his or her professional colleagues. To wit, most societies have established, maintain and publicize *regulatory mechanisms* to set, monitor and enforce standards and requirements so when a "hurting, in trouble, vulnerable, unknowing and uninformed" citizen goes to a professional for help, they can trust and have confidence in the assistance and help provided to them.

HUMAN SERVICE REGULATORY MECHANISMS

There are four regulatory mechanisms pertinent to the provision of human services by professionals: (1) certification; (2) licensure; (3) registration; (4) accreditation; and (5) Diplomate Status.

Certification. If a professional is "certified," it means that some formal body has assessed the professional and, based on a review of his or her credentials and often an examination, has issued a "certificate" of competency within their specialty. In the best cases, it means that the public can feel assured that he or she has met minimum published standards of competency in his or her discipline as evidenced by formal education, experience, supervisory evaluation and, typically, the passing of a state or nationally standardized examination. Thus, for example, if a rehabilitation counselor has "CRC" after his or her name, it means that he or she is a "Certified Rehabilitation Counselor."

In recent years, unfortunately, many bodies with questionable motives and expertise have established themselves as certification authorities that are deemed by other experienced professionals to offer little of value in establishing the professional's qualifications. Such

---

[6] More recently, and in no small part due to the Internet (see Chapter 13), therapists are finding increasing sophistication among their clients. We estimate that between one third and one half of our current clients have researched their symptoms on sites such as "WebMD" and arrive with a self-diagnosis, whether accurate or otherwise, prior to their first session.

certificates are called "junk certifications" and represent a growing problem for both consumers and regulatory authorities. For example, suppose you learned that a psychotherapist had attended a single weekend seminar on the use of some new type of treatment approach (let's call it "emotional bonding techniques"). After having sat through several lectures and demonstrations of such techniques, they had passed a 20-question, multiple-choice test and had, as a result, received a document that labeled him or her as a "certified emotional bonding expert." Would you feel they were now qualified in some important way that they previously were not? (Your authors would not!) On the other hand, the term "Certified Rehabilitation Counselor" *does* imply rigorous training, supervised internship and assessment of qualifications via national examination.

Our advice is, "when in doubt, contact your state's regulatory body (i.e., Department of Professional Regulation or Department of Consumer Affairs) to obtain more information." In addition, we recommend seeking the advice of licensed practitioners who you trust. In and of itself, certification unfortunately no longer carries the value it once did.

Licensure. Licensure to practice a profession or trade is regulated by state legislation, and typically is operationally under the auspices of a state board of professional regulation. Some licensure boards also regulate non-professional occupations as well (e.g., plumbers, electricians). Importantly, if a professional is "licensed," he or she is able to: (1) go into private practice; (2) function autonomously (i.e., without required, direct supervision); and (3) qualify for "third party funding" (i.e., he or she not only can charge and get paid by clients directly, but also can charge for services to be paid for by a third party, such as an insurance company). Penalties associated with licensure typically are severe and restrictive (e.g., in most states, a person cannot even refer to himself or herself as a "psychologist" unless he or she is licensed as a psychologist in that state). Thus, for example, if a professional has "LMHC," "LPC" or "LMFT" after his or her name, it means that he or she is a "Licensed Mental Health Counselor," "Licensed Professional Counselor" or "Licensed Marriage and Family Therapist" – licensed by his or her state regulatory body. Fortunately, licensure by a State governing body remains a guarantee of at least minimal competency and professionalism. Unfortunately, because licensure is typically issued at the state (rather than the national) level, there may be highly qualified professionals who are unable to practice in a given jurisdiction due to local guidelines. More often than not, it has been our experience that licensing at the state level, at least in the health care area, to a large extent has persisted in order to protect salaries and third-party reimbursement rates rather than to provide any additional protection to consumers. Such "turf wars" are an unfortunate aspect of the human service professions.

Registration. Most states have a list, or "registry," of certified and/or licensed professionals who have met state and/or national requirements to practice their respective profession. For example, nurses may have "R.N." after their names, signifying that they are "registered nurses." Many national level registries also exist. For example, a psychologist who is registered with the National Register of Health Care Providers in Psychology is very likely to meet demanding qualifications as a psychologist regardless of the state in which he or she is licensed.

Accreditation. In the human services arena, accreditation includes two main areas: (1) the accreditation of organizations, service agencies, facilities, and institutions; and (2) the accreditation of professional preparation programs. Regarding the former, if a rehabilitation facility such as a sheltered workshop is "CARF Accredited," it means that that facility has demonstrated high quality service-delivery standards and practices to the Commission on Accreditation or Rehabilitation Facilities. A person could have trust and confidence in the services provided at a CARF Accredited facility. Regarding the latter, if a doctoral program in clinical psychology at a university is "APA Approved," it means that academic program has met the quality standards set by the American Psychological Association. Likewise, if a psychologist earns a doctoral degree from an APA Approved psychology program, he or she can trust that they received a high quality education; furthermore, prospective employers would have confidence in the graduate's knowledge, skills and expertise.

Diplomate Status. A "Diplomate" is a medical or health care specialist whose competence has been certified by a diploma granted by an appropriate professional group. In medicine, this may mean the same as "Board Certified." In Psychology, the American Board of Professional Psychologists (ABPP) awards Diplomate status to specialists within various sub-fields of clinical psychology that are considered the highest level of certification available. Although technically a certification, such Boards have thus far remained free from repudiation and association with issuers of so-called "junk certificates."

Our readers may be wondering what one is to take away from this discussion. Our opinion is that both your profession and your clients are best served by the maintenance of strict standards of licensure at the appropriate levels of jurisdiction, requirements for continuing professional education, and actively prosecuting unqualified individuals who practice fraudulently. Personally, we find it difficult in today's climate to justify the unconditional state-level licensure of most health care providers, particularly when many States lack adequate providers. At best, a requirement for a "laws and rules" exam to practice within a State is defensible, but beyond this we feel that the United States would be better served if health care providers were subject to national-level licensure. How, when the world is becoming increasingly "flat" (Friedman, 2006), is the interest or protection of the consumer advanced by an ever growing number of incompatible local licensing authorities? That rhetorically asked, we urge you, our readers to remember that no matter how you are credentialed, it ultimately remains your responsibility to maintain currency and practice within your competencies, and otherwise to act professionally at all times and in every way.

AUTONOMY AND PROFESSIONAL BEHAVIOR

It is of conscientious importance to underscore the critical nature of "autonomous functioning" and "professional behavior" on behalf of a professional. A few years ago, Bill Emener received a phone call from another licensed psychologist asking if she could refer a client to him. Further discussion revealed that the referring psychologist had completed two sessions with a male client who was in recovery from alcoholism, and she realized that: (1) the client closely resembled the man from whom she was recently divorced; and (2) at this particular time in her life due to newness of her emotionally challenging and difficult divorce, she was unable to be totally objective and "professional" with her client. Two of the critical "autonomous functioning" attributes in this example are (a) she was aware of her own issues and recognized her lack of objectivity, and (b) she did the right thing and referred the client to another psychologist who could be objective and professional with that particular client.

About a year ago, Bill Lambos was attending a grand opening of a friend's newly remodeled restaurant, and during a conversation with a small group of attendees was asked, "Dr. Lambos, I would appreciate it if you would talk with me for a few minutes and tell me if you think I have an anxiety problem." With genuine warmth, care, and professionalism, Bill replied, "It sounds like you are concerned about feeling nervous and anxious. Here is one of my business cards, and if you would call me at my office we could arrange an appointment at my office to evaluate you for anxiety. I'm sure you would agree this is not the time or place to do that." She smiled and acknowledged her agreement with his well-made point.

A professional colleague of ours, a certified rehabilitation counselor and a licensed mental health counselor, has had numerous examples of chronic pain patients who, in their best efforts, attempt to persuade him to sign off on disability applications due to lack of functioning and severity of their condition. However, he usually requires a thorough assessment and evaluation in order to rule out malingering, substance dependence/addiction issues and other maladaptive behavior patterns often seen among people with chronic pain conditions. Recognition of these maladaptive behaviors is crucial in order to prevent enabling maladaptive coping responses, but also to make sure that those with legitimate conditions receive the proper care and support.

It is important to note that in all three of these illustrative situations, the professional was aware of what was going on, knew what to do and did what was needed – with class, concern and consideration for the client (or potential client). Among other things, it is this self-awareness, self-monitoring and self-direction that substantiate the public's confidence and trust in professionals.

PROFESSIONAL CODES OF ETHICS

Among the attributes of any professional is the fact that his or her behavior is guided by a code of ethics (Corey, Corey & Callahan, 1988). Every human service profession has its own code of ethics. Furthermore, each profession's code of ethics is known, endorsed and practiced by its members. Selected sources of human service professional codes of ethics are listed in Table 15.1.

Ethical codes are not designed to tell respective professionals what is right or wrong, or what to do or not do, in a given situation. They are not rules or laws; rather, they are philosophical principles designed to guide the professional in making the best decision for each individual client and/or each individual situation. Like every human being, every situation is different, unique, and requires a decision befitting the individual circumstance.

Fittingly, inherent to any code of ethics are the following five guiding philosophical principles (examples of pertinent statements on behalf of a couples or marriage therapist are included for each principle):

- Principle 1. Beneficence and Nonmaleficence

Human service professionals strive to benefit those with whom they work and take care to do no harm. In their professional actions, they seek to safeguard the welfare and rights of those with whom they interact professionally and other affected persons. When conflicts occur among their obligations or concerns, they attempt to resolve these conflicts in a responsible fashion that avoids or minimizes harm. Because their scientific and professional judgments and actions may affect the lives of others, they are alert to and guard against personal, financial, social, organizational or political factors that might lead to misuse of their influence. Moreover, they strive to be aware of the possible effect of their own physical and mental health on their ability to help those with whom they work.

"I will act in a manner that respects and facilitates my client's freedom of choice."

Table 15.1.

Selected Sources of Professional Human Service Ethical Codes.

American Association for Marriage and Family Therapy AAMFT Code of Ethics http://www.aamft.org/resources/lrm_plan/Ethics/ethicscode2001.asp American Counseling Association ACA Code of Ethics http://www.counseling.org/Resources/CodeOfEthics/TP/Home/CT2.aspx American Psychological Association Ethical Principles of Psychologists and Code of Conduct http://www.apa.org/ethics/code2002.html#intro National Association of Social Workers NASW Code of Ethics http://ncsss.cua.edu/Docs/NASWCodeofEthics.pdf Association for Conflict Resolution Model Standards of Practice for Family and Divorce Mediation http://www.acrnet.org/about/committees/ethics.htm#family

- Principle 2. Fidelity and Responsibility

Human service professionals establish relationships of trust with those with whom they work. They are aware of their professional and scientific responsibilities to society and to the specific communities in which they work. They also uphold professional standards of conduct, clarify their professional roles and obligations, accept appropriate responsibility for their behavior, and seek to manage conflicts of interest that could lead to exploitation or harm. Human service professionals consult with, refer to, or cooperate with other professionals and institutions to the extent needed to serve the best interests of those with whom they work. They are concerned about the ethical compliance of their colleagues' scientific and professional conduct. They strive to contribute a portion of their professional time for little or no compensation or personal advantage.

"I will act in a manner that promotes the growth and well-being of my client."

- Principle 3. Integrity

Human service professionals seek to promote accuracy, honesty and truthfulness in the science, teaching and practice of their profession. In these respective activities, they do not steal, cheat or engage in fraud, subterfuge or intentional misrepresentation of fact. Furthermore, they strive to keep their promises and to avoid unwise or unclear commitments. In situations in which deception may be ethically justifiable to maximize benefits and minimize harm, they have a serious obligation to consider the need for, the possible consequences of, and their responsibility to correct any resulting mistrust or other harmful effects that arise from the use of such techniques.

> "I will act in a manner that keeps promises and commitments to my clients, colleagues and agencies, both stated and implied."

- Principle 4. Justice

Human service professionals recognize that fairness and justice entitle all persons to access, and benefit from, the contributions of their profession and to equal quality in the processes, procedures and services being conducted by their fellow professionals. They exercise reasonable judgment and take precautions to ensure that their potential biases, the boundaries of their competence and the limitations of their expertise do not lead to or condone unjust practices.

> "I will act in a manner that will treat my clients fairly."

- Principle 5. Respect for People's Rights and Dignity

Human service professionals respect the dignity and worth of all people, and the rights of individuals to privacy, confidentiality and self-determination. They are aware that special safeguards may be necessary to protect the rights and welfare of persons or communities whose vulnerabilities impair autonomous decision-making. Also, they are aware of and respect cultural, individual and role differences, including those based on age, gender, gender identity, race, ethnicity, culture, national origin, religion, sexual orientation, disability, language and socioeconomic status, and consider these factors when working with members of such groups. Overall, human service professionals try to eliminate the effect on their work of biases based on those factors, and they do not knowingly participate in or condone activities of others based upon such prejudices.

> "I will act in a manner that does not cause harm to my clients or prevents harm to my clients."

As you may have noticed, these principles are intentionally competing. For example, facilitating a client's "freedom of choice" may not guarantee that the client will act in a manner that will assure his or her "growth and well-being." But, as previously stated, every client with whom a professional works and every situation in which they find themselves are unique and different. By design every client and every situation calls for a unique decision.

Codes of ethics do not provide the answers – they provide the professional philosophical guidelines and principles with which to make the best possible decision. Consulting with others, both with in-the-same profession colleagues and other pertinent colleagues, is highly recommended. For example, the Preamble of the American Association for Marriage and Family Therapy's Code of Ethics states, "The standards are not exhaustive. Marriage and family therapists who are uncertain about the ethics of a particular course of action are encouraged to seek counsel from consultants, attorneys, supervisors, colleagues or other appropriate authorities."

Ethics and Morality. As you easily can appreciate, there is a very close relationship between ethics and morality – phenomena such as beneficence, nonmaleficence, fidelity, responsibility, integrity, justice, respect, rights and dignity clearly are moral issues. With regard to the role of morality, the ethical considerations of couples and marriage counseling – where the counselor assists clients in making adjustments not only within themselves but also within their relationship – Silverman (1967) poignantly stated,

> …the concept of marital adjustment, in terms of the moral issues involved, in the counseling process, refers essentially to the art of living effectively and wholesomely within the framework of responsibilities, relations and expectations that constitute the state of marriage, coupled with appropriate and intelligent compatibility of sexual, psychological and religious factors, consistently requiring continuous personal growth, predicated on respect, love, trust, autonomy, recognition and integrity in the lives of each of us as human beings. (p. 445)

When counseling couples, direct and indirect considerations of "right and wrong" and "good and bad," are always in the room.

As demonstrated in the two following case examples, our professional ethics also can be of great assistance to us when our client's morality is different from our own, and this is true – be it an individual client or a couple.

Individual Client. About 10 years ago, a self-pay client came to see Bill Emener because, as he said, "I've been feeling down and depressed for a few months now and need to talk with someone. You were highly recommended." When Bill looked at the man's Intake Form, he noticed that there were only two pieces of information supplied: name (John) and state (Florida). Within a few minutes, however, Bill realized why – John made a living as a professional hit man. "I make a lot of money and only work one or two days a month and do some nice traveling," were part of the clues.

A few minutes later, John said, "I think part of my problem is that I've been feeling bad about what I do to earn a living. Maybe a little regret too… it's really been bothering me a lot lately." Bill put down his note pad, looked at John and said, "I have to ask you a very important question: are you wanting to see me so I can help you not feel guilty about what you do to earn a living or is it because you'd like me to help you find another way to earn a living?" John silently looked away and then back. "Because," Bill furthered, "if it's the former I will not work with you." Bill believed that John understood why he said what he said, graciously adding, "Bill, I respect you for that."

John never called to schedule another appointment, and Bill didn't try to contact him (for obvious reasons). And while there are only two innocuous lines in his notes from that session, Bill was comforted by the thought, based on his professional ethics and personal sense of morality, that he did the right thing for the right reasons.

Couple. A colleague of ours, a licensed clinical social worker who has a reputation as being an excellent couples and marriage counselor, shared with us that she recently transferred a couple to another therapist. She admitted to us that she tends to be a rather conservative person and lives a relatively conservative lifestyle. But when this particular couple came to see her – "Because we want to decide whether or not to adopt a child" – she was doing fine until they casually mentioned, "We go to a clothing optional resort two or three times a month and are 'swingers' – we have a regular group who we hook up with at least once a month."

She told us that toward the end of her intake session with the couple that because she was concerned that her personal values and beliefs might preclude her from being at her professional best if she worked with them, she told them she would not charge them for that session and recommended two other couples therapists for them to choose from and see.

It was comforting to her that the couple understood why she was not going to work with them and respected her for it. She also felt comforted by the fact that based on her keen awareness of her personal morality, and especially her professional ethics, she did the right thing for the right reasons.

Three Sources of Counter-transference. When counseling an individual client, there always is the possibility for your client to experience *transference* with you – basically transferring his or her thoughts, feelings and behavior associated with someone else onto and toward you. Counter-transference is when you, the counselor, have a similar experience with or toward your client. Thus, for a counselor working with one client, there is *one* possible target of counter-transference. However, when working with a couple – two individuals – there are *three* possible targets of counter-transference. The following examples of a male counselor working with a married couple illustrate this:

1) The counselor has counter-transference with the husband – thinking, Jack, you remind me of the SOB my ex-wife divorced me for.
2) The counselor has counter-transference with the wife – thinking, Susan, you are so beautiful in every way; you're exactly the kind of woman I've been looking for.
3) The counselor has counter-transference with the couple's relationship – thinking, when they argue like that it so vividly reminds me of how my ex-wife and I use to fight for those three months before our divorce.

As we said in Chapter 1 and throughout this book, "our focus is on the couple – on the *dyad* and its constituents." Pointedly, Anand (1967) said, "The focus throughout, in marriage counseling, is the couple *and* the marriage as a unit, not the individual as such" (p. 153). Thus, as the previous three examples illustrate, when counseling with a couple, you have three opportunities for counter-transference. If you are keenly aware of your ethics, nonetheless, you indeed are in a much better position: (1) to recognize when counter-transference possibilities such as these surface within you; and (2) to self-monitor your thinking and behavior, and respond – not just appropriately, but also professionally and ethically.

THE ROLE(S) OF KNOWLEDGE IN A PROFESSIONAL'S DECISION-MAKING

Human service professionals constantly make decisions and assist others in making decisions. Usually, "good decisions" are not made by data or information alone; "poor decisions" usually are made in the absence of data and information. Having accurate, complete, valid and relevant information is critical in good decision-making. Simply said, it is important for you – as a human service professional doing couples counseling – to know what information you have (and/or don't have), as well as the source and validity of it.

There are many sources of knowledge, such as: (a) tradition; (b) expert opinion; (c) documentation; (d) individuals in position of authority; (e) common sense; (f) faith; (g) intuition; (h) logical reasoning; (i) personal experience; and (j) habit. Do not assume that any of these or any other sources of knowledge is more important, pertinent or meaningful than the others. What is important is to *know the source(s) of all information you have*. Don't suffer from the transgression of *secondary ignorance*. As Bill Emener frequently has said in lectures, "Primary ignorance is when you don't know nothin'; secondary ignorance is when you don't even know that you don't know nothin'." In your role as a professional couples counselor, there are four crucial things you need to know about "your" knowledge:

1) Know What You Know. Knowledge is critical in decision-making – you should know what you know.
2) Know What You Don't Know. This refers to the above discussed "secondary ignorance" notion – knowing what you don't know, is equally important information.
3) Know the Source of What You Know. Be critical of your knowledge and its source. The frequently heard "They say...." source of information is contingent upon who they are. An illustration of this postulate is another light-hearted expression Bill Emener uses in his lectures on professional decision-making: "All Indians walk in single file – at least the one I saw did."
4) Know How What You Know Affects What You Do. Our knowledge affects and influences most aspects of our lives – our feelings, attitudes, perceptions and decisions, and especially our behavior. As professional couples counselors, appreciating how knowledge (and a lack of knowledge) affects us is very important.

Professionals' "Ultimate" Decisions. Pertinent to professionals' decision-making, Saad Nagi (1977) suggested three "ultimate" decisions that professionals make (if they truly are professionals). The following will briefly discuss these "ultimate decisions" with representative illustrations:

1) Who Do I Serve? Professionals ultimately decide who they serve and who they do not serve. For example, if you look closely at courses listed in college and university catalogues, the term "Instructor's consent required" explicitly means that the professor has the right (and responsibility) to determine who will and who will not be allowed to take his or her course. If a floor nurse in a hospital were to discover that a family member was a patient on his or her floor, he or she would have the right (and the responsibility) to request that another nurse attend to the family member. (This

principle also was illustrated in our social worker colleague's decision not to work with the "swingers.")

2) How Do I Serve? For a professor, this refers to the issue of "academic freedom" – no administrator at a college or university should dictate or tell a professor how to teach a course. Likewise, an agency or company may establish goals for clients receiving services but should not dictate to the professionals employed by the agency (e.g., counselors, psychologists, social workers) how to serve the clients on their caseload.

3) When Do I Terminate Services? When students complete a degree in higher education and attend their graduation ceremony, the appropriate academic officer, such as a dean, will introduce the graduating students by name and then say, "Mr. (or Madam) President, based on the recommendation of the faculty, I request that these students receive their aforementioned degrees." It is the faculty who decides when students have completed degree requirements – not the Dean, etc. Likewise, the only person other than yourself who can sign you out of a hospital is your attending physician. Thus, as a professional, you should be the person with the authority and responsibility of determining (in consultation with your client) when a he, she or they have completed their program with you (e.g., counseling, treatment plan).

For almost a decade, numerous professionals have suggested that the rise in the managed care model of human service delivery has eroded some of these areas of professionals' ultimate decision-making (Janes & Emener, 1999). Fittingly, it behooves professionals to work hard to preserve their capacity to make such decisions – the decisions that define their professionalism.

YOUR "PROFESSIONAL SELF-CONCEPT"

The phenomenon of self-concept could be expanded to include a person's concept of himself or herself in more than a general or overall sense. For example, a person could think about his or her "self" as a parent, an athlete, etcetera, and as a professional – his or her *professional self-concept*. Nonetheless, how an individual's professional self-concept significantly interfaces with an employer or a job ultimately offers an insight into their primary source of identification – as an employee or as a professional. Consider, for example, the following illustration:

Mary has a master's degree in Mental Health Counseling from an accredited master's degree program, is a Licensed Mental Health Counselor and also a Licensed Marriage and Family Therapist, and is a member of numerous professional counseling associations. She is employed by a state human services agency and one of her job titles is "Marriage and Family Therapist." Her professional self-concept, however, can be interestingly analyzed by finding out her primary source of professional- versus employer-affiliation. From an analytical perspective:

- does Mary think to herself: "I am an employee of the state, and I am working as a marriage and family therapist." *OR*

- does Mary think: "I am a professional marriage and family therapist, and I am employed by the state."

Central to Mary's or anyone's way of thinking about themselves is whether their primary sense of affiliation and identification is with their employer or with their profession.

CHAPTER SUMMARY

In this chapter, we gave serious consideration to, and discussion of, six pivotal considerations of ethics and professionalism – specifically in terms of how they interface with the provision of professional couples and marriage counseling: (1) professionalism in human services; (2) human service regulatory bodies; (3) autonomy and professional behavior; (4) professional codes of ethics; (5) the role(s) of knowledge in a professional's decision-making; and (6) your professional self-concept.

Winston Churchill said, "The best indication of the civilness of any society is in the way it treats its vulnerable citizens." This tradition primarily has included children, the elderly and individuals with disabilities. It could be argued when working as a professional that caring for and helping vulnerable individuals (who also may be hurting, in trouble and/or uninformed and unable to meaningfully help themselves), that you have a professional obligation to offer them the best help and assistance available. We suggest that this is not just a professional obligation; you also have a moral obligation to do so. If you believe in this challenge (to offer your clients the best help and assistance available), then you are obligated to be the best you can be. And, á la

Former Associate Chief Justice Potter Stewart's tenet of "…knowing the difference between what you have a right to do and what is right to do," when counseling couples, it is your ethical, moral and professional obligation to remain aware of:

- what you do;
- what you don't do; and
- why you are doing (and not doing) what you are doing.

And above all – do the right things for the right reasons.

CHAPTER 15 DISCUSSION QUESTIONS

1) In your own words, what does it mean to be a "professional?"
2) What specific regulatory bodies have been, are and will continue to be pertinent to your former, current and continuing development as a professional human service professional sanctioned to provide couples and marriage counseling in your state?
3) How, why and in what ways is "autonomy" critical to the essence of your existence as a professional?
4) What are the codes of ethics directly and indirectly pertinent to your existence as a human service professional offering couples and marriage counseling?

5) As a human service professional providing couples and marriage counseling, how and in what ways is "knowledge" critical to your decision-making?

6) To what extent are you "an employee who happens to be a professional" and "a professional who happens to be an employee?"

7) In your own opinion, what would be the "best" way to credential healthcare professionals in the United States?

EPILOGUE

At the end of a counseling, therapy or mediation session, it is not uncommon for two things to occur: (1) the helping professional may reflect on what was discussed and experienced in the session and offer a "last minute thought" or "it may be important for you to remember" kind of statement; and/or (2) the client(s) may offer what therapists refer to as a "doorknob issue."[7] These typically are phrased as "One last thing I thought I should mention to you..." or "Oh by the way, I thought you also should know that..." and "Something that I wanted to tell you but forgot was..." After reading the previous 15 chapters of this book – our own book – we found ourselves reflecting on the book's content in a similar way. We were reminded of some general issues that we felt were important for our readers to remember as you finish this book. The following briefly discusses a few of the more poignant reflections we have regarding the topics and the existence and essence of this book.

WHAT IS A RELATIONSHIP?

Good question. And just when we think we are in a position to answer that question definitively, we read another book, talk to another person or experience something new, and our conceptualization changes. In many ways, we then feel like we have to start all over again. It is often said, "The journey is as important as or even more important than the destination." Maybe helping our clients discover what a loving relationship is, constitutes a major overall goal of our journey with them. Similarly, "There is no perfect relationship." Just when things appear to be going great, something happens. A "good" relationship is something that needs constant attention. It is akin to heating a house in the wintertime. No house is perfectly insulated from the elements. A good thermostat monitors the temperature and signals the heater when it needs to kick in to heat the house. When the house is warm again, the heater shuts off. But eventually the temperature will drop and the cycle continues. When something goes awry or something interferes with a relationship, the two individuals hopefully become aware of it and attend to the problem in order to return their relationship to the level of comfort and meaningfulness they both want and enjoy. Fittingly, as in the analogy

---

[7] The term "doorknob issue" is used in two very different ways. The first, and the way we use it here, is as a parting thought that the client offers as he or she is leaving the therapist's office. The second way this term is used refers to a different situation, one in which the client uses the act of leaving the office to communicate essential or volatile information that he or she was unwilling or felt unable to communicate during the session. Most therapists are familiar with these "bombshell" statements; similarly, mediators are trained to counsel their clients to avoid making such statements following the formal close of a mediation session.

of the house, the cycle continues. As we have illustrated numerous times throughout this book, it is imperative that we help clients appreciate that it is the *process* of the relationship that is important, not just the outcome. Like happiness, a good loving relationship is not a station you arrive at, it is a manner of traveling.

LOVING RELATIONSHIPS

The establishment, development and maintenance of a loving relationship are exciting yet intriguing mysteries. In addition to many other considerations, a relationship involves constant attention to competing, juxtaposed values. For example:

1) *Now vs. forever.* A person can look at his or her loving relationship from a perspective of temporality versus a value of eternity: "The most important issue is how we feel about each other at this moment" versus "It is critical for me to feel that this relationship will last forever."

2) *Love vs. friendship (with sex).* One person may decide that unless he or she can experience a deep feeling of love for a significant other, the relationship is not worth having. A different person may take the perspective that "what really matters is that my significant other is my best friend; romance and sex, when they happen, are added rewards."

3) *All or none vs. good enough.* An individual can look at his or her personal happiness, as it interfaces with his or her loving relationship, from a perspective of "Having what you want" versus "Wanting what you have." One individual may say, "I will never stay in a relationship with another person unless he or she is the kind of person I want, and we have the kind of relationship that I want." While another person may say, "The person I am with and my relationship with him/her may not be what I want, but I am willing to do whatever I can do to learn to want what I have."

4) *It's about me vs. it's about us.* A person may look at his or her being in a loving relationship from a position of "wanting my own individual autonomy and freedom" versus a position of "wanting a connected, interdependent and committed loving relationship with another person."

5) *Pain vs. emotional investment.* One person may see relationship struggles or failure as sources of intolerable pain that seem impossible to overcome. A different person may have a "no regrets" perspective that every relationship carries with it the risk of failure, but as long as the majority of experiences are good, it is worth the ride.

Of course with each of these juxtaposed value sets, a person can hold an *either/or* attitude or a *both* attitude. And as one uncovers the delicate and intricate root system beneath most loving relationships, the mystery becomes more mysterious. "Sally and I are very successful *workmates* as well as wonderful and fun loving *playmates*, but I wonder if we ever could be *soul mates*?" Greg, a client, once asked Bill Emener. "I don't know," Bill replied. "Do you have to be good workmates and good playmates in order to be soul mates? Or put another way, Greg, could two people be good soul mates yet not be good workmates or good playmates?"

After pondering Bill's retort, Greg said, "I don't know. Those are intriguing questions. It would be interesting and helpful for us to discuss them." Bill responded, "That indeed would be interesting, Greg, but it may be more important for you and Sally to discuss them."

You may have noticed that throughout this book, on numerous occasions when individuals came to see one of us about a relationship issues, we eventually talked at length about them – the person himself or herself. Many of our clients realize this. When you think about it, it makes sense. In many ways, a loving relationship is like a reflecting pool or a mirror. It vividly reveals to us many aspects about ourselves. Intuitively, it is reasonable to believe constructs such as:

- My ability to trust another individual is an indication of the extent to which I can trust myself.
- If I am not comfortable with myself, then I probably will have difficulties feeling and being comfortable with another person and my relationship with that person, and
- My ability to love another person is an indication of the extent to which I can love myself.

As a rule of thumb, whenever we sense that a client is having a difficulty with a significant other, the first question we typically ask him or her is: "What is going on within you?"

Every human being is unique in a myriad of ways – different from anyone else. Moreover, every human being is constantly changing. Thus, every loving relationship is unique and constantly changing. What may appear "right" or "good" for one couple may not be "right" or "good" for another, and what working for them today may not work tomorrow. Facilitating our client's understanding and appreciation of their uniqueness and differences, and remaining flexible, postured for and attentive to constant change, are critical aspects of professional counseling. We often help our clients to understand this with the following principle:

True loving relationships never end, they just change their form.

In the process of developing a good loving relationship, "you and I" also becomes "us." And typically, that does not happen until "You" and "I" are no longer exclusive, independent realities. In a meaningful relationship, we find the comingling of intertwined lives, the genuine sharing of fears, wants and desires, the simultaneous struggling for togetherness and oneness, the preservation of two unique, individual lives in the presence of a shared relationship lifestyle, and the simultaneous awareness of, appreciation of, and respect for our relationship's beginning, temporal existence and never-ending essence. We do not "have" a relationship. Rather, a relationship is an *interdependent process of being* – a process that translates into, or "becomes," a relationship. In this sense, the term "relationship" is not just a noun or an adjective – it is also a verb.

A relationship involves many risks. Two of these seem particularly salient to us: freedom and comfort. First, every relationship implicitly requires a risk to our freedom. When given further thought, nonetheless, it is only the free person who can take risks in the first place. If you are free, then you can risk freedom. But if you truly are free, then you may not actually be risking anything. *Freedom is not a place in life – it is a manner of being.* And from a spiritual or philosophical perspective, one can be free no matter where one is. Thus, it is no wonder that some people will say, "I am free *and* I am in a wonderful, enjoyable and meaningful loving relationship."

Second, relationships explicitly force us out of our comfort zone. A person cannot develop a new relationship without doing a myriad of things, and experiencing many emotions, they otherwise would not. To experience such things forces people to alter their routines and make changes to their lifestyles that can seem daunting, even overwhelming. In a nutshell, as with most aspects of life, *the only constant in the relationship process is change.*

In view of the above postulates, remember: you and your clients are human beings – you have a lot in common.

You – The Counselor, The Student, The Person

As we said in the book's Prologue, our intention was for this book to have an impact on you – as a counselor, as a student and as a person.

In your role as a professional counselor working with couples, it is your goal to have an impact on each of the partners you are seeing so that their individual feelings, thoughts and behaviors change – change that then translates into changes in their relationship. Helping couples change, moreover, not only affects them and their relationships – frequently it also affects their children, families, friends and many others in their life space.

If you read this book because you are taking a graduate course in couples and marriage counseling, you obviously are a student. However, if you read this book as a practicing counselor wanting to improve and expand your knowledge and expertise, you also are a student. Learning never is completed – it never ends. As a professional counselor or therapist, you not only are a student of life – you are a student for life.

In terms of "you – the person," when your clients meet you and work with you, they know you for who you are, not only what you are. For a multitude of reasons, the importance of your own self-awareness can never be overestimated.

Like the three legs of a tripod, your clients know or will know you – you the professional counselor, you the student of and for life, and you the person. And while these individual attributes of yourself can be looked at individually, their interrelatedness as a gestalt is the most important thing you offer your clients: yourself.

Doorknob Issues

We assume that now that you have finished reading this book and bounced its ideas, principles and considerations off of your life and experiences as a counselor, you have some ideas, principles and considerations of your own that the book has not addressed. We would greatly appreciate knowing what your doorknob issues are for us. Thus, please take a few moments of your time to share them with us. You probably have some good suggestions and criticisms that we would all benefit from knowing.

Please write to us and share:

William A. Lambos, Ph.D.
Licensed Clinical Neuropsychologist and Mental Health Counselor Intern
CNS Wellness Florida, LLC.
5201 W. Kennedy Blvd.
Suite 615
Tampa, Florida 33609
Email: walambos@eegscience.com

William G. Emener, Ph.D.
Distinguished Research Professor Emeritus
Department of Rehabilitation and Mental Health Counseling
College of Behavioral and Community Sciences
University of South Florida
Tampa, Florida 33620
Email: emener@bcs.usf.edu

Thank-you!
Bill and Bill

REFERENCES

Aanstoos, C., Serlin, I., & Greening, T. (2000). *History of division 32 (Humanistic Psychology) of the American Psychological Association.* In D. Dewsbury (ed.), Unification through Division: Histories of the divisions of the American Psychological Association, Vol. V. Washington, DC: American Psychological Association.

Ackerman, N. W. (1958). *The psychodynamics of family life.* New York: Basic Books.

Ackerman, N.W. (1982). In D. Bloch, R. Simon & N.W. Ackerman (eds.) *The Strength of family therapy.* New York: Taylor & Francis/Routledge.

Adler, A. (1999). *Practice and theory of individual psychology.* London: Taylor & Francis, Inc.

American Psychological Association (1992). *Ethical principles of psychologists and code of conduct.* American Psychologist, 47, 1597-1611.

American Psychological Association (2007). *Summary report of journal operations.* American Psychologist, *62,* 543-544.

Anand, U. (1967). *Objective of marriage counseling: Family unity versus individual happiness.* In H.L. Silverman (ed.) Marital counseling: Psychology, ideology, science (pp. 151-163). Springfield, IL: Charles C. Thomas.

Anderson, H. (1996). *Conversation language and possibilities*: A postmodern approach to therapy. New York: Basic Books.

Arden, J., & Linford, L. (2009). *Brain-based therapy for adults*: Evidence-based treatment for everyday practice. Hoboken, NJ: John Wiley & Sons.

Bagarozzi, D. (1982). *The family therapist's role in treating families in rural communities: A general systems approach.* Journal of Marital and Family Therapy, *8,* 51-58.

Bandura, A. (1986). *Social foundations of thought and action:* A social cognitive theory. Englewood Cliffs, NJ: Prentice-Hall.

Bandura, A. (1997). *Self-efficacy:* The exercise of control. New York: Worth Publishers.

Beattie, M. (1992). *Codependent no more:* How to stop controlling others and start caring for yourself. Center City, MN: Hazelden Publishing.

Beauregard, M., & O'Leary, D. (2007). *The spiritual brain*: A neuroscientist's case for the existence of the soul. New York: Harper One.

Beck, A. T. (1976). *Cognitive therapy and the emotional disorders.* New York: New American Library.

Bernard, J. M., & Goodyear, R. K. (2003). *Fundamentals of clinical supervision* (3rd ed.) Needham Heights, MA: Allyn & Bacon.

Berne, E. (1964). *Games people play:* The psychology of human relationships. New York: Ballantine Books.

Berry, J. W. (2001). *A psychology of immigration.* Journal of Social Issues, *57*, 615-631.

Berry, J. W. (2007). *Acculturation.* In J. E. Grusec & P. D. Hastings (eds.) Handbook of socialization: Theory and research (pp. 543-558). New York: Guilford.

Bertalanffy, L. von. (1968) *General system theory* (rev.). New York: George Braziller.

Betz, N. E., & Hackett, G. (1981). *The relationship of career-related self-efficacy expectations to perceived career options in college women and men.* Journal of Counseling Psychology, 28, 399-410.

Bordin, E. S. (1979). T*he generalizability of the psychoanalytic concept of the working alliance.* Psychotherapy: Theory, Research & Practice, 16, 252-260.

Boscolo, L., Cecchin, G., Hoffman, L., & Penn, P. (1987). *Milan systemic family therapy.* New York: Basic Books.

Bowen, M. (1988). *Family therapy in clinical practice.* Northvale, NJ: Jason Aronson.

Bowlby, J. (1983). *Attachment* (2nd ed.). New York: Basic Books.

Bowlby, J. (1990). *A secure base*: Parent-child attachment and healthy human development. New York: Basic Books.

Broderick, C.B., & Schrader, S.S. (1981). *The history of professional marriage and family therapy.* In A.S. Gurman & D.P. Kniskern, (eds.), Handbook of family therapy (pp. 5-35). New York: Brunner/Mazel.

Brown, L. S. (in press). *Feminist therapy*: Not for women only. Washington, DC: American Psychological Association.

Busby, D.M., Glenn, E., Steggell, G.L., & Adamson, D.W. (1993). *Treatment issues for survivors of physical and sexual abuse.* Journal of Marital and Family Therapy, 19, 377-392.

Butler, A.C., Chapman, J.E., Forman, E.M., & Beck, A.T. (2006). *The empirical status of cognitive-behavioral therapy: A review of meta-analyses.* Clinical Psychology Review, 26, 17-31.

Chabot, D.R. (1983). *Historical perspective on working with the individual in family therapy.* In E.G. Pendagast (ed.), Compendium II: The best of the Family 1978-1983 (pp. 40-44). New Rochelle, NY: The Center for Family Learning.

Chapman, G. (2008). *The five love languages:* How to express heartfelt commitment to your mate. New York: Walker & Co.

Collins, D. (2008). *An expert on the roles people play.* New York Times. http://query.nytimes.com/gst/fullpage.html?sec=health&res=9A0CE4D91739F930A1575 1C0A967948260, retrieved December 27, 2008.

Constantine, M. G., & Sue, D. W. (2007). *Perceptions of racial microaggressions among black supervisees in cross-racial dyads.* Journal of Counseling Psychology, 54, 142-153.

Corey, G., Corey, M.S., & Callahan, P. (1988). *Issues and ethics in the helping professions.* (3rd ed.) Pacific Grove, CA: Brooks/Cole.

Cozolino, L. (2002). *The neuroscience of psychotherapy.* New York: W. W. Norton & Co. de Shazer, S. (1988). Clues: Investigating solutions in brief therapy. New York: W.W. Norton & Company.

DeAngelis, T. (2008). *Psychology's growth careers.* Monitor on Psychology, 39, 64-71.

DeFrain, J. (1991). *Learning about grief from normal families: SIDS, stillbirth, and miscarriage.* Journal of Marital and Family Therapy, 17, 215-232.

Dennett, D. (1995). *Darwin's dangerous Idea*. New York: Simon & Schuster.

Denton, W.H., Walsh, S.R., & Daniel, S.S. (2002). *Evidence-based practice in family therapy: Adolescent depression as an example.* Journal of Marital and Family Therapy, 28, 39-45.

Dobson, K.S. (1989). *A meta-analysis of the efficacy of cognitive therapy for depression.* Journal of Consulting and Clinical Psychology, 57, 414-419.

Dollard, J., & Miller, N.E. (1979). *Social learning and imitation.* Westport, CT: Greenwood Press Reprint.

Edelman, G. (1987). *Neural Darwinism* The theory of neuronal group selection. New York: Basic Books.

Elliott, R., Watson, J. C., Goldman, R. N., & Greenberg, L. S. (2004). *Learning emotion-focused therapy: The process-experiential approach to change.* Washington DC: American Psychological Association.

Ellis, A. (1996). *Better, deeper, and more enduring brief psychotherapy:* The rational emotive behavior therapy approach. New York: Brunner/Mazel, Inc.

Ellis, A. (2000*). How to stubbornly refuse to make yourself miserable about anything*: Yes, anything. New York: Lyle Stuart.

Ellis, A. (2005). *The myth of self-esteem*: How rational emotive behavior therapy can change your life forever. Amherst, NY: Prometheus Books.

Emener, W.G. (1975). *The rehabilitation counselor: A student of life.* Journal of Rehabilitation, 41(1), 16-17, 43.

Emener, W.G. (1987). *Ethical standards for rehabilitation counseling: A brief review of critical historical developments.* Journal of Applied Rehabilitation Counseling, 18(4), 5-8.

Emener, W.G., & Lambos, W.A. (2009). *My Loving Relationships.* Hauppauge, NY: Nova Science Publishers. (a)

Emener, W.G., & Lambos, W.A. (2009). *Our Loving Relationship.* Hauppauge, NY: Nova Science Publishers. (b)

Emener, W.G., Richard, M.A., & Bosworth, J.J. (2009. *A Guidebook to human service professions:* Helping college students explore opportunities in the human services field. Springfield, IL: Charles C. Thomas, Publisher. (a)

Emener, W.G., Richard, M.A., & Bosworth, J.J. (2009) *Ethics and professionalism.* In W. G. Emener, M. A. Richard, & John J. Bosworth (eds.) A guidebook to human service professions: Helping college students explore opportunities in the human services field (pp. 257-262). Springfield, IL: Charles C. Thomas. (b)

Ferro, G. (2007. *Tell-All PCs and Phones Transforming Divorce.* New York: New York Times. http://www.nytimes.com/2007/09/15/business/15divorce.html?_r=1, retrieved April 21, 2009.

Fisher, H. (2004). *Why we love:* The nature and chemistry of romantic love. New York: Henry Holt & Co.

Fleck, C. (2001). *Faculty retirement: The issue, the predictions, and the effects on campuses.* Briefing papers, Association of American Colleges and Universities. http://www.greaterexpectations.org/briefing_papers/FacultyRetirement.html, retrieved June 17, 2008.

Frank, R. (2007). *Richistan:* A journey through the American wealth boom and the lives of the new rich. New York: Crown Publishers.

Frankl, V. (1946). *Man's Search for Meaning*. Boston: Beacon Press.

Frankl, V. E. (1984). *Man's search for meaning* (Revised and updated). New York: Washington Square Press/Pocket Books.

Freud, S. (1961). *The ego and the id and other works*. (Standard Edition, vol. A9). London: Hogarth.

Freud, S. (1964). *New introductory lectures on psycho-analysis* (standard edition, vol. 22). London: Hogarth.

Frey, J. (2005). *A million little pieces*. New York: Anchor.

Friedlander, M.L. (1999). *Ethnic identity development of internationally adopted children and adolescents: Implication for family therapists*. Journal of Marital and Family Therapy, 25 43-60.

Friedman, T. L. (2006) *The world is flat:* A brief history of the twenty-first century. New York: Farrar, Straus and Giroux.

Friedman, T. L. (2008). *Hot, flat and crowded:* Why we need a green revolution--and how it can renew America. New York: Farrar, Straus and Giroux.

Frisbie, D., & Frisbie, L (2005). *Happily remarried:* Making decisions together * Blending families successfully * Building a love that will last. Eugene, OR: Harvest House Publishers.

Gelso, C. J., & Fretz, B. R. (2001). *Counseling psychology* (2nd ed.) Fort Worth, TX: Harcourt College.

Gilbran, K. (1965). *The prophet*. New York: Alfred A. Knopf.

Gladwell, M. (2007). *Blink:* The power of thinking without thinking. New Port Beach, CA: Back Bay Books, Inc.

Gloaguen, V., Cottraux, J., Cucherat, M., & Blackburn, I.M. (1998). *A meta-analysis of the effects of cognitive therapy in depressed patients*. Journal of Affective Disorders, 49, 59-72.

Goldenberg, I., & Goldenberg, H. (2004). *Family therapy:* An overview (6th ed.). Pacific Grove, CA: Books/Cole – Thomson Learning.

Goldberg, E. (2002). *The Executive Brain:* Frontal Lobes and the Civilized Mind. New York: Oxford University Press.

Goldberg, E. (2005). *The wisdom paradox*: How your mind can grows stronger as your brain grows older. Gotham: New York.

Goldenberg, I., & Goldenberg, H. (2004). *Family therapy:* An overview (6th ed.). Pacific Grove, CA: Books/Cole – Thomson Learning.

Goldman, D. (1995). *Emotional intelligence*: How it can matter more than IQ. New York: Random House.

Goodwin, C. J. (2005). *A history of modern psychology* (2nd ed.). Hoboken, NJ: John Wiley & Sons.

Goodyear, R. K., Murdock, N., Lichtenberg, J. W., McPherson, R., Koetting, K., & Petren, S. (2008). *Stability and change in counseling psychologists' identities, roles, functions, and career satisfaction across 15 years*. The Counseling Psychologist, 36, 220-249.

Gordon, S.B., & Davidson, N. (1981*). Behavioral parent training*. In A.S. Gurman & D.P. Gurman, N.S., & Jacobson, A.S. (eds.) (2002). Clinical handbook of couple therapy. New York: Guilford.

Gottman, J., & Silver, N. (1999). *The seven principles for making marriage work:* A practical guide from the country's foremost relationship expert. New York: Three Rivers Press.

Gurman, A.S., & Kniskern, D.P. (eds.). (1981). *Handbook of family therapy*. New York: Brunner/Mazel.

Haley, J. (1984). *Ordeal therapy*. San Francisco: Jossey-Bass.

Haley, J. (1987). *Problem solving therapy* (2nd ed.). San Francisco: Jossey-Bass.

Hall, C. S. (1954). *A primer of Freudian psychology*. New York: Mentor.

Haselton, M.G., & Gangestad, S.W. (2006). *Conditional expression of women's desires and men's mate guarding across the ovulatory cycle*. Hormones and Behavior, 49, 509–518.

Hawkins, J., & Blakeslee, S. (2004). *On intelligence*. New York: Henry Holt & Co. Held, B.S. (1995). *Back to reality:* A critique of postmodern theory in psychotherapy. New York: W.W. Norton and Company.

Hazan C., & Shaver P.R. (1987). *Romantic love conceptualized as an attachment process*. Journal of Personality and Social Psychology, 52, 511–24.

Helms, J. E., & Cook, D. A. (1999). *Using race and culture in counseling and psychotherapy: Theory and process*. Upper Saddle River, NJ: Prentice Hall.

Heppner, P. P., Witty, T. E., & Dixon, W. A. (2004). *Problem-solving appraisal: Helping normal people lead better lives*. The Counseling Psychologist, 32, 466-472.

Herek, G. M., & Garnets, L. D. (2007). *Sexual orientation and mental health*. Annual Review of Clinical Psychology, 353-375.

Hoffman, L. (1992). *A reflexive stance for family therapy*. In S. McNamee, & K. Gergen (eds.). Therapy as social construction (pp. 7-24). London: Sage.

Hoffsteader, D.R. (2007). *I am a strange loop*. New York: Basic Books.

Horvath, A. O., & Greenberg, L. S. (eds.) (1994*). The working alliance*: Theory, research and practice. New York: Wiley.

Hothersall, D. (2003). *History of psychology* (4th ed.). New York: McGraw-Hill

Jacobson, N.S. (1981). *Behavioral marital therapy*. In A.S. Gurman & D.P. Kniskern, (eds.), Handbook of family therapy (pp. 556-591). New York: Brunner/Mazel, Inc.

Janes, M.W., & Emener, W.G. (1999). *The human side of health care in the new millennium*. In C.G. Dixon, & W.G. Emener (eds.). Professional counseling: Transitioning into the next millennium. Springfield, IL: Charles C. Thomas.

Johnson, S. (1992). *The Laocoon: Systemic concepts in a work of art*. Journal of Marital and Family Therapy, 18(2), 113-124.

Johnson, S. (1996). *Family of the forest: Fatal enmeshment and other systems issues in the animal world*. Contemporary Family Therapy: An International Journal, 18(3), 447-461.

Johnson, S. (2001) *Emergence:* The connected lives of ants, cities and software. New York: Scribner.

Johnson, S. (2009). *Marriage and Family Therapy*. In W. G. Emener, M. A. Richard, & John J. Bosworth (eds*.) A guidebook to human service professions: Helping college students explore opportunities in the human services field* (pp. 128-141). Springfield, IL: Charles C. Thomas.

Jones, W.H.S. (1923). *Hippocrates, Volume II*. London: Loeb Classical Library, Harvard University Press.

Jung, C.G. (1972). *C.G. Jung: Psychological reflections:* A new anthology of his writings, 1905 -1961. Bollingen, Switzerland: Bollingen Foundation.

Keitner, G.I. (2005). *Family therapy in the treatment of depression*. Psychiatric Times. Available online at http://www.psychiatrictimes.com/display/article/10168/52636.

Kiley, D. (1983). *The Peter Pan syndrome*: Men who have never grown up. New York: Dodd, Mead and Co.

Kniskern, (Eds.), *Handbook of family therapy* (pp. 517-555). New York: Brunner/Mazel.

Koertge, N. (ed.). (1998). *A house built on sand:* Exposing postmodern myths about science. New York: Oxford University Press.

Krugman, P. (2008). *The return of depression economics and the crisis of 2008.* New York: W. W. Norton.

Kurzweil, R. (2006). *The singularity is near:* When humans transcend biology. New York: Penguin.

Lakoff, G., & Johnson, M. (1999). *Philosophy in the flesh:* The embodied mind and its challenge to western thought. New York: Basic Books.

Lambos. W.A. (2009). *Mediation: A collaborative approach to dispute resolution.* In W. G. Emener, M. A. Richard, & John J. Bosworth (eds.) A guidebook to human service professions: Helping college students explore opportunities in *the human services field* (pp. 142-153). Springfield, IL: Charles C. Thomas.

Lent, R. W., Brown, S. D., & Hackett, G. (2000*). Contextual supports and barriers to career choice: A Social cognitive analysis. Journal of Counseling Psychology, 47*, 36-49.

Lerner, R. (1995). *Living in the comfort zone:* The gift of boundaries in relationships. Deerfield Beach, FL: Heath Communications, Inc.

Levitsky, A., & Simkin, J. (1972). *Gestalt therapy.* In Solomon & Gerzon (eds.) New perspectives on encounter groups. San Francisco, CA: Jossey-Bass.

Lewis, M. (2008). *Panic:* The story of modern financial insanity. New York: W. W. Norton.

Lidz, T. (1975). *Hamlet's enemy.* New York: Basic Books.

Lindley, D. (2007). *Uncertainty:* Einstein, Heisenberg, Bohr, and the struggle for the soul of science. New York: Doubleday.

Lipton, A. (1984). *"Death of a Salesman": A family systems point of view. The Family, 11*, 55-67.

Lipton, B. (2005). *The biology of belief:* Unleashing the power of consciousness, matter and miracles. San Francisco: Mountain of Love/Elite Books.

Lopez, F. G., & Brennan, K. A. (2000). *Dynamic processes underlying adult attachment organization: Toward an attachment theoretical perspective on the healthy and effective self. Journal of Counseling Psychology, 47*, 283-300.

Mackintosh, N. J. (1983). *Conditioning and associative learning.* New York: Oxford University Press.

Maconis, J. (2007). *Sociology.* (12th ed.). Upper Saddle River, NJ: Prentice Hall.

Mallinckrodt, B., Porter, M. J., & Kivlighan, D. M. Jr. (2005*). Client attachment to therapist, depth of in-session exploration, and object relations in brief psychotherapy.* Psychotherapy: Theory, Research, Practice, and Training, 42, 85-100.

Marshall, S. (1997). *Cognitive behavior therapy*: An introduction to theory and practice. Philadelphia: W.B Saunders.

Maslow, A. (1943). *A Theory of Human Motivation.* Psychological Review, 50, 370-396.

Maslow, A. (1954). *Motivation and Personality.* Harper: New York.

Maslow, A. (1970). *Motivation and Personality* (2nd Ed.). Harper Collins: Detroit, MI.

May, R. (1992). *Man's Search for Himself.* New York: Bantam Dell Pub Group.

McGoldrick, M. (1998). *Re-Visioning family therapy*: Race, culture, and gender in clinical practice. New York: Guilford Press.

McGoldrick, M., & Gerson, R. (1985). *Genograms in family assessment.* New York: W.W. Norton.

McNamee, S., & Gergen, K. (eds.) (1992). *Therapy as social construction.* London: Sage.

McTaggert, L. (2003). *The field:* The quest for the secret force of the universe. New York: Harper Collins.

Meichenbaum, D. (1977). *Cognitive-behavior modification:* An integrative approach. New York: Springer.

Mendez, C.L., Coddou, F., & Maturana, H.R. (1988). *The bringing forth of pathology.* The Irish Journal of Psychology, 9, 144-172.

Meyer, I. H. (2003). *Prejudice, social stress, and mental health in lesbian, gay and bisexual populations: Conceptual issues and research evidence. Psychological Bulletin, 129,* 674-697.

Minuchin S., & Fishman, H.C. (1981). *Family therapy techniques.* Cambridge, MA: Harvard University Press.

Minuchin, S., Montalvo, B., Guerney, B.G. Jr., Rosman, B.L., & Schumer, F. (1967). *Families of the slums:* An exploration of their structure and treatment. New York: Basic Books.

Molina, B., Agudelo, M.A., de los Réos, A., Builes, M.V., Ospina, A., Arroyave, R., Lopez, O.L., Vásquez, M., & Navia, C.E. (2005*). Kidnapping: Its effects on the beliefs and the structure of relationships in a group of families in Antioquia. Journal of Family Psychotherapy, 16, 39-55.*

Morris, M. (2006). *A cybernetic analysis of the United States of America's relationship with Iraq* [electronic resource]. Available at: http://scholar.lib.vt.edu/theses/available/etd-12232006-234249/

Munley, P. H., Pate, W. E., & Duncan, L. E. (2008). *Demographic, educational, employment, and professional characteristics of counseling psychologists.* The Counseling Psychologist, 36, 250-280.

Murdock, N. L. (2009). *Theories of counseling and psychotherapy*: A case study approach. Upper Saddle River, NJ: Merrill/Pearson.

Nagi, S. (1977). *Disability concepts and implications to the structure of services.* An address to the American Rehabilitation Counseling Association, Dallas, TX.

Nichols, W. (1992). *Fifty years of marital & family therapy.* Alexandria, VA: American Association for Marriage and Family Therapy.

Patterson, C. H., & Watkins, C.E. (1997). *Theories of counseling and psychotherapy* (5th ed.). New York: Harper & Row.

Paul, J, & Paul, M. (2002). *Do I have to give up me to be loved by you?* (2nd ed.) Center City, MN: Hazelden Publishing.

Pear, R. (2008). *House approves bill on mental health parity.* New York Times. http://www.nytimes.com/2008/03/06/washington/06health.html?_r=1&scp=2&sq=mental%20health%20parity&st=cse, retrieved April 18, 2009.

Phelps, R., Eisman, E. J., & Kohout, J. (1998). *Psychological practice and managed care: Results of the CAPP practitioner survey.* Professional Psychology: Research and Practice, 29, 31-36.

Pipkin, M. (Producer). (1989). *Family therapy [television episode].* The Simpsons. Century City, CA: Twentieth Century Fox Broadcasting.

Potter-Efron, R., & Potter-Efron, P. *Letting go of shame:* Understanding how shame affects your life. (1989). Center City, MN: Hazelden Publishing.

Psychotherapy Networker. (2007*). The most influential therapists of the past quarter century.* Retrieved on 29 June 2008 from http://www.psychotherapynetworker.com/index.php? category=magazine&sub_cat=articles&type=article&id=The%20Top%2010&page=6.

Rogers, C. R. (1951). *Client-centered therapy.* Boston: Houghton-Mifflin.

Rogers, C. (1961). *On becoming a person*: A therapist's view of psychotherapy. Boston: Houghton Mifflin.

Rotter, J.B. (1972). *Applications of a social learning theory of personality.* Geneva, IL: Holt McDougal.

Russell, B. (1967). *Autobiography (vol. 1). New York: George Allen and Unwin, 1967.*

Sanger, M. (2004). *The autobiography of Margaret Sanger.* Mineola, NY: Dover Publications.

Satir, V. (1968). *Conjoint family therapy.* Palo Alto, CA: Science and Behavior Books.

Searle, J. (2004*). Mind: A brief introduction (fundamentals of philosophy).* New York: Oxford University Press.

Seligman, M. (2006). *Positivistic psychology.* Washington, DC: American Psychological Association.

Selye, H. (1956). *The stress of life.* New York: McGraw-Hill.

Shalay, N., & Brownlee, K. (2007*). Narrative family therapy with blended families.* Journal of Family Psychotherapy, 18, 17-30.

Schultz, D.P., & Schultz, S.E. (1987). *A history of modern psychology.* New York: Harcourt Brace Jovanovich Publications.

Schwartz, J. (2002). *The mind and the brain*: Neuroplasticity and the power of mental force. New York: Harper.

Silverman, H.L. (1967). *Morality and marital counseling.* In H.L. Silverman (ed.) Marital counseling: Psychology, ideology, science (pp. 443-446). Springfield, IL: Charles C. Thomas.

Skinner, B.F. (1969). *Contingencies of reinforcement*: A theoretical analysis. New York: Appleton-Century-Crofts.

Skinner, B.F. (1991). *Verbal behavior.* Acton, MA: Copley Publishing Group.

Skynner, R., & Cleese, J. (1984). *Families and how to survive them.* New York: Oxford University Press.

Spinelli, E. (2005) *The interpreted world, an introduction to phenomenological psychology (2nd ed.).* London, UK: Sage Publications.

Staub, D. (1997). *The heart of leadership:* 12 practices of courageous leaders. West Valley City, Utah: Covey Leadership Center.

Sternberg, R. (2003). *Cognitive psychology (3rd ed.).* Florence, KY: Thomson/Wadsworth.

Stith, S.M., Williams, M.B., & Rosen, K.H. (eds.) (1990). Violence hits home: Comprehensive treatment approaches to domestic violence. New York: Springer Publications.

Strong, S. R., Claiborne, C. D. (1982). *Change through interaction:* Social psychological processes of counseling and psychotherapy. New York: Wiley.

Strupp, H. H., & Binder, J. L. (1984). *Psychotherapy in a new key*: A guide to time-limited dynamic psychotherapy. New York: Basic Books.

Substance Abuse and Mental Health Services Administration (SAMSHA). (2007). Minority fellowship program. Washington, DC: Author.

Sue, D. W., Arredondo, P., & McDavis, R. J. (1992*). Multicultural counseling competencies and standards: A call to the profession*. Journal of Multicultural Counseling and Development, 20, 64-88.

Taleb, N. N. (2007). *The black swan:* The impact of the highly improbable. New York: Random House.

Teyber, E. (2005). *Interpersonal process in therapy:* An integrative model. (5th ed.). Brooks Cole.

Thomas, J.H. (2000). *Tillich.* New York: Continuum International Publishing Group.

Thornhill, R., Gangestad, S.W., Miller, R., Scheyd, G., McCollough, J.K., & Franklin, M. (2003). *Major histocompatibility complex genes, symmetry, and body scent attractiveness in men and women.* Behavioral Ecology, 14, 668–678.

Toffler, A. (1970). *Future shock.* New York: Penguin.

Toporek, R. L., Gerstein, R. H., Fouad, N. A., Boysircar, G., & Israel, T. (2006) (eds.) *Handbook for social justice counseling psychology:* Leadership, vision and action. Thousand Oaks, CA: Sage.

Tracey, T. J. (1993). *An interpersonal stage model of the therapeutic process.* Journal of Counseling Psychology, 40, 396-409.

Wampold, B. E. (2001). *The great psychotherapy debate:* Models, methods, and findings. Mahwah, NJ: Erlbaum.

Waters, H., Hyder, A., Rajkotia, Y., Basu, S., Rehwinkel, J.A., & Butchart, A. (2004). *The economic dimensions of interpersonal violence.* Department of Injuries and Violence Prevention, World Health Organization, Geneva.

Watson, J.B. (1924/1925). *Behaviorism.* New York: People's Institute Publishing Company;

Watson, J.B. (1928). *The ways of behaviorism.* New York: Harper & Brothers

Weisberg, J. (2008). *The Bush tragedy.* New York: Random House.

Whitaker, C. (1972). *We became family therapists.* In A. Ferber, M. Mendelsohn, & A. Napier (eds.). The book of family therapy. Boston: Houghton Mifflin Company.

Whitaker, C., & Bumberry, W.A. (1988). *Dancing with the family:* A symbolic-experiential approach. New York: Brunner-Mazel, Inc.

White, M., & Epston, D. (1990). *Narrative means to therapeutic ends.* New York: W.W. Norton.

Wilson, E. O. (1975). *Sociobiology:* The new synthesis. Cambridge, MA: Harvard University Press, (Twenty-fifth Anniversary Edition, 2000).

Woldt, A. L., & Toman, S. M. (eds.) (2005). *Gestalt therapy:* History, theory, and practice. Thousand Oaks, CA: Sage Publications.

World Health Organization. (2004). *The economic dimensions of interpersonal violence.*

Worthington, R. L., Soth-McNett, A. M., & Moreno, M. V. (2007*). Multicultural counseling competencies research: A 20-year content analysis.* Journal of Counseling Psychology, *54*, 351-361.

APPENDIX A. A CATEGORICAL/ANNOTATED LIST OF BIBLIOTHERAPEUTIC SELF-HELP BOOKS

The following includes 10 categorical listings of a total of 86 self-help books, published since 2000, that can be very helpful to counselors and students; moreover, some of the books can be helpful for individuals struggling with specific issues – issues that also are interfering and/or troublesome in their loving relationships.

ADDICTION/ALCOHOLISM AND RELATIONSHIPS

Barnard, M. (2007). *Drug addiction and families*. London: Jessica Kingsley Publishers. Maria Barnard seeks to address both the family experience and professional implications of this increasingly pressing problem for social policy and direct practice. She does this by drawing on findings from three linked qualitative research studies undertaken with colleagues in Glasgow between the late 1990s and 2002.

Conyers, B. (2003). *Addict in the family: Stories of loss, hope, and recovery*. Center City, MN: Hazelden. Through compelling testimonials, along with the latest research and information on addiction and recovery, Conyers combines a personal and compassionate voice with one of authority. She takes a step even further revealing her own daughter's addiction and how she learned to lovingly detach herself and become more helpful.

Hornik-Beer, E. L. (2001). *For teenagers living with a parent who abuses alcohol/drugs*. Lincoln, NE: IUniverse.com, Inc. This books answers questions about alcoholism asked by teenagers. Included are: What causes alcoholism? Where can I get help? What do I do about the abuse? Should I stay at home? Where can I go? How can anyone expect me to concentrate in school? Why do I fight with my parents even when they are sober?

Jay, J., & Jay, D. (2008). *Love first: A family's guide to intervention*. Center City, MN: Hazelden. This top-selling updated edition helps readers create a loving and effective plan for helping those who suffer from addiction. While dispelling two damaging myths – that an addict has to hit bottom and that intervention must be confrontational – it contains many new chapters and new material on meeting the specific needs of adolescents, aging adults and professionals.

Martinez, S. E. (2001). *Last call for alcohol: Healing a marriage harmed by alcohol abuse*. Edina, MN: Tjsusan.com. This book is the author's straightforward story of her tumultuous life with an active alcoholic, their climatic downfall and their subsequent healing. It also includes spiritual and metaphysical healing concepts and suggestions.

Staal, S. (2001). *The love they lost: Living with the legacy of our parents' Divorce*. New York: Random House/Delta. This book shows a divorce's effects on children as they grow into adults and attempt to forge their own romantic and familial relationships. The path to healing for these children, Stall believes, lies in recognizing the far-reaching effects of their parents' marriage and in bringing them together in the first place.

Woititz, J. G. (2002). *The complete ACOA sourcebook: Adult children of alcoholics at home, at work, and in love*. Deerfield Beach, FL: Health Communications. This is a compilation of three of Dr. Woititz's classic books, addressing head-on the symptoms of The Adult Children of Alcoholics syndrome and providing strategies for living a normal life as an adult, finding help for themselves at home, in intimate relationships and on the job, and feeling good about themselves.

AFFAIRS AND LOVING RELATIONSHIPS

Alan, R. (2006). *First aid for the betrayed: Recovering from the devastation of an affair: A personal guide to healing*. Victoria, B.C.: Trafford. Written by a man whose wife had an affair, this book contains some of the rawest honesty about the pain of an affair and provides a great deal of hard-earned wisdom about the whole issue of affairs, particularly in healing from the devastation.

Barnes, H. C. (2005). *Affair! How to manage every aspect of your extramarital relationship with passion, discretion and dignity*. London: Metro. This is a thoughtful, detailed discussion of every aspect of considering, preparing for, beginning and conducting a successful and emotionally fulfilling extramarital affair, including advice, case histories, numerous first-person narratives, humorous anecdotes and step-by-step guidance for every facet of the process.

Glass, S. P., & Staeheli, J. C. (2003). *Not "just friends": Rebuilding trust and recovering your sanity after infidelity*. New York: Free Press. Drawing on research studies and clinical cases, this book scrutinizes affairs and offers well-defined guidelines, tips for determining how vulnerable individuals and relationships are to temptation, prescriptions for keeping relationships "safe," and repairing betrayal-induced damages and recovering from the trauma.

Judah, S. M. (2006). *Staying together: When an affair pulls you apart*. Downers Grove, IL: IVP Books. With clear and helpful analysis of the relational science behind infidelity, the author delivers a tested way back toward a meaningful marriage, including: How did we get here? Where do we go from here? and Can this relationship survive? It is a practical and hopeful guide for couples to find their way back to one another.

Kirshenbaum, M. (2008). *When good people have affairs: Inside the hearts & minds of people in two relationships*. New York: St. Martin's Press. Kirshenbaum puts her unsurpassed experience into one clear, calming place and gives readers everything they need to cut through the thickets of fear, hurt and confusion to find their ways to happier, more solid relationships with the person who's right for them.

Ortman, D. C. (2009). *Transcending post-infidelity stress disorder (PISD: The six stages of healing*. Berkeley, CA: Ten Speed Press. The author, a psychologist, uses post-traumatic stress disorder as a model for the partner wounded by infidelity to explore rage and emotional pain and to learn the secrets of recovery.

Snyder, D. K., Baucom, D. H., & Gordon , K. C. (2007). *Getting past the affair: A program to help you cope, heal, and move on together or apart.* New York: The Guilford Press. The book is considered a 'must read' for anyone trying to recover from the trauma of an affair and make good decisions about the future, and offers wisdom, compassion, and practical advice from a dynamite team of therapists and researchers.

Spring, J. A., & Spring, M. (2006). *After the affair: Healing the pain and rebuilding trust when a partner has been unfaithful.* New York: Harper. This tough-minded, insightful manual urges both partners to probe the deeper meaning of the affair, to explore why it happened and to accept responsibility for it, and includes exercises, concise case studies and checklists of suggestions to guide readers through the difficult task of healing.

BLENDED FAMILIES

Becnel, M. (2000). *God breathes on blended families.* Baton Rouge, La.: Healing Place Productions. This is the story of a blended family coming together in fullness, and is a handbook for other blended families who are pursuing a solid, loving family. The book identifies several crucial problem areas that blended families, children of divorce and stepparents face today, and how to overcome to make a family complete.

Bjornsen, S. (2005). *The single girl's guide to marrying a man, his kids, and his ex-wife.* New York: New American Library. This is a funny, honest, and empathetic resource for the novice stepmother, which includes advice on the kids, the ex-wife, the holidays, and the sex, and includes an invaluable list of resources, websites, publications, and organizations specifically for the new stepmother.

Burns, C. (2001). *Stepmotherhood: How to survive without feeling frustrated, left out, or wicked.* New York: Three Rivers Press. The author, a stepmother herself and humorous writer, has written what is considered a vital guide for any woman who is either contemplating stepmotherhood or who is already there.

Chedekel, D. (2001). *The blended family sourcebook: A guide to negotiating change.* New York: McGraw-Hill. This practical guide offers proactive solutions for integrating new family relationships--from the classic stepfamily to gay and lesbian families, adopted and foster families, interracial and interfaith families, grandparents raising grandchildren, and adult children taking in elderly parents.

Clark, T. (2004). *Tying the family knot: Meeting the challenges of a blended family.* Nashville, Tenn. Broadman & Holman. Tying the Family Knot is a very practical and Biblical book, specifically for Christian women, on an occurrence that is more common and that affects more people today than ever before, and can help make a blended family situation work, and it is written by someone who has done just that for 12 years.

Deal, R. L. (2006). *The smart stepfamily: Seven steps to a healthy family.* Minneapolis, MN: Bethany House. This book provides seven effective, achievable steps toward building a healthy marriage and a workable and peaceful stepfamily, and helps parents recognize the unique personality and place of each family member, honoring the families of origin while establishing new traditions.

Frisbie, D. (2005). *Happily remarried: Making decisions together: Blending families successfully: Building a love that will last*. Eugene, OR: Harvest House Publishers. The author uses many real-life examples and speaks with hope and humor about the challenges of re-marriage and offers four strategies to help bring long–term unity: forgive everyone, including yourself; regard remarriage as permanent and irreversible; use conflict to get better acquainted; and form a spiritual connection centered on serving God.

Marsolini, M. (2006). *Raising children in blended families: Helpful insights, expert opinions, and true stories*. Grand Rapids, MI: Kregel Publications. The author, who has a blended family herself, includes many stories from her counseling background to illustrate each chapter. The book would be helpful to any blended family with children from preschool to adulthood.

Norwood, P. K., & Wingender, P. (2001). *Enlightened stepmother: Revolutionizing the role*. New York: HarperCollins World. Becoming a stepmother is a life-altering event in any woman's life – the issues are extraordinarily complex and women are overwhelmingly unprepared, and concerns usually focus on the effect remarriage has on the children. This book offers helpful insights and suggestions from the perspective of a stepmother.

Parrott, L. (2001). *Saving your second marriage before it starts*. Grand Rapids, MI: Zondervan Publishing House. This book includes 28 self tests, group discussion guide, and workbooks for men and women to help couples uncover and understand the unique shaping factors they bring into their second marriage both as men and women and as individuals.

Thoele, S. P. (2003). *The courage to be a stepmom: Finding your place without losing yourself*. Tulsa, OK: Wildcat Canyon Press. This practical handbook, considered a comforting friend, addresses stepmothers' commonly felt emotions – guilt, shame, grief, frustration, and fear – and offers hands-on advice for acknowledging and dealing with them.

Wisdom, S., & Green, J. (2002). *Stepcoupling: Creating and sustaining a strong marriage in today's blended family*. New York: Three Rivers Press. This book offers advice for step-couples on how to do just that while strengthening their blended family with a healthy marriage and provides tips and strategies on dealing with the issues remarried couples face, with a wealth of advice from real-life step-couples.

Wooding, G. S. (2008). *Step parenting and the blended family: Recognizing the problems and overcoming the obstacles*. Markham, Ont.: Fitzhenry & Whiteside. The author offers a comprehensive look at the challenges faced by couples starting over again – starting with the breakup itself, outlining the pitfalls and hurdles surrounding the couple's love, and presents a comprehensive roadmap, a one step-at-a-time guide to successful remarriage for parents and children alike.

COURTSHIP

Browne, J. (2006). *Dating for dummies*. Hoboken, NJ: Wiley. In keeping with the excellent "For Dummies" treatment of complicated subjects, psychologist Browne's book offers a professional, insightful, and very readable examination of dating and thoroughly covers every aspect of the basic mechanics of dating in the 1990s.

Cloud, H. (2005). *Boundaries in dating*. Grand Rapids, MI: Zondervan. This book helps readers bridge the pitfalls of dating and unfolds a wise, biblical path to developing self-control, freedom, and intimacy in the dating process, and helps singles to think, solve problems, and enjoy the benefits of dating to the hilt, increasing their abilities to find and commit to a marriage partner.

Givens, D. B. (2006). *Love signals: A practical field guide to the body language of courtship*. New York: St. Martin's Press. The author explores the nonverbal signs, signals, and cues human beings exchange to attract and keep their mates through five distinct phases – attracting attention, recognition phase, conversation phase, touching phase and making love – to increase the likelihood of finding a loving, lasting partner.

Grenier, G. (2007). *The 10 conversations you must have before you get married (and how to have them)*. Toronto, Ont.: Key Porter Books. Written in an accessible style and illustrated with real-life case studies from the author's practice, this book arms couples with practical and effective strategies for forging a lifetime pattern of excellent communication and enhancing the chances for long-term marital bliss.

Munroe, M. (2004). *Waiting and dating: A sensible guide to a fulfilling love relationship*. Shippensburg, PA: Destiny Image. This book offers a balanced, biblical view for every believer who wants a prosperous and fulfilling marriage relationship, and offers advice on the subject of finding the one with whom you will spend the rest of your life.

Murray, C. E. (2008). *Just engaged: Prepare for your marriage before you say "I do."* Avon, MA: Adams Media. Designed to learn how to prepare for your marriage, even as you plan your wedding, the author offers practical guidance, exercises, case studies, and discussion questions to help you both build realistic, positive expectations for your marriage, laying the foundation for a satisfying partnership.

Santagati, S., & Cohen, A. (2007). *The manual: A true bad boy explains how men think, date, and mate – and what women can do to come out on top*. New York: Crown Publishers. Santagati, a former model, wrote this guidebook to dating and taming the wild male, taking women through every step of the bad boy's process, from hunt to sex to relationship to "endgame," through his short, easy-to-digest chapters.

Steele, R. D. (2002). *Body language secrets: A guide during courtship and dating*. Whittier, CA: Steele Balls Press. The author asserts that sexual signals help you find, meet, talk with and date Mister or Ms Right using secrets of nonverbal communication. Forty photographs clearly show what to watch out for – amid the position that the essence of courtship and dating conversations is to communicate, with and without words.

Young, B. (2008). *The ten commandments of dating: Time-tested laws for building successful relationships*. Nashville, TN: Thomas Nelson. This work, completely revised and updated, offers hope and sanity to singles who are sick and tired of the dating scene, and offers hard-hitting, black-and-white, practical guidelines that will address their questions and frustrations about dating to help avoid dating pitfalls move toward finding and building lasting relationships.

Ziglar, Z. (2004). *Courtship after marriage*. Nashville: Oliver Nelson. This book offers six steps for "starting over" – no matter how long you've been married – strategies to avoid the "Three A's of Divorce," and advice to revive romance and keep sexuality sizzling, as well as a unique sixty-six question survey to evaluate the state of your marriage – both before and after you read the book.

DIVORCE

Finnamore, S. (2008). *Split: A memoir of divorce*. New York: Dutton. The author, a California journalist, wrote this sharp, cut-to-the-quick account of her painful divorce after five years of marriage, facilitated by what is considered her supreme vulnerability and bravery.

Fisher, B. (2005). *Rebuilding: When your relationship ends* (3rd edition). Atascadero, CA: Impact Publishers, Inc. This revised and updated 3rd Edition continues the author's tradition of straight-to-the-heart response to the needs of those who are divorcing or divorced. The book's divorce process rebuilding blocks offer a supportive 19-step process for putting one's life back together after divorce.

Lankston, K. (2001). *Self-help for healing from divorce*. St. Meinrad, IN: Abbey Press. This book was written to give people a caring aid as they go through the divorce process, and discusses the pressures and struggles of going through a divorce and helpful bits of wisdom to help facilitate the healing process.

Lynn, T. (2008). *How to heal your heart and soul from divorce: A quick, easy to read guide to healing*. Denver, CO: Outskirts Press. The book's author, having been through the pain, and through diligent effort emerged victorious, addresses the fears and challenges the reader may be facing, and provides tools to take back all the pieces of yourself that you have lost.

Torres, D., & Torres-Alvarez, J. (2008). *Married to me: How committing to myself led to triumph after divorce*. New York: Celebra. Torres, a former Miss Universe, with a big assist from sister Jinny – a mental health counselor with several degrees – delivers this well-written guide to post-divorce recovery; the famous ex of singer Marc Anthony isn't remarkably original in her debut publication (yet the book is reported to be interesting and helpful).

INTERRACIAL MARRIAGE

Amato, P. R. (2007). *Alone together: How marriage in America is changing*. Cambridge, MA: Harvard University Press. This book draws on a unique data set, analyzes and interprets the data in a very sophisticated fashion, and presents the results in clear, straightforward prose. The text is dense with useful and interesting information.

Childs, E. C. (2005). *Navigating interracial borders: Black-white couples and their social worlds*. New Brunswick, NJ: Rutgers University Press. Drawing upon personal accounts, in-depth interviews, focus group responses and cultural analysis of media sources, the book provides compelling evidence that sizable opposition still exists toward black-white unions. Well-researched, the book offers important insights into racial hierarchies of contemporary society in the U.S.

Douglas, D., & Douglas, B. (2002). *Marriage beyond black and white: An interracial family portrait*. Wilmette, IL: Bahá'í Pub. A powerful story about the marriage of a black man and a white woman, this book provides a poignant look at what it was like to be an interracial couple in the U.S. from the early 1940s to the mid-1990s, and offers invaluable perspective on the roles of faith and spiritual transformation in combating prejudice and racism.

Kennedy, R. (2004). *Interracial intimacies: Sex, marriage, identity, and adoption*. New York: Vintage. With focus on black and white relationships, this comprehensive and well-researched book details the U.S.'s shameful history of racial classification and the phenomenon of racial passing as portrayed in movies and literature and as practiced in real life, and takes an in-depth look at the intersection of race and sex in the U.S.

Palmer, S. (2004). *Marrying Roque: Memoir of an interracial marriage*. New York: iUniverse. Set against a background of an intolerant society and conflicting cultural values, this chronicled marriage between a young Jewish girl and a Filipino immigrant that later becomes problematic. With insight and compassion, the author narrates the couple's struggles with honesty and adventuresome spirit.

Persaud, R. (2004). *Why black men love white women: Going beyond sexual politics to the heart of the matter*. New York: Pocket Books. This book's over-arching question is answered in this illuminating, no-holds-barred work that will have you laughing while fundamentally changing the way you see just about everything – from sex and marriage to your own gender and race in all its foibles, pretensions, and ultimate possibilities.

Root, M. P. P. (2001). *Love's revolution: Interracial marriage*. Philadelphia, PA: Temple University Press. Via a careful, social and psychological study of the growing phenomenon of interracial marriage, this book examines ideas about factors that have been thought to encourage or discourage interracial marriages, to make them more or less successful than other sorts of marriages and offers helpful practical guidelines.

Sue, J. A. (2004). *Cornbread and dim sum: A memoir of a heart glow romance*. Corte Madera, CA: Khedcanron. This book tells the story of an interracial courtship and marriage between an African-American woman and an American born Chinese man in San Francisco during the 1960s civil rights era. It is an authentic, delightful romance with dynamic honesty.

Wallenstein, P. (2004). *Tell the court I love my wife: Race, marriage, and law: An American history*. New York: Palgrave Macmillan. The author scholarly and compellingly traces the legal intersection between race and sex from the pre-Civil War to later concerns, and examines the social intricacies affecting the evolution of the legal meaning of black to the current state of increasing racial and ethnic diversity that defies easy definition.

INTIMACY

Hanson, R. Ph. D., Hanson, J., & Pollycove, R. (2002). *Mother nurture: A mother's guide to health in body, mind, and intimate relationships*. New York: Penguin Books. The authors offer hundreds of practical ways a mother can lift her mood, stay energetic and healthy, build teamwork and intimacy with her partner, and be at her best for her family, during the stressful and crucial first three to five years of her child's life – basically taking care of herself while she takes care of her family.

Kerner, I. (2008). *Sex detox: Recharge desire, revitalize intimacy, rejuvenate your love life*. New York: Collins. Based on the premise – when it comes to sex, dating, and relationships, sometimes we get in so deep the only way out is to start over again – this book suggests that for some people their love lives have become a source of toxicity. Sex Detox offers a revolutionary way to start fresh and take helpful action.

Osho. (2008). *Being in love: How to love with awareness and relate without fear*. New York: Harmony Books. Replete with wit, humor and understanding, this book challenges us to question what we think we know about love and opens us to the possibility of a love that is natural, fulfilling and free of possessiveness and jealousy, and inspire you to welcome love into your life anew and experience the joy of being truly alive by sharing it.

Perel, E. (2006). *Mating in captivity: Reconciling the erotic and the domestic*. New York: HarperCollins. With references to case studies of couples both heterosexual and gay, spanning all ages, with kids and without, the author offers cures to what ails an individual's sex life, specifically for the rekindling of eroticism, and in short: sanctions fantasy and play and offers the estranged modern couple a unique richness of experience.

MARRIAGE

Bloom, L., & Bloom, C. (2004). *101 things I wish I knew when I got married: Simple lessons to make love last*. Novato, CA: New World Library. Psychotherapists Linda and Charlie Bloom present 101 techniques delivering practical guidance and demonstrates how anyone can find ways out of a painful relationship – specifically how couples can enrich their own relationships through working through love's challenges.

Gafni, L. (2001). *Living a blissful marriage: 24 steps to happiness*. Rancho Palos Verdes, CA: Lifeline Publications. This book guides couples step by step on how to take control of their relationship, how to create the marriage they hoped it would be, how to avoid trouble spots, to rekindle love and sexual passion in the marriage, and to set a foundation for trust between the partners.

Gray, J. (2008). *Why Mars & Venus collide: Improving relationships by understanding how men and women cope differently with stress*. New York: Collins. A highly-acclaimed author, Dr. John Grey focuses on the ways that men and women misinterpret and mismanage the stress in their daily lives, and how these reactions ultimately affect their relationships.

Gungor, M. (2008). *Laugh your way to a better marriage: Unlocking the secrets to life, love, and marriage*. New York: Atria Books. Using a unique blend of humor and tell-it-like-it-is honesty, the author helps couples get along and have fun doing it. He also explores a variety of subjects including the myth of a "soul mate," the different ways men and women think, the conflicting levels of libido, and the necessity to forgive.

Larson, J. H. (2003). *The great marriage tune-up book: A proven program for evaluating and renewing your relationship*. San Francisco, CA: Jossey-Bass. This practical book includes helpful and easy-to-use quizzes, self-tests and personal assessments that reveal why you're feeling this way, explain the underlying issues, and provide solutions to specific issues and problems. It also highlights strengths and weaknesses, and focuses on goals for improvement.

Louden, J. (2004). *The couple's comfort book: A creative guide for renewing passion, pleasure & commitment*. San Francisco: HarperSanFrancisco. This book, considered a "must-read for anyone who wants to live and love more fully" and "a comprehensive compendium of coupledom," offers a vast array of ways for couples to stay connected in a busy world, including playful rituals and reliable recipes for making the most of a couple's time together.

Stosny, S. (2006). *Love without hurt: Turn your resentful, angry, or emotionally abusive relationship into a compassionate, loving one: You don't have to take it anymore.* Philadelphia, PA: Da Capo Press. The author draws examples and exercises from his experience working with couples as he discusses core values, anger management, power struggles and reconstruction. While the approach may provide false hope if the reader's reality is too complex for self-help, it nonetheless could foster important life changes.

Whyte, D. (2009). *The three marriages: Reimagining work, self and relationship.* New York: Riverhead Books. Drawing from his own experience and the lives of some of the world's great writers and poets, the author brings compelling insights to our three most important commitments (to another, to our work and to ourselves) to frame a complete picture of a satisfying life, and investigates captivating ideas for bringing a deeper satisfaction to our lives, one that goes beyond our previously held ideas of balance.

ROMANCE

Bassil, J. (2008). *Askmen.com presents the guy's guide to romance: The 11 rules for finding a woman and keeping her happy.* New York: HarperCollins. Considered "an indispensable handbook filled with fundamentals that every man can use to enter into or maintain a happy, healthy relationship," this book presents 11 rules for every man who wants to get a great girl – and keep her.

Brisben, P. (2008). *Pure romance between the sheets: Find your best sexual self and enhance your intimate relationship.* New York: Atria Books. Designed to help you learn the secrets behind your body's sexuality and revitalize your intimate relationship with your partner, and teaches how to overcome your insecurities, understand your libido, and learn the ins and outs of orgasm.

Kroll, K., & Klein, E. L. (2001). *Enabling romance: A guide to love, sex, and relationships for people with disabilities (and the people who care about them).* Horsham, PA: No Limits Communications. The authors candidly cover: shattering sexual stereotypes; building self-esteem; creative sexual variations; reproduction and contraception for people with disabilities; specific information on several different physical and sensory disabilities, including spinal cord injury, multiple sclerosis, and others.

Rainey, D., Rainey, B., & DeMoss, R. G. (2004). *Rekindling the romance: Loving the love of your life.* Nashville, TN: Thomas Nelson. This book is organized into a collection of short, easy-to-digest, biblically-based chapters. Packed with practical insight, this tastefully candid and inviting resource provides the Christian couple with the keys to unlock their relational and sexual intimacy.

Sanna, L., & Miller-Vejtasa, K. (2001). *How to romance the woman you love – the way she wants you to!* New York: Three Rivers Press. Based on substantial research, this book reveals the most intimate desires of women from across the country, helping the reader gain a new understanding of romance, suggesting that you can easily develop a deeper, more fulfilling relationship with your own partner in imaginative and often fantastically fun ways.

Smith, D. W. (2008). *A little book of romance: 101 ways to romance your marriage.* Eugene, OR: Harvest House Publishers. Spice up your love life with over 100 creative ideas, this book is on ideas and small in size. It has been said, "This compact guide will soon have your marriage sizzling. For husbands: how about buying a flower a month? For wives: Pack a gift box with your husband's favorite CD and a note saying, 'I've made plans for us tonight'."

Smith, D. W., & Smith, D. W. (2005). *Romancing your wife: A little effort can spice up your marriage*. Eugene, OR: Harvest House Publishers. Debra White Smith and her husband, Daniel, show husbands how to make their marriages sparkle – exploring how to woo their wives and turn their marriages into ardent romances, men will discover things such as that helping with housework without being asked is as romantic as bringing her flowers, among others.

Westheimer, R. K., & Lehu, P. (2001). *Rekindling romance for dummies*. Philadelphia, PA: Running Press. In this friendly guide, Dr. Ruth shows you how to "embrace the art of romance," and "discover how rate the romance in your relationship, renew respect and commitment, spice up your sex life, find time for romance in everyday situations, and plan a romantic getaway."

SINGLE PARENTING

Aldrich, S. P. (2005). *From one single mother to another*. Ventura, CA: Gospel Light. The author shares her experiences and answers questions for single mothers. Her overall message is: "Single mom, you and your children do have bright tomorrows. And they can start today if you will lean on the Lord and ask Him for the strength you need."

Canfield, J. (2005). *Chicken soup for the single parent's soul*. Deerfield Beach, FL: Health Communications. The author shares the joys, challenges and humorous moments of single parents, who cope daily with the unique pressures, constraints and sacrifices their role brings. It also offers inspiration and advice for getting through the difficult times, reassurance for those days when you worry you're not living up to expectations and reminders of the unique influence you have on your children's lives.

Chisholm, D. S. (2007). *Single moms raising sons*. Kansas City, MO: Beacon Hill Press of Kansas City. Speaking from her own experience as a single mother of two boys, the author inspires other single moms to partner with God – the Father of the fatherless – and offers honest insight, unifying encouragement, and practical applications to guide mothers as they raise their boys to be the solid, Christian men they want them to be.

Colopy, E. K. (2006). *The single mom's guide to finding joy in the chaos*. Grand Rapids, MI: Fleming H. Revell. The author, a single mom for 12 years, discusses what a struggle it is to raise young children alone but also knows that it's full of tender moments, happy tears and downright crazy fun. In brief, practical chapters, the book addresses a host of everyday issues from nutrition to discipline and more.

Ellis, C. B. (2007). *The 7 pitfalls of single parenting*. New York: iUniverse, Inc. Drawing from her own experiences as well as from in-depth studies on personal development, the author offers what has been said is "the ultimate 'how-to' guide for successful single parenting," and includes inspiration and advice for getting through the difficult times, reassurance and important reminders.

Ellison, S. (2002). *The courage to be a single mother*. San Francisco: HarperSanFrancisco. This book discusses four steps important for divorced mothers facing the realities of raising children, and is considered an excellent source of understanding, encouragement, and strength that will help single women to nurture their children, resurrect their spirits, and create the life they want.

Engber, A., & Klungness, L. (2000). *The complete single mother: Reassuring answers to your most challenging concerns*. Holbrook, MA: Adams Media. The authors, single mothers whose state was unexpectedly thrust upon them by departing partners, wrote this frank and unabashedly feminist guide, including tips on how not to fall to pieces when the baby starts saying "da-da" to what to do when teenagers start worrying that mom will be old maid.

Leman, K. (2006). *Single parenting that works: Six keys to raising happy, healthy children in a single-parent home*. Carol Stream, IL: Tyndale House Publishers. Using his trademark quirky, no-nonsense approach, the author shows parents how to build healthy, mature relationships with their former spouses, how to develop their children's self-esteem, and how to discipline and relate to their kids in accordance with their unique God-given personalities.

Morrissette, M. (2008). *Choosing single motherhood: The thinking woman's guide*. Boston: Houghton Mifflin. Written in a lively style that never sugarcoats or sweeps problems under the rug, this is a comprehensive guide for single women interested in proactively becoming and being a mother, and includes the essential tools needed to decide whether to take this step, helpful information, and insight about children's questions and needs.

Noel, B. (2005). *The single parent resource*. Belgium, WI: Champion Press. This very readable handbook covers important concerns of single parents, economically presenting the issues and helpful tips, techniques and strategies. Key issues include: getting organized, managing the household, balancing family and work, creating a financial plan, dealing with difficult emotions, etc.

Passley, J. A. (2006). *Single parenting in the 21st century and beyond: A single mother's guide to rearing sons without fathers*. Victoria, BC: Trafford. The author, Dr. Passley, describes parenting practices that have not worked well for the single mother and describes more effective ways to handle difficult situations that lead to improved and strengthened mother-son relationships including building self-esteem, establishing boundaries and establishing male role models for her son.

Peterson, M., & Warner, D. (2003). *Single parenting for dummies*. New York: Wiley, Baker & Taylor. Along with insightful, inspiring real-life single parent success stories, this encouraging and practical book offers helpful solutions to balancing work and family life, developing strong relationships with your kids, managing your time (and money), and dealing with such challenges as dating and remarriage.

Shimberg, E. F. (2007). *The complete single father: Reassuring answers to your most challenging situations*. Avon, MA: Adams Media. This comprehensive guide, offers the tips and advice to show you how to: make your house (or apartment) a home; juggle your work and personal schedule with that of your kids; co-parent with your ex for the kids' sake; handle special circumstances if you're a widower; and date again (among others).

Yates, C. (2006). *Living well as a single mom: A practical guide to managing your money, your kids, and your personal life*. Eugene, OR: Harvest House Publishers. With empathy and biblical wisdom and combining her own experiences as a single mom with the insight of other moms, the author shares the practical and emotional way to live life well when a woman is raising her children alone. The book includes numerous suggestions, guidance and "How To" topics.

APPENDIX B. A CATEGORICAL/ANNOTATED LIST OF VIDEOTHERAPEUTIC MOVIES

The following includes 10 categorical listings of a total of 42 movies; except for some "classics," most of the movies are relatively new. The movies can be very helpful to counselors and students as well as for individuals (clients) struggling with specific issues – issues that also are interfering and/or troublesome in their loving relationships.

ADDICTION/ALCOHOLISM AND RELATIONSHIPS

Barfly (R) (1987) This film concentrates on alcoholic writer Mickey Rourke who carries on a hate-hate relationship with bartender Frank Stallone and makes the acquaintance of another of society's castaways, Faye Dunaway, who in addition to being a souse is said to be crazy. They move in together, even though Dunaway all but promises to be unfaithful for the price of a drink. Rourke has a chance to clean up his act when offered a large commission for his writings by publisher Alice Krige. They too end up in bed, each trying to change the other. The clarion call of the cheap wine bottle overrides Rourke's half-hearted efforts to enter the mainstream.

Days of Wine and Roses (NR) (1962) In this classic addiction melodrama, Joe Clay (Jack Lemmon), a promising adman, meet his future wife Kirsten (Lee Remick) at a party. Once married, the pressures of his business lead Joe to seek solace in liquor. Kirsten joins him in his nocturnal drinking sessions, and before long both are confirmed alcoholics. After several frightening episodes, Joe is able to shake the habit thanks to AA, but Kirsten finds it impossible to get through the day without liquor. The two split up, although Joe clings to the hope that someday he and Kirsten will be reunited, if for no reason other than the sake of their young daughter.

Even Money (R) (2007) Forest Whitaker, Kim Basinger, Danny DeVito and Nick Cannon star in this ensemble addiction drama detailing the manner in which gambling and drugs affect a variety of people's lives leading up to a championship college basketball game. Carolyn's (Basinger), addictions to the slots drives her to deceive her husband Tom (Liotta). Clyde (Whitaker) stands at the sidelines of the basketball court cheering for his little brother Godfrey (Cannon) while keeping his lingering gambling debts a well-guarded secret. As the big game draws near and casino magician Walter (DeVito) befriends gambling-addicted Carolyn, all on a tragic collision course.

28 Days (PG-13) (2000) In this romantic comedy, a journalist finds a new lease on life in a drug and alcohol treatment center. Newspaper columnist Gwen Cummings (Sandra Bullock) has a fondness for liquor, a boyfriend (Dominic West) with a similar taste, a party girl image and plenty of emotional baggage. At the wedding of her sister, Gwen's pursuit of a good time goes a bit too far. The result is a court-ordered, 28-day stay in a rehabilitation facility for drug and alcohol abusers. She fails to get with the program, but her attitude begins to change when she meets Eddie Boone (Viggo Mortensen), a baseball player trying to deal with his substance abuse problems.

AFFAIRS AND LOVING RELATIONSHIPS

Bridges Over Madison County (PG-13) (1995) Francesca (Meryl Streep), who meets a traveling photographer, Robert Kincaid (Clint Eastwood), who has arrived in Madison County, Iowa to shoot its covered bridges. They begin a four-day affair while her husband and children are out of town, that reawakening long-lost passions and yearnings in Francesca. Kincaid confronts his own roving, rootless nature; he asks Francesca to come with him, but they both know that after their brief interlude, they can never be together again. A framing story follows Francesca's children after her death that builds the film into a deeply moving reflection on the choices one must make in both life and love.

Falling in Love (PG-13) (1984) This movie, described as an urban American Brief Encounter, features a married couple. Thing of it is, they're not married to each other. While Christmas shopping for their respective families, architect Frank Raftis (Robert DeNiro) and graphic artist Molly Gilmore (Meryl Streep) "meet cute" – their holiday packages becoming mixed up. What starts as a pleasant chance acquaintance blossoms into romance. Inevitably, however, both parties realize that what they're doing is wrong – a shade too late to save their marriages, as it turns out. The film ends with a bittersweet "one year later" coda.

Fatal Attraction (R) (1987) Dan (Michael Douglas) is a family man whose one-night affair with Alex (Glenn Close) turns into a nightmare when she insists on continuing the relationship, claiming to be carrying his baby. Alex systematically terrorizes Dan, even temporarily kidnapping his daughter to win back his affection. Dan guiltily tries to preserve his marriage and family from the consequences of his own indiscretion. Close's performance as the love-struck psycho-siren (aka Borderline Personality Disorder) remains her signature role, conveying the buried feminist message of the film in her challenge to Dan to take responsibility for his sexual behavior.

The Graduate (PG) (1967) College graduate Benjamin Braddock (Dustin Hoffman) would rather float in his parents' pool than follow adult advice about his future. But the exhortation of Mr. Robinson to seize every possible opportunity inspires Ben to accept an offer of sex from icily feline Mrs. Robinson (Anne Bancroft). However, Ben is pushed to go out with the Robinsons' daughter Elaine (Katharine Ross) and he falls in love with her. Mrs. Robinson sabotages the relationship and Elaine runs back to college. Ben follows her to school and then disrupts her family-sanctioned wedding. None too happy about her pre-determined destiny, Elaine flees with Ben – but to what?

Something to Talk About (R) (1995) Julia Roberts stars as Grace King Bichon, a prim small-town wife who learns that her husband Eddie Bichon (Dennis Quaid) is having an affair, not his first dalliance. Grace embarrasses her husband publicly, and then moves in with her wise-mouthed little sister Emma Rae (Kyra Sedgwick). Grace becomes even angrier when her mother Georgia (Gena Rowlands) and wealthy father, horse breeder Wyly King (Robert Duvall), side with Eddie in the conflict. However, when Georgia finds that Wyly has been a long-term philanderer as well, she kicks him out, embroiling the entire King family in a war between the sexes.

Twice in a Lifetime (R) (1985) On the occasion of his 50th birthday, blue-collar family man Gene Hackman is possessed "The Mid-Life Crisis." Visiting a local tavern, Hackman becomes enchanted by gorgeous barmaid Ann-Margret. In less time than it takes to down his beer, he has resolved to leave his wife Ellen Burstyn, and his daughters Ally Sheedy and Amy Madigan, in favor of a fresh start with his sexy new "conquest." The film deals not so much with Hackman's impulsive decision as with the genuine pain he leaves in his wake. Madigan's vituperative lash-out at her father is one of many heartbreaking moments of truth in this refreshingly cliché-free domestic drama.

Unfaithful (R) (2002) Diane Lane is a wayward wife and Richard Gere is her suspicious husband. On a trash-strewn Soho street, she literally runs into Paul Martel (Olivier Martinez) and gets a bad scrape on her knee; unable to get a cab, Paul invites her up to his apartment. Paul is quietly flirtatious; Connie phones home and explains that she's running late. She mentions the encounter to Edward (Gere), but it's clear that she's obsessing about Paul. Soon, they are lovers and grow bolder and bolder in their passion. Edward begins to suspect, and hires a private investigator. His worst fears confirmed, Edward decides to confront Paul, a decision that will come to haunt him.

BLENDED FAMILIES

Yours, Mine & Ours (PG) (2005) In this comedy, two big families merge into one super-sized brood. Frank (Dennis Quaid) is a naval officer who has been raising eight children on his own after the death of his wife, and agrees to be set up on a blind date. His date turns out to be Helen North (Rene Russo), a girl he dated years ago and lost her spouse not long ago. The old chemistry clicks anew and he asks her to marry him. However, there's just a bit of a problem — Helen is caring for 10 children of her own, six of whom were adopted. The 18 siblings don't get along at all well at first, until they decide to set aside their differences and unite against a common foe — their folks.

Stepmom (PG-13) (1998) Family turmoil of divorce pits a birth mother against the new mother. Jackie (Susan Sarandon), juggling the schedules of her two kids and her ex-husband Luke (Ed Harris), who gets weekend custody of the kids, is living with a woman half his age, Isabel (Julia Roberts), a younger, devil-may-care woman. The burden of getting the kids ready for school falls on Isabel, and she just isn't the nurturing type. The story heats up when Jackie learns that she has cancer and realizes that her kids will be left with this irresponsible Isabel as their mother. What ensues is part parenting lesson and part competitive parenting, but 100% family bonding.

COURTSHIP

Meet the Parents (PG-13) (2000) In this comedy, Greg Focker (Ben Stiller) plays a young man who endures a disastrous weekend at the home of his girlfriend's parents. Greg is in love with Pam Byrnes (Teri Polo) and plans to ask her to marry him. Things stampede steadily downhill when Pam's father, Jack (Robert De Niro), takes an instant and obvious dislike to his daughter's boyfriend, lambasting him for his job as a nurse and the differences between their families. Things go from bad to worse, with Greg incurring the wrath of both Pam's father and the rest of her family, almost single-handedly destroying their house and the wedding in the process.

When Harry Met Sally (R) (2000) This romantic comedy stars Billy Crystal and Meg Ryan who share a car trip from Chicago to New York, eventually deciding it is impossible for men and women to be "just friends." They go their separate ways and then meet a few years later when Harry reveals he is married. They meet again a few years after that where Harry reveals he is now divorced. From that point on, the two form a friendship. Eventually their closeness results in their respective best friends meeting and falling in love with each other. Nonetheless, at a New Year's Eve party Harry and Sally confront the complex tangle of emotions they feel for each other.

Hitch (PG-13) (2005) A man who teaches dateless wonders how to become irresistible to women learns just how hard it can be to do it yourself in this romantic comedy. Alex "Hitch" Hitchens (Will Smith) has made a career out of coordinating a man's first three dates so that they'll show him to his best advantage (for a price, of course), and more than a few have taken women to the altar. But Hitch discovers his own romantic limitations when he falls for Sara (Eva Mendes) who has her own ideas about romance. In the midst of all this, Hitch has his hands full with Albert, a socially inept man who has enlisted Hitch's services.

My Big Fat Greek Wedding (PG) (2002) Toula (Nia Vardalos) is committed to remaining a single Greek-American which distresses her mother (Lainie Kazan) and father (Michael Constantine), who want to send her to Greece in hopes of finding a husband. After seeing a handsome stranger, Toula spruces herself up with a new look and a new attitude. She meets another handsome stranger, Ian Miller (John Corbett), who is soon in love with Toula – except that he's not Greek and a vegetarian, both of which horrify Toula's family. When Ian pops the question, she has to negotiate a meeting between Ian's upper-class parents and her own working-class family. There's also the matter of the wedding – aka, quantity IS quality.

DIVORCE

Diary of a Mad Black Woman (PG-13) (2005) Helen McCarter (Kimberly Elise) would seem to have it all – married for 18 years to Charles (Steve Harris), one of Atlanta's most successful attorneys. But despite wealth and prestige, things are not as they should be, and on their anniversary Charles tells Helen he's divorcing her for another woman. Helen moves in with her grandmother Madea (Tyler Perry), a sassy woman who helps Helen get back on her feet emotionally, and makes the acquaintance of Orlando (Shemar Moore), a handsome man who is obviously attracted to her. But after her experiences with Charles, Helen isn't sure if she's ready to trust a man again.

Heartburn (R) (1986) Meryl Streep plays Rachel, an influential food critic who marries charismatic columnist Mark (Jack Nicholson) after a whirlwind courtship. Warned that Mark is constitutionally incapable of settling down with any one woman, Rachel gives up her own job to make certain that her marriage works. When Rachel announces that she's pregnant, Mark virtually jumps out of his skin with delight. But as the news sinks in, Mark chafes at the impending responsibilities of fatherhood, and the philandering begins – as if it had ever really stopped!

Kramer vs. Kramer (PG) (1979) Joanna Kramer (Meryl Streep) walks out on her workaholic husband Ted (Dustin Hoffman), leaving their young son Billy in his less than capable hands. Ted learns how to take care of Billy, but Joanna returns with her own lucrative job and the intent to take custody of Billy. Ted proves that he can do it all, yet Joanna still wins in court. Joanna, however, rethinks her desires when she finally grasps how close father and son have become. Addressing the male side of the self-actualization question, the movie focuses on Ted's evolution as he learns to balance domestic and professional lives in the shifting late-1970s social landscape.

Mrs. Doubtfire (PG-13) (1993) Daniel Hillard (Robin Williams) is a kind man and a loving father, yet a poor disciplinarian and a shaky role model. His wife, Miranda (Sally Field), reaches the end of her patience and files for divorce. Daniel is heartbroken when Miranda is given custody of the children. Determined to stay in contact with his kids, Daniel learns that Miranda is looking for a housekeeper, and with help from a makeup artist, Daniel gets the job disguised as Mrs. Iphegenia Doubtfire, a stern but caring Scottish nanny. Daniel pulls off the ruse and in the process learns how to be the good parent he should have been all along.

Under the Tuscan Sun (PG-13) (2003) In this romantic comedy drama, Frances (Diane Lane) feels emotionally derailed after her divorce and isn't sure what to do with her life. Her best friend Patti (Sandra Oh) gives Frances a ticket for a two-week tour of the Tuscany region of Italy where Frances finds a dilapidated old villa. Frances impulsively decides to buy the villa, thinking she can fix it up herself. The home repairs prove to be more than she imagined, but as she slowly gets the hang of household maintenance, Italian style, Frances develops a new confidence as she makes friends with her neighbors and finds love with a handsome local named Marcello (Raoul Bova).

War of the Roses (R) (1989) In this slapstick tragedy, divorce lawyer Danny De Vito warns his prospective client that the story he's about to tell isn't a pretty one, but the client listens with eager intensity. After 17 years, Oliver (Michael Douglas) and Barbara (Kathleen Turner) Rose want a divorce. Not for this couple is there anything resembling a "civilized understanding" – e.g., Barbara wants their opulent house and Oliver isn't about to part with the domicile – culminating in a disastrous showdown around, about and under the living room's fancy chandelier. The movie never lets us forget that the couple's self-indulgent imbroglio exacts an awful price upon their children.

INTERRACIAL MARRIAGE

Guess Who's Coming To Dinner (NR) (1967) Matt and Christina Drayton (Spencer Tracy and Katharine Hepburn) have raised their daughter Joey (Katharine Houghton) to think for herself and not blindly conform to the conventional – until she returns home with a new fiancé: African-American doctor John Prentice (Sidney Poitier). While they come to grips with their own prejudices, they must also contend with John's parents (Roy Glenn Sr. and Beah Richards), who are dead-set against the union. While Joey is determined to go ahead with the wedding, John refuses to consider marriage until he receives the unqualified approval of all concerned. The closing monologue delivered by Spencer Tracy turned out to be the last scene ever played by the veteran film luminary.

Mississippi Masala (R) (1991) In 1972 Indian Jay (Roshan Seth), a resident of Uganda, is forced by the bigoted Amin regime to take his family and flee the country. He vows to hate and distrust all blacks. Flash-forward to 1990: Jay and his family have settled in Mississippi. Jay's daughter Mina (Sarit Choudhury) makes the acquaintance of African-American Demetrius (Denzel Washington), a prosperous businessman. At first attracted to Mina because he is fascinated by her African background, Demetrius slowly falls in love with her, causing Jay to exercise the same racial prejudice by which he was himself victimized. Both Jay and Demetrius must learn to bury their pasts and their prejudices to go on with their lives.

Something New (PG-13) (2006) In this romantic comedy-drama, Kenya (Sanaa Lathan), a successful African-American lawyer in her mid-30s thirties, has rather high standards and isn't willing to settle for a man who isn't everything she wants. Then she's introduced to Brian (Simon Baker), a White, landscape architect. Brian is immediately and obviously attracted to Kenya, though she doesn't feel the same way at all, yet likes his work and hires him to refurbish her garden. He asks her out on a date. While they have little in common, in time they hit it off and a romance begins to blossom. However, Kenya's friends and family try to find her a more suitable, African-American suitor.

INTIMACY

About Last Night (R) (1986 Danny (Rob Lowe) and Debbie (Demi Moore) meet and engage in a torrid sexual relationship, but then slowly negotiate if there is anything more between them. Danny seeks advice from his loudmouthed friend Bernie (James Belushi), who offers little more than outrageous tales of his randy exploits. Debbie confides in her best friend Joan (Elizabeth Perkins), a bitter, single kindergarten teacher who has lost any hope of finding the right person on the dating scene. Although Danny and Debbie talk, they have trouble communicating. The film ends on a coda that suggests they are still unsure as to where their relationship may be headed.

Bliss (R) (1997) In their marriage, Joseph (Craig Sheffer) and Maria (Sheryl Lee) are in serious trouble – Maria has difficulty opening up to Joseph and unable to have an orgasm with him. Joseph is shocked to see Maria visiting a building where an unlicensed sex therapist, (Terence Stamp) teaches about the mind as much as the body – less concerned with orgasm than with "bliss" – an emotional and spiritual as well as physical state. Before long, Joseph convinces Balthazar to teach him what he knows about tantric healing and sex, in the hope that he can help heal Maria's emotional scars, as well as help himself become a better man.

Children of a Lesser God (R) (1986) James Leeds (William Hurt), a teacher, meets the attractive custodian, Sarah (Marlee Matlin). An exceptionally intelligent yet bitter young woman, Sarah feels safer with her "own people" rather than to face what she perceives as a cruel and uncaring world. She hardly seems interested in James and will only communicate with him through signing. James learns that Sarah was sexually molested as a teenager, explaining why she is so wary of James' attempts to form a relationship with her and so full of fear. Eventually, James does get through to Sarah and the two fall in love – having to learn new ways to communicate their feelings.

Good Will Hunting (R) (1997) A gifted, 20-year-old, gifted MIT janitor, Will Hunting (Matt Damon), hangs out with his South Boston bar buddies, best friend Chuckie (Ben Affleck) and his British girlfriend Skylar (Minnie Driver). When Professor Lambeau tries to stump students with a challenging math formula, Will anonymously leaves the correct solution. As Will's problems escalate, Lambeau offers an out, but with two conditions – visits to a therapist and weekly math sessions – and contacts his former classmate, therapist Sean McGuire (Robin Williams). Both are equally stubborn, but Will is finally forced to deal with both his past and his future.

MARRIAGE

Coast to Coast (R) (2005) This movie features a couple whose marriage is on the rocks. Barnaby (Richard Dreyfuss) and Maxine (Judy Davis) are attempting to salvage what might be left of their broken marriage by taking a road trip together. As they stop at various places and interact with a variety of people, they begin to bridge the wide gap that had taken its toll on their relationship.

Dinner with Friends (2001) A happily married couple discovers their friends are not happy. A decade previously, Gabe (Dennis Quaid) and Karen (Andie MacDowell) introduced their close friends Tom (Greg Kinnear) and Beth (Toni Collette) who fell in love and got married. But one night Gabe and Karen receive startling news from Beth – Tom has left her for another woman, and the two are filing for divorce. Feeling as if they are being forced to take sides as the combative couple separates and both parties move on to new relationships, Gabe and Karen find themselves taking a long, hard look at their own marriage, not sure how happy they are with what they find.

Eyes Wide Shut (R) (1999) The Hartford's, William (Tom Cruise) and Alice (Nicole Kidman), are a physician and a gallery manager who are wealthy, successful, and travel in a sophisticated social circle. However, a certain amount of decadence crosses their paths on occasion and a visit to a formal-dress party leads them into sexual temptation when William is drafted into helping a beautiful girl who has overdosed on drugs while Alice is charmed by a man bent on seduction. While neither William nor Alice act on their adulterous impulses, once the issue has been brought into the open it begins a dangerous season of erotic gamesmanship for the couple.

Mr. and Mrs. Smith (PG-13) (2005) Many married couples have secrets, but one pair of lovebirds discovers they've both been living dangerous secret lives in this action thriller laced with comedy. Jane (Angelina Jolie) and John (Brad Pitt), a suburban couple whose marriage has started to go a bit stale after five or six years, actually are world-class assassins who will take on perilous missions for the right price, but neither is aware of the other's secret life. When John and Jane are both assigned to take out the same target, one Benjamin Danz (Adam

Brody), they become aware of each other's secret lives, and suddenly both their careers and their marriage go through some dramatic changes.

The Story of US (R) (1999) Bruce Willis and Michelle Pfeiffer star in this romantic comedy as Ben and Katie Jordan, a couple who have been married for 15 years. They have two great kids, a nice home, and a comfortable life, but somewhere down the line, the spark went out of their marriage, and they find that they don't really love each other anymore. With their relationship at a crossroads, Ben and Katie, two different people who have never felt more different, have to decide if they want to try to salvage their marriage, or if it's time to move on. The movie, directed by Rob Reiner, addresses the meaning of "marriage" and portrays the many dysfunctional "dances" couples can get into.

Who's Afraid of Virginia Woolf? (NR) (1966) First staged on Broadway in 1962, Edward Albee's play was adapted for this movie classic. George (Richard Burton) is an alcoholic college professor, and Martha (Elizabeth Taylor) is his virago of a wife. They both know just how to push each other's buttons, with George having a special advantage – he need only mention the couple's son to send Martha into orbit. This evening, the couple's guests are Nick (George Segal), a junior professor, and Honey (Sandy Dennis), Nick's child-like wife. After an evening of sadistic (and sometimes perversely hilarious) "fun and games," the truth about George and Martha's son comes to light.

ROMANCE

50 First Dates (PG-13) (2004) Re-teaming Adam Sandler with Drew Barrymore, his co-star from *The Wedding Singer*, this movie finds the funnyman (Sandler) playing veterinarian Henry Roth. More than content with a life of one-night-stands, Henry decides to give up his noncommittal lifestyle when he meets and falls for Lucy (Barrymore). However, when he discovers that Lucy has no short term memory, Henry finds himself having to win her heart again with every new day. Sean Astin and Rob Schneider also star.

Moonstruck (PG) (1987) Loretta Castorini (Cher) agrees to marry a man she does not love, Johnny Cammareri (Danny Aiello). Before the wedding, Johnny must visit his dying mother in Sicily; Loretta is supposed to try to patch up the differences between Johnny and his brother, Ronny (Nicolas Cage) who has never forgiven Johnny for indirectly causing the accident that crippled him. Ronny does, however, fall for Loretta like a ton of bricks. Loretta tries to avoid Ronny, but he's just too fascinating to resist. Meanwhile, Loretta's father is fooling around with his mistress while her mother is being wooed by a college professor. These brief flings are forgiven, but there's still the delicate situation of Loretta being in love with her future brother-in-law.

Sleepless in Seattle (PG) (1993) In this light romantic comedy, Sam (Tom Hanks) is as a widower and single father. When his son, Jonah (Ross Malinger), calls into a talk radio program looking for a new mother, Sam ends up getting on the phone and laments about his lost love. Thousands of miles away, Annie (Meg Ryan) hears the program and immediately falls in love with Sam, despite the fact that she has never met him and that she is engaged to humdrum Walter (Bill Pullman). Believing they are meant to be together, Annie sets out for Seattle to meet Sam, who, meanwhile, contends with an onslaught of letters from available women equally touched by his phone call.

Something's Gotta Give (PG13) (2003) Harry Langer (Jack Nicholson) is a swinging 60-something entertainment executive. His latest romance is young petite sophisticate Marin (Amanda Peet), who takes him to her mother's beach house in the Hamptons for the weekend. However, Marin's mother, Erica (Diane Keaton) is already vacationing at the house. Marin and Harry stay anyway, and Harry ends up having a heart attack and is looked after by 30-something doctor Julian Mercer (Keanu Reeves). While Marin returns to Manhattan, Erica agrees to stay on and look after Harry. Repulsed by each other at first, they end up falling in love throughout Harry's recovery process.

Somewhere in Time (PG) (1980) In 1972, Richard Collier (Christopher Reeve) is approached by an elderly woman – all she says to him is "Come back to me" and leaves him with a picture of a ravishing young woman. Eight years later, he discovers she was an actress who made an appearance at a hotel in 1912. He becomes obsessed and falls in love with her image. Then hears that time travel may in fact be possible, using an extreme form of self-hypnosis. Collier's feelings for the woman are so strong that he succeeds, bringing himself back to the hotel in 1912. He meets the actress, Elise McKenna (Jane Seymour), and the two fall in love despite the machinations of her obsessive, autocratic manager (Christopher Plummer), who feels threatened.

While You Were Sleeping (PG) (1995) In this latter-day romantic screwball comedy, Lucy (Sandra Bullock), a love-starved subway toll booth operator, pines for regular customer Peter (Peter Gallagher), but the self-absorbed attorney pays her no heed. One day, Peter is beaten by a gang of thugs and tossed onto the tracks. Lucy rescues him from death. While he is comatose in the hospital, a comment she makes at his bedside is misinterpreted – his family members, who haven't seen Peter in awhile, believe that she is his fiancée. Peter's parents take a liking to Lucy. But Lucy takes a liking to Peter's brother Jack (Bill Pullman), though Jack is suspicious about her claim to be Peter's intended.

SINGLE-PARENTING

One Fine Day (PG) (1996) When Melanie Parker (Michelle Pfeiffer) suddenly decides to elope, Jack Taylor (George Clooney), her ex-husband, is left totally responsible for their daughters. As Jack attempts to link corruption with city hall, his reporting job unhappily demands 100% commitment. Melanie must not only somehow prepare a complex multimillion-dollar real-estate development presentation, but also must keep up the pretense that she doesn't have a son because her boss loathes children. When Jack flubs his assignment of getting the two children off on a school day-trip, he and Melanie have to take turns caring for the kids. Mishap follows mishap, as the initially antagonistic Jack and Melanie get to know one another.

ABOUT THE AUTHORS

William A. Lambos, Ph.D., is Chief Cognitive Neuroscientist and a Partner of CNS Wellness, Florida, L.L.C. (d/b/a Cognitive Neuro Sciences, or CNS), a multi-site integrated healthcare practice with headquarters in Tampa, Florida. CNS's approach to health care is based on a combining leading-edge neuropsychological assessment, EEG-based brain mapping and EEG biofeedback treatment approaches within a philosophy of wellness, self-regulation, and healthy interpersonal dynamics. Dr. Lambos possesses a post-doctoral certification in Clinical Neuropsychology from Fielding Graduate University, master's and doctoral degrees in Experimental Psychology from McMaster University, a master's degree in Rehabilitation and Mental Health Counseling, and has satisfied the coursework requirements for a post-masters certificate in Marriage and Family Therapy, both of the latter from the University of South Florida. In addition, he is certified as a family mediator by the Supreme Court of the State of Florida and provides dispute resolution services in divorce, childcare and healthcare quality assurance cases.

Dr. Lambos' recognitions include certifications in EEG-biofeedback and QEEG analysis by both the Biofeedback Certification Institute of America (BCIA) and The Society for the Advancement of Brain Analysis (SABA), on whose Board he sits.

While Dr. Lambos' B.A. degree from Vassar, with honors, and membership in Phi Beta Kappa and his publications in scientific journals clearly reveal his revered acumen and scholarly prowess, his quick wit, hearty laugh and overall enjoyment of life are among the reasons he enjoys a reputation of "a life of the party" kind of person.

William G. Emener, Ph.D., is a Distinguished Research Professor Emeritus in, and the former Chair of, the Department of Rehabilitation and Mental Health Counseling, and a former Associate Dean, at the University of South Florida, Tampa. Additionally, he has worked as a rehabilitation counselor and supervisor as well as a rehabilitation counselor educator and program director at Murray State University, Florida State University and the University of Kentucky. Dr. Emener's publications and writings include seven research monographs, twenty-seven books, numerous book chapters in twenty-six different books, over fifty nonpublished professional papers, over 100 authored/coauthored articles in seventeen different professional refereed journals, and over a hundred professional papers presented at professional association meetings. He also has been an editor/coeditor of over twenty special publications (including the *American Rehabilitation Counseling Association Newsletter*) and was Coeditor of the *Journal of Applied Rehabilitation Counseling* from

1978-1982. While many of his books have been textbooks and professional readings, his more recent books are pop-psych books, self-help books, and contemporary romance novels.

Dr. Emener's recognitions include being a recipient of the 1980 *American Rehabilitation Counseling Association Research Award*, a recipient of the National Rehabilitation Administration Association's 1982 *The Advancement of Research in Rehabilitation Administration Award*, and in 1988 was honored with the title of *Fellow* by the American Psychological Association. He was the 1983-1984 President of the National Rehabilitation Administration Association and the 1989-1990 President of the National Council on Rehabilitation Education.

For 33 years, Dr. Emener also had a part-time private practice as a licensed psychologist in Florida and Kentucky, with specializations in employee assistance programs, marriage/couples counseling and addictions/substance abuse counseling. A former college basketball player, Bill's hobbies and interests now include playing his guitar and piano, fishing, boating, scuba diving, motorcycle riding, slow pitch softball, reading contemporary novels, playing golf, and occasionally walking a sandy beach with a six pack.

SUBJECT INDEX

A

A-B-C's of Happiness, The, viii, 105
A, B, C's of Loving Relationships (The), 96
A-B-C model, 22, 96, 106, 107
A-B-C's of Communication (The), 233
About this Book, xxviii
abuse, 241, 357
   exposure to, 92
   kinds of, 241
Abusive Relationship, viii, 92
abusiveness, 93
accreditation, 331
Active and Passive Control, xiv, 153, 154
Active Listening, 263
addictions, ix, xvii, 181, 182, 223, 224
Adlerian, 1
adult (defined), 78
Adult Adjustment Group, 87
advocational counseling, 209
Affair Person (The), 145
affairs, 146
   three questions, 146
   two questions, 147
affect, 96, 129, 233
agape, 4, 30
   love, 4
Albert Ellis Institute, 77, 195
All or Nothing Relationships, xiv, 119, 120
Alone – Lonesome – Lonely, 207
alternative dispute resolution, 320
American Association for Marriage and Family Therapy, 5, 334, 336, 355
American Psychological Association, 20, 332, 334, 349, 350, 351, 356, 382
amygdala, xxiv, 14, 121, 122, 198

analysis, 1, 4, 5, 12, 20, 35, 50, 55, 56, 57, 68, 69, 75, 95, 103, 137, 181, 212, 236, 250, 310, 351, 352, 354, 355, 356, 357, 360, 364, 381
anger, ix, 220, 221, 222, 223, 224, 254, 296
   management programs, 222
   post-divorce, 254
anxiety, ix, 123, 198, 205, 211, 224, 296
   reduction, 123
aphasia, 139
archetypes, 14
Aristotelian logic, 42
arousal, 7, 8, 13, 22, 29, 30, 44, 45
assistive technology, 140
associative learning, 14, 354
attachment theory, 199
attention, iii
   sustained versus divided, 47
attention deficit disorder, 238
attraction and mate selection, 32
authenticity, 19, 313
Autonomy and Professional Behavior, x, 332
Avoidant and Escape Behavior, 39
avoidant behavior, 40, 41

B

Babel: If You Want to be Heard – Listen, 181
balance, viii, xiv, 95, 100, 101
behavior, ii, iii, viii, xiii, 15, 35, 36, 38, 39, 40, 41, 43, 52, 96, 105, 129, 152, 180, 315, 353, 356
   behavior analysis, viii, 35
   Perception, and, 38
behavior analysis, 41
Behavioral and Ethological Theories, vii, 14
Behaviorism, 15, 357
Being
   alone, 208
   lonely, 208

lonesome, 208
Loved and Feeling Loved, viii, 67
bereavement, 144, 213, 214, 220, 249
Bibliotherapy
    dovetail reading, 319
    Videotherapy, and, 318
Biology of Belief, The, 189
birth order, 14, 91
blame of self, 194
Blended Families, 134, 361, 373
    misconceptions about..., 135
    research on, 135
Blink: The Power of Thinking Without Thinking,
    180
boundaries, ix, 148, 151, 362
    limits, and, 50, 151, 152
Boundaries and Control, ix, 148
boundary conditions, 131, 132, 137, 148, 149, 151,
    157
brain, xxiv, xxvii, xxviii, 1, 2, 5, 6, 7, 9, 11, 13, 14,
    18, 22, 23, 24, 28, 29, 30, 31, 44, 47, 62, 78, 115,
    121, 126, 139, 172, 173, 181, 198, 206, 211, 224,
    227, 259, 260, 293, 349, 352, 356, 381
Browning, Elizabeth Barrett, 34

C

cardiocentric view (Aristotle), 5
catastrophize, 198
catastrophizing, 39, 198
cephalocentric view (Hippocrates), 6
Certification, 330, 381
Children, 92, 135, 136, 138, 167, 197, 360, 376
Clients
    present problems - examples, 294
    questions they may have, 298
    six stages of change, 310
    "They're here!", 326
    Willingness to Work, 309
Co-, In-, and Inter-Dependence, ix, 258, 268
cognitions, 2, 9, 21, 23, 96, 100, 121
cognitive, i, iii, v, vi, vii, 1, 12, 20, 28, 115, 121,
    206, 349, 354, 355, 356, 381
Cognitive Behavioral Movement, 121
Cognitive-Behavioral Theories, vii, 20
Cognitive-Behavioral Therapy, 20, 21
Commitment Phobia, xiv, 202, 204
Communication Styles, xv, 233, 234
compulsions, ix, 223, 225
confidentiality, 297
conflict habituated, 222
Confronting the Fear and Pain, xiv, 126, 128

congruence, 95, 96, 97, 101, 128, 129, 131, 230, 232,
    233
consistency, 36, 37
contempt, 180
contra- question(s), 247
control intrusive behavior, 224
Controlling the Relationship Lifestyle: Putting
    Partners First, 233
controls, 148, 152
coping skills, ix, 264, 268
Counseling
    costs, 297
    homework, 316
    Intervention Strategies, ix, 316
    Progress May be Slow and Gradual, 312
    Respect Your Client's Options, 325
counter-transference - three possible targets of, 337
Couples and Marriage Counseling Intake Form, xv,
    299, 300, 301, 302, 303, 304
criticism, 180

D

Defense Advanced Research Projects Agency, 277
defensiveness, 19, 180, 181
denial, 55, 213, 214, 215, 220, 249, 251, 264, 295
dependence, 55, 58, 60, 61, 75, 76, 92, 95, 223, 224,
    270, 313, 333
Dependence and Independence, viii, xvii, 60, 61
depression, ix, 205, 206, 211, 224, 288
Diagnostic and Statistical Manual of Mental
    Disorders, 211
Dichotomous Thinking, viii, xiv, 115, 116
differences among the theories, 23
Differences Between
    Needs and Wants, 107
    Rational and Irrational Beliefs, xiv, 107
Diplomate Status, 330, 332
Dirty Sexy Money, 33
disability, xiv, 139, 140, 355
Dissociative Identity Disorder, 78
distance, 138
distancer, 50
distress (and eustress), 265
divorce, xv, 244, 245, 249, 253, 254, 275, 334, 351,
    360, 363, 364, 374
    kinds of, 249
    post-divorce anger, 254
    stages of, 245
Divorce and separation - nine questions, 245
Do I Have to Give Up Me to be Loved by You?, 51

domestic violence, 92, 221, 222, 223, 241, 257, 299, 308, 356
Don't Expect Immediate Results, 314
Don't Give Up You, 55
doorknob issue, 343, 346
downside of an upswing, 315, 316
DR BOLL, 106, 152
During the Ending Stage, 267
Dysfunctional Relationships, viii, 87

E

EEG-biofeedback, 176
ELF, 106, 113
Emener Formula (The), 39
Emotional Intelligence: How it Can Matter More than IQ, 121
emotional scar tissue, 239
Emotional Shutdown, 124
emotions, 2, 5, 7, 8, 9, 23, 24, 28, 31, 44, 96, 97, 106, 115, 120, 121, 122, 124, 125, 126, 127, 129, 146, 171, 177, 191, 197, 205, 211, 212, 222, 223, 243, 314, 315, 317, 325, 346, 362, 369, 374
empathy (defined), 260
empathy and listening skills, ix, xvii, 258, 259, 261, 271
Ending Stage, 265, 267, 272
ennui, 175
Equitable Equity, xvii, 163
eros, 4
escape behavior, 36, 40
Establishing Stage, 266
ethical behaior - two case examples, 336
ethics, x, 329, 333, 334, 336, 351
    consumer protection, 329
    five guiding philosophical principles, 333
    Morality, and, 336
executive brain, 6, 29
executive functions (of the brain), 259
Existential and Humanistic Approaches, vii, 17
Existential Guilt, xvii, 191
experiential family therapy, 4

F

failure of
    being, 197
    doing, 197
family counseling, xxviii, 21, 199, 257
family mediator and a family therapist - differences between, 320

fear, ii, xiii, xiv, 86, 122, 126, 197, 198, 199, 200, 201, 202, 203
    abandonment, of, 87, 123, 138, 179, 183, 197, 199, 200, 201, 204, 307
    anxiety, and, 198
    change, of, 199
    change or the unknown, of, 198
    ending a relationship, of, 201
    getting hurt, of, 264
    intimacy, of, 200, 201
    Losing Individuality, of, 202
    perceived reality,of a, 205
Fears and Phobias, ix, 197, 224
Feelings and Emotions, viii, 120
Feelings, Thoughts and Actions, xiii, xiv, 99, 100
Fighting Well - Ten Recommendations, 242
financial
    advice - 23
    issues, 166
Florida Lottery, 229
Florida Supreme Court Certified Family Mediator, 126
fMRI imaging, 30
Forgetting and Forgiving, viii, 73
four blocks to happiness, 106, 191, 206, 209
Four Horsemen (The), 180, 181
freedom, 346
Functional and Dysfunctional Controls, 152
Functional and Dysfunctional Lifestyles, 232
Future Shock, 273, 290

G

Games People Play, 19
Gestalt and Phenomenological Theories, vii, 18
Gestalt Psychology, 18
Gestalt Therapy, 18
Good and Bad, 118
Great Recession of 2008 (The), 288
gridlock, 240
grieving, 214
    A Process, 214
guilt, ix, xiv, xvii, 134, 190, 191, 192, 193, 194, 195, 196, 197, 224, 296
    rational versus irrational guilt, 196

H

Hamlet, 55, 354
Have Something to Take Care Of, 218
Health Insurance Portability and Accountability Act (HIPAA), 297

Healthy Interdependent Loving Relationships, 270
healthy shame, 194
    toxic shame, and, xvii, 193, 195
Helplessness and Hopelessness, xvii, 209, 210
High Maintenance and Low Maintenance People,
    xvii, 48, 49
History of the Internet, Electronic Communications
    and Social, 276
House Built on One or Many Stilts (A) , xvii, 58
*How to Stubbornly Refuse to Make Yourself
    Miserable About Anything: Yes, Anything*, 98
How We Spend Our Time, xiv, 116, 117
Human Service Regulatory Mechanisms, x, 330
humanistic psychology, 17, 349

I

I Don't Know How to Act, 206
Ideal Self, xiv, 104
identified client (the), 57, 308
Importance of Feeling "Safe", The, 121
Importance of Me (The), 42
In or Outside the Relationship, 111
incongruence, 97, 100, 101
independence, 55, 58, 60, 61, 75, 76, 78, 95, 142,
    268, 271
Individual Lifestyles and Relationship Lifestyles,
    xvii, 230
Intake Information, ix, 299
Interaction Effect of Your Pasts (The), 80
interdependent loving relationship (An), 270, 271,
    272
interdependent process of being, 345
Internal and External Control, xiv, xvii, 154, 155
Internet Dating, xvii, 281
    recommendations, 279, 282
    the Good, the Bad and the Ugly, 278
    tips, 282
Internet romance, 280
interpersonal, ii, vii, 1, 12, 84, 357
intimacy, passion and commitment, 58, 69, 71, 72,
    75, 76
irrational beliefs, 20, 42, 52, 106, 108, 196, 209, 213,
    222
isolation, 92, 173, 220
Issues of Agency, 121

J

jealousy, 123
journaling, 316, 317, 318

K

Know thyself. (Socrates), 55
knowledge,
    four things counselors need to know, 338
    sources of, 338

L

learned avoidant behavior, 41
Learned Interpersonal Needs, viii, xvii, 84
Learned Response Patterns, xiv, 177, 178
*Letting Go of Shame: Understanding How Shame
    Affects Your Life*, 98
licensure, 331
lifestyle, 48, 49, 118, 120, 143, 171, 175, 228, 229,
    230, 231, 232, 233, 234, 235, 255, 256, 285, 305,
    313, 322, 337, 345, 378
    congruence, 232, 233
    defined, 229
    Functional and Dysfunctional Lifestyles, 232
    Individual Lifestyles and Relationship
        Lifestyles, 230
    transition, 171
limbic system, 7, 13, 22, 24, 29, 30, 44, 206
Limited Assumptions, 112
linkages
    Feelings, Thoughts and Actions, xvii, 97
Little Child Within (The), 51
Living a Lie, 235
locus of control, 154, 155, 156
Logical Consequences, 113
Logotherapy, 17
loneliness, 208
long-distance loving relationship - questions, 138
Long-Term Trade Off (A), 174
Loss of a Child or Another Loved One (The), 219
love, v, vi, vii, viii, xiii, 8, 27, 28, 29, 30, 32, 67, 69,
    70, 71, 73, 75, 93, 135, 163, 344, 354, 359, 363,
    365, 367, 372
    defined, 28, 29
Love Story, 29
Love Triangle, viii, xiii, 69, 70, 71
loving, vii, viii, xiii, xiv, xv, xvii, 5, 8, 27, 64, 65, 96,
    108, 150, 227, 266, 269, 270, 285, 344, 351, 360,
    367, 372
Loving Roles We Play, xiii, 64, 65
LovingThings - two lists, xxi, 68, 309, 320
lust, 30, 53, 54

M

Maintenance Person (The), 147
Maintenance Stage, 265, 266, 272
Man's Search for Meaning, 17, 219
Marriage and Couples Counseling, i, v, vii, xxvii, 4
Marriage and Family Therapy, vii, xxv, 4, 5, 21, 336, 353, 381
Matching Our Roles with Our Needs, 109
Me and You – Self and You, 50
mediation, iii, 320, 334, 354
mediator - defined, 320
Meeting Relationship Needs and Wants - three questions, 108
Men, Love & Sex, 163
message consistency, 36
meta-analysis, 236, 351, 352
Million Little Pieces, A, 268
Mind and The Brain, The, 32
mistaken forward reasoning, 81
Mixed Anxiety and Depression, 211
mixed depression, 211
Mom and Dads – Our Primary Teachers, viii, 82
Monetary and Equity Issues, ix, 159, 160, 166, 186
    common signs of, 160
    Long-Term Relationships, in, 166
monetary issues - advice to clients, 165
money, 33, 160, 161, 162, 167, 168, 371
Mr. Data, 7, 28, 44
Mr. Spock, 7, 44
Multi-Dimensional Approach, A, vii, 23
Multi-trackers and Uni-trackers, 46, 47
Murphy's Law, 173
My Big Fat Greek Wedding, 5, 374

N

natural selection, 14
Need for Resolution and Serenity, A, 124
Need for Someone in One's Life, A, 52
Need to be Fought For, A ,53
Need to Feel Special, A, 53
Negative and Positive Compensatory Behavior, 41
Negotiating Boundaries and Limits, 151
network operations center, 277
neurofunctional areas, 22, 29, 30, 31, 44
neuroscientific, i, iii, v, vii, 1, 28
New Experiences – Old Feelings, xvii, 101, 102
New York Times, 64, 275, 350, 351, 355
Not-So-Secret Secret, 90

O

obsessions, ix, 223, 225
obsessive-compulsive spectrum disorders, 223
Old Patterns with New People, 179
On Death and Dying, 214
One Therapist, One Identified Client, 307
Only One "Should", 151
Only-Child Issues, viii, 91
operant (voluntary) behavior, 15
Other People, viii, 142
Our Parents (three questions), 83
outside factors, 131, 132, 138, 141, 148, 157, 159, 186
    cross-cultural factors, 141
    Extended Family Issues, 142
    Inter-racial Factors, 142
    other, 141
    relatives, 141
    social status, 142
    socio-economic factors, 141
Over-Estimating Our Expectations of Each Other, 112

P

Paradigm Shifts, 183
Parallel Lives, viii, 87
paralysis of analysis, 212
Patterns and Trends, ix, 176, 186
    five considerations, 176
Patterns are Like Addictions, 181
Pavlovian conditioning, xxvii
People Are Either "Good" or "Bad", 118
perception(s), 6, 17, 18, 24, 38, 39, 74, 118, 129, 154, 163, 175, 221, 229, 238, 239, 258, 259, 263, 289, 312, 320, 326, 338
    Behavioral Analysis, of, 41
    difficulties, and, 39
Phenomenological Approaches, 18
pheromones, 33
philio, 4, 30
phobia, 197, 202, 203, 204, 225, 306
Physical Attributes and Attractiveness, xiii, 45, 46
Physiological and Emotional Considerations, 44
physiological arousal, 44
Poor Communications Patterns, 180
Positivistic Psychology, 17
Post-Traumatic Stress Disorder, 78
predictability, 36, 37, 79, 92
    comfort of, 92
primary blocks to happiness, 134

primary reactive depression, 211
Primary-Immediate Family, 133
Priorities Change Over Time, xiv, 171, 172
Problems
    Making Clients' Problems Less Problematic,
        239
    "sage advice" to clients, 239
    solvable problems, 236
    unsolvable problems, 238
professional - criteria, 330
Professional Decision-Making - three "ultimate"
    decisions, 338
Professional helper - defined, 295
Professional Human Service Ethical Codes, xi, 334
Professional Self-Concept, x, 339
Professionalism in Human Services, x, 329
Promoting Relationship Happiness, viii, 73, 74
    Questions, 74
Prophet, The, 138
Psychodynamic Theories, vii, 13
psychotherapy, 3, 4, 350, 354, 355, 356
Public Space and Private Space, viii, 62
public space, private space and together space, 58,
    62, 63, 75, 76
pursuer, 50
Pursuers and Distancers, 50

R

Rational Emotive Behavior Therapy, 43, 52, 105,
    152, 180
Rational Emotive Behavioral Therapy, xxii, 191, 219
Rational-Emotive Therapy, 20
razor's edge, 220
real self, xiv, 104
Real versus Social Recovery, 324
Realistic Expectations
    Behavior and Emotions, 313
registration, 331
relationship, viii, ix, xiii, xiv, xv, 38, 57, 62, 68, 69,
    74, 86, 100, 108, 111, 140, 150, 184, 185, 189,
    201, 227, 240, 257, 258, 265, 266, 268, 309, 326,
    343, 351
relationship counseling - suggestions to guide
    clients, 287
relationship distracter, 143
relationship enders, 68
relationship enhancer, 143
relationship health, 53, 95, 128, 162
Relationship Paradox (The), 185
Relationship Patterns - five questions, 184
Relationship Pros and Cons, viii, xiii, 68, 69
Relationship Stages, ix, xv, 265, 266

advice to clients, 267
relationship-issue questions, 58
Relationships,
    Guilt-Based and Shame-Based, 196
    impact of social changes, 286
    Twenty-Four Hour Work Cycle, and the, ix, xvii,
        283, 284
Relationship's Past, Present and Future, A, viii, 78
Rocking in the Comfort Zone, 253
Rogerian Bailout, The, 326
role conflict and role strain, 64
romance, vii, 27, 367, 378
routinization, 198

S

Sabotage (Roles of), 178
secondary depression, 211
secrets, viii, 88, 89
    secret-secrets and not-so-secret secrets, 88
    six questions, 88
Secret-Secret (A), 89
Self Analysis, viii, 42
Self Identity, viii, 51
self-destructive behavior, 220, 223
self-efficacy, 93, 154, 211, 268, 269, 350
    defined, 268
Self-Fulfilling Prophecy, viii, 85
self-fulfilling relationship prophecy, 86
Self-Inflation, 45
Self-Protection, 250
    Some Do's and Don't-Do's, 250
separation, ix, 242, 244
    Divorce, and, ix, 244
Shakespeare, William, 28, 29, 32
shame, 197
Shame-Based Fear, 201
Shoulds - in relationships, 152
Sick or sorry?, 305
Similar Wants and Needs - two questions, 109
simple stimulus-driven processes, 14
Singularity is Near, The, 274
Social Self, xiv, 104
sociobiological studies, 16
Socrates, 55, 76
Solvable Problems, 236
soul mates, 344
Stages of Change Efforts, xv, 310, 311
Stalls in Your Barn (The), 216
Staying in "The Now.", 175
stonewalling, 180, 181, 185
strategic family therapy, 4

Support Groups, 321
systemic family therapy, 4, 350
Systems Theories, 21
systems theory, 2, 32

T

taboos, 89
texting, 273
Theories of Counseling and Couples Counseling, vii, 11
theory of mind, 62, 259, 260, 261
Third Person in a "Two-Seater", A, 143
thoughts, 2, 5, 6, 14, 44, 50, 54, 62, 72, 74, 85, 96, 97, 98, 99, 100, 101, 102, 113, 118, 121, 129, 132, 174, 231, 234, 235, 246, 247, 264, 295, 312, 318, 319, 322, 337, 346
time, ix, xiv, xv, 116, 123, 168, 169, 170, 171, 186, 207, 252, 253, 254, 285, 287, 363, 379
 A Precious Commodity, 169
 You Can't Create it – Just Allocate *it*, 170
 effects of, 252
 Timing, and, ix, 168, 186
Time: A Precious Commodity, 169
Timing is Everything, 172
Toxic shame, 194
transactional analysis, 19, 181
Transactional and Interpersonal Models, vii, 19
Transference and Counter-transference, 337
transition assistance or maintenance assistance, 143
Transition Person (The), 144
transtheoretical model of change, 310
Triple-A Rating (A), 54
trust issues, 161, 162

U

Unconditional Love, viii, 72
unconditional self-acceptance, 191

Unhealthy Dependent and Codependent Loving Relationships, 269
Unsolvable Problems, 238

V

values (from four different perspectives), 149
Values and Attitudes, 161
Values: Foundations for Boundaries, 149
Verbal Behavior, 36

W

Walk a Mile in My Shoes, 261
Wall Street Journal, The, 270
We Help You Help Yourself, 310
Wellstone Mental Health and Addiction Equity Act of 2008, 274
What I am" versus "Who I am, 43
What I Want You to See, 103
What to Do with Your Feelings, 127
When a Loved One Dies, 219
Why We Love: The Nature and Chemistry of Romantic Love, 30
Wired, 276
World Health Organization, 221, 357
World of Warcraft, 287
World Wide Web, 278
Worth and Meaning, 162

Y

Yellow Pages, The, 297

To Further Help You Help Your Clients.....

Two New Self Help Books by Your Authors

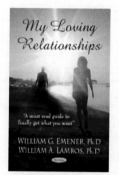

For any individual who has wondered how a perfectly sane person in today's crazy world is supposed to figure out what is expected of them when navigating a loving relationship (and who hasn't?), *My Loving Relationships* is a must-read. The primary focus is on those issues most pertinent to the *individual* – "I," "me," and "you" issues – relevant to the quest for satisfying, loving relationships.

Using case vignettes from the authors' clinical experiences as psychologists, the book's first 15 chapters address the topics of *Self Analysis, Relationship Analysis, My Past, Behavior Analysis, Dichotomous Thinking, Patterns and Trends, Divorce and Separation, Guilt and Shame, Fears and Phobias, Depression, Grieving, Time and Timing, Happiness and Joy,* and *The Internet (the Good, the Bad, and the Ugly).* The last three address where to look for more help when serious situations arise: *Seeing a Professional Counselor, Therapist or Family Mediator, How a Professional Counselor or Therapist Can be Helpful to You,* and *Some Suggestions About Getting Help from a Professional.* The book is very reader-friendly, solution-focused and down to earth, and also includes 43 Figures from the author's case files that graphically display the issues and helpful recommendations.

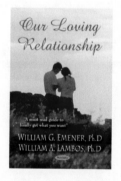

For any healthy individual or couple experiencing a difficult, problematic or less than enjoyable loving relationship in today's crazy world (and who hasn't?) – *Our Loving Relationship* is perfect for you. The primary focus is on mutual ("us," "we," and "me and you") issues pertinent to loving relationships – the couple and their relationship.

Using case vignettes from the authors' clinical experiences as psychologists, the first 14 chapters address the loving relationship topics of *Love, Loving, Our Pasts, Relationship Analysis, Congruence and Balance, Outside Factors and Features, Other People, Needs and Wants, Expectations and Dependence, Boundaries and Control, Lifestyles, Monetary and Equity Issues,* and *Problems, and Relationship Skills.* The last three address where to look for more help when serious situations arise: *Seeing a Professional Counselor, Therapist or Family Mediator, How a Professional Counselor or Therapist Can be Helpful to You,* and *Some Suggestions About Getting Help from a Professional.* The book is very reader-friendly, simplistic, solution-focused and down to earth, and also includes 39 Figures from their case files that graphically display the issues and helpful recommendations.

Available from: novapublishers.com *OR* your local bookseller